THOMAS PAINE

THOMAS PAINE

COLLECTED WRITINGS

*Common Sense, The Crisis,
and Other Pamphlets,
Articles, and Letters*

Rights of Man

The Age of Reason

THE LIBRARY OF AMERICA

Letter to Thomas Jefferson on page 368 reprinted from *The
Papers of Thomas Jefferson*, Vol 13: *March 1780 –October 1788*,
Julian P. Boyd, ed. Copyright © 1956 by Princeton University
Press. © renewed 1984 by PUP. Used with permission. Letters
to George Washington on pages 370 and 374 reprinted from
The Papers of George Washington, Presidential Series, Volume 4,
W. W. Abbot and Dorothy Twohig, eds. Used with permission
of the University Press of Virginia.

The paper used in this publication meets the
minimum requirements of the American National Standard for
Information Sciences—Permanence of Paper for Printed
Library Materials, ANSI z39.48—1984.

Distributed to the trade in the United States
by Penguin Books USA Inc
and in Canada by Penguin Books Canada Ltd.

Library of Congress Catalog Number: 94–25756
For cataloging information, see end of Index.
ISBN 1–883011–03–5

Second Printing
The Library of America–76

Manufactured in the United States of America

Eric Foner

selected the contents and
wrote the notes for this volume

Contents

COMMON SENSE,
THE CRISIS,
AND
OTHER PAMPHLETS,
ARTICLES, AND LETTERS

Contents

Common Sense

Addressed to the
Inhabitants of America

Man knows no Master save creating HEAVEN,
Or those whom Choice and common Good ordain.
THOMSON.

February 14, 1776

INTRODUCTION.

PERHAPS the sentiments contained in the following pages, are
not *yet* sufficiently fashionable to procure them general favor;
a long habit of not thinking a thing *wrong*, gives it a super-
ficial appearance of being *right*, and raises at first a formidable
outcry in defence of custom. But the tumult soon subsides.
Time makes more converts than reason.

As a long and violent abuse of power, is generally the
Means of calling the right of it in question (and in Matters
too which might never have been thought of, had not the
Sufferers been aggravated into the inquiry) and as the King of
England hath undertaken in his *own Right*, to support the
Parliament in what he calls *Theirs*, and as the good people of
this country are grievously oppressed by the combination,
they have an undoubted privilege to inquire into the pretensions of both, and equally to reject the usurpation of either.

In the following sheets, the author hath studiously avoided
every thing which is personal among ourselves. Compliments
as well as censure to individuals make no part thereof. The
wise, and the worthy, need not the triumph of a pamphlet;
and those whose sentiments are injudicious, or unfriendly,
will cease of themselves unless too much pains are bestowed
upon their conversion.

The cause of America is in a great measure the cause of all
mankind. Many circumstances hath, and will arise, which are
not local, but universal, and through which the principles of
all Lovers of Mankind are affected, and in the Event of which,

5

their Affections are interested. The laying a Country desolate with Fire and Sword, declaring War against the natural rights of all Mankind, and extirpating the Defenders thereof from the Face of the Earth, is the Concern of every Man to whom Nature hath given the Power of feeling; of which Class, regardless of Party Censure, is the

AUTHOR

P. S. The Publication of this new Edition hath been delayed, with a View of taking notice (had it been necessary) of any Attempt to refute the Doctrine of Independance: As no Answer hath yet appeared, it is now presumed that none will, the Time needful for getting such a Performance ready for the Public being considerably past.

Who the Author of this Production is, is wholly unnecessary to the Public, as the Object for Attention is the *Doctrine itself*, not the *Man*. Yet it may not be unnecessary to say, That he is unconnected with any Party, and under no sort of Influence public or private, but the influence of reason and principle.

Philadelphia, February 14, 1776.

COMMON SENSE.

OF THE ORIGIN AND DESIGN OF GOVERNMENT IN GENERAL. WITH CONCISE REMARKS ON THE ENGLISH CONSTITUTION.

SOME writers have so confounded society with government, as to leave little or no distinction between them; whereas they are not only different, but have different origins. Society is produced by our wants, and government by our wickedness; the former promotes our happiness *positively* by uniting our affections, the latter *negatively* by restraining our vices. The one encourages intercourse, the other creates distinctions. The first is a patron, the last a punisher.

Society in every state is a blessing, but government even in its best state is but a necessary evil; in its worst state an intolerable one; for when we suffer, or are exposed to the same miseries *by a government*, which we might expect in a country *without government*, our calamity is heightened by reflecting that we furnish the means by which we suffer. Government, like dress, is the badge of lost innocence; the palaces of kings are built on the ruins of the bowers of paradise. For were the impulses of conscience clear, uniform, and irresistably obeyed, man would need no other lawgiver; but that not being the case, he finds it necessary to surrender up a part of his property to furnish means for the protection of the rest; and this he is induced to do by the same prudence which in every other case advises him out of two evils to choose the least. *Wherefore*, security being the true design and end of government, it unanswerably follows that whatever *form* thereof appears most likely to ensure it to us, with the least expence and greatest benefit, is preferable to all others.

In order to gain a clear and just idea of the design and end of government, let us suppose a small number of persons settled in some sequestered part of the earth, unconnected with the rest, they will then represent the first peopling of any country, or of the world. In this state of natural liberty, society will be their first thought. A thousand motives will excite them thereto, the strength of one man is so unequal to his wants, and his mind so unfitted for perpetual solitude, that he is soon obliged to seek assistance and relief of another, who in his turn requires the same. Four or five united would be able to raise a tolerable dwelling in the midst of a wilderness, but *one* man might labour out the common period of life without accomplishing any thing; when he had felled his timber he could not remove it, nor erect it after it was removed; hunger in the mean time would urge him from his work, and every different want call him a different way. Disease, nay even misfortune would be death, for though neither might be mortal, yet either would disable him from living, and reduce him to a state in which he might rather be said to perish than to die.

Thus necessity, like a gravitating power, would soon form our newly arrived emigrants into society, the reciprocal blessings of which, would supersede, and render the obligations of law and government unnecessary while they remained perfectly just to each other; but as nothing but heaven is impregnable to vice, it will unavoidably happen, that in proportion as they surmount the first difficulties of emigration, which bound them together in a common cause, they will begin to relax in their duty and attachment to each other; and this remissness, will point out the necessity, of establishing some form of government to supply the defect of moral virtue.

Some convenient tree will afford them a State-House, under the branches of which, the whole colony may assemble to deliberate on public matters. It is more than probable that their first laws will have the title only of REGULATIONS, and be enforced by no other penalty than public disesteem. In this first parliament every man, by natural right, will have a seat.

But as the colony increases, the public concerns will increase likewise, and the distance at which the members may be separated, will render it too inconvenient for all of them to meet on every occasion as at first, when their number was small, their habitations near, and the public concerns few and trifling. This will point out the convenience of their consenting to leave the legislative part to be managed by a select number chosen from the whole body, who are supposed to have the same concerns at stake which those have who appointed them, and who will act in the same manner as the whole body would act were they present. If the colony continue increasing, it will become necessary to augment the number of the representatives, and that the interest of every part of the colony may be attended to, it will be found best to divide the whole into convenient parts, each part sending its proper number; and that the *elected* might never form to themselves an interest separate from the *electors*, prudence will point out the propriety of having elections often; because as the *elected* might by that means return and mix again with the general body of the *electors* in a few months, their fidelity to the public will be secured by the prudent reflexion of not making a rod for themselves. And as this frequent interchange will establish a common interest with every part of the community, they will mutually and naturally support each other, and on this (not on the unmeaning name of king) depends the *strength of government, and the happiness of the governed*.

Here then is the origin and rise of government; namely, a mode rendered necessary by the inability of moral virtue to govern the world; here too is the design and end of government, viz. freedom and security. And however our eyes may be dazzled with show, or our ears deceived by sound; however prejudice may warp our wills, or interest darken our understanding, the simple voice of nature and of reason will say, it is right.

I draw my idea of the form of government from a principle in nature, which no art can overturn, viz. that the more simple any thing is, the less liable it is to be disordered, and the easier repaired when disordered; and with this maxim in view, I offer a few remarks on the so much boasted constitution of England. That it was noble for the dark and slavish times in which it was erected, is granted. When the world was over run with tyranny the least remove therefrom was a glorious rescue. But that it is imperfect, subject to convulsions, and incapable of producing what it seems to promise, is easily demonstrated.

Absolute governments (tho' the disgrace of human nature) have this advantage with them, that they are simple; if the people suffer, they know the head from which their suffering springs, know likewise the remedy, and are not bewildered by a variety of causes and cures. But the constitution of England is so exceedingly complex, that the nation may suffer for years together without being able to discover in which part the fault lies, some will say in one and some in another, and every political physician will advise a different medicine.

I know it is difficult to get over local or long standing prejudices, yet if we will suffer ourselves to examine the component parts of the English constitution, we shall find them to be the base remains of two ancient tyrannies, compounded with some new republican materials.

First.—The remains of monarchical tyranny in the person of the king.

Secondly.—The remains of aristocratical tyranny in the persons of the peers.

Thirdly.—The new republican materials, in the persons of the commons, on whose virtue depends the freedom of England.

The two first, by being hereditary, are independent of the people; wherefore in a *constitutional sense* they contribute nothing towards the freedom of the state.

To say that the constitution of England is a *union* of three powers reciprocally *checking* each other, is farcical, either the words have no meaning, or they are flat contradictions.

To say that the commons is a check upon the king, presupposes two things.

First.—That the king is not to be trusted without being looked after, or in other words, that a thirst for absolute power is the natural disease of monarchy.

Secondly.—That the commons, by being appointed for that purpose, are either wiser or more worthy of confidence than the crown.

But as the same constitution which gives the commons a power to check the king by withholding the supplies, gives afterwards the king a power to check the commons, by empowering him to reject their other bills; it again supposes that the king is wiser than those whom it has already supposed to be wiser than him. A mere absurdity!

There is something exceedingly ridiculous in the composition of monarchy; it first excludes a man from the means of information, yet empowers him to act in cases where the highest judgment is required. The state of a king shuts him from the world, yet the business of a king requires him to know it thoroughly; wherefore the different parts, by unnaturally opposing and destroying each other, prove the whole character to be absurd and useless.

Some writers have explained the English constitution thus; the king, say they, is one, the people another; the peers are an house in behalf of the king; the commons in behalf of the people; but this hath all the distinctions of an house divided against itself; and though the expressions be pleasantly arranged, yet when examined they appear idle and ambiguous; and it will always happen, that the nicest construction that words are capable of, when applied to the description of some thing which either cannot exist, or is too incomprehensible to be within the compass of description, will be words of sound only, and though they may amuse the ear, they cannot inform the mind, for this explanation includes a previous question, viz. *How came the king by a power which the people are afraid to trust, and always obliged to check?* Such a power could not be the gift of a wise people, neither can any power, *which needs checking*, be from God; yet the provision, which the constitution makes, supposes such a power to exist.

But the provision is unequal to the task; the means either cannot or will not accomplish the end, and the whole affair is a felo de se; for as the greater weight will always carry up the less, and as all the wheels of a machine are put in motion by one, it only remains to know which power in the constitution has the most weight, for that will govern; and though the others, or a part of them, may clog, or, as the phrase is, check the rapidity of its motion, yet so long as they cannot stop it, their endeavors will be ineffectual; the first moving power will at last have its way, and what it wants in speed is supplied by time.

That the crown is this overbearing part in the English constitution needs not be mentioned, and that it derives its whole consequence merely from being the giver of places and pensions is self-evident, wherefore, though we have been wise enough to shut and lock a door against absolute monarchy, we at the same time have been foolish enough to put the crown in possession of the key.

The prejudice of Englishmen, in favour of their own government by king, lords and commons, arises as much or more from national pride than reason. Individuals are undoubtedly safer in England than in some other countries, but the *will* of the king is as much the *law* of the land in Britain as in France, with this difference, that instead of proceeding directly from his mouth, it is handed to the people under the more formidable shape of an act of parliament. For the fate of Charles the first, hath only made kings more subtle—not more just.

Wherefore, laying aside all national pride and prejudice in favour of modes and forms, the plain truth is, that *it is wholly owing to the constitution of the people, and not to the constitution of the government* that the crown is not as oppressive in England as in Turkey.

An inquiry into the *constitutional errors* in the English form of government is at this time highly necessary, for as we are never in a proper condition of doing justice to others, while we continue under the influence of some leading partiality, so neither are we capable of doing it to ourselves while we remain fettered by any obstinate prejudice. And as a man, who is attached to a prostitute, is unfitted to choose or judge of a wife, so any prepossession in favour of a rotten constitution of government will disable us from discerning a good one.

OF MONARCHY AND HEREDITARY SUCCESSION.

MANKIND being originally equals in the order of creation, the equality could only be destroyed by some subsequent circumstance; the distinctions of rich, and poor, may in a great measure be accounted for, and that without having recourse to the harsh ill sounding names of oppression and avarice. Oppression is often the *consequence*, but seldom or never the *means* of riches; and though avarice will preserve a man from being necessitously poor, it generally makes him too timorous to be wealthy.

But there is another and greater distinction for which no truly natural or religious reason can be assigned, and that is, the distinction of men into KINGS and SUBJECTS. Male and female are the distinctions of nature, good and bad the distinctions of heaven; but how a race of men came into the world so exalted above the rest, and distinguished like some new species, is worth enquiring into, and whether they are the means of happiness or of misery to mankind.

In the early ages of the world, according to the scripture chronology, there were no kings; the consequence of which was there were no wars; it is the pride of kings which throw mankind into confusion. Holland without a king hath enjoyed more peace for this last century than any of the monarchical governments in Europe. Antiquity favors the same remark; for the quiet and rural lives of the first patriarchs hath a happy something in them, which vanishes away when we come to the history of Jewish royalty.

Government by kings was first introduced into the world by the Heathens, from whom the children of Israel copied the custom. It was the most prosperous invention the Devil ever set on foot for the promotion of idolatry. The Heathens paid divine honors to their deceased kings, and the christian world hath improved on the plan by doing the same to their living ones. How impious is the title of sacred majesty applied to a worm, who in the midst of his splendor is crumbling into dust!

As the exalting one man so greatly above the rest cannot be justified on the equal rights of nature, so neither can it be defended on the authority of scripture; for the will of the Almighty, as declared by Gideon and the prophet Samuel, expressly disapproves of government by kings. All anti-monarchical parts of scripture have been very smoothly glossed over in monarchical governments, but they undoubtedly merit the attention of countries which have their governments yet to form. *"Render unto Cæsar the things which are Cæsar's"* is the scripture doctrine of courts, yet it is no support of monarchical government, for the Jews at that time were without a king, and in a state of vassalage to the Romans.

Near three thousand years passed away from the Mosaic account of the creation, till the Jews under a national delusion requested a king. Till then their form of government (except in extraordinary cases, where the Almighty interposed) was a kind of republic administred by a judge and the elders of the tribes. Kings they had none, and it was held sinful to acknowledge any being under that title but the Lord of Hosts. And when a man seriously reflects on the idolatrous homage which is paid to the persons of Kings, he need not wonder, that the Almighty ever jealous of his honor, should disapprove of a form of government which so impiously invades the prerogative of heaven.

Monarchy is ranked in scripture as one of the sins of the Jews, for which a curse in reserve is denounced against them. The history of that transaction is worth attending to.

The children of Israel being oppressed by the Midianites, Gideon marched against them with a small army, and victory, thro' the divine interposition, decided in his favour. The Jews elate with success, and attributing it to the generalship of Gideon, proposed making him a king, saying, *Rule thou over us, thou and thy son and thy son's son.* Here was temptation in its fullest extent; not a kingdom only, but an hereditary one, but Gideon in the piety of his soul replied, *I will not rule over you, neither shall my son rule over you.* THE LORD SHALL RULE OVER YOU. Words need not be more explicit; Gideon doth not *decline* the honor, but denieth their right to give it; neither doth he compliment them with invented declarations of his thanks, but in the positive stile of a prophet charges them with disaffection to their proper Sovereign, the King of heaven.

About one hundred and thirty years after this, they fell again into the same error. The hankering which the Jews had for the idolatrous customs of the Heathens, is something exceedingly unaccountable; but so it was, that laying hold of the misconduct of Samuel's two sons, who were entrusted with some secular concerns, they came in an abrupt and clamorous manner to Samuel, saying, *Behold thou art old, and thy sons walk not in thy ways, now make us a king to judge us like all the other nations.* And here we cannot but observe that their motives were bad, viz. that they might be *like* unto other nations, i. e. the Heathens, whereas their true glory laid in being as much *unlike* them as possible. *But the thing displeased Samuel when they said, Give us a king to judge us; and Samuel prayed unto the Lord, and the Lord said unto Samuel, Hearken unto the voice of the people in all that they say unto thee, for they have not rejected thee, but they have rejected me,* THAT I SHOULD NOT REIGN OVER THEM. *According to all the works which they have done since the day that I brought them up out of Egypt, even unto this day; wherewith they have forsaken me and served other Gods; so do they also unto thee. Now therefore hearken unto their voice, howbeit, protest solemnly unto them and shew them the manner of the king that shall reign over them,* i. e. not of any particular king, but the general manner of the kings of the earth, whom Israel was so eagerly copying after. And notwithstanding the great distance of time and difference of manners, the character is still in fashion. *And Samuel told all the words of the Lord unto the people, that asked of him a king. And he said, This shall be the manner of the king that shall reign over you; he will take your sons and appoint them for himself, for his chariots, and to be his horsemen, and some shall run before his chariots* (this description agrees with the present mode of impressing men) *and he will appoint him captains over thousands and captains over fifties, and will set them to ear his ground and to reap his harvest, and to make his instruments of war, and instruments of his chariots; and he will take your daughters to be confectionaries, and to be cooks and to be bakers* (this describes the expence and luxury as well as the oppression of kings) *and he will take your fields and your olive yards, even the best of them, and give them to his servants; and he will take the tenth of your feed, and of your vineyards, and give them to his officers and to his servants* (by which we see that bribery, corruption and favoritism are the standing vices of kings) *and he will take the tenth of your men servants, and your maid servants, and your goodliest young men and your asses, and put them to his work; and he will take the tenth of your sheep, and ye shall be his servants, and ye shall cry out in that day because of your king which ye shall have chosen,* AND THE LORD WILL NOT HEAR YOU IN THAT DAY. This accounts for the continuation of monarchy; neither do the characters of the few good kings which have lived since, either sanctify the title, or blot out the sinfulness of the origin; the high enco- mium given of David takes no notice of him *officially as a king,* but only as a *man* after God's own heart. *Nevertheless the People refused to obey the voice of Samuel, and they said, Nay, but we will have a king over us, that we may be like all the nations, and that our king may judge us, and go out before us, and fight our battles.* Samuel continued to reason with them, but to no purpose; he set before them their ingratitude, but all would not avail; and seeing them fully bent on their folly, he cried out, *I will call unto the Lord, and he shall send thun- der and rain* (which then was a punishment, being in the time of wheat harvest) *that ye may perceive and see that your wickedness is great which ye have done in the sight of the Lord,* IN ASKING YOU A KING. *So Samuel called unto the Lord, and the Lord sent thunder and rain that day, and all the people greatly feared the Lord and Samuel. And all the people said unto Samuel, Pray for thy servants unto the Lord thy God that we die not, for* WE HAVE ADDED UNTO OUR SINS THIS EVIL, TO ASK A KING. These portions of scripture are direct and positive. They admit of no equivocal construction. That the Almighty hath here entered his protest against monarchical government is true, or the scripture is false. And a man hath good reason to believe that there is as much of king-craft, as priest-craft, in withholding the scripture from the public in Popish countries. For monarchy in every instance is the Popery of government.

To the evil of monarchy we have added that of hereditary succession; and as the first is a degradation and lessening of ourselves, so the second, claimed as a matter of right, is an insult and an imposition on posterity. For all men being originally equals, no *one* by *birth* could have a right to set up his own family in perpetual preference to all others for ever, and though himself might deserve *some* decent degree of honors of his cotemporaries, yet his descendants might be far too unworthy to inherit them. One of the strongest *natural* proofs of the folly of hereditary right in kings, is, that nature disapproves it, otherwise she would not so frequently turn it into ridicule by giving mankind an *ass for a lion*.

Secondly, as no man at first could possess any other public honors than were bestowed upon him, so the givers of those honors could have no power to give away the right of posterity, and though they might say "We choose you for *our* head," they could not, without manifest injustice to their children, say "that your children and your childrens children shall reign over *ours* for ever." Because such an unwise, unjust, unnatural compact might (perhaps) in the next succession put them under the government of a rogue or a fool. Most wise men, in their private sentiments, have ever treated hereditary right with contempt; yet it is one of those evils, which when once established is not easily removed; many submit from fear, others from superstition, and the more powerful part shares with the king the plunder of the rest.

This is supposing the present race of kings in the world to have had an honorable origin; whereas it is more than probable, that could we take off the dark covering of antiquity, and trace them to their first rise, that we should find the first of them nothing better than the principal ruffian of some restless gang, whose savage manners or pre-eminence in subtility obtained him the title of chief among plunderers; and who by increasing in power, and extending his depredations, overawed the quiet and defenceless to purchase their safety by frequent contributions. Yet his electors could have no idea of giving hereditary right to his descendants, because such a perpetual exclusion of themselves was incompatible with the free and unrestrained principles they professed to live by. Wherefore, hereditary succession in the early ages of monarchy could not take place as a matter of claim, but as something

casual or complimental; but as few or no records were extant
in those days, and traditionary history stuffed with fables, it
was very easy, after the lapse of a few generations, to trump
up some superstitious tale, conveniently timed, Mahomet like,
to cram hereditary right down the throats of the vulgar. Perhaps the disorders which threatened, or seemed to threaten,
on the decease of a leader and the choice of a new one (for
elections among ruffians could not be very orderly) induced
many at first to favor hereditary pretensions; by which means
it happened, as it hath happened since, that what at first was
submitted to as a convenience, was afterwards claimed as a
right.

England, since the conquest, hath known some few good
monarchs, but groaned beneath a much larger number of bad
ones; yet no man in his senses can say that their claim under
William the Conqueror is a very honorable one. A French
bastard landing with an armed banditti, and establishing himself king of England against the consent of the natives, is in
plain terms a very paltry rascally original.—It certainly hath
no divinity in it. However, it is needless to spend much time
in exposing the folly of hereditary right, if there are any so
weak as to believe it, let them promiscuously worship the ass
and lion, and welcome. I shall neither copy their humility, nor
disturb their devotion.

Yet I should be glad to ask how they suppose kings came at
first? The question admits but of three answers, viz. either by
lot, by election, or by usurpation. If the first king was taken
by lot, it establishes a precedent for the next, which excludes
hereditary succession. Saul was by lot, yet the succession was
not hereditary, neither does it appear from that transaction
there was any intention it ever should. If the first king of any
country was by election, that likewise establishes a precedent
for the next; for to say, that the *right* of all future generations
is taken away, by the act of the first electors, in their choice
not only of a king, but of a family of kings for ever, hath no
parallel in or out of scripture but the doctrine of original sin,
which supposes the free will of all men lost in Adam; and
from such comparison, and it will admit of no other, hereditary succession can derive no glory. For as in Adam all sinned,

and as in the first electors all men obeyed; as in the one all mankind were subjected to Satan, and in the other to Sovereignty; as our innocence was lost in the first, and our authority in the last; and as both disable us from reassuming some former state and privilege, it unanswerably follows that original sin and hereditary succession are parellels. Dishonorable rank! Inglorious connexion! Yet the most subtile sophist cannot produce a juster simile.

As to usurpation, no man will be so hardy as to defend it; and that William the Conqueror was an usurper is a fact not to be contradicted. The plain truth is, that the antiquity of English monarchy will not bear looking into.

But it is not so much the absurdity as the evil of hereditary succession which concerns mankind. Did it ensure a race of good and wise men it would have the seal of divine authority, but as it opens a door to the *foolish*, the *wicked*, and the *improper*, it hath in it the nature of oppression. Men who look upon themselves born to reign, and others to obey, soon grow insolent; selected from the rest of mankind their minds are early poisoned by importance; and the world they act in differs so materially from the world at large, that they have but little opportunity of knowing its true interests, and when they succeed to the government are frequently the most ignorant and unfit of any throughout the dominions.

Another evil which attends hereditary succession is, that the throne is subject to be possessed by a minor at any age; all which time the regency, acting under the cover of a king, have every opportunity and inducement to betray their trust. The same national misfortune happens, when a king worn out with age and infirmity, enters the last stage of human weakness. In both these cases the public becomes a prey to every miscreant, who can tamper successfully with the follies either of age or infancy.

The most plausible plea, which hath ever been offered in favour of hereditary succession, is, that it preserves a nation from civil wars; and were this true, it would be weighty; whereas, it is the most barefaced falsity ever imposed upon mankind. The whole history of England disowns the fact. Thirty kings and two minors have reigned in that distracted kingdom since the conquest, in which time there have been (including the Revolution) no less than eight civil wars and nineteen rebellions. Wherefore instead of making for peace, it makes against it, and destroys the very foundation it seems to stand on.

The contest for monarchy and succession, between the houses of York and Lancaster, laid England in a scene of blood for many years. Twelve pitched battles, besides skirmishes and sieges, were fought between Henry and Edward. Twice was Henry prisoner to Edward, who in his turn was prisoner to Henry. And so uncertain is the fate of war and the temper of a nation, when nothing but personal matters are the ground of a quarrel, that Henry was taken in triumph from a prison to a palace, and Edward obliged to fly from a palace to a foreign land; yet, as sudden transitions of temper are seldom lasting, Henry in his turn was driven from the throne, and Edward recalled to succeed him. The parliament always following the strongest side.

This contest began in the reign of Henry the Sixth, and was not entirely extinguished till Henry the Seventh, in whom the families were united. Including a period of 67 years, viz. from 1422 to 1489.

In short, monarchy and succession have laid (not this or that kingdom only) but the world in blood and ashes. 'Tis a form of government which the word of God bears testimony against, and blood will attend it.

If we inquire into the business of a king, we shall find that in some countries they have none; and after sauntering away their lives without pleasure to themselves or advantage to the nation, withdraw from the scene, and leave their successors to tread the same idle round. In absolute monarchies the whole weight of business, civil and military, lies on the king; the children of Israel in their request for a king, urged this plea "that he may judge us, and go out before us and fight our battles." But in countries where he is neither a judge nor a general, as in England, a man would be puzzled to know what *is* his business.

The nearer any government approaches to a republic the less business there is for a king. It is somewhat difficult to find a proper name for the government of England. Sir William Meredith calls it a republic; but in its present state it is unworthy of the name, because the corrupt influence of the crown, by having all the places in its disposal, hath so effectually swallowed up the power, and eaten out the virtue of the house of commons (the republican part in the constitution) that the government of England is nearly as monarchical as that of France or Spain. Men fall out with names without understanding them. For it is the republican and not the monarchical part of the constitution of England which Englishmen glory in, viz. the liberty of choosing an house of commons from out of their own body—and it is easy to see that when republican virtue fails, slavery ensues. Why is the constitution of England sickly, but because monarchy hath poisoned the republic, the crown hath engrossed the commons?

In England a king hath little more to do than to make war and give away places; which in plain terms, is to impoverish the nation and set it together by the ears. A pretty business indeed for a man to be allowed eight hundred thousand sterling a year for, and worshipped into the bargain! Of more worth is one honest man to society and in the sight of God, than all the crowned ruffians that ever lived.

THOUGHTS ON THE PRESENT STATE OF AMERICAN AFFAIRS.

IN the following pages I offer nothing more than simple facts, plain arguments, and common sense; and have no other preliminaries to settle with the reader, than that he will divest himself of prejudice and prepossession, and suffer his reason and his feelings to determine for themselves; that he will put *on*, or rather that he will not put *off*, the true character of a man, and generously enlarge his views beyond the present day.

Volumes have been written on the subject of the struggle between England and America. Men of all ranks have embarked in the controversy, from different motives, and with various designs; but all have been ineffectual, and the period of debate is closed. Arms, as the last resource, decide the contest; the appeal was the choice of the king, and the continent hath accepted the challenge.

It hath been reported of the late Mr. Pelham (who tho' an

able minister was not without his faults) that on his being attacked in the house of commons, on the score, that his measures were only of a temporary kind, replied *"they will last my time."* Should a thought so fatal and unmanly possess the colonies in the present contest, the name of ancestors will be remembered by future generations with detestation.

The sun never shined on a cause of greater worth. 'Tis not the affair of a city, a country, a province, or a kingdom, but of a continent—of at least one eighth part of the habitable globe. 'Tis not the concern of a day, a year, or an age; posterity are virtually involved in the contest, and will be more or less affected, even to the end of time, by the proceedings now. Now is the seed time of continental union, faith and honor. The least fracture now will be like a name engraved with the point of a pin on the tender rind of a young oak; the wound will enlarge with the tree, and posterity read it in full grown characters.

By referring the matter from argument to arms, a new æra for politics is struck; a new method of thinking hath arisen. All plans, proposals, &c. prior to the nineteenth of April, *i. e.* to the commencement of hostilities, are like the almanacks of the last year; which, though proper then, are superceded and useless now. Whatever was advanced by the advocates on either side of the question then, terminated in one and the same point, viz. a union with Great-Britain; the only difference between the parties was the method of effecting it; the one proposing force, the other friendship; but it hath so far happened that the first hath failed, and the second hath withdrawn her influence.

As much hath been said of the advantages of reconciliation, which, like an agreeable dream, hath passed away and left us as we were, it is but right, that we should examine the contrary side of the argument, and inquire into some of the many material injuries which these colonies sustain, and always will sustain, by being connected with, and dependant on Great-Britain. To examine that connexion and dependance, on the principles of nature and common sense, to see what we have to trust to, if separated, and what we are to expect, if dependant.

I have heard it asserted by some, that as America hath

flourished under her former connexion with Great-Britain, that the same connexion is necessary towards her future happiness, and will always have the same effect. Nothing can be more fallacious than this kind of argument. We may as well assert that because a child has thrived upon milk, that it is never to have meat, or that the first twenty years of our lives is to become a precedent for the next twenty. But even this is admitting more than is true, for I answer roundly, that America would have flourished as much, and probably much more, had no European power had any thing to do with her. The commerce, by which she hath enriched herself are the necessaries of life, and will always have a market while eating is the custom of Europe.

But she has protected us, say some. That she hath engrossed us is true, and defended the continent at our expence as well as her own is admitted, and she would have defended Turkey from the same motive, viz. the sake of trade and dominion.

Alas, we have been long led away by ancient prejudices, and made large sacrifices to superstition. We have boasted the protection of Great-Britain, without considering, that her motive was *interest* not *attachment*; that she did not protect us from *our enemies* on *our account*, but from *her enemies* on *her own account*, from those who had no quarrel with us on any *other account*, and who will always be our enemies on the *same account*. Let Britain wave her pretensions to the continent, or the continent throw off the dependance, and we should be at peace with France and Spain were they at war with Britain. The miseries of Hanover last war ought to warn us against connexions.

It hath lately been asserted in parliament, that the colonies have no relation to each other but through the parent country, *i. e.* that Pennsylvania and the Jerseys, and so on for the rest, are sister colonies by the way of England; this is certainly a very round-about way of proving relationship, but it is the nearest and only true way of proving enemyship, if I may so call it. France and Spain never were, nor perhaps ever will be our enemies as *Americans*, but as our being the *subjects of Great-Britain*.

But Britain is the parent country, say some. Then the more

shame upon her conduct. Even brutes do not devour their young, nor savages make war upon their families; wherefore the assertion, if true, turns to her reproach; but it happens not to be true, or only partly so, and the phrase *parent* or *mother country* hath been jesuitically adopted by the king and his parasites, with a low papistical design of gaining an unfair bias on the credulous weakness of our minds. Europe, and not England, is the parent country of America. This new world hath been the asylum for the persecuted lovers of civil and religious liberty from *every part* of Europe. Hither have they fled, not from the tender embraces of the mother, but from the cruelty of the monster; and it is so far true of England, that the same tyranny which drove the first emigrants from home, pursues their descendants still.

In this extensive quarter of the globe, we forget the narrow limits of three hundred and sixty miles (the extent of England) and carry our friendship on a larger scale; we claim brotherhood with every European christian, and triumph in the generosity of the sentiment.

It is pleasant to observe by what regular gradations we surmount the force of local prejudice, as we enlarge our acquaintance with the world. A man born in any town in England divided into parishes, will naturally associate most with his fellow parishioners (because their interests in many cases will be common) and distinguish him by the name of *neighbour*; if he meet him but a few miles from home, he drops the narrow idea of a street, and salutes him by the name of *townsman*; if he travel out of the county, and meet him in any other, he forgets the minor divisions of street and town, and calls him *countryman*, i. e. *county-man*; but if in their foreign excursions they should associate in France or any other part of *Europe*, their local remembrance would be enlarged into that of *Englishmen*. And by a just parity of reasoning, all Europeans meeting in America, or any other quarter of the globe, are *countrymen*; for England, Holland, Germany, or Sweden, when compared with the whole, stand in the same places on the larger scale, which the divisions of street, town, and county do on the smaller ones; distinctions too limited for continental minds. Not one third of the inhabitants, even of this province, are of English descent. Wherefore I reprobate the phrase of parent or mother country applied to England only, as being false, selfish, narrow and ungenerous.

But admitting, that we were all of English descent, what does it amount to? Nothing. Britain, being now an open enemy, extinguishes every other name and title: And to say that reconciliation is our duty, is truly farcical. The first king of England, of the present line (William the Conqueror) was a Frenchman, and half the Peers of England are descendants from the same country; wherefore, by the same method of reasoning, England ought to be governed by France.

Much hath been said of the united strength of Britain and the colonies, that in conjunction they might bid defiance to the world. But this is mere presumption; the fate of war is uncertain, neither do the expressions mean any thing; for this continent would never suffer itself to be drained of inhabitants, to support the British arms in either Asia, Africa, or Europe.

Besides, what have we to do with setting the world at defiance? Our plan is commerce, and that, well attended to, will secure us the peace and friendship of all Europe; because, it is the interest of all Europe to have America a *free port*. Her trade will always be a protection, and her barrenness of gold and silver secure her from invaders.

I challenge the warmest advocate for reconciliation, to shew, a single advantage that this continent can reap, by being connected with Great Britain. I repeat the challenge, not a single advantage is derived. Our corn will fetch its price in any market in Europe, and our imported goods must be paid for buy them where we will.

But the injuries and disadvantages we sustain by that connection, are without number; and our duty to mankind at large, as well as to ourselves, instruct us to renounce the alliance: Because, any submission to, or dependance on Great-Britain, tends directly to involve this continent in European wars and quarrels; and sets us at variance with nations, who would otherwise seek our friendship, and against whom, we have neither anger nor complaint. As Europe is our market for trade, we ought to form no partial connection with any part of it. It is the true interest of America to steer clear of European contentions, which she never can do, while by her dependance on Britain, she is made the make-weight in the scale of British politics.

Europe is too thickly planted with kingdoms to be long at peace, and whenever a war breaks out between England and any foreign power, the trade of America goes to ruin, *because of her connection with Britain*. The next war may not turn out like the last, and should it not, the advocates for reconciliation now will be wishing for separation then, because, neutrality in that case, would be a safer convoy than a man of war. Every thing that is right or natural pleads for separation. The blood of the slain, the weeping voice of nature cries, 'TIS TIME TO PART. Even the distance at which the Almighty hath placed England and America, is a strong and natural proof, that the authority of the one, over the other, was never the design of Heaven. The time likewise at which the continent was discovered, adds weight to the argument, and the manner in which it was peopled encreases the force of it. The reformation was preceded by the discovery of America, as if the Almighty graciously meant to open a sanctuary to the persecuted in future years, when home should afford neither friendship nor safety.

The authority of Great-Britain over this continent, is a form of government, which sooner or later must have an end: And a serious mind can draw no true pleasure by looking forward, under the painful and positive conviction, that what he calls "the present constitution" is merely temporary. As parents, we can have no joy, knowing that *this government* is not sufficiently lasting to ensure any thing which we may bequeath to posterity: And by a plain method of argument, as we are running the next generation into debt, we ought to do the work of it, otherwise we use them meanly and pitifully. In order to discover the line of our duty rightly, we should take our children in our hand, and fix our station a few years farther into life; that eminence will present a prospect, which a few present fears and prejudices conceal from our sight.

Though I would carefully avoid giving unnecessary offence, yet I am inclined to believe, that all those who espouse the doctrine of reconciliation, may be included within the following descriptions. Interested men, who are not to be trusted;

weak men, who *cannot* see; prejudiced men, who *will not* see; and a certain set of moderate men, who think better of the European world than it deserves; and this last class, by an ill-judged deliberation, will be the cause of more calamities to this continent, than all the other three.

It is the good fortune of many to live distant from the scene of sorrow; the evil is not sufficiently brought to *their* doors to make *them* feel the precariousness with which all American property is possessed. But let our imaginations transport us for a few moments to Boston, that seat of wretchedness will teach us wisdom, and instruct us for ever to renounce a power in whom we can have no trust. The inhabitants of that unfortunate city, who but a few months ago were in ease and affluence, have now, no other alternative than to stay and starve, or turn out to beg. Endangered by the fire of their friends if they continue within the city, and plundered by the soldiery if they leave it. In their present condition they are prisoners without the hope of redemption, and in a general attack for their relief, they would be exposed to the fury of both armies.

Men of passive tempers look somewhat lightly over the offences of Britain, and, still hoping for the best, are apt to call out, *"Come, come, we shall be friends again, for all this."* But examine the passions and feelings of mankind, Bring the doctrine of reconciliation to the touchstone of nature, and then tell me, whether you can hereafter love, honour, and faithfully serve the power that hath carried fire and sword into your land? If you cannot do all these, then are you only deceiving yourselves, and by your delay bringing ruin upon posterity. Your future connection with Britain, whom you can neither love nor honour, will be forced and unnatural, and being formed only on the plan of present convenience, will in a little time fall into a relapse more wretched than the first. But if you say, you can still pass the violations over, then I ask, Hath your house been burnt? Hath your property been destroyed before your face? Are your wife and children destitute of a bed to lie on, or bread to live on? Have you lost a parent or a child by their hands, and yourself the ruined and wretched survivor? If you have not, then are you not a judge of those who have. But if you have, and still can shake hands with the murderers, then are you unworthy the name of husband, father, friend, or lover, and whatever may be your rank or title in life, you have the heart of a coward, and the spirit of a sycophant.

This is not inflaming or exaggerating matters, but trying them by those feelings and affections which nature justifies, and without which, we should be incapable of discharging the social duties of life, or enjoying the felicities of it. I mean not to exhibit horror for the purpose of provoking revenge, but to awaken us from fatal and unmanly slumbers, that we may pursue determinately some fixed object. It is not in the power of Britain or of Europe to conquer America, if she do not conquer herself by *delay* and *timidity*. The present winter is worth an age if rightly employed, but if lost or neglected, the whole continent will partake of the misfortune; and there is no punishment which that man will not deserve, be he who, or what, or where he will, that may be the means of sacrificing a season so precious and useful.

It is repugnant to reason, to the universal order of things to all examples from former ages, to suppose, that this continent can longer remain subject to any external power. The most sanguine in Britain does not think so. The utmost stretch of human wisdom cannot, at this time, compass a plan short of separation, which can promise the continent even a year's security. Reconciliation is *now* a falacious dream. Nature hath deserted the connexion, and Art cannot supply her place. For, as Milton wisely expresses, "never can true reconcilement grow where wounds of deadly hate have pierced so deep."

Every quiet method for peace hath been ineffectual. Our prayers have been rejected with disdain; and only tended to convince us, that nothing flatters vanity, or confirms obstinacy in Kings more than repeated petitioning—and nothing hath contributed more than that very measure to make the Kings of Europe absolute: Witness Denmark and Sweden. Wherefore, since nothing but blows will do, for God's sake, let us come to a final separation, and not leave the next generation to be cutting throats, under the violated unmeaning names of parent and child.

To say, they will never attempt it again is idle and visionary, we thought so at the repeal of the stamp-act, yet a year or two undeceived us; as well may we suppose that nations, which have been once defeated, will never renew the quarrel.

As to government matters, it is not in the power of Britain to do this continent justice: The business of it will soon be too weighty, and intricate, to be managed with any tolerable degree of convenience, by a power, so distant from us, and so very ignorant of us; for if they cannot conquer us, they cannot govern us. To be always running three or four thousand miles with a tale or a petition, waiting four or five months for an answer, which when obtained requires five or six more to explain it in, will in a few years be looked upon as folly and childishness—There was a time when it was proper, and there is a proper time for it to cease.

Small islands not capable of protecting themselves, are the proper objects for kingdoms to take under their care; but there is something very absurd, in supposing a continent to be perpetually governed by an island. In no instance hath nature made the satellite larger than its primary planet, and as England and America, with respect to each other, reverses the common order of nature, it is evident they belong to different systems: England to Europe, America to itself.

I am not induced by motives of pride, party, or resentment to espouse the doctrine of separation and independance; I am clearly, positively, and conscientiously persuaded that it is the true interest of this continent to be so; that every thing short of *that* is mere patchwork, that it can afford no lasting felicity, —that it is leaving the sword to our children, and shrinking back at a time, when, a little more, a little farther, would have rendered this continent the glory of the earth.

As Britain hath not manifested the least inclination towards a compromise, we may be assured that no terms can be obtained worthy the acceptance of the continent, or any ways equal to the expence of blood and treasure we have been already put to.

The object, contended for, ought always to bear some just proportion to the expence. The removal of North, or the whole detestable junto, is a matter unworthy the millions we have expended. A temporary stoppage of trade, was an inconvenience, which would have sufficiently ballanced the repeal of all the acts complained of, had such repeals been obtained; but if the whole continent must take up arms, if every man must be a soldier, it is scarcely worth our while to fight against a contemptible ministry only. Dearly, dearly, do we pay for the repeal of the acts, if that is all we fight for; for in a just estimation, it is as great a folly to pay a Bunker-hill price for law, as for land. As I have always considered the independancy of this continent, as an event, which sooner or later must arrive, so from the late rapid progress of the continent to maturity, the event could not be far off. Wherefore, on the breaking out of hostilities, it was not worth the while to have disputed a matter, which time would have finally redressed, unless we meant to be in earnest; otherwise, it is like wasting an estate on a suit at law, to regulate the trespasses of a tenant, whose lease is just expiring. No man was a warmer wisher for reconciliation than myself, before the fatal nineteenth of April 1775*, but the moment the event of that day was made known, I rejected the hardened, sullen tempered Pharoah of England for ever; and disdain the wretch, that with the pretended title of FATHER OF HIS PEOPLE can unfeelingly hear of their slaughter, and composedly sleep with their blood upon his soul.

But admitting that matters were now made up, what would be the event? I answer, the ruin of the continent. And that for several reasons.

First. The powers of governing still remaining in the hands of the king, he will have a negative over the whole legislation of this continent. And as he hath shewn himself such an inveterate enemy to liberty, and discovered such a thirst for arbitrary power; is he, or is he not, a proper man to say to these colonies, *"You shall make no laws but what I please."* And is there any inhabitant in America so ignorant, as not to know, that according to what is called the *present constitution*, that this continent can make no laws but what the king gives leave to; and is there any man so unwise, as not to see, that (considering what has happened) he will suffer no law to be made

*Massacre at Lexington.

here, but such as suit *his* purpose. We may be as effectually enslaved by the want of laws in America, as by submitting to laws made for us in England. After matters are made up (as it is called) can there be any doubt, but the whole power of the crown will be exerted, to keep this continent as low and humble as possible? Instead of going forward we shall go backward, or be perpetually quarrelling or ridiculously petitioning.—We are already greater than the king wishes us to be, and will he not hereafter endeavour to make us less? To bring the matter to one point. Is the power who is jealous of our prosperity, a proper power to govern us? Whoever says *No* to this question is an *independant*, for independancy means no more, than, whether we shall make our own laws, or, whether the king, the greatest enemy this continent hath, or can have, shall tell us *"there shall be no laws but such as I like."*

But the king you will say has a negative in England; the people there can make no laws without his consent. In point of right and good order, there is something very ridiculous, that a youth of twenty-one (which hath often happened) shall say to several millions of people, older and wiser than himself, I forbid this or that act of yours to be law. But in this place I decline this sort of reply, though I will never cease to expose the absurdity of it, and only answer, that England being the King's residence, and America not so, makes quite another case. The king's negative *here* is ten times more dangerous and fatal than it can be in England, for *there* he will scarcely refuse his consent to a bill for putting England into as strong a state of defence as possible, and in America he would never suffer such a bill to be passed.

America is only a secondary object in the system of British politics, England consults the good of *this* country, no farther than it answers her *own* purpose. Wherefore, her own interest leads her to suppress the growth of *ours* in every case which doth not promote her advantage, or in the least interferes with it. A pretty state we should soon be in under such a second-hand government, considering what has happened! Men do not change from enemies to friends by the alteration of a name: And in order to shew that reconciliation *now* is a dangerous doctrine, I affirm, *that it would be policy in the king at this time, to repeal the acts for the sake of reinstating himself in the government of the provinces;* in order, that HE MAY AC-COMPLISH BY CRAFT AND SUBTILTY, IN THE LONG RUN, WHAT HE CANNOT DO BY FORCE AND VIOLENCE IN THE SHORT ONE. Reconciliation and ruin are nearly related.

Secondly. That as even the best terms, which we can expect to obtain, can amount to no more than a temporary expedi-ent, or a kind of government by guardianship, which can last no longer than till the colonies come of age, so the general face and state of things, in the interim, will be unsettled and unpromising. Emigrants of property will not choose to come to a country whose form of government hangs but by a thread, and who is every day tottering on the brink of com-motion and disturbance; and numbers of the present inhabit-ants would lay hold of the interval, to dispose of their effects, and quit the continent.

But the most powerful of all arguments, is, that nothing but independance, i. e. a continental form of government, can keep the peace of the continent and preserve it inviolate from civil wars. I dread the event of a reconciliation with Britain now, as it is more than probable, that it will be followed by a revolt somewhere or other, the consequences of which may be far more fatal than all the malice of Britain.

Thousands are already ruined by British barbarity; (thou-sands more will probably suffer the same fate) Those men have other feelings than us who have nothing suffered. All they *now* possess is liberty, what they before enjoyed is sacri-ficed to its service, and having nothing more to lose, they disdain submission. Besides, the general temper of the colo-nies, towards a British government, will be like that of a youth, who is nearly out of his time; they will care very little about her. And a government which cannot preserve the peace, is no government at all, and in that case we pay our money for nothing; and pray what is it that Britain can do, whose power will be wholly on paper, should a civil tumult break out the very day after reconciliation? I have heard some men say, many of whom I believe spoke without thinking, that they dreaded an independance, fearing that it would pro-duce civil wars. It is but seldom that our first thoughts are truly correct, and that is the case here; for there are ten times more to dread from a patched up connexion than from independance. I make the sufferers case my own, and I protest, that were I driven from house and home, my property destroyed, and my circumstances ruined, that as a man, sensible of injuries, I could never relish the doctrine of reconciliation, or consider myself bound thereby.

The colonies have manifested such a spirit of good order and obedience to continental government, as is sufficient to make every reasonable person easy and happy on that head. No man can assign the least pretence for his fears, on any other grounds, than such as are truly childish and ridiculous, viz. that one colony will be striving for superiority over another.

Where there are no distinctions there can be no superiority, perfect equality affords no temptation. The republics of Europe are all (and we may say always) in peace. Holland and Swisserland are without wars, foreign or domestic: Monarchical governments, it is true, are never long at rest; the crown itself is a temptation to enterprizing ruffians at *home*; and that degree of pride and insolence ever attendant on regal authority, swells into a rupture with foreign powers, in instances, where a republican government, by being formed on more natural principles, would negociate the mistake.

If there is any true cause of fear respecting independance, it is because no plan is yet laid down. Men do not see their way out—Wherefore, as an opening into that business, I offer the following hints; at the same time modestly affirming, that I have no other opinion of them myself, than that they may be the means of giving rise to something better. Could the straggling thoughts of individuals be collected, they would frequently form materials for wise and able men to improve into useful matter.

Let the assemblies be annual, with a President only. The representation more equal. Their business wholly domestic, and subject to the authority of a Continental Congress.

Let each colony be divided into six, eight, or ten, convenient districts, each district to send a proper number of delegates to Congress, so that each colony send at least thirty. The whole number in Congress will be least 390. Each Congress to sit   and to choose a president by the following method. When the delegates are met, let a colony be taken from the whole thirteen colonies by lot, after which, let the whole Congress choose (by ballot) a president from out of the delegates of *that* province. In the next Congress, let a colony be taken by lot from twelve only, omitting that colony from which the president was taken in the former Congress, and so proceeding on till the whole thirteen shall have had their proper rotation. And in order that nothing may pass into a law but what is satisfactorily just, not less than three fifths of the Congress to be called a majority. — He that will promote discord, under a government so equally formed as this, would have joined Lucifer in his revolt.

But as there is a peculiar delicacy, from whom, or in what manner, this business must first arise, and as it seems most agreeable and consistent that it should come from some intermediate body between the governed and the governors, that is, between the Congress and the people, let a CONTINENTAL CONFERENCE be held, in the following manner, and for the following purpose.

A committee of twenty-six members of Congress, viz. two for each colony. Two members from each House of Assembly, or Provincial Convention; and five representatives of the people at large, to be chosen in the capital city or town of each province, for, and in behalf of the whole province, by as many qualified voters as shall think proper to attend from all parts of the province for that purpose; or, if more convenient, the representatives may be chosen in two or three of the most populous parts thereof. In this conference, thus assembled, will be united, the two grand principles of business, *knowledge* and *power*. The members of Congress, Assemblies, or Conventions, by having had experience in national concerns, will be able and useful counsellors, and the whole, being impowered by the people, will have a truly legal authority.

The conferring members being met, let their business be to frame a CONTINENTAL CHARTER, or Charter of the United Colonies; (answering to what is called the Magna Charta of England) fixing the number and manner of choosing members of Congress, members of Assembly, with their date of sitting, and drawing the line of business and jurisdiction between them: (Always remembering, that our strength is continental, not provincial:) Securing freedom and property to all men, and above all things, the free exercise of religion, according to the dictates of conscience; with such other matter as is necessary for a charter to contain. Immediately after which, the said Conference to dissolve, and the bodies which shall be chosen comformable to the said charter, to be the legislators and governors of this continent for the time being: Whose peace and happiness, may God preserve, Amen.

Should any body of men be hereafter delegated for this or some similar purpose, I offer them the following extracts from that wise observer on governments *Dragonetti*. "The science" says he "of the politician consists in fixing the true point of happiness and freedom. Those men would deserve the gratitude of ages, who should discover a mode of government that contained the greatest sum of individual happiness, with the least national expense.

Dragonetti on virtue and rewards."

But where says some is the King of America? I'll tell you Friend, he reigns above, and doth not make havoc of mankind like the Royal Brute of Britain. Yet that we may not appear to be defective even in earthly honors, let a day be solemnly set apart for proclaiming the charter; let it be brought forth placed on the divine law, the word of God; let a crown be placed thereon, by which the world may know, that so far as we approve of monarchy, that in America THE LAW IS KING. For as in absolute governments the King is law, so in free countries the law *ought* to be King; and there ought to be no other. But lest any ill use should afterwards arise, let the crown at the conclusion of the ceremony be demolished, and scattered among the people whose right it is.

A government of our own is our natural right: And when a man seriously reflects on the precariousness of human affairs, he will become convinced, that it is infinitely wiser and safer, to form a constitution of our own in a cool deliberate manner, while we have it in our power, than to trust such an interesting event to time and chance. If we omit it now,

some * Massanello may hereafter arise, who laying hold of
popular disquietudes, may collect together the desperate and
the discontented, and by assuming to themselves the powers
of government, may sweep away the liberties of the continent
like a deluge. Should the government of America return again
into the hands of Britain, the tottering situation of things, will
be a temptation for some desperate adventurer to try his fortune; and in such a case, what relief can Britain give? Ere she
could hear the news, the fatal business might be done; and
ourselves suffering like the wretched Britons under the oppression of the Conqueror. Ye that oppose independance
now, ye know not what ye do; ye are opening a door to eternal tyranny, by keeping vacant the seat of government. There
are thousands, and tens of thousands, who would think it
glorious to expel from the continent, that barbarous and
hellish power, which hath stirred up the Indians and Negroes
to destroy us, the cruelty hath a double guilt, it is dealing
brutally by us, and treacherously by them.

To talk of friendship with those in whom our reason forbids
us to have faith, and our affections wounded through a thousand pores instruct us to detest, is madness and folly. Every
day wears out the little remains of kindred between us and
them, and can there be any reason to hope, that as the relationship expires, the affection will increase, or that we shall
agree better, when we have ten times more and greater concerns to quarrel over than ever?

Ye that tell us of harmony and reconciliation, can ye restore
to us the time that is past? Can ye give to prostitution its
former innocence? Neither can ye reconcile Britain and
America. The last cord now is broken, the people of England
are presenting addresses against us. There are injuries which
nature cannot forgive; she would cease to be nature if she did.
As well can the lover forgive the ravisher of his mistress, as the
continent forgive the murders of Britain. The Almighty hath
implanted in us these unextinguishable feelings for good and

*Thomas Anello, otherwise Massanello, a fisherman of Naples, who after
spiriting up his countrymen in the public market place, against the oppression
of the Spaniards, to whom the place was then subject, prompted them to
revolt, and in the space of a day became king.

wise purposes. They are the guardians of his image in our hearts. They distinguish us from the herd of common animals. The social compact would dissolve, and justice be extirpated from the earth, or have only a casual existence were we callous to the touches of affection. The robber, and the murderer, would often escape unpunished, did not the injuries which our tempers sustain, provoke us into justice.

O ye that love mankind! Ye that dare oppose, not only the tyranny, but the tyrant, stand forth! Every spot of the old world is overrun with oppression. Freedom hath been hunted round the globe. Asia, and Africa, have long expelled her.— Europe regards her like a stranger, and England hath given her warning to depart. O! receive the fugitive, and prepare in time an asylum for mankind.

OF THE PRESENT ABILITY OF AMERICA, WITH SOME MISCELLANEOUS REFLEXIONS.

I HAVE never met with a man, either in England or America, who hath not confessed his opinion, that a separation between the countries, would take place one time or other: And there is no instance, in which we have shewn less judgment, than in endeavouring to describe, what we call, the ripeness or fitness of the Continent for independance.

As all men allow the measure, and vary only in their opinion of the time, let us, in order to remove mistakes, take a general survey of things, and endeavour, if possible, to find out the *very* time. But we need not go far, the inquiry ceases at once, for, the *time hath found us.* The general concurrence, the glorious union of all things prove the fact.

It is not in numbers, but in unity, that our great strength lies; yet our present numbers are sufficient to repel the force of all the world. The Continent hath, at this time, the largest body of armed and disciplined men of any power under Heaven; and is just arrived at that pitch of strength, in which, no single colony is able to support itself, and the whole, when united, can accomplish the matter, and either more, or, less than this, might be fatal in its effects. Our land force is already sufficient, and as to naval affairs, we cannot be insensible, that Britain would never suffer an American man of war to be built, while the continent remained in her hands. Wherefore, we should be no forwarder an hundred years hence in that branch, than we are now; but the truth is, we should be less so, because the timber of the country is every day diminishing, and that, which will remain at last, will be far off and difficult to procure.

Were the continent crowded with inhabitants, her sufferings under the present circumstances would be intolerable. The more sea port towns we had, the more should we have both to defend and to loose. Our present numbers are so happily proportioned to our wants, that no man need be idle. The diminution of trade affords an army, and the necessities of an army create a new trade.

Debts we have none; and whatever we may contract on this account will serve as a glorious memento of our virtue. Can we but leave posterity with a settled form of government, an independant constitution of it's own, the purchase at any price will be cheap. But to expend millions for the sake of getting a few vile acts repealed, and routing the present ministry only, is unworthy the charge, and is using posterity with the utmost cruelty; because it is leaving them the great work to do, and a debt upon their backs, from which, they derive no advantage. Such a thought is unworthy a man of honor, and is the true characteristic of a narrow heart and a pedling politician.

The debt we may contract doth not deserve our regard if the work be but accomplished. No nation ought to be without a debt. A national debt is a national bond; and when it bears no interest, is in no case a grievance. Britain is oppressed with a debt of upwards of one hundred and forty millions sterling, for which she pays upwards of four millions interest. And as a compensation for her debt, she has a large navy; America is without a debt, and without a navy; yet for the twentieth part of the English national debt, could have a navy as large again. The navy of England is not worth, at this time, more than three millions and an half sterling.

The first and second editions of this pamphlet were published without the following calculations, which are now given as a proof that the above estimation of the navy is a just one. *See Entic's naval history, intro.* page 56.

The charge of building a ship of each rate, and furnishing

her with masts, yards, sails and rigging, together with a proportion of eight months boatswain's and carpenter's sea-
stores, as calculated by Mr. Burchett, Secretary to the navy.

		£.
For a ship of a 100 guns	. . . .	35,553
90	. . . .	29,886
80	. . . .	23,638
70	. . . .	17,785
60	. . . .	14,197
50	. . . .	10,606
40	. . . .	7,558
30	. . . .	5,846
20	. . . .	3,710

And from hence it is easy to sum up the value, or cost
rather, of the whole British navy, which in the year 1757, when
it was at its greatest glory consisted of the following ships and
guns.

Ships.	Guns.	Cost of one.	Cost of all.
6 100	. . . .	35,553 *l.*	. . . . 213,318 *l.*
12 90	. . . .	29,886	 358,632
12 80	. . . .	23,638	 283,656
43 70	. . . .	17,785	 764,755
35 60	. . . .	14,197	 496,895
40 50	. . . .	10,606	. . . 424,240
45 40	. . . .	7,558	 340,110
58 20	. . . .	3,710	 215,180
85 Sloops, bombs, and fireships, one with another, at		2,000	 170,000

Cost 3,266,786

Remains for guns 233,214

3,500,000

No country on the globe is so happily situated, or so internally capable of raising a fleet as America. Tar, timber, iron,
and cordage are her natural produce. We need go abroad for
nothing. Whereas the Dutch, who make large profits by

hiring out their ships of war to the Spaniards and Portuguese, are obliged to import most of the materials they use. We ought to view the building a fleet as an article of commerce, it being the natural manufactory of this country. It is the best money we can lay out. A navy when finished is worth more than it cost. And is that nice point in national policy, in which commerce and protection are united. Let us build; if we want them not, we can sell; and by that means replace our paper currency with ready gold and silver.

In point of manning a fleet, people in general run into great errors; it is not necessary that one fourth part should be sailors. The Terrible privateer, Captain Death, stood the hottest engagement of any ship last war, yet had not twenty sailors on board, though her complement of men was upwards of two hundred. A few able and social sailors will soon instruct a sufficient number of active landmen in the common work of a ship. Wherefore, we never can be more capable to begin on maritime matters than now, while our timber is standing, our fisheries blocked up, and our sailors and shipwrights out of employ. Men of war, of seventy and eighty guns were built forty years ago in New-England, and why not the same now? Ship-building is America's greatest pride, and in which, she will in time excel the whole world. The great empires of the east are mostly inland, and consequently excluded from the possibility of rivalling her. Africa is in a state of barbarism; and no power in Europe, hath either such an extent of coast, or such an internal supply of materials. Where nature hath given the one, she has withheld the other; to America only hath she been liberal of both. The vast empire of Russia is almost shut out from the sea; wherefore, her boundless forests, her tar, iron, and cordage are only articles of commerce.

In point of safety, ought we to be without a fleet? We are not the little people now, which we were sixty years ago; at that time we might have trusted our property in the streets, or fields rather; and slept securely without locks or bolts to our doors or windows. The case now is altered, and our methods of defence, ought to improve with our increase of property. A common pirate, twelve months ago, might have come up the Delaware, and laid the city of Philadelphia under instant contribution, for what sum he pleased; and the same might have happened to other places. Nay, any daring fellow, in a brig of fourteen or sixteen guns, might have robbed the whole Continent, and carried off half a million of money. These are circumstances which demand our attention, and point out the necessity of naval protection.

Some, perhaps, will say, that after we have made it up with Britain, she will protect us. Can we be so unwise as to mean, that she shall keep a navy in our harbours for that purpose? Common sense will tell us, that the power which hath endeavoured to subdue us, is of all others, the most improper to defend us. Conquest may be effected under the pretence of friendship; and ourselves, after a long and brave resistance, be at last cheated into slavery. And if her ships are not to be admitted into our harbours, I would ask, how is she to protect us? A navy three or four thousand miles off can be of little use, and on sudden emergencies, none at all. Wherefore, if we must hereafter protect ourselves, why not do it for ourselves? Why do it for another?

The English list of ships of war, is long and formidable, but not a tenth part of them are at any one time fit for service, numbers of them not in being; yet their names are pompously continued in the list, if only a plank be left of the ship: and not a fifth part, of such as are fit for service, can be spared on any one station at one time. The East, and West Indies, Mediterranean, Africa, and other parts over which Britain extends her claim, make large demands upon her navy. From a mixture of prejudice and inattention, we have contracted a false notion respecting the navy of England, and have talked as if we should have the whole of it to encounter at once, and for that reason, supposed, that we must have one as large; which not being instantly practicable, have been made use of by a set of disguised Tories to discourage our beginning thereon. Nothing can be farther from truth than this; for if America had only a twentieth part of the naval force of Britain, she would be by far an over match for her; because, as we neither have, nor claim any foreign dominion, our whole force would be employed on our own coast, where we should, in the long run, have two to one the advantage of those who had three or four thousand miles to sail over, before they could attack us, and the same distance to return in order to refit and recruit.

And although Britain by her fleet, hath a check over our trade to Europe, we have as large a one over her trade to the West-Indies, which, by laying in the neighbourhood of the Continent, is entirely at its mercy.

Some method might be fallen on to keep up a naval force in time of peace, if we should not judge it necessary to support a constant navy. If premiums were to be given to merchants, to build and employ in their service, ships mounted with twenty, thirty, forty, or fifty guns, (the premiums to be in proportion to the loss of bulk to the merchants) fifty or sixty of those ships, with a few guard ships on constant duty, would keep up a sufficient navy, and that without burdening ourselves with the evil so loudly complained of in England, of suffering their fleet, in time of peace to lie rotting in the docks. To unite the sinews of commerce and defence is sound policy; for when our strength and our riches, play into each other's hand, we need fear no external enemy.

In almost every article of defence we abound. Hemp flourishes even to rankness, so that we need not want cordage. Our iron is superior to that of other countries. Our small arms equal to any in the world. Cannon we can cast at pleasure. Saltpetre and gunpowder we are every day producing. Our knowledge is hourly improving. Resolution is our inherent character, and courage hath never yet forsaken us. Wherefore, what is it that we want? Why is it that we hesitate? From Britain we can expect nothing but ruin. If she is once admitted to the government of America again, this Continent will not be worth living in. Jealousies will be always arising; insurrections will be constantly happening; and who will go forth to quell them? Who will venture his life to reduce his own countrymen to a foreign obedience? The difference between Pennsylvania and Connecticut, respecting some unlocated lands, shews the insignificance of a British government, and fully proves, that nothing but Continental authority can regulate Continental matters.

Another reason why the present time is preferable to all others, is, that the fewer our numbers are, the more land there is yet unoccupied, which instead of being lavished by the king on his worthless dependants, may be hereafter applied, not only to the discharge of the present debt, but to the constant support of government. No nation under heaven hath such an advantage as this.

The infant state of the Colonies, as it is called, so far from being against, is an argument in favor of independance. We are sufficiently numerous, and were we more so, we might be less united. It is a matter worthy of observation, that the more a country is peopled, the smaller their armies are. In military numbers, the ancients far exceeded the moderns: and the reason is evident, for trade being the consequence of population, men become too much absorbed thereby to attend to any thing else. Commerce diminishes the spirit, both of patriotism and military defence. And history sufficiently informs us, that the bravest atchievements were always accomplished in the non-age of a nation. With the increase of commerce, England hath lost its spirit. The city of London, notwithstanding its numbers, submits to continued insults with the patience of a coward. The more men have to lose, the less willing are they to venture. The rich are in general slaves to fear, and submit to courtly power with the trembling duplicity of a Spaniel.

Youth is the seed time of good habits, as well in nations as in individuals. It might be difficult, if not impossible, to form the Continent into one government half a century hence. The vast variety of interests, occasioned by an increase of trade and population, would create confusion. Colony would be against colony. Each being able might scorn each other's assistance: and while the proud and foolish gloried in their little distinctions, the wise would lament, that the union had not been formed before. Wherefore, the *present time* is the *true time* for establishing it. The intimacy which is contracted in infancy, and the friendship which is formed in misfortune, are, of all others, the most lasting and unalterable. Our present union is marked with both these characters: we are young, and we have been distressed; but our concord hath withstood our troubles, and fixes a memorable æra for posterity to glory in.

The present time, likewise, is that peculiar time, which never happens to a nation but once, *viz.* the time of forming itself into a government. Most nations have let slip the opportunity, and by that means have been compelled to receive laws from their conquerors, instead of making laws for themselves.

First, they had a king, and then a form of government; whereas, the articles or charter of government, should be formed first, and men delegated to execute them afterward: but from the errors of other nations, let us learn wisdom, and lay hold of the present opportunity — *To begin government at the right end*.

When William the Conqueror subdued England, he gave them law at the point of the sword; and until we consent, that the seat of government, in America, be legally and authoritatively occupied, we shall be in danger of having it filled by some fortunate ruffian, who may treat us in the same manner, and then, where will be our freedom? where our property?

As to religion, I hold it to be the indispensible duty of all government, to protect all conscientious professors thereof, and I know of no other business which government hath to do therewith. Let a man throw aside that narrowness of soul, that selfishness of principle, which the niggards of all professions are so unwilling to part with, and he will be at once delivered of his fears on that head. Suspicion is the companion of mean souls, and the bane of all good society. For myself, I fully and conscientiously believe, that it is the will of the Almighty, that there should be diversity of religious opinions among us: It affords a larger field for our Christian kindness. Were we all of one way of thinking, our religious dispositions would want matter for probation; and on this liberal principle, I look on the various denominations among us, to be like children of the same family, differing only, in what is called, their Christian names.

In page thirty-three, I threw out a few thoughts on the propriety of a Continental Charter, (for I only presume to offer hints, not plans) and in this place, I take the liberty of re-mentioning the subject, by observing, that a charter is to be understood as a bond of solemn obligation, which the whole enters into, to support the right of every separate part, whether of religion, personal freedom, or property. A firm bargain and a right reckoning make long friends.

In a former page I likewise mentioned the necessity of a large and equal representation; and there is no political matter which more deserves our attention. A small number of electors, or a small number of representatives, are equally dangerous. But if the number of the representatives be not only small, but unequal, the danger is increased. As an instance of this, I mention the following; when the Associators petition was before the House of Assembly of Pennsylvania; twenty-eight members only were present, all the Bucks county members, being eight, voted against it, and had seven of the Chester members done the same, this whole province had been governed by two counties only, and this danger it is always exposed to. The unwarrantable stretch likewise, which that house made in their last sitting, to gain an undue authority over the Delegates of that province, ought to warn the people at large, how they trust power out of their own hands. A set of instructions for the Delegates were put together, which in point of sense and business would have dishonored a schoolboy, and after being approved by a *few*, a *very few* without doors, were carried into the House, and there passed *in behalf of the whole colony*, whereas, did the whole colony know, with what ill-will that House hath entered on some necessary public measures, they would not hesitate a moment to think them unworthy of such a trust.

Immediate necessity makes many things convenient, which if continued would grow into oppressions. Expedience and right are different things. When the calamities of America required a consultation, there was no method so ready, or at that time so proper, as to appoint persons from the several Houses of Assembly for that purpose; and the wisdom with which they have proceeded hath preserved this continent from ruin. But as it is more than probable that we shall never be without a CONGRESS, every well wisher to good order, must own, that the mode for choosing members of that body, deserves consideration. And I put it as a question to those, who make a study of mankind, whether *representation and election* is not too great a power for one and the same body of men to possess? When we are planning for posterity, we ought to remember, that virtue is not hereditary.

It is from our enemies that we often gain excellent maxims, and are frequently surprised into reason by their mistakes. Mr. Cornwall (one of the Lords of the Treasury) treated the petition of the New-York Assembly with contempt, because *that*

House, he said, consisted but of twenty-six members, which trifling number, he argued, could not with decency be put for the whole. We thank him for his involuntary honesty.*

To CONCLUDE, however strange it may appear to some, or however unwilling they may be to think so, matters not, but many strong and striking reasons may be given, to shew, that nothing can settle our affairs so expeditiously as an open and determined declaration for independance. Some of which are,

First.—It is the custom of nations, when any two are at war, for some other powers, not engaged in the quarrel, to step in as mediators, and bring about the preliminaries of a peace: but while America calls herself the Subject of Great-Britain, no power, however well disposed she may be, can offer her mediation. Wherefore, in our present state we may quarrel on for ever.

Secondly.—It is unreasonable to suppose, that France or Spain will give us any kind of assistance, if we mean only, to make use of that assistance for the purpose of repairing the breach, and strengthening the connection between Britain and America; because, those powers would be sufferers by the consequences.

Thirdly.—While we profess ourselves the subjects of Britain, we must, in the eye of foreign nations, be considered as rebels. The precedent is somewhat dangerous to *their peace*, for men to be in arms under the name of subjects; we, on the spot, can solve the paradox: but to unite resistance and subjection, requires an idea much too refined for common understanding.

Fourthly.—Were a manifesto to be published, and despatched to foreign courts, setting forth the miseries we have endured, and the peaceable methods we have ineffectually used for redress; declaring, at the same time, that not being able, any longer, to live happily or safely under the cruel disposition of the British court, we had been driven to the necessity of breaking off all connections with her; at the same time, assuring all such courts of our peaceable disposition towards

---

*Those who would fully understand of what great consequence a large and equal representation is to a state, should read Burgh's political Disquisitions.

them, and of our desire of entering into trade with them: Such a memorial would produce more good effects to this Continent, than if a ship were freighted with petitions to Britain.

Under our present denomination of British subjects, we can neither be received nor heard abroad: The custom of all courts is against us, and will be so, until, by an independance, we take rank with other nations.

These proceedings may at first appear strange and difficult; but, like all other steps which we have already passed over, will in a little time become familiar and agreeable; and, until an independance is declared, the Continent will feel itself like a man who continues putting off some unpleasant business from day to day, yet knows it must be done, hates to set about it, wishes it over, and is continually haunted with the thoughts of its necessity.

APPENDIX.

SINCE the publication of the first edition of this pamphlet, or rather, on the same day on which it came out, the King's Speech made its appearance in this city. Had the spirit of prophecy directed the birth of this production, it could not have brought it forth, at a more seasonable juncture, or a more necessary time. The bloody mindedness of the one, shew the necessity of pursuing the doctrine of the other. Men read by way of revenge. And the Speech, instead of terrifying, prepared a way for the manly principles of Independance.

Ceremony, and even, silence, from whatever motive they may arise, have a hurtful tendency, when they give the least degree of countenance to base and wicked performances; wherefore, if this maxim be admitted, it naturally follows, that the King's Speech, as being a piece of finished villany, de-served, and still deserves, a general execration both by the Congress and the people. Yet, as the domestic tranquillity of a nation, depends greatly, on the *chastity* of what may properly be called NATIONAL MANNERS, it is often better, to pass some things over in silent disdain, than to make use of such new methods of dislike, as might introduce the least innovation, on that guardian of our peace and safety. And, perhaps, it is chiefly owing to this prudent delicacy, that the King's Speech, hath not, before now, suffered a public execution. The Speech if it may be called one, is nothing better than a wilful audacious libel against the truth, the common good, and the existence of mankind; and is a formal and pompous method of offering up human sacrifices to the pride of tyrants. But this general massacre of mankind, is one of the privileges, and the certain consequence of Kings; for as nature knows them *not*, they know *not her*, and although they are beings of our *own* creating, they know not *us*, and are become the gods of their creators. The Speech hath one good quality, which is, that it is not calculated to deceive, neither can we, even if we would, be deceived by it. Brutality and tyranny appear on the face of it. It leaves us at no loss: And every line convinces, even in the moment of reading, that He, who hunts the woods for prey, the naked and untutored Indian, is less a Savage than the King of Britain.

Sir John Dalrymple, the putative father of a whining jesuitical piece, fallaciously called, *"The Address of the people of* ENGLAND *to the inhabitants of* AMERICA,*"* hath, perhaps, from a vain supposition, that the people *here* were to be frightened at the pomp and description of a king, given, (though very unwisely on his part) the real character of the present one: "But," says this writer, "if you are inclined to pay compliments to an administration, which we do not complain of," (meaning the Marquis of Rockingham's at the repeal of the Stamp Act) "it is very unfair in you to withhold them from that prince, *by whose* NOD ALONE *they were permitted to do any thing.*" This is toryism with a witness! Here is idolatry even without a mask: And he who can calmly hear, and digest such doctrine, hath forfeited his claim to rationality—an apostate from the order of manhood; and ought to be considered—as one, who hath not only given up the proper dignity of man, but sunk himself beneath the rank of animals, and contemptibly crawls through the world like a worm.

However, it matters very little now, what the king of England either says or does; he hath wickedly broken through every moral and human obligation, trampled nature and conscience beneath his feet; and by a steady and constitutional spirit of insolence and cruelty, procure for himself an universal hatred. It is *now* the interest of America to provide for herself. She hath already a large and young family, whom it is more her duty to take care of, than to be granting away her property, to support a power who is become a reproach to the names of men and christians—YE, whose office it is to watch over the morals of a nation, of whatsoever sect or denomination ye are of, as well as ye, who, are more immediately the guardians of the public liberty, if ye wish to preserve your native country uncontaminated by European corruption, ye must in secret wish a separation—But leaving the moral part to private reflection, I shall chiefly confine my farther remarks to the following heads.

First. That it is the interest of America to be separated from Britain.

Secondly. Which is the easiest and most practicable plan, RECONCILIATION or INDEPENDANCE? with some occasional remarks.

In support of the first, I could, if I judged it proper, produce the opinion of some of the ablest and most experienced men on this continent; and whose sentiments, on that head, are not yet publicly known. It is in reality a self-evident position: For no nation in a state of foreign dependance, limited in its commerce, and cramped and fettered in its legislative powers, can ever arrive at any material eminence. America doth not yet know what opulence is; and although the progress which she hath made stands unparalleled in the history of other nations, it is but childhood, compared with what she would be capable of arriving at, had she, as she ought to have, the legislative powers in her own hands. England is, at this time, proudly coveting what would do her no good, were she to accomplish it; and the Continent hesitating on a matter, which will be her final ruin if neglected. It is the commerce and not the conquest of America, by which England is to be benefited, and that would in a great measure continue, were the countries as independant of each other as France and Spain; because in many articles, neither can go to a better market. But it is the independance of this country of Britain or any other, which is now the main and only object worthy of contention, and which, like all other truths discovered by necessity, will appear clearer and stronger every day.

First. Because it will come to that one time or other.

Secondly. Because, the longer it is delayed the harder it will be to accomplish.

I have frequently amused myself both in public and private companies, with silently remarking, the specious errors of those who speak without reflecting. And among the many which I have heard, the following seems the most general, viz. that had this rupture happened forty or fifty years hence, instead of *now*, the Continent would have been more able to have shaken off the dependance. To which I reply, that our military ability, *at this time*, arises from the experience gained in the last war, and which in forty or fifty years time, would have been totally extinct. The Continent, would not, by that time, have had a General, or even a military officer left; and we, or those who may succeed us, would have been as ignorant of martial matters as the ancient Indians: And this single position, closely attended to, will unanswerably prove, that the present time is preferable to all others. The argument turns thus—at the conclusion of the last war, we had experience, but wanted numbers; and forty or fifty years hence, we should have numbers, without experience; wherefore, the proper point of time, must be some particular point between the two extremes, in which a sufficiency of the former remains, and a proper increase of the latter is obtained: And that point of time is the present time.

The reader will pardon this digression, as it does not properly come under the head I first set out with, and to which I again return by the following position, viz.

Should affairs be patched up with Britain, and she to remain the governing and sovereign power of America, (which, as matters are now circumstanced, is giving up the point intirely) we shall deprive ourselves of the very means of sinking the debt we have, or may contract. The value of the back lands which some of the provinces are clandestinely deprived of, by the unjust extention of the limits of Canada, valued only at five pounds sterling per hundred acres, amount to upwards of twenty-five millions, Pennsylvania currency; and the quit-rents at one penny sterling per acre, to two millions yearly.

It is by the sale of those lands that the debt may be sunk, without burthen to any, and the quit-rent reserved thereon, will always lessen, and in time, will wholly support the yearly expence of government. It matters not how long the debt is in paying, so that the lands when sold be applied to the discharge of it, and for the execution of which, the Congress for the time being, will be the continental trustees.

I proceed now to the second head, viz. Which is the easiest and most practicable plan, RECONCILIATION or INDEPENDANCE; with some occasional remarks.

He who takes nature for his guide is not easily beaten out of his argument, and on that ground, I answer *generally —That* INDEPENDANCE *being a* SINGLE SIMPLE LINE, *contained within ourselves; and reconciliation, a matter exceedingly perplexed and complicated, and in which, a treacherous capricious court is to interfere, gives the answer without a doubt.*

The present state of America is truly alarming to every man who is capable of reflexion. Without law, without government, without any other mode of power than what is founded on, and granted by courtesy. Held together by an unexampled concurrence of sentiment, which, is nevertheless subject to change, and which, every secret enemy is endeavouring to dissolve. Our present condition, is, Legislation without law; wisdom without a plan; constitution without a name; and, what is strangely astonishing, perfect Independance contending for dependance. The instance is without a precedent; the case never existed before; and who can tell what may be the event? The property of no man is secure in the present unbraced system of things. The mind of the multitude is left at random, and seeing no fixed object before them, they pursue such as fancy or opinion starts. Nothing is criminal; there is no such thing as treason; wherefore, every one thinks himself at liberty to act as he pleases. The Tories dared not have assembled offensively, had they known that their lives, by that act, were forfeited to the laws of the state. A line of distinction should be drawn, between, English soldiers taken in battle, and inhabitants of America taken in arms. The first are prisoners, but the latter traitors. The one forfeits his liberty, the other his head.

Notwithstanding our wisdom, there is a visible feebleness in some of our proceedings which gives encouragement to dissentions. The Continental Belt is too losely buckled. And if something is not done in time, it will be too late to do any thing, and we shall fall into a state, in which, neither *Reconciliation* nor *Independance* will be practicable. The king and his worthless adherents are got at their old game of dividing the Continent, and there are not wanting among us, Printers, who will be busy in spreading specious falsehoods. The artful and hypocritical letter which appeared a few months ago in two of the New-York papers, and likewise in two others, is an evidence that there are men who want either judgment or honesty.

It is easy getting into holes and corners and talking of reconciliation: But do such men seriously consider, how difficult the task is, and how dangerous it may prove, should the Continent divide thereon. Do they take within their view, all the various orders of men whose situation and circumstances, as well as their own, are to be considered therein. Do they put themselves in the place of the sufferer whose *all* is *already* gone, and of the soldier, who hath quitted *all* for the defence of his country. If their ill judged moderation be suited to their own private situations *only*, regardless of others, the event will convince them, that "they are reckoning without their Host."

Put us, say some, on the footing we were on in sixty-three: To which I answer, the request is not *now* in the power of Britain to comply with, neither will she propose it; but if it were, and even should be granted, I ask, as a reasonable question, By what means is such a corrupt and faithless court to be kept to its engagements? Another parliament, nay, even the present, may hereafter repeal the obligation, on the pretence, of its being violently obtained, or unwisely granted; and in that case, Where is our redress?—No going to law with nations; cannon are the barristers of Crowns; and the sword, not of justice, but of war, decides the suit. To be on the footing of sixty-three, it is not sufficient, that the laws only be put on the same state, but, that our circumstances, likewise, be put on the same state; Our burnt and destroyed towns repaired or built up, our private losses made good, our public debts (contracted for defence) discharged; otherwise, we shall be millions worse than we were at that enviable period. Such a request, had it been complied with a year ago, would have won the heart and soul of the Continent—but now it is too late, "The Rubicon is passed."

Besides, the taking up arms, merely to enforce the repeal of a pecuniary law, seems as unwarrantable by the divine law, and as repugnant to human feelings, as the taking up arms to enforce obedience thereto. The object, on either side, doth not justify the means; for the lives of men are too valuable to be cast away on such trifles. It is the violence which is done and threatened to our persons; the destruction of our property by an armed force; the invasion of our country by fire and sword, which conscientiously qualifies the use of arms: And the instant, in which such a mode of defence became necessary, all subjection to Britain ought to have ceased; and the independancy of America, should have been considered, as dating its æra from, and published by, *the first musket that was fired against her*. This line is a line of consistency; neither drawn by caprice, nor extended by ambition; but produced by a chain of events, of which the colonies were not the authors.

I shall conclude these remarks, with the following timely and well intended hints. We ought to reflect, that there are three different ways, by which an independancy may hereafter be effected; and that *one* of those *three*, will one day or other, be the fate of America, viz. By the legal voice of the people in Congress; by a military power; or by a mob: It may not always happen that our soldiers are citizens, and the multitude a body of reasonable men; virtue, as I have already remarked, is not hereditary, neither is it perpetual. Should an independancy be brought about by the first of those means, we have every opportunity and every encouragement before us, to form the noblest purest constitution on the face of the earth. We have it in our power to begin the world over again. A situation, similar to the present, hath not happened since the days of Noah until now. The birthday of a new world is at hand, and a race of men, perhaps as numerous as all Europe contains, are to receive their portion of freedom from the event of a few months. The Reflexion is awful—and in this point of view, How trifling, how ridiculous, do the little, paltry cavellings, of a few weak or interested men appear, when weighed against the business of a world.

Should we neglect the present favorable and inviting period, and an Independance be hereafter effected by any other means, we must charge the consequence to ourselves, or to those rather, whose narrow and prejudiced souls, are habitually opposing the measure, without either inquiring or reflecting. There are reasons to be given in support of Independance, which men should rather privately think of, than be publicly told of. We ought not now to be debating whether we shall be independant or not, but, anxious to accomplish it on a firm, secure, and honorable basis, and uneasy rather that it is not yet began upon. Every day convinces us of its necessity. Even the Tories (if such beings yet remain among us) should, of all men, be the most solicitous to promote it; for, as the appointment of committees at first, protected them from popular rage, so, a wise and well established form of government, will be the only certain means of continuing it securely to them. *Wherefore*, if they have not virtue enough to be WHIGS, they ought to have prudence enough to wish for Independance.

In short, Independance is the only BOND that can tye and keep us together. We shall then see our object, and our ears will be legally shut against the schemes of an intriguing, as well, as a cruel enemy. We shall then too, be on a proper footing, to treat with Britain; for there is reason to conclude, that the pride of that court, will be less hurt by treating with the American states for terms of peace, than with those, whom she denominates, "rebellious subjects," for terms of accommodation. It is our delaying it that encourages her to hope for conquest, and our backwardness tends only to prolong the war. As we have, without any good effect therefrom, withheld our trade to obtain a redress of our grievances, let us *now* try the alternative, by *independantly* redressing them ourselves, and then offering to open the trade. The mercantile and reasonable part in England, will be still with us; because, peace *with* trade, is preferable to war *without* it. And if this offer be not accepted, other courts may be applied to.

On these grounds I rest the matter. And as no offer hath yet been made to refute the doctrine contained in the former editions of this pamphlet, it is a negative proof, that either the doctrine cannot be refuted, or, that the party in favour of it are too numerous to be opposed. WHEREFORE, instead of gazing at each other with suspicious or doubtful curiosity, let each of us, hold out to his neighbour the hearty hand of friendship, and unite in drawing a line, which, like an act of oblivion shall bury in forgetfulness every former dissention. Let the names of Whig and Tory be extinct; and let none other be heard among us, than those of *a good citizen, an open and resolute friend, and a virtuous supporter of the* RIGHTS *of* MANKIND *and of the* FREE AND INDEPEN-DANT STATES OF AMERICA.

To the Representatives of the Religious Society of the People called Quakers, or to so many of them as were concerned in publishing a late piece, entitled "The ANCIENT TESTIMONY AND PRINCIPLES *of the People called* QUAKERS *renewed, with Respect to the* KING *and* GOVERNMENT, *and touch-ing the* COMMOTIONS *now prevailing in these and other parts of* AMERICA *addressed to the* PEOPLE IN GENERAL."

THE Writer of this, is one of those few, who never dis-honors religion either by ridiculing, or cavilling at any denom-ination whatsoever. To God, and not to man, are all men accountable on the score of religion. Wherefore, this epistle is not so properly addressed to you as a religious, but as a political body, dabbling in matters, which the professed Quietude of your Principles instruct you not to meddle with.

As you have, without a proper authority for so doing, put yourselves in the place of the whole body of the Quakers, so, the writer of this, in order to be on an equal rank with your-selves, is under the necessity, of putting himself in the place of all those, who, approve the very writings and principles, against which, your testimony is directed: And he hath chosen this singular situation, in order, that you might discover in him that presumption of character which you cannot see in yourselves. For neither he nor you can have any claim or title to *Political Representation*.

When men have departed from the right way, it is no wonder that they stumble and fall. And it is evident from the manner in which ye have managed your testimony, that politics, (as a religious body of men) is not your proper Walk; for however well adapted it might appear to you, it is, nevertheless, a jumble of good and bad put unwisely together, and the conclusion drawn therefrom, both unnatural and unjust.

The two first pages, (and the whole doth not make four) we give you credit for, and expect the same civility from you, because the love and desire of peace is not confined to Quakerism, it is the *natural*, as well the religious wish of all denominations of men. And on this ground, as men laboring to establish an Independant Constitution of our own, do we exceed all others in our hope, end, and aim. *Our plan is peace for ever*. We are tired of contention with Britain, and can see no real end to it but in a final separation. We act consistently, because for the sake of introducing an endless and uninterrupted peace, do we bear the evils and burthens of the present day. We are endeavoring, and will steadily continue to endeavor, to separate and dissolve a connexion which hath already filled our land with blood; and which, while the name of it remains, will be the fatal cause of future mischiefs to both countries.

We fight neither for revenge nor conquest; neither from pride nor passion; we are not insulting the world with our fleets and armies, not ravaging the globe for plunder. Beneath the shade of our own vines are we attacked; in our own houses, and on our own lands, is the violence committed against us. We view our enemies in the character of Highwaymen and Housebreakers, and having no defence for ourselves in the civil law, are obliged to punish them by the military one, and apply the sword, in the very case, where you have before now, applied the halter—Perhaps we feel for the ruined and insulted sufferers in all and every part of the continent, with a degree of tenderness which hath not yet made it's way into some of your bosoms. But be ye sure that ye mistake not the cause and ground of your Testimony. Call not coldness of soul, religion; nor put the *Bigot* in the place of the *Christian.*

O ye partial ministers of your own acknowledged principles. If the bearing arms be sinful, the first going to war must be more so, by all the difference between wilful attack and unavoidable defence. Wherefore, if ye really preach from conscience, and mean not to make a political hobby-horse of your religion, convince the world thereof, by proclaiming your doctrine to our enemies, *for they likwise bear* ARMS. Give us proof of your sincerity by publishing it at St. James's, to the commanders in chief at Boston, to the Admirals and Captains who are piratically ravaging our coasts, and to all the murdering miscreants who are acting in authority under HIM whom ye profess to serve. Had ye the honest soul of * *Barclay* ye would preach repentance to *your* king; Ye would tell the Royal Wretch his sins, and warn him of eternal ruin. Ye would not spend your partial invectives against the injured and the insulted only, but, like faithful ministers, would cry aloud and *spare none.* Say not that ye are persecuted, neither endeavour to make us the authors of that reproach, which, ye are bringing upon yourselves; for we testify unto all men, that we do not complain against you because ye are *Quakers*, but because ye pretend to *be* and are NOT Quakers.

Alas! it seems by the particular tendency of some part of your testimony, and other parts of your conduct, as if, all sin was reduced to, and comprehended in, *the act of bearing arms*, and that by the *people only.* Ye appear to us, to have mistaken party for conscience; because, the general tenor of

---

*"Thou hast tasted of prosperity and adversity: thou knowest what it is to be banished thy native country, to be over-ruled as well as to rule, and set upon the throne; and being *oppressed* thou hast reason to know how *hateful* the *oppressor* is both to God and man: If after all these warnings and advertisements, thou dost not turn unto the Lord with all thy heart, but forget him who remembered thee in thy distress, and give up thyself to follow lust and vanity, surely great will be thy condemnation.—Against which snare, as well as the temptation of those who may or do feed thee, and prompt thee to evil, the most excellent and prevalent remedy will be, to apply thyself to that light of Christ which shineth in thy conscience, and which neither can, nor will flatter thee, nor suffer thee to be at ease in thy sins."

Barclay's Address to Charles II.

your actions wants uniformity: And it is exceedingly difficult
to us to give credit to many of your pretended scruples; because, we see them made by the same men, who, in the very
instant that they are exclaiming against the mammon of this
world, are nevertheless, hunting after it with a step as steady
as Time, and an appetite as keen as Death.

The quotation which ye have made from Proverbs, in the
third page of your testimony, that, "when a man's ways please
the Lord, he maketh even his enemies to be at peace with
him"; is very unwisely chosen on your part; because, it
amounts to a proof, that the king's ways (whom ye are so
desirous of supporting) do *not* please the Lord, otherwise, his
reign would be in peace.

I now proceed to the latter part of your testimony, and
that, for which all the foregoing seems only an introduction,
viz.

"It hath ever been our judgment and principle, since we
were called to profess the light of Christ Jesus, manifested in
our consciences unto this day, that the setting up and putting
down kings and governments, is God's peculiar prerogative;
for causes best known to himself: And that it is not our business to have any hand or contrivance therein; nor to be busy
bodies above our station, much less to plot and contrive the
ruin, or overturn of any of them, but to pray for the king, and
safety of our nation, and good of all men: That we may live a
peaceable and quiet life, in all godliness and honesty; *under
the government which God is pleased to set over us.*"—If these
are *really* your principles why do ye not abide by them? Why
do ye not leave that, which ye call God's Work, to be managed by himself? These very principles instruct you to wait
with patience and humility, for the event of all public measures, and to receive *that event* as the divine will towards you.
Wherefore, what occasion is there for your *political testimony* if
you fully believe what it contains: And the very publishing it
proves, that either, ye do not believe what ye profess, or have
not virtue enough to practise what ye believe.

The principles of Quakerism have a direct tendency to
make a man the quiet and inoffensive subject of any, and
every government *which is set over him*. And if the setting up
and putting down of kings and governments is God's peculiar

prerogative, he most certainly will not be robbed thereof by us; wherefore, the principle itself leads you to approve of every thing, which ever happened, or may happen to kings as being his work. OLIVER CROMWELL thanks you. CHARLES, then, died not by the hands of man; and should the present Proud Imitator of him, come to the same untimely end, the writers and publishers of the Testimony, are bound, by the doctrine it contains, to applaud the fact. Kings are not taken away by miracles, neither are changes in governments brought about by any other means than such as are common and human; and such as we are now using. Even the dispersion of the Jews, though foretold by our Saviour, was effected by arms. Wherefore, as ye refuse to be the means on one side, ye ought not to be meddlers on the other; but to wait the issue in silence; and unless ye can produce divine authority, to prove, that the Almighty who hath created and placed this *new* world, at the greatest distance it could possibly stand, east and west, from every part of the old, doth, nevertheless, disapprove of its being independent of the corrupt and abandoned court of Britain, unless I say, ye can shew this, how can ye on the ground of your principles, justify the exciting and stirring up the people "firmly to unite in the *abhorrence* of all such *writings*, and *measures*, as evidence of desire and design to break off the *happy* connexion we have hitherto enjoyed, with the kingdom of Great-Britain, and our just and necessary subordination to the king, and those who are lawfully placed in authority under him." What a slap of the face is here! the men, who in the very paragraph before, have quietly and passively resigned up the ordering, altering, and disposal of kings and governments, into the hands of God, are now, recalling their principles, and putting in for a share of the business. Is it possible, that the conclusion, which is here justly quoted, can any ways follow from the doctrine laid down? The inconsistency is too glaring not to be seen; the absurdity too great not to be laughed at; and such as could only have been made by those, whose understandings were darkened by the narrow and crabby spirit of a dispairing political party; for ye are not to be considered as the whole body of the Quakers but only as a factional and fractional part thereof.

Here ends the examination of your testimony; (which I call

upon no man to abhor, as ye have done, but only to read and judge of fairly;) to which I subjoin the following remark; "That the setting up and putting down of kings," most certainly mean, the making him a king, who is yet not so, and the making him no king who is already one. And pray what hath this to do in the present case? We neither mean to *set up* nor to *put down*, neither to *make* nor to *unmake*, but to have nothing to *do* with them. Wherefore, your testimony in whatever light it is viewed serves only to dishonor your judgement, and for many other reasons had better have been let alone than published.

First, Because it tends to the decrease and reproach of all religion whatever, and is of the utmost danger to society, to make it a party in political disputes.

Secondly, Because it exhibits a body of men, numbers of whom disavow the publishing political testimonies, as being concerned therein and approvers thereof.

Thirdly, Because it hath a tendency to undo that continental harmony and friendship which yourselves by your late liberal and charitable donations hath lent a hand to establish; and the preservation of which, is of the utmost consequence to us all.

And here without anger or resentment I bid you farewell. Sincerely wishing, that as men and christians, ye may always fully and uninterruptedly enjoy every civil and religious right; and be, in your turn, the means of securing it to others; but that the example which ye have unwisely set, of mingling religion with politics, *may be disavowed and reprobated by every inhabitant of* AMERICA.

The Forester's Letters

LETTER I

April 1, 1776

TO CATO

To be *nobly wrong* is more manly than to be *meanly right*. Only let the error be disinterested—let it wear, *not the mask*, but the *mark* of principle and 'tis pardonable. It is on this large and liberal ground, that we distinguish between men and their tenets, and generously preserve our friendship for the one, while we combat with every prejudice of the other. But let not Cato take this compliment to himself; he stands excluded from the benefit of the distinction; he deserves it not—And if the sincerity of disdain can add a cubit to the stature of my sentiments, it shall not be wanting.

It is indifferent to me who the writers of Cato's letters are, and sufficient for me to know, that they are gorged with absurdity, confusion, contradiction, and the most notorious and willful falsehoods. Let Cato and his faction be against Independance and welcome; their consequence will not *now* turn the scale: But let them have regard to justice, and pay some attention to the plain doctrine of reason. Where these are wanting, the sacred cause of truth applauds our anger, and dignifies it with the name of Virtue.

Four letters have already appeared under the specious name of Cato. What pretensions the writer of them can have to the signature, the Public will best determine; while, on my own part, I prophetically content myself with contemplating the similarity of their exits. The first of those letters promised a second, the second a third, the third a fourth; the fourth hath since made its appearance and still the writer keeps wide of the question. Why doth he thus loiter in the suburbs of the dispute? Why hath he not shewn us what the numerous blessings of reconciliation are, and *proved them practicable*? But he cunningly avoids the point. He cannot but discover the rock he is driving on. The fate of the Roman Cato is before his eyes: And that the Public may be prepared for his funeral, and for his funeral oration, I will venture to predict the time and the manner of his exit. The moment he explains his terms of reconciliation the typographical Cato dies. If they be calculated to please the Cabinet they will not go down with the Colonies; and if they be suited to the Colonies they will be rejected by the Cabinet: The line of no-variation is yet unfound; and, like the philosophers stone, doth not exist. "I am bold," says Cato, "to declare and yet hope to make it evident to every honest man, that the true interest of America lies in *reconciliation* with Great-Britain on *constitutional principles.*"

This is a curious way of lumping the business indeed! And Cato may as well attempt to catch lions in a mouse-trap as to hope to allure the Public with such general and unexplained expressions. It is now a meer bug-bear to talk of *reconciliation* on *constitutional principles*, unless the terms of the first be produced and the sense of the other be defined; and unless he does this he does nothing.

To follow Cato through every absurdity and falshood in the compass of a * letter is impossible; neither is it *now* necessary. *Cassandra* (and I thank him) hath saved me much trouble; there is a spirit in his remarks which honesty only can inspire, and a uniformity in the conduct of his letter which the want of principle can never arrive at. Mark that, Cato.

One observation which I cannot help making on Cato's letters, is, that they are addressed *"To the People of Pennsylvania" only*: In almost any other writer this might have passed unnoticed, but we know it hath mischief in its meaning. The particular circumstance of a Convention is undoubtedly Provincial, but the great business of the day is Continental. And he who dares to endeavour to withdraw this province from the glorious union by which all are supported, deserves the reprobation of all men. It is the true interest of the whole to go hand in hand; and dismal in every instance would be the fate of that Colony which should retreat from the protection of the rest.

The first of Cato's letters is insipid in its stile, language and substance; crouded with personal and private innuendues, and directly levelled against *"the Majesty of the People of Penn-*

---

*The writer intended at first to have contained his remarks in one letter.

sylvania." The Committee could only call, propose, or recommend a Convention; but, like all other public measures, it still rested with the people at large, whether they would approve it or not; and Cato's reasoning on the right or wrong of that choice is contemptible; because, if the body of the people had thought, or should still think, that the Assembly (or any of their Delegates in Congress) by setting under the embarrassment of *oaths*, and entangled with *Government* and *Governors*, are not so perfectly free as they ought to be, they undoubtedly had, and still have, both the *right* and the *power* to place even the whole authority of the Assembly in any body of men they please; and whoever is hardy enough to say to the contrary is an enemy to mankind. The constitution of Pennsylvania hath been twice changed through the cunning of former Proprietors; surely, the people, whose right, power and property is greater than that of any single man, may make such alterations in their mode of government as the change of times and things require. Cato is exceedingly fond of impressing us with the importance of our *"chartered constitution."* Alas! We are not now, Sir, to be led away by the jingle of a phrase. Had we framed our conduct by the contents of the present charters, we had, ere now, been in a state of helpless misery. That *very assembly* you mention hath broken it, and been obliged to break it, in almost every instance of their proceedings. Hold it up to the Public and it is transparent with holes; pierced with as many deadly wounds as the body of McLeod. Disturb not its remains, Cato, nor dishonour it with another funeral oration.

There is nothing in Cato's first letter worthy of notice but the following insinuating falshood: "Grievous as the least restraint of the press must always be, to a *people* entitled to freedom, it must be the more so, when it is not only unwarranted by *those* to whom *they* have committed the care of *their* liberties, but cannot be warranted by *them*, consistent with liberty itself."—The rude and unscholastical confusion of persons in the above paragraph, though it throws an obscurity on the meaning, still leaves it discoverable. Who, Sir, hath laid any restraint on the liberty of the press? I know of no instance, in which the press hath been even the object of notice, in this province, except on account of the Tory letter from

Kent County which was published last spring in the *Pennsyl-vania Ledger*, and which it was the duty of every good man to detect, because the *honesty* of the press is as great an object to society as the *freedom* of it. If this is the restraint you com-plain of we know your true character at once; and that it is so, appears evident from the expression which immediately fol-lows the above quotation; your words are, "Nevertheless, *we* readily submitted to it, while the least colourable pretence could be offered for requiring such a submission." Who sub-mitted, Cato? *we* Whigs or *we* Tories? Until you clear up this, Sir, you must content yourself with being ranked among the rankest of the *writing* Tories; because, no other body of men can have any pretence to complain of want of freedom of the press. It is not your throwing out, now and then, a little popular phrase, which can protect you from suspicion; they are only the gildings under which the poison is conveyed, and without which you dared not to renew your attempts on the virtue of the people.

Cato's second letter, or the greatest part thereof, is taken up with the reverence due from us to the persons and author-ity of the Commissioners, whom Cato vainly and ridiculously stiles AMBASSADORS *coming to negociate a peace*. How came Cato not to be let a little better into the secret? The act of Parliament which describes the powers of these men, hath been in this city upwards of a month, and in the hands too of Cato's friends. No, Sir, they are not the *Ambassadors of peace*, but the distributors of pardons, mischief and insult. Cato discovers a gross ignorance of the British constitution, in supposing that these men *can* be empowered to act as Ambas-sadors. To prevent his future errors I will set him right. The present war differs from every other, in this instance, viz. that it is not carried on under the prerogative of the Crown as other wars have always been, but under the authority of the whole legislative power united, and as the barriers which stand in the way of a negociation, are not proclamations but acts of Parliament, it evidently follows, that were even the King of England here in person, he could not ratify the terms or conditions of a reconciliation; because, in the single char-acter of King he could not stipulate for the repeal of any *acts* of Parliament, neither can the Parliament stipulate for him.

There is no body of men more jealous of their privileges than the Commons: because they sell them. Mark that, Cato.

I have not the least doubt upon me but that their business (exclusive of granting us pardons) is downright bribery and corruption. It is the machine by which they effect all their plans. We ought to view them as enemies of a most dangerous species, and he who means not to be corrupted by them will enter his protest in time. Are they not the very men who are paid for voting in every measure against us, and ought we not to suspect their designs? Can we view the barbarians as friends? Would it be prudent to trust the viper in our very bosoms? Or to suffer them to ramble at large among us while such doubtful characters as Cato have a being upon the Continent? Yet let their persons be safe from injury and outrage— but trust them not. Our business with them is short and explicit, viz. We are desirous of peace, Gentlemen; we are ready to ratify the terms, and will virtuously fulfil the conditions thereof; but we should deserve all and every misery which tyranny can inflict, were we, after suffering such a repetition of savage barbarities, to come under your government again.

Cato, by way of stealing into credit, says, that "the contest we are engaged in is founded on the most noble and virtuous principles which can animate the mind of man. We are contending, (says he) against an arbitrary Ministry for the rights of Englishmen." No, Cato, we are *now* contending against an arbitrary King to get clear of his tyranny. While the dispute rested in words only, it might be called "contending with the Ministry," but since it is broken out into open war, it is high time to have done with such silly and water-gruel definitions. But it suits not Cato to speak the truth. It is his interest to dress up the sceptered savage in the mildest colours. Cato's patent for a large tract of land is yet unsigned. Alas poor Cato!

Cato proceeds very importantly to tell us, *"that the eyes of all Europe are upon us."* This stale and hackneyed phrase, hath had a regular descent, from many of the King's speeches down to several of the speeches in Parliament; from thence, it took a turn among the little wits and bucks of St. James's; till after suffering all the torture of senseless repetition, and being reduced to a state of vagrancy, was charitably picked up to embellish the second letter of Cato. It is truly of the bug-bear kind, contains no meaning, and the very using it discovers a barrenness of invention. It signifies nothing to tell us "that the eyes of all Europe are upon us," unless he had likewise told us what they are looking at us *for*; which, as he hath not done, I will: They are looking at us, Cato, in hopes of seeing a final separation between Britain and the Colonies, that they, the *lookers on*, may partake of a free and uninterrupted trade with the whole Continent of America. Cato! thou reasonest *wrong*.

For the present, Sir, farewell. I have seen thy soliloquy and despise it. Remember, thou hast thrown me the glove, Cato, and either thee or I must tire. I fear not the field of fair debate, but thou hast stepped aside and made it personal— Thou hast tauntingly called on me by name; and if I cease to hunt thee from every lane and lurking-hole of mischief, and bring thee not a trembling culprit before the public bar, then brand me with reproach, by naming me in the list of your confederates.

Philadelphia, March 28, 1776.   THE FORESTER.

LETTER II

April 10, 1776

TO CATO

BEFORE I enter on the more immediate purpose of this letter; I think it necessary, once for all, to endeavour to settle as clearly as I can the following point, viz. How far personality is concerned in any political debate. The general maxim is, that measures, and not men, is the thing in question; and the maxim is undeniably just, when rightly understood. Cato, as a refuge for himself, hath quoted the author of *Common Sense*, who, in his preface, says, "That the object for attention is the *doctrine itself*, not the *man*;" that is, not the *rank* or *condition* of the man; for whether he is with those whose fortune is *already* made, or with those whose fortune is *yet* to make, or among those who seldom think or care whether they make *any*, is a matter wholly out of the question, and entirely confined to himself. But the political characters, political dependencies, and political Connections of men, being of a public nature, differ exceedingly from the circumstances of private life: And they are in many instances so nearly related to the measures they propose, that, to prevent our being deceived by the last, we *must* be acquainted with the first. A total ignorance of men lays us under the danger of mistaking plausibility for principle. Could the wolf bleat like the lamb, the flock would soon be inticed into ruin; wherefore, to prevent the mischief, he ought to be *seen*, as well as *heard*. There never was, nor ever will be, nor ever ought to be, any important political debate carried on, in which a total separation in all cases between men and measures could be admitted with sufficient safety. When hypocrisy shall be banished from the earth, the knowledge of men will be unnecessary, because, their measures cannot then be fraudulent; but until that time come (which never will come) they ought, under proper limitations, to go together. We have already too much secrecy in some things; and too little in others;—were men more known, and measures more concealed, we should have fewer hypocrites, and more security.

As the chief design of these letters is to detect and expose the falshoods and fallacious reasonings of Cato, he must not expect (when detected) to be treated like one who had debated fairly; for I will be bold to say, and to prove, that a grosser violation of truth and reason scarcely ever came from the pen of a writer; And the explanations which he hath endeavoured to impose on the passages which he hath quoted from *Common Sense*, are such as never existed in the mind of the author, nor can they be drawn from the words themselves. Neither must Cato expect to be spared, where his carelessness of expression, and visible want of compassion and sentiment, shall give occasion to raise any moral or philosophical reflection thereon. These things being premised, I now proceed to review the latter part of Cato's second letter.

In this place, Cato begins his first attack on *Common Sense*; but as he only discovers his ill-will, and neither offers any arguments against it, nor makes any quotation from it, I should in this place pass him by, were it not for the following strange assertion. "If little notice, says Cato (*little opposition he means*) has yet been taken of the publications concerning Independence, it is neither owing to the popularity of the doctrine, the unanswerable nature of the arguments, nor the fear of opposing them as the vanity of the author would suggest." As Cato hath given us the *negative* reasons, he ought to have given us the *real* ones; for as he *positively* tells what it was *not* owing to, he undoubtedly knows what it *was* owing to, that *he* delayed *his* answers so long; but instead of telling us that (which perhaps is not proper to be told) he flies from the argument with the following plump declaration—"nine tenths of the people of Pennsylvania (says he) yet abhor the doctrine." But stop, Cato! not quite so fast friend. If this be true, how came they, so late as the 2d of March last, to elect for a Burgess of this City a Gentleman of known *independent principles*, and one of the very few to whom the author of Common Sense shewed some part thereof while in manuscript.

Cato is just as unfortunate in the following paragraph. "Those, says he, who made the appeal (that is, published the pamphlet) have but little cause to triumph in its success. Of this they seem sensible, and, like true quacks, are constantly pestering us with additional doses, till the stomachs of their patients *begin wholly* to revolt." It is Cato's hard fate to be always detected: For perhaps there never was a pamphlet, since the use of letters were known, about which so little pains were taken, and of which so great a number went off in so short a time; I am certain that I am within compass when I say one hundred and twenty thousand. The book was turned upon the world like an orphan, to shift for itself; no plan was formed to support it, neither hath the author ever published a syllable on the subject from that time, till after the appearance of Cato's fourth letter; wherefore, what Cato says of additional doses administered by the author is an absolute falsity. Besides which, it comes with an ill-grace from one, who frequently publishes two letters in a week, and often puts them both into one paper. Cato here, Cato there, look where you will.

At the distance of a few lines from the above quotations, Cato presents us with a retrospective view of our former state, in which, says he, "we considered our connection with Great-Britain as our chief happiness. We flourished, grew rich and populous, to a degree not to be paralleled in history." This assertion is truly of the legerdemain kind, appearing at once both right and wrong. All writers on Cato's side have used the same argument, and conceived themselves invincible; nevertheless, a single expression, properly placed, dissolves the charm, for the cheat lies in putting the *consequence* for the *cause*; for had we not *flourished* the *connexion* had never *existed*, or never been *regarded*, and this is fully proved by the neglect shewn to the first settlers, who had every difficulty to struggle with, unnoticed and unassisted by the British Court.

Cato proceeds very industriously to sum up the former declarations of Congress and other public bodies, some of which were made upwards of a year ago, to prove that the doctrine of Independence hath no sanction from them. To this I shall give Cato one general answer, which is, that had he produced a thousand more such authorities they would *now* amount to nothing. They are out of date. Times and things are altered. The true character of the King was but little known among the body of the people a year ago, — willing to believe him good, they fondly called him so, but have since found, that Cato's Royal Sovereign is a Royal Savage.

Cato hath introduced the above-mentioned long quotation of authorities against independency with the following curious preface. "Nor have many weeks, says he, yet elapsed, since the first open proposition for independence was published to the world. By what men of consequence this scheme is supported, or whether by any, may possibly be the subject of future enquiry. Certainly it hath no countenance from the Congress, to whose sentiments we look up with reverence. On the contrary, it is *directly repugnant to every* declaration of that respectable body." Now Cato thou hast nailed thyself with a witness! directly repugnant to every declaration of that respectable body! mind that Cato, and mark what follows. It appears by an extract from the Resolves of the Congress, printed in the front of the Oration delivered by Dr. Smith, in honour of that brave man General Montgomery, that he (the

Doctor) was appointed by that honourable body to compose and deliver the same, in the *execution* of which, the orator exclaimed loudly against the doctrine of independence, but when a motion was afterwards made in Congress (according to former usage) to return the *Orator* thanks, and request a copy for the press, the motion was rejected from every part of the house, and thrown out without a division.

I now proceed to Cato's third letter, in the opening of which he deserts the subject of independence, and renews his attack on the Committee. Cato's manner of writing has as much order in it as the motion of a squirrel; he frequently writes as if he knew not what to write next, just as the other and jumps about only because he cannot stand still; though I am sometimes angry with him for his unprincipled method of writing and reasoning, I cannot help laughing at him at other times for his want of ingenuity: an instance of which he gives us, in kindly warning us against *"the foul pages of interested writers and strangers intermeddling in our affairs."* Were I to reply seriously, my answer would be this, thou seemest then ignorant, Cato, of that ancient and numerous order which are related to each other in all and every part of the globe, with whom the kindred is not formed by place or accident, but in principle and sentiment. A freeman, Cato, is a stranger no where, a slave, every where. But were I disposed to answer merrily, I should tell him, that as his notions of friendship were so very narrow and local, he obliges me to understand, that when he addresses the people with the tender title of *"my dear countrymen"* which frequently occurs in his letters, that he particularly means the long list of Mac's published in Donald MacDonald's commission.

In this letter Cato recommends the pamphlet called *Plain Truth*, a performance, which hath withered away like a sickly unnoticed weed, and which, even its advocates are displeased at, and the author ashamed to own. About the middle of this third letter Cato gives notice of his being ready to take the field. "I now proceed says he to give my reasons." How Cato hath managed the attack we are now to examine; and the first remark I shall offer on his conduct, is, that he hath most unluckily entered the list on the wrong side, and discharged his first fire among the Tories.

In order to prove this I shall give the paragraph entire—
"AGRICULTURE and COMMERCE, says Cato, have hitherto
been the happy employments by which these middle colonies
have risen into wealth and importance. By *them* the face of the
country have been changed from a barren wilderness into the
hospitable abodes of peace and plenty. Without *them*, we had
either never existed as Americans, or existed only as savages.
—The oaks would still have possessed their *native spots of
earth*, and never have *appeared in the form of ships and
houses*. What are now well cultivated fields, or flourishing
cities, would have remained only the solitary haunts of wild
beasts, or of men equally wild." The reader cannot help perceiving that through this whole paragraph, *our connection*
with Britain is left entirely out of the question, and our
present greatness attributed to internal causes *agriculture* and
commerce. This is a strange way, Cato, of overturning *Common Sense*, which says, "I challenge the warmest advocate for
reconciliation, to shew a single advantage which this continent can reap by being connected with Great-Britain; I repeat, says he, the challenge, not a single advantage is derived.
*Our corn will fetch its price in any market in Europe, and our
imported goods must be paid for, buy them where we will*." Cato
introduces his next paragraph with saying "that much of our
former felicity was owing to the protection of England *is not
to be denied*;" yes Cato, I deny it wholly, and for the following
clear and simple reasons, viz. that our being connected with,
and submitting to be protected by her, made and will still make
all "*her* enemies *our* enemies, or as *Common Sense* says,
sets us at variance with nations who would otherwise seek
our friendship, and against whom we have neither anger nor
complaint."

The following passage is so glaringly absurd, that I shall
make but a short comment upon it. "And if hereafter, says
Cato, in the fulness of time, it shall be necessary to separate
from the land that gave birth to (*some of*) our ancestors, it will
be in a state of perfect manhood, when we can fully wield our
own arms, and *protect our commerce and coasts by our own
fleets*." But how are we to come by *fleets* Cato, while Britain
hath the government of the continent? unless, we are to suppose, as you have hinted in the former paragraph, that our

oaks are to *grow* into ships, and be launched self-built from their "native spots of earth." It is Cato's misfortune, as a writer, not to distinguish justly between magic and imagination; while on the other hand there are many passages in his letters so seriously and deliberately false, that nothing but the most hardened effrontery, and a cast of mind bordering upon impiety would have uttered. He frequently forces me out of the common tract of civil language, in order, to do him justice; moderation and temper being really unequal to the task of exposing him.

Cato, unless he meant to destroy the ground he stood upon, ought not to have let the following paragraph been seen. "If our present *differences,* says he, can be accommodated, there is *scarce a probability* that Britain will ever *renew* her late fatal system of policy, or attempt again to employ force against us." How came Cato to admit the *probability* of our being brought *again* into the same bloody and expensive situation? but it is worth remarking, that those who write without principle, cannot help sometimes blundering upon truth. Then there is no *real security*, Cato, in this *reconciliation* of yours on *constitutional principles*? It still amounts to nothing, and after all this expence of life and wealth, we are to rest at last upon hope, hazard and uncertainty. Why then, by all that is sacred, *"it is time to part."*

But Cato, after admitting the *probability* of our being brought *again* into the same situation, proceeds to tell us, how we are to conduct ourselves in the second quarrel; and that is, by the very same methods we have done the present one, viz. to expend millions of treasure, and thousands of lives, in order to patch up a second *re-union*, that the way may be open for a *third quarrel*; and in this endless and chequered round of blood and treacherous peace hath Cato disposed of the continent of America.—That I may not be thought to do Cato injustice, I have quoted the whole passage; "But should Britain be so infatuated, says he, at any future period, as to think of subjugating us, either by the arts of corruption, or oppressive exertions of power, can we entertain a doubt but we shall AGAIN, with a virtue equal to the present, and with the *weapons of defence in our hands* (when necessary) convince her that we are willing, by a *constitutional connection* with her, to afford and receive reciprocal benefits; but although subjects of the same King we will not consent to be her slaves."—Come hither ye *little ones*, whom the poisonous hand of Cato is rearing for destruction, and remember the page that warns ye of your ruin!

Cato, in many of his expressions, discovers all that calm command over the passions and feelings, which always distinguishes the man who hath expelled them from his heart. Of this careless kind is the before mentioned phrase "our present differences," and the same unpardonable negligence is conveyed in the following one—"*Although* I consider her, says he, as having in her late conduct towards us, acted the part of a cruel step-dame." Wonderful sensibility indeed! All the havoc and desolation of unnatural war; the destruction of thousands; the burning and depopulating of towns and cities; the ruin and separation of friends and families, are just sufficient to extort from Cato, *this one* callous confession. But the cold and creeping soul of Cato is a stranger to the manly powers of sympathetic sorrow. He *moves* not, nor *can* he move in so pure an element. Accustomed to lick the hand that hath made him visible, and to breathe the gross atmosphere of servile and sordid dependance, his soul would *now* starve on virtue, and suffocate in the clear region of disinterested friendship.

Surely when Cato sat down to write, he either did not expect to be called to an account, or was totally regardless of reputation; otherwise, he would not have endeavoured to persuade the public, that the doctrine of independence was broached in a kind of seditious manner, at a time *"when says he, some gleams of reconciliation began first to break in upon us."* Come forth Cato, and prove the assertion! where do these gleams of reconciliation spring from? Are they to be found in the King's speech—in the address of either House of Parliament;—or in the act which lets loose a whole kennel of pirates upon our property, and commissions another sett to insult with pardons, the very men, whom their own measures had sought to ruin? Either prove the assertion, Cato, or take the reward of it, for it is the part of an incendiary to endeavour with specious falshoods, to mislead the credulity of unwary readers.—Cato likewise says, that while we continue united, and renounce all thoughts of independence, "that we have the *utmost assurance* of obtaining a *full redress* of our *grievances*, and an *ample security* against any *future violation* of our *just rights.*" If Cato means to insinuate that we have *received* such an assurance, let him read the conclusion of the preceding paragraph again, the same answer will serve for both.

Perhaps, when we recollect the long and unabated cruelty of the British Court toward us, and remember the many prayers which we have put up both *to* them and *for* them, that the following piece of declamation of Cato can hardly be equalled, either for absurdity or insanity: "If we now effect independence, says he, we must be considered as a *faithless people in the sight of all mankind, and could scarcely expect the confidence of any nation upon earth, or look up to heaven for its approving sentence.*" Art thou mad, Cato, or art thou foolish —or art thou *both*—or art thou *worse* than both? In *this passage* thou hast fairly gone beyond me. I have not language to bring thee back. Thou art safely entrenched indeed!—Rest therefore in thy strong-hold till HE who fortified thee in it shall come and fetch thee out.

Cato seems to be possessed of that jesuitical cunning, which always endeavours to disgrace what it cannot disprove; and this he sometimes effects, by unfairly introducing *our* terms into *his* arguments, and thereby begets a monster which he sends round the country for a show, and tells the good people that the name of it is *independance.* Of this character are several passages in his fourth and fifth letters, particularly where he quotes the term *"foreign assistance,"* which he ungenerously explains into a surrender of the continent to France and Spain. Such an unfair and sophistical reasoner doth not deserve the civility of good manners. He creates, likewise, the same confusion, by frequently using the word *peace* for *union*, and thereby charges us falsly by representing us as being determined to "reject all propositions of *peace*:" Whereas our wish is *peace*, but *not re-union*; and though we would gladly listen to the former, we are determined to resist every proposal for the latter, *come from where it will*; being fully persuaded, that in the present state of affairs *separation of governments is the only and best thing that can be done for both countries.*

The following case is unjustly put. "There never was a war, says Cato, so implacable, even among states naturally rivals and enemies, or among savages themselves, as not to have *peace* for its object as well as end." But was there ever a war, Cato, which had *union* for its object? No. What Cato means by states naturally rivals and enemies, I shall not enquire into, but this I know (for myself at least) that it was not in the power of France or Spain, or all the other powers in Europe, to have given such a wound or raised up such a mortal hatred Britain hath done. We feel the same kind of undescribed anger at her conduct, as we would at the sight of an animal devouring its young: And this particular species of anger is not generated in the transitory temper of the man, but in the chaste undefiled womb of nature.

Cato, towards the conclusion of his third letter (at which place I shall leave him for the present) compares the state of Britain and America to the quarrels of lovers, and from thence infers a probability that our affections will be renewed thereby. This I cannot help looking on as one of the most unnatural and distorted similes that can be drawn. Come hither ye that are lovers, or ye that *have been* lovers and decide the controversy between us! What comparison is there between the soft murmurs of an heart mourning in secret, and the loud horrors of war—between the silent fears of pensive sorrow, and rivers of wasted blood—between the *sweet* strife of affection, and the *bitter* strife of death—between the curable calamities of pettish lovers, and the sad sight of a thousand slain. "Get thee behind me," Cato, for thou hast not the feelings of a man.

THE FORESTER.

LETTER III

April 22, 1776

TO CATO

CATO's partizans may call me furious; I regard it not. There are men too, who have not virtue enough to be angry, and that crime perhaps is Cato's—He who dares not offend cannot be honest. Having thus balanced the charge, I proceed to Cato's fourth, fifth, sixth and seventh letters, all of which as they contain but little matter, I shall dismiss with as little trouble and less formality.

His fourth letter is introduced with a punning soliloquy — Cato's title to soliloquies is indisputable; because no man cares for his company*. However, he disowns the writing it, and assures his readers that it "was *really* put into his hands." I always consider this confirming mode of expression, as betraying a suspicion of one's self; and in this place, it amounts to just as much as if Cato had said, "you know my *failing*, Sirs, but what I tell you now is really true." Well! be it so, Cato; you shall have all the credit you ask for, and as to when, or where, or how you got it, who was the author, or who the giver, I shall not enquire after; being fully convinced, by the poetical merit of the performance, that tho' the writer of it may be an *Allen*, he'll never be a *Ramsay*†. Thus much for the soliloquy; and if this gentle chastisement should be the means of preventing Cato or his colleagues from mingling their punning nonsense with subjects of such a serious nature as the present one truly is, it will answer *one* of the ends it was intended for.

Cato's fourth, and the greatest part of his fifth letter, are constructed on a false meaning uncivilly imposed on a passage quoted from *Common Sense*; and for which, the author of that pamphlet hath a right to expect from Cato the usual concessions. I shall quote the passage entire, with Cato's additional meaning, and the inferences which he draws therefrom.

He introduces it with saying, "In my remarks on the pamphlet before me, I shall first consider those arguments on which he (the author) appears to lay his chief stress; and these are collected under four heads in his conclusion:" one of which is, *"It is the custom of nations when any two are at war, for some other powers, not engaged in the quarrel, to step in by way of mediators, and bring about the preliminaries of a peace; but while America calls herself the subject of Great-Britain, no*

---

*As this piece may possibly fall into the hands of some who are not acquainted with the word Soliloquy, for *their* information the sense of it is given, viz. *"talking to one's self."*

†*Allan Ramsay*, a famous Scotch poet of *genuine* wit and humour.

power, however well-disposed she may be, can offer her mediation." The meaning contained in this passage is so exceedingly plain, and expressed in such easy and familiar terms, that it scarcely admits of being made plainer. No one, I think, could have understood it any other wise, than that, while we continue to call ourselves British subjects, the quarrel between us can only be called a *family quarrel*, in which it would be just as indelicate for any other nation to advise, or any ways to meddle or make, even with their offers of mediation, as it would be for a third person to interfere in a quarrel between a man and his wife. Whereas, were we to make use of that natural right which all other nations have done before us, and erect a government of our own, *independent of all the world*, the quarrel could then be no longer called a *family quarrel*, but a *regular war* between the two powers of Britain and America, in the same manner as one carried on between England and France; and in this state of political separation, the neutral powers might kindly tender their mediation, (as hath always been the practice) and bring about the preliminaries of a *peace*. Not a *union*, Cato, that is quite another thing. But instead of Cato's taking it in this easy and natural sense, he flies away on a wrong scent, *charges the author with proposing to call in foreign assistance*; and, under this wilful falshood, raises up a mighty cry after nothing at all. He begins his wild and unintelligible comment in the following manner: "Is this" says he, (meaning the passage already quoted) "*common sense*, or *common nonsense*? Surely peace * with Great Britain cannot be the object of this writer, after the horrible character he has given of the people of that country, and telling us, that reconciliation with them would be our ruin. The latter part of the paragraph seems to cast some light upon the former, altho' it contradicts it; for these mediators are not to interfere for making up the quarrel, but to widen it, by supporting us in a declaration, that we are not the subjects of Great-Britain: a new sort of business truly for mediators! But this," continues Cato, "leads us directly to the *main enquiry, what foreign*

---

*It is a strange thing that Cato cannot be taught to distinguish between *peace* and *union*.

power is able to give us this support?" What support, Cato? the passage you have quoted neither says a syllable, nor insinuates a hint about support: It speaks *only* of neutral powers in the neighbourly character of mediators between those which are at war; and says it is the custom of European Courts to do so. Cato hath already raised Commissioners into Ambassadors, but how he could transform mediators into men in arms, and mediation into military alliance, is surpassingly strange. Read the part over again, Cato; if you find I have charged you wrongfully and will point it out, I will engage that the author of *Common Sense* shall ask your pardon in the public papers with his name to it, but if the error be yours, the concession on your part follows as a duty.

Though I am fully persuaded that Cato does not believe one half of what himself has written, he, nevertheless, takes amazing pains to *frighten* his readers into a belief of the whole: Tells them of foreign troops (which he supposes we are going to send for) ravaging up and down the country; of their "bloody massacres, unrelenting persecutions which would *harrow up* (says he) the *very souls of protestants and freemen*." Were they coming, Cato, which no one ever dreamed of but yourself (for thank God we want them not) it would be impossible for them to exceed, or even to equal the cruelties practised by the British army in the East-Indies: The tying men to the mouths of cannon and *"blowing them away,"* was never acted by any but an English General, or approved by any but a British Court*—read the proceeding of the Select Committee on India affairs.

From temporal fears Cato proceeds to spiritual ones, and in a hypocritical panic, asks, "To whose share will Pennsylvania fall—that of his most Catholic, or his most Christian King? I confess, continues he, that these questions stagger me." I dont wonder at it, Cato—I am glad to hear that some kind of remorse hath overtaken you—that you begin to *feel* that you are "heavy laden"—you have had a long run; and the stoutest heart must fail at last.

---

*Lord Clive, the chief of Eastern plunderers, received the thanks of Parliament for *"his honourable conduct in the East-Indies."*

Cato perceiving that the falsehoods in his fourth letter passed unreproved, ventured boldly on a fifth, in which he continues enlarging on the same convenient bug-bear. "In my last," says he "some notice was taken of the dangerous proposition held up by the author of *Common Sense*, for having recourse to foreign assistance." When will Cato learn to speak the truth! The assistance which we hope for from France, is not armies, (we want them not) but arms and ammunition. We have already received into this province only, near two hundred tons of salt-petre and gun-powder, besides muskets. Surely! we may continue to cultivate a useful acquaintance, without such malevolent beings as Cato raising his barbarous slander thereon. At *this time*, it is not only illiberal, but impolitic, and perhaps dangerous, to be pouring forth such torrents of abuse as his fourth and fifth letters contain, against the only power, that, in articles of defence, hath supplied our hasty wants.

Cato after expending near two letters in beating down an idol which himself *only* had set up, proudly congratulates himself on the defeat, and marches off to new exploits, leaving behind him the following proclamation. "Having thus," says Cato, "*dispatched* his" (the author of *Common Sense*'s) "*main argument* for *independence*, which he founds on the necessity of calling in *foreign assistance*, I proceed to examine some other parts of his work." Not a syllable, Cato, doth any part of the pamphlet in question, say of calling in foreign assistance, or even forming military alliances. The dream is wholly your own; and is directly repugnant both to the letter and spirit of every page in the piece. The idea which *Common Sense*, constantly holds up, is, to have nothing to do with the political affairs of Europe. "As Europe, says the pamphlet, is our market for trade, we ought to form no political connections with *any part of it*. It is the true interest of America to steer clear of all European contentions." And where it proposes sending a manifesto to foreign courts (which it is high time to do) it recommends it, only, for the purpose of announcing to them the *impossibility of our living any longer under the British government, and of "assuring such Courts, of our peaceable disposition towards them, and of our desire of entering into trade with them."* Learn to be an honest man,

Cato, and then thou wilt not be thus exposed.—I have been the more particular in detecting Cato here, because it is on this *bubble* that his air-built battery against independance is raised—a poor foundation indeed! which even the point of a pin, or a pen if you please, can demolish with a touch, and bury the formidable Cato beneath the ruins of a vapour.

From this part of his fifth letter to the end of his seventh, he entirely deserts the subject of independance, and sets up the proud standard of Kings, in preference to a Republican form of government. My remarks on this part of the subject will be general and concise.

In this part of the debate, Cato shelters himself chiefly in quotations from other authors, without reasoning much on the matter himself;* in answer to which, I present him with a string of maxims and reflexions, drawn from the nature of things, without borrowing from any one. Cato may observe, that I scarcely ever quote; the reason is, I always think. But to return.

Government should always be considered as a matter of convenience, not of right. The scripture institutes no particular form of government, but it enters a protest against the monarchical form; and a negation on *one* thing, where *two only* are offered, and *one* must be chosen, amounts to an affirmative on the *other*. Monarchical government was first set up by the Heathens, and the Almighty permitted it to the Jews as a punishment. *"I gave them a King in mine anger."* Hosea xiii. 11. A Republican form of government is pointed out by nature—Kingly governments by an unequality of power. In Republican governments, the leaders of the people, if improper, are removeable by vote; Kings only by arms: an unsuccessful vote in the first case, leaves the voter safe; but an unsuccessful attempt in the latter, is death. Strange! that, that

---

*The following is an instance of Cato's method of conducting an argument, "If hereditary succession, says *Common Sense*, (meaning succession of monarchical governments) did ensure a race of good and wise men, it would have the seal of divine authority," *"thus we find him,"* says Cato, *"with his own hand affixing the seal of heaven to what he before told us the Devil invented and the Almighty entered his protest against."* Cato's 7th letter.—This is a strange argument indeed, Cato! or rather it is no argument at all, for hereditary succession does *not* ensure a race of good and wise men, consequently has *not* the *seal of divine authority.*

which is our *right* in the *one*, should be our *ruin* in the *other*—from which reflexion follows this maxim, That that mode of government in which our *right* becomes our *ruin*, cannot be the *right one*. If all human nature be corrupt, it is needless to strengthen the corruption by establishing a succession of Kings, who, be they ever so base are still to be obeyed; for the manners of a Court will always have an influence over the morals of a people. A Republican government hath more *true grandeur* in it than a Kingly one: On the part of the public it is more consistent with freemen to appoint their rulers than to have them born; and on the part of those who preside, it is far nobler to be a ruler by the choice of the people, than a King by the chance of birth. Every honest Delegate is more than a Monarch. Disorders will unavoidably happen in all States, but monarchical governments are the most subject thereto, because the balance hangs uneven. *"Nineteen rebellions and eight civil wars in England since the conquest."* Whatever commotions are produced in Republican States, are not produced by a Republican spirit, but by those who seek to extinguish it. A Republican State cannot produce its own destruction, it can only suffer it. No nation of people, in their true senses, when seriously reflecting on the rank which God hath given them, and the reasoning faculties he hath blessed them with, would ever, of their own consent, give any *one man* a negative power over the whole: No man since the fall hath ever been equal to the trust; wherefore, 'tis insanity in us to entrust them with it; and in this sense, all those who have had it have done us right by abusing us into reason. Nature seems sometimes to laugh at mankind, by giving them so many fools for Kings; at other times, she punishes their folly by giving them tyrants; but England must have offended highly to be curst with both in one. *Rosseau* proposed a plan for establishing a perpetual European peace; which was, for every State in Europe to send Ambassadors to form a General Council, and when any difference happened between any two nations, to refer the matter to arbitration instead of going to arms. This would be forming a kind of European Republic: But the proud and plundering spirit of Kings hath not peace for its object.—They look not at the good of mankind—They set not out upon that plan: And if the history of the Creation, and the history of Kings be compared together, the result will be this — that God hath made a world, and Kings have robbed him of it.

But that which sufficiently establishes the Republican mode of government, in preference to a Kingly one, even when all other arguments are left out, is this simple truth, that all men are Republicans by nature and Royalists only by fashion. And this is fully proved by that passionate adoration, which all men shew to that great and almost only remaining bulwark of natural rights, *trial by juries*, which is founded on a pure Republican basis. Here the power of Kings is shut out. No Royal negative can enter this Court. The Jury, which is here, supreme, is a *Republic*, a body of *Judges chosen from among the people*.

The charter which secures this freedom in England, was formed, not in the senate, but in the field; and insisted on by the people, not granted by the crown; the crown in that instance *granted nothing*, but only renounced its former tyrannies, and bound itself over to its future good behaviour. — It was the compromise, by which the wearer of it made his peace with the people, and the condition on which he was suffered to reign.

Here ends my reply to all the letters which have at present appeared under the signature of Cato, being at this time seven in number. I have made no particular remarks on his two last, which treats only of the mode of government, but answered to them generally. In one place I observe, he accuses the writer of *Common Sense* with inconsistency, in having declared, "That no man was a warmer wisher for reconciliation than himself, before the fatal 19th of April, 1775;" "that is, (says Cato) reconciliation to monarchical government:" to which I reply, that *war* ought to be no man's *wish*, neither ought any man to perplex a state, already formed, with his private opinions; "the mode of government being a proper consideration for those countries" only "which have their governments yet to form." *Common Sense*.

On a review of the ground which I have gone over in Cato's letters, (exclusive of what I have omitted) I find the following material charges against him:

First. He hath accused the Committee with crimes generally; stated none, nor proved, nor attempted to prove any. *N. B.* The pretence of charging the acts of a body of men on individuals, is too slender to be admitted*.

Secondly. He hath falsly complained to the public of the restraint of the press.

Thirdly. He hath wickedly asserted that "gleams of reconciliation had lately broken in upon us," thereby grossly deceiving the people.

Fourthly. He hath insinuated as if he wished the public to believe, that we had *received* "the utmost assurance of having all our grievances redressed, and an ample security against any future violation of our just rights.

Fifthly. He hath spread false alarms of calling in foreign troops.

Sixthly. He hath turned the scripture into a jest. Ez. 35.

These falsehoods, if uncontradicted, might have passed for truths, and the minds of persons remote from better intelligence might have been greatly embarrassed thereby. Let our opinions be what they will, truth as to facts should be strictly adhered to. It was this affecting consideration that drew out the *Forester* (a perfect volunteer) to the painful task of writing three long letters, and occasioned to the public the trouble of reading them.

Having for the present closed my correspondence with Cato, I shall conclude this letter with a well-meant, affectionate address—

TO THE PEOPLE.

It is not a time to triffle. Men, who know they deserve nothing from their country, and whose hope is on the arm that hath sought to enslave ye, may hold out to you, as Cato hath done, the false light of reconciliation—There is no such thing. 'Tis gone! 'Tis past!—The grave hath parted us—and

---

*Cato and I differ materially in our opinion of Committees; I consider them as the *only constitutional* bodies at present in this province, and that for the following reason; they were duly elected by the people, and chearfully and faithfully do the service for which they were elected. The House of Assembly were likewise elected by the people, but do the business for which they *were not* elected. Their authority is truly unconstitutional, being self created. My charge is as a body, and *not* as individuals.

death, in the persons of the slain, hath cut the thread of life between Britain and America.

Conquest, and not reconciliation is the plan of Britain. But admitting even the last hope of the Tories to happen, which is, that our enemies after a long succession of losses, wearied and disabled, should despairingly throw down their arms and propose a re-union; in that case, what is to be done? Are defeated and disappointed tyrants, to be considered like mistaken and converted friends? Or would it be right, to receive those for Governors, who, had they been conquerors, would have hung us up for traitors? Certainly not. Reject the offer then, and propose another; which is, *we will make peace with you as with enemies, but we will never re-unite with you as friends.* This effected, and ye secure to yourselves the pleasing prospect of an eternal peace. America, remote from all the wrangling world, may live at ease. Bounded by the ocean and backed by the wilderness, what hath she to fear, but her GOD?

Be not deceived. — It is not a little that is at stake. Reconciliation will not now go down, even if it were offered. 'Tis a dangerous question; for the eyes of all men begin to open. There is now no secret in the matter; there ought to be none. It is a case that concerns every man, and every man ought to lay it to heart. He that *is* here and he that was *born* here are alike concerned. It is needless too, to split the business into a thousand parts, and perplex it with endless and fruitless investigations, in the manner that a writer signed a *Common Man* hath done. This unparalleled contention of nations is not to be settled like a school-boy's task of pounds, shillings, pence, and fractions. *That writer*, though he may mean well, is strangely below the mark: For the first and great question, and that which involves every other in it, and from which every other will flow, is *happiness.* Can this continent be happy under the government of Great-Britain or not? Secondly, can she be happy under a government of our own? To live beneath the authority of those whom we cannot love, is misery, slavery, or what name you please. In that case, there will never be peace. Security will be a thing unknown, because, a treacherous friend in power, is the most dangerous of enemies. The answer to the second question, can America be happy under a government of her own is short and simple, viz. as happy as she please; she hath a blank sheet to write upon. Put it not off too long.*

Painful as the task of speaking truth must sometimes be, yet I cannot avoid giving the following hint, because much, nay almost every thing depends upon it; and that is, *a thorough knowledge of the persons whom we trust*. It is the duty of the public, at this time, to scrutinize closely into the conduct of their Committee Members, Members of Assembly, and Delegates in Congress; to know *what* they do, and their motives for so doing. Without knowing this, we shall never know who to confide in; but shall constantly mistake friends for enemies, and enemies for friends, till in the confusion of persons we sacrifice the cause.—I am led to this reflexion by the following circumstance, That the Gentleman to whom the unwise and arbitrary instructions to the Delegates of this province owe their being, and who hath bestowed all his power to support them, is said to be the same person who, when the ships now on the stocks were wanting timber, *refused to sell it*, and thus by preventing our strength to cry out of our insufficiency.—But his hour of fame is past—he is hastening to his political exit.

THE FORESTER.

REPLY TO CATO'S EIGHTH LETTER

April 30, 1776

TO CATO.

WHEREAS Cato, in his eighth letter, and some of his partizans since, have made free with the Forester as having neither *"character nor connexion."* To which I answer, first, "better to have none than bad ones." Secondly, that the person supposed by some, and known by others, to be the author of Common Sense, and the Forester's letters, came a cabin passenger in Jeremiah Warder's ship, the London Packet, last Christmas twelvemonth, bringing with him two unsealed letters of introduction from Dr. Franklin to his friends here, in

*Forget not the hapless African.

which he says, *"I recommend the bearer hereof, Mr. ——, as a worthy ingenious, &c."*

I have published this at the request, and for the sake of those gentlemen whose acquaintance I am honored with—and in my turn call on Cato and his confederates to set forth, as I have done, what rank and recommendation they or their originals made their first appearance in ——

THE FORESTER.

LETTER IV

May 8, 1776

WHOEVER will take the trouble of attending to the progress and changeability of times and things, and the conduct of mankind thereon, will find that *extraordinary circumstances* do sometimes arise before us, of a species, either so purely natural or so perfectly original, that none but the man of nature can understand them. When precedents fail to assist us, we must return to the first principles of things for information; and *think*, as if we were the *first men* that *thought*. And this is the true reason, that in the present state of affairs, the wise are become foolish, and the foolish wise. I am led to this reflection by not being able to account for the conduct of the Quakers on any other; for although they do not seem to perceive it themselves, yet, it is amazing to hear with what unanswerable ignorance many of that body, wise in other matters, will discourse on the present one. Did they hold places or commissions under the King, were they Governors of provinces, or had they any interest apparently distinct from us, the mystery would cease; but as they have not, their folly is best attributed, to that superabundance of *worldly knowledge*, which in original matters is too cunning to be wise. Back to the first plain path of nature friends, and begin anew, for in this business your first footsteps were wrong. You have now travelled to the summit of inconsistency, and that, with such accelerated rapidity as to acquire autumnal ripeness by the first of May. Now your *resting time comes on*. You have done your utmost and must abide the consequences. Yet who can reflect on such conduct without feeling concern; Who can look unaffected, on a body of *thoughtfull* men, undoing in *one rash hour* the labour of seventy years: Or what can be said in their excuse, more, than that they have arrived at their second childhood, the infancy of threescore and ten.*

But my chief design, in this letter, is to set forth the inconsistency, partiality, and injustice of the *dependant faction*, and like an honest man, who courts no favor, to shew to them the dangerous ground they stand upon; in order to do which, I must refer to the *business, event,* and *probable consequences* of the late election.

The business of that day was to do what? Why, to elect four burgesses to assist those already elected, in conducting the military proceedings of this province, against the power of *that crown* by whose authority they pretend to sit: And those gentlemen when elected, are according to the rules of that house (as the rest have done) to take an oath of allegiance to serve the same King against whom this province, with themselves at the head thereof, are at war: And a necessary qualification required of many voters, was, that they likewise should swear allegiance to the same King against whose power the same house of assembly had just before obliged them, either, to fine or take up arms. Did ever national hypocrisy arise to such a pitch as this! Under the pretence of moderation we are running into the most damnable sins. It is now the duty of every man from the pulpit and from the press, in his family and in the street to cry out against it. Good God! Have we no remembrance of duty left to the King of Heaven! No conscientious awe to restrain this sacrifice of sacred things? Is this our chartered priviledge? This our boasted constitution, that

---

*The Quakers in 1704 who then made up the whole house of assembly, zealously guarded their own and the peoples rights against the encroaching power of the proprietor, who nevertheless, outwitted them by finding means to abolish the original charter and introduce another, of which they complained in the following words. "And then by a subtle contrivance and artifice, 'of thine,' laid deeper than the capacities of some could fathom, or the circumstances of many could admit time then to consider of, a way was found out, to lay the first charter aside and introduce another." — *Query,* Would these men have elected the proprietary persons which you have done?

we can sin and feel it not? The clergy of the English church, of which I profess myself a member, complain of *their* situation, and wish relief; in short, every *thinking man* must feel distress. — Yet, to the credit of the people be it spoken, the sin lies not at their door. We can trace the iniquity in this province to the fountain head, and see by what delusions it has imposed on others. The guilt centers in a few, and flows from the same source, that a few years ago avariciously suffered the frontiers of this province to be deluged in blood; and though the vengeance of Heaven hath slept since, it may awake too soon for their repose.

A motion was sometime ago made to elect a convention to take into consideration the state of the province, a more judicious proposal could not be thought of. Our present condition is alarming. We are worse off then other provinces — and such an enquiry is highly necessary. The House of Assembly in its present form is disqualified for such business, because it is a branch from that power against whom we are contending. Besides, they are in intercourse with the King's representative, and the members which compose the house have, as *members thereof*, taken an oath to discover to the King of England the very business, which, in that inquiry would unavoidably come before them. Their minds too are warped and prejudiced by the provincial instructions they have arbitrarily and without right issued forth. They are again improper, because, the enquiry would necessarily *extend to them as a body*, to see how far it is proper to trust men with such unlimited power as they have lately assumed. In times like these, we must trace to the root and origin of things; It being the only way to become right, when we are got systematically wrong. The motion for a Convention, alarmed the crown and proprietary dependants; but to every man of reflection, it had a cordial and restorative quality. The case is, first, we are got wrong — Secondly, how shall we get right? — Not by an House of Assembly; because they cannot sit as *Judges in a case*, where their *own existence* under their *present form and authority is to be judged of.* However, the objectors found out a way, as they thought, to supercede the necessity of a Convention, by promoting a bill for augmenting the number of representatives; not perceiving at the same time, that such an augmentation would *encrease* the *necessity* of a convention; because, the more any power is augmented, which derives it's authority from our enemies, the more unsafe and dangerous it becomes to us. Far be it from the writer of this to censure the individuals which compose that house; his aim being only against the chartered authority under which it acts. However the bill passed into a law (which shews, that in Pennsylvania, as well as in England, there is *no constitution*, but only *a temporary form of government**) While in order to shew the inconsistency of the house in its present state, the motion for a convention was postponed, and four conscientious independant gentlemen were proposed as candidates, on the augmentation, who, had they been elected would not have taken the oaths necessary to admit a person as member of that assembly. And in that case, the house would have had neither one kind of authority nor another. While the old part remained sworn to divulge to the King, what the new part thought it their duty to declare against him. Thus matters stood on the morning of the election.

On our side we had to sustain the loss of those gallant citizens who are now before the walls of Quebec, and other parts of the continent; while the tories by never stirring out, remain at home to take the advantage of elections; and this evil prevails more or less from the Congress down to the Committees. A numerous body of Germans, of property, zealots in the cause of freedom, were likewise excluded for non-allegiance: Notwithstanding which, the tory non-conformists, that is, those who are advertised as enemies to their country, were admitted to vote on the other side. A strange contradiction indeed! To which were added the testimonizing Quakers, who, after suffering themselves to be duped by the meanest of all passion, religious spleen, endeavoured in a vague uncharitable manner to possess the Roman Catholics of the same disease. These parties, with such others as they could influence, were headed by the proprietary dependants, to support the British and Proprietary power against the public. They had pompously given out that nine tenths of the people were on their side. A vast majority truly! But it so happened,

*This distinction will be more fully explained in some future letter.

that notwithstanding the disadvantages we laid under, of having many of our voters rejected, others disqualified for non-allegiance, with the great loss sustained by absentees, the manœuvre of shutting up the doors between seven and eight o'clock, and circulating the report of adjourning and finishing the next morning, by which, several were deceived, it so happened, I say, that on casting up the tickets, that the first, in numbers, on the dependant side, and the first on the independant side, viz. Clymer and Allen, were a tye 923 each.*

To the description which I have already given of those who are against us, I may add, that they have neither associated nor assisted, or but very few of them; that they are a collection of different bodies blended by accident, having no natural relation to each other; that they have agreed rather out of spite than right; and that, as they met by chance, they will dissolve away again for the want of a cement.

On our side, our object was *single*, our cause was *one*; wherefore, we *cannot* separate, neither *will* we separate. We have stood the experiment of the election, for the sake of knowing the men who were against us. Alass what are they! One half of them ought to be now asking public pardon for their former offences; and the other half may think themselves well off that they are let alone. When the enemy enters the country, *can* they defend themselves? Or *will* they defend themselves? And if not, are they so foolish as to think, that in times like these, when it is our duty to search the corrupted wound to the bottom, that we, with ten times their strength and number (if the question were put to the people at large) will submit to be governed by cowards and tories.

He that is wise will reflect, that the safest asylum, especially in times of general convulsion when no settled form of government prevails, is, *the love of the people*. All property is safe under their protection. Even in countries where the lowest and most licentious of them have risen into outrage, they have never departed from the path of *natural* honour. Volunteers unto death in defence of the person or fortune of those who had served or defended them. Division of property never

---

*Mr. Samuel Howell, though in their ticket, was never considered by us a proprietary dependant.

entered the mind of the populace.—It is incompatible with that spirit which impels them into action. An avaricious mob was never heard of; nay, even a miser put in the midst of them, and catching their spirit, would, for that instant, cease to be covetous.

I shall conclude this letter with remarking, that the English fleet and army have of late gone upon a different plan of operation to what they first set out with; for instead of going against those Colonies where independance prevails *most*, they go against *those only* where they suppose it prevails *least*. They have quitted Massachusetts-Bay and gone to North-Carolina; supposing they had many friends there. Why are they expected at New-York? But because they imagine the inhabitants are *not* generally independants, (yet that province hath a large share of virtue, notwithstanding the odium which its House of Assembly brought upon it.) From which I argue, that the electing the King's Attorney for a Burgess of this city, is a fair invitation for them to come here; and in that case, will those who have invited them turn out to repulse them; I suppose not, for in their 923 votes there will not be found more than sixty armed men, perhaps not so many. Wherefore, should such an event happen, which probably will, I here give my *first vote* to levy the expence attending the expedition against them, *on the estates of those who have invited them.*

THE FORESTER.

The American Crisis

NUMBER I

December 19, 1776

THESE are the times that try men's souls: The summer soldier and the sunshine patriot will, in this crisis, shrink from the service of his country; but he that stands it NOW, deserves the love and thanks of man and woman. Tyranny, like hell, is not easily conquered; yet we have this consolation with us, that the harder the conflict, the more glorious the triumph. What we obtain too cheap, we esteem too lightly:—'Tis dearness only that gives every thing its value. Heaven knows how to set a proper price upon its goods; and it would be strange indeed, if so celestial an article as FREEDOM should not be highly rated. Britain, with an army to enforce her tyranny, has declared, that she has a right (*not only to* TAX) but "*to* BIND *us in* ALL CASES WHATSOEVER," and if being *bound in that manner* is not slavery, then is there not such a thing as slavery upon earth. Even the expression is impious, for so unlimited a power can belong only to GOD.

Whether the Independence of the Continent was declared too soon, or delayed too long, I will not now enter into as an argument; my own simple opinion is, that had it been eight months earlier, it would have been much better. We did not make a proper use of last winter, neither could we, while we were in a dependent state. However, the fault, if it were one, was all our own; we have none to blame but ourselves*. But no great deal is lost yet; all that Howe has been doing for this month past is rather a ravage than a conquest, which the spirit of the Jersies a year ago would have quickly repulsed, and which time and a little resolution will soon recover.

*"The present winter" (meaning the last) "is worth an age, if rightly employed, but if lost, or neglected, the whole Continent will partake of the evil; and there is no punishment that man does not deserve, be he who, or what, or where he will, that may be the means of sacrificing a season so precious and useful."   COMMON SENSE.

I have as little superstition in me as any man living, but my secret opinion has ever been, and still is, that GOD almighty will not give up a people to military destruction, or leave them unsupportedly to perish, who had so earnestly and so repeatedly sought to avoid the calamities of war, by every decent method which wisdom could invent. Neither have I so much of the infidel in me, as to suppose, that HE has relinquished the government of the world, and given us up to the care of devils; and as I do not, I cannot see on what grounds the king of Britain can look up to heaven for help against us: A common murderer, a highwayman, or a housebreaker, has as good a pretence as he.

'Tis surprising to see how rapidly a panic will sometimes run through a country. All nations and ages have been subject to them: Britain has trembled like an ague at the report of a French fleet of flat bottomed boats; and in the fourteenth century the whole English army, after ravaging the kingdom of France, was driven back like men petrified with fear; and this brave exploit was performed by a few broken forces collected and headed by a woman, Joan of Arc. Would, that Heaven might inspire some Jersey maid to spirit up her countrymen, and save her fair fellow-sufferers from ravage and ravishment! Yet panics, in some cases, have their uses; they produce as much good as hurt. Their duration is always short; the mind soon grows thro' them, and acquires a firmer habit than before. But their peculiar advantage is, that they are the touchstones of sincerity and hypocrisy, and bring things and men to light, which might otherwise have lain for ever undiscovered. In fact, they have the same effect on secret traitors, which an imaginary apparition would upon a private murderer. They sift out the hidden thoughts of man, and hold them up in public to the world. Many a disguised Tory has lately shewn his head, that shall penitentially solemnize with curses the day on which Howe arrived upon the Delaware.

As I was with the troops at fort Lee, and marched with them to the edge of Pennsylvania, I am well acquainted with many circumstances, which those, who lived at a distance, know but little or nothing of. Our situation there was exceedingly cramped, the place being on a narrow neck of land between the North river and the Hackensack. Our force was inconsiderable, being not one fourth so great as Howe could bring against us. We had no army at hand to have relieved the garrison, had we shut ourselves up and stood on the defence. Our ammunition, light artillery, and the best part of our stores, had been removed upon the apprehension that Howe would endeavour to penetrate the Jersies, in which case fort Lee could be of no use to us; for it must occur to every thinking man, whether in the army or not, that these kind of field forts are only for temporary purposes, and last in use no longer than the enemy directs his force against the particular object, which such forts are raised to defend. Such was our situation and condition at fort Lee on the morning of the 20th of November, when an officer arrived with information, that the enemy with 200 boats had landed about seven or eight miles above: Major General Green, who commanded the garrison, immediately ordered them under arms, and sent express to his Excellency General Washington at the town of Hackensack, distant by the way of the ferry six miles. Our first object was to secure the bridge over the Hackensack, which laid up the river between the enemy and us, about six miles from us and three from them. General Washington arrived in about three quarters of an hour, and marched at the head of the troops towards the bridge, which place I expected we should have a brush for; however they did not chuse to dispute it with us, and the greatest part of our troops went over the bridge, the rest over the ferry, except some which passed at a mill on a small creek, between the bridge and the ferry, and made their way through some marshy grounds up to the town of Hackensack, and there passed the river. We brought off as much baggage as the waggons could contain, the rest was lost. The simple object was to bring off the garrison, and to march them on till they could be strengthened by the Jersey or Pennsylvania militia, so as to be enabled to make a stand. We staid four days at Newark, collected in our outposts with some of the Jersey militia, and marched out twice to meet the enemy on information of their being advancing, though our numbers were greatly inferiour to theirs. Howe, in my little opinion, committed a great error in generalship, in not throwing a body of forces off from Staaten Island through Amboy, by which means he might have seized all our stores at Brunswick, and intercepted our march into Pennsylvania: But, if we believe the power of hell to be limited, we must likewise believe that their agents are under some providential controul.

I shall not now attempt to give all the particulars of our retreat to the Delaware; suffice it for the present to say, that both officers and men, though greatly harassed and fatigued, frequently without rest, covering, or provision, the inevitable consequences of a long retreat, bore it with a manly and a martial spirit. All their wishes were one, which was, that the country would turn out and help them to drive the enemy back. Voltaire has remarked, that king William never appeared to full advantage but in difficulties and in action; the same remark may be made on General Washington, for the character fits him. There is a natural firmness in some minds which cannot be unlocked by triffles, but which, when unlocked, discovers a cabinet of fortitude; and I reckon it among those kind of public blessings, which we do not immediately see, that GOD hath blest him with uninterrupted health, and given him a mind that can even flourish upon care.

I shall conclude this paper with some miscellaneous remarks on the state of our affairs; and shall begin with asking the following question, Why is it that the enemy hath left the New-England provinces, and made these middle ones the seat of war? The answer is easy: New-England is not infested with Tories, and we are. I have been tender in raising the cry against these men, and used numberless arguments to shew them their danger, but it will not do to sacrifice a world to either their folly or their baseness. The period is now arrived, in which either they or we must change our sentiments, or one or both must fall. And what is a Tory? Good GOD! what is he? I should not be afraid to go with a hundred Whigs against a thousand Tories, were they to attempt to get into arms. Every Tory is a coward, for a servile, slavish, self-interested fear is the foundation of Toryism; and a man under such influence, though he may be cruel, never can be brave.

But before the line of irrecoverable separation be drawn between us, let us reason the matter together: Your conduct is an invitation to the enemy, yet not one in a thousand of you has heart enough to join him. Howe is as much deceived by you as the American cause is injured by you. He expects you will all take up arms, and flock to his standard with muskets on your shoulders. Your opinions are of no use to him, unless you support him personally; for 'tis soldiers, and not Tories, that he wants.

I once felt all that kind of anger, which a man ought to feel, against the mean principles that are held by the Tories: A noted one, who kept a tavern at Amboy, was standing at his door, with as pretty a child in his hand, about eight or nine years old, as most I ever saw, and after speaking his mind as freely as he thought was prudent, finished with this unfatherly expression, *"Well! give me peace in my day."* Not a man lives on the Continent but fully believes that a seperation must some time or other finally take place, and a generous parent would have said, *"If there must be trouble, let it be in my day, that my child may have peace;"* and this single reflection, well applied, is sufficient to awaken every man to duty. Not a place upon earth might be so happy as America. Her situation is remote from all the wrangling world, and she has nothing to do but to trade with them. A man may easily distinguish in himself between temper and principle, and I am as confident, as I am that GOD governs the world, that America will never be happy till she gets clear of foreign dominion. Wars, without ceasing, will break out till that period arrives, and the Continent must in the end be conqueror; for, though the flame of liberty may sometimes cease to shine, the coal never can expire.

America did not, nor does not, want force; but she wanted a proper application of that force. Wisdom is not the purchase of a day, and it is no wonder that we should err at first sitting off. From an excess of tenderness, we were unwilling to raise an army, and trusted our cause to the temporary defence of a well meaning militia. A summer's experience has now taught us better; yet with those troops, while they were collected, we were able to set bounds to the progress of the enemy, and, thank GOD! they are again assembling. I always considered a militia as the best troops in the world for a sudden exertion, but they will not do for a long campaign. Howe, it is probable, will make an attempt on this city; should he fail on this side the Delaware, he is ruined; if he succeeds, our cause is not ruined. He stakes all on his side against a part of ours; admitting he succeeds, the consequence will be, that armies from both ends of the Continent will march to assist their suffering friends in the middle States; for he cannot go every where, it is impossible. I consider Howe as the greatest enemy the Tories have; he is bringing a war into their country, which, had it not been for him and partly for themselves, they had been clear of. Should he now be expelled, I wish, with all the devotion of a Christian, that the names of Whig and Tory may never more be mentioned; but should the Tories give him encouragement to come, or assistance if he come, I as sincerely wish that our next year's arms may expell them from the Continent, and the Congress appropriate their possessions to the relief of those who have suffered in well doing. A single successful battle next year will settle the whole. America could carry on a two years war by the confiscation of the property of disaffected persons, and be made happy by their expulsion. Say not that this is revenge, call it rather the soft resentment of a suffering people, who, having no object in view but the GOOD of ALL, have staked their OWN ALL upon a seemingly doubtful event. Yet it is folly to argue against determined hardness; eloquence may strike the ear, and the language of sorrow draw forth the tear of compassion, but nothing can reach the heart that is steeled with prejudice.

Quitting this class of men, I turn with the warm ardour of a friend to those who have nobly stood, and are yet determined to stand the matter out: I call not upon a few, but upon all; not on THIS State or THAT State, but on EVERY State; up and help us; lay your shoulders to the wheel; better have too much force than too little, when so great an object is at stake. Let it be told to the future world, that in the depth of winter, when nothing but hope and virtue could survive, that the city and the country, alarmed at one common danger, came forth to meet and to repulse it. Say not, that thousands are gone, turn out your tens of thousands; throw not the burthen of the day upon Providence, but *"shew your faith by your works,"* that GOD may bless you. It matters not where you live, or what rank of life you hold, the evil or the blessing will reach you all. The far and the near, the home counties and the back, the rich and the poor, shall suffer or rejoice alike. The heart that feels not now, is dead: The blood of his children shall curse his cowardice, who shrinks back at a time when a little might have saved the whole, and made *them* happy. I love the man that can smile in trouble, that can gather strength from distress, and grow brave by reflection. 'Tis the business of little minds to shrink; but he whose heart is firm, and whose conscience approves his conduct, will pursue his principles unto death. My own line of reasoning is to myself as strait and clear as a ray of light. Not all the treasures of the world, so far as I believe, could have induced me to support an offensive war, for I think it murder; but if a thief break into my house, burn and destroy my property, and kill or threaten to kill me, or those that are in it, and to *"bind me in all cases whatsoever,"* to his absolute will, am I to suffer it? What signifies it to me, whether he who does it, is a king or a common man; my countryman or not my countryman? whether it is done by an individual villain, or an army of them? If we reason to the root of things we shall find no difference; neither can any just cause be assigned why we should punish in the one case, and pardon in the other. Let them call me rebel, and welcome, I feel no concern from it; but I should suffer the misery of devils, were I to make a whore of my soul by swearing allegiance to one, whose character is that of a sottish, stupid, stubborn, worthless, brutish man. I conceive likewise a horrid idea in receiving mercy from a being, who at the last day shall be shrieking to the rocks and mountains to cover him, and fleeing with terror from the orphan, the widow and the slain of America.

There are cases which cannot be overdone by language, and this is one. There are persons too who see not the full extent of the evil that threatens them; they solace themselves with hopes that the enemy, if they succeed, will be merciful. It is the madness of folly to expect mercy from those who have refused to do justice; and even mercy, where conquest is the object, is only a trick of war: The cunning of the fox is as murderous as the violence of the wolfe; and we ought to guard equally against both. Howe's first object is partly by threats and partly by promises, to terrify or seduce the people to deliver up their arms, and receive mercy. The ministry recommended the same plan to Gage, and this is what the Tories call making their peace; *"a peace which passeth all understanding" indeed!* A peace which would be the immediate forerunner of a worse ruin than any we have yet thought of. Ye men of Pennsylvania, do reason upon those things! Were the back counties to give up their arms, they would fall an easy prey to the Indians, who are all armed: This perhaps is what some Tories would not be sorry for. Were the home counties to deliver up their arms, they would be exposed to the resentment of the back counties, who would then have it in their power to chastise their defection at pleasure. And were any one State to give up its arms, THAT State must be garrisoned by all Howe's army of Britons and Hessians to preserve it from the anger of the rest. Mutual fear is a principal link in the chain of mutual love, and woe be to that State that breaks the compact. Howe is mercifully inviting you to barbarous destruction, and men must be either rogues or fools that will not see it. I dwell not upon the vapours of imagination; I bring reason to your ears; and in language, as plain as A, B, C, hold up truth to your eyes.

I thank GOD that I fear not. I see no real cause for fear. I know our situation well, and can see the way out of it. While our army was collected, Howe dared not risk a battle, and it is no credit to him that he decamped from the White Plains, and waited a mean opportunity to ravage the defenceless Jersies; but it is great credit to us, that, with an handful of men, we sustained an orderly retreat for near an hundred miles, brought off our ammunition, all our field-pieces, the greatest part of our stores, and had four rivers to pass. None can say that our retreat was precipitate, for we were near three weeks in performing it, that the country might have time to come in. Twice we marched back to meet the enemy and remained out till dark. The sign of fear was not seen in our camp, and had not some of the cowardly and disaffected inhabitants spread false alarms thro' the country, the Jersies had never been ravaged. Once more we are again collected and collecting; our new army at both ends of the Continent is recruiting fast, and we shall be able to open the next campaign with sixty thousand men, well armed and cloathed. This is our situation, and who will may know it. By perseverance and fortitude we have the prospect of a glorious issue; by cowardice and submission, the sad choice of a variety of evils—a ravaged country—a depopulated city—habitations without safety, and slavery without hope—our homes turned into barracks and baudy-houses for Hessians, and a future race to provide for whose fathers we shall doubt of. Look on this picture, and weep over it!—and if there yet remains one thoughtless wretch who believes it not, let him suffer it unlamented.

The American Crisis

NUMBER II

January 13, 1777

TO LORD HOWE.

"What's in the name of LORD that I should fear,
    To bring my grievance to the public ear."   CHURCHILL.

UNIVERSAL empire is the prerogative of a writer. His concerns are with all mankind, and though he cannot command their obedience, he can assign them their duty. The Republic of Letters is more ancient than monarchy, and of far higher character in the world than the vassal court of Britain; he that rebels against reason is a real rebel, but he that in defence of reason, rebels against tyranny, has a better title to "DEFENDER OF THE FAITH" than George the Third.

As a military man your Lordship may hold out the sword of war, and call it the "ULTIMA RATIO REGUM:" *The last Reason of Kings;* we in return can show you the sword of justice, and call it, "The best Scourge of Tyrants." The first of these two may threaten, or even frighten, for a while, and cast a sickly languor over an insulted people, but reason will soon recover the debauch, and restore them again to tranquil fortitude. Your Lordship, I find, has now commenced author and published a proclamation; I too have published a crisis; as they stand, they are the antipodes of each other; both cannot rise at once, and one of them must descend: And so quick is the revolution of things, that your Lordship's performance, I see, has already fallen many degrees from its first place, and is now just visible on the edge of the political horizon.

It is surprising to what pitch of infatuation blind folly and obstinacy will carry mankind, and your Lordship's drowsy proclamation is a proof that it does not even quit them in their sleep. Perhaps you thought America too was taking a nap, and therefore, chose, like satan to Eve, to whisper the delusion softly, lest you should awaken her. This Continent, Sir, is too extensive to sleep all at once, and too watchful, even in its slumbers, not to startle at the unhallowed foot of an invader. You may issue your proclamations, and welcome, for we have learned to *"reverence ourselves"* and scorn the insulting ruffian that employs you. America for your deceased brother's sake would gladly have shown you respect, and it is a new aggravation to her feelings that *Howe* should be forgetful, and raise his sword against those, who at their own charge raised a monument to his brother. But your master has commanded, and you have not enough of nature left to refuse. Surely! there must be something strangely degenerating in the love of monarchy, that can so completely wear a man down to an ingrate, and make him proud to lick the dust that kings have trod upon. A few more years, should you survive them, will bestow on you the title of an old man, and in some hour of future reflection you may probably find the fitness of Woolsey's despairing penitence, *"Had I served my God as faithfully as I have served my king, he would not thus have forsaken me in my old age."*

The character you appear to us in is truly ridiculous. Your friends, the Tories, announced your coming with high descriptions of your unlimited powers; but your proclamation has given them the lie, by shewing you to be a Commissioner without authority. Had your powers been ever so great, they were nothing to us, farther than we pleased; because we had the same right which other nations had, to do what we thought was best. "THE UNITED STATES OF AMERICA," will sound as pompously in the world or in history as *"The Kingdom of Great-Britain;"* The character of *General Washington* will fill a page with as much luster as that of *Lord Howe*; and the *Congress* have as much right to command the *King and Parliament* of London, to desist from legislation, as *they* or *you* have to command the Congress. Only suppose how laughable such an edict would appear from us, and then, in that merry mood, do but turn the tables upon yourself, and you will see how your proclamation is received here. Having thus placed you in a proper position in which you may have a full view of folly and learn to despise it, I hold up to you, for that purpose, the following quotation from your own lunarian proclamation. "And We (Lord Howe and General Howe) do command, (and in his Majesty's name forsooth) all such persons as are assembled together under the name of general or provincial Congresses, Committees, Conventions, or other Associations, by whatever name or names known or distinguished, to desist and cease from all such treasonable actings and doings."

You introduce your proclamation by referring to your declarations of the 14th of July and 19th of September. In the last of these, you sunk yourself below the character of a private gentleman. That I may not seem to accuse you unjustly I shall state the circumstance: By a verbal invitation of yours communicated to Congress by General Sullivan, then a prisoner on his parole, you signified your desire of conferring with some members of that body as private gentlemen. It was beneath the dignity of the American Congress to pay any regard to a message that at best was but a genteel affront, and had too much of the ministerial complexion of tampering with private persons; and which might probably have been the case, had the gentlemen who were deputed on that business, possessed that easy kind of virtue which an English courtier is so truly distinguished by. Your request however was complied with, for honest men are naturally more tender of their civil than their political fame. The interview ended as every sensible man thought it would; for your Lordship knows, as well as the writer of the Crisis, that it is impossible for the king of England to promise the repeal, or even the revisal, of any acts of parliament; wherefore, on your part, you had nothing to say, more than to request, in the room of demanding, the entire surrender of the Continent; and then, if that was complied with, to promise that the inhabitants should escape with their lives. This was the upshot of the conference. You informed the conferees that you were two months in soliciting these powers. We ask, what powers? for as Commissioner you have none. If you mean the power of pardoning, it is an oblique proof that your master was determined to sacrifice all before him; and that you were two months in dissuading him from his purpose. Another evidence of his savage obstinacy! From your own account of the matter we may justly draw these two conclusions; first, that you serve a monster; and secondly, that never was a commissioner sent on a more foolish errand than yourself. This plain language may perhaps sound uncoothly to an ear viciated by courtly refinements; but words were made for use, and the fault lies in deserving them, or the abuse in applying them unfairly.

Soon after your return to New-York you published a very illiberal and unmanly hand bill against the Congress; for it was certainly stepping out of the line of common civility, first to screen your national pride by soliciting an interview with them as private gentlemen, and in the conclusion to endeavour to deceive the multitude by making an hand bill attack on the whole body of the Congress; you got them together under one name, and abused them under another. But the king you serve and the cause you support afford you so few instances of acting the gentleman, that out of pity to your situation the Congress pardoned the insult by taking no notice of it.

You say in that hand bill, "that they, the Congress, disavowed every purpose for reconciliation not consonant with their extravagant and inadmissible claim of Independence." Why, God bless me! what have you to do with our Independence? we ask no leave of yours to set it up; we ask no money of yours to support it; we can do better without your fleets and armies than with them; you may soon have enough to do to protect yourselves without being burthened with us. We are very willing to be at peace with you, to buy of you and sell to you, and, like young beginners in the world, to work for our own living; therefore, why do you put yourselves out of cash, when we know you cannot spare it, and we do not desire you to run into debt? I am willing, Sir, you should see your folly in every view I can place it, and for that reason descend sometimes to tell you in jest what I wish you to see in earnest. But to be more serious with you, why do you say "their" Independence? To set you right, Sir, we tell you, that the Independency is *ours* not *theirs*. The Congress were authorised by every State on the Continent to publish it to all the world, and in so doing are not to be considered as the inventors, but only as the heralds that proclaimed it, or the office from which the sense of the people receive a legal form; and it was as much as any or all their heads were worth, to have treated with you on the subject of submission under any name whatever. But we know the men in whom we have trusted; can England say the same of her parliament?

I come now more particularly to your proclamation of the 30th of November last. Had you gained an entire conquest over all the armies of America, and then put forth a proclamation, offering (what you call) mercy, your conduct would have had some specious show of humanity; but to creep by surprise into a province, and there endeavour to terrify and seduce the inhabitants from their just allegiance to the rest by promises, which you neither meant nor were able to fulfil, is both cruel and unmanly: Cruel in its effects; because, unless you can keep all the ground you have marched over, how are you, in the words of your proclamation, to secure to your proselytes "the enjoyment of their property?" What are to become either of your new adopted subjects, or your old friends the Tories, in Burlington, Bordentown, Trenton, Mountholly, and many other places, where you proudly lorded it for a few days, and then fled with the precipitation of a pursued thief? What, I say, are to become of those wretches? What are to become of those who went over to you from this city and State? What more can you say to them than *"Shift for yourselves?"* Or what more can they hope for than to wander like vagabonds over the face of the earth? You may now tell them to take their leave of America and all that once was theirs. Recommend them, for consolation, to your master's court; there perhaps they may make a shift to live on the scraps of some dangling parasite, and choose companions among thousands like themselves. A traitor is the foulest fiend on earth!

In a political sense we ought to thank you for thus bequeathing estates to the Continent; we shall soon, at this rate, be able to carry on a war without expence, and grow rich by the ill policy of Lord Howe and the generous defection of the Tories. Had you set your foot into this city you would have bestowed estates upon us which we never thought of, by bringing forth traitors we were unwilling to suspect. But these men, you'll say, *"are his majesty's most faithful subjects;"* let that honour then be all their fortune, and let his majesty take them to himself.

I am now thoroughly disgusted with them; they live in ungrateful ease and bend their whole minds to mischief. It seems as if GOD had given them over to a spirit of infidelity, and that they are open to conviction in no other line but that of punishment. It is time to have done with tarring, feathering, carting, and taking securities for their future good behaviour; every sensible man must feel a conscious shame at seeing a poor fellow hawked for a show about the streets, when it is known that he is only the tool of some principal villain, biased into his offence by the force of false reasoning, or bribed thereto through sad necessity. We dishonour ourselves by attacking such trifling characters, while greater ones are suffered to escape; 'tis our duty to find *them* out, and their proper punishment would be to exile them from the Continent for ever. The circle of them is not so great as some imagine; the influence of a few have tainted many who are not naturally corrupt. A continual circulation of lies among those who are not much in the way of hearing them contradicted, will in time pass for truth; and the crime lies not in the believer but the inventor. I am not for declaring war against every man that appears not so warm as myself: Difference of constitution, temper, habit of speaking and many other things will go a great way in fixing the outward character of a man, yet simple honesty may remain at bottom. Some men have naturally a military turn, and can brave hardships and the risk of life with a chearful face; others have not, no slavery appears to them so great as the fatigue of arms, and no terror so powerful as that of personal danger: What can we say? We cannot alter nature, neither ought we to punish the son because the father begot him in a cowardly mood. However, I believe most men have more courage than they know of, and that a little at first is enough to begin with. I knew the time when I thought that the whistling of a cannon ball would have frightened me almost to death; but I have since tried it, and find I can stand it with as little discomposure, and (I believe) with a much easier conscience than your Lordship. The same dread would return to me again were I in your situation, for my solemn belief of your cause is, that it is hellish and damnable, and under that conviction every thinking man's heart *must* fail him.

From a concern that a good cause should be dishonoured by the least disunion among us, I said in my former paper, No. 1. "That should the enemy now be expelled, I wish, with all the sincerity of a Christian, that the names of Whig and

Tory might never more be mentioned;" but there is a knot of men among us of such a venomous cast that they will not admit even one's good wishes to act in their favour. Instead of rejoicing that Heaven had, as it were, providentially preserved this city from plunder and destruction, by delivering so great a part of the enemy into our hands with so little effusion of blood, they stubbornly affected to disbelieve it till within an hour, nay half an hour, of the prisoners arriving: And the Quakers put forth a testimony, dated the 20th of December, signed *"John Pemberton,"* declaring their attachment to the British government.* These men are continually harping on the great sin of *our* bearing arms, but the king of Britain may lay waste the world in blood and famine, and they, poor fallen souls, have nothing to say.

In some future paper I intend to distinguish between the different kind of persons who have been denominated *Tories*; for this I am clear in, that all are not so who have been called so, nor all men Whigs who were once thought so; and as I mean not to conceal the name of any true friend when there shall be occasion to mention him, neither will I that of an enemy who ought to be known, let his rank, station or religion be what it may. Much pains have been taken by some to set your Lordship's private character in an amiable light, but as it has chiefly been done by men who know nothing about you, and who are no ways remarkable for their attachment to us, we have no just authority for believing it. George the Third was imposed upon us by the same arts, but TIME, at length, has done him justice, and the same fate may probably attend your Lordship. Your avowed purpose here, is to kill, conquer, plunder, pardon and enslave; and the ravages of your army through the Jersies have been marked with as much barbarism as if you had openly professed yourself the

---

*I have ever been careful of charging offences upon whole societies of men, but as the paper referred to is put forth by an unknown set of men, who claim to themselves the right of representing the whole; and while the whole society of Quakers admit its validity by a silent acknowledgment, it is impossible that any distinction can be made by the public; and the more so because the New-York paper, of the 30th of December, printed by permission of our enemies, says that *"the Quakers begin to speak openly of their attachment to the British constitution."* We are certain that we have many friends among them, and wish to know them.

prince of ruffians; not even the appearance of humanity has been preserved either on the march or the retreat of your troops; no general order, that I could ever learn, has ever been issued to prevent or even forbid your troops from robbery wherever they came, and the only instance of justice, if it can be called such, which has distinguished you for impartiality, is, that you treated and plundered all alike; what could not be carried away have been destroyed, and mohogony furniture have been deliberately laid on the fire for fuel, rather than the men should be fatigued with cutting wood.* There was a time when the Whigs confided much in your supposed candour, and the Tories rested themselves on your favour; the experiments have now been made, and failed; and every town, nay every cottage, in the Jersies, where your arms have been, is a testimony against you. How you may rest under this sacrifice of character I know not, but this I know, that you sleep and rise with the daily curses of thousands upon you; perhaps the misery which the Tories have suffered by your proffered mercy may give them some claim to their country's pity, and be in the end the best favour you could show them.

In a folio general order book belonging to Colonel Rohl's battalion, taken at Trenton, and now in the possession of the Council of Safety for this State, the following barbarous order is frequently repeated, *"His Excellency the* COMMANDER IN CHIEF *orders, that all inhabitants which shall be found with arms, not having an officer with them, shall be immediately taken and hung up."* How many you may thus have privately sacrificed we know not, and the account can only be settled in another world. Your treatment of prisoners, in order to distress them to enlist into your infernal service, is not to be equalled by any instance in Europe. Yet this is the humane Lord Howe and his brother, whom the Tories and their three quarter kindred the Quakers, or some of them at least, have been holding up for patterns of justice and mercy!

A bad cause will ever be supported by bad means and bad

*As some people may doubt the truth of such wanton destruction, I think it necessary to inform, that one of the people called Quakers, who lives at Trenton, gave me this information at the house of Mr. Michael Hutchinson (one of the same profession) who lives near to Trenton ferry, on the Pennsylvania side; Mr. Hutchinson being present.

men, and whoever will be at the pains of examining strictly into things, will find that one and the same spirit of oppression and impiety, more or less, governs through your whole party in both countries: Not many days ago I accidently fell in company with a person of this city, noted for espousing your cause, and on my remarking to him, "that it appeared clear to me, by the late providential turn of affairs, that GOD Almighty was visibly on our side," he replied, "We care nothing for that, you may have HIM, and welcome; if we have but enough of the devil on our side we shall do." However carelessly this might be spoken matters not, 'tis still the insensible principle that directs all your conduct, and will at last most assuredly deceive and ruin you.

If ever a nation was mad and foolish, blind to its own interest and bent on its own destruction, it is Britain. There are such things as national sins, and though the punishment of individuals may be reserved to *another* world, national punishment can only be inflicted in *this* world. Britain, as a nation, is in my inmost belief the greatest and most ungrateful offender against GOD on the face of the whole earth: Bless'd with all the commerce she could wish for, and furnished by a vast extension of dominion with the means of civilizing both the eastern and western world, she has made no other use of both than proudly to idolize her own "Thunder," and rip up the bowels of whole countries for what she could get;—like Alexander she has made war her sport, and inflicted misery for prodagality sake. The blood of India is not yet repaid, nor the wretchedness of Africa yet requitted. Of late she has enlarged her list of national cruelties by her butcherly destruction of the Caribbs of St. Vincents, and in returning an answer by the sword to the meek prayer for *"Peace, Liberty and Safety."* These are serious things; and whatever a foolish tyrant, a debauched court, a trafficing legislature or a blinded people may think, the national account with Heaven must some day or other be settled: All countries have sooner or later been called to their reckoning; the proudest empires have sunk when the balance was struck; and Britain, like an individual penitent, must undergo her day of sorrow, and the sooner it happens to her the better. As I wish it over, I wish it to come, but withal wish that it may be as light as possible.

Perhaps your Lordship has no taste for serious things; by your connexions in England I should suppose not: Therefore I shall drop this part of the subject, and take it up in a line in which you will better understand me.

By what means, may I ask, do you expect to conquer America? If you could not effect it in the summer when our army was less than yours, nor in the winter when we had none, how are you to do it? In point of generalship you have been outwitted, and in point of fortitude outdone; your advantages turn out to your loss, and show us that it is in our power to ruin you by gifts: Like a game of drafts we can move out of *one* square to let you come in, in order that we may afterwards take two or three for one; and as we can always keep a double corner for ourselves, we can always prevent a total defeat. You cannot be so insensible as not to see that we have two to one the advantage of you, because we conquer by a drawn game, and you lose by it. Burgoyne might have taught your Lordship this knowledge; he has been long a student in the doctrine of chances.

I have no other idea of conquering countries than by subduing the armies which defend them: Have you done this, or can you do this? If you have not, it would be civil in you to let your proclamations alone for the present; otherwise, you will ruin more Tories by your grace and favour than you will Whigs by your arms.

Were you to obtain possession of this city, you would not know what to do with it more than to plunder it. To hold it, in the manner you hold New-York, would be an additional dead weight upon your hands; and if a general conquest is your object, you had better be without the city than with it. When you have defeated all our armies, the cities will fall into your hands of themselves; but to creep into them in the manner you got into Princetown, Trenton, &c. is like robbing an orchard in the night before the fruit be ripe, and running away in the morning. Your experiment in the Jersies is sufficient to teach you that you have something more to do than barely to get into other people's houses; and your new converts, to whom you promised all manner of protection, and seduced into new guilt by pardoning them from their former virtues, must begin to have a very contemptible opinion both of your power and your policy. Your authority in the Jersies is now reduced to the small circle which your army occupies, and your proclamation is no where else seen unless it be to be laughed at. The mighty subduers of the Continent are retreated into a nutshell, and the proud forgivers of our sins are fled from those they came to pardon; and all this at a time when they were dispatching vessel after vessel to England with the great news of every day. In short, you have managed your Jersey expedition so very dexterously that the dead only are conquerors, because none will dispute the ground with them.

In all the wars you have formerly been concerned in, you had only armies to contend with; in this case you have both an army and a country to combat with. In former wars, the countries followed the fate of their capitals; Canada fell with Quebec, and Minorca with Port Mahon or St. Philips; by subduing those, the conquerors opened a way into, and became masters of the country: here it is otherwise; if you get possession of a city here, you are obliged to shut yourselves up in it, and can make no other use of it, than to spend your country's money in. This is all the advantage you have drawn from New-York; and you would draw less from Philadelphia, because it requires more force to keep it, and is much farther from the sea. A pretty figure you and the Tories would cut in this city, with a river full of ice, and a town full of fire; for the immediate consequence of your getting here would be, that you would be cannonaded out again and the Tories be obliged to make good the damage; and this, sooner or later, will be the fate of New-York.

I wish to see the city saved, not so much from military as from natural motives. 'Tis the hiding-place of women and children, and Lord Howe's proper business is with our armies. When I put all the circumstances together which ought to be taken, I laugh at your notion of conquering America. Because you lived in a little country where an army might run over the whole in a few days, and where a single company of soldiers might put a multitude to the route, you expected to find it the same here. It is plain that you brought over with you all the narrow notions you were bred up with, and imagined that a proclamation in the king's name was to do great things; but Englishmen always travel for knowledge, and your Lordship, I hope, will return, if you return at all, much wiser than you came.

We may be surprised by events we did not expect, and in that interval of recollection you may gain some temporary advantage: Such was the case a few weeks ago, but we soon ripen again into reason, collect our strength, and while you are preparing for a triumph we came upon you with a defeat. Such it has been, and such it would be were you to try it an hundred times over. Were you to garrison the places you might march over, in order to secure their subjection, (for remember you can do it by no other means) your army would be like a stream of water running to nothing. By the time you reached from New-York to Virginia you would be reduced to a string of drops not capable of hanging together; while we, by retreating from State to State, like a river turning back upon itself, would acquire strength in the same proportion as you lost it, and in the end be capable of overwhelming you. The country in the mean time would suffer, but 'tis a day of suffering, and we ought to expect it. What we contend for is worthy the affliction we may go through. If we get but bread to eat, and any kind of rayment to put on, we ought, not only to be contented, but thankful. More than *that* we ought not to look for, and less than *that* Heaven has not yet suffered us to want. He that would sell his Birthright for a little *salt*, is as worthless as he who sold it for *porridge* without salt. And he that would part with it for a gay coat, or a *plain* coat, ought for ever to be a slave in buff. What are salt, sugar and finery to the inestimable blessings of "Liberty and Safety?" Or what are the inconveniencies of a few months to the tributary bondage of ages? The meanest peasant in America, bless'd with these sentiments, is a happy man compared with a New-York Tory; he can eat his morsel without repining, and when he has done, can sweeten it with a repast of wholesome air; he can take his child by the hand and bless it, without feeling the conscious shame of neglecting a parent's duty.

In publishing these remarks I have several objects in view: On your part they are, to expose the folly of your pretended authority as a Commissioner; the wickedness of your cause in general; and the impossibility of your conquering us at any rate. On the part of the public my meaning is, to show them their true and solid interest; to encourage them to their own good, to remove the fears and falsities which bad men had spread and weak men had encouraged; and to excite in all men a love for union, and a chearfulness for duty.

I shall submit one more case to you respecting your conquest of this country, and then proceed to new observations:

Suppose our armies in every part of the Continent were immediately to disperse, every man to his home, or where else he might be safe, and engage to re-assemble again on a certain future day; it is clear that you would then have no army to contend with, yet you would be as much at a loss in that case as you are now; you would be afraid to send your troops in parties over the Continent, either to disarm, or prevent us from assembling, lest they should not return; and while you kept them together, having no army of ours to dispute with, you could not call it a conquest; you might furnish out a pompous page in the London Gazette or the New-York paper, but when we returned at the appointed time, you would have the same work to do you had at first.

It has been the folly of Britain to suppose herself more powerful than she really is, and by that means have arrogated to herself a rank in the world she is not entitled to; for more than this century past she has not been able to carry on a war without foreign assistance. In Marlborough's campaigns, and from that day to this, the number of German troops and officers assisting her have been about equal with her own; ten thousand Hessians were sent to England last war to protect her from a French invasion; and she would have cut but a poor figure in her Canadian and West-Indian expeditions, had not America been lavish both of her money and men to help her along. The only instance in which she was engaged singly, that I can recollect, was against the rebellion in Scotland in forty-five and forty-six, and in that, out of three battles, she was twice beaten, till by thus reducing their numbers (as we shall yours) and taking a supply-ship that was coming to Scotland with cloaths, arms and money (as we have often done) she was at last enabled to defeat them. England was never famous by land; her officers have generally been suspected of cowardice, have more of the air of a dancing-master than a soldier, and by the sample we have taken prisoners we begin to give the preference to ourselves. Her strength of late has laid in her extravagance; but as her finances and her credit are now low, her sinews in that line begin to fail fast. As a nation she is the poorest in Europe; for were the whole kingdom, and all that is in it, to be put up to sale like the estate of a bankrupt, it would not fetch as much as she owes: Yet this thoughtless wretch must go to war, and with the avowed design too of making us beasts of burthen, to support her in riot and debauchery, and to assist her afterwards in distressing those nations who are now our best friends. This ingratitude may suit a Tory, or the unchristian peevishness of a fallen Quaker, but none else.

'Tis the unhappy temper of the English to be pleased with any war, right or wrong, be it but successful; but they soon grow discontented with ill fortune, and it is an even chance that they are as clamorous for peace next summer, as the king and his ministers were for war last winter. In this natural view of things, your Lordship stands in a very ugly critical situation: Your whole character is staked upon your laurels; if they wither, you wither with them; if they flourish, you cannot live long to look at them; and at any rate, the black account hereafter is not far off. What lately appeared to us misfortunes, were only blessings in disguise; and the seeming advantages on your side have turned out to our profit. Even our loss of this city, as far as we can see, might be a principal gain to us: The more surface you spread over, the thinner you will be, and the easier wiped away; and our consolation under that apparent disaster would be, that the estates of the Tories would become securities for the repairs. In short, there is no old ground we can fail upon, but some new foundation rises again to support us. *"We have put,* Sir, *our hands to the plough, and cursed be he that looketh back."*

Your king, in his speech to parliament last spring, declared to them, *"That he had no doubt but the great force they had enabled him to send to America, would effectually reduce the rebellious Colonies."* It has not, neither can it; but it has done just enough to lay the foundation of its own next year's ruin. You are sensible that you left England in a divided distracted state of politics, and, by the command you had here, you became a principal prop in the court party; their fortunes rest on yours; by a single express you can fix their value with the public, and the degree to which their spirits shall rise or fall; they are in your hands as stock, and you have the secret of the ally with you. Thus situated and connected, you become the unintentional mechanical instrument of your own and their overthrow. The king and his ministers put conquest out of doubt, and the credit of both depended on the proof. To support them in the interim, it was necessary you should make the most of every thing; and we can tell by Hugh Gaine's New-York paper what the complexion of the London Gazette is. With such a list of victories the nation cannot expect you will ask new supplies; and to confess your want of them, would give the lie to your triumphs, and impeach the king and his ministers of treasonable deception. If you make the necessary demand at home, your party sinks; if you make it not, you sink yourself; to ask it now is too late, and to ask it before was too soon, and unless it arrive quickly will be of no use. In short, the part you have to act, cannot be acted; and I am fully persuaded that all you have to trust to, is to do the best you can with what force you have got, or little more. Though we have greatly excelled you in point of generalship and bravery of men, yet, as a people, we have not entered into the full soul of enterprize; for I, who know England and the disposition of the people well; am confident that it is easier for us to effect a revolution there, than you a conquest here: A few thousand men landed in England with the declared design of deposing the present king, bringing his ministers to trial, and setting up the duke of Gloucester in his stead, would assuredly carry their point, while you were groveling here ignorant of the matter. As I send all my papers to England, this, like COMMON SENSE, will find its way there; and though it may put one party on their guard, it will inform the other and the nation in general of our design to help them.

Thus far, Sir, I have endeavoured to give you a picture of present affairs: You may draw from it what conclusions you please. I wish as well to the true prosperity of England as you can, but I consider *Independence as America's natural Right and Interest*, and never could see any real disservice it would be to Britain. If an English merchant receives an order and is paid for it, it signifies nothing to him who governs the country—This is my creed of politics. If I have any where expressed myself overwarmly, 'tis from a fixt immovable hatred I have, and ever had, to cruel men and cruel measures. I have likewise an aversion to monarchy, as being too debasing to the dignity of man; but I never troubled others with my notions till very lately, nor ever published a syllable in England in my life. What I write is pure nature, and my pen and my soul have ever gone together. My writings I have always given away, reserving only the expence of printing and paper, and sometimes not even that. I never courted either fame or interest, and my manner of life, to those who know it, will justify what I say. My study is to be useful, and if your Lordship love mankind as well I do, you would, seeing you cannot conquer us, cast about and lend your hand towards accomplishing a peace. Our Independence, with GOD's blessing, we will maintain against all the world; but as we wish to avoid evil ourselves, we wish not to inflict it on others. I am never overinquisitive into the secrets of the Cabinet, but I have some notion, that if you neglect the present opportunity, that it will not be in our power to make a separate peace with you afterwards; for whatever treaties or alliances we form, we shall most faithfully abide by; wherefore you may be deceived if you think you can make it with us at any time. A lasting independent peace is my wish, end and aim; and to accomplish that *"I pray God the"* Americans *"may never be defeated, and I trust while they have good officers, and are well commanded,"* and willing to be commanded, *"that they* NEVER WILL.*"*

COMMON SENSE.

Philadelphia, January 13, 1777.

The American Crisis

NUMBER III

April 19, 1777

IN the progress of politics, as in the common occurrences of life, we are not only apt to forget the ground we have travelled over, but frequently neglect to gather up experience as we go. We expend, if I may so say, the knowledge of every day on the circumstances that produce it, and journey on in search of new matter and new refinements: But as it is pleasant, and sometimes useful, to look back, even to the first periods of infancy, and trace the turns and windings through which we have passed, so we may likewise derive many advantages by halting a while in our political career, and taking a review of the wondrous complicated labyrinth of little more than yesterday.

Truly, may we say, that never did man grow old in so short a time! We have crouded the business of an age into the compass of a few months, and have been driven through such a rapid succession of things, that, for the want of leisure to think, we unavoidably wasted knowledge as we came, and have left nearly as much behind us as we brought with us: But the road is yet rich with the fragments, and, before we fully lose sight of them, will repay us for the trouble of stopping to pick them up.

Were a man to be totally deprived of memory, he would be incapable of forming any just opinion; every thing about him would seem a chaos; he would have even his own history to ask from every one; and by not knowing how the world went on in his absence, he would be at a loss to know how it *ought* to go on when he recovered, or rather, returned to it again. In like manner, tho' in a less degree, a too great inattention to past occurrences retards and bewilders our judgment in every thing; while, on the contrary, by comparing what is past with what is present, we frequently hit on the true character of both, and become wise with very little trouble. It is a kind of countermarch, by which we get into the rear of Time, and mark the movements and meaning of things as we make our return. There are certain circumstances, which, at the time of their happening, are kind of riddles, and as every riddle is to be followed by its answer, so those kind of circumstances will be followed by their events, and those events are always the true solution. A considerable space of time may lapse between, and unless we continue our observations from the one to the other, the harmony of them will pass away unnoticed: But the misfortune is, that partly from the pressing necessity of some instant things, and partly from the impatience of our own tempers, we are frequently in such a hurry to make out the meaning of every thing as fast as it happens, that we thereby never truly understand it; and not only start new difficulties to ourselves by so doing, but, as it were, embarrass Providence in her good designs.

I have been civil in stating this fault on a large scale, for, as it now stands, it does not appear to be levelled against any particular set of men; but were it to be refined a little farther, it might afterwards be applied to the Tories with a degree of striking propriety: Those men have been remarkable for drawing sudden conclusions from single facts. The least apparent mishap on our side, or the least seeming advantage on the part of the enemy, have determined with them the fate of a whole campaign. By this hasty judgment they have converted a retreat into a defeat; mistook generalship for error; while every little advantage purposely given the enemy, either to weaken their strength by dividing it, embarrass their councils by multiplying their objects, or to secure a greater post by the surrender of a less, has been instantly magnified into a conquest. Thus, by quartering ill policy upon ill principles, they have frequently promoted the cause they designed to injure, and injured that which they intended to promote.

It is probable the campaign may open before this Number comes from the press. The enemy have long lain idle and amused themselves with carrying on the war by proclamations only. While they continue their delay our strength encreases, and were they to move to action now, it is a circumstantial proof they have no reinforcement coming; wherefore, in either case, the comparative advantage will be ours. Like a wounded disabled whale they want only time and room to die in; and though in the agony of their exit, it may be unsafe to live within the flapping of their tail, yet every hour shortens their date and lessens their power of mischief. If any thing happens while this Number is in the press, it will afford me a subject for the last pages of it. At present I am tired of waiting; and as neither the enemy, nor the state of politics, have *yet* produced any thing new, I am thereby left in the field of general matter undirected by any striking or particular object. This Crisis, therefore, will be made up rather of variety than novelty, and consist more of things useful than things wonderful.

The success of the cause, the union of the people, and the means of supporting and securing both, are points which cannot be too much attended to. He who doubts of the former is a desponding coward, and he who wilfully disturbs the latter is a traitor. Their characters are easily fixt, and under these short descriptions I leave them for the present.

One of the greatest degrees of sentimental union which America ever knew, was in denying the right of the British parliament *"to bind the Colonies in all cases whatever."* The declaration is in its form an almighty one, and is the loftiest stretch of arbitrary power that ever one set of men, or one country claimed over another. Taxation was nothing more than the putting the declared right into practice; and this failing, recourse was had to arms, as a means to establish both the right *and* the practice, or to answer a worse purpose, which will be mentioned in the course of this Number. And in order to repay themselves the expence of an army, and to profit by their own injustice, the Colonies were, by another law, declared to be in a state of actual rebellion, and of consequence all property therein would fall to the conquerors.

The Colonies, on their part, FIRST, denied the right; SECONDLY, they suspended the use of taxable articles, and petitioned against the practice of taxation: and these failing, they, THIRDLY, defended their property by force, as soon as it was forcibly invaded, and in answer to the declaration of rebellion and non-protection, published their declaration of Independence and right to self-protection.

These, in a few words, are the different stages of the quarrel; and the parts are so intimately and necessarily connected with each other as to admit of no separation. A person, to use a trite phrase, must be a Whig or a Tory in the lump. His feelings, as a man, may be wounded; his charity, as a Christian, may be moved; but his political principles must go through all the cases on one side or the other. He cannot be a Whig in *this* stage, and a Tory in *that*. If he says he is against the United Independence of the Continent, he is to all intents and purposes against her in all the rest; because THIS LAST comprehends the whole. And he may just as well say, that Britain was right in declaring us rebels; right in taxing us; and right in declaring her *"right to bind the Colonies in all cases whatsoever."* It signifies nothing what neutral ground, of his own creating, he may skulk upon for shelter, for the quarrel in no stage of it hath afforded any such ground; and either we or Britain are absolutely right or absolutely wrong through the whole.

Britain, like a gamester nearly ruined, hath now put all her losses into one bet, and is playing a desperate game for the total. If she win it, she wins from *me* my life; she wins the Continent as the forfeited property of rebels; the right of taxing those that are left as reduced subjects; and the power of binding them as slaves: And the single die which determines this unparalleled event is, Whether we support our Independence or she overturn it. This is coming to the point at once. Here is the touch-stone to try men by. *He that is not a supporter of the Independent States of America, in the same degree that his religious and political principles would suffer him to support the government of any other country, of which he called himself a subject, is, in the American sense of the word,* A TORY; *and the instant that he endeavours to bring his Toryism into practice, he becomes* A TRAITOR. The first can only be detected by a general test, and the law hath already provided for the latter.

It is unnatural and impolitic to admit men who would root up our Independence to have any share in our legislation, either as electors or representatives; because the support of our Independence rests in a great measure on the vigour and purity of our public bodies. Would Britain, even in time of peace, much less in war, suffer an elector to be carried by men who professed themselves not to be her subjects, or allow such to sit in parliament? Certainly not.

But there are a certain species of Tories with whom conscience or principle hath nothing to do, and who are so from avarice only. Some of the first fortunes in the Continent, on the part of the Whigs, are staked on the issue of our present measures. And shall disaffection only be rewarded with security? Can any thing be a greater inducement to a miserly man, than the hope of making his mammon safe? And though the scheme be fraught with every character of folly, yet, so long as he supposes, that by doing nothing materially criminal against America on one part, and by expressing his private disapprobation against Independence, as a palliative with the enemy on the other part, he stands thereby in a safe line between both, while, I say, this ground be suffered to remain, craft and the spirit of avarice will point it out, and men will not be wanting to fill up this most contemptible of all characters.

These men, ashamed to own the sordid cause from whence their disaffection springs, add thereby meanness to meanness, by endeavouring to shelter themselves under the mask of hypocrisy; that is, they had rather be thought to be Tories from *some kind of principle*, than Tories by having *no principle at all*. But till such time as they can show some real reason, natural, political or conscientious, on which their objections to Independence are founded, we are not obliged to give them credit for being Tories of the first stamp, but must set them down as Tories of the last.

In the Second Number of the Crisis I endeavoured to show the impossibility of the enemy making any conquest of America; that nothing was wanting on our part but patience and perseverance, and that, with these virtues, our success, as far as human speculation could discern, seemed as certain as fate. But as there are many among us, who, influenced by others, have regularly gone back from the principles they once held, in proportion as we have gone forward; and as it is the unfortunate lot of many a good man to live within the neighbourhood of disaffected ones; I shall therefore, for the sake of confirming the one and recovering the other, endeavour, in the space of a page or two, to go over some of the leading principles in support of Independence. It is a much pleasanter task to prevent vice than to punish it; and however our tempers may be gratified by resentment, or our national expences

eased by forfeited estates, harmony and friendship is nevertheless the happiest condition a country can be blest with.

The principal arguments in support of Independence may
be comprehended under the four following heads,

FIRST,—The natural right of the Continent to Independence.

SECONDLY,—Her interest in being independent.

THIRDLY,—The necessity.—And

FOURTHLY,—The moral advantages arising therefrom.

I. The NATURAL RIGHT of the Continent to Independence,
is a point which never yet was called in question. It will not
even admit of a debate. To deny such a right, would be a kind
of atheism against nature: And the best answer to such an
objection would be, *"The fool hath said in his heart, There is
no God."*

II. The INTEREST of the Continent in being independent is
a point as clearly right as the former. America, by her own
internal industry, and unknown to all the powers of Europe,
was at the beginning of the dispute, arrived at a pitch of
greatness, trade and population, beyond which it was the interest of Britain not to suffer her to pass, lest she should grow
too powerful to be kept subordinate. She began to view this
country with the same uneasy malicious eye, with which a
covetous guardian would view his ward whose estate he had
been enriching himself by for twenty years, and saw him just
arriving at manhood. And America owes no more to Britain
for her present maturity, than the ward would to his guardian
for being twenty-one years of age. That America hath flourished *at the time* she was under the government of Britain, is
true; but there is every natural reason to believe, that had she
been an independent country from the first settlement
thereof, uncontrouled by any foreign power, free to make her
own laws, regulate and encourage her own commerce, she
had by this time been of much greater worth than now. The
case is simply this, The first settlers in the different Colonies
were left to shift for themselves, unnoticed and unsupported
by any European government; but as the tyranny and persecution of the old world daily drove numbers to the new, and,
as by the favour of Heaven on their industry and perseverance, they grew into importance, so, in a like degree, they

became an object of profit to the greedy eyes of Europe. It was impossible in this state of infancy, however thriving and promising, that they could resist the power of any armed invader that should seek to bring them under his authority. In this situation Britain thought it worth her while to claim them, and the Continent received and acknowledged the claimer. It was, in reality, of no very great importance who was her master, seeing, that from the force and ambition of the different powers of Europe she must, till she acquired strength enough to assert her own right, acknowledge some one. As well, perhaps, Britain as another; and it might have been as well to have been under the States of Holland as any. The same hopes of engrossing and profiting by her trade, by not oppressing it too much, would have operated alike with any master, and produced to the Colonies the same effects. The clamor of protection, likewise, was all a farce; because, in order to make *that* protection necessary, she must first, by her own quarrels create us enemies. Hard terms, indeed!

To know whether it be the interest of the Continent to be independent, we need only ask this easy, simple question: Is it the interest of a man to be a boy all his life? The answer to one will be the answer to both. America hath been one continued scene of legislative contention from the first king's representative to the last; and this was unavoidably founded in the natural opposition of interest between the old country and the new. A governor sent from England, or receiving his authority therefrom, ought never to have been considered in any other light than that of a genteel commissioned spy, whose private business was information, and his public business a kind of civilized oppression. In the first of these characters he was to watch the tempers, sentiments and disposition of the people, the growth of trade, and the encrease of private fortunes; and in the latter, to suppress all such acts of the Assemblies, however beneficial to the people, which did not directly or indirectly throw some encrease of power or profit into the hands of those who sent him.

America, till now, could never be called a *free country*, because her legislation depended on the will of a man three thousand miles distant, whose interest was in opposition to ours, and who, by a single "NO," could forbid what law he pleased.

The freedom of trade, likewise, is, to a trading country, an article of such vast importance, that the principal source of wealth depends upon it; and it is impossible that any country can flourish, as it otherwise might do, whose commerce is engrossed, cramped and fettered by the laws and mandates of another—yet these evils, and more than I can here enumerate, the Continent has suffered by being under the government of Great-Britain. By an Independence we clear the whole at once—put an end to the business of unanswered petitions and fruitless remonstrances—exchange Britain for Europe—shake hands with the world—live at peace with mankind—and trade to any market where we best can buy and sell.

III. The NECESSITY, likewise, of being independent, even before it was declared, became so evident and important, that the Continent ran the risk of being ruined every day she delayed it. There were reasons to believe that Britain would endeavour to make a European matter of it, and rather than lose the whole, would dismember it like Poland, and dispose of her several claims to the highest bidder. Genoa, failing in her attempts to reduce Corsica, made a sale of it to the French, and such traffics have been common in the old world. We had at that time no Ambassador in any part of Europe, to counteract her negociations, and by that means she had the range of every foreign Court uncontradicted on our part. We even knew nothing of the treaty for the Hessians till it was concluded, and the troops ready to embark. Had we been independent before, we had probably prevented her obtaining them. We had no credit abroad, because of our rebellious dependency. Our ships could claim no protection in foreign ports, because we afforded them no justifiable reason for granting it to us. The calling ourselves subjects, and at the same time fighting against the power we acknowledged, was a dangerous precedent to all Europe. If the grievances justified our taking up arms, they justified our separation; if they did not justify our separation, neither could they justify our taking up arms. All Europe was interested in reducing us as

rebels, and all Europe (or the greatest part at least) is interested in supporting us as Independent States. At home our
condition was still worse: Our currency had no foundation,
and the fall of it would have ruined Whig and Tory alike. We
had no other law than a kind of moderated passion; no other
civil power than an honest mob; and no other protection than
the temporary attachment of one man to another. Had Independence been delayed a few months longer, this Continent
would have been plunged into irrecoverable confusion: Some
violent for it, some against it, till in the general cabal the rich
would have been ruined, and the poor destroyed. It is to Independence that every Tory owes the present safety he lives
in; for by *that*, and *that only*, we emerged from a state of
dangerous suspense, and became a regular people.

The necessity likewise of being independent, had there
been no rupture between Britain and America, would in a
little time have brought one on. The encreasing importance
of commerce, the weight and perplexity of legislation, and the
entangled state of European politics, would daily have shewn
to the Continent the impossibility of continuing subordinate;
for, after the coolest reflections on the matter, *this must* be
allowed, that Britain was too jealous of America, to govern it
justly; too ignorant of it, to govern it well; and too distant
from it, to govern it at all.

IV. But, what weigh most with all men of serious reflection
are the MORAL ADVANTAGES arising from Independence: War
and desolation are become the trades of the old world; and
America neither could, nor can be under the government of
Britain without becoming a sharer of her guilt, and a partner
in all the dismal commerce of death. The spirit of duelling,
extended on a national scale, is a proper character for European wars. They have seldom any other motive than pride, or
any other object than fame. The conquerors and the conquered are generally ruined alike, and the chief difference at
last is, that the one marches home with his honours, and the
other without them. 'Tis the natural temper of the English to
fight for a feather, if they suppose *that feather* to be an affront; and America, without the right of asking why, must
have abetted in every quarrel and abided by its fate. It is a
shocking situation to live in, that one country must be

brought into all the wars of another, whether the measure be right or wrong, or whether she will or not; yet this, in the fullest extent, was, and ever would be, the unavoidable consequence of the connection. Surely! the Quakers forgot their own principles, when in their late testimony they called *this connection* with these military and miserable appendages hanging to it, *"The happy constitution."*

Britain, for centuries past, have been nearly fifty years out of every hundred at war with some power or other. It certainly ought to be a conscientious as well as political consideration with America, not to dip her hands in the bloody work of Europe. Our situation affords us a retreat from their cabals, and the present happy union of the States bids fair for extirpating the future use of arms from one quarter of the world; yet such have been the irreligious politics of the present leaders of the Quakers, that, for the sake of they scarce know what, they would cut off every hope of such a blessing by tying this Continent to Britain, like Hector to the chariot-wheel of Achilles, to be dragged through all the miseries of endless European wars.

The connection, viewed from this ground, is distressing to every man who has the feelings of humanity. By having Britain for our master, we became enemies to the greatest part of Europe, and they to us; and the consequence was war inevitable. By being our own masters, independent of any foreign one, we have Europe for our friends, and the prospect of an endless peace among ourselves. Those who were advocates for the British government over these Colonies, were obliged to limit both their arguments and their ideas to the period of a European peace only: The moment Britain became plunged in war, every supposed convenience to us vanished away, and all we could hope for was *not to be ruined*. Could this be a desirable condition for a young country to be in?

Had the French pursued their fortune immediately after the defeat of Braddock last war, this city and province had then experienced the woful calamities of being a British subject. A scene of the same kind might happen again; for America, considered as a subject to the crown of Britain, would ever have been the seat of war and the bone of contention between the two powers.

On the whole, If the future expulsion of arms from one quarter of the world be a desirable object to a peaceable man;—if the freedom of trade to every part of it can engage the attention of a man of business,—if the support or fall of millions of currency can affect our interest;—if the entire possession of estates, by cutting off the lordly claims of Britain over the soil, deserves the regard of landed property;—and if the right of making our own laws, uncontrouled by royal or ministerial spies or mandates, be worthy our care as freemen;—then are all men interested in the support of Independence, and may he that supports it not, be driven from the blessing, and live unpitied beneath the servile sufferings of scandalous subjection!

We have been amused with the tales of ancient wonders; we have read, and wept over, the histories of other nations; applauded, censured, or pitied, as their cases affected us.—The fortitude and patience of the sufferers—the justness of their cause—the weight of their oppressions and oppressors—the object to be saved or lost—with all the consequences of a defeat or a conquest—have, in the hour of sympathy, bewitched our hearts and chained it to their fate: But where is the power that ever made war upon petitioners? Or where is the war on which a world was staked till now?

We may not, perhaps, be wise enough to make all the advantages we ought of our Independence; but they are, nevertheless, marked and presented to us with every character of GREAT and GOOD, and worthy the hand of Him who sent them. I look through the present trouble to a time of tranquillity, when we shall have it in our power to set an example of peace to all the world. Were the Quakers really impressed and influenced by the quiet principles they profess to hold, they would, however they might disapprove the means, be the first of all men to approve of INDEPENDENCE, because, by separating from the cities of Sodom and Gomorrah, it affords an opportunity, never given to man before, of carrying their favourite principle of peace into general practice, by establishing governments that shall hereafter exist without wars. Oh ye fallen, cringing priest- and Pemberton-ridden people! what more can we say of ye than that a religious Quaker is a valuable character, and a political Quaker a real Jesuit.

Having thus gone over some of the principal points in support of Independence, I must now request the reader to return back with me to the period when it first began to be a public doctrine, and examine the progress it has made among the various classes of men. The era I mean to begin at, is the breaking out of hostilities, April 19th, 1775. Until this event happened, the Continent seemed to view the dispute as a kind of lawsuit for a matter of right, litigating between the old country and the new; and she felt the same kind and degree of horror, as if she had seen an oppressive plaintiff, at the head of a band of ruffians, enter the court, while the cause was before it, and put the judge, the jury, the defendant and his council to the sword. Perhaps a more heart-felt convulsion never reached a country with the same degree of power and rapidity before, and never may again. Pity for the sufferers, mixt with indignation at the violence and heightened with apprehensions of undergoing the same fate, made the affair of Lexington the affair of the Continent. Every part of it felt the shock, and all vibrated together. A general promotion of sentiment took place: Those who had drank deeply into Whiggish principles, that is, the right and necessity not only of opposing, but wholly setting aside the power of the Crown as soon as it became practically dangerous (for in theory it was always so) stept into the first stage of Independence; while another class of Whigs, equally sound in principle, but not so sanguine in enterprize, attached themselves the stronger to the cause and fell close in with the rear of the former; their partition was a mere point. Numbers of the moderate men, whose chief fault, *at that time*, arose from their entertaining a better opinion of Britain than she deserved, convinced now of their mistake, gave her up and publicly declared themselves good Whigs. While the Tories, seeing it was no longer a laughing matter, either slunk into silent obscurity, or contended themselves with coming forth and abusing General Gage: Not a single advocate appeared to justify the action of that day; it seemed to appear to every one with the same magnitude, struck every one with the same force, and created in every one the same abhorrence. From this period we may date the growth of Independence.

If the many circumstances, which happened at this memorable time, be taken in one view, and compared with each other, they will justify a conclusion which seems not to be attended to, I mean a fixt design in the king and ministry of driving America into arms, in order that they might be furnished with a pretence for seizing the whole Continent as the immediate property of the Crown. A noble plunder for hungry courtiers!

It ought to be remembered, that the first petition from the Congress was at this time unanswered on the part of the British king. That the motion, called Lord North's motion, of the 20th of February, 1775, arrived in America the latter end of March. This motion was to be laid by the several governors, then in being, before the Assembly of each province; and the first Assembly before which it was laid, was the Assembly of Pennsylvania in *May* following. This being a just state of the case, I then ask, why were hostilities commenced between the time of passing the resolve in the House of Commons, of the 20th of February, and the time of the Assemblies meeting to deliberate upon it? Degrading and infamous as that motion was, there is, nevertheless, reason to believe, that the king and his adherents were afraid the Colonies would agree to it, and lest they should, took effectual care they should not, by provoking them with hostilities in the interim. They had not the least doubt at that time of conquering America at one blow; and what they expected to get by a conquest being infinitely greater than any thing they could hope to get either by taxation or accommodation, they seemed determined to prevent even the possibility of hearing each other, lest America should disappoint their greedy hopes of the whole, by listening even to their own terms. On the one hand they refused to hear the petition of the Continent, and on the other hand took effectual care the Continent should not hear them.

That the motion of the 20th of February and the orders for commencing hostilities were both concerted by the same PERSON or persons, and not the latter by General Gage, as was falsely imagined at first, is evident from an extract of a letter of his to administration, read among other papers in the House of Commons; in which he informs his masters, *That though their idea of his disarming certain counties was a right one, yet it required him to be master of the country, in order to enable him to execute it.* This was prior to the commencement of hostilities, and consequently before the motion of the 20th of February could be deliberated on by the several Assemblies.

Perhaps it may be asked, why was the motion past, if there was at the same time a plan to aggravate the Americans not to listen to it? Lord North assigned one reason himself, which was, *a hope of dividing them.* This was publicly tempting them to reject it; that if, in case, the injury of arms should fail of provoking them sufficiently, the insult of such a declaration might fill it up. But by passing the motion and getting it afterwards rejected in America, it enabled them, in their wretched idea of politics, among other things, to hold up the Colonies to foreign powers with every possible mark of disobedience and rebellion. They had applied to those powers not to supply the Continent with arms, ammunition, &c. and it was necessary they should incense them against us, by assigning on their own part some seeming reputable reason why. By dividing, it had a tendency to weaken the States, and likewise to perplex the adherents of America in England. But the principal scheme, and that which has marked their character in every part of their conduct, was a design of precipitating the Colonies into a state which they might afterwards deem rebellion, and under that pretence put an end to all future complaints, petitions or remonstrances, by seizing the whole at once. They had ravaged one part of the globe, till it could glut them no longer; their prodigality required new plunder, and through the East-India article TEA they hoped to transfer their rapine from that quarter of the world to this.—Every designed quarrel has its pretence; and the same barbarian avarice accompanied the *Plant* to America, which ruined the country that produced it.

That men never turn rogues without turning fools, is a maxim, sooner or later, universally true. The commencement of hostilities, being in the beginning of April, was, of all times, the worst chosen: The Congress were to meet the tenth of May following, and the distress the Continent felt at this unparalleled outrage gave a stability to *That Body*, which no other circumstance could have done. It suppressed too all inferior debates, and bound them together by a necessitous affection, without giving them time to differ upon trifles. The suffering likewise, softened the whole body of the people into a degree of pliability, which laid the principal foundation stone of union, order and government; and which, at any other time, might only have fretted and then faded away unnoticed and unimproved: But Providence, who best knows how to time her misfortunes as well as her immediate favours, chose this to be the time: And who dares dispute it?

It did not seem the disposition of the people at this crisis to heap petition upon petition, while the former remained unanswered: The measure, however, was carried in Congress, and a second petition was sent; of which I shall only remark, that it was submissive even to a dangerous fault, because the prayer of it appealed solely to, what is called, the prerogative of the Crown, while the matter in dispute was confessed to be constitutional. But even this Petition, flattering as it was, was still not so harmonious as the chink of cash, and consequently not sufficiently grateful to the tyrant and his ministry. From every circumstance it is evident, that it was the determination of the British court to have nothing to do with America but to conquer it fully and absolutely. They were certain of success, and the field of battle was to be the only place of treaty. I am confident there are thousands and tens of thousands in America who wonder *now* they should ever think otherwise; but the sin of that day was the sin of Civility, yet it operated against our present good in the same manner that a civil opinion of the devil would against our future peace.

Independence was a doctrine scarce and rare even towards the conclusion of the year Seventy-five: All our politics had been founded on the hope or expectation of making the matter up—a hope, which, though general on the side of America, had never entered the head or heart of the British court. Their hope was conquest and confiscation. Good Heavens! what volumes of thanks does America owe to Britain! What infinite obligations to the fool, that fills, with paradoxical vacancy, the throne! Nothing but the sharpest essence of villany, compounded with the strongest distillation of folly, could have produced a menstruum that would have effected a separation. The Congress in Seventy-four administered an abortive medicine to Independence, by prohibiting the importation of goods, and the succeeding Congress rendered the dose still more dangerous by continuing it. Had Independence been a settled system with America (as Britain has advanced) she ought to have *doubled* her importation, and prohibited in some degree her exportation. And this single circumstance is sufficient to acquit America before any jury of nations of having a Continental plan of Independence in view: A charge, which had it been true, would have been honourable, but is so grossly false, that either the amazing ignorance, or the wilful dishonesty, of the British court is effectually proved by it.

The second petition like the first produced no answer; it was scarcely acknowledged to be received; the British court were too determined in their villany even to act it artfully, and in their rage for conquest neglected the necessary subtleties for obtaining it. They might have divided, distracted and played a thousand tricks with us had they been as cunning as they were cruel.

This last indignity gave a new spring to Independence. Those who knew the savage obstinacy of the king and the jobbing gambling spirit of the court predicted the fate of the petition as soon as it was sent from America; for the men being known, their measures were easily foreseen. As politicians we ought not so much to ground our hope on the reasonableness of the thing we ask, as on the reasonableness of the person of whom we ask it: Who would expect discretion from a fool, candour from a tyrant, or justice from a villain?

As every prospect of an accommodation seemed now to fail fast, men began to think seriously on the matter; and their reason being thus stript of the false hope which had long encompassed it, became approachable by fair debate; yet still the bulk of the people hesitated; they startled at the novelty of Independence, without once considering that our getting into arms at first was a more extraordinary novelty, and that all other nations had gone through the work of Independence before us. They doubted, likewise, the ability of the Continent to support it, without reflecting, that it required the same force to obtain an accommodation by arms as an Independence. If the one was acquireable, the other was the same; because, to accomplish either, it was necessary that our strength should be too great for Britain to subdue; and it was too unreasonable to suppose, that with the power of being masters, we should submit to be servants.* Their caution, at this time, was exceedingly misplaced; for if they were able to defend their property and maintain their rights by arms, they consequently were able to defend and support their Independence; and in proportion as these men saw the necessity and rightness of the measure, they honestly and openly declared and adopted it, and the part they have acted since, have done them honour, and fully established their characters. Error in opinion has this peculiar advantage with it, that the foremost point of the contrary ground may at any time be reached by the sudden exertion of a thought; and it frequently happens in sentimental differences that some striking circumstance, or some forcible reason, quickly conceived, will effect in an instant what neither argument nor example could produce in an age.

I find it impossible in the small compass I am limited to, to trace out the progress which Independence has made on the minds of the different classes of men, and the several reasons by which they were moved. With some, it was a passionate abhorrence against the king of England and his ministry as a set of savages and brutes; and these men, governed by the agony of a wounded mind, were for trusting every thing to

---

*In this state of political suspense the pamphlet *Common Sense* made its appearance, and the success it met with does not become me to mention. Dr. Franklin, Mr. Samuel and John Adams were severally spoken of as the supposed Author. I had not, at that time, the pleasure either of personally knowing or being known to the two last Gentlemen. The favour of Dr. Franklin's friendship I possessed in England, and my introduction to this part of the world was through his patronage. I happened, when a school boy, to pick up a pleasing natural history of Virginia, and my inclination from that day of seeing the western side of the atlantic never left me. In October, Seventy-five, Dr. Franklin proposed giving me such materials as were in his hands, towards compleating a history of the present transaction, and seemed desirous of having the first volume out by the next spring. I had then formed the outlines of Common Sense, and finished nearly the first part; and as I supposed the Doctor's design in getting out a history, was to open the new year with a new system, I expected to surprize him with a production on that subject much earlier than he thought of; and without informing him of what I was doing, got it ready for the press as fast as I conveniently could, and sent him the first pamphlet that was printed off.

hope and Heaven and bidding defiance at once. With others, it was a growing conviction that the scheme of the British court was to create, ferment and drive on a quarrel for the sake of confiscated plunder: Men of this cast ripened into Independence in proportion as the evidence encreased. While a third class, conceiving it was the true interest of America, internally and externally, to be her own master, gave their support to Independence, step by step, as they saw her abilities to maintain it enlarge. With many it was a compound of all these reasons; while those, who were too callous to be reached by neither, remained, and still remain Tories.

The *legal necessity* of being independent, with several collateral reasons, is pointed out in an elegant, masterly manner, in a charge to the grand jury for the district of Charlestown, by the Hon. WILLIAM HENRY DRAYTON, Esq; Chief Justice of South-Carolina. This performance, and the ADDRESS of the CONVENTION of New-York, are pieces, in my humble opinion, of the first rank in America.

The principal causes why Independence has not been so universally supported as it ought, are, *fear* and *indolence*, and the causes why it has been opposed, are, *avarice, downright villany*, and *lust of personal power*. There is not such a Being in America as a Tory from conscience: Some secret defect or other is interwoven in the character of all those, be they men or women, who can look with patience on the brutality, luxury and debauchery of the British court, and the violations of their army here. A woman's virtue must sit very lightly on her who can even hint a favourable sentiment in their behalf. It is remarkable that the whole race of prostitutes in New-York were Tories; and the schemes for supporting the Tory cause, in this city, for which several are now in jail, and one hanged, were concerted and carried on in common baudy-houses, assisted by those who kept them.

The connection between vice and meanness is a fit object for satire, but when the satire is a fact, it cuts with the irresistible power of a diamond. If a Quaker, in defence of his just rights, his property and the chastity of his house, takes up a musket, he is expelled the meeting; but the present king of England, who reduced and took into keeping a sister of their society, is reverenced and supported with repeated testimonies, while the friendly noodle from whom she was taken, (and who is now in this city) continues a drudge in the service of his rival, as if proud of being cuckolded by a creature called a king.

Our support and success depend on such a variety of men and circumstances, that every one, who does but wish well, is of some use: There are men who have a strange awkwardness to arms, yet have hearts to risk every shilling in the cause, or in support of those who have better talents for defending it. Nature, in the arrangement of mankind, has fitted some for every service in life: Were all soldiers, all would starve and go naked, and were none soldiers, all would be slaves. As *disaffection* to Independence is the badge of a Tory, so *affection* to it is the mark of a Whig; and the different services of the Whigs down from those who nobly contribute every thing, to those who have nothing to render but their wishes, tend all to the same centre, though with different degrees of merit and ability. The larger we make the circle, the more we shall harmonize, and the stronger we shall be. All we want to shut out, is disaffection, and *that excluded*, we must accept from each other such duties as we are best fitted to bestow. A narrow system of politics, like a narrow system of religion, is calculated only to sour the temper, and live at variance with mankind.

All we want to know in America is simply this, Who is for Independence, and who is not? Those who are for it, will support it, and the remainder will undoubtedly see the reasonableness of their paying the charges; while those who oppose, or seek to betray it, must expect the more rigid fate of the jail and the gibbet. There is a kind of bastard generosity, which, by being extended to all men, is as fatal to society, on one hand, as the want of true generosity is on the other. A lax manner of administring justice, falsely termed moderation, has a tendency both to dispirit public virtue and promote the growth of public evils. Had the late Committee of Safety taken cognizance of the last testimony of the Quakers, and proceeded against such delinquents as were concerned therein, they had, probably, prevented the treasonable plans which have been concerted since. When one villain is suffered to escape, it encourages another to proceed, either from a hope of escaping likewise, or an apprehension that we dare not punish. It has been a matter of general surprise, that no notice was taken of the incendiary publication of the Quakers, of the 20th of November last: A publication evidently intended to promote sedition and treason, and encourage the enemy, who were then within a day's march of this city, to proceed on and possess it. I here present the reader with a memorial, which was laid before the Board of Safety a few days after the testimony appeared. Not a member of that Board, that I conversed with but expressed the highest detestation of the perverted principles and conduct of the Quaker junto, and that the Board would take the matter up; notwithstanding which, it was suffered to pass away unnoticed, to the encouragement of new acts of treason, the general danger of the cause, and the disgrace of the State.

To the HONOURABLE *the* COUNCIL OF SAFETY
of the State of Pennsylvania.

At a meeting of a reputable number of the inhabitants of the city of Philadelphia, impressed with a proper sense of the justice of the cause which this Continent is engaged in, and animated with a generous fervor for supporting the same, it was resolved, that the following be laid before the Board of Safety:

"WE profess liberality of sentiment to all men; with this distinction *only*, that those who do *not* deserve it, would become wise and *seek* to deserve it. We hold the pure doctrine of universal liberty of conscience, and conceive it our duty to endeavour to secure that sacred right to others, as well as to defend it for ourselves; for we undertake not to judge of the religious rectitude of tenets, but leave the whole matter to Him who made us.

"We persecute no man, neither will we abet in the persecution of any man for religion sake; our common relation to others being that of fellow-citizens and fellow-subjects of one civil community; and in this line of connection we hold out the right hand of fellowship to all men. But we should conceive ourselves to be unworthy members of the FREE AND INDEPENDENT STATES OF AMERICA, were we unconcernedly to see or suffer any treasonable wound, public or private, directly or indirectly, to be given against the peace and safety of the same. We enquire not into the rank of the offenders, nor their religious persuasion; we have no business with either, our part being only to find them out, and exhibit them to justice.

"A printed paper, dated the 20th of November, and signed '*John Pemberton,*' whom we suppose to be an inhabitant of this city, has lately been dispersed abroad, a copy of which accompanies this. Had the framers and publishers of that paper conceived it their duty to exhort the youth, and others, of their society, to a patient submission under the present trying visitations, and humbly to wait the event of Heaven towards them, they had therein shewn a Christian temper, and we had been silent; but the anger and political virulence with which their instructions are given, and the abuse with which they stigmatize all ranks of men, not thinking like themselves, leave no doubt on our minds from what spirit their publication proceeded: And it is disgraceful to the pure cause of truth, that men can dally with words of the most sacred import, and play them as mechanically off as if religion consisted only in contrivance. We know of no instance, in which the Quakers have been compelled to bear arms, or do any thing which might strain their conscience; wherefore their advice '*to withstand and refuse to submit to the arbitrary instructions and ordinances of men,*' appear to us a false alarm, and could only be treasonably calculated to gain favour with our enemies, when they were seemingly on the brink of invading this State, or, what is still worse, to weaken the hands of our defence, that their entrance into this city might be made practicable and easy.

"We disclaim all tumult and disorder in the punishment of offenders; and wish to be governed, not by temper but by reason, in the manner of treating them. We are sensible that our cause has suffered by the two following errors; first, by an ill-judged lenity to traiterous persons in some cases; and secondly, by only a passionate treatment of them in others. For the future we disown both, and wish to be steady in our proceedings, and serious in our punishments.

"Every State in America has by the repeated voice of its

inhabitants, directed and authorised the Continental Congress to publish a formal Declaration of Independence of, and Separation from, the oppressive king and parliament of Great-Britain; and we look on every man an enemy who does not in some line or other give his assistance towards supporting the same; at the same time we consider the offence to be heightened to a degree of unpardonable guilt, when such persons, under the shew of religion, endeavour, either by writing, speaking, or otherwise, to subvert, overturn, or bring reproach upon the Independence of this Continent as declared by Congress.

"The publishers of the paper, signed *'John Pemberton,'* have called in a loud and passionate manner on their friends and connections, to *'withstand and refuse'* obedience to whatever *'instructions or ordinances'* may be published, not warranted by (what they call) 'THAT HAPPY CONSTITUTION UNDER WHICH THEY AND OTHERS LONG ENJOYED TRANQUILLITY AND PEACE.' If this be not treason, we know not what may properly be called by that name.

"To us it is a matter of surprise and astonishment, that men with the word *'peace, peace'* continually on their lips, should be so fond of living under, and supporting a government and at the same time calling it *'happy,'* which is never better pleased than when at war—that hath filled India with carnage and famine—Africa with slavery—and tampered with Indians and Negroes to cut the throats of the freemen of America. We conceive it a disgrace to this State to harbour or wink at such palpable hypocrisy. But as we seek not to hurt the hair of any man's head, when we can make ourselves safe without, we with such persons to restore peace to themselves and us, by removing themselves to some part of the king of Britain's dominions, as by that means they may live unmolested by us or we by them; for our fixt opinion is, that those who do not deserve a place among us, ought not to have one.

"We conclude, with requesting the Council of Safety to take into their consideration the paper signed *'John Pemberton;'* and if it shall appear to them to be of a dangerous tendency, or of a treasonable nature, that they would commit the signer, together with such other persons as they can discover were concerned therein, into custody, until such time as some mode of trial shall ascertain the full degree of their guilt and punishment; in the doing of which, we wish their judges, whoever they may be, to disregard the man, his connections, interest, riches, poverty or principles of religion, and to attend to the nature of his offence only."

The most cavilling sectarian cannot accuse the foregoing with containing the least ingredient of persecution. The free spirit on which the American cause is founded, disdains to mix with such an impurity, and leave it a rubbish fit only for narrow and suspicious minds to grovel in: Suspicion and persecution are weeds of the same dunghill, and flourish best together. Had the Quakers minded their religion and their business, they might have lived through this dispute in enviable ease, and none would have molested them. The common phrase with these people is, *"Our principles are peace."* To which may be replied, *and your practices are the reverse*; for never did the conduct of men oppose their own doctrine more notoriously than the present race of the Quakers. They have artfully changed themselves into a different sort of people to what they used to be, and yet have the address to persuade each other they are not altered; like antiquated virgins they see not the havoc deformity hath made upon them, but pleasantly mistaking wrinkles for dimples, conceit themselves yet lovely, and wonder at the stupid world for not admiring them.

Did no injury arise to the public by this apostacy of the Quakers from themselves, the public would have nothing to do with it; but as both the design and consequences are pointed against a cause in which the whole community are interested, it is therefore no longer a subject confined to the cognizance of the meeting only, but comes as a matter of criminality before either the authority of the particular State *in which* it is acted, or of the Continent *against which* it operates. Every attempt now to support the authority of the king or parliament of Great-Britain over America, is treason against *every* State; therefore it is impossible that any *one* can pardon or screen from punishment an offender against *all*.

But to proceed: While the infatuated Tories of this and other States were last spring talking of Commissioners, accommodation, making the matter up and the Lord knows what stuff and nonsense, their *good* king and ministry were glutting themselves with the revenge of reducing America to an *unconditional submission*, and solacing each other with the certainty of conquering it in *one campaign*. The following quotations are from the Parliamentary Register of the debates of the House of Lords, March 5th, 1776.

"The Americans," says Lord *Talbot**, "have been obstinate, undutiful and ungovernable from the very beginning, from their first early and infant settlements; and I am every day more and more convinced that this people will never be brought back to their duty, and the subordinate relation they stand in to this country, till *reduced to an unconditional effectual submission; no concession on our part, no lenity, no endurance,* will have any other effect but that of encreasing their insolence."

"'The struggle," says Lord *Townsend*†, "is now a struggle for power; the die is cast, and the ONLY POINT which now remains to be determined, is, in what manner the war can be most effectually prosecuted and speedily finished, in order to procure that *unconditional submission*, which has been so ably stated by the noble Earl with the white staff" (meaning Lord Talbot); "and I have no reason to doubt that the measures now pursuing will put an end to the war in the course of a SINGLE CAMPAIGN. Should it linger longer, we shall then have reason to expect that some foreign power will interfere, and take advantage of our domestic troubles and civil distractions."

Lord *Littleton*, "My sentiments are pretty well known. I shall only observe now, that lenient measures have had no other effect than to produce insult after insult; that the more we conceded, the higher America rose in her demands, and the more insolent she has grown. It is for this reason that I am now for the most effective and decisive measures; and am of opinion, that no alternative is left us, but to relinquish America for ever, or finally determine to compel her to acknowledge the legislative authority of this country; and it is

*Steward of the king's houshold.

†Formerly General Townsend at Quebec, and late Lord Lieutenant of Ireland.

the principle of an *unconditional submission* I would be for maintaining."

Can words be more expressive than these? Surely the Tories will believe the Tory Lords! The truth is, they *do believe them*, and know as fully as any Whig on the Continent knows, that the king and ministry never had the least design of an accommodation with America, but an absolute unconditional conquest. And the part which the Tories were to act, was, by downright lying, to endeavour to put the Continent off its guard, and to divide and sow discontent in the minds of such Whigs as they might gain an influence over. In short, to keep up a distraction here, that the force sent from England might be able to conquer in *"one campaign."* They and the ministry were, by a different game, playing into each other's hands. The cry of the Tories in England was, *"No reconciliation, no accommodation,"* in order to obtain the greater military force; while those in America were crying nothing but *"reconciliation and accommodation,"* that the force sent might conquer with the less resistance.

But *this "single campaign"* is over, and America not conquered. The whole work is yet to do, and the force much less to do it with. Their condition is both despicable and deplorable: Out of cash—out of heart—and out of hope. A country furnished with arms and ammunition, as America now is, with three millions of inhabitants, and three thousand miles distant from the nearest enemy that can approach her, is able to look and laugh them in the face.

Howe appears to have two objects in view, either to go up the North river, or come to Philadelphia.

By going up the North river, he secures a retreat for his army thro' Canada, but the ships must return, if they return at all, the same way they went; and as our army would be in the rear, the safety of their passage down is a doubtful matter. By such a motion he shuts himself from all supplies from Europe but thro' Canada, and exposes his army and navy to the danger of perishing. The idea of his cutting off the communication between the eastern and southern States, by means of the North river, is merely visionary. He cannot do it by his shipping; because no ship can lay long at anchor in any river within reach of the shore; a single gun would drive a first rate from such a station: This was fully proved last October at fort Washington and Lee, where one gun only, on each side the river, obliged two frigates to cut and be towed off in an hour's time. Neither can he cut it off by his army; because the several posts they must occupy, would divide them almost to nothing, and expose them to be picked up by ours like pebbles on a river's bank; but admitting he could, where is the injury? Because while his whole force is cantoned out, as centries over the water, they will be very innocently employed, and the moment they march into the country, the communication opens.

The most probable object is Philadelphia, and the reasons are many. Howe's business in America is to conquer it, and in proportion as he finds himself unable to the task, he will employ his strength to distress women and weak minds, in order to accomplish through *their* fears what he cannot effect by his *own* force. His coming or attempting to come to Philadelphia is a circumstance that proves his weakness: For no general, that felt himself able to take the field and attack his antagonist, would think of bringing his army into a city in the summer time; and this mere shifting the scene from place to place, without effecting any thing, has feebleness and cowardice on the face of it, and holds him up in a contemptible light to any one who can reason justly and firmly. By several informations from New-York, it appears that their army in general, both officers and men, have given up the expectation of conquering America; their eye, now, is fixt upon the spoil. They suppose Philadelphia to be rich with stores, and as they think to get more by robbing a town than by attacking an army, their movement towards this city is probable. We are not now contending against an army of soldiers, but against a band of thieves, who had rather plunder than fight, and have no other hope of conquest than by cruelty.

They expect to get a mighty booty and strike another general panic by making a sudden movement and getting possession of this city, but unless they can march *out* as well as *in*, or get the entire command of the river, to remove off their plunder, they may probably be stopt with the stolen goods upon them. They have never yet succeeded wherever they have been opposed but at fort Washington. At Charlestown their defeat was effectual. At Ticonderoga they ran away. In every skirmish at Kingsbridge and the White Plains they were obliged to retreat, and the instant our arms were turned upon them in the Jersies, they turned likewise, and those that turned not were taken.

The necessity of always fitting our internal police to the circumstances of the times we live in, is something so strikingly obvious that no sufficient objection can be made against it. The safety of all societies depend upon it; and where this point is not attended to, the consequence will either be a general languor or a tumult. The encouragement and protection of the good subjects of any State, and the suppression and punishment of bad ones, are the principal objects for which all authority is instituted, and the line in which it ought to operate. We have in this city a strange variety of men and characters, and the circumstances of the times require they should be publicly known; it is not the number of Tories that hurt us, so much, as the not finding out who they are; men must now take one side or the other, and abide by the consequences: The Quakers, trusting to their short sighted sagacity, have, most unluckily for them, made their declaration in their last testimony, and we ought *now* to take them at their word. They have voluntarily read themselves out of the Continental meeting, and cannot hope to be restored to it again, but by payment and penitence. Men whose political principles are founded on avarice, are beyond the reach of reason, and the only cure for Toryism of this cast, is to tax it. A substantial good drawn from a real evil, is of the same benefit to society, as if drawn from a virtue; and where men have not public spirit to render themselves serviceable, it ought to be the study of government to draw the best use possible from their vices. When the governing passion of any man or set of men is once known, the method of managing them is easy; for even misers, whom no public virtue can impress, would become generous, could a heavy tax be laid upon covetousness.

The Tories have endeavoured to insure their property with the enemy, by forfeiting their reputation with us; from which may be justly inferred, that their governing passion is avarice. Make them as much afraid of losing on one side as the other, and you stagger their Toryism; make them more so, and you reclaim them; for their principle is to worship any power they are most afraid of.

This method of considering men and things together, opens into a large field for speculation, and affords me opportunity of offering some observations on the state of our currency, so as to make the support of it go hand in hand, with the suppression of disaffection and the encouragement of public spirit.

The thing which first presents itself in inspecting the state of the currency, is, that we have too much of it, and that there is a necessity of reducing the quantity, in order to encrease the value. Men are daily growing poor by the very means they take to get rich, for in the same proportion that the prices of all goods on hand are raised, the value of all money laid by is reduced. A simple case will make this clear: Let a man have one hundred pounds cash, and as many goods on hand as will to-day sell for £ 20, but not content with the present market-price, he raises them to 40, and by so doing, obliges others in their own defence to raise cent per cent likewise; in this case, it is evident that his hundred pounds laid by is reduced fifty pounds in value; whereas, had the markets dropt cent per cent, his goods would have sold but for ten, but his hundred pounds would have risen in value to two hundred; because it would then purchase as many goods again, or support his family as long again as before. And strange as it may seem, he is one hundred and fifty pounds the poorer for raising his goods, to what he would have been had he lowered them; because the forty pounds his goods sold for, is by the general rise of the markets, cent per cent, rendered of no more value than the ten pounds would be had the market fallen in the same proportion; and consequently the whole difference of gain or loss is on the different values of the hundred pounds laid by, viz. from fifty to two hundred. This rage for raising goods is for several reasons much more the fault of the Tories than the Whigs; and yet the Tories (to their shame and confusion ought they to be told of it) are by far the most noisy and discontented. The greatest part of the Whigs, by being now either in the army or employed in some public service, are *buyers* only and not *sellers*, and as this evil has its origin in trade, it cannot be charged on those who are out of it.

But the grievance is now become too general to be remedied by partial methods, and the only effectual cure is to reduce the quantity of money; with half the quantity we should be richer than we are now, because the value of it would be doubled, and consequently our attachment to it increased; for it is not the number of dollars a man has, but how far they will go, that makes him either rich or poor.

These two points being admitted, viz. that the quantity of money is too great, and that the prices of goods can be only effectually reduced by reducing the quantity of the money, the next point to be considered is, The method how to reduce it?

The circumstances of the times, as before observed, require that the public characters of all men should *now* be fully understood, and the only general method of ascertaining it is by an oath or affirmation, renouncing all allegiance to the king of Great-Britain, and to support the Independency of the United States as declared by Congress. Let, at the same time, a tax of ten, fifteen or twenty per cent per annum, to be collected quarterly, be levied on all property. These alternatives, by being perfectly voluntary, will take in all sorts of people. Here is the test; here is the tax. He who takes the former, conscientiously proves his affection to the cause, and binds himself to pay his quota by the best *services* in his power, and is thereby justly exempt from the latter; and those who chuse the latter, pay their quota in money, to be excused from taking the former, or rather 'tis the price paid to us for their supposed, though mistaken, insurance with the enemy.

But this is only a part of the advantage which would arise by knowing the different characters of men. The Whigs stake every thing on the issue of their arms, while the Tories, by their disaffection, are sapping and undermining their strength, and, of consequence, the property of the Whigs is the more exposed thereby; and whatever injury their estates may sustain by the movements of the enemy, must either be borne by themselves, who have done every thing which have *yet* been done, or by the Tories, who have not only done nothing, but have by their disaffection, invited the enemy on.

In the present crisis we ought to know square by square, and house by house, who are in real allegiance with the United Independent States, and who are not. Let but the line be made clear and distinct, and all men will then know what they are to trust to. It would not only be good policy, but strict justice, to raise fifty or an hundred thousand pounds, or more, if it is necessary, out of the estates and property of the king of England's votaries, resident in Philadelphia, to be distributed, as a reward to those inhabitants of the city and State, who should turn out and repulse the enemy, should they attempt their march this way; and likewise, to bind the property of all such persons to make good the damages which that of the Whigs might sustain. In the undistinguishable mode of conducting a war, we frequently make reprisals at sea, on the vessels of persons in England who are friends to our cause compared with the residentiary Tories among us.

In every former publication of mine, from Common Sense down to the last Crisis, I have generally gone on the charitable supposition, that the Tories were rather a mistaken than a criminal people, and have applied argument after argument with all the candour and temper I was capable of, in order to set every part of the case clearly and fairly before them, and if possible to reclaim them from ruin to reason. I have done my duty by them and have now done with that doctrine, taking it for granted, that those who yet hold their disaffection, are, either a set of avaricious miscreants, who would sacrifice the Continent to save themselves, or a banditti of hungry traitors, who are hoping for a division of the spoil. To which may be added, a list of Crown or Proprietary dependents, who, rather than go without a portion of power, would be content to share it with the devil. Of such men there is no hope; and their obedience will only be according to the danger that is set before them, and the power that is exercised over them.

A time will shortly arrive, in which, by ascertaining the characters of persons now, we shall be guarded against their mischiefs then; for in proportion as the enemy despair of conquest, they will be trying the arts of seduction and the force of fear by all the mischiefs they can inflict. But in war we may be certain of these two things, viz. that cruelty in an enemy, and motions made with more than usual parade, are always signs of weakness. He that can conquer, finds his mind too free and pleasant to be brutish; and he that intends to conquer, never makes too much show of his strength.

We now know the enemy we have to do with. While drunk with the certainty of victory they disdained to be civil; and in proportion as disappointment makes them sober, and their apprehensions of an European war alarm them, they will become cringing and artful; honest they cannot be. But our answer to them, in either condition they may be in, is short and full, "As Free and Independent States we are willing to make peace with you to-morrow, but we can neither hear nor reply in any other character."

If Britain cannot conquer us, it proves, that she is neither able to govern or protect us, and our particular situation now is such, that any connection with her would be unwisely exchanging a half defeated enemy for two powerful ones. Europe, by every appearance and information, is now on the eve, nay, on the morning twilight of a war, and any alliance with *George the Third* brings *France* and *Spain* upon our backs; a separation from him attach them to our side; therefore, the only road to *Peace, Honour* and *Commerce* is INDEPENDENCE.

COMMON SENSE.

Philadelphia, April 19, 1777.

And in the Fourth year of the UNION, *which GOD preserve!*

The American Crisis

NUMBER IV

September 12, 1777

THOSE who expect to reap the blessings of Freedom, must, like men, undergo the fatigue of supporting it. The event of yesterday is one of those kind of alarms, which is just sufficient to rouse us to duty, without being of consequence enough to depress our fortitude. It is not a field of a few acres of ground, but a cause that we are defending, and whether we defeat the enemy in one battle, or by degrees, the consequence will be the same.

Look back at the events of last winter and the present year, there you will find that the enemy's successes have always contributed to reduce them. What they have gained in ground, they paid so dearly for in numbers, that their victories have in the end amounted to defeats. We have always been masters at the last push, and always shall while we do our duty. Howe has been once on the banks of the Delaware, and from thence driven back with loss and disgrace; and why not be again driven from the Schuylkill? His condition and ours are very different. He has every body to fight, we have only his *one* army to cope with and which wastes away at every engagement; we can not only reinforce, but can redouble our numbers; he is cut off from all supplies, and must sooner or later inevitably fall into our hands.

Shall a band of ten or twelve thousand robbers, who are this day fifteen hundred or two thousand men less in strength than they were yesterday, conquer America, or subdue even a single state? The thing cannot be, unless we sit down and suffer them to do it. Another such a brush, notwithstanding we lost the ground, would, by still reducing the enemy, put them in a condition to be afterwards totally defeated.

Could our whole army have come up to the attack at one time, the consequences had probably been otherwise; but our having different parts of the Brandywine creek to guard, and the uncertainty which road to Philadelphia the enemy would attempt to take, naturally afforded them an opportunity of passing with their main body at a place where only a part of ours could be posted; for, it must strike every thinking man with conviction, that it requires a much greater force to oppose an enemy in several places, than is sufficient to defeat them in any one place.

Men who are sincere in defending their freedom, will always feel concern at every circumstance, which seems to make against them; it is the natural and honest consequence of all affectionate attachments, and the want of it is a vice. But the dejection lasts only for a moment; they soon rise out of it with additional vigor; the glow of hope, courage and fortitude, will, in a little time, supply the place of every inferior passion, and kindle the whole heart into heroism.

There is a mystery in the countenance of some causes, which we have not always present judgment enough to explain. It is distressing to see an enemy advancing into a country, but it is the only place in which we can beat them, and in which we have always beaten them, whenever they made the attempt. The nearer any disease approaches to a crisis, the nearer it is to a cure: Danger and deliverance make their advances together, and it is only at the last push, that one or the other takes the lead.

There are many men who will do their duty when it is not wanted; but a genuine Public spirit always appears most when there is most occasion for it. Thank GOD! our army, though fatigued, is yet entire. The attack made by us yesterday was under many disadvantages, naturally arising from the uncertainty of knowing which route the enemy would take; and from that circumstance, the whole of our force could not be brought up together time enough to engage all at once. Our strength is yet reserved; and it is evident that Howe does not think himself a gainer by the affair, otherwise, he would this morning have moved down and attacked General Washington.

Gentlemen of the city and country, It is in your power, by a spirited improvement of the present circumstance, to turn it to a real advantage: Howe is now weaker than before, and every shot will contribute to reduce him. You are more immediately interested than any other part of the Continent; your

All is at stake; it is not so with the general cause; you are devoted by the enemy to plunder and destruction: It is the encouragement which Howe, the chief of plunderers, has promised his army. Thus circumstanced, you may save yourselves by a manly resistance, but you can have no hope in any other conduct. I never yet knew our brave General, or any part of the army, officers or men, out of heart, and I have seen them in circumstances a thousand times more trying than the present. It is only those that are not in action, that feel languor and heaviness, and the best way to rub it off is to turn out, and make sure work of it.

Our army must undoubtedly feel fatigue, and want a reinforcement of rest, though not of valour. Our own interest and happiness call upon us to give them every support in our power, and make the burden of the day, on which the safety of this city depends, as light as possible. Remember, Gentlemen, that we have forces both to the Northward and Southward of Philadelphia, and if the enemy be but stopt till those can arrive, this city will be saved, and the enemy finally routed. You have too much at stake to hesitate. You ought not to think an hour upon the matter, but to spring to action at once. Other States have been invaded, and have likewise driven off the invaders. Now OUR time and turn is come, and perhaps the finishing stroke is reserved for us. When we look back on the dangers we have been saved from, and reflect on the successes we have been blest with, it would be sinful either to be idle or despair.

I close this paper with a short address to General Howe. You, sir, are only lingering out the period that shall bring with it your defeat. You have yet scarce began upon the war; and the farther you enter, the faster will your troubles thicken. What you now enjoy is only a respite from ruin; an invitation to destruction; a something, that will lead on to our deliverance at your expence. We know the cause we are engaged in, and though a passionate fondness for it may make us grieve at every injury which threatens it, yet, when the moment of concern is over, the determination to duty returns. We are not the hireling slaves of a beggarly tyrant, nor the cringing flatterers of an infamous court. We are not moved by the gloomy smile of a worthless king, but by the ardent glow of generous patriotism. We fight, not to enslave, but to set a country free, and to make room upon the earth for honest men to live in. In such a cause we are sure we are right; and we leave to you the despairing reflection of being the tool of a miserable tyrant.

COMMON SENSE

Philadelphia, Sept. 12, at Noon.

The American Crisis

NUMBER V

March 21, 1778

TO GENERAL SIR WILLIAM HOWE.

To argue with a man who has renounced the use and authority of reason, and whose philosophy consists in holding humanity in contempt, is like administring medicine to the dead, or endeavouring to convert an Atheist by scripture. Enjoy, Sir, your insensibility of feeling and reflecting. It is the prerogative of animals. And no man will envy you those honours, in which a savage only can be your rival and a bear your master.

As the generosity of this country rewarded your brother's services last war with an elegant monument in Westminster Abbey, it is consistent that she should bestow some mark of distinction upon you. You certainly deserve her notice, and a conspicuous place in the catalogue of extraordinary persons. Yet it would be a pity to pass you from the world in state, and consign you to magnificent oblivion among the tombs, without telling the future beholder why. Judas is as much known as John, yet history ascribes their fame to very different actions.

Sir William hath undoubtedly merited a monument: But of what kind, or with what inscription, where placed or how embellished, is a question that would puzzle all the Heralds of St James's in the profoundest mood of historical deliberation. We are at no loss, Sir, to ascertain your real character, but somewhat perplexed how to perpetuate it's identity, and preserve it uninjured from the transformations of time or mistake. A statuary may give a false expression to your bust, or decorate it with some equivocal emblems, by which you may happen to steal into reputation and impose upon the hereafter traditionary world. Ill nature or ridicule may conspire, or a variety of accidents combine, to lessen, enlarge, or change Sir William's fame; and no doubt but he who has taken so much pains to be singular in his conduct, would choose to be just as singular in his exit, his monument and his epitaph.

The usual honours of the dead, to be sure, are not sufficiently sublime to escort a character like you to the republic of dust and ashes; for however men may differ in their ideas of grandeur or government here, the grave is nevertheless a perfect republic. Death is not the monarch of the dead, but of the dying. The moment he obtains a conquest he loses a subject, and, like the foolish King you serve, will, in the end, war himself out of all dominion.

As a proper preliminary towards the arrangement of your funeral honors, we readily admit your new rank of *Knighthood*. The title is perfectly in character, and is your own, more by merit than creation. There are Knights of various orders from the Knight of the Windmill to the Knight of the Post. The former is your patron for exploits, and the latter will assist you in settling your accounts. No honorary title could be more happily applied! The ingenuity is sublime! And your royal master hath discovered more genius in fitting you therewith, than in generating the most finished figure for a button, or discanting on the properties of a button-mould.

But how, Sir, shall we dispose of you? The invention of a Statuary is exhausted, and Sir William is yet unprovided with a monument. America is anxious to bestow her funeral favors upon you, and wishes to do it in a manner that shall distinguish you from all the deceased heroes of the last war. The *Egyptian method of embalming* is not known to the present age, and hieroglyphical pageantry hath out-lived the science of decyphering it. Some other method, therefore, must be thought of to immortalize the new Knight of the Windmill and Post. Sir William, thanks to his stars, is not oppressed with very delicate ideas. He has no ambition of being wrapt up and handed about in myrrh, aloes and cassia. Less chargeable odors will suffice; and it fortunately happens, that the simple genius of America hath discovered the art of preserving bodies and embellishing them too, with much greater frugality than the ancients. In a balmage, Sir, of humble tar, you will be as secure as Pharoah, and in a hieroglyphic of feathers rival in finery all the mummies of Egypt.

As you have already made your exit from the moral world, and by numberless acts both of passionate and deliberate injustice engraved an "HERE LYETH" on your deceased honor, it must be meer affectation in you to pretend concern at the humours or opinions of mankind respecting you. What remains of you may expire at any time. The sooner the better. For he who survives his reputation, lives out of spite to himself, like a man listening to his own reproach.

Thus entombed and ornamented I leave you to the inspection of the curious, and return to the history of your yet surviving actions. — The character of Sir William hath undergone some extraordinary revolutions since his arrival in America. It is now fix'd and known; and we have nothing to hope from your candor or to fear from your capacity. Indolence and inability have too large a share in your composition ever to suffer you to be any thing more than the hero of little villainies and unfinished adventures. That, which to some persons appeared moderation in you at first, was not produced by any real virtue of your own, but by a contrast of passions dividing and holding you in perpetual irresolution. One vice will frequently expel another without the least merit in the man, as powers in contrary directions reduce each other to rest.

It became you, to have supported a dignified solemnity of character; to have shewn a superior liberality of soul; to have won respect by an obstinate perseverance in maintaining order, and to have exhibited, on all occasions, such an unchangeable graciousness of conduct, that while we beheld in you the resolution of an enemy we might admire in you the sincerity of a man. You came to America under the highsounding titles of Commander and Commissioner; not only to suppress what you call rebellion by arms, but to shame it out of countenance by the excellence of your example. Instead of which, you have been the patron of low and vulgar frauds, the encourager of Indian cruelties; and have imported a cargo of vices blacker than those you pretended to suppress.

Mankind are not universally agreed in their determination of right and wrong; but there are certain actions which the consent of all nations and individuals hath branded with the unchangeable name of MEANNESS. In the list of human vices we find some of such a refined constitution, that they cannot be carried into practice without seducing some virtue to their assistance; but *meanness* hath neither alliance nor apology. It is generated in the dust and sweepings of other vices, and is of such a hateful figure that all the rest conspire to disown it. Sir William, the Commissioner of George the Third, hath at last vouchsafed to give it rank and pedigree. He has placed the fugitive at the Council Board, and dubbed it companion of the order of knighthood.

The particular act of meanness which I allude to in this description, is forgery. You, Sir, have abetted and patronised the forging and uttering counterfeit continental bills. In the same New-York news-papers in which your own proclamation under your master's authority was published, offering, or pretending to offer, pardon and protection to the inhabitants of these States, there were repeated advertisements of counterfeit money for sale, and persons who have come officially from you and under the sanction of your flag, have been taken up in attempting to put them off.

A conduct so basely mean in a public character is without precedent or pretence. Every nation on earth, whether friends or enemies, will unite in despising you. 'Tis an incendiary war upon society which nothing can excuse or palliate—An improvement upon beggarly villainy—and shews an inbred wretchedness of heart made up between the venomous malignity of a serpent and the spiteful imbecility of an inferior reptile.

The laws of any civilized country would condemn you to the gibbet without regard to your rank or titles, because it is an action foreign to the usage and custom of war; and should you fall into our hands, which pray God you may, it will be a doubtful matter whether we are to consider you as a military prisoner or a prisoner for felony.

Besides, it is exceedingly unwise and impolitic in you, or any persons in the English service, to promote, or even encourage, or wink at, the crime of forgery in any case whatever. Because, as the riches of England, as a nation, is chiefly in paper, and the far greater part of trade among individuals is carried on by the same medium, that is, by notes and drafts on one another, they, therefore, of all people in the world ought to endeavour to keep forgery out of sight, and, if possible, not to revive the idea of it. It is dangerous to make men familiar with a crime which they may afterwards practise to much greater advantage against those who first taught them. Several officers in the English army have made their exit at the gallows for forgery on their agents; for we all know, who know any thing of England, that there is not a more necessitous body of men, taking them generally, than what the English officers are. They contrive to make a shew at the expence of the taylor, and appear clean at the charge of the washer-woman.

England hath at this time nearly two hundred millions pounds sterling of public money in paper, for which she hath no real property, besides a large circulation of bank notes, bank post bills, and promissary notes and drafts of private bankers, merchants and tradesmen. She hath the greatest quantity of paper currency and the least quantity of gold and silver of any nation in Europe; the real specie, which is about sixteen millions sterling, serve only as change in large sums, which are always made in paper, or for payment in small ones. Thus circumstanced, the nation is put to its wit's ends, and obliged to be severe almost to criminality, to prevent the practice and growth of forgery. Scarcely a session passes at the Old Bailey, or an execution at Tyburn, but witnesseth this truth. Yet you, Sir, regardless of the policy which her necessity obliges her to adopt, have made your whole army intimate with the crime. And as all armies, at the conclusion of a war, are too apt to carry into practice the vices of the campaign, it will probably happen, that England will hereafter abound in forgeries, to which Art, the practitioners were first initiated under your authority in America. You, Sir, have the honor of adding a new vice to the military catalogue; and the reason, perhaps, why the invention was reserved for you, is, because no General before was mean enough even to think of it.

That a man whose soul is absorbed in the low traffic of vulgar vice, is incapable of moving in any superior region, is clearly shewn in you by the event of every campaign. Your military exploits have been without plan, object or decision. Can it be possible that you or your employers can suppose the possession of Philadelphia to be any ways equal to the expence or expectation of the nation which supports you? What advantages does England derive from any atchievements of yours? To *her* it is perfectly indifferent what place you are in, so long as the business of conquest is unperformed and the charge of maintaining you remains the same.

If the principal events of the three campaigns be attended to, the balance will appear strongly against you at the close of each; but the last, in point of importance to us, hath exceeded the former two. It is pleasant to look back on dangers past, and equally as pleasant to meditate on present ones when the way out begins to appear. *That* period is now arrived, and the long doubtful winter of war is changing to the sweeter prospects of victory and joy. At the close of the campaign in seventy-five, you were obliged to retreat from Boston. In the summer of seventy-six, you appeared with a numerous fleet and army in the harbour of New-York. By what miracle the Continent was preserved in that season of danger is a subject of admiration! If instead of wasting your time against Long-Island, you had run up the North River and landed any where above New-York, the consequence must have been, that either you would have compelled General Washington to fight you with very unequal numbers, or he must have suddenly evacuated the city with the loss of nearly all the stores of the army, or have surrendered for want of provisions, the situation of the place naturally producing one or other of these events.

The preparations made to defend New-York were, nevertheless, wise and military; because your forces were then at sea, their numbers uncertain; storms, sickness, or a variety of accidents might have disabled their coming, or so diminished them on their passage, that those which survived would have been incapable of opening the campaign with any prospect of success; in which case the defence would have been sufficient and the place preserved; for cities that have been raised from nothing with an infinitude of labor and expence, are not to be thrown away on the bare probability of their being taken. On these grounds, the preparations made to maintain New-York were as judicious as the retreat afterwards. While you, in the interim, let slip the *very* opportunity which seemed to put conquest in your power.

Through the whole of that campaign you had nearly double the forces which General Washington immediately commanded. The principal plan, at that time, on our part, was to wear away the season with as little loss as possible, and to raise the army for the next year. Long-Island, New-York, Forts Washington and Lee were not defended, after your superior force was known, under any expectation of their being finally maintained, but as a range of out works, in the attacking of which, your time might be wasted, your numbers reduced, and your vanity amused by possessing them on our retreat. It was intended to have withdrawn the garrison from Fort Washington after it had answered the former of those purposes, but the fate of that day put a prize into your hands without much honour to yourselves.

Your progress through the Jerseys was accidental; you had it not even in contemplation, or you would not have sent so principal a part of your force to Rhode-Island before-hand. The utmost hope of America in the year seventy-six reached no higher than that she might not *then* be conquered. She had no expectation of defeating you in that campaign. Even the most cowardly Tory allowed, that, could she withstand the shock of *that* summer her independence would be past a doubt. You had *then* greatly the advantage of her. You were formidable. Your military knowledge was supposed to be compleat. Your fleets and forces arrived without an accident. You had neither experience nor reinforcements to wait for. You had nothing to do but to begin, and your chance lay in the first vigorous onset.

America was young and unskilled. She was obliged to trust her defence to time and practice; and hath, by meer dint of perseverance, maintained her cause, and brought her enemy to a condition, in which, she is now capable of meeting him on any grounds.

It is remarkable that in the campaign of seventy-six, you gained no more, notwithstanding your great force, than what was given you by consent of evacuation, except Fort Washington: While every advantage obtained by us was by fair and hard fighting. The defeat of Sir Peter Parker was compleat. The conquest of the Hessians at Trenton by the remains of a retreating army, which, but a few days before, you affected to despise, is an instance of heroic perseverance very seldom to be met with. And the victory over the British troops at

Princeton, by a harrassed and wearied party, who had been engaged the day before and marched all night without refreshment, is attended with such a scene of circumstances and superiority of Generalship, as will ever give it a place on the first line in the history of great actions.

When I look back on the gloomy days of last winter and see America suspended by a thread, I feel a triumph of joy at the recollection of her delivery, and a reverence for the characters which snatched her from destruction. To doubt *now* would be a species of infidelity, and to forget the instruments which saved us *then* would be ingratitude.

The close of that campaign left us with the spirits of conquerors. The Northern districts were relieved by the retreat of General Carleton over the lakes. The army under your command were hunted back and had their bounds prescribed. The Continent began to feel its military importance, and the winter passed pleasantly away in preparations for the next campaign.

However confident you might be on your first arrival, the course of the year seventy-six gave you some idea of the difficulty, if not impossibility, of conquest. To this reason I ascribe your delay in opening the campaign in seventy-seven. The face of matters, on the close of the former year, gave you no encouragement to pursue a discretionary war as soon as the spring admitted the taking the field; for though conquest, in that case, would have given you a double portion of fame, yet the experiment was too hazardous. The Ministry, had you failed, would have shifted the whole blame upon you, charged you with having acted without orders, and condemned at once both your plan and execution.

To avoid those misfortunes, which might have involved you and your money accounts in perplexity and suspicion, you prudently waited the arrival of a plan of operations from England, which was, that you should proceed for Philadelphia by way of Chesapeak, and that Burgoyne, after reducing Ticonderoga, should take his route by Albany, and, if necessary, join you.

The splendid laurels of the last campaign have flourished in the North. In that quarter America hath surprized the world, and laid the foundation of her this year's glory. The conquest of Ticonderoga (if it may be called a conquest) has, like all your other victories, led on to ruin. Even the provisions taken in that fortress, (which by General Burgoyne's return was sufficient in bread and flour for nearly 5000 men for ten weeks, and in beef and pork for the same number of men for one month) served only to hasten his overthrow, by enabling him to proceed for Saratoga the place of his destruction. A short review of the operations of the last campaign will shew the condition of affairs on both sides.

You have taken Ticonderoga and marched into Philadelphia. These are all the events which the year hath produced on your part. A trifling campaign indeed, compared with the expences of England and the conquest of the Continent. On the other side, a considerable part of your Northern force has been routed by the New-York militia under General Herkimer. Fort Stanwix hath bravely survived a compounded attack of soldiers and savages, and the besiegers have fled. The battle of Bennington has put a thousand prisoners into our hands, with all their arms, stores, artillery and baggage. General Burgoyne in two engagements has been defeated; himself, his army, and all that were his and theirs are now ours. Ticonderoga and Independence are retaken, and not the shadow of an enemy remains in all the Northern districts. At this instant we have upwards of eleven thousand prisoners, between sixty and seventy pieces of brass ordnance, besides small arms, tents, stores, &c. &c.

In order to know the real value of those advantages we must reverse the scene, and suppose General Gates, and the force he commanded, to be at your mercy as prisoners, and General Burgoyne with his army of soldiers and savages to be already joined to you in Pennsylvania. So dismal a picture can scarcely be looked at. It hath all the traces and colourings of horror and despair; and excites the most swelling emotions of gratitude by exhibiting the miseries we are so graciously preserved from.

I admire this distribution of laurels around the Continent. It is the earnest of future union. South-Carolina has had her day of suffering and of fame; and the other Southern States have exerted themselves in proportion to the force that invaded or insulted them. Towards the close of the campaign in seventy-six, these middle States were called upon and did their duty nobly. They were witnesses to the almost expiring flame of human freedom. It was the close struggle of life and death. The line of invisible division; and on which, the unabated fortitude of a Washington prevailed, and saved the spark, that has since blazed in the North with unrivalled lustre.

Let me ask, Sir, what great exploits have you performed? Through all the variety of changes and opportunities which this war hath produced, I know no one action of yours that can be stiled masterly. You have moved in and out, backward and forward, round and round, as if valor consisted in a military jig. The history and figure of your movements would be truly ridiculous could they be justly delineated. They resemble the labors of a puppy pursuing his tail; the end is still at the same distance, and all the turnings round must be done over again.

The first appearance of affairs at Ticonderoga wore such an unpromising aspect, that it was necessary, in July, to detach a part of the forces to the support of that quarter, which were otherwise destined or intended to act against you, and this, perhaps, has been the means of postponing your downfal to another campaign. The destruction of one army at a time is work enough. We know, Sir, what we are about, what we have to do, and how to do it.

Your progress from Chesapeak was marked by no capital stroke of policy or heroism. Your principal aim was to get General Washington between the Delaware and Schuylkill and between Philadelphia and your army. In that situation, with a river on each of his flanks, which united about five miles below the city, and your army above him, you could have intercepted his reinforcements and supplies, cut off all his communication with the country, and, if necessary, have dispatched assistance to open a passage for General Burgoyne. This scheme was too visible to succeed, for had General Washington suffered you to command the open country above him, I think it a very reasonable conjecture that the conquest of Burgoyne would not have taken place, because you could, in that case, have relieved him. It was therefore necessary, while that important victory was in suspense, to trepan *you* into a situation, in which you could only be on the defensive without the power of affording him assistance. The manœuvre had its effect and Burgoyne was conquered.

There has been something unmilitarily passive in you from the time of your passing the Schuylkill and getting possession of Philadelphia to the close of the campaign. You mistook a trap for a conquest, the probability of which has been made known to Europe, and the edge of your triumph taken off by our own information long before.

Having got you into this situation, a scheme for a general attack upon you at Germantown was carried into execution on the fourth of October, and though the success was not equal to the excellence of the plan, yet the attempting it proved the genius of America to be on the rise and her power approaching to superiority. The obscurity of the morning was your best friend, for a fog is always favorable to a hunted enemy. Some weeks after this, you, likewise, planned an attack on General Washington while at Whitemarsh, marched out with infinite parade, but on finding him preparing to attack you the next morning, you prudently cut about and retreated to Philadelphia with all the precipitation of a man conquered in imagination.

Immediately after the battle of Germantown, the probability of Burgoyne's defeat gave a new policy to affairs in Pennsylvania, and it was judged most consistent with the general safety of America to wait the issue of the Northern campaign. Slow and sure is sound work. The news of that victory arrived in our camp on the 18th of October, and no sooner did the shout of joy, and the report of the thirteen cannon reach your ears, than you resolved upon a retreat, and the next day, that is, on the 19th, you withdrew your drooping army into Philadelphia. This movement was evidently dictated by fear; and carried with it a positive confession that you dreaded a second attack. It was hiding yourself among women and children, and sleeping away the choicest part of the campaign in expensive inactivity. An army in a city can never be a conquering army. The situation admits only a defence. It is meer shelter; and every military power in Europe will conclude you to be eventually defeated.

The time when you made this retreat was the very time you ought to have fought a battle, in order to put yourself in a condition of recovering in Pennsylvania what you had lost at Saratoga. And the reason why you did not, must be either prudence or cowardice; the former supposes your inability, and the latter needs no explanation. I draw no conclusions, Sir, but such as are naturally deduced from known and visible facts, and such as will always have a being while the facts which produced them remain unaltered.

After this retreat a new difficulty arose which exhibited the power of Britain in a very contemptible light, which was the attack and defence of Mud-Island. For several weeks did that little unfinished fortress stand out against all the attempts of Admiral and General Howe. It was the fable of Bender realized on the Delaware. Scheme after scheme and force upon force were tried and defeated. The garrison, with scarce any thing to cover them but their bravery, survived in the midst of mud, shot and shells, and were at last obliged to give it up more to the powers of time and gun-powder than to the military superiority of the besiegers.

It is my sincere opinion that matters are in much worse condition with you than what is generally known. Your master's speech at the opening of Parliament is like a soliloquy on ill luck. It shews him to be coming a little to his reason, for sense of pain is the first symptom of recovery in profound stupefactions. His condition is deplorable. He is obliged to submit to all the insults of France and Spain without daring to know or resent them, and thankful for the most trivial evasions to the most humble remonstrances. The time *was* when he could not *deign* an answer to a petition from America, and the time now *is* when he dare not *give* an answer to an affront from France. The capture of Burgoyne's army will sink his consequence as much in Europe as in America. In his speech he expresses his suspicions at the warlike preparations of France and Spain, and as he has only the one army which you command to support his character in the world with, it remains very uncertain when, or in what quarter, it will be most wanted or can be best employed, and this will partly account for the great care you take to keep it from action and attacks, for should Burgoyne's fate be yours, which it probably will, England may take her endless farewell not only of all America but of all the West-Indies.

Never did a nation invite destruction upon itself with the eagerness and the ignorance with which Britain has done. Bent upon the ruin of a young and unoffending country, she hath drawn the sword that hath wounded herself to the heart, and in the agony of her resentment hath applied a poison for a cure. Her conduct towards America is a compound of rage and lunacy; she aims at the government of it, yet preserves neither dignity nor character in her methods to obtain it. Were government a mere manufacture or article of commerce immaterial by whom it should be made or sold, we might as well employ her as another, but when we consider it as the fountain from whence the general manners and morality of a country take their rise, that the persons entrusted with the execution thereof are by their serious example an authority to support these principles, how abominably absurd is the idea of being hereafter governed by a set of men who have been guilty of forgery, perjury, treachery, theft, and every species of villainy which the lowest wretches on earth could practise or invent. What greater public curse can befal any country than to be under such authority, and what greater blessing than to be delivered therefrom. The soul of any man of sentiment would rise in brave rebellion against them and spurn them from the earth.

The malignant and venemous tempered Gen. Vaughan has amused his savage fancy in burning the whole town of Kingston, in York government, and the late Governor of that State, Mr. Tryon, in his letter to General Parsons, has endeavoured to justify it, and declared his wish to burn the houses of every Committee-man in the country. Such a confession from one who was once entrusted with the powers of civil government, is a reproach to the character. But it is the wish and the declaration of a man whom anguish and disappointment have driven to despair, and who is daily decaying into the grave with constitutional rottenness.

There is not in the compass of language a sufficiency of words to express the baseness of your King, his Ministry and his Army. They have refined upon villainy till it wants a name. To the fiercer vices of former ages they have added the dregs and scummings of the most finished rascality, and are so completely sunk in serpentine deceit, that there is not left among them *one* generous enemy.

From such men and such masters may the gracious hand of Heaven preserve America! And though the sufferings she now endures are heavy and severe, they are like straws in the wind compared to the weight of evils she would feel under the government of your King, and his pensioned Parliament.

There is something in meanness which excites a species of resentment that never subsides, and something in cruelty which stirs up the heart to the highest agony of human hatred; Britain hath filled up both these characters till no addition can be made, and hath not reputation left with us to obtain credit for the slightest promise. The will of God hath parted us, and the deed is registered for eternity. When she shall be a spot scarcely visible among the nations, America shall flourish the favorite of Heaven and the friend of mankind.

For the domestic happiness of Britain and the peace of the world I wish she had not a foot of land but what is circumscribed within her own island. Extent of dominion hath been her ruin, and instead of civilizing others hath brutalized herself. Her late reduction of India under Clive and his successors, was not so properly a conquest as an extermination of mankind. She is the only power who could practise the prodigal barbarity of tying men to mouths of loaded cannon and blowing them away. It happens that General Burgoyne, who made the report of that horrid transaction in the House of Commons, is now a prisoner with us, and though an enemy, I can appeal to him for the truth of it, being confident that he neither can nor will deny it. Yet Clive received the approbation of the last Parliament.

When we take a survey of mankind we cannot help cursing the wretch, who, to the unavoidable misfortunes of nature shall wilfully add the calamities of war. One would think there were evils enough in the world without studying to increase them, and that life is sufficiently short without shaking the sand that measures it. The histories of Alexander, and Charles of Sweden, are the histories of human devils; a good man cannot think of their actions without abhorrence nor of their deaths without rejoicing. To see the bounties of Heaven destroyed, the beautiful face of nature laid waste, and the choicest works of creation and art tumbled into ruin, would fetch a curse from the soul of piety itself. But in this country the aggravation is heightened by a new combination of affecting circumstances. America was young, and, compared with other countries, was virtuous. None but a Herod of uncommon malice would have made war upon infancy and innocence, and none but a people of the most finished fortitude dared, under those circumstances, have resisted the tyranny. The natives, or their ancestors, had fled from the former oppressions of England, and with the industry of bees had changed a wilderness into a habitable world. To Britain they were indebted for nothing. The country was the gift of Heaven, and God alone is their Lord and Sovereign.

The time, Sir, will come when you, in a melancholy hour, shall reckon up your miseries by your murders in America. Life, with you, begins to wear a clouded aspect. The vision of pleasurable delusion is wearing away, and changing to the barren wild of age and sorrow. The poor reflection of having served your King will yield you no consolation in your parting moments. He will crumble to the same undistinguished ashes with yourself, and have sins enough of his own to answer for. It is not the farcical benedictions of a Bishop, nor the cringing hypocrisy of a court of Chaplains, nor the formality of an act of Parliament, that can change guilt into innocence, or make the punishment *one* pang the less. You may, perhaps, be unwilling to be serious, but this destruction of the goods of Providence, this havoc of the human race, and this sowing the world with mischief, must be accounted for to him who made and governs it. To us they are only present sufferings, but to him they are deep rebellions.

If there is a sin superior to every other it is that of willful and offensive war. Most other sins are circumscribed within narrow limits, that is, the power of *one* man cannot give them a very general extension, and many kind of sins have only a mental existence from which no infection arises; but he who is the author of a war, lets loose the whole contagion of Hell, and opens a vein that bleeds a nation to death. We leave it to England and Indians to boast of these honors; we feel no thirst for such savage glory; a nobler flame, a purer spirit animates America. She hath taken up the sword of virtuous defence; she hath bravely put herself between Tyranny and

Freedom, between a curse and a blessing, determined to expel the one, and protect the other.

It is the object only of war that makes it honorable. And if there were ever *a just* war since the world began, it is this which America is now engaged in. She invaded no land of yours. She hired no mercenaries to burn your towns, nor Indians to massacre their inhabitants. She wanted nothing from you and was indebted for nothing to you; and thus circumstanced, her defence is honorable and her prosperity certain.

Yet it is not on the *justice* only, but likewise on the *importance* of this cause that I ground my seeming enthusiastical confidence of our success. The vast extension of America makes her of too much value in the scale of Providence, to be cast, like a pearl before swine, at the feet of a European island; and of much less consequence would it be that Britain were sunk in the sea than that America should miscarry. There has been such a chain of extraordinary events in the discovery of this country at first, in the peopling and planting it afterwards, in the rearing and nursing it to its present State, and in the protection of it through the present war, that no man can doubt, but Providence hath some nobler end to accomplish than the gratification of the petty Elector of Hanover or the ignorant and insignificant King of Britain.

As the blood of the martyrs hath been the seed of the Christian Church, so the political persecutions of England will, and hath already enriched America with industry, experience, union and importance. Before the present æra she was a meer chaos of uncemented Colonies, individually exposed to the ravages of the Indians and the invasion of any power that Britain should be at war with. She had nothing that she could call her own. Her felicity depended upon accident. The convulsions of Europe might have thrown her from one conqueror to another, till she had been the slave of all and ruined by every one; for until she had spirit enough to become her own master, there was no knowing to which master she should belong. *That* period, thank God, is past, and she is no longer the dependent, disunited Colonies of Britain, but the independent and united States of America, knowing no master but Heaven and herself. You or your King may call this "Delusion," "Rebellion," or what name you please. To us it is perfectly indifferent. The issue will determine the character and Time will give it a name as lasting as his own.

You have now, Sir, tried the fate of three campaigns, and can fully declare to England, that nothing is to be got on your part but blows and broken bones, and nothing on hers but waste of trade and credit and an encrease of poverty and taxes. You are now only where you might have been two years ago without the loss of a single ship, and yet not a step the forwarder towards the conquest of the Continent; because, as I have already hinted, "An army in a city can never be a conquering army." The full amount of your losses since the beginning of the war exceeds twenty thousand men, besides millions of treasure for which you have nothing in exchange. Our expences, though great, are circulated within ourselves. Yours is a direct sinking of money, and that from both ends at once; first in hiring troops out of the nation, and in paying them afterwards, because the money in neither case can return to Britain. We are already in possession of the prize, you only in suit for it. To us it is a real treasure, to you it would be only an empty triumph. Our expences will repay themselves with ten fold interest, while yours entail upon you everlasting poverty.

Take a review, Sir, of the ground you have gone over, and let it teach you policy, if it cannot honesty. You stand but on a very tottering foundation. A change of the Ministry in England may probably bring your measures into question and your head to the block. Clive, with all his successes, had some difficulty in escaping, and yours being all a war of losses, will afford you less pretensions and your enemies more grounds for impeachment.

Go home, Sir, and endeavor to save the remains of your ruined country by a just representation of the madness of her measures. A few moments well applied may yet preserve her from political destruction. I am not one of those who wish to see Europe in a flame, because I am persuaded such an event will not shorten the war. The rupture, at present, is confined between the two powers of America and England. England finds she cannot conquer America, and America has no wish to conquer England. You are fighting for what you can never obtain, and we defending what we mean never to part with. A few words, therefore, settle the bargain. Let England mind her own business and we will mind ours. Govern yourselves and we will govern ourselves. You may then trade where you please unmolested by us, and we will trade where we please unmolested by you; and such articles as we can purchase of each other better than elsewhere may be mutually done. If it were possible that you could carry on the war for twenty years you must still come to this point at last, or worse, and the sooner you think of it the better it will be for you.

My official situation enables me to know the repeated insults which Britain is obliged to put up with from foreign powers, and the wretched shifts she is driven to, to gloss them over. Her reduced strength and exhausted coffers in a three years war with America have given a powerful superiority to France and Spain. She is not now a match for them—But if neither counsels can prevail on her to think, nor sufferings awaken her to reason, she must e'en go on, till the honor of England becomes a proverb of contempt, and Europe dub her the Land of Fools.

I am, Sir,

With every wish for an honorable peace,

Your friend, enemy, and countryman,

COMMON SENSE.

YORK-TOWN,
March 18, 1778.

TO THE INHABITANTS OF AMERICA.

WITH all the pleasure with which a man exchanges bad company for good, I take my leave of Sir William and return to you. It is now nearly three years since the tyranny of Britain received its first repulse by the arms of America. A period, which has given birth to a new world and erected a monument to the folly of the old.

I cannot help being sometimes surprised at the complimentary references which I have seen and heard made to antient histories and transactions. The wisdom, civil governments, and sense of honor of the States of Greece and Rome, are frequently held up as objects of excellence and imitation. Mankind have lived for very little purpose, if, at this period of the world, they must go two or three thousand years back for lessons and examples. We do dishonorary injustice to ourselves by placing them in such a superior line. We have no just authority for it, neither can we tell why it is that we should suppose ourselves inferior.

Could the mist of antiquity be taken away, and men and things viewed as they then really were, it is more than probable that they would admire us, rather than we them. America has surmounted a greater variety and combination of difficulties than, I believe, ever fell to the share of any one people, in the same space of time, and has replenished the world with more useful knowledge and sounder maxims of civil government than were ever produced in any age before. Had it not been for America there had been no such thing as freedom left throughout the whole universe. England hath lost hers in a long chain of right reasoning from wrong principles, and it is from this country now she must learn the resolution to redress herself, and the wisdom how.

The Grecians and Romans were strongly possessed of the *spirit* of liberty but *not* the *principle*, for at the time they were determined not to be slaves themselves, they employed their power to enslave the rest of mankind. But this distinguished era is blotted by no one misanthropical vice. In short, if the principle on which the cause is founded, the universal blessings that are to arise from it, the difficulties that accompanied it, the wisdom with which it has been debated, the fortitude by which it has been supported, the strength of the power we had to oppose, and the condition in which we undertook it, be all taken in one view, we may justly stile it the most virtuous and illustrious revolution that ever graced the history of mankind.

A good opinion of ourselves is exceedingly necessary in private life, but absolutely necessary in public life, and of the utmost importance in supporting national character. I have no notion of yielding the palm of the United States to any Grecians or Romans that were ever born. We have equalled the bravest in times of danger, and excelled the wisest in the construction of civil governments, *no one in America excepted.*

From this agreeable eminence let us take a review of present affairs. The spirit of corruption is so inseparably interwoven with British politics, that their Ministry suppose all mankind are governed by the same motive. They have no idea of a people submitting even to temporary inconvenience from an attachment to rights and privileges. Their plans of business are calculated *by* the hour and *for* the hour, and are uniform in nothing but the corruption which gives them birth. They never had, neither have they at this time, any regular plan for the conquest of America by arms. They know not how to go about it, neither have they power to effect it if they could know. The thing is not within the compass of human practicability, for America is too extensive either to be fully conquered or *passively* defended. But she may be *actively* defended by defeating or making prisoners of the army that invades her. And this is the only system of defence that can be effectual in a large country.

There is something in a war carried on by invasion which makes it differ in circumstances from any other mode of war, because he who conducts it cannot tell whether the ground he gains, be for him, or against him, when he first makes it. In the winter seventy six General Howe marched with an air of victory through the Jerseys, the consequence of which was his defeat, and General Burgoyne at Saratoga experienced the same fate from the same cause. The Spaniards about two years ago were defeated by the Algerines in the same manner, that is, their first triumphs became a trap in which they were totally routed. And whoever will attend to the circumstances and events of a war carried on by invasion, will find, that any invader, in order to be finally conquered must first begin to conquer.

I confess myself one of those who believe the loss of Philadelphia to be attended with more advantages than injuries. The case stood thus. The enemy imagined Philadelphia to be of more importance to us than it really was; for we all know that it had long ceased to be a port, not a cargo of goods had been brought into it for near a twelve-month, nor any fix'd manufactories, nor even ship building carried on in it; yet as the enemy believed the conquest of it to be practicable, and to that belief added the absurd idea that the soul of all

America was centered there and would be conquered there, it naturally follows, that their possession of it, by not answering the end proposed, must break up the plans they had so foolishly gone upon, and either oblige them to form a new one, for which their present strength is not sufficient, or to give over the attempt.

We never had so small an army to fight against, nor so fair an opportunity of final success as *now*. The death wound is already given. The day is ours if we follow it up. The enemy by his situation is within our reach, and by his reduced strength is within our power. The Ministers of Britain may rage as they please, but our part is to conquer their armies. Let them wrangle and welcome, but let it not draw our attention from the *one* thing needful. *Here*, in *this* spot is our business to be accomplished, our felicity secured. What we have now to do is as clear as light, and the way to do it is as strait as a line. It needs not to be commented upon, yet, in order to be perfectly understood, I will put a case that cannot admit of a mistake.

Had the armies under the Generals Howe and Burgoyne been united and taken post at Germantown, and had the Northern army under General Gates been joined to that under General Washington at Whitemarsh, the consequence would have been a general action; and if in that action we had killed and taken the same number of officers and men, that is, between nine and ten thousand, with the same quantity of artillery, arms, stores, &c. as have been taken to the Northward, and obliged General Howe with the remains of his army, that is, with the same number he now commands, to take shelter in Philadelphia, we should certainly have thought ourselves the greatest heroes in the world; and should, as soon as the season permitted, have collected together all the force of the Continent and laid siege to the city, for it requires a much greater force to besiege an enemy in a town than to defeat them in the field. The case *now* is just the same as if it had been produced by the means I have here supposed. Between nine and ten thousand have been killed and taken, all their stores are in our possession, and General Howe, in consequence of that victory, has thrown himself for shelter into Philadelphia. He, or his trifling friend Galloway, may form what pretences they please, yet no just reason can be given for their going into winter quarters so early as the 19th of October, but their apprehension of a defeat if they continued out, or their conscious inability of keeping the field with safety. I see no advantage which can arise to America by hunting the enemy from State to State. It is a triumph without a prize, and wholly unworthy the attention of a people determined to conquer. Neither can any State promise itself security while the enemy remain in a condition to transport themselves from one part of the Continent to another. Howe, likewise, cannot conquer where we have no army to oppose, therefore any such removals in him are mean and cowardly, and reduces Britain to a common pilferer. If he retreats from Philadelphia, he will be despised; if he stays, he may be shut up and starved out, and the country, if he advances into it, may become his Saratoga. He has his choice of evils and we of opportunities. If he moves early, it is not only a sign but a proof that he expects no reinforcement, and his delays will prove that he either waits for the arrival of a plan to go upon, or force to execute it, or both; in *which* case, our strength will encrease more than his, therefore in *any* case we cannot be wrong if we do but proceed.

The particular condition of Pennsylvania deserves the attention of all the other States. Her military strength must not be estimated by the number of inhabitants. Here are men of all nations, characters, professions and interests. Here are the firmest Whigs, surviving, like sparks in the ocean, unquenched and uncooled in the midst of discouragement and disaffection. Here are men losing their all with chearfulness, and collecting fire and fortitude from the flames of their own estates. Here are others skulking in secret, many making a market of the times, and numbers who are changing Whig and Tory with the circumstances of every day.

It is by meer dint of fortitude and perseverance that the Whigs of this State have been able to maintain so good a countenance, and do even what they have done. We want help, and the sooner it can arrive the more effectual it will be. The invaded State, be it which it may, will always feel an additional burthen upon its back, and be hard set to support its civil power with sufficient authority; and this difficulty will always rise or fall, in proportion as the other States throw in their assistance to the common cause.

The enemy will most probably make many manœuvres at the opening of this campaign, to amuse and draw off the attention of the several States from the *one thing needful*. We may expect to hear of alarms and pretended expeditions to *this* place and *that* place, to the Southward, the Eastward and the Northward, all intended to prevent our forming into one formidable body. The less the enemy's strength is, the more subtleties of this kind will they make use of. Their existence depends upon it, because the force of America, when collected, is sufficient to swallow their present army up. It is therefore our business to make short work of it, by bending our whole attention to *this one principal point*, for the instant that the main body under General Howe is defeated, all the inferior alarms throughout the Continent, like so many shadows, will follow his downfall.

The only way to finish a war with the least possible bloodshed, or perhaps without any, is to collect an army, against the power of which, the enemy shall have no chance. By not doing this, we prolong the war, and double both the calamities and expences of it. What a rich and happy country would America be, were she, by a vigorous exertion, to reduce Howe as she has reduced Burgoyne. Her currency would rise to millions beyond its present value. Every man would be rich, and every man would have it in his power to be happy. And why not do these things? What is there to hinder? America is her own mistress and can do what she pleases.

If we had not at this time a man in the field, we could, nevertheless, raise an army in a few weeks sufficient to overwhelm all the force which General Howe at present commands. Vigor and determination will do any thing and every thing. We began the war with this kind of spirit, why not end it with the same? Here, Gentlemen, is the enemy. Here is the army. The interest, the happiness, of all America is centered in this half ruined spot. Come on and help us. Here are laurels, come and share them. Here are Tories, come and help us to expel them. Here are Whigs that will make you welcome, and enemies that dread your coming.

The worst of all policy is that of doing things by halves.

Penny-wise and pound foolish has been the ruin of thousands. The present spring, if rightly improved, will free us from all our troubles, and save us the expence of millions. We have now only one army to cope with. No opportunity can be fairer; no prospect more promising. I shall conclude this paper with a few outlines of a plan either for filling up the battalions with expedition, or for raising an additional force for any limited time, on any sudden emergency.

That in which every man is interested is every man's duty to support. And any burthen which falls equally on all men, and, from which every man is to receive an equal benefit, is consistent with the most perfect ideas of liberty. I would wish to revive something of that virtuous animation which first called America into the field. Then every man was eager to do his part, and perhaps the principal reason why we have in any degree fallen therefrom, is, because we did not set a sufficient value by it at first, but left it to blaze out of itself, instead of regulating and preserving it by just proportions of rest and service.

Suppose any State whose number of effective inhabitants were 80,000, should be required to furnish 3200 men towards the defence of the Continent on any very sudden emergency.

First, Let the whole number of effective inhabitants be divided into hundreds; then if each of those hundreds turn out four men, the whole number of 3200 will be had.

2dly, Let the names of each hundred men be entered in a book, and let four dollars be collected from each man, with as much more as any of the gentlemen whose abilities can afford it shall please to throw in, which gifts shall likewise be entered against the donors names.

3dly, Let the sums so collected be offered as a present, over and above the bounty of twenty dollars, to any four who may be inclined to propose themselves as volunteers; if more than four offer, the majority of the subscribers present shall determine which; if none offers, then four out of the hundred shall be taken by lot, who shall be entitled to the said sums, and shall either go, or provide others that will, in the space of six days.

4thly, As it will always happen, that in the space of ground on which any hundred men shall live, there will always be a number of persons who, by age and infirmity, are incapable of doing personal service, and as such persons are generally possessed of the greatest part of property in any country, their portion of service, therefore, will be to furnish each man with a blanket, which will make a regimental coat jacket and breeches, or cloaths in lieu thereof, and another for a watch cloak, and two pair of shoes—for however choice people may be of these things matters not in cases of this kind—Those who live always in houses can find many ways to keep themselves warm, but it is a shame and a sin to suffer a soldier in the field to want a blanket while there is one in the country.

Should the cloathing not be wanted, the superannuated or infirm persons possessing property, may, in lieu thereof, throw in their money subscriptions towards encreasing the bounty, for though age will naturally exempt a person from personal service, it cannot exempt him from his share of the charge, because the men are raised for the defence of property and liberty jointly.

There never was a scheme against which objections might not be raised. But this alone is not a sufficient reason for rejection. The only line to judge truly upon, is, to draw out and admit all the objections which can fairly be made, and place against them all the contrary qualities, conveniences and advantages, then by striking a balance you come at the true character of any scheme, principle or position.

The most material advantages of the plan here proposed are ease, expedition, and cheapness; yet the men so raised get a much larger bounty than is any where at present given; because all the expences, extravagance, and consequent idleness of recruiting are saved or prevented. The country incurs no new debt, nor interest thereon; the whole matter being all settled at once and entirely done with. It is a subscription answering all the purposes of a tax, without either the charge or trouble of collecting. The men are ready for the field with the greatest possible expedition, because it becomes the duty of the inhabitants themselves, in every part of the country, to find up their proportion of men, instead of leaving it to a recruiting Serjeant, who, be he ever so industrious, cannot know always where to apply.

I do not propose this as a regular digested plan, neither will the limits of this paper admit of any further remarks upon it. I believe it to be a hint capable of much improvement, and as such submit it to the Public.

COMMON SENSE.

Lancaster, March 21, 1778.

Prospects for War Between Britain and France

June 10, 1778

TO THE PEOPLE OF AMERICA.

As the country appears greatly amused with expectations of the enemy quitting Philadelphia, and lest that amusement should lull us into some unlooked for misfortune, I take the liberty, thro' the channels of the several news-papers, to point out the grounds upon which the politics of the enemy may, I think, be understood, or at least ought to be considered.

Whether they will quit Philadelphia or not is a question, which neither we, nor the General who commands there, can determine. He acts by orders from England, and we can judge only by appearances. He may expect to receive such, and may, nevertheless, receive orders to the contrary.

The state of European affairs, after the treaty with France was signed, rendered a war between France and England probable; and under that expectation, the Commander of the British troops would consequently pack up, and hold himself in readiness to obey *any* orders he might receive, upon a supposition that such orders would be sudden and peremptory. He must know that Philadelphia is no station for him, in case of an European war. He cannot help seeing that he is subject to an attack from France and America unitedly, and that the army he commands will be wanted elsewhere. Should such an event take place, he will move instantly, and therefore will, in the interim, always hold himself in readiness to move. And this, I presume, accounts for his preparations, which rather indicates his apprehensions than his intentions.

As I would not be misunderstood by using an undefined nicety of expression, I choose therefore to say, that we have a sett of as vile and treacherous characters to deal with, as were ever permitted to work out their own destruction, or suffered to live as a scourge to mankind. I mean the present King of England and his Ministers. As there is no act of baseness they would not commit, so there is no meanness they will not submit to. They would, I believe, suffer themselves to be kicked by every power in Europe, if by that submission they could go on unmolested with their schemes against America. *Here* they have fixed their object, and their eyes and ears are shut against every other.

There is *one* and *only* one way, by which they may creditably avoid a rupture with France, and likewise put themselves in a condition of making peace with America; and which if they omit doing, we may be sure there is mischief lurking behind, viz. *To acknowledge, on their part, the Independence of America.* Because such an acknowledgment admits France to the undisturbed enjoyment of her treaty with us as a matter of *right*, and consequently no quarrel can take place on the part of Britain. In this case, the capture of French vessels will be confined to those laden with military stores and cloathing made up, which likewise, according to the custom of nations, is not a legal cause for a declaration of war on the part of France.

Should this be their conduct, they will keep clear of a war with France, and consequently their apprehensions of immediate danger from their situation in Philadelphia will subside; after which, they will think themselves at liberty to hold or evacuate it as *future* occasions may arise. They know that their strongest fortification is their being mixed among the inhabitants, who must be exposed to the same mischief with themselves by an attack.

So if they do not accede to the Independence of America, and yet avoid a rupture with France, we may justly attribute such conduct to a mixture of secret villainy and public meanness, and may likewise be sure they have no intentions of quitting Philadelphia, and will have none, unless forced to it; and every expectation of their voluntarily doing it, tends only to lull us into a state of drowsiness and danger. I have here stated three cases, which are all that can happen.

First. A war with France.

Secondly. An acknowledgment of our independence, on the part of Britain, by which such a war may be *creditably* avoided. And,

Thirdly. Her submission to every indignity which France

has or may show, by which submission a war may be *meanly* avoided.

The first leads to an immediate evacuation of Philadelphia, and perhaps New-York. The second and third do not. And tho' I may possibly be wrong in my conjecture, yet I think it more than probable that the *last* of the three will be the Ministry's line of conduct. The character of the men favours this supposition.

But taking either of the two last to happen, we shall be exposed to consequences that we ought immediately to prepare against. The apparent probability of a war with France has given the British King and Ministry *new and popular pretensions for raising more troops,* which they may yet employ against us, if they can *any ways* avoid employing them against France; while we, amused with delusive appearances, may be most unwarily taken in.

This is not a time to trifle, neither are these trifling matters. I do not undertake to say what *will* happen, I only state what *may* happen; and as one of these three *must* happen, it is our part to be guarded against all. Not a man now ought to be absent from his proper post; and I submit it to the judgment of every State, whether the present time is not as politically critical, and may, by remissness, be as distressing as any which has yet happened. A reinforcement of eight hundred men has very lately arrived at New-York, which does not look much like an evacuation. They are yet tampering with the Indians. The burning Col. Kirkbride's and Mr. Borden's is but a recent affair, since which they have burnt a considerable number of houses in the state of Rhode-Island, and all these at the time they are pretending to negociate. If any thing can determine what confirmed villainy is, it must be conduct like this.

On our part we cannot be wrong, but by mistake or delusion. A fairer prospect we need not wish for, if we do but improve it. We have at present steered with safety thro a rough sea, and are bringing the ship into port, let us take care she is not shipwreck'd in the harbour.

The danger arising to Britain by the mean policy which I suppose she will adopt is, that by sending her forces to America, and failing at the same time in making fair weather with France, she will expose herself to be conquered at home, while she aims at conquest abroad. But as there is no act of absurdity she is not capable of committing, we should, therefore, not depend on the *wise* things she *ought* to do, but prepare against the *mad* things she will *most probably* do.

COMMON SENSE.

York-Town, June 10, 1778.

N. B. *The* CRISIS, *No. 6, which is ready for the press, will be published as soon as possible. It has been delayed in order to take in a larger compass of affairs than was at first intended. The author cannot promise the exact time, as it is lengthy and the printers very busy. Such News-papers as choose to publish the above remarks, are desired to insert this note.*

C. S.

The Crisis

TO THE EARL OF CARLISLE, GENERAL
CLINTON, AND WILLIAM EDEN, ESQ; BRITISH
COMMISSIONERS, AT NEW-YORK.

THERE is a dignity in the warm passions of a whig, which is never to be found in the cold malice of a tory. In the one, nature is only heated—in the other she is poisoned. The instant the former has it in his power to punish, he feels a disposition to forgive; but the canine venom of the latter knows no relief but in revenge. This general distinction will, I believe, apply in all cases, and suit as well the meridian of England as America.

As I presume your last proclamation will undergo the strictures of other pens, I shall confine my remarks to only a few parts thereof. All that you have said might have been comprised in half the compass. It is tedious and unmeaning, and only a repetition of your former follies, with here and there an offensive aggravation. Your cargo of pardons will have no market—It is unfashionable to look at them—Even speculation is at an end. They are become a perfect drug, and no ways calculated for the climate.

In the course of your proclamation you say, "The policy as well as the *benevolence of Great-Britain*, have thus far checked the extremes of war, when they tended to distress a people still considered as our fellow subjects, and to desolate a country shortly to become again a source of mutual advantage." What you mean by "the *benevolence* of Great-Britain," is to me inconceivable. To put a plain question: Do you consider yourselves men or devils? For until this point is settled, no determinate sense can be put upon the expression. You have already equalled, and in many instances excelled, the savages of either Indies; and if you have yet a cruelty in store, you must have imported it, unmixed with every human material, from the original ware-house of Hell.

To the interposition of Providence, and her blessings on our endeavours, and not to *British benevolence*, are we indebted for the short chain that limits your ravages. Remember you do not, at this time, command a foot of land on the Continent of America. Staten-Island, York-Island, a small part of Long-Island, and Rhode-Island, circumscribe your power; and even those you hold at the expence of the West-Indies. To avoid a defeat and prevent a desertion of your troops, you have taken up your quarters in holes and corners of inaccessible security; and in order to conceal what every one can conceive, you now endeavour to impose your weakness upon us for an act of mercy. If you think to succeed by such shadowy devises, you are but infants in the political world; you have the A, B, C, of stratagem yet to learn; and are wholly ignorant of the people you have to contend with. Like men in a state of intoxication, you forget that the rest of the world have eyes, and that the same stupidity which conceals you from yourselves, exposes you to their satire and contempt.

The paragraph I have quoted, stands as an introduction to the following, "But when that country (America) professes the unnatural design, not only of estranging herself from us, but of mortgaging herself and her resources to our enemies, the whole contest is changed; and the question is, how far Great-Britain may, by every means in her power, destroy or render useless, a connection contrived for her ruin and the aggrandizement of France. Under such circumstances, the laws of self-preservation must direct the conduct of Britain, and if the British Colonies are to become an accession to France, will direct her to render that accession of as little avail as possible to her enemy."

I consider you in this declaration like madmen biting in the hour of death. It contains likewise a fraudulent meanness; for, in order to justify a barbarous conclusion, you have advanced a false position. The treaty we have formed with France is open, noble and generous. It is true policy founded on sound philosophy, and neither a surrender or mortgage, as you would scandalously insinuate. I have seen every article, and speak from positive knowledge. In France we have found an affectionate friend and a faithful ally; from Britain nothing but tyranny, cruelty and infidelity.

But the happiness is, that the mischief you threaten is not in your power to execute; and if it were, the punishment would return upon you in a tenfold degree. The humanity of America hath hitherto restrained her from acts of retaliation, and the affection she retains for many individuals in England, who have fed, cloathed, and comforted her prisoners, has, to the present day, warded off her resentment, and operated as a screen to the whole. But even these considerations must cease when national objects interfere and oppose them. Repeated aggravations will provoke a retort, and policy justify the measure. We mean now to take you seriously up upon your own ground and principle, and as you do so shall you be done by.

You ought to know, gentlemen, that England and Scotland are far more exposed to incendiary desolation than America in her present State can possibly be. We occupy a country with but few towns, and whose riches consists in land and annual produce. The two last can suffer but little, and that only within a very limited compass. In Britain it is otherwise. Her wealth lies chiefly in cities and large towns, the repositories of manufactures, and fleets of merchant men. There is not a Nobleman's country seat but may be laid in ashes by a single person. Your own may probably contribute to the proof: In short, there is no evil which cannot be returned when you come to incendiary mischief. The ships in the Thames may certainly be as easily set on fire as the temporary bridge was a few years ago; yet of that affair no discovery was ever made; and the loss you would sustain by such an event, executed at a proper season, is infinitely greater than any you can inflict. The East-India house and the Bank, neither are nor can be secure from this sort of destruction, and as Doctor Price justly observes, a fire at the latter would bankrupt the nation. It has never been the custom of France and England, when at war, to make those havocs on each other, because the ease with which they could retaliate, rendered it as impolitic as if each had destroyed his own.

But think not gentlemen that our distance secures you, or our invention fails us. We can much easier accomplish such a point than any nation in Europe. We talk the same language, dress in the same habit, and appear with the same manners as yourselves. We can pass from one part of England to another unsuspected, many of us are as well acquainted with the country as you are, and should you impoliticly provoke our will, you will most assuredly lament the effects of it. Mischiefs of this kind require no army to execute them. The means are obvious, and the opportunities unguardable. I hold up a warning piece to your senses, if you have any left, and *"to the unhappy people likewise whose affairs are committed to you."** I call not with the rancour of an enemy, but with the earnestness of a friend on the deluded people of England, lest between your blunders and theirs, they sink beneath the evils contrived for us.

"He who lives in a glass house, says the Spanish proverb, should never begin throwing stones." This, gentlemen, is exactly your case; and you must be the most ignorant of mankind, or suppose us so, not to see on which side the balance of accounts will fall. There are many other modes of retaliation, which for several reasons I choose not to mention. But be assured of this, that the instant you put a threat in execution, a counter blow will follow it. If you *openly* profess yourselves savages, it is high time we should treat you as such, and if nothing but distress can recover you to reason, to punish will become an office of charity.

While your fleet lay last Winter in the Delaware I offered my service to the Pennsylvania Navy Board then at Trenton, as one who would make a party with them, or any four or five gentlemen on an expedition down the river to set fire to it, and though it was not then accepted, nor the thing *personally* attempted, it is more than probable, that your own folly will provoke a much heavier stroke in some more vulnerable part. Say not when the mischief is done that you had not warning, and remember that we do not begin it, but mean to repay it. Thus much for your savage and impolitic threat.

In another part of your proclamation you say, "But if the honours of a military life are become the object of the Americans, let them seek those honours under the banners of their *rightful Sovereign,* and in fighting the battles of the united British empire, against our late *mutual and natural enemies."* Surely! The union of absurdity with madness was never

*General Clinton's letter to Congress.

marked in more distinguishable lines than those. Your *rightful Sovereign* as you call him may do well enough for you, who dare not enquire into the humble capacities of the man; but we who estimate persons and things by their real worth, cannot suffer our judgments to be so imposed upon; and unless it is your wish to see him exposed, it ought to be your endeavour to keep him out of sight. The less you have to say about him the better. We have *done with him*, and that ought to be answer enough. You have been often told so. Strange! that the answer must be so often repeated. You go a begging with your King as with a brat, or with some unsaleable commodity you were tired of; and though every body tells you no, no, still you keep hawking him about. But there is *one* that will have him in a little time, and as we have no inclination to disappoint you of a customer we shall bid nothing for him.

The impertinent folly of the paragraph I have just quoted, deserves no other notice than to be laughed at and thrown by, but the principle on which it is founded is detestable. *We are invited to submit to a man who has attempted by every cruelty to destroy us, and to join him in making war against France, who is already at war against him for our support.* Can Bedlam in concert with Lucifer form a more mad and devilish request? Were it possible that a people could sink into such apostacy, they would deserve to be swept from the earth like the inhabitants of Sodom and Gomorrah. The proposition is an universal affront to the rank which man holds in the creation. An indignity to him who placed him there. It supposes him made up without a spark of honour, and under no obligation to God or man.

What sort of men or christians must you suppose the Americans to be, who after seeing their most humble petitions insultingly rejected; the most grievous laws passed to distress them in every quarter; an undeclared war let loose upon them, and Indians and Negroes invited to the slaughter: Who after seeing their kindred murdered, their fellow citizens starved to death in prisons, and their houses and property destroyed and burned: Who after the most serious appeals to Heaven, the most solemn abjuration by oath of all government connection with you, and the most heart-felt pledges and protestations of faith to each other; and who after soliciting the friendship and entering into alliances with other nations, should at last break through all these obligations civil and divine, by complying with your horrid and infernal proposal. Ought we ever after to be considered as a part of the human race? Or ought we not rather to be blotted from the society of mankind and become a spectacle of misery to the world?—But there is something in corruption, which, like a jaundiced eye, transfers the colour of itself to the object it looks upon, and sees every thing stained and impure; for unless you were capable of such conduct yourselves, you would never have supposed such a character in us. The offer fixes your infamy. It exhibits you as a nation without faith; with whom oaths and treaties are considered as trifles, and the breaking them as the breaking of a bubble. Regard to decency or to rank might have taught you better, or pride inspired you though virtue could not. There is not left a step in the degradation of character to which you can now descend; you have put your foot on the ground floor and the key of the dungeon is turned upon you.

That the invitation may want nothing of being a complete monster, you have thought proper to finish it with an assertion which has no foundation either in fact or philosophy; and as Mr. Ferguson your Secretary, is a man of letters, and has made civil society his study and published a treatise on that subject, I address this part to him.

In the close of the paragraph which I last quoted, France is stiled the *"natural enemy"* of England, and by way of lugging us into some strange idea, she is likewise stiled the *late mutual and natural enemy* of both countries. I deny that she ever was the natural enemy of either, and that there does not exist in nature such a principle. The expression is an unmeaning barbarism, and wholly unphilosophical when applied to beings of the same species, let their rank in the creation be what it may. We have a perfect idea of a *natural* enemy when we think of the *Devil*, because the enmity is perpetual, unalterable and unabateable. It admits of neither peace, truce or treaty; consequently the warfare is eternal, and therefore it is natural. But man with man cannot arrange in the same opposition. Their quarrels are accidental and equivocally created.

They become friends or enemies as the change of temper or the cast of interest inclines them. The Creator of man did not constitute him the natural enemy of each other. He has not made any one order of beings so. Even wolves may quarrel, still they herd together. If any two nations are so, then must all nations be so, otherwise it is not nature but custom, and the offence frequently originates with the accuser. England is as truly the natural enemy of France as France is of England, and perhaps more so. Separated from the rest of Europe she has contracted an unsociable habit of manners, and imagines in others the jealousy she creates in herself. Never long satisfied with peace, she supposes the discontent universal, and buoyed up with her own importance, conceives herself the only object pointed at. The expression has been often used, and always with a fraudulent design, for when the idea of a *natural enemy* is conceived it prevents all other enquiries, and the real cause of the quarrel is hidden in the universality of the conceit. Men start at the notion of a natural enemy and ask no other questions. The cry obtains credit like the alarm of a mad dog, and is one of those kind of tricks, which, by operating on the common passions, secures their interest through their folly.

But we, Sir, are not to be thus imposed upon. We live in a large world, and have extended our ideas beyond the limits and prejudices of an island. We hold out the right hand of fellowship to all the universe, and we conceive there to be a sociality in the manners of France, which is much better disposed to peace and negociation than that of England, and until the latter become more civilized she cannot expect to live long at peace with any power. Her common language is vulgar and offensive, and children with their milk suck in the rudiments of insult *"The arm of Britain! The mighty arm of Britain! Britain that shakes the earth to its center and its poles! The scourge of France! The terror of the world! That governs with a nod and pours down vengeance like a God!"* This language neither makes a nation great or little, but it shews a savageness of manners, and has a tendency to keep national animosity alive. The entertainments of the stage are calculated to the same end, and almost every publick exhibition is tinctured with insult. Yet England is always in dread of France. Terrified at the apprehension of an invasion. Suspicious of being outwitted in a treaty, and privately cringing though she is publickly offending. Let her, therefore, reform her manners and do justice, and she will find the idea of a *natural enemy* to be only a phantom of her own imagination.

Little did I think, at this period of the war, to see a proclamation which could promise you no one useful purpose whatever, and tend only to expose you. One would think that you were just awakened from a four years dream, and knew nothing of what had passed in the interval. Is this a time to be offering pardons, or renewing the long forgotten subjects of charters and taxation? Is it worth your while, after every force has failed you, to retreat under the shelter of argument and persuasion? Or can you think that we, with nearly half your army prisoners, and in alliance with France, are to be begged or threatened into submission by a piece of paper? But as Commissioners, at a hundred pounds sterling a week each, you conceived yourselves bound to do something, and the genius of ill fortune told you you must write.

For my own part, I have not put pen to paper these several months. Convinced of our superiority by the issue of every campaign, I was inclined to hope, that that, which all the rest of the world can see, would become visible to you, and therefore felt unwilling to ruffle your temper by fretting you with repetitions or discoveries. There have been intervals of hesitation in your conduct, from which it seemed a pity to disturb you, and a charity to leave you to yourselves. You have often stopt, as if you intended to think, but your thoughts have ever been too early or too late.

There was a time when Britain disdained to answer, and even to hear a petition from America. *That* time is past, and she in her turn is petitioning our acceptance. We now stand on higher ground and offer her peace; and the time will come when she, perhaps in vain, will ask it from *us*. The latter case is as probable as the former ever was. She cannot refuse to acknowledge our Independence with greater obstinacy than she before refused to repeal her laws, and if America alone could bring her to the one, united with France she will reduce her to the other. There is something in obstinacy which differs from every other passion, whenever it fails it never re-covers, but either breaks like iron or crumbles sulkily away like a fractured arch. Most other passions have their periods of fatigue and rest; their suffering and their cure; but obstinacy has no resource, and the first wound is mortal. You have al-ready began to give it up, and you will, from the natural con-struction of the vice, find yourselves both obliged and inclined to do so.

If you look back you see nothing but loss and disgrace. If you look forward the same scene continues, and the close is an impenetrable gloom. You may plan and execute little mis-chiefs, but are they worth the expence they cost you, or will such partial evils have any effect on the general cause? Your expedition to Egg-Harbour will be felt at a distance like an attack upon a hen roost, and expose you in Europe with a sort of childish phrensy. Is it worth while to keep an army to protect you in writing proclamations, or to get once a year into winter quarters? Possessing yourselves of towns is not conquest, but convenience, and in which you will one day or other be trepanned. Your retreat from Philadelphia was only a timely escape, and your next expedition may be less fortunate.

It would puzzle all the politicians in the universe to con-ceive what you stay for, or why you have staid so long. You are prosecuting a war in which you confess you have neither object nor hope, and that conquest, could it be effected, would not repay the charge: In the mean while the rest of your affairs are running to ruin, and a European war kindling against you. In such a situation there is neither doubt or dif-ficulty; the first rudiments of reason will determine the choice, for if peace can be procured with more advantages than even a conquest can be obtained, he must be an ideot indeed that hesitates.

But you are probably buoyed up by a set of wretched mor-tals, who, having deceived themselves, are cringing with the duplicity of a spaniel for a little temporary bread. Those men will tell you just what you please. It is their interest to amuse in order to lengthen out their protection. They study to keep you amongst them for that very purpose; and in proportion as

you disregard their advice and grow callous to their complaints, they will stretch into improbability, and pepper off
their flattery the higher. Characters like these are to be found
in every country, and every country will despise them.

COMMON SENSE.

Philadelphia, October 20th, 1778.

The Crisis

NUMBER VII

November 11, 1778

TO THE PEOPLE OF ENGLAND.

THERE are stages in the business of serious life in which to amuse is cruel, but to deceive is to destroy; and it is of little consequence, in the conclusion, whether men deceive themselves, or submit, by a kind of mutual consent, to the impositions of each other. That England has been long under the influence of delusion or mistake, needs no other proof than the unexpected and wretched situation she is now involved in: And so powerful has been the influence, that no provision was ever made or thought of against the misfortune, because the possibility of its happening was never conceived.

The general and successful resistance of America, the conquest of Burgoyne, and a war with France, were treated in Parliament as the dreams of a discontented opposition, or a distempered imagination. They were beheld as objects unworthy of a serious thought, and the bare intimation of them afforded the Ministry a triumph of laughter. Short triumph indeed! For every thing which has been predicted has happened, and all that was promised have failed. A long series of politics so remarkably distinguished by a succession of misfortunes, without one alleviating turn, must certainly have something in it systematically wrong. It is sufficient to awaken the most credulous into suspicion, and the most obstinate into thought. Either the means in your power are insufficient, or the measures ill planned; either the execution has been bad, or the thing attempted impracticable; or to speak more emphatically, either you are not able, or Heaven is not willing. For, why is it that you have not conquered us? Who, or what has prevented you? You have had every opportunity you could desire, and succeeded to your utmost wish in every preparatory means. Your fleets and armies have arrived in America without an accident. No uncommon misfortune hath intervened. No foreign nation hath interfered until the time you had allotted for victory was past. The opposition either in or out of Parliament, neither disconcerted your measures, retarded or diminished your force. They only foretold your fate. Every ministerial scheme was carried with as high a hand as if the whole nation had been unanimous. Every thing wanted was asked for, and every thing asked for was granted. A greater force was not within the compass of your abilities to send, and the time you sent it was of all others the most favourable. You were then at rest with the whole world beside. You had the range of every court in Europe uncontradicted by us. You amused us with a tale of Commissioners of Peace, and under that disguise collected a numerous army and came almost unexpectedly upon us. The force was much greater than we looked for; and that which we had to oppose it with, was unequal in numbers, badly armed, and poorly disciplined; beside which, it was embodied only for a short time, and expired within a few months after your arrival. We had governments to form; measures to concert; an army to raise and train, and every necessary article to import or to create. Our non-importation scheme had exhausted our stores, and your command by sea intercepted our supplies. We were a people unknown, and unconnected with the political world, and strangers to the disposition of foreign powers. Could you possibly wish for a more favourable conjunction of circumstances? Yet all these have happened and passed away, and as it were left you with a laugh. They are likewise events of such an original nativity as can never happen again, unless a new world should arise from the ocean.

If any thing can be a lesson to presumption, surely the circumstances of this war will have their effect. Had Britain been defeated by any European power, her pride would have drawn consolation from the importance of her conquerors; but in the present case, she is excelled by those she affected to despise, and her own opinions, retorting on herself, become an aggravation of her disgrace. Misfortune and experience are lost upon mankind when they produce neither reflection nor reformation. Evils, like poisons, have their uses, and there are diseases which no other remedy can reach. It has been the crime and folly of England to suppose herself invincible, and *that*, without acknowledging or perceiving that a full third of her strength was drawn from the country she is now at war with. The arm of Britain has been spoken of as the arm of the Almighty, and she has lived of late as if she thought the whole world created for her diversion. Her politics, instead of civilizing, has tended to brutalize mankind, and under the vain unmeaning title of *"Defender of the Faith,"* she has made war like an Indian against the religion of humanity. Her cruelties in the East-Indies will *never, never* be forgotten; and it is somewhat remarkable that the produce of that ruined country, transported to America, should there kindle up a war to punish the destroyer. The chain is continued, though with a kind of mysterious uniformity, both in the crime and the punishment. The latter runs parallel with the former; and time and fate will give it a perfect illustration.

Where information is with-held, ignorance becomes a reasonable excuse; and one would charitably hope that the people of England do not encourage cruelty from choice but from mistake. Their recluse situation, surrounded by the sea, preserves them from the calamities of war, and keeps them in the dark as to the conduct of their own armies. They see not, therefore they feel not. They tell the tale that is told them and believe it, and accustomed to no other news than their own, they receive it, stript of its horrors and prepared for the palate of the nation, through the channel of the London Gazette. They are made to believe that their Generals and armies differ from those of other nations, and have nothing of rudeness or barbarity in them. They suppose them what they wish them to be. They feel a disgrace in thinking otherwise, and naturally encourage the belief from a partiality to themselves. There was a time when I felt the same prejudices and reasoned from the same errors; but experience, sad and painful experience has taught me better. What the conduct of former armies was I know not, but what the conduct of the present is I well know. It is low, cruel, indolent, and profligate; and had the people of America no other cause for separation than what the army has occasioned, *that alone* is cause enough.

The field of politics in England is far more extensive than that of news. Men have a right to reason for themselves, and though they cannot contradict the intelligence in the London Gazette, they may frame upon it what sentiments they please.

But the misfortune is, that a general ignorance has prevailed over the whole nation respecting America. The Ministry and the Minority have both been wrong. The former was always so; the latter only lately so. Politics to be executively right, must have a unity of means and time, and a defect in either overthrows the whole. The Ministry rejected the plans of the Minority while they were practicable, and joined in them when they became impracticable. From wrong measures they got into wrong time, and have now compleated the circle of absurdity by closing it upon themselves.

It was my fate to come to America a few months before the breaking out of hostilities. I found the disposition of the people such, that they might have been led by a thread and governed by a reed. Their suspicion was quick and penetrating, but their attachment to Britain was obstinate, and it was, at that time, a kind of treason to speak against it. They disliked the Ministry, but they esteemed the nation. Their ideas of grievance operated without resentment, and their single object was reconciliation. Bad as I believed the Ministry to be, I never conceived them capable of a measure so rash and wicked as the commencing of hostilities; much less did I imagine the nation would encourage it. I viewed the dispute as a kind of law-suit, in which I supposed the parties would find a way either to decide or settle it. I had no thoughts of independence or of arms. The world could not then have persuaded me that I should be either a soldier or an author. If I had any talents for either they were buried in me, and might ever have continued so, had not the necessity of the times dragged and driven them into action. I had formed my plan of life, and conceiving myself happy, wished every body else so. But when the country, into which I had but just put my foot, was set on fire about my ears it was time to stir. It was time for every man to stir. Those who had been long settled had something to defend; those who were just come had something to pursue; and the call and the concern was equal and universal. For in a country where all men were once adventurers, the difference of a few years in their arrival could make none in their right.

The breaking out of hostilities opened a new suspicion in

the politics of America, which though at that time very rare, has been since proved to be very right. What I allude to is, *a secret and fixt determination in the British Cabinet to annex America to the Crown of England as a conquered country*. If this be taken as the object, then the whole line of conduct pursued by the Ministry, though rash in its origin, and ruinous in its consequences, is nevertheless uniform and consistent in its parts. It applies to every case and resolves every difficulty. But if taxation of any thing else be taken in its room, then is there no proportion between the object and the charge. Nothing but the whole soil and property of the country can be placed as a possible equivalent against the millions which the Ministry expended. No taxes raised in America could possibly repay it. A revenue of two millions sterling a year would not discharge the sum and interest accumulating thereon, in twenty years.

Reconciliation never appear to have been the wish or the object of administration, they looked on conquest as certain and infallible, and under that persuasion, sought to drive the Americans into what they might stile a general rebellion, and then crushing them with arms in their hands, reap the rich harvest of a general confiscation and silence them forever. The dependants at Court were too numerous to be provided for in England. The market for plunder in the East-Indies was over; and the profligacy of government required that a new mine should be opened, and that mine could be no other than America conquered and forfeited. They had no where else to go. Every other channel was drained, and extravagance, with the thirst of a drunkard, was gaping for supplies.

If the Ministry deny this to have been their plan, it becomes them to explain what was their plan. For either they have abused us in coveting property they never laboured for, or they have abused you in expending an amazing sum upon an incompetent object. Taxation, as I mentioned before could never be worth the charge of obtaining it by arms, and any kind of formal obedience which America could have made, would have weighed with the lightness of a laugh against such a load of expence. It is therefore most probable, that the Ministry will at last justify their policy by their dishonesty, and openly declare that their original design was conquest: And in this case it well becomes the people of England to consider how far the nation would have been benefited by the success.

In a general view there are very few conquests that repay the charge of making them, and mankind are pretty well convinced that it can never be worth their while to go to war for profit sake. If they are made war upon, their country invaded, or their existence at stake, it is their duty to defend and preserve themselves, but in every other light and from every other cause is war inglorious and detestable. But to return to the case in question—

When conquests are made of foreign countries, it is supposed that the *commerce* and *dominion* of the country which made them are extended. But this could neither be the object nor the consequence of the present war. You enjoyed the whole commerce before. It could receive no possible addition by a conquest, but on the contrary, must diminish as the inhabitants were reduced in numbers and wealth. You had the same *dominion* over the country which you used to have, and had no complaint to make against her for breach of any part of the compact between you and her, or contending against any established custom commercial, political, or territorial. The country and the commerce were both your own when you *began* to conquer, in the same manner and form as they had been your own a hundred years before. Nations have sometimes been induced to make conquests for the sake only of reducing the power of their enemies, or bringing it to a balance with their own. But this could be no part of your plan. No foreign authority was claimed here, neither was any such authority suspected by you, or acknowledged, or imagined by us. What then, in the name of Heaven, could you go to war for? or what chance could you possibly have in the event, but either to hold the same country which you held before, and that in a much worse condition, or to lose with an amazing expence what you might have retained without a farthing charge?

War never can be the interest of a trading nation, any more than quarreling can be profitable to a man in business. But to make war upon those who trade with us, is like setting a bulldog upon a customer at the shop door. The least degree of common sense shews the madness of the latter, and it will apply with the same force of conviction to the former. Piratical nations, having neither commerce or commodities of their own to lose, may make war upon all the world and lucratively find their account in it. But it is quite otherwise with Britain. For besides the stoppage of trade in time of war, she exposes more of her own property to be lost, than she has the chance of taking from others. Some ministerial gentlemen in Parliament have mentioned the greatness of her trade as an apology for the greatness of her loss. This is miserable politics indeed! because it ought to have been given as a reason for her not engaging in war at first. The coast of America commands the West India trade almost as effectually as the coast of Africa does that of the Streights, and England can no more carry on the former without the consent of America, than she can the latter without a Mediterranean pass.

In whatever light the war with America is considered upon commercial principles, it is evidently the interest of the people of England not to support it; and why it has been supported so long against the clearest demonstrations of truth and national advantage, is to me, and must be to all the reasonable world, a matter of astonishment. Perhaps it may be said that I live in America, and write this from interest. To this I reply, that my principles are universal. My attachment is to all the world and not to any particular part, and if what I advance is right, no matter where or who it comes from. We have given the proclamation of your Commissioners a currency in our news-papers, and I have no doubt but you will give this a place in yours. To oblige and be obliged is fair.

Before I dismiss this part of my address I shall mention one more circumstance in which I think the people of England have been equally mistaken; and then proceed to other matter.

There is such an idea existing in the world as that of *national honor*, and this, falsly understood, is oftentimes the cause of war. In a christian and philosophical sense mankind seem to have stood still at individual civilization, and to retain as nations all the original rudeness of nature. Peace, by treaty, is only a cessation of violence, not a reformation of sentiment. It is a substitute for a principle that is wanting, and ever will be wanting till the idea of *national honor* be rightly understood. As individuals we profess ourselves christians, but as nations we are heathens, Romans, and what not. I remember the late Admiral Saunders declaring in the House of Commons, and that in the time of peace *"that the city of Madrid laid in ashes was not a sufficient atonement for the Spaniards taking off the rudder of an English sloop of war."* I do not ask whether this is christianity or morality, I ask whether it is decency? whether it is proper language for a nation to use? In private life we should call it by the plain name of bullying, and the elevation of rank cannot alter its character. It is I think exceedingly easy to define what ought to be understood by *national honour*, for *that* which is the best character for an individual is the best character for a nation; and wherever the latter exceeds or falls beneath the former, there is a departure from the line of true greatness.

I have thrown out this observation with a design of applying it to Great-Britain. Her idea of national honour seems devoid of that benevolence of heart, that universal expansion of philanthropy, and that triumph over the rage of vulgar prejudice, without which man is inferior to himself, and a companion of common animals. To know whom she shall regard or dislike, she asks what country they are of, what religion they profess, and what property they enjoy. Her idea of national honour seems to consist in national insult, and that to be a great people, is to be neither a christian, a philosopher, or a gentleman, but to threaten with the rudeness of a bear, and to devour with the ferocity of a lion. This perhaps may sound harsh and uncourtly, but it is too true, and the more is the pity.

I mention this only as her general character. But towards America she has observed no character at all, and destroyed by her conduct what she assumed in her title. She set out with the stile of *Parent* or *Mother Country*. The association of ideas which naturally accompany this expression are filled with every thing that is fond, tender, and forbearing. They have an energy particular to themselves, and overlooking the accidental attachment of common affections, apply with peculiar softness to the first feelings of the heart. It is a political term which every mother can feel the force of, and every child can judge of. It needs no painting of mine to set it off, for nature only can do it justice.

But has any part of your conduct to America corresponded with the title you set up? If in your general national character you are unpolished and severe, in this you are inconsistent and unnatural; and you must have exceeding false notions of national honour, to suppose that the world can admire a want of humanity, or that national honour depends on the violence of resentment, the inflexibility of temper, or the vengeance of execution.

I would willingly convince you, and that with as much temper as the times will suffer me to do, that as you opposed your own interest by quarreling with us, so likewise your national honour, rightly conceived and understood, was no ways called upon to enter into a war with America. Had you studied true greatness of heart, the first and fairest ornament of mankind, you would have acted directly contrary to all that you have done, and the world would have ascribed it to a generous cause, besides which, you had (*though with the assistance of this country*) secured a powerful name by the last war. You were known and dreaded abroad; and it would have been wise in you to have suffered the world to have slept undisturbed under that idea. It was to you, a force existing without expence. It produced to you all the advantages of real power; and you were stronger through the universality of *that charm* than any future fleets and armies may probably make you. Your greatness was so secured and interwoven with your silence that you ought never to have awakened mankind, and had nothing to do but to be quiet. Had you been true politicians you would have seen all this, and continued to draw from the magic of a name, the force and authority of a nation.

Unwise as you were in breaking the charm, you were still more unwise in the manner of doing it. *Sampson* only *told the secret*, but *you* have *performed the operation*; you have shaven your own head, and wantonly thrown away the locks. America was the hair from which the charm was drawn that infatuated the world. You ought to have quarrelled with *no* power; but with *her* upon *no* account. You had nothing to fear from any condescension you might make. You might have humoured her, even if there had been no justice in her claims, without any risk to your reputation; for Europe fascinated by your fame, would have ascribed it to your beneficence, and America, intoxicated by the grant, would have slumbered in her fetters.

But this method of studying the progress of the passions, in order to ascertain the probable conduct of mankind, is a philosophy in politics, which those who preside at St. James's have no conceptions of. They know no other influence than corruption, and reckon all their probabilities from precedent. A new case is to them a new world, and while they are seeking for a parallel they get lost. The talents of Lord Mansfield can be estimated at best no higher than those of a Sophist. He understands the subtleties but not the elegance of nature; and by continually viewing mankind through the cold medium of the law, never thinks of penetrating into the warmer region of the mind. As for Lord North, it is his happiness to have in him more philosophy than sentiment, for he bears flogging like a top and sleeps the better for it. His punishment becomes his support, for while he suffers the lash for his sins, he keeps himself up by twirling about. In politics, he is a good arithmetician, and in every thing else nothing at all.

There is one circumstance which comes so much within Lord North's province as a financer, that I am surprised it should escape him, which is, the different abilities of the two countries in supporting the expence; for, strange as it may seem, England is not a match for America in this particular. By a curious kind of revolution in accounts, the people of England seem to mistake their poverty for their riches, that is, they reckon their national debt as a part of their national wealth. They make the same kind of error which a man would do, who after mortgaging his estate, should add the money borrowed, to the full value of the estate in order to count up his worth, and in this case he would conceit that he got rich by running into debt. Just thus it is with England. The Government owed at the beginning of this war One Hundred and Thirty-five millions sterling, and though the individuals to whom it was due, had a right to reckon their shares as so much private property yet to the nation collectively it was so much poverty. There is as effectual limits to public debts as to private ones, for when once the money borrowed is so great as to require the whole yearly revenue to discharge the interest thereon, there is an end to all farther borrowing; in the same manner as when the interest of a man's debts amounts to the yearly income of his estate there is an end to his credit. This is nearly the case with England, the interest of her present debt being at least equal to one half of her yearly revenue, so that out of Ten Million annually collected by taxes, she has but Five she can call her own.

The very reverse of this was the case with America. She began the war without any debt upon her, and in order to carry it on, she neither raised money by taxes, nor borrowed it upon interest, but *created* it, and her situation, at this time, continues so much the reverse of yours, that taxing would make her rich, whereas it would make you poor. When we shall have sunk the sum which we have created, we shall then be out of debt, be just as rich as when we began, and all the while we are doing it, shall feel no difference, because the value will rise as the quantity decreases.

There was not a country in the world so capable of bearing the expence of a war as America; not only because she was not in debt when she began, but because the country is young and capable of infinite improvement, and has an almost boundless tract of new lands in store; whereas England has got to her extent of age and growth, and has no unoccupied lands or property in reserve. The one is like a young heir coming to a large improveable estate; the other like an old man whose chances are over, and his estate mortgaged for half its worth.

In the second number of the Crisis, which I find has been re-published in England, I endeavoured to set forth the impracticability of conquering America. I stated every case, that I conceived could possibly happen, and ventured to predict its consequences. As my conclusions were drawn not artfully but naturally, they have all proved to be true. I was upon the spot; knew the politics of America, her strength and resources, and by a train of services, the best in my power to render, was honoured with the friendship a Congress, the army and the people. I considered the cause a just one. I know and feel it a just one, and under that confidence never made my own profit or loss an object. My endeavour was to have the matter well understood on both sides, and I conceived myself rendering a general service, by setting forth to the one the impossibility of being conquered, and to the other the impossibility of conquering. Most of the arguments made use of by the Ministry for supporting the war, are the very arguments that ought to have been used against supporting it; and the plans, by which they thought to conquer, are the very plans in which they were sure to be defeated. They have taken every thing up at the wrong end. Their ignorance is astonishing, and were you in my situation you would see it. They may perhaps have your confidence, but I am persuaded they would make very indifferent Members of Congress. I know what England is, and what America is, and from this compound of knowledge, am better enabled to judge of the issue, than what the King or any of his Ministers can be.

In this number I have endeavoured to shew the ill policy and disadvantages of the war. I believe many of my remarks are new. Those which are not so, I have studied to improve and place in a manner that may be clear and striking. Your failure is, I am persuaded, as certain as fate. America is above your reach. She is at least your equal in the world, and her Independence neither rests upon your consent, or can be prevented by your arms. In short, you spend your substance in vain, and impoverish yourselves without a hope.

But suppose you had conquered America, what advantage, collectively or individually, as merchants, manufacturers, or conquerors, could you have looked for. This is an object you never seem to have attended to. Listening for the sound of victory, and led away by the phrensy of arms, you neglected to reckon either the cost or the consequences. You must all pay towards the expence; the poorest among you must bear his share, and it is both your right and your duty to weigh seriously the matter. Had America been conquered, she might have been parcelled out in grants to the favourites at court, but no share of it would have fallen to you. Your taxes would not have been lessened, because she would have been in no condition to have paid any towards your relief. We are rich by a contrivance of our own, which would have ceased as soon as you became masters. Our paper money will be of no use in England, and gold and silver we have none. In the last war you made many conquests, but were any of your taxes lessened thereby? On the contrary, were you not taxed to pay for the charge of making them, and have not the same been the case in every war?

To the Parliament I beg to address myself in a particular manner. They appear to have supposed themselves partners in the chace, and to have hunted with the lion from an expectation of a right in the booty; but in this it is most probable they would, as legislators, have been disappointed. The case is quite a new one, and many unforeseen difficulties would have arisen thereon. The Parliament claimed a legislative right over America, and the war originated from that pretence. But the army is supposed to belong to the crown, and if America had been conquered through their means, the claim of the Legislature would have been suffocated in the conquest. Ceded or conquered countries are supposed to be out of the authority of Parliament. Taxation is exercised over them by prerogative and not by law. It was attempted to be done in the Granades a few years ago, and the only reason why it was not done was because the crown had made a prior relinquishment of its claim. Therefore, Parliament have been all this while supporting measures for the establishment of their authority, in the issue of which, they would have been triumphed over by the prerogative. This might have opened a new and interesting opposition between the Parliament and the Crown. The Crown would have said that it conquered for itself, and that to conquer for Parliament was an unknown case. The Parliament might have replied, that America not being a *foreign* country, but only a country in *rebellion*, could not be said to be *conquered*, but *reduced*; and thus continued their claim by disowning the term. The Crown might have rejoined, that however America might be considered at *first*, she became foreign at *last* by a declaration of Independence and a *treaty with France*; and that her case being, by *that treaty*, put within the law of nations, was out of the law of Parliament. The Parliament might have maintained, that as their claim over America had never been *surrendered*, so neither could it be *taken away*. The Crown might have insisted, that though the claim of Parliament could *not be taken away*, yet being an *inferior* it might be *superceded*; and that, whether the claim was withdrawn from the object, or the object taken from the claim, the same separation ensued; and that America being subdued after a treaty with France, was to all intents and purposes a regal conquest, and of course the sole property of the King. The Parliament, as the legal delegates of the people, might have contended against the term *"inferior"* and rested the case upon the antiquity of power, and this would have brought on a set of interesting and rational questions.

First, What is the original fountain of power and honour in any country?

Secondly, Whether the prerogative does not belong to the people?

Thirdly, Whether there is any such a thing as the English constitution?

Fourthly, Of what use is the Crown to the people?

Fifthly, Whether he who invented a crown was not an enemy to mankind?

Sixthly, Whether it is not a shame for a man to spend a million a year and do no good for it, and whether the money might not be better applied?

Seventhly, Whether such a man is not better dead than alive?

Eighthly, Whether a Congress, constituted like that of America, is not the most happy and consistent form of government in the world?—With a number of others of the same import.

In short, the contention about the dividend might have distracted the nation; for nothing is more common than to agree in the conquest and quarrel for the prize; therefore it is, perhaps, a happy circumstance that our successes have prevented the dispute.

If the Parliament had been thrown out in *their* claim, which it is most probable they would, the nation likewise would have been thrown out in *their* expectation; for as the taxes would have been laid on by the Crown without the Parliament, the revenue arising therefrom, if any could have arose, would not have gone into the Exchequer, but into the privy purse, and so far from lessening their taxes, would not even have been added to them, but served only as pocket money to the Crown. The more I reflect on this matter the more am I astonished at the blindness and ill policy of my countrymen, whose wisdom seem to operate without discernment, and their strength without an object.

To the great bulwark of the nation, I mean the mercantile and manufacturing part thereof, I likewise present my address. It is your interest to see America an independent country and *not* a conquered one. If conquered, she is ruined; and if ruined, poor; consequently the trade will be a trifle, and her credit doubtful. If independent she flourish, and from *her flourishing* must *your profits* arise. It matters nothing to you who governs America, if your manufactures find a consumption there. Some articles will consequently be obtained from other places, and right they should, but the demand of others will encrease by the great influx of inhabitants which a state of independence and peace will occasion, and on the final event you may be enriched. The commerce of America is perfectly free, and ever will be so. She will consign away no part of it to any nation. She has not to her friends, and certainly will not to her enemies, though it is probable that your narrow minded politicians, thinking to please you thereby, may some time or other make such an unnecessary proposal. Trade flourishes best when it is free, and it is weak policy to attempt to fetter it. Her treaty with France is on the most liberal and generous principles, and the French in their conduct towards her has proved themselves to be philosophers, politicians and gentlemen.

To the Ministry I likewise address myself. You, gentlemen, have studied the ruin of your country, from which it is not within your abilities to rescue her. Your attempts to recover are as ridiculous as your plans which involved her are detestable. The Commissioners being about to depart, will probably bring you this, and with it my sixth number to them; and in so doing they carry back more *Common Sense* than they brought, and you likewise will have more than when you sent them.

Having thus addressed you severally, I conclude by addressing you collectively. It is a long lane that has no turning. A period of sixteen years of misconduct and misfortune, is certainly long enough for any one nation to suffer under; and upon a supposition that war is not declared between France and you, I beg to place a line of conduct before you that will easily lead you out of all your troubles. It has been hinted before, and cannot be too much attended to.

Suppose America had remained unknown to Europe till the present year, and that Mr. Banks and Dr. Solander, in another voyage round the world, had made the first discovery of her, in the self same condition she is now in of arts, arms, numbers, and civilization. What I ask in that case, would have been your conduct towards her, for *that* will point out what it ought to be now? The problems and their solutions are equal, and the right line of the one is the parallel of the other. The question takes in every circumstance that can possibly arise. It reduces politics to a simple thought, and is moreover a mode of investigation, in which, while you are studying your interest, the simplicity of the case will cheat you into good temper. You have nothing to do but to suppose you have found America and she appears sound to your hand, and while in the joy of your heart you stand still to admire her, the path of politics rises strait before you.

Were I disposed to paint a contrast, I could easily set off what you *have done* in the *present case* against what you *would have done* in *that case*, and by justly opposing them, conclude a picture that would make you blush. But as when any of the prouder passions are hurt, it is much better philosophy to let a man slip into a good temper than to attack him in a bad one: for that reason therefore, I only state the case and leave yourselves to reflect upon it.

To go a little back into politics, it will be found, that the true interest of Britain lay in proposing and promoting the independence of America immediately after the last peace, for the expence which Britain had then incurred by defending America as HER OWN DOMINIONS, ought to have shewn her the policy and necessity of changing the *stile* of the country, as the *best* probable method of preventing future wars and expence, and the *only* method by which she could hold the commerce without the charge of sovereignty. Besides which, the title she assumed of *Parent country* naturally led to, and pointed out, the propriety, wisdom and advantage of a separation; for as in private life children grow into men, and by setting up for themselves extend and secure the interest of the whole family, so in the settlement of colonies large enough to admit of maturity, the same policy should be pursued and the same consequences would follow. Nothing hurts the affections both of parents and children so much, as living too closely connected, and keeping up the distinction too long. Domineering will not do over those, who by a progress in life are become equal in rank to their parents, that is, when they have families of their own; and though they may conceive themselves the subjects of their advice, will not suppose themselves the objects of their government. I do not, by drawing this parallel, mean to admit the title of *Parent country*, because, if due any where, it is due to Europe collectively and the first settlers from England were driven here by persecution. I mean only to introduce the term for the sake of the policy, and to show from your title, the line of your interest.

When you saw the state of strength and opulence, and that by her own industry, which America had arrived at, you ought to have advised her to have set up for herself, and proposed an alliance of interest with her, and in so doing, you would have drawn, and that at her *own* expence, more real advantage, and more military supplies and assistance both of ships and men, than from any weak and wrangling government you could exercise over her. In short, had you studied only the domestic politics of a family, you would have learned how to govern the state; but instead of this easy and natural line, you flew out into every thing which was wild and outrageous, till by following the passion and stupidity of the pilot you wrecked the vessel within sight of the shore.

Having shown what you *ought to have done*, I now proceed to shew the reason why it was *not done*. The caterpillar circle of the Court, had an interest to pursue distinct from, and opposed to yours, for though by the independence of America and an alliance therewith, the trade would have continued if not encreased, as in many articles neither country can go to a better market, and though by defending and protecting herself, she would have been no expence to you, and consequently your national charges would have decreased and your taxes might have been proportionably lessened thereby, yet the striking off so many places from the Court Calendar was put in opposition to the interests of the nation. The loss of thirteen governmentships with their appendages here and in England is a shocking sound to the ear of a hungry courtier. Your present King and Ministry will be the ruin of you; and you had better risk a revolution and call a Congress than be thus led on from madness to despair, and from despair to ruin. America has set you the example, and may you follow it and be free.

I now come to the last part, *a war with France.* This is what no man in his senses will advise you to, and all good men would wish to prevent. Whether France will declare war against you, is not for me in this place to mention or to hint even if I knew it, but it must be madness in you to do it first. The matter is now come to a *full crisis*, and peace is easy if willingly set about. Whatever you may think, France has behaved handsomely to you. She would have been unjust to herself to have acted otherwise than she did; and having accepted our offer of alliance, she gave you genteel notice of it. There was nothing in her conduct reserved or indelicate, and while she announced her determination to support her treaty she left you to give the first offence. America, on her part, has exhibited a character of firmness to the world. Unprepared and unarmed, without form or government she singly opposed a nation that domineered over half the globe. The greatness of the deed demands respect; and though you may feel resentment, you are compelled both to WONDER and ADMIRE.

HERE I rest my arguments and finish my address. Such as it is, it is a gift and you are welcome. It was always my design to dedicate a *Crisis* to you, when the time should come that would properly *make it a Crisis*; and when, likewise, I should catch myself in a temper to write it, and suppose you in a condition to read it. *That* time is now arrived, and with it, the opportunity of conveyance. For the Commissioners—*poor Commissioners!*—having proclaimed, that *"yet forty days and Ninevah shall be overthrown,"* have waited out the date, and discontented with their God, are returning to their goard. And all the harm I wish them is, that it may not *wither* about their ears, and that they may not make their exit in the belly of a Whale.

COMMON SENSE.

Philadelphia, November 11, 1778.

P. S. Though in the tranquility of my mind I have concluded with a laugh, yet I have something to mention to the *Commissioners*, which to them is serious and worthy their attention. Their authority is derived from an act of Parliament which likewise describes and *limits* their *official* powers. Their commission, therefore, is only a recital, and personal investiture, of those powers, or a nomination and description of the persons who are to execute them. Had it contained any thing contrary to, or gone beyond the line of, the written law from which it is derived and by which it is bound, it would, by the English constitution, have been treason in the Crown, and the King been subject to an impeachment. He dared not, therefore, have put in his commission what you have put into your proclamation, that is, he dared not have authorised you in that commission to burn and destroy, or to threaten to burn and destroy, any thing in America. You are both in the *Act* and in the *Commission* stiled *Commissioners for restoring peace,* and the methods for doing it are there pointed out. Your last proclamation is signed by you as Commissioners *under that Act.* You make Parliament the patron of its contents. Yet in the body of it, you insert matters contrary both to the spirit and letter of the Act, and what likewise your King dared not have put in his commission to you. The state of things in England, Gentlemen, is too ticklish for you to run hazards. You are *accountable to Parliament for the execution of that Act according to the letter of it.* Your heads may pay for breaking it, for you certainly have broke it by exceeding it. And as a friend, who would wish you to escape the paw of the Lion as well as the belly of the Whale, I civilly hint to you, *to keep within compass.*

Sir Harry Clinton, strictly speaking, is as accountable as the rest; for though a General, he is likewise a Commissioner, acting under a superior authority. His first obedience is to the Act; and his plea of being a General will not and cannot clear him as a Commissioner, for that would suppose the Crown, in its single capacity, to have a power of dispensing with an Act of Parliament. Your situations, Gentlemen, are nice and critical, and the more so because England is unsettled. Take heed! Remember the times of Charles the first! For Laud and Strafford fell by trusting to a hope like yours.

Having thus shewn you the danger of your proclamation, I now shew you the folly of it. The means contradict the design. You threatened to lay waste in order to render America a useless acquisition of alliance to France. I reply, that the more destruction you commit (if you could do it) the more valuable to France would you make that alliance. You can destroy only houses and goods; and by so doing you encrease our demand upon her for materials and merchandize, for the wants of one nation, provided it has FREEDOM and CREDIT, naturally produces riches to the other; and as you can neither ruin the land nor prevent the vegitation, you would encrease the exportation of our produce as payment, which to her would be a new fund of wealth. In short, had you cast about for a plan on purpose to enrich your enemies you could not have hit upon a better.

C. S.

Portion of a Letter to Henry Laurens

1778?

As we are forming Government on a new system, *that of representation*, I will give you my thoughts on the various classes and merits of men in society so far as relates to each other.

The first useful class of citizens are the farmers and cultivators. These may be called citizens of the first necessity, because every thing comes originally from the earth.

After these follow the various orders of manufacturers and mechanics of every kind. These differ from the first class in this particular, that they contribute to the accommodation rather than to the first necessities of life.

Next follow those called merchants and shopkeepers. These are occasionally convenient but not important. They produce nothing themselves as the two first classes do, but employ their time in exchanging one thing for another and living by the profits.

Perhaps you will say that in this classification of citizens I have marked no place for myself; that I am neither farmer, manufacturer, mechanic, merchant nor shopkeeper. I believe, however, I am of the first class. I am *a Farmer of thoughts*, and as all the crops I raise I give away, I please myself with making you a present of the thoughts in this letter.

Response to "Observations on the American Revolution"

March 20, 1779

FOR THE PENNSYLVANIA PACKET.

MR. DUNLAP,

THROUGH the channel of your paper, I take the liberty of remarking on a passage in a pamphlet just come into my hands, entitled, *"Observations on the American Revolution, published according to a Resolution of Congress. By their Committee."*

The gentlemen who, principally, if not wholly, conducted this work were Governeur Morriss, Esq; Delegate from the state of New-York, and W. H. Drayton, Esq; late Delegate from South-Carolina; and of those two Mr. Morriss had the chief share. Consequently, the honours or errors it contain, are claimable by, or chargeable on, the compilers and conductors only.

The work consists of a collection of the principal state papers, which are connected with the rise and progress of the present revolution, and are arranged in the following order:

A part of the proceedings of Congress in 1774. The motion, commonly called Lord North's conciliatory motion, in February, 1775, and the resolution of Congress thereon. A paper delivered to Congress by a British emissary. Resolutions of Congress respecting the defence of New York. Declaratory reasons of Congress for taking up arms, dated July 6th, 1775. Petition of Congress to the King of England July 8th, 1775. Address to the people of Great-Britain, July 8th, 1775. Resolutions of Congress, for granting commissions to privateers, of November 29th, 1775, and March 23d, 1776. Resolution of Congress recommending the taking up new governments, May 15th, 1776. Declaration of Independence, July 4th, 1776. Conference on Staten-Island with Lord Howe, reported September 17th, by the Committee of Congress appointed on that business. Draught of the bills of the British Parliament, received by Congress at York-Town April the 21st, 1778, and the resolutions of Congress thereon, April 22d, 1778. Address of Congress to the people of America, May 4th, 1778. Collection of letters, &c. &c. which passed between Congress and the British Commissioners. The work closes with the Proclamation and Manifesto of the said British Commissioners, dated New-York, October 3d, 1778, and the Manifesto of Congress in answer thereto, October 30th, 1778. The greatest part, if not the whole, of those publications, have, at different times, appeared in most of the Newspapers on the continent.

The above making up the substance of the work, the only thing that is new in it is the historical connection by which the several declarations, resolutions, &c. are formed into a continued chain, and in this part there is an evident defect amounting to injustice.

It cannot be supposed that the historical part should be compleat in so short a compass, but that is no reason that it should be unjust in the gross; and as Mr. Morriss and Mr. Drayton are the only persons accountable for the defect I shall here take notice of, to them, only, I address these remarks.

The reader, by casting his eye on the arrangement of papers in the order in which I have placed them, which is the order they stand in in the pamphlet, will see there is a skip (a flying over I may call it) from the conference on Staten Island, September 1776, to the receipt of the British bills at York-Town, April 21st, 1778. I shall give the paragraph entire, (for there is but one) which unites those two events so widely distant in time, and, on the part of the enemy, so different in complexion.

Page 6: "From this moment," that is, from the conference on Staten-Island, "the war raged with the utmost violence, and was prosecuted by the enemy with unabated vigour and barbarity. To recite the numerous instances in which their faith, solemnly pledged, hath been broken, would be tedious and perhaps useless: Victory declared herself for a long time in favour of their superior numbers and superior discipline, and their insolence was equal to their success. Unable to comprehend the whole of the object they had undertaken, and overjoyed at the acquisition of the minuter parts, already the needy, greedy parasites of a voluptuous court had, in imagination, carved out our possessions among them, and wantoned in the prospect of enjoying the fruits of our laborious industry. Every thing, therefore, which looked like conciliation was treated as a concession flowing from feebleness of soul. The spirit of despotism, flushed with hope and inured to guilt, turned a *hard, unfeeling eye* upon the miseries of human nature, and directed, well pleased, the storm of vengeance on the head of freedom. *But that full tide of success which had carried their expectations so high, began to ebb away: The gallant army, commanded by Burgoyne, checked by impediments which nature had thrown in his course,* at length submitted, notwithstanding the efforts of their accomplished General, to the determined bravery of their foes. The splendor of our success in that quarter called the attention of Europe to our fortitude and perseverance. The weight and importance of a country which could resist the astonishing efforts made by Great-Britain, were evident to the most careless observation. The acknowledgment of our Independence became therefore an object of serious deliberation. Awakened from their dream of glory to a view of their danger, the Ministry of England determined, if possible, to recover what they had wantonly thrown away.

"On the 21st day of April, 1778, the Congress, then sitting at York-Town, received a letter from the General inclosing a printed paper from Philadelphia to the following effect:

"Draught of a bill for declaring the intentions of the Parliament of Great-Britain," &c. &c. &c.

I have marked the exceptionable parts in italics. The first, which is immaterial to the history, though of some moment to the writer, is a false rhetorical figure, for "*hard* and *unfeeling*" are not, in any case, properties of the eye, but sentimentally, of the heart. A hard unfeeling—heart; a deaf—ear; and a scornful—eye; are epithets expressive of possible qualities in the parts they are applied to: But according to this gentleman's derangement of them, he might as well say a scornful ear or a deaf eye. A man must be but little acquainted with feelings, not to know which is their place of residence.

As the sense of the reader would have supplied the above defect in the writer, I should not have gone out of my way to have made the remark, had it been in any other paragraph than that which I have quoted, on account of a more important inattention.

The insolence of the enemy after the engagement on Long Island, and their barbarity after taking Fort Washington, were far greater than their vigor at any one time of that campaign. I speak this from better knowledge than either Mr. Morriss or Mr. Drayton can have, as I was out with the army from the first marching of the associators early in August, and after their return was with General Green at Fort Lee till the evacuation and continued with the army till after their passing the Delaware on the eighth of December. I had began the first number of the Crisis while on the retreat at Newark, with a design of publishing it in the Jersies, as it was Gen. Washington's intentions to have made a stand at Newark, could he have been timely reinforced instead of which, near half the army left him at that place, or soon after, their time being out.

To use a plain phrase, the enemy were then masters of the field, and had it in their power to carry every thing before them. "Flushed with hope and inured to guilt," and in full expectation of conquest, their confidence betrayed them into carelessness, and enabled General Washington to defeat them by a spirited and judicious improvement of their neglects: And I ask Mr. Morriss and Mr. Drayton, *when it was* that their, the enemy's, "*full tide of success began to ebb away?*" Truth will, and history ought to say, that it turned at Trenton and was additionally impelled by the subsequent, and more masterly, stroke at Princeton. These two actions disabled and laid the enemy dormant for more than six months afterwards; and by throwing a spirit of joy into the continent gave life and vigor to the recruiting service for the next campaign. They were hard bought victories, under every disadvantage of winter and misfortune. But the tide, once turned, went on, and the conquest of Burgoyne was, properly speaking, the high water mark of our successes.

Why Mr. Morriss and Mr. Drayton have, in utter silence, passed over the affairs of Trenton and Princeton, and taken a flight from Staten-Island to Saratoga, I cannot conceive. As historians they have reversed the line of facts, and as writers they have not made the most of their metaphor; for had they given honor where it was justly due, and shewn where the tide *began* to turn in *our* favor, it would have enabled them to have shewn its full encrease in the reduction of Burgoyne, where they have only placed its beginning.

The remains of the army which at that time continued with Gen. Washington, and the citizens of this state and of Jersey, who turned out to repel the torrent which threatened distruction to America, must feel themselves injured by such a partial representation, published under the authority of a Committee of Congress. Their services are done away, as if they had never been; and an omission, amounting to oblivion, stands as a contradiction to the fact. This could not unintentionally happen, as the natural order both of time and circumstances threw the whole in their way, and half a page, judiciously compiled, would have united the several links of the chain. I wonder that the metaphor of a tide should not revive in Mr. Drayton an idea of its progress; as he has, I am told, been an *Admiral*—of the *yellow*, I suppose.

But this is not the only injustice in the paragraph I have quoted. The compilers say, that "the gallant army commanded by Burgoyne, checked by impediments *which nature had thrown in his course*, at length submitted, notwithstanding the efforts of their accomplished General, to the determined bravery of their foes."

The conquest at Bennington by General Stark, which laid the foundation of Burgoyne's defeat, is here unjustly buried under a general description of *impediments which nature threw in his course.*

There is no part in the pamphlet, where half a dozen pages might have been employed to more honour and advantage, than in concisely setting forth the principal circumstances which passed between the conference on Staten-Island and the arrival of the draughts of the British bills at York-Town; for the want of which, the circumstantial connection is lost, and that which is omitted, as well as that which is told, have an appearance of injustice.

Mr. Morriss and Mr. Drayton have each of them been so exceedingly industrious in supporting Mr. Deane's impositions, that they seem not to have had time to attend any other kind of duty, and as, I believe, Mr. Deane is now looked on by half that House as a dishonest man, and the other half dare not support him, it will become these two gentlemen to show on what grounds they have abetted him. The suspicions against Mr. Deane are now too strong to be suffocated, and the evidence too full to be rejected or explained away, and he can but perceive that his character is every day sinking with the public—That he negociated a profered present into a purchase, and either stole, or was privy to the stealing the dispatches to cover the imposition, are circumstances which I have no reason to disbelieve.

COMMON SENSE.

P. S. As the pamphlet I have referred to is sent to all the states, the Printers in each will do an act of justice to those whose merits are in that performance so greatly neglected, by inserting this piece in their papers.

C— S—.

Response to the Riot Outside
James Wilson's House

October 16, 1779

TO THE PRINTER OF
THE PENNSYLVANIA PACKET.

SIR,

WHEN passion and mistake give way to candor and benevolence, we sensibly forget the injury in contemplating the effect, and pay a reverence to virtue tho' provoked into action by a fault. The late unfortunate affair of the fourth inst. will, to different minds, administer a different medicine. Surviving relations will feel as nature teaches, their part requires no invention, needs no apology, and whoever were to blame they are to be pitied. Those who unfortunately fell on either side, have paid a martyrdom to mistake, and distinguished themselves as the lamented victims of wasted bravery. In the softer sentiments of a thoughtful world, the whole affair will become a subject of concern; and the only consolation it affords is the hope of seeing the same degree of spirit exerted against the enemy, which, warped by error and aggravated by passion, produced a tumult in which no one enemy fell.

The countenance of the city during that affair, wore an unusual contemplative gloominess. It had nothing of that heated appearance which accompanies the disturbances of other countries, and was totally void of that eagerness of enterprise which takes place against a known enemy. Neither Whig nor Tory could rejoice; all were at a stand; concern produced in the one what dread created in the other; and for once the city was afflictedly united.

Neither can I see any hope the enemy can derive, when they learn the story with its causes and consequences. As a misfortune which we lament, it may to them become a matter of malignant joy; but it promises them nothing; it neither gives encouragement to their arms, nor invitation to their artifice; it neither indicates unwillingness to the field, nor wariness in resisting. On the contrary, it holds out to them a redundancy of zeal, a vehemence of spirit, which, however injudicious in its plans, or unfortunate in its effects, was intentionally aimed at their abettors.

It was the fourth of October. The anniversary of the action at Germantown. A day, distinguished by perplexities and consigned to misfortune. Whether the circumstance occurred at the time the matter was concerted, is what I have not authority even to guess upon, but be that as it may, we cannot but lament that the events of the evening should, in both instances, close with a tear the spirits of the morning.

As it is one of those occurrences which it is unpleasant to enquire into, I wish not to know more than I already know, nor indulge any other thoughts on the subjects than what may tend to abate the painfulness of remembrance, and extinguish the acrimony which error may have kindled. It is over, and thank God it was no worse. But were nothing said the matter might suffer abroad by aggravated misrepresentation. The deaths of three men might be multiplied into as many hundreds, and perpetuity be added to the contention of an hour.

That nothing more was meant by those who assembled on the Commons than to remove persons suspected of disaffection, is universally consented to, and in this light their design was naturally prompted by an attachment to the cause of an injured country. The difficulty of attempting such a measure, the hazard of executing it, and the consequences which might probably ensue, without first obtaining an authoritative sanction and consent, were matters which do not always accompany an excess of zeal. Those whose talent it is to act, are seldom much devoted to deliberate thinking; and feeling that they mean well they suppose it impossible to be wrong, and in the confidence of success overlook the trouble that lies concealed. Where is the man who has not, in his turn, exclaimed, that the Tories ought to be removed; and who had those men laid hold of, that could be deemed a Whig? The measure, while it existed in words, was a measure of popularity; and every one who has promoted it in conversation, has prompted them on.

On what occasion, or by what contrivance a number of Gentlemen were brought together in Mr. Wilson's house, makes up the most mysterious part of the business. As far as I can discover, I cannot find the least trace whereon to conclude that any one who went there had the least reason to be apprehensive of his own safety. They must, in general, have been induced by misrepresentation tho' some, I am well assured, were led by a generous intention of preventing mischief; and pity it is their advice was not taken. That Mr. Wilson is not a favourite in the State, is a matter which, I presume, he is fully sensible of, yet the difference is exceedingly great, between not being in favor and being considered as an enemy. But that he who never armed when the country was in danger, should arm his house to provoke danger, and draw to it a number of Gentlemen at the hazard of their lives, when a timely application to the Civil Power might have prevented every thing, was at once both unconstitutional and unfriendly, a disregard to the laws of the State and the peace of the city. By this imprudent conduct, parties became pitted who knew not each other; and that which had the appearance of a challenge, produced an action.

The affliction which followed, soon extended itself over the city. Every one asked what was the matter; how it began; who were the persons, with every other question of curiosity concern, and still the matter was inveloped in darkness; some supposed one thing, and some another, without being able to satisfy themselves or those who enquired. But when the parties in and out of the house were known, and became known to each other, the animosity began to subside; and the whole, exclusive of the imprudence, explained itself into a tragedy of errors.

It generally happens that distress is the forerunner of benevolence; at least it serves to quicken into action that which might otherwise take a longer time to awake. The sickness which has so generally prevailed through the city, added to the misfortune already mentioned, has been the means of setting on foot two well intended subscriptions; the one for the relief of the families of those who were killed or wounded on the fourth instant, the other for relief of the sick and distressed in the several wards. Both of them have been liberally supported; and most of the persons both in and out of the house, who could afford it, have been ample contributors.

How different this, to that spirit of rancor which generally accompanies, and most assuredly succeeds, premeditated domestic feuds. It calls back the mind to a state of serenity; and shews, by the most convincing proofs, that the affair, now too late to be remedied, was not the quarrel of enemies or of parties, but the unfortunate blunder of friends.

C—— S——.

The Crisis

NUMBER VIII

February 26, 1780

ADDRESSED TO THE PEOPLE OF ENGLAND,
BY THE AUTHOR OF COMMON SENSE.

"Trusting, (says the King of England in his speech of November last) in the Divine Providence, and in the justice of my cause, I am firmly resolved to prosecute the war with vigor, and to make every exertion in order to compel our enemies to equitable terms of peace and accommodation." To this declaration the United States of America and the Confederated Powers of Europe, will reply, *If Britain will have war, she shall have enough of it.*

Five years have nearly elapsed since the commencement of hostilities, and every campaign, by a gradual decay, has lessened your ability to conquer, without producing in you a serious thought on your condition or your fate. Like a prodigal lingering in an habitual consumption, you feel the relicks of life and mistake them for recovery. New schemes, like new medicines, have administered fresh hopes and prolonged the disease instead of curing it. A change of Generals, like a change of physicians, served only to keep the flattery alive, and furnish new pretences for new extravagance.

*"Can Britain fail?"** has been proudly asked at the commencement of every enterprize, and that *"whatever she wills is fate,"*† has been given with the solemnity of prophetic confidence, and tho' the question has been constantly replied to by disappointment, and the prediction falsified by misfortune, yet still the insult continued, and your catalogue of national evils encreased therewith. Eager to persuade the world of her power, she considered destruction as the minister of greatness, and conceived that the glory of a nation, like that of

---

*Whitehead's new-years ode for 1776.

†Ode at the installation of Lord North for Chancellor of the University of Oxford.

an Indian, lay in the number of its scalps and the miseries it inflicts.

Fire, sword and want, as far as the arms of Britain could extend them, have been spread with wanton cruelty along the coast of America; and while you, remote from the scene of suffering, had nothing to lose and as little to dread, the information reached you like a tale of antiquity, in which the distance of time defaces the conception, and changes the severest sorrows into conversable amusement.

This makes the second paper, addressed perhaps in vain, to the people of England. That advice should be taken where example has failed, or precept be regarded where warning is ridiculed, is like a picture of hope resting on dispair: But when time shall stamp with universal currency, the facts you have long encountered with a laugh, and the irresistible evidence of accumulated losses, like the hand writing on the wall, shall add terror to distress, you will then, in a conflict of sufferings, learn to sympathise with others by feeling for yourselves.

The triumphant appearance of the combined fleets in the channel and at your harbour's mouth, and the expedition of Captain Paul Jones on the western and eastern coast of England and Scotland, will, by placing you in the condition of an endangered country, read to you a stronger lecture on the calamities of invasion, and bring to your minds a truer picture of promiscuous distress, than the most finished rhetoric can describe or the keenest imagination conceive.

Hitherto you have experienced the expences, but nothing of the miseries of war. Your disappointments have been accompanied with no immediate suffering, and your losses came to you only by intelligence. Like fire at a distance, you heard not even the cry; you felt not the danger, you saw not the confusion. To you every thing has been foreign but the taxes to support it. You knew not what it was to be alarmed at midnight with an armed enemy in the streets. You were strangers to the distressing scene of a family in flight, and to the thousand restless cares and tender sorrows that incessantly arose. To see women and children wandering in the severity of winter with the broken remains of a well furnished house, and seeking shelter in every crib and hut, were matters you had no conception of. You knew not what it was to stand by and see your goods chopt up for fuel, and your beds ript to pieces to make packages for plunder. The misery of others, like a tempestuous night, added to the pleasures of your own security. You even enjoyed the storm, by contemplating the difference of conditions; and that which carried sorrow into the breasts of thousands, served but to heighten in you a species of tranquil pride. Yet these are but the fainter sufferings of war, when compared with carnage and slaughter, the miseries of a military hospital, or a town in flames.

The people of America by anticipating distress had fortified their minds against every species you could inflict. They had resolved to abandon their homes, to resign them to destruction, and to seek new settlements rather than submit. Thus familiarised to misfortune, before it arrived, they bore their portion with the less regret: The justness of their cause was a continual source of consolation, and the hope of final victory, which never left them, served to lighten the load and sweeten the cup alloted them to drink.

But when their sufferings shall become yours, and invasion be transferred upon the invaders, you will have neither their extended wilderness to fly to, their cause to comfort you, nor their hopes to rest on. Distress with them was sharpened by no self-reflection. They had not brought it on themselves. On the contrary, they had by every proceeding endeavoured to avoid it, and had descended even below the mark of congressional character to prevent a war. The national honor or the advantages of independence are matters, which at the commencement of the dispute, they had never studied, and it was only at the last moment that the measure was resolved on. Thus circumstanced, they naturally and conscientiously felt a dependence upon Providence. They had a clear pretension to it, and had they failed therein, infidelity had gained a triumph.

But your condition is the reverse of theirs. Every thing you suffer you have sought; nay, had you created mischiefs on purpose to inherit them, you could not have secured your title by a firmer deed. The world awakens with no pity at your complaints. You felt none for others; you deserve none for yourselves. Nature does not interest herself in cases like yours, but on the contrary turns from them with dislike and abandons them to punishment. You may now present memorials to what Court you please, but so far as America is the object, none will listen. The policy of Europe and the propensity there is in every mind to curb insulting ambition, and bring cruelty to judgment, are unitedly against you; and where nature and interest reinforces each other, the compact is too intimate to be dissolved.

Make but the case of others your own, and your own theirs, and you will then have a clear idea of the whole. Had France acted towards her Colonies as you have done, you would have branded her with every epithet of abhorrence; and had you, like her, stept in to succour a struggling people, all Europe must have echoed with your own applauses. But entangled in the passion of dispute, you see it not as you ought, and form opinions thereon which suit with no interest but your own. You wonder America does not rise in union with you to impose on herself a portion of your taxes and reduce herself to unconditional submission. You are amazed that the Southern Powers of Europe do not assist you in conquering a country which is afterwards to be turned against themselves; and that the northern ones do not contribute to reinstate you in America, who already enjoy the market for naval stores by the separation. You seem surprised that Holland does not pour in her succours to maintain you mistress of the seas, when her own commerce is suffering by your Act of navigation, or that any country should study her own interests while yours is on the carpet.

Such excesses of passionate folly, and unjust as well as unwise resentment, have driven you on, like Pharoah, to unpitied miseries, and while the importance of that quarrel shall perpetuate your disgrace, the flag of America will carry it round the world. The natural feelings of every rational being will take against you, and wherever the story shall be told, you will have neither excuse nor consolation left. With an unsparing hand and an unsatiable mind, you have havocked the world, both to gain dominion and to lose it, and while, in a frenzy of avarice and ambition, the east and west were doomed to tributary bondage, you rapidly earned destruction as the wages of a nation.

At the thoughts of a war at home every man amongst you

ought to tremble. The prospect is far more dreadful there than in America. Here the party that was against the measures of the continent were in general a kind of neutrals who added strength to neither army. There does not exist a being so devoid of sense and sentiment as to covet *"unconditional submission,"* and therefore no man in America could be with you in principle. Several might from a cowardice of mind, *prefer* it to the hardships and dangers of *opposing* it; but the same disposition that gave them such a choice, unfitted them to act either for or against. But England is rent into parties, with equal shares of resolution. The principle which produced the war, divides the nation. Their animosities are in the highest state of fermentation, and both sides by a call of the militia, are in arms. No human foresight can discern, no conclusion can be formed, what turn a war might take, if once set on foot by an invasion. She is not now in a fit disposition, to make a common cause of her own affairs, and having no conquests to hope for abroad, and nothing but expences arising at home, her every thing is staked upon a defensive combat, and the further she goes the worse she is off.

There are situations a nation may be in, in which peace or war, abstracted from every other consideration, may be politically right or wrong. When nothing can be lost by a war, but what must be lost without it, war is then the policy of that country; and such was the situation of America at the commencement of hostilities: But when no security can be gained by a war, but what may be accomplished by a peace, the case becomes reversed, and such now is the situation of England.

That America is beyond the reach of conquest, is a fact which experience has shewn and time confirmed, and this admitted, what, I ask, is now the object in contention? If there be any honor in pursuing self-destruction with inflexible passion; if national suicide be the perfection of national glory, you may, with all the pride of criminal happiness, expire unenvied and unrivalled.—But when the tumult of war shall cease, and the tempest of present passions be succeeded by calm reflection, or when those who surviving its fury, shall inherit from you a legacy of debts and misfortunes, when the yearly revenue shall scarcely be able to discharge the interest of the one, and no possible remedy be left for the other;

ideas, far different to the present, will arise, and embitter the remembrance of former follies. A mind disarmed of its rage, feels no pleasure in contemplating a frantic quarrel. Sickness of thought, the sure consequence of conduct like yours, leaves no ability for enjoyment, no relish for resentment; and tho' like a man in a fit, you feel not the injury of the struggle, nor distinguish between strength and disease, the weakness will nevertheless be proportioned to the violence, and the sense of pain encrease with the recovery.

To what persons or to whose system of politics you owe your present state of wretchedness is a matter of total indifference to America. They have contributed, however unwillingly, to set her above themselves, and she in the tranquility of conquest resigns the enquiry. The case now is not so properly who began the war, as who continues it. That there are men in all countries to whom a state of war is a mine of wealth, is a fact never to be doubted. Characters like these naturally breed in the putrefaction of distempered times, and after fattening on the disease they perish with it, or impregnated with the stench retreat into obscurity.

But there are several erroneous notions to which you likewise owe a share of your misfortunes, and which if continued will only increase your trouble and your losses. An opinion hangs about the gentlemen of the minority, that America would relish measures under *their* administration, which she would not from the present cabinet. On this rock Lord Chatham would have split had he gained the helm, and several of his survivors are steering the same course. Such distinctions in the infancy of the argument had some degree of foundation, but they now serve no other purpose than to lengthen out a war, in which the limits of the dispute, being fixt by the fate of arms, and guaranteed by treaties, are not to be changed or altered by trivial circumstances.

The Ministry and many of the minority sacrifice their time in disputing on a question with which they have nothing to do, namely, whether America shall be independant or not? Whereas the only question that can come under their determination, is, whether they will accede to it or not? They confound a military question with a political one, and undertake to supply by a vote what they lost by a battle. Say, she shall not be independant, and it will signify as much as if they voted against a decree of fate, or say that she shall, and she will be no more independant than before. Questions, which when determined, cannot be executed, serve only to shew the folly of dispute and the weakness of disputants.

From a long habit of calling America your own, you suppose her governed by the same prejudices and conceits which govern yourselves. Because you have set up a particular denomination of religion to the exclusion of all others, you imagine she must do the same, and because you, with an unsociable narrowness of mind, have cherished animosity against France and Spain, you suppose her alliance must be defective in friendship. Copying her notions of the world from you, she formerly thought as you instructed, but now feeling herself free, and the prejudice removed, she thinks and acts upon a different system. It frequently happens that in proportion as we are taught to dislike persons and countries not knowing why, we feel an ardor of esteem upon a removal of the mistake; It seems as if something was to be made amends for, and we eagerly give into every office of friendship to attone for the injury of the error.

But perhaps there is something in the extent of countries, which among the generality of people, insensibly communicates extention to the mind. The soul of an Islander in its native State, seems bounded by the foggy confines of the water's edge, and all beyond, affords to him matter only for profit or curiosity, not for friendship. His island is to him his world, and fixt to that his every thing centers in it; while those, who are inhabitants of a continent, by casting their eye over a larger field, takes in likewise a larger intellectual circuit, and thus approaching nearer to an acquaintance with the universe, their atmosphere of thought is extended, and their liberality fills a wider space. In short, our minds seem to be measured by countries when we are men, as they are by places, when we are children, and until something happens to disentangle us from the prejudice, we serve under it without perceiving it.

In addition to this, it may be remarked, that men who study any universal science, the principles of which are universally known, or admitted, and applied without distinction to the common benefit of all countries, obtain thereby a larger share of philanthropy than those who only study national arts and improvements. Natural philosophy, mathematics and astronomy, carry the mind from the country to the creation, and give it a fitness suited to the extent. It was not Newton's honor, neither could it be his pride, that he was an Englishman, but that he was a philosopher: The Heavens had liberated him from the prejudices of an island, and science had expanded his soul as boundless as his studies.

(To be concluded in a subsequent paper.)

The Crisis

NUMBER IX

June 9, 1780

HAD America pursued her advantages with half the spirit she resisted her misfortunes, she would, before now, have been a conquering and a peaceful people; but lulled in the lap of soft tranquility she rested on her hopes, and adversity only has convulsed her into action. Whether subtilty or sincerity at the close of the last year, induced the enemy to an appearance for peace, is a point not material to know; it is sufficient that we see the effects it has had on our politics, and that we sternly rise to resent the delusion.

The war on the part of America, has been a war of natural feeling. Brave in distress; serene in conquest; drowsy when at rest; and in every situation generously disposed to peace. A dangerous calm, and the most heightened zeal, have, as circumstances varied, succeeded each other. Every passion, but that of dispair, has been called to a tour of duty; and so mistaken has been the enemy of our abilities and disposition, that when she supposed us conquered, we rose the conquerors. The extensiveness of the United States and the variety of their resources; the universality of their cause, the quick operation of their feelings, and the similarity of their sentiments, have, in every trying situation, produced a *something*, which favoured by Providence, and pursued with ardour, has accomplished in an instant the business of a campaign. We have never deliberately sought victory, but snatched it; and bravely undone in an hour, the plotted operations of a season.

The reported fate of Charlestown, like the misfortunes of seventy-six, has at last called forth a spirit, and kindled up a flame, which perhaps no other event could have produced. If the enemy has circulated a falsehood, they have unwisely aggravated us into life, and if they have told us a truth, they have unintentionally done us a service. We were returning with folded arms from the fatigues of war and thinking, and sitting leisurely down to enjoy repose. The dependence that has been put upon Charlestown, threw a drowsiness over America. We looked on the business done—the conflict over—the matter settled—or that all which remained unfinished would follow of itself. In this state of dangerous relax, exposed to the poisonous infusions of the enemy, and having no common danger to attract our attention, we were extinguishing by stages the ardour we began with, and surrendering by peacemeals the virtue that defended us.

Afflicting as the loss of Charlestown may be, yet if it universally rouse us from the slumber of a twelve months past, and renew in us the spirit of former days, it will produce an advantage more important than its loss. America ever *is* what she *thinks* herself to be. Governed by sentiment, and acting her own mind, she becomes as she pleases the victor or the victim.

It is not the conquest of towns, nor the accidental capture of garrisons, that can reduce a country so extensive as this. The sufferings of one part can ever be relieved by the exertions of another, and there is no situation the enemy can be in, that does not afford to us, the same advantages she seeks herself. By dividing her force, she leaves every post attackable. It is a mode of war, that carries with it a confession of weakness, and goes on the principle of distress, rather than conquest.

The decline of the enemy is visible not only in their operations but in their plans; Charlestown originally made but a secondary object in their system of attack, and it is now become their principal one, because they have not been able to succeed else where. It would have carried a cowardly appearance in Europe, had they formed their grand expedition in seventy-six, against a part of the Continent, where there was no army, or not a sufficient one to oppose them; but failing year after year, in their impression here, and to the eastward and northward, they deserted their first capital design, and prudently contenting themselves with what they can get, give a flourish of honor to conceal disgrace.

But this piece meal work is not conquering the Continent. It is discredit in them to attempt it, and in us to suffer it. It is now full time to put an end to a war of aggravations, which on one side, has no possible object, and on the other, has every inducement which honor, interest, safety and happiness, can inspire. If we suffer them much longer to remain among us, we shall become as bad as themselves. An association of vices will reduce us more than the sword. A nation hardened in the practice of iniquity, knows better how to profit by it, than a young country newly corrupted. We are not a match for them in the line of advantageous guilt, nor they to us, on the principles we bravely set out with. Our first days were our days of honor. They have marked the character of America wherever the story of her wars are told; and convinced of this, we have nothing to do, but wisely and unitedly to tread the well known track.

The progress of a war, is often as ruinous to individuals, as the issue of it is to a nation; and it is not only necessary that our force be such, that we be conquerors in the end, but that by timely exertions, we be secure in the interim. The present campaign will afford an opportunity which has never presented itself before, and the preparation for it, are equally necessary, whether Charlestown stand or fall. Suppose the first, it is in that case, only a failure of the enemy, not a defeat. All the conquest a besieged town can hope for, is not to be conquered; and compelling an enemy to raise the siege is to the besieged a victory. But there must be a probability amounting almost to certainty, that would justify a garrison marching out to attack a retreat. Therefore should Charlestown *not* be taken, and the enemy abandon the siege, every other part of the Continent should prepare to meet them; and on the contrary, *should it be taken*, the same preparations are necessary, to balance the loss, and put ourselves in a condition to co-operate with our allies, immediately on their arrival.

We are not now fighting our battles alone, as we were in seventy-six. England, from a malicious disposition to America, has *not* only not declared war against France and Spain, but the better to prosecute her passions here, has afforded those Powers no military object, and avoids them, to distress us. She will suffer her West-India Islands to be over run by France, and her southern settlements taken by Spain, rather than quit the object that gratifies revenge. This conduct, on the part of Britain, has pointed out the propriety of France sending a naval and land force to co-operate with America on the spot.

Their arrival cannot be very distant, nor the ravages of the enemy long. In the mean time the part necessary to us, needs no illustration. The recruiting the army, and procuring the supplies, are the two things needful, and a capture of either of the enemy's divisions, will restore to America peace and plenty.

At a Crisis, big, like the present, with expectation and events, the whole country is called to unanimity and exertion. Not an ability ought now to sleep that can produce but a mite to the general good, nor even a whisper suffered to pass that militates against it. The necessity of the case, and the importance of the consequences, admit no delay from a friend, no apology from an enemy. To spare now, would be the height of extravagance, and to consult present ease, would sacrifice it, perhaps, for ever.

America, rich in patriotism and produce, can want neither men nor supplies, when a serious necessity calls them forth. The slow operation of taxes, owing to the extensiveness of collection, and their depreciated value before they arrived in the Treasury, have, in many instances, thrown a burthen upon Government, which has been artfully interpreted by the enemy into a general decline throughout the country. Yet this, inconvenient as it may at first appear, is not only remediable, but may be turned to an immediate advantage; for it makes no real difference, whether a certain number of men, or company of militia, (and in this country every man is a militia man) are directed by law, to send a recruit at their own expence, or whether a tax is laid on them for that purpose and the man hired by government afterwards. The first, if there is any difference, is both cheapest and best, because it saves the expence which would attend collecting it as a tax, and brings the man sooner into the field, than the modes of recruiting formerly used: And on this principle, a law has been passed in this State, for recruiting two men from each company of militia, which will add upwards to a thousand to the force of the country.

But the flame, which has broke forth in this city, since the report from New-York, of the loss of Charlestown, not only does honor to the place, but like the blaze of seventy-six, will kindle into action, the scattered sparks throughout America. The valour of a country may be learned by the bravery of its soldiery, and the general cast of its inhabitants, but confidence of success is best discovered by the active measures pursued by men of property; and when the spirit of enterprize becomes so universal, as to act at once on all ranks of men, a war may then, and not till then, be stiled truly popular.

In seventy-six the ardour of the enterprising part was considerably checked by the real revolt of some, and the coolness of others. But in the present case there is a firmness in the substance and property of the country to the public cause. An association has been entered into by the merchants, tradesmen, and principal inhabitants of the city, to receive and support the new State money at the value of gold and silver; a measure, which, while it does them honour, will likewise contribute to their interest, by rendering the operations of the campaign convenient and effectual.

Neither has the spirit of exertion stopt here. A voluntary subscription is likewise began to raise a fund of hard money, to be given as bounties to fill up the full quota of the Pennsylvania line. It has been the remark of the enemy, that every thing in America has been done by the force of government; but when she sees the individuals throwing in their voluntary aids, and facilitating the public measures in concert with the established powers of the country, it will convince her that the cause of America stands not on the will of a few but on the broad foundation of property and popularity.

Thus aided and thus supported, disaffection will decline, and the withered head of tyranny expire in America. The ravages of the enemy will be short and limited, and like all their former ones will produce a victory over themselves.

COMMON SENSE.

Philadelphia, June 9, 1780.

At the time of writing this number of the Crisis, the loss of Charlestown, though believed by some, was more confidently disbelieved by others. But there ought to be no longer a doubt on the matter. Charlestown is gone, and I believe for the want of a sufficient supply of provisions. The man that does not now feel for the honor of the best and noblest cause that ever a country engaged in and exert himself accordingly, is no longer worthy a peacable residence among a people determined to be free.
C. S.

The Crisis Extraordinary

October 4, 1780

IT is impossible to sit down and think seriously on the affairs of America, but the original principles on which she resisted, and the glow and ardor they inspired, will occur like the un-defaced remembrance of a lovely scene. To trace over in imagination the purity of the cause, the voluntary sacrifices made to support it, and all the various turnings of the war in its defence, is at once both paying and receiving respect. The principles deserve to be remembered, and to remember them rightly is repossessing them. In this indulgence of generous recollection we become gainers by what we seem to give, and the more we bestow the richer we become.

So extensively right was the ground on which America pro-ceeded, that it not only took in every just and liberal senti-ment which could impress the heart, but made it the direct interest of every class and order of men to defend the country. The war, on the part of Britain, was originally a war of covet-ousness. The sordid and not the splendid passions gave it being. The fertile fields and prosperous infancy of America appeared to her as mines for tributary wealth. She viewed the hive, and disregarding the industry that had enriched it, thirsted for the honey. But in the present stage of her affairs, the violence of temper is added to the rage of avarice; and therefore, that which, at our first setting out, proceeded from purity of principle and public interest, is now heightened by all the obligations of necessity; for it requires but little knowl-edge of human nature to discern what would be the conse-quence, were America again reduced to the subjection of Britain. Uncontrouled power, in the hands of an incensed, imperious and rapacious conqueror, is an engine of dreadful execution; and woe be to that country over which it can be exercised. The names of Whig and Tory would then be sunk in the general term of Rebel, and the oppression, whatever it might be, would, with very few instances of exception, light equally on all.

Britain did not go to war with America for the sake of dominion, because she was then in possession; neither was it for the extension of trade and commerce, because she had monopolized the whole and the country had yielded to it; neither was it to extinguish what *she* might call rebellion, because before she began no resistance existed. It could then be from no other motive than avarice, or a design of establishing, in the first instance, the same taxes in America as are paid in England (which, as I shall presently show, are above eleven times heavier than the taxes we now pay for the present year 1780) or, in the second instance, to confiscate the whole property of America, in case of resistance and conquest, of the latter of which she had then no doubt.

I shall now proceed to show what the taxes in England are, and what the yearly expence of the present war is to her— What the taxes of this country amount to, and what the annual expence of defending it effectually will be to us; and shall endeavor concisely to point out the cause of our difficulties, and the advantages on one side, or the consequences on the other, in case we do, or do not, put ourselves in an effectual state of defence. I mean to be open, candid and sincere. I see a universal wish to expel the enemy from the country, a murmuring because the war is not carried on with more vigour, and my intention is to show as shortly as possible both the reason and the remedy.

The number of souls in England (exclusive of Scotland and Ireland) is seven millions*, and the number of souls in America is three millions.

The amount of the taxes in England (exclusive of Scotland and Ireland) was, before the present war commenced, eleven millions six hundred and forty two thousand six hundred and fifty three pounds sterling, which on an average is no less a sum than one pound thirteen shillings and threepence sterling per head per annum men, women, and children; besides county taxes, taxes for the support of the poor, and a tenth of all the produce of the earth for the support of the bishops and clergy†. Nearly five millions of this sum went annually to pay

---

*This is taking the highest number that the people of England have been or can be rated at.

†The following is taken from Dr. Price's state of the taxes of England, pages 96, 97, 98.

the interest of the national debt contracted by former wars, and the remaining sum of six millions six hundred and forty two thousand six hundred pounds was applied to defray the yearly expence of government, the peace establishment of the army and navy, placemen pensioners, &c. consequently the whole of her enormous taxes being thus appropriated, she had nothing to spare out of them towards defraying the expences of the present war or any other. Yet had she not been in debt at the beginning of the war as we were not, and like us had only a land and not a naval war to carry on, her then revenue of eleven millions and a half pounds sterling would defray all her annual expences of war and government within each year.

But this not being the case with her, she is obliged to borrow about ten million pounds sterling yearly, to prosecute the war she is now engaged in (this year she borrowed twelve) and lay on new taxes to discharge the interest; and allowing that the present war has cost her only fifty millions sterling, the interest thereon at five per cent. will be two millions and

---

"An account of the money drawn from the public by taxes annually, being the medium of three years before the year 1776.

Amount of customs in England, ... £.	2,528,275
Amount of the excise in England, ...	4,649,892
Land tax at 3 s.	1,300,000
Land tax at 1 s. in the pound, ...	450,000
Salt duties, ...	218,739
Duties on stamps, cards, dice, advertisements, bonds, leases, indentures, newspapers, almanacks, &c.	280,788
Duties on houses and windows, ...	385,369
Post office, seizures, wine licences, hackney coaches, &c. . . .	250,000
Annual profit from lotteries, ...	150,000
Expence of collecting the excises in England, ...	297,887
Expence of collecting the customs in England, ...	468,703
Interest of loans on the land tax at 4 s. expences of collection, militia, &c.	250,000
Perquisites, &c. to custom house officers, &c. supposed	250,000
Expence of collecting the salt duties in England, 10 d. 1-2 per cent.	27,000
Bounties on fish exported	18,000
Expence of collecting the duties on stamps, cards, advertisements, &c. 5 and 1-4 per cent.	18,000
Total, £.	11,642,653

an half, therefore the amount of her taxes now must be four-teen millions, which on an average is no less than forty shillings sterling per head, men, women and children throughout the nation. Now as this expence of fifty millions was borrowed on the hopes of conquering America, and as it was avarice which first induced her to commence the war, how truly wretched and deplorable would the condition of this country be, were she, by her own remissness, to suffer an enemy of such a disposition, and so circumstanced, to reduce her to subjection.

I now proceed to the revenues of America.

I have already stated the number of souls in America to be three millions, and by a calculation I have made, which I have every reason to believe is sufficiently right, the whole expence of the war, and the support of the several governments, may be defrayed for two million pounds sterling, annually; which, on an average, is thirteen shillings and four pence per head, men, women and children, and the peace establishment at the end of the war will be but three quarters of a million, or five shillings sterling per head. Now throwing out of the question every thing of honor, principle, happiness, freedom, and repu-tation in the world, and taking it up on the simple ground of interest, I put the following case.

Suppose Britain was to conquer America, and as con-querors was to lay her under no other conditions than to pay the same proportions toward her annual revenue which the people of England pay; our share, in that case, would be six million pounds sterling yearly; can it then be a question, whether it is best to raise two millions to defend the country, and govern it ourselves, and only three quarters of a million afterwards, or pay six millions to have it conquered, and let the enemy govern it.

Can it be supposed that conquerors would chuse to put themselves in a worse condition than what they granted to the conquered. In England, the tax on rum is five shillings and one penny sterling per gallon, which is one silver dollar and fourteen coppers. Now would it not be laughable to imagine, that after the expence they have been at, they would let either Whig or Tory in America drink it cheaper than themselves. Coffee which is so considerable an article of consumption and support here is there loaded with a duty, which makes the price between five and six shillings sterling a pound, and a penalty of fifty pounds sterling on any person detected in roasting it in his own house. There is scarce an article of life you can eat, drink, wear, or enjoy that is not there loaded with a tax; even the light from heaven is only permitted to shine into their dwellings by paying eighteen pence sterling per window annually; and the humblest drink of life, small beer, cannot there be purchased without a tax of nearly two coppers a gallon, besides a heavy tax upon the malt, and another on the hops before it is brewed, exclusive of a land tax on the earth which produces them. In short, the condition of that country in point of taxation is so oppressive, the number of her poor so great, and the extravagance and rapaciousness of the court so enormous, that were they to effect a conquest of America, it is then only that the distresses of America would begin. Neither would it signify any thing to a man whether he be what we call a Whig or a Tory. The people of England and the ministry of that country know us by no such distinctions. What they want is clear solid revenue, and the modes they would take to procure it, would operate alike on all. Their manner of reasoning would be short, because they would naturally infer that if we were able to carry on a war of five or six years against them, we are able to pay the same taxes which they do.

I have already stated that the expence of conducting the present war, and the government of the several states, may be done for two millions sterling, and the establishment in time of peace, for three quarters of a million*.

As to navy matters, they flourish so well, and are so well attended to, in the hands of individuals, that I think it consistent on every principle of real use and œconomy, to turn the navy into hard money (keeping only three or four packets) and apply it to promote the service of the army. We shall not have a ship the less; the use of them, and the benefit from them, will be greatly increased, and their expences saved. We

---

*I have made the calculations in sterling, because it is a rate generally known in all the states, and because likewise it admits of an easy comparison between our expences to support the war and those of the enemy. Four silver dollars and an half is one pound sterling and threepence over.

are now allied with a formidable naval power, from whom we derive the assistance of a navy. And the line in which we can prosecute the war, so as to reduce the common enemy and benefit the alliance most effectually, will be by attending closely to the land service.

I estimate the charge of keeping up and maintaining an army, officering them, and all expences included, sufficient for the defence of the country, to be equal to the expence of forty thousand men at thirty pounds sterling per head, which is one million two hundred thousand pounds.

I likewise allow four hundred thousand pounds for Continental expences at home and abroad.

And four hundred thousand pounds for the support of the several state governments, the amount then will be,

For the army,	1,200,000
Continental expences at home and abroad,	400,000
Government of the several states,	400,000
Total	2,000,000

I take the proportion of this state, Pennsylvania, to be an eighth part of the Thirteen United States, the quota then for us to raise will be two hundred and fifty thousand pounds sterling; two hundred thousand of which will be our share for the support and pay of the army and Continental expences at home and abroad, and fifty thousand pounds for the support of state government.

In order to gain an idea of the proportion in which the raising such a sum will fall, I make the following calculation:

Pennsylvania contains three hundred and seventy five thousand inhabitants, men, women and children, which is likewise an eighth part of the whole inhabitants of the United States: therefore two hundred and fifty thousand pounds sterling to be raised among three hundred and seventy five thousand persons, is, on an average, thirteen shillings and fourpence sterling per head per annum, or something more than one shilling sterling per month. And our proportion of three quarters of a million for the government of the country, in time of peace, will be ninety three thousand seven hundred and fifty pounds sterling, fifty thousand of which will be for the government expences of the state, and forty three thousand seven hundred and fifty pounds for Continental expences at home and abroad.

The peace establishment then will, on an average, be five shillings sterling per head. Whereas was England now to stop, and the war cease, her peace establishment would continue the same as it is now, viz. forty shillings per head; therefore was our taxes necessary for carrying on the war as much per head as hers now is, and the difference to be only whether we should, at the end of the war, pay at the rate of five shillings per head, or forty shillings per head, the case needs no thinking of. But as we can securely defend and keep the country for one third less than what our burthen would be if it was conquered, and support the governments afterward for an eighth of what Britain would levy on us, and could I find a miser whose heart never felt the emotion of a spark of principle, even that man, uninfluenced by every love but the love of money, and capable of no attachment but to his interest, would, and must, from the frugality which govern him contribute to the defence of the country, or he ceases to be a miser and becomes an ideot. But when we take in with it every thing that can ornament mankind; when the line of our interest becomes the line of our happiness; when all that can chear and animate the heart; when sense of honor, fame, character, at home and abroad, are interwoven not only with the security but the increase of property, there exists not a man in America, unless he be a hired emissary, who does not see that his good is connected with keeping up a sufficient defence.

I do not imagine that an instance can be produced in the world, of a country putting herself to such an amazing charge to conquer and enslave another as Britain has done. The sum is too great for her to think of with any tolerable degree of temper; and when we consider the burthen she sustains as well as the disposition she has shewn, it would be the height of folly in us to suppose that she would not reimburse herself by the most rapid means, had she once more America within her power. With such an oppression of expence, what would an empty conquest be to her! what relief under such circumstances could she derive from a victory without a prize? It was money, it was revenue, she first went to war for, and nothing but *that* would satisfy her. It is not the nature of avarice to be satisfied with any thing else. Every passion that acts upon mankind has a peculiar mode of operation. Many of them are temporary and fluctuating; they admit of cessation and variety: But avarice is a fixed uniform passion. It neither abates of its vigour nor changes its object; and the reason why it does not is founded in the nature of things, for wealth has not a rival where avarice is a ruling passion. One beauty may excel another, and extinguish from the mind of a man the pictured remembrance of a former one: But wealth is the phœnix of avarice, and therefore cannot seek a new object, because there is not another in the world.

I now pass on to shew the value of the present taxes, and compare them with the annual expence; but this I shall preface with a few explanatory remarks.

There are two distinct things which make the payment of taxes difficult; the one is the large and real value of the sum to be paid, and the other is the scarcity of the thing in which the payment is to be made; and although these appear to be one and the same, they are in several instances not only different, but the difficulty springs from different causes.

Suppose a tax was to be laid equal to one half of what every man's yearly income is, such a tax could not be paid because the property could not be spared; and on the other hand, suppose a very trifling tax was laid to be collected in *pearls,* such a tax likewise could not be paid, because it could not be had. Now any person may see that these are distinct cases, and the latter of them is a representation of ours.

That the difficulty cannot proceed from the former, that is, from the real value or weight of the tax, is evident at first view to any person who will consider it.

The amount of the quota of taxes for this state for the present year, 1780 (and so in proportion for every other state) is twenty millions of dollars, which at seventy for one is but sixty four thousand two hundred and eighty pounds three shillings sterling, and on an average is no more than three shillings and five pence sterling per head per annum men, women and children, or five pence per head per month. Now here is a clear positive fact, that cannot be contradicted, and which proves that the difficulty cannot be in the weight of the tax, for in itself it is a trifle and far from being adequate to our quota of the expence of the war. The quit rents of one penny sterling per acre on only one half the state, come to upwards of fifty thousand pounds, which is almost as much as all the taxes of the present year, and as those quit rents made no part of the taxes then paid, and are now discontinued, the quantity of money drawn for public service this year, exclusive of the militia fines, which I shall take notice of in the process of this work, is less than what was paid and payable in any year preceding the revolution, and since the last war; what I mean is that the quit rents and taxes taken together came to a larger sum then than the present taxes without the quit rents do now.

My intention by these arguments and calculations is to place the difficulty to the right cause, and shew that it does not proceed from the weight or worth of the tax, but from the scarcity of the medium in which it is paid; and to illustrate this point still farther, I shall now shew, that if the tax of twenty millions of dollars was of four times the real value it now is or nearly so, which would be about two hundred and fifty thousand pounds sterling, and would be our full quota, that this sum would have been raised with more ease, and less felt, than the present sum of only sixty four thousand two hundred and eighty pounds.

The convenience or inconvenience of paying a tax in money arises from the quantity of money that can be spared out of trade.

When the emissions stopt, the continent was left in possession of two hundred millions of dollars, perhaps as equally dispersed as it was possible for trade to do it. And as no more was to be issued, the rise or fall of prices could neither increase nor diminish the quantity. It therefore remained the same through all the fluctuations of trade and exchange.

Now had the exchange stood at twenty for one, which was the rate congress calculated upon when they quoted the states the latter end of last year, trade would have been carried on for nearly four times less money than it is now, and consequently the twenty millions would have been spared with much greater ease, and when collected would have been of almost four times the value they now are. And on the other hand, was the depreciation to be at ninety or one hundred for one, the quantity required for trade would be more than at sixty or seventy for one, and though the value of the tax would be less, the difficulty of sparing the money out of trade would be greater. And on these facts and arguments I rest the matter, to prove, that it is not the want of property, but the scarcity of the medium by which the proportion of property for taxation is to be measured out, that makes the embarrassment we lie under. There *is not* money enough, and what is equally as true, the people will not let there be money enough.

While I am on the subject of the currency, I shall offer one remark which will appear true to every body, and can be accounted for by nobody, which is, that the better the times were, the worse the money grew; and the worse the times were, the better the money stood. It never depreciated by any advantage obtained by the enemy. The troubles of seventy six, and the loss of Philadelphia in seventy seven, made no sensible impression on it, and every one knows that the surrender of Charlestown did not produce the least alteration in the rate of exchange, which for long before, and for more than three months after, stood at sixty for one. It seems as if the certainty of its being our own made us careless of its value, and that the most distant thoughts of losing it made us hug it the closer, like something we were loth to part with; or that we depreciate it for our pastime, which, when called to seriousness by the enemy, we leave off to renew again at our leisure. In short our good luck seem to break us, and our bad make us whole.

Passing on from this digression, I shall now endeavor to bring into one view the several parts I have already stated, and form thereon some propositions, and conclude.

I have placed before the reader, the average tax per head paid by the people in England; which is forty shillings sterling.

And I have shewn the rate on an average per head, which will defray all the expence of the war to us, and support the several governments without running the country into debt, which is thirteen shillings and fourpence.

I have shewn what the peace establishment may be conducted for, viz. an eighth part of what it would be, if under the government of Britain.

And I have likewise shewn what the average per head of the

present taxes are, namely, three shillings and five pence sterling or five pence per month; and that their whole yearly value in sterling is only sixty four thousand two hundred and eighty pounds. Whereas our quota to keep the payments equal with the expences, is two hundred and fifty thousand pounds. Consequently there is a deficiency of one hundred and eighty five thousand seven hundred and twenty pounds, and the same proportion of defect, according to the several quotas, happens in every other state. And this defect is the cause why the army has been so indifferently fed, cloathed and paid. It is the cause, likewise, of the nerveless state of the campaign, and the insecurity of the country. Now if a tax equal to thirteen and fourpence per head will remove all these difficulties, make people secure in their homes, leave them to follow the business of their stores and farms unmolested, and not only keep out, but drive out the enemy from the country; and if the neglect of raising this sum will let them in, and produce the evils which might be prevented, on which side, I ask, does the wisdom, interest and policy lie? Or rather would it not be an insult to reason to put the question. The sum when portioned out according to the several abilities of the people, can hurt no one, but an inroad from the enemy ruins hundreds of families.

Look at the destruction done in this city. The many houses totally destroyed, and others damaged; the waste of fences in the country round it, besides the plunder of furniture, forage and provision. I do not suppose that half a million sterling would reinstate the sufferers, and does this, I ask, bear any proportion to the expence that would make us secure. The damage on an average is at least ten pound sterling per head, which is as much as thirteen shillings and fourpence per head comes to for fifteen years. The same has happened on the frontiers, and in the Jersies, New York, and other places, where the enemy has been, Carolina and Georgia is likewise suffering the same fate.

That the people generally do not understand the insufficiency of the taxes to carry on the war, is evident, not only from common observation, but from the construction of several petitions, which were presented to the assembly of this state, against the recommendation of congress of the 18th of

March last, for taking up and funding the present currency at forty for one, and issuing new money in its stead. The prayer of the petitions was, *That the currency might be appreciated by taxes* (meaning the present taxes) *and that part of the taxes be applied to the support of the army, if the army could not be otherwise supported.* Now it could not have been possible for such a petition to have been presented, had the petitioners known, that so far from *part* of the taxes being sufficient for the support of the army, the *whole* of them falls three fourths short of the year's expences.

Before I proceed to propose methods by which a sufficiency of money may be raised, I shall take a short review of the general state of the country.

Notwithstanding the weight of the war, the ravages of the enemy, and the obstructions she has thrown in the way of trade and commerce, so soon does a young country outgrow misfortune, that America has already surmounted many that once heavily oppressed her. For the first year or two of the war, we were shut up within our ports, scarce venturing to look towards the ocean. Now our rivers are beautified with large and valuable vessels, our stores filled with merchandize, and the produce of the country has a ready market, and an advantageous price. Gold and silver, that for a while seemed to have retreated again within the bowels of the earth, is once more risen into circulation, and every day adds new strength to trade, commerce, and agriculture. In a pamphlet written by Sir John Dalrymple, and dispersed in America in the year 1775, he asserted, that, *two twenty gun ships, nay,* says he, *the tenders of those ships, stationed between Albermarle sound and Chesapeak bay, would shut up the trade of America for 600 miles.* How little did Sir John Dalrymple know of the abilities of America!

While under the government of Britain, the trade of this country was loaded with restrictions. It was only a few foreign ports she was allowed to sail to. Now it is otherwise; and allowing that the quantity of trade is but half what it was before the war, the case must shew the vast advantage of an open trade, because the present quantity under her restrictions could not support itself; from which I infer, that if half the quantity without the restrictions can bear itself up nearly, if not quite, as well as the whole when subject to them, how prosperous must the condition of America be when the whole shall return open with all the world. By trade I do not mean the employment of a merchant only, but the whole interest and business of the country taken collectively.

It is not so much my intention, by this publication, to propose particular plans for raising money, as it is to shew the necessity and the advantages to be derived from it. My principal design is to form the disposition of the people to such measures which I am fully persuaded is their interest and duty to adopt, and which needs no other force to accomplish them than the force of being felt. But as every hint may be useful, I shall throw out a sketch, and leave others to make such improvements upon it as to them may appear reasonable.

The annual sum wanted is two millions, and the average rate in which it falls is thirteen shillings and fourpence per head.

Suppose then that we raise half the sum and sixty thousand pounds over. The average rate thereof will be seven shillings per head.

In this case we shall have half the supply we want, and an annual fund of sixty thousand pounds whereon to borrow the other million; because sixty thousand pounds is the interest of a million at six per cent. and if at the end of another year we should be obliged, by the continuance of the war, to borrow another million, the taxes will be increased to seven shillings and sixpence; and thus for every million borrowed, an additional tax equal to sixpence per head must be levied.

The sum then to be raised next year will be one million and sixty thousand pounds: One half of which I would propose should be raised by duties on imported goods and prize goods, and the other half by a tax on landed property and houses, or such other means as each state may devise.

But as the duties on imports and prize goods must be the same in all the states, therefore the rate per cent. or in what other form the duty shall be laid, must be ascertained and regulated by congress, and ingrafted in that form into the law of each state; and the monies arising therefrom carried into the treasury of each state. The duties to be paid in gold or silver.

There are many reasons why a duty on imports is the most convenient duty or tax that can be collected, one of which is, because the whole is payable in a few places in a country, and it likewise operates with the greatest ease and equality, because as every one pays in proportion to what he consumes, so people in general consume in proportion to what they can afford, and therefore the tax is regulated by the abilities which every man supposes himself to have, or in other words every man becomes his own assessor, and pays by a little at a time when it suits him to buy. Besides, it is a tax which people may pay or let alone by not consuming the articles; and though the alternative may have no influence on their conduct, the power of choosing is an agreeable thing to the mind. For my own part, it would be a satisfaction to me, was there a duty on all sorts of liquors during the war, as in my idea of things, it would be an addition to the pleasure of society, to know, that when the health of the army goes round, a few drops from every glass become theirs. How often have I heard an emphatical wish almost accompanied with a tear, *"Oh, that our poor fellows in the field had some of this!"* Why then need we suffer under a fruitless sympathy, when there is a way to enjoy both the wish and the entertainment at once?

But the great national policy of putting a duty upon imports is, that it either keeps the foreign trade in our own hands or draws something for the defence of the country from every foreigner who participates it with us.

Thus much for the first half of the taxes, and as each state will best devise means to raise the other half, I shall confine my remarks to the resources of this state.

The quota then of this state of one million and sixty thousand pounds will be one hundred and thirty-three thousand two hundred and fifty pounds, the half of which is sixty-six thousand six hundred and twenty-five pounds; and supposing one fourth part of Pennsylvania inhabited, then a tax of one bushel of wheat on every twenty acres of land, one with another, would produce the sum, and all the present taxes to cease. Whereas the tythes of the bishops and clergy in England, exclusive of the taxes, are upwards of half a bushel of wheat on *every single* acre of land, good and bad, throughout the nation.

In a former part of this paper I mentioned the militia fines, but reserved speaking to the matter, which I shall now do: The ground I shall put it upon is, that two millions sterling a year will support a sufficient army, and all the expences of war, and government, without having recourse to the inconvenient method of continually calling men from their employments, which of all others is the most expensive and the least substantial. I consider the revenue created by taxes as the first and principal thing, and fines only as secondary and accidental things. It was not the intention of the militia law to apply the militia fines to any thing else but the support of the militia, neither do they produce any revenue to the state, yet these fines amount to more than all the taxes; for taking the muster roll to be sixty thousand men, the fine on forty thousand who may not attend, will be sixty thousand pounds sterling, and those who muster, will give up a portion of time equal to half that sum, and if the eight classes should be called within the year, and one third turn out, the fine on the remaining forty thousand would amount to seventy two millions of dollars, besides the fifteen shillings on every hundred pounds property, and the charge of seven and a half per cent for collecting in certain instances, which on the whole would be upwards of two hundred and fifty thousand pounds sterling.

Now if those very fines disable the country from raising a sufficient revenue without producing an equivalent advantage, would it not be to the ease and interest of all parties to encrease the revenue, in the manner I have proposed, or any better, if a better can be devised, and cease the operation of the fines. I would still keep the militia as an organized body of men, and should there be a real necessity to call them forth, pay them out of the proper revenues of the state, and encrease the taxes a third or fourth per cent. on those who did not attend. My limits will not allow me to go farther into this matter, which I shall therefore close with this remark; that fines are, of all modes of revenue, the most unsuited to the mind of a free country. When a man pays a tax, he knows the public necessity requires it, and therefore feels a pride in discharging his duty; but a fine seems an attonement for neglect of duty, and of consequence is paid with discredit, and frequently levied with severity.

I have now only one subject more to speak to, with which I shall conclude, which is, the resolve of congress of the 18th of March last, for taking up and funding the present currency at forty for one, and issuing new money in its stead.

Every one knows I am not the flatterer of congress, but in this instance *they are right*; and if that measure is supported, the currency will acquire a value, which without it, it will not. But this is not all: It will give relief to the finances until such time as they can be properly arranged, and save the country from being immediately double taxed under the present mode. In short, support that measure, and it will support you.

I have now waded through a tedious course of difficult business, and over an untrodden path. The subject on every point it could be viewed was entangled with perplexities, and inveloped in obscurity, yet such are the resources of America, that she wants nothing but system to insure success.

COMMON SENSE.

Philadelphia, October 4, 1780.

P. S. While this paper was preparing for the press, the treachery of General Arnold became known, and engrossed the attention and conversation of the public; and that, not so much on account of the traitor as the magnitude of the treason, and the providence evident in the discovery. The matter, as far as is at present known, is thus briefly related.

General Arnold about six weeks before had obtained the command of the important post of West Point, situated on the North river, about sixty miles above New York, and an hundred below Albany, there being no other defenceable pass between it and the last mentioned place. At what time, or in what manner, he first entered into a negociation with the enemy for betraying the fort and garrison into their hands, does not yet appear.

While Arnold commanded at West Point, General Washington and the minister of France went to Hartford in Connecticut, to consult on matters, in concert with Admiral Terney commander of the French fleet stationed at Rhode Island. In the mean time Arnold held a conference with major Andre, Adjutant General to General Clinton, whom he traiterously furnished with plans of the fort, state of the garrison, minutes of the last council of war, and the manner in which he would post the troops when the enemy should attempt a surprise; and then gave him a pass, by the name of Mr. John Anderson, to go to the lines at the White Plains or lower, if he Mr. Anderson thought proper, he being (the pass said) on public business.

Thus furnished, Andre parted from Arnold, set off for New York, and had nearly arrived at the extent of our lines, when he was stopped by a party of militia, to whom he produced his pass, but they, not being satisfied with his account, insisted on taking him before the commanding officer Lieut. Col. Jamieson. Finding himself in this situation, and hoping to escape by a bribe, he offered them his purse, watch and a promise of any quantity of goods they would accept, which these honest men nobly and virtuously scorned, and consistent with their duty took him to the proper officer. On examination there was found on him the above mentioned papers and several others, all in the hand writing of General Arnold, and finding himself thus detected, he confessed his proper name and character; he was accordingly made a close prisoner, and the papers sent off by express to West Point, at which place General Washington had arrived soon after the arrival of the packet. On this disclosure, he went in quest of Arnold, whom he had not seen that day, but all that could be learned was, that Arnold had received a letter some short time before, which had much confused him, since which he had disappeared. Colonel Hamilton, one of General Washington's aids, with some others were sent after him, but he having the start eluded the pursuit, took boat under pretence of a flag, and got on board the Vulture sloop of war lying in the North river; on which it may be truly said, that one vulture was receiving another. From on board this vessel he addressed a letter to General Washington, which, in whatever light it may be viewed, confirms him a finished villain.

The true character of Arnold is that of a desperado. His whole life has been a life of jobbs; and where either plunder or profit was the object, no danger deterred, no principle restrained him. In his person he was smart and active, somewhat diminutive, weak in his capacities and trifling in his conversation; and though gallant in the field, was defective in the talents necessary for command. The early convulsion of the times afforded him an introduction into life, to the elegance of which he was before a stranger, and the eagerness of the public, to reward and encourage enterprize, procured him at once both applause and promotion. His march to Quebec gave him fame, and the plunder of Montreal put the first stamp to his public character. His behaviour at Danbury and Saratoga once more covered over his crimes, which again broke forth in the plunder of Philadelphia, under pretence of supplying the army. From this time, the true spring of his conduct being known, he became both disregarded and disesteemed, and this last instance of his treachery has proved the public judgment right.

When we take a review of the history of former times, it will turn out to the honor of America, that, notwithstanding the trying variety of her situation, this is the only instance of defection in a general officer; and even in this case the unshaken honesty of those who detected him heightens the national character, to which his apostacy serves as a foil. From the nature of his crime, and his disposition to monopolize, it is reasonable to conclude he had few or no *direct* accomplices. His sole object was to make a monied bargain; and to be consistent with himself, he would as readily betray the side he has deserted to, as that he deserted from.

But there is one reflection results from this black business, that deserves notice, which is, that it shows the declining power of the enemy. An attempt to bribe is a sacrifice of military fame, and a confession of inability to conquer; as a proud people they ought to be above it, and as soldiers to despise it; and however they may feel on the occasion, the world at large will despise them for it, and consider America superior to their arms.

C. S.

Public Good

BEING AN EXAMINATION
INTO THE CLAIM OF VIRGINIA
TO THE VACANT WESTERN TERRITORY,
AND
OF THE RIGHT OF
THE UNITED STATES TO THE SAME.

TO WHICH IS ADDED,
PROPOSALS FOR LAYING OFF A NEW STATE,
TO BE APPLIED AS A FUND
FOR CARRYING ON THE WAR,
OR REDEEMING THE NATIONAL DEBT.

—————

December 30, 1780

—————

THE PREFACE.

THE following pages are on a subject hitherto little understood, but highly interesting to the United States.

They contain an investigation of the claims of Virginia to the vacant western territory, and of the right of the United States to the same; with some outlines of a plan for laying out a new state, to be applied as a fund, for carrying on the war, or redeeming the national debt.

The reader, in the course of this publication, will find it studiously plain, and, as far as I can judge, perfectly candid. What materials I could get at I have endeavoured to place in a clear line, and deduce such arguments therefrom as the subject required. In the prosecution of it, I have considered myself as an advocate for the right of the states, and taken no other liberty with the subject than what a counsel would, and ought to do, in behalf of a client.

I freely confess that the respect I had conceived, and still preserve, for the character of Virginia, was a constant check upon those sallies of imagination, which are fairly and advantageously indulged against an enemy, but ungenerous when against a friend.

If there is any thing I have omitted or mistaken, to the injury of the intentions of Virginia or her claims, I shall gladly rectify it; or if there is any thing yet to add, should the subject require it, I shall as chearfully undertake it; being fully convinced, that to have matters fairly discussed, and properly understood, is a principal means of preserving harmony and perpetuating friendship.

THE AUTHOR.

PUBLIC GOOD, &c.

WHEN we take into view the mutual happiness and united interests of the states of America, and consider the important consequences to arise from a strict attention of each, and of all, to every thing which is just, reasonable and honourable; or the evils that will follow from an inattention to those principles; there cannot, and ought not, to remain a doubt, but that the governing rule of *right* and mutual good must in all public cases finally preside.

The hand of providence has cast us into one common lot, and accomplished the independence of America, by the unanimous consent of the several parts, concurring at once in time, manner and circumstances. No superiority of interest, at the expence of the rest, induced the one, more than the other, into the measure. Virginia and Maryland, it is true, might foresee, that their staple commodity, tobacco, by being no longer monopolized by Britain, would bring them a better price abroad: for as the tax on it in England was treble its first purchase from the planter, and they being now no longer compelled to send it under that obligation, and in the restricted manner they formerly were; it is easy to see, that the article, from the alteration of the circumstances of trade, will, and daily does, turn out to them with additional advantages.

But this being a natural consequence, produced by that common freedom and independence of which all are partakers, is therefore an advantage they are intitled to, and on which the rest of the states can congratulate them without feeling a wish to lessen, but rather to extend it. To contribute to the encreased prosperity of another, by the same means which occasion our own, is an agreeable reflection; and the more valuable any article of export becomes, the more riches will be introduced into and spread over the continent.

Yet this is an advantage which those two states derive from the independence of America superior to the local circumstances of the rest; and of the two it more particularly belongs to Virginia than Maryland, because the staple commodity of a considerable part of Maryland is flour, which, as it is an article that is the growth of Europe as well as of America, cannot obtain a foreign market but by under selling, or at least by limiting it to the current price abroad. But tobacco commands its own price. It is not a plant of almost universal growth, like wheat. There are but few soils and climes that produce it to advantage, and before the cultivation of it in Virginia and Maryland, the price was from four to sixteen shillings sterling a pound in England.*

But the condition of the vacant western territory of America makes a very different case to that of the circumstances of trade in any of the states. Those very lands, formed, in contemplation, the fund by which the debt of America would in a course of years be redeemed. They were considered as the common right of all; and it is only till lately that any pretension of claims has been made to the contrary.

That difficulties and differences will arise in communities ought always to be looked for. The opposition of interests, real or supposed; the variety of judgments; the contrariety of temper; and, in short, the whole composition of man, in his individual capacity, is tinctured with a disposition to contend; but in his social capacity there is either a right which, being proved, terminates the dispute, or a reasonableness in the measure, where no direct right can be made out, which decides or compromises the matter.

As I shall have frequent occasion to mention the word *right*, I wish to be clearly understood in my definition of it. There are various senses in which this term is used, and custom has, in many of them, afforded it an introduction contrary to its true meaning. We are so naturally inclined to give

---

*See sir Dalby Thomas's historical account of the rise and growth of the West-India colonies.

the utmost degree of force to our own case, that we call every pretension, however founded, *a right*; and by this means the term frequently stands opposed to justice and reason.

After Theodore was elected king of Corsica, not many years ago, by the meer choice of the natives, for their own convenience in opposing the Genoese, he went over into England, run himself into debt, got himself into jail, and on his release therefrom by the benefit of an act of insolvency, he surrendered up, what he called, *his* kingdom of Corsica, as a part of his personal property, for the use of his creditors; some of whom may hereafter call this a charter, or by any other name more fashionable, and ground thereon what they may term a *right* to the sovereignty and property of Corsica. But does not justice abhor such an action, both in him and them, under the prostituted name of a *right*, and must not laughter be excited where ever it is told.

A right, to be truly so, must be right in itself; yet many things have obtained the name of rights, which are originally founded in wrong. Of this kind are all rights by meer conquest, power or violence. In the cool moments of reflection we are obliged to allow, that the mode by which such right is obtained, is not the best suited to that spirit of universal justice which ought to preside equally over all mankind. There is something in the establishment of such a right that we wish to flip over as easily as possible, and say as little about as can be. But in the case of a *right founded in right* the mind is carried chearfully into the subject, feels no compunction, suffers no distress, subjects its sensations to no violences, nor sees any thing in its way which requires an artificial smoothing.

From this introduction I proceed to examine into the claims of Virginia; first as to the right, secondly as to the reasonableness, and lastly as to the consequences.

The name, *Virginia*, originally bore a different meaning to what it does now. It stood in the place of the word North-America, and seems to have been intended as a name comprehensive of all the English settlements or colonies on the continent, and not descriptive of any one as distinguishing it from the rest. All to the southward of Chesapeak, as low as the Gulf of Mexico, was called South-Virginia, and all to the northward North-Virginia, in a similar line of distinction, as we now call the whole continent North and South-America.*

The first character or patent was to sir Walter Rawleigh by Queen Elizabeth, of England, in the year 1583, and had neither name nor bounds. Upon sir Walter's return, the name *Virginia*, was given to the whole country, including the now United States. Consequently the present Virginia, either as a province or a state, can sit up no exclusive claim to the western territory under this patent, and that for two reasons; first, because the words of the patent run *to sir Walter Rawleigh, and such persons as he should nominate, themselves and their successors*; which is a line of succession Virginia does not pretend to stand in; and secondly, because a prior question would arise, namely, who are to be understood by Virginians under this patent? and the answer would be, all the inhabitants of America, from New-England to Florida.

This patent, therefore, would destroy their exclusive claim, and invest the right collectively in the thirteen states.

But it unfortunately happened, that the settlers under this patent, partly from misconduct, the opposition of the Indians, and other calamities, discontinued the process, and the patent became extinct.

After this James the first, who, in the year 1602, succeeded Elizabeth, issued a new patent, which I come next to describe.

This patent differed from the former in this essential point, that it had limits, whereas the other had none: the former was intended to promote discoveries where ever they could be made, which accounts why no limits were affixed, and this to settle discoveries already made, which likewise assigns a reason why limits should be described.

In this patent were incorporated two companies, called the South-Virginia company, and the North-Virginia company, and sometimes the London company, and the Plymouth company.

The South-Virginia or London company was composed chiefly of London adventurers; the North-Virginia or Ply-

*Oldmixon's history of Virginia.

mouth company was made up of adventurers from Plymouth in Devonshire, and other persons of the western parts of England.

Tho' they were not to fix together, yet they were allowed to chuse their places of settlement any where on the coast of America, then called Virginia, between the latitudes of 34 and 45 degrees, which was a range of 760 miles: the south company was not to go below 34 degrees, nor the north company above 45 degrees. But the patent expressed, that as soon as they had made their choice, each was to become limited to 50 miles each way on the coast, and 100 up the country; so that the grant to each company was a square of 100 miles, and no more. The North-Virginia or Plymouth company settled to the eastward, and in the year 1614 changed the name, and called that part New-England. The South-Virginia or London company settled near cape Henry.

This then cannot be the patent of boundless extent, and that for two reasons; first, because the limits are described, namely, a square of 100 miles; and secondly, because there were two companies of equal rights included in the same patent.

Three years after this, that is, in the year 1609, the South-Virginia company applied for new powers from the Crown of England, which were granted them in a new patent, and the boundaries of the grant enlarged; and this is the charter or patent on which some of the present Virginians ground their pretension to boundless territory.

The first reflection that presents itself on this enlargement of the grant is, that it must be supposed to bear some intended degree of reasonable comparison to that which it superceded. The former could not be greater than a square of one hundred miles; and this new one being granted in the lieu of that, and that within the space of three years, and by the same person, James the first, who was never famed either for profusion or generosity, cannot, on a review of the time and circumstances of the grant, be supposed a very extravagant or very extraordinary one. If a square of one hundred miles was not sufficiently large, twice that quantity was as much as could well be expected or solicited: but to suppose that he, who had caution enough to confine the first grant within moderate bounds, should in so short a space as three years, supercede it by another grant of many million times greater content, is, on the face of the affair, a circumstantial nullity.

Whether this patent of charter was in existence or not at the time the revolution commenced, is a matter I shall hereafter speak to, and confine myself in this place to the limits which the said patent or charter lays down.

The words are as follows:

"Beginning from the cape or point of land called cape or point Comfort, thence all along the sea coast to the NORTHWARD 200 miles; and from the said point or cape Comfort all along the sea coast to the *southward* 200 miles; and all that space or circuit of land lying from the sea coast of the precinct aforesaid up into the land throughout, from sea to sea, WEST and *north-west*."

The first remark I shall offer on the words of this grant is, that they are uncertain, obscure and unintelligible, and may be construed into such a variety of contradictory meanings as to leave at last no meaning at all.

Whether the 200 miles each way, from cape Comfort, were to be on a *straight* line, or ascertained by following the indented *line of the coast*, that is, *"all along the sea coast,"* in and out as the coast lay, cannot now be fully determined; because, as either will admit of supposition, and nothing but supposition can be produced, therefore neither can be taken as positive. Thus far may be said, that had it been intended to be a straight line, the word *straight* ought to have been inserted, which would have made the matter clear; but as no inference can well be drawn to the advantage of that which does *not appear* against that which *does*, therefore the omission implies negatively in favour of the coast indented line, or that the 400 miles were to be traced on the windings of the coast that is *"all along the sea coast."*

But what is meant by the words *"west and north-west"* is still more unintelligible. Whether they mean a west line and a north-west line, or whether they apply to the general lying of the land from the Atlantic, without regard to lines, cannot again be determined. But if they are supposed to mean lines to be run, then a new difficulty of more magnitude than all the rest arises; namely, From which end of the extent on the coast is the west line and the north-west line to be set off; as the difference in the content of the grant, occasioned by transposing them is many hundred million of acres; and either includes or excludes a far greater quantity of land than the whole thirteen United States contain?

In short, there is not a boundary in this grant that is clear, fixt and defined. The coast line is uncertain, and that being the base on which the others are to be formed, renders the whole uncertain. But even if this line was admitted, in either shape, the other boundaries would still be on supposition, till it might be said there is no boundary at all, and consequently no charter; for words which describe nothing can give nothing.

The advocates for the Virginia claim, laying hold of these ambiguities, have explained the grant thus:

Four hundred miles on the sea coast, and from the south point a west line to the great south sea, and from the north point a north-west line to the said south sea. The figure which these lines produce will be thus:

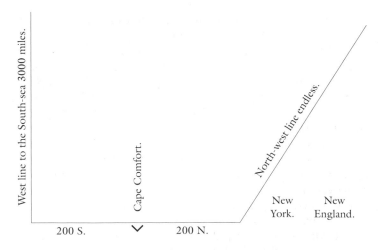

But why, I ask, must the west land line be set off from the south point, any more than from the north point? The grant or patent does not say from which it shall be, neither is it clear that a line is the thing intended by the words: but admitting it is, on what grounds do the claimants proceed in making this choice? the answer, I presume, is easily given, namely, because it is the most beneficial explanation to themselves they can possibly make; as it takes in many thousand times more extent of country than any other explanation would. But this, tho' it be a very good reason to them, is a very bad reason to us; and tho' it may do for the claimants to hope upon, will not answer to plead upon; especially to the very people, who, to confirm the partiality of the claimants choice, must relinquish their own right and interest.

Why not set off the west land line from the north end of the coast line, and the north-west line from the south end of the same? there is some reason why this should be the construction and none why the other should.

First, because, if the line of two hundred miles each way from cape Comfort, be traced by following the indented line of the coast, which seems to be the implied intention of the words, and a west line be set off from the north end, and a north-west line from the south end, these lines will all unite, (which the other construction never can) and form a compleat triangle, the content of which will be about twenty nine or thirty millions of acres, or something larger than Pennsylvania: and

Secondly, because this construction is following the order of the lines as expressed in the grant; for the *first* mentioned *coast* line, which is that to the *northward* of cape Comfort, and the *first* mentioned *land* line, which is the *west* line, have a numerical relation, being the *first mentioned of each*; and implies, that the *west* line was to be set off from the *north* point and *not* from the south point: and consequently the two *last* mentioned of each have the same numerical relation, and again implies that the *north-west* line was to be set off from the *south* point, and *not* from the *north* point. But why the claimants should break thro' the order of the lines, and, contrary to implication, join the *first* mentioned of the *one*, to the *last* mentioned of the *other*, and thereby produce a shapeless monster, for which there is no name nor any parallel in the world, either as to extent of soil or sovereignty, is a construction that cannot be supported.

The figure produced by following the order of the lines is as under.

N. B.   If the reader will cast his eye again over the words of the patent on page 259 he will perceive the numerical relation alluded to, by observing, that the first mentioned coast line and the first mentioned land line are distinguished by CAPITALS. And the last mentioned of each by *italics*, which I have chosen to do to illustrate the explanation.

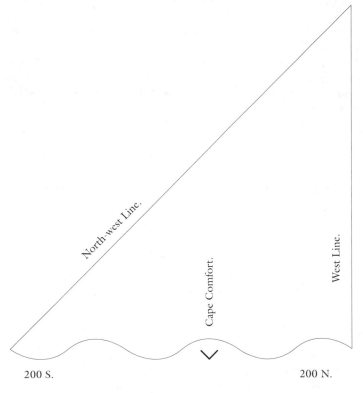

North-west Line.

Cape Comfort.

West Line.

200 S.   200 N.

I presume that if four hundred miles be traced by following the inflexes of any sea shore, that the two extremes will not be more than three hundred miles distant from each other, on a straight line. Therefore to find the content of a triangle whose base is three hundred miles, multiply the length of the base into half the perpendicular, which, in this case is the west line, and the product will be the answer:

300 miles length of the base.
150 half the perpendicular (supposing a right angled triangle)
━━━━━━
15000
300
━━━━━━
45,000 contents of the grant in square miles.
640 acres in a square mile.
━━━━━━
1800000
270000
━━━━━━
28,800,000 contents in square acres.

Now will any one undertake to say, that this explanation is not as fairly drawn, (if not more so) from the words themselves, as any other that can be offered, because it is not only justified by the exact words of the patent, grant, or charter, or any other name by which it may be called, but by their implied meaning; and is likewise of such a content, as may be supposed to have been intended; whereas the claimants explanation is without bounds, and beyond every thing that is reasonable. Yet after all, who can say what were the precise meaning of terms and expressions so loosely formed, and capable of such a variety of contradictory interpretations!

Had the order of the lines been otherwise than they are in the patent, the reasonableness of the thing must have directed the manner in which they should be connected: but as the claim is founded in unreasonableness, and that unreasonableness endeavoured to be supported by a transposition of the lines, there remains no pretence for the claim to stand on.

Perhaps those who are interested in the claimants explanation will say, that as the south sea is spoken of, the lines must be as they explain them, in order to reach it.

To this I reply; first, that no man then knew how far it was from the Atlantic to the south sea, as I shall presently show, but believed it to be but a short distance: and,

Secondly, that the uncertain and ambiguous manner in which the south sea is alluded to, (for it is not mentioned by name, but only *"from sea to sea"*) serves to perplex the patent, and not to explain it: and as no right can be founded on an ambiguity, but on some proof cleared of ambiguity, therefore the allusive introduction of "sea to sea," can yield no service to the claim.

There is likewise an ambiguous mention made of *two lands* in this patent, as well as of two *seas*; viz. "and all that *space or circuit of land* lying from the sea coast of the precinct afore-said up into the *land throughout from sea to sea*."

On which I remark, that the two *lands* here mentioned have the appearance of a major and a minor, or the greater out of which the less is to be taken: and the term from *"sea to sea"* may be said to apply descriptively to the *land throughout*, and not to the *space or circuit of land patented to the company*: in a similar manner that the former patent described a major of 760 miles extent, out of which the minor, or square of one hundred miles, was to be chosen.

But to suppose, that because the south sea is darkly alluded to, it must therefore, (at whatever distance it might be, which then nobody knew, or for whatever purpose it might be intro-duced) be made a certain boundary, and that without regard to the reasonableness of the matter, or the order in which the lines are arranged, which is the only implication the patent gives for setting off the land lines, is a supposition that con-tradicts every thing which is reasonable.

The figure produced by following the order of the lines will be compleat in itself, let the distance to the south sea be more or less: because, if the *land throughout from sea to sea* had not been sufficiently extensive to admit the west land line and the north west land line to close, the south sea, in that case, would have eventually become a boundary: but if the extent of the *land throughout from sea to sea*, was so great, that the lines closed without reaching the said south sea, the figure was compleat without it.

Wherefore, as the order of the lines, when raised on the indented coast line, produces a regular figure of reasonable dimensions, and of about the same content, tho' not of the same shape, which Virginia now holds within the Allegany Mountains; and by transposing them another figure is pro-duced, for which there is no name, and cannot be com-pleated, as I shall presently explain, and of an extent greater

than one half of Europe, it is needless to offer any other arguments to shew that the order of the lines must be the rule, if
any rule can be drawn from the words, for ascertaining from
which point the west line and north-west line were to be set
off. Neither is it possible to suppose any other rule could be
followed; because a north-west line set off two hundred miles
above cape Comfort, would not only never touch the south
sea, but would form a spiral line of infinite windings round
the globe, and after passing over the northern parts of
America and the frozen ocean, and then into the northern
parts of Asia, would, when eternity should end and not before, terminate in the north pole.

This is the only manner in which I can express the effect of
a north-west line, set off as above; because as its direction
must always be between the north and the west, it consequently can never get into the pole nor yet come to a rest;
and on the principle, that matter or space is capable of being
eternally divided, must proceed on for ever.

But it was a prevailing opinion, at the time this patent was
obtained, that the South sea was at no great distance from the
Atlantic, and therefore it was needless, under that supposition, to regard which way the lines should be run; neither
need we wonder at this error in the English government respecting America then, when we see so many and such glaring
ones now, for which there are less excuse.

Some circumstances favoured this mistake. Admiral sir
Francis Drake not long before this, had, from the top of a
mountain in the Isthmus of Darien, which is the center of
North and South America, seen both the South sea and the
Atlantic; the width of the part of the continent where he then
was, not being above 70 miles, whereas its width opposite
Chesapeak bay is as great, if not greater, than in any other
part, being from *sea to sea*, about the distance it is from
America to England. But this could not then be known, because only two voyages had been made across the South sea;
the one by the ship in which Magellan sailed, who died in his
passage, and which was the first ship that sailed round the
world, and the other by sir Francis Drake: but as neither of
these sailed into a northern latitude in that ocean, high
enough to fix the longitude of the western coast of America

from the eastern, the distance across was intirely on supposition, and the errors they then ran into appear laughable to us who now know what the distance is.

That the company expected to come at the South sea without much trouble or travelling, and that the great body of land which intervened, so far from being their view in obtaining the charter, became their disappointment, may be collected from a circumstance mentioned in Stith's history of Virginia.

He relates, that, in the year 1608, which was at the time the company were soliciting this patent, they fitted up in England "a barge for captain Newport," (who was afterwards one of the joint deputy governors under the very charter we are now treating of) "which, for convenience of carriage, might be taken into five pieces, and with which he and his company were instructed to go up James River as far as the falls thereof, to discover the country of the Monakins, and from thence they were to proceed, *carrying their barge beyond the falls to convey them to the south sea;* being ordered not to return without a lump of gold, or a certainty of the said sea."

And Hutchinson, in his history of New England, which was called North-Virginia at the time this patent was obtained, says, "the geography of this part of America was less understood than at present. A line to the Spanish settlements was imagined much shorter than it really was. Some of Champlain's people, in the beginning of the last century, who had been but a few days march from Quebec, returned with great joy, supposing that from the top of a high mountain they had *discovered the South-Sea*."

From these matters, which are evidences on record, it appears that the adventurers had no knowledge of the distance it was to the South-Sea, but supposed it to be no great way from the Atlantic; and also, that great extent of territory was not their object, but a short communication with the southern ocean, by which they might get into the neighbourhood of the Gold Coast, and likewise carry on a commerce with the East Indies.

Having thus shewn the confused and various interpretations this charter is subject to, and that it may be made to mean any thing and nothing; I now proceed to show, that, let the limits of it be more or less, the present Virginia does not, and cannot, as a matter of right, inherit under it.

I shall open this part of the subject by putting the following case:

Either Virginia stands in succession to the London company, to whom the charter was granted, or to the Crown of England. If to the London company, then it becomes her, as an outset in the matter, to shew who they were, and likewise that they were in possession at the commencement of the revolution.—If to the Crown, then the charter is of consequence superseded; because the Crown did not posses territories by charter, but by prerogative without charter. The notion of the Crown chartering to itself is a nullity; and in this case, the unpossessed lands, be they little or much, are in the same condition as if they never had been chartered at all; and the sovereignty of them devolves to the sovereignty of the United States.

The charter or patent of 1609 as well as that of 1606 was to Sir Thomas Gates, Sir George Summers, the reverend Richard Hackluit, prebend of Westminster, and others; and the government was then proprietary. Those proprietors, by virtue of the charter of 1609, chose Lord Delaware for their governor, and Sir Thomas Gates, Sir George Summers, and captain Newport, (the person who was to go with a boat to the South sea,) joint deputy governors.

Was this the form of government either as to soil or constitution at the time the present revolution commenced? if not, the charter was not in *being*; for it matters not to us how it came to be *out of being*, so long as the present Virginians, or their ancestors, neither are nor were sufferers by the change then made.

But suppose it could be proved to be in being, which it cannot, because *being* in a charter is power, it would only prove a right in behalf of the London company of adventurers, but how that right is to be disposed of is another question. We are not defending the right of the London company deceased 150 years ago, but taking up the matter at the place where we found it, and so far as the authority of the Crown of England was exercised when the revolution commenced.

The charter was a contract between the Crown of England

and those adventurers for their own emolument, and not between the Crown and the people of Virginia; and whatever was the occasion of the contract becoming void, or surrendered up, or superceded, makes no part of the question now. It is sufficient that when the United States succeeded to sovereignty they found no such contract in existence or even in litigation. They found Virginia under the authority of the Crown of England, both as to soil and government, subject to quit-rents to the Crown and not to the company, and had been so for upwards of 150 years: and that an instrument or deed of writing, of a private nature, as all proprietary contracts are so far as land is concerned, and which is now only historically known, and in which Virginia was no party, and to which no succession in any line can be proved, and have ceased for 150 years, should now be raked from oblivion and held up as a charter whereon to assume a right to boundless territory, and that by a perversion of the order of it, is something very singular and extraordinary.

If there was any innovation on the part of the crown, the contest rested between the crown and the proprietors, the London company, and not between Virginia and the said crown. It was not her charter; it was the company's charter, and the only parties in the case were the crown and the company.

But why, if Virginia contends for the immutability of charters, has she selected this in preference to the two former ones? All her arguments arising from this principle must go to the first charter and not to the last; but by placing them to the last, instead of the first, she admits a fact against her principle; because, in order to establish the last, she proves the first to be vacated by the second in the space of 23 years, the second to be vacated by the third in the space of 3 years; and why the third should not be vacated by the fourth form of government, issuing from the same power with the former two, and which took place about 25 years after, and continued in being for 150 years since, and under which all her public and private business was transacted, her purchases made, her warrants for survey and patents for land obtained, is too mysterious to account for.

Either the re-assumption of the London company's charter

into the hands of the crown was an usurpation, or it was not. If it was, then, strictly speaking, is every thing which Virginia has done under that usurpation illegal, and she may be said to have lived in the most curious species of rebellion ever known; rebellion against the London company of adventurers. For if the charter to the company (for it was not to the Virginians) ought to be in being now, it ought to have been in being then; and why she should admit its vacation then, and reject it now, is unaccountable; or why she should esteem her purchases of lands good which were *then* made contrary to this charter, and now contend for the operation of the same charter to possess new territory by, are circumstances which cannot be reconciled.

But whether the charter, as it is called, ought to be extinct or not, cannot make a question with us. All the parties concerned in it are deceased, and no successors, in any regular line of succession, appear to claim. Neither the London company of adventurers, their heirs or assigns, were in possession of the exercise of this charter at the commencement of the revolution; and therefore the state of Virginia does not, in point of fact, succeed to and inherit from the company.

But say they, we succeed to and inherit from the Crown of England, which was the immediate possessor of the sovereignty at the time we entered, and had been so for 150 years.

To say this, is to say there is no charter at all. A charter is an assurance from one party to another, and cannot be from the same party to itself.

But before I enter further on this case I shall concisely state how this charter came to be re-assumed by the power which granted it, the Crown of England.

I have already stated that it was a proprietary charter, or grant, to sir Thomas Gates and others, who were called the London company, and sometimes the South-Virginia company, to distinguish them from those who settled to the eastward (now New-England) and were then called the North-Virginia or Plymouth company.

Oldmixon's history of Virginia (in his account of the British empire in America) published in the year 1708, gives a concise progress of the affair. He attributes it to the misconduct, contentions and mismanagement of the proprietors, and their innovations upon the Indians, which had so exasperated them, that they fell on the settlers and destroyed at one time 334 men, women, and children.

"Some time after this massacre, says he, several gentlemen in England procured grants of land from the company, and others came over on their private accounts to make settlements; among the former was one captain Martin, who was named to be of the council. This man raised so many differences among them, that new distractions followed, which the Indians observing, took heart and once more fell upon the settlers on the borders, destroying, without pitying either age, sex, or condition.

"These and other calamities, being chiefly imputed to the mismanagement of the proprietors, whose losses had so discouraged most of their best members, that they sold their shares, and Charles the first on his accession to the throne dissolved the company, and took the colony into his own immediate direction. He appointed the governor and council himself, ordered all patents and process to issue in his own name, and reserved a quit-rent of two shillings sterling for every hundred acres."

Thus far our author. Now it is impossible for us at this distance of time to say what were all the exact causes of the change; neither have we any business with it. The company might surrender it, or they might not, or they might forfeit it by not fulfilling conditions, or they might sell it, or the Crown might, as far as we know, take it from them. But what are either of these cases to Virginia, or any other which can be produced. She was not a party in the matter. It was not her charter, neither can she ingraft any right upon it or suffer any injury under it.

If the charter was vacated it must have been by the London company; if it was surrendered it must be by the same; If it was sold nobody else could sell it, and if it was taken from them nobody else could lose it; and yet Virginia calls this her charter, which it was not within her power to hold, to sell, to vacate, or to lose.

But if she puts her right upon the ground that it never was sold, surrendered, lost, or vacated, by the London company, she admits that if they *had* sold, surrendered, lost, or vacated it, that it would have become extinct, and to her no charter at all. And in this case, the only thing to prove is the fact, which is, Has this charter been the rule of government, and of purchasing or procuring unappropriated lands in Virginia, from the time it was granted to the time of the revolution? Answer, the charter has not been the rule of government, nor of purchasing or procuring lands, neither has any lands been purchased or procured under its sanction or authority for upwards of 150 years.

But if she goes a step further, and says that they could not vacate, surrender, sell, or lose it, by any act they could do, so neither could they vacate, surrender, sell, or lose that of 1606, which was three years prior to this; and this argument, so far from establishing the charter of 1609, would destroy it; and in its stead confirm the preceding one which limited the company to a square of 100 miles. And if she still goes back to that of sir Walter Rawleigh, *that* only places her in the light of Americans in common with all.

The only fact that can be clearly proved, is, that the Crown of England exercised the power of dominion and government of Virginia, and of the disposal of the lands, and that the charter had neither been the rule of government or purchasing lands for upwards of 150 years, and this places Virginia in succession to the Crown and not to the Company. Consequently it proves a lapse of the charter into the hands of the crown by some means or other.

Now to suppose that the charter could return into the hands of the crown and yet remain in force, is to suppose that a man could be bound by a bond of obligation to himself.

Its very *being* in the hands of the crown from which it issued is a cessation of its existence; and an effectual unchartering all that part of the Grant which was not before disposed of. And consequently the state of Virginia standing thus in succession to the crown, can be intitled to no more extent of country as a state under the union, than what it possessed as a province under the crown. And all lands exterior to these bounds as well of Virginia as the rest of the states, devolve, in the order of succession to the sovereignty of the United States for the benefit of all.

And this brings the case to what were the limits of Virginia as a province under the crown of England.

Charter it had none. It's limits then rested at the discretion of the authority to which it was subject. Maryland and Pennsylvania became it's boundary to the eastward and northward and North-Carolina to the southward, therefore the boundary to the westward was the only principal line to be ascertained.

As Virginia from a proprietary soil and government was become what then bore the name of a royal one, the extent of the province, as the order of things then stood (for something must always be admitted whereon to form a beginning) was wholly at the disposal of the crown of England, who might enlarge, or diminish, or erect new governments to the westward, by the same authoritative right that Virginia now can divide a county into two; if too large, or too inconvenient.

To say, as has been said, that Pennsylvania, Maryland and North-Carolina, were taken out of Virginia, is no more than to say, they were taken out of America; because Virginia was the common name of all the country, north and south: and to say they were taken out of the chartered limits of Virginia, is likewise to say nothing; because after the dissolution or extinction of the proprietary company, there was nobody to whom any provincial limits became chartered. The extinction of the company was the extinction of the chartered limits. The patent could not survive the company, because it was to them a right, which, when they expired ceased to be any body's else in their stead.

But to return to the western boundary of Virginia at the commencement of the revolution.

Charters, like proclamations, were the sole act of the crown, and if the former were adequate to fix limits to the lands which it gave away, sold, or otherways disposed of, the latter were equally adequate to fix limits or divisions to those which it retained; and therefore, the western limits of Virginia, as the proprietary company was extinct and consequently the patent with it, must be looked for in the line of proclamations.

I am not fond of quoting these old remains of former arrogance, but as we must begin somewhere, and as the states have agreed to regulate the right of each state to territory, by the condition each stood in with the crown of England at the commencement of the revolution, we have no other rule to go by; and any rule which can be agreed on is better than none.

From the proclamation then of 1763, the western limits of Virginia, as a province under the crown of England, are described so as not to extend beyond the heads of any of the rivers which empty themselves into the Atlantic, and consequently the limits did not pass over the Allegany Mountain.

Extract from the proclamation of 1763 so far as respects boundary:

"AND WHEREAS it is *just* and *reasonable*, and *essential to our interest*, and the security of our colonies, that the several nations or tribes of Indians, with whom we are connected, and who live under our protection, should not be molested or disturbed in the possession of such parts of our dominions and territories, *as, not having been ceded to, or purchased by us, are reserved to them or any of them as their hunting grounds*; we do therefore, with the advice of our privy council, declare it to be our royal will and pleasure, that no governor, or commander in chief, in any of our colonies of Quebec, east Florida, or west Florida, do presume, upon any pretence whatever, to grant warrants of survey, or pass any patents for lands beyond the bounds of their respective governments, as described in their commissions: As ALSO that no governor or commander in chief of our other colonies or plantations in America, do presume, for the present, and until our further pleasure be known, to grant warrants of survey, or pass patents for any lands *beyond the heads or sources of any of the rivers which fall into the Atlantic ocean from the west or north-west*, or upon any lands whatever, *which not having been ceded to, or purchased by us, as aforesaid, are reserved unto the said Indians or any of them.*

"And we do further declare it to be our royal will and pleasure, for the present, as aforesaid, to reserve under our sovereignty, protection, and dominion, *for the use of the said Indians all the lands and territories*, not included within the limits of our said three new governments, or within the limits of the territory granted to the Hudson's-Bay company; as also, *all the lands and territories lying to the westward of the sources of the rivers, which fall into the sea from the west and north-west as aforesaid*; and we do hereby strictly forbid, on pain of our displeasure, all our loving subjects from making any purchases or settlements whatever, or taking possession of any of the lands above reserved, without our especial leave and licence for that purpose first obtained:

"And we do further strictly enjoin and require all persons whatever, who have either wilfully or inadvertently seated themselves upon any lands within the countries above described, or upon any other lands, *which, not having been ceded to, or purchased by us*, are still reserved to the said Indians, as aforesaid, forthwith to remove themselves from such settlements."

It is easy for us to understand, that the frequent and plausible mention of the Indians was only speciousness to create an idea of the humanity of government. The object and intention of the proclamation was the western boundary, which is here signified not to extend beyond the heads of the rivers: and these, then, are the western limits which Virginia had as a province under the crown.

And agreeable to the intention of this proclamation and the limits described thereby, lord Hilsborough, then secretary of state in England, addressed an official letter of the 31st of July, 1770, to lord Bottetourt, at that time governor of Virginia, which letter was laid before the council of Virginia by Mr. president Nelson, and by him answered on the 18th of October in the same year, of which the following are extracts:

"On the evening of the day your lordship's letter to the governor was delivered to me, and as it contains matters of great variety and importance, it was read in council, and, together with the several papers inclosed, it hath been maturely considered, and I now trouble your lordship with theirs as well as my own opinion upon the subject of them.

"We do not presume to say to whom our gracious sovereign shall grant his vacant lands," and "with respect to the establishment of a *new colony on the back of Virginia*, it is a subject of too great political importance for me to presume to give an opinion upon, however, permit me, my lord, to observe, that when that part of the country shall become sufficiently populated it may be a wise and prudent measure."

On the death of lord Bottetourt, lord Dunmore was appointed to the government, and he, either from ignorance of the subject, or other motives, made a grant of some lands on the Ohio to certain of his friends and favorites, which produced the following letter from lord Dartmouth, who succeeded lord Hilsborough as secretary of state:

"I think fit to inclose your lordship a copy of lord Hilsborough's letter to lord Bottetourt, of the 31st of July, 1770, the receipt of which was acknowledged by Mr. president Nelson, a few days after lord Bottetourt's death, and appears by his answer to it, to have been laid before the council. That board, therefore, could not be ignorant of what has passed here upon Mr. Walpole's application, nor of the king's express command, contained in lord Hilsborough's letter, that no lands should be granted beyond the limits of the royal proclamation of 1763, until the king's further pleasure was signified; and I have only to observe, that it must have been a very extraordinary neglect in them not to have informed your lordship of that letter and those orders."

On these documents I shall make no remarks. They are their own evidence, and shew what the limits of Virginia were while a British province; and as there was then no other authority by which they could be fixed, and as the grant to the London company could not be a grant to any but themselves, and of consequence ceased to be when they ceased to exist, it remained a matter of choice in the crown, on its reassumption of the lands, to limit or divide them into separate governments, as it judged best, and from which there was not, and could not in the order of government, be any appeal. Neither was Virginia, as a province, affected by it, because the monies, in any case, arising from the sale of lands, did not go into her treasury; and whether to the crown or to the proprietors was to her indifferent. And it is likewise evident, from the secretary's letter, and the president's answer, that it was in contemplation to lay out a new colony on the *back* of Virginia, between the Allegany Mountains and the Ohio.

Having thus gone thro' the several charters, or grants, and their relation to each other, and shewn that Virginia cannot stand in succession to a private Grant, which has been extinct for upwards of 150 years; and that the western limits of Virginia, at the commencement of the revolution, were at the heads of the rivers emptying themselves into the Atlantic, none of which are beyond the Allegany Mountains; I now proceed to the second part, namely,

The reasonableness of her claims:

Virginia, as a British province, stood in a different situation with the crown of England to any of the other provinces, because she had no ascertained limits, but such as arose from the laying off new provinces and the proclamation of 1763. For the name, Virginia, as I have before mentioned, was the general name of all the country, and the dominion out of which the several governments were laid off: and in strict propriety, conformable to the origin of names, the province of Virginia was taken out of the dominion of Virginia. For the term, *dominion*, could not appertain to the province, which retained the name of Virginia, but to the crown, and from thence was applied to the whole country, and signified its being an appendage to the crown of England, as they now say *"our dominion of Wales."*

It is not possible to suppose there could exist an idea, that Virginia, as a British province, was to be extended to the south sea at the distance of three thousand miles. The dominion, as appertaining at that time to the crown, might be claimed to extend so far, but as a province the thought was not conceiveable, nor the practice possible. And it is more than probable, that the deception made use of to obtain the patent of 1609, by representing the south sea to be near where the Allegany Mountains are, was one cause of its becoming extinct; and it is worthy of remarking, that no history (at least that I have met with) mentions any dispute or litigation, between the crown and the company in consequence of the extinction of the patent, and the re-assumption of the lands; and therefore the negative evidence corroborating with the positive, make it, as certain as such a case can possibly be, that either the company received a compensation for the patent, or quitted it quietly, ashamed of the imposition they had acted, and their subsequent mal-administration. Men are not inclined to give up a claim where there is any ground to contend on, and the silence in which the patent expired is a presumptive proof that its fate, from whatever cause, was just.

There is one general policy which seems to have prevailed with the English in laying off new governments, which was, not to make them larger than their own country, that they might the easier hold them manageable: this was the case with every one except Canada, the extension of whose limits was for the political purpose of recognizing new acquisition of territory, not immediately convenient for colonization.

But, in order to give this matter a chance thro' all its cases, I will admit what no man can suppose, which is, that there is an English charter that fixes Virginia to extend from the Atlantic to the south sea, and contained within a due west line, set off two hundred miles below cape Comfort, and a north west line, set off two hundred miles above it. Her side, then, on the Atlantic (according to an explanation given in Mr. Bradford's Paper of September 29th, 1779, by an advocate for the Virginia claims) will be four hundred miles; her side to the south three thousand; her side to the west four thousand; and her north-west line about five thousand; and the quantity of land contained within these dimensions will be almost 4,000,000,000, that is, four thousand million of acres, which is more than ten times the quantity contained within the present United States, and above an hundred times greater than the kingdom of England.

To reason on a case like this is such a waste of time, and such an excess of folly that it ought not to be reasoned upon. It is impossible to suppose that any patent to private persons could be so intentionally absurd, and the claim grounded thereon is as wild as any thing the imagination of man ever conceived.

But if, as I before mentioned, there was a charter which bore such an explanation, and that Virginia stood in succession to it, what would that be to us any more than the will of Alexander, had he taken it in his head to have bequeathed away the world? Such a charter or grant must have been obtained by imposition and a false representation of the country, or granted in error, or both; and in any of, or all, these cases, the United States must reject the matter as something they can know nothing of, for the merits will not bear an argument, and the pretention of right stands upon no better ground.

Our case is an original one; and many matters attending it must be determined on their own merits and reasonableness. The territory of the rest of the states is in general, within known bounds of moderate extent, and the quota which each state is to furnish towards the expence and service of the war, must be ascertained upon some rule of comparison. The number of inhabitants of each state formed the first rule; and it was naturally supposed that those numbers bore nearly the same proportion to each other, which the territory of each state did. Virginia, on this scale, would be about one fifth larger than Pennsylvania, which would be as much dominion as any state could manage with happiness and convenience.

When I first began this subject, my intention was to be extensive on the merits, and concise on the matter of right; instead of which, I have been extensive on the matter of right, and concise on the merits or reasonableness: and this alteration in my design arose, consequentially, from the nature of the subject; for as a reasonable thing the claim can be supported by no argument, and therefore needs none to refute it; but as there is a strange propensity in mankind to shelter themselves under the sanction of a right, however unreasonable that supposed right may be, I found it most conducive to the interest of the case, to shew, that the right stands upon no better grounds than the reason. And shall therefore proceed to make some observations on,

The consequences of the claim.

The claim being unreasonable in itself and standing on no ground of right, but such as, if true, must from the quarter it is drawn be offensive, has a tendency to create disgust and sour the minds of the rest of the states. Those lands are capable, under the management of the United States, of repaying the charges of the war, and some of them, as I shall hereafter show, may, I presume, be made an immediate advantage of.

I distinguish three different descriptions of lands in America at the commencement of the revolution. Proprietary or chartered lands, as was the case in Pennsylvania. Crown lands, within the described limits of any of the crown governments; and crown residuary lands that were without, or beyond, the limits of any province; and those last were held in reserve whereon to erect new governments and lay out new provinces; as appears to have been the design by lord Hillsborough's letter and the president's answer, wherein he says "with respect to the establishment of a *new* colony on the *back* of Virginia, it is a subject of too great political importance for me to presume to give an opinion upon; however, permit me, my lord, to observe, that when that part of the country shall become populated it may be a wise and prudent measure."

The expression is a "*new colony* on the *back* of Virginia"; and referred to lands between the heads of the rivers and the Ohio. This is a proof that those lands were not considered within, but beyond, the limits of Virginia as a colony; and the other expression in the letter is equally descriptive, namely, *"We do not presume to say to whom our gracious sovereign shall grant his vacant lands"*. Certainly then, the same right, which, at that time, rested in the crown, rests now in the more supreme authority of the United States; and therefore, addressing the president's letter to the circumstances of the revolution it will run thus,

"We do not presume to say to whom the *sovereign United States* shall grant their vacant lands, and with respect to the settlement of a *new colony* on the *back* of Virginia, it is a matter of too much political importance for me to give an opinion upon; however, permit me to observe, that when that part of the country shall become populated it may be a wise and prudent measure."

It must occur to every person, on reflection, that those lands are too distant to be within the government of any of the present states; and, I may presume to suppose, that were a calculation justly made, Virginia has lost more by the decrease of taxables, than she has gained by what lands she has made sale of; therefore, she is not only doing the rest of the states wrong in point of equity, but herself and them an injury in point of strength, service and revenue.

It is only the United States, and not any single State, that can lay off new states and incorporate them in the union by representation; therefore, the situation which the settlers on those lands will be in, under the assumed right of Virginia, will be hazardous and distressing, and they will feel themselves at last like aliens to the common wealth of Israel, their habitations unsafe and their title precarious.

And when men reflect on that peace, harmony, quietude, and security, which is necessary to prosperity, especially in making new settlements, and think that when the war shall be ended, their happiness and safety will depend on a union with the states, and not a scattered people, unconnected with, and politically unknown to, the rest, they will feel but little inclination to put themselves in a situation, which, however solitary and recluse, it may appear, at present, will then be uncertain and unsafe, and their troubles will have to begin where those of the United States shall end.

It is probable that some of the inhabitants of Virginia may be inclined to suppose, that the writer of this, by taking up the subject in the manner he has done, is arguing unfriendly against their interest. To this he wishes to reply;

That the most extraordinary part of the whole is, that Virginia should countenance such a claim. For it is worthy of observing, that, from the beginning of the contest with Britain, and long after, there was not a people in America who discovered, thro' all the variety and multiplicity of public business, a greater fund of true wisdom, fortitude, and disinterestedness, than the then colony of Virginia. They were loved—They were reverenced. Their investigation of the assumed rights of Britain had a sagacity which was uncommon. Their reasonings were piercing, difficult to be equalled and impossible to be refuted, and their public spirit was exceeded by none. But since this unfortunate land scheme has taken place, their powers seem to be absorbed. A Torpor has overshaded them, and every one asks what is become of Virginia?

It seldom happens that the romantic schemes of extensive dominion are of any service to a government, and never to a people. They assuredly end at last in loss, trouble, division, and disappointment. And was even the title of Virginia good, and the claim admissible, she would derive more lasting and real benefit by participating it, than by attempting the management of an object so infinitely beyond her reach. Her share with the rest, under the supremacy of the United States, which is the only authority adequate to the purpose, would be worth more to her, than what the whole would produce under the management of herself alone, and that for several reasons.

First, because her claim not being admissible nor yet manageable, she cannot make a good title to the purchasers, and consequently can get but little for the lands.

Secondly, because the distance the settlers will be at from her, will immediately put them out of all government and protection, so far, at least, as relates to Virginia: and by this means she will render her frontiers a refuge to desperadoes, and a hiding place from justice; and the consequence will be perpetual unsafety to her own peace and that of the neighbouring states.

Thirdly, Because her quota of expence for carrying on the war, admitting her to engross such an immensity of territory, would be greater than she can either support or supply, and could not be less, upon a reasonable rule of proportion, than nine tenths of the whole. And

Lastly, because she must sooner or later relinquish them, and therefore to see her own interest wisely at first, is preferable to the alternative of finding it out by misfortune at last.

I have now gone thro' my examination of the claims of Virginia in every case which I proposed; and for several reasons wish the lot had fallen to another person.

But as this is a most important matter, in which all are interested, and the substantial good of Virginia not injured but promoted, and as few men have leisure, and still fewer have inclination, to go into intricate investigation, I have at last ventured on the subject.

The succession of the United States to the vacant western territory is a right they originally sat out upon, and in the pamphlet, *Common Sense*, I frequently mentioned those lands as a national fund for the benefit of all; therefore, resuming the subject, where I then left off, I shall conclude with concisely reducing to system what I then only hinted.

In my last piece, the *Crisis Extraordinary*, I estimated the annual amount of the charge of the war and the support of the several governments at two millions pounds sterling, and the peace establishment at three quarters of a million, and, by a comparison of the taxes of this country with those of England, proved that the whole yearly expence to us, to defend the country, is but a third of what Britain would have drawn from us by taxes, had she succeeded in her attempt to conquer; and our peace establishment only an eighth part; and likewise shewed, that it was within the ability of the states to carry on the whole of the war by taxation without having recourse to any other modes or funds. To have a clear idea of taxation is necessary to every country, and the more funds we can discover and organize the less will be the hope of the enemy, and the readier their disposition to peace, which it is now *their* interest more than *ours* to promote.

I have already remarked that only the United States and not any particular state can lay off new states and incorporate them in the union by representation; keeping, therefore, this idea in view, I ask, might not a substantial fund be quickly created by laying off a new state, so as to contain between twenty and thirty million of acres, and opening a land office in all the countries in Europe for hard money, and in this country for supplies in kind at a certain price.

The tract of land that seems best adapted to answer this purpose is contained between the Allegany Mountain and the river Ohio, as far north as the Pennsylvania line, thence extending down the said river to the falls thereof, thence due south into the latitude of the North-Carolina line, and thence east to the Allegany Mountain aforesaid—I, the more readily, mention this tract, because it is fighting the enemy at their own weapons, as it includes the same ground on which a new colony would have been erected, for the emolument of the crown of England, as appears by lord Hilsborough's and Dartmouth's letters, had not the revolution prevented its being carried into execution.

It is probable there may be some spots of private property within this tract, but to incorporate them into some government will render them more profitable to the owners, and the condition of the scattered settlers more eligible and happy than at present.

If twenty millions of acres of this new state be patented and sold at twenty pounds sterling per hundred acres, they will produce four million pounds sterling, which, if applied to continental expences only, will support the war for three years, should Britain be so unwise to herself to prosecute it against her own direct interest and against the interest and policy of all Europe. The several states will then have to raise taxes for their internal government only, and the continental taxes as soon as the fund begins to operate, will lessen, and if sufficiently productive will cease.

Lands are the real riches of all the habitable world and the natural funds of America. The funds of other countries are, in general, artificially constructed; the creatures of necessity and contrivance; dependent upon credit, and always exposed to hazard and uncertainty. But lands can neither be annihilated nor lose their value; on the contrary, they universally rise with population, and rapidly so, when under the security of effectual government. But this it is impossible for Virginia to give, and, therefore, that which is capable of defraying the expences of the empire, will, under the management of any single state, produce only a fugitive support to wandring individuals.

I shall now enquire into the effects which the laying out a new state, under the authority of the United States, will have upon Virginia.

It is the very circumstance she ought to, and must, wish for, when she examines the matter thro' all its case and consequences.

The present settlers being beyond her reach, and her supposed authority over them remaining in herself, they will appear to her as revolters, and she to them as oppressors; and this will produce such a spirit of mutual dislike, that in a little time a total disagreement will take place, to the disadvantage of both.

But under the authority of the United States the matter is

manageable, and Virginia will be eased of a disagreeable consequence.

Besides this, a sale of the lands, continentally, for the purpose of supporting the expence of the war, will save her a greater share of taxes, than what the small sale she could make herself, and the small price she could get for them, would produce.

She would likewise have two advantages which no other state in the union enjoys, first, a frontier state for her defence against the incursions of the Indians; and the second is, that the laying out and peopling a new state on the back of an old one, situated as she is, is doubling the quantity of its trade.

The new state, which is here proposed to be laid out, may send its exports down the Missisippi, but its imports must come thro' Chesapeak Bay, and consequently Virginia will become the market for the new state; because, tho' there is a navigation from it, there is none into it, on account of the rapidity of the Missisippi.

There are certain circumstances that will produce certain events whether men think of them or not. The events do not depend upon thinking, but are the natural consequence of acting; and according to the system which Virginia has gone upon, the issue will be, that she will get involved with the back settlers in a contention about *rights* till they dispute with her own claims, and, soured by the contention, will go to any other state for their commerce; both of which may be prevented, a perfect harmony established, the strength of the states encreased, and the expences of the war defrayed, by settling the matter now on the plan of a general right; and every day it is delayed the difficulty will be encreased and the advantages lessened.

But if it should happen, as it possibly may that the war should end before the money which the new state may produce be expended, the remainder of the lands therein may be set apart to reimburse those, whose houses have been burnt by the enemy, as this is a species of suffering which it was impossible to prevent, because houses are not moveable property: and it ought not to be, that because we cannot do every thing, that we ought not to do what we can.

Having said thus much on the subject, I think it necessary to remark, that the prospect of a new fund, so far from abating our endeavours in making every immediate provision for the supply of the army, ought to quicken us therein; for should the states see it expedient to go upon the measure, it will be at least a year before it can be productive. I the more freely mention this, because, there is a dangerous species of popularity, which, I fear, some men are seeking from their constituents by giving them grounds to believe, that if they are elected they will lighten the taxes; a measure, which, in the present state of things, cannot be done without exposing the country to the ravages of the enemy by disabling the army from defending it.

Where knowledge is a duty ignorance is a crime; and if any man whose duty it was to know better has encouraged such an expectation, he has either deceived himself or them: besides, no country can be defended without expence, and let any man compare his portion of temporary inconveniences arising from taxations, with the real distresses of the army for the want of supplies, and the difference is not only sufficient to strike him dumb, but make him thankful that worse consequences have not followed.

In advancing this doctrine, I speak with an honest freedom to the country; for as it is their good to be defended, so it is their interest to provide that defence, at least, till other funds can be organized.

As the laying out new states will some time or other be the business of the country, and as it is yet a new business to us; and as the influence of the war has scarcely afforded leisure for reflecting on distant circumstances, I shall throw together a few hints for facilitating that measure, whenever it may be proper for adopting it.

The United States now standing on the line of sovereignty, the vacant territory is their property collectively, but the persons by whom it may hereafter be peopled will have an equal right with ourselves; and therefore, as new states shall be laid off and incorporated with the present, they will become partakers of the remaining territory with us who are already in possession. And this consideration ought to heighten the value of lands to new emigrants; because, in making purchases, they not only gain an immediate property, but become initiated into the right and heirship of the states to a property in reserve, which is an additional advantage to what any purchasers under the late government of England enjoyed.

The setting off the boundary of any new state will naturally be the first step, and as it must be supposed not to be peopled at the time it is laid off, a constitution must be formed, by the United States, as the rule of government in any new state, for a certain term of years, (perhaps ten) or until the state become peopled to a certain number of inhabitants; after which, the whole and sole right of modelling their government to rest with themselves.

A question may arise, whether a new state should immediately possess an equal right with the present ones in all cases which may come before Congress.

This, experience will best determine; but at first view of the matter it appears thus; That it ought to be immediately incorporated into the union on the ground of a family right, such a state standing in the line of a younger child of the same stock; but as new emigrants will have something to learn when they first come to America, and a new state requiring aid rather than capable of giving it, it might be most convenient to admit its immediate representation into Congress, there to sit, hear, and debate, on all questions and matters, but not to vote on any till after the expiration of seven years.

I shall in this place take the opportunity of renewing a hint which I formerly threw out in the pamphlet *Common Sense*, and which the several states will, sooner or later, see the convenience, if not the necessity, of adopting; which is, that of electing a Continental Convention, for the purpose of forming a Continental Constitution, defining and describing the powers and authority of Congress.

Those of entering into treaties, and making peace, they naturally possess, in behalf of the states, for their separate as well as their united good: but the internal control and dictatorial powers of Congress are not sufficiently defined, and appear to be too much in some cases, and too little in others; and therefore, to have them marked legally out will give additional energy to the whole, and new confidence to the several parts.

Common Sense, on the King of England's Speech

February 19 and 28, 1782

OF all the innocent passions which actuate the human mind, there is none more universally prevalent than curiosity. It reaches all mankind, and in matters which concern us, or concern us not, it alike provokes in us a desire to know.

Altho' the situation of America, superior to every effort to enslave her, and daily rising into importance and oppulence hath placed her above the region of anxiety, it still left her within the circle of curiosity; and her fancy to see the speech of a man who had proudly threatened to bring her at his feet, was visibly marked with that tranquil confidence which cared nothing about its contents. It was enquired after with a smile, read with a laugh, and dismissed with disdain.

But, as justice is due, even to an enemy, it is right to say, that the speech is as well managed as the embarrassed condition of their affairs could well admit of; and though scarce a line of it is true, except the mournful story of Cornwallis, it may serve to amuse the deluded commons and people of England, for whom it was calculated.

"The war," says the speech, "is still unhappily prolonged by that restless ambition which first excited our enemies to commence it, and which still continues to disappoint my earnest wishes and diligent exertions to restore the public tranquility."

How easy is it to abuse truth and language, when men, by habitual wickedness, have learned to set justice at defiance. That the very man who began the war, who, with the most sullen insolence refused to answer, and even to hear the humblest of all petitions, who hath encouraged his officers and his army in the most savage cruelties, and the most scandalous plunderings, who hath stirred up the Indians on one side, and the Negroes on the other, and invoked every aid of Hell in his behalf, should now with an air of affected pity turn the tables from himself, and charge on another the wickedness that is his own, can only be equalled by the baseness of the heart that spoke it.

TO BE NOBLY WRONG IS MORE MANLY THAN TO BE MEANLY RIGHT, is an expression I once used on a former occasion, and it is equally applicable now. We feel something like respect for consistency even in error. We lament the virtue that is debauched into a vice, but the vice that affects a virtue becomes the more detestable: and amongst the various assumptions of character, which hypocrisy has taught, and men have practised, there is none that raises a higher relish of disgust, than to see disappointed inveteracy twisting itself, by the most visible falshoods, into an appearance of piety it has no pretentions to.

"But I should not," continues the speech, "answer the trust committed to the sovereign of a FREE PEOPLE, nor make a suitable return to my subjects for their constant, zealous, and affectionate attachment to my person, family and government, if I consented to sacrifice, either to my own desire of peace, or to their temporary ease and relief, THOSE ESSENTIAL RIGHTS AND PERMANENT INTERESTS, upon the maintainance and preservation of which, the future strength and security of this country must principally depend."

That the man whose ignorance and obstinacy first involved and still continues the nation in the most hopeless and expensive of all wars, should now meanly flatter them with the name of a FREE PEOPLE, and make a merit of his crime, under the disguise of their essential rights and permanent interests, is something which disgraces even the character of perverseness. Is he afraid they will send him to Hanover, or what does he fear? Why is the sycophant thus added to the hypocrite, and the man who pretends to govern, sunk into the humble and submissive memorialist?

What those essential rights and permanent interests are, on which the future strength and security of England must principally DEPEND, are not so much as alluded to. They are words which impress nothing but the ear, and are calculated only for the sound.

But if they have any reference to America, then do they amount to the disgraceful confession, that England, who once assumed to be her protectress, is now become her

DEPENDENT. The British king and ministry are constantly holding up the vast importance which America is of to England, in order to allure the nation to carry on the war: now whatever ground there is for this idea, it ought to have operated as a reason for not beginning it; and therefore they support their present measures at their own disgrace, because the arguments they now use, are a direct reflection on their former policy.

"The favourable appearance of affairs," continues the speech "in the East Indies and the safe arrival of the numerous commercial fleets of my kingdom must have given you satisfaction."

That things are not QUITE so bad every where as in America may be some cause of consolation, but can be none for triumph. One broken leg is better than two, but still it is not joy: and let the appearance of affairs in the East-Indies be ever so favourable, they are nevertheless worse than at first, without a prospect of their ever being better. But the mournful story of Cornwallis was yet to be told, and it was necessary to give it the softest introduction possible.

"But in the course of this year," continues the speech "my assiduous endeavours to guard the extensive dominions of my crown, have not been attended with success equal to the justice and uprightness of my views"—what justice and uprightness there was in beginning a war with America the world will judge of, and the unequalled barbarity with which it has been conducted is not to be worn from the memory by the cant of snivelling hypocrisy.

"And it is with GREAT CONCERN that I inform you that the events of war have been very unfortunate to my arms in Virginia, having ended in the loss of my forces in that province."—And OUR great concern is that they are not all served in the same manner.

"No endeavours have been wanting on my part" says the speech "to extinguish that spirit of rebellion which our enemies have found means to foment and maintain in the colonies; and to restore to my DELUDED SUBJECTS in America that happy and prosperous condition which they formerly derived from a due obedience to the laws."

The expression of DELUDED SUBJECTS is become so hacknied and contemptable, and the more so when we see them making prisoners of whole armies at a time, that the pride of not being laughed at would induce a man of common sense to leave it off. But the most offensive falshood in the paragraph, is the attributing the prosperity of America to a wrong cause. It was the unremitted industry of the settlers and their descendants, the hard labour and toil of persevering fortitude that were the true causes of the prosperity of America. The former tyranny of England served to people it, and the virtue of the adventurers to improve it. Ask the man who with his axe hath cleared a way in the wilderness and now possesses an estate, what made him rich, and he will tell you the labour of his hands, the sweat of his brow and the blessing of heaven. Let Britain but leave America to herself and she asks no more. She has risen into greatness without the knowlege and against the will of England, and has a right to the unmolested enjoyment of her own created wealth.

"I will order" says the speech "the estimates of the ensuing year to be laid before you. I rely on your wisdom and public spirit for such supplies as the circumstances of our affairs shall be found to require. Among the many ill consequences which attend the continuation of the present war, I must sincerely regret the additional burthens which it must unavoidably bring upon my faithful subjects."

Strange! That a nation must run thro' such a labyrinth of trouble, and expend such a mass of wealth to gain the wisdom which an hour's reflection might have taught. The final superiority of America over every attempt which an island might make to conquer her, was as naturally marked in the constitution of things, as the future ability of a giant over a dwarf is delineated in his features while an infant. How far Providence, to accomplish purposes, which no human wisdom could foresee, permitted such extraordinary errors, will be believed by some and doubted by others, and still a secret in the womb of time, must rest till futurity shall give it birth.

"In the prosecution of this great and important contest," says the speech, "in which we are engaged, I retain a firm confidence in the PROTECTION OF DIVINE PROVIDENCE, and a perfect conviction in the justice of my cause, and I have no doubt, but, that by the concurrence and support of my parliament, by the valour of my fleets and armies, and by a vigorous, animated, and united exertion of the faculties and resources of my people, I shall be enabled to restore the blessings of a safe and honorable peace to all my dominions."

The king of England is one of the readiest believers in the world. In the beginning of the contest he passed an act to put America out of the protection of the crown of England, and though Providence, for seven years together hath put him out of HER protection, still the man has no doubt. Like Pharoah on the edge of the Red sea, he sees not the plunge he is making, and precipitately drives across the flood that is closing over his head.

I think it is a reasonable supposition, that this part of the speech was composed before the arrival of the news of the capture of Cornwallis; for it certainly has no relation to their condition at the time it was spoken. But, be this as it may, it is nothing to us. Our line is fixt. Our lot is cast. And America, the child of fate, is arriving at maturity. We have nothing to do but by a spirited and quick exertion, to stand prepared for war or peace. Too great to yield, and too noble to insult; superior to misfortune, and generous in success, let us untaintedly preserve the character we have gained, and show to future ages, an example of unequalled magnanimity. There is something in the cause and consequence of America that has drawn on her the attention of all mankind. The world has seen her brave. Her love of liberty; her ardour in supporting it; the justice of her claims, and the constancy of her fortitude has won her the esteem of Europe, and attached to her interest the first power of that country.

Her situation now is such, that to whatever point, past, present or to come she cast her eyes, new matter rises to convince her she is right. In her conduct towards her enemy, no reproachful sentiment lurks in secret. No sense of injustice is left upon the mind. Untainted with ambition and a stranger to revenge, her progress hath been marked by providence, and she, in every stage of the conflict has blest her with success.

But let not America wrap herself up in delusive hope and suppose the business done. The least remissness in preparation, the least relax in execution, will only serve to prolong

the war and increase expences. If our enemies can draw consolation from misfortune, and exert themselves upon dispair,
how much more ought we, who are to win a continent by the
conquest and have already an earnest of success.

[To be continued in a future paper.]

————————

[Continued from our Paper of the 19th Instant.]
Having in the preceding part made my remarks on the several
matters which the speech contains, I shall now make my remarks on what it does not contain.

There is not a syllable in it respecting alliances. Either the
injustice of Britain is too glaring, or her condition too desperate, or both, for any neighbouring power to come to her
support. In the beginning of the contest, when she had only
America to contend with, she hired assistance from Hesse and
other smaller States of Germany, and for nearly three years
did America, young, raw, undisciplined and unprovided,
stand against the power of Britain, aided by twenty thousand
foreign troops, and made a compleat conquest of one entire
army. The remembrance of those things ought to inspire us
with confidence and greatness of mind, and carry us through
every remaining difficulty with content and chearfulness.
What are the little sufferings of the present day, compared
with the hardships that are past. There was a time, when we
had neither house nor home in safety; when every hour was
the hour of alarm and danger; when the mind, tortured with
anxiety, knew no repose, and every thing but hope and fortitude was bidding us farewel.

It is of use to look back upon these things; to call to mind
the times of trouble and the scenes of complicated anguish
that are past and gone. Then every expence was cheap, compared with the dread of conquest and the misery of submission. We did not stand debating upon trifles, nor contending
about the necessary and unavoidable charges of defence.
Every one bore his lot of suffering, and looked forward to
happier days and scenes of rest.

Perhaps one of the greatest dangers which any country can
be exposed to arises from a kind of trifling, which sometimes
steals upon the mind when it supposes the danger past; and

this unsafe situation marks at this time the peculiar crisis of America. What would she once have given, to have known that her condition at this day should be what it now is? and yet we do not seem to place a proper value upon it, nor vigorously pursue the necessary measures to secure it. We know we cannot be defended, nor yet defend ourselves, without trouble and expence. We have no right to expect it; neither ought we even to look for it. We are a people, who, in our situation, differ from all the world. We form one common floor of public good and, whatever is our charge, it is paid for our own interest and upon our own account.

Misfortune and experience have now taught us system and method; and the arrangements for carrying on the war are reduced to rule and order. The quota of the several States are ascertained, and I intend in a future publication to shew what they are, and the necessity as well as the advantages of vigorously providing them.

In the mean time, I shall conclude this paper with an instance of *British clemency*, from Smollet's History of England, volume the 11th, page 239, printed in London. It will serve to show how dismal is the situation of a conquered people, and that the only security is in effectual defence.

We all know that the Stuart family and the House of Hanover opposed each other for the Crown of England. The Stuart family stood first in the line of succession, but the other was the most successful.

In July, 1745, Charles, the son of the exiled king, landed in Scotland, collected a small force, at no time exceeding five or six thousand men, and made some attempts to re-establish his claim. The late Duke of Cumberland, uncle to the present King of England, was sent against him, and on the sixteenth of April following Charles was totally defeated at Culloden, in Scotland. Success and power are the only situations in which clemency can be shewn, and those who are cruel, because they are victorious, can, with the same facility, act any other degenerate characters.

"Immediately after the decisive action at Culloden, the Duke of Cumberland took possession of Inverness; where six and thirty deserters, convicted by a court-martial, were ordered to be executed: then he detached several parties to ravage the country. One of these apprehended the lady Mackintosh, who was sent prisoner to Inverness, plundered her house, and drove away her cattle, though her husband was actually in the service of the government. The castle of lord Lovat was destroyed. The French prisoners were sent to Carlisle and Penrith: Kilmarnock, Balmerino, Cromartie, and his son the lord Macleod, were conveyed by sea to London; and those of an inferior rank were confined in different prisons. The marquis of Tullibardine, together with a brother of the earl of Dunmore, and Murray the pretender's secretary, were seized and transported to the Tower of London, to which the earl of Traquair had been committed on suspicion; and the eldest son of lord Lovat was imprisoned in the castle of Edinburgh. In a word, all the goals of Great-Britain, from the capital northwards, were filled with those unfortunate captives; and great numbers of them were crowded together in the holds of ships, where they perished in the most deplorable manner, for want of air and exercise. Some rebel chiefs escaped in two French frigates that arrived on the coast of Lochaber about the end of April, and engaged three vessels belonging to his Britannic majesty, which they obliged to retire. Others embarked on board of a ship on the coast of Buchan, and were conveyed to Norway, from whence they travelled to Sweden. In the month of May, the duke of Cumberland advanced with the army into the Highlands, as far as Fort-Augustus, where he encamped; and sent off detachments on all hands, to hunt down the fugitives, and lay waste the country with fire and sword. The castles of Glengary and Lochiel were plundered and burned; every house, hutt, or habitation, met with the same fate, without distinction; and all the cattle and provision were carried off; the men were either shot upon the mountains, like wild beasts, or put to death in cold blood, without form of trial; the women, after having seen their husbands and fathers murdered, were subjected to brutal violation, and then turned out naked, with their children, to starve on the barren heaths. One whole family was inclosed in a barn, and consumed to ashes. Those ministers of vengeance were so alert in the execution of their office, that in a few days there was neither house, cottage, man, nor beast, to be seen within the compass of fifty miles; all was ruin, silence and desolation."

I have here presented the reader with one of the most shocking instances of cruelty ever practised, and I leave it to rest on his mind, that he may be fully impressed with a sense of the destruction he has escaped in case Britain had conquered America; and likewise, that he may see and feel the necessity, as well for his own personal safety, as for the honor, the interest, the happiness of the whole community, to omit or delay no one preparation necessary to secure the ground we so happily stand upon.

Common Sense, on Financing the War

March 5, 1782

TO THE PEOPLE OF AMERICA.

ON THE EXPENCES, ARRANGEMENTS AND DISBURSEMENTS FOR CARRYING ON THE WAR, AND FINISHING IT WITH HONOUR AND ADVANTAGE.

WHEN any necessity or occasion has pointed out the convenience of addressing the public, I have never made it a consideration whether the subject was popular or unpopular, but whether it was right or wrong; for that which is right will become popular, and that which is wrong, though by mistake it may obtain the cry or fashion of the day, will soon lose the power of delusion, and sink into disesteem.

A remarkable instance of this happened in the case of Silas Deane; and I mention this circumstance with the greater ease, because the poison of his hypocrisy spread over the whole country, and every man, almost without exception, thought me wrong in opposing him. The best friends I then had, except Mr. Laurens, stood at a distance, and this tribute, which is due to his constancy, I pay to him with respect, and that the readier, because he is not here to hear it. If it reaches him in his imprisonment, it will afford him an agreeable reflection.

"As he rose like a rocket, he would fall like the stick," is a metaphor which I applied to Mr. Deane in the first piece which I published respecting him, and he has exactly fulfilled the description. The credit he so unjustly obtained from the public, he lost in almost as short a time. The delusion perished as it fell, and he soon saw himself stripped of popular support. His more intimate acquaintance began to doubt and to desert him long before he left America, and at his departure he saw himself the object of general suspicion. When arrived in France, he endeavoured to effect by treason what he had failed to accomplish by fraud. His plans, schemes and projects, together with his expectation of being sent to Holland to negociate a loan of money, had all miscarried. He then began traducing and accusing America of every crime,

which could injure her reputation. "That she was a ruined country; that she only meant to make a tool of France, to get what money she could out of her, and then to leave her, and accommodate with Britain." Of all which, and much more, Colonel Laurens and myself, when in France, informed Dr. Franklin, who had not before heard of it. And to compleat the character of a traitor, he has, by letters to this country since, some of which, in his own hand writing, are now in the possession of Congress, used every expression and argument in his power to injure the reputation of France, and to advise America to renounce her alliance, and surrender up her independence.* Thus, in France, he abuses America, and in his letters to America he abuses France; and is endeavouring to create disunion between the two countries, by the same arts of double-dealing by which he caused dissensions among the Commissioners in Paris, and distractions in America. But his life has been fraud, and his character is that of a plodding, plotting, cringing mercenary, capable of any disguise that suited his purpose. His final detection has very happily cleared up those mistakes, and removed those uneasinesses, which his unprincipled conduct occasioned. Every one now sees him in the same light; for towards friends or enemies he acted with the same deception and injustice, and his name, like that of *Arnold*, ought now to be forgotten among us. As this is the first time I have mentioned him since my return from France, it is my intention it shall be the last. — From this digression, which for several reasons I thought necessary to give, I now proceed to the purport of my address.

I consider the war of America against Britain as the country's war, the public's war, or the war of the people in their own behalf, for the security of their natural rights, and the protection of their own property. It is not the war of Congress, the war of the Assemblies, or the war of Govern-

---

*Mr. William Marshal, of this city, formerly a pilot, who had been taken at sea and carried to England, and got from thence to France, brought over letters from Mr. Deane to America, one of which was directed to *"Robert Morris, Esq."* Mr. Morris sent it unopened to Congress, and advised Mr. Marshal to deliver the others there, which he did. The letters were of the same purport with those which have been already published under the signature of *S. Deane*, to which they had frequent reference.

ment, in any line whatever. The country first, by a mutual compact, resolved to defend their rights and maintain their independance, *at the hazard of their lives and fortunes.* They elected their Representatives, by whom they appointed their members to Congress, and said, *act you for us, and we will support you.* This is the true ground and principle of the war on the part of America, and, consequently, there remains nothing to do, but for every one to fulfil his obligation.

It was next to impossible that a new country, engaged in a new undertaking, could set off systematically right at first. She saw not the extent of the struggle she was involved in, neither could she avoid the beginning. She supposed every step she took, and every resolution she formed, would bring her enemy to reason, and close the contest. Those failing, she was forced into new measures; and these, like the former, being fitted to her expectations, and failing in their turn, left her continually unprovided and without system. The enemy likewise was induced to prosecute the war, from the temporary expedients we adopted for carrying it on. We were continually expecting to see their credit exhausted, and they were looking to see our currency fail; and thus, between their watching us and we them, the hopes of both have been deceived, and the childishness of the expectation has served to encrease the expence.

Yet who, through this wilderness of error, has been to blame? where is the man who can say, the fault has not in part been his? They were the natural unavoidable errors of the day. They were the errors of a whole country, which nothing but experience could detect, and time remove. Neither could the circumstances of America admit of system, till either the paper currency was fixed or laid aside. No calculation of finance could be made on a medium falling without reason, and fluctuating without rule.

But there is one error which might have been prevented, and was not; and as it is not my custom to flatter, but to serve mankind, I will speak it freely. It certainly was the duty of every assembly on the continent to have known, at all times, what was the condition of its treasury, and to have ascertained at every period of depreciation, how much the real worth of the taxes fell short of their nominal value. This knowledge, which might have been easily gained, would have enabled them to have kept their constituents well informed, which is one of the greatest duties of representation. They ought to have studied and calculated the expences of the war, the quota of each State, and the consequent proportion that would fall on each man's property for his defence; and this must easily have shewn to them, that a tax of an hundred pounds could not be paid by a bushel of apples or an hundred of flour, which was often the case two or three years ago. But instead of this, which would have been plain and upright dealing, the little line of temporary popularity, the feather of an hour's duration, was too much pursued; and in this involved condition of things, every State, for the want of a little thinking, or a little information, supposed that it supported the whole expences of the war, when in fact it fell, by the time the tax was levied and collected, above three fourths short of its own quota.

Impressed with a sense of the danger to which the country was exposed by this lax method of doing business, and the prevailing errors of the day, I published, last October was a twelvemonth, *The Crisis Extraordinary*, on the revenues of America, and the yearly expence of carrying on the war. My estimation of the latter, together with the civil list of Congress, and the civil list of the several States, was Two Million Pounds sterling, which is very nearly Nine Millions of Dollars.

Since that time, Congress have gone into a calculation, and have estimated the expences of the war department and the civil list of Congress (exclusive of the civil list of the several governments) at Eight Millions of Dollars; and as the remaining million will be fully sufficient for the civil list of the several States, the two calculations are exceedingly near each other.

This sum of Eight Millions of Dollars they have called upon the States to furnish, and their quotas are as follows, which I shall preface with the resolution itself.

By the United States in Congress assembled,
October 30th, 1781.
RESOLVED,
THAT the respective States be called upon to furnish the Treasury of the United States with their quotas of eight

millions of dollars, for the war department and civil list for the ensuing year, to be paid quarterly, in equal proportions, the first payment to be made on the first day of April next.

Resolved, That a Committee, consisting of a member from each State, be appointed to apportion to the several States the quota of the above sum.

November 2d.

The Committee, appointed to ascertain the proportions of the several States of the monies to be raised for the expences of the ensuing year, report the following resolutions:

That the sum of Eight Millions of Dollars, as required to be raised by the resolutions of the 30th of October last, be paid by the States in the following proportion.

New-Hampshire	373,598
Massachusetts.	1,307,596
Rhode-Island	216,684
Connecticut	747,196
New-York.	373,598
New-Jersey	485,679
Pennsylvania	1,120,794
Delaware	112,085
Maryland	933,996
Virginia	1,307,594
North-Carolina	622,677
South-Carolina	373,598
Georgia	<u>24,905</u>
	8,000,000 Dollars

Resolved,

That it be recommended to the several States to lay taxes for raising their quotas of money for the United States, separate from those laid for their own particular use.

On these resolutions I shall offer several remarks.

First. On the sum itself, and the ability of the country.

Secondly. On the several quotas, and the nature of a union. And

Thirdly. On the manner of collection and expenditure.

First. On the sum itself, and the ability of the country. As I know my own calculation is as low as possible, and as the sum called for by Congress, according to their calculation, agrees very nearly therewith, I am sensible it cannot possibly be lower. Neither can it be done for that, unless there is ready money to go to market with; and even in that case, it is only by the utmost management and œconomy that it can be made to do.

By the accounts which were laid before the British parliament last spring, it appeared that the charge of only subsisting, that is feeding, their army in America, cost annually Four Millions Pounds sterling, which is very nearly Eighteen Millions of Dollars. Now if, for Eight Millions, we can feed, clothe, arm, provide for and pay an army sufficient for our defence, the very comparison shows that the money must be well laid out.

It may be of some use, either in debate or conversation, to attend to the progress of the expences of an army, because it will enable us to see on what part any deficiency will fall.

The first thing is, to feed them and provide for the sick.

Secondly, to clothe them.

Thirdly, to arm and furnish them.

Fourthly, to provide means for removing them from place to place. And,

Fifthly, to pay them.

The first and second are absolutely necessary to them as men. The third and fourth are equally as necessary to them as an army. And the fifth is their just due. Now if the sum which shall be raised should fall short, either by the several acts of the States for raising it, or by the manner of collecting it, the deficiency will fall on the fifth head, the soldiers pay, which would be defrauding them, and eternally disgracing ourselves. It would be a blot on the Councils, the country, and the revolution of America, and a man would hereafter be ashamed to own he had any hand in it.

But if the deficiency should be still shorter, it would next fall on the fourth head, *the means of removing the army from place to place*; and in this case, the army must either stand still where it can be of no use, or seize on horses, carts, waggons, or any means of transportation it can lay hold of; and in this instance the country suffers. In short, every attempt to do a thing for less than it can be done for, is sure to become at last both a loss and a dishonour.

But the country cannot bear it say some. This has been the most expensive doctrine that ever was held out, and cost America millions of money for nothing. Can the country bear to be over-run, ravaged and ruined by an enemy, which will immediately follow where defence is wanting, and defence will ever be wanting where sufficient revenues are not provided. But this is only one part of the folly. The second is, that when the danger comes, invited in part by our not preparing against it, we have been obliged, in a number of instances, to expend double the sums, to do that which at first might have been done for half the money. But this is not all. A third mischief has been, that grain of all sorts, flour, beef, fodder, horses, carts, waggons, or whatever was absolutely or immediately wanted, have been taken without pay. Now, I ask, why was all this done, but from that extremely weak and expensive doctrine, *that the country could not bear it?* that is, that she could not bear, in the first instance, that which would have saved her twice as much at last; or, in proverbial language, that she could not bear to pay a penny to save a pound; the consequence of which has been, that she has paid a pound for a penny. Why are there so many unpaid certificates in almost every man's hands, but from the parsimony of not providing sufficient revenues? Besides, the doctrine contradicts itself; because, if the whole country cannot bear it, how is it possible that a part should; and yet this has been the case. For those things have been had, and they must be had; but the misfortune is, they have been had in a very unequal manner and upon expensive credit, whereas with ready money they might have been purchased for half the price, and no body distressed.

But there is another thought which ought to strike us, which is, — How is the army to bear the want of food, cloathing and other necessaries? The man who is at home can turn himself a thousand ways, and find as many means of ease, convenience or relief: But a soldier's life admits of none of those: Their wants cannot be supplied from themselves: For an army, though it is the defence of a State, is at the same time the child of a country, and must be provided for in every thing.

And lastly, The doctrine is false. There are not three millions of people, in any part of the universe, who live so well, or have such a fund of ability as in America. The income of a common labourer, who is industrious, is equal to that of the generality of tradesmen in England. In the mercantile line, I have not heard of one who could be said to be a bankrupt since the war began, and in England they have been without number. In America almost every farmer lives on his own lands, and in England not one in a hundred does. In short, it seems as if the poverty of that country had made them furious, and they were determined to risk all to recover all.

Yet, notwithstanding those advantages on the part of America, true it is, that had it not been for the operation of taxes for our necessary defence, we had sunk into a state of sloth and poverty: For there was more wealth lost by neglecting to till the earth in the years 1776, 77 and 78, than the quota of the tax amounts to. That which is lost by neglect of this kind, is lost for ever; whereas that which is paid, and continues in the country, returns to us again; and at the same time that it provides us with defence, it operates not only as a spur but as a premium to our industry.

I shall now proceed to the second head, viz. ON THE SEVERAL QUOTAS, AND THE NATURE OF A UNION.

There was a time when America had no other bond of union, than that of common interest and affection. The whole country flew to the relief of Boston, and, making her cause their own, participated her cares and administred to her wants. The fate of war, since that day, has carried the calamity in a ten-fold proportion to the southward; but in the mean time the union has been strengthened by a legal compact of the States, jointly and severally ratified, and that which before was choice, or the duty of affection, is now likewise the duty of legal obligation.

The union of America is the foundation-stone of her independence; the rock on which it is built; and is something so sacred in her constitution, that we ought to watch every word we speak, and every thought we think, that we injure it not, even by mistake. When a multitude, extended, or rather scattered, over a continent, in the manner we are, mutually agree to form one common centre whereon the whole shall move, to accomplish a particular purpose, all parts must act together and alike, or act not at all, and a stoppage in any one is a stoppage of the whole, at least for a time.

Thus the several States have sent Representatives to assemble together in Congress, and they have empowered that body, which thus becomes their centre, and are no other than themselves in representation, to conduct and manage the war, while their constituents at home attend to the domestic cares of the country, their internal legislation, their farms, professions or employments: For it is only by reducing complicated things to method and orderly connection that they can be understood with advantage, or pursued with success. — Congress, by virtue of this delegation, estimates the expence, and apportions it out to the several parts of the empire according to their several abilities; and here the debate must end, because each State has already had its voice, and the matter has undergone its whole portion of argument, and can no more be altered by any particular State, than a law of any State, after it has passed, can be altered by an individual. For with respect to those things which immediately concern the union, and for which the union was purposely established and is intended to secure, each State is to the United States what each individual is to the State he lives in. And it is on this grand point, this movement upon one centre, that our existence as a nation, our happiness as a people, and our safety as individuals, depend.

It may happen that some State or other may be somewhat over or under rated, but this cannot be much. The experience which has been had upon the matter has nearly ascertained their several abilities. But even in this case, it can only admit of an appeal to the United States, but cannot authorise any State to make the alteration itself, any more than our internal government can admit an individual to do so in the case of an act of assembly; for if one State can do it, then may another do the same, and the instant this is done the whole is undone.

Neither is it supposeable that any single State can be a judge of all the comparative reasons which may influence the collective body in quoating out the continent. The circumstances of the several States are frequently varying, occasioned by the accidents of war and commerce, and it will often fall upon some to help others, rather beyond what their exact proportion at another time might be; but even this assistance is as naturally and politically included in the idea of a union, as that of any particular assigned proportion; because we know not whose turn it may be next to want assistance; for which reason, that is the wisest State which sets the best example.

Though in matters of bounden duty and reciprocal affection, it is rather a degeneracy from the honesty and ardour of the heart to admit any thing selfish to partake in the government of our conduct, yet in cases where our duty, our affections, and our interest all coincide, it may be of some use to observe their union. The United States will become heir to an extensive quantity of vacant land, and their several titles to shares and quotas thereof will naturally be adjusted according to their relative quotas during the war, exclusive of that inability which may unfortunately arise to any State by the enemy holding possession of a part; but as this is a cold matter of interest, I pass it by, and proceed to my third head, viz,

On the manner of Collection and Expenditure.

It hath been our error, as well as our misfortune, to blend the affairs of each State, especially in money matters, with those of the United States; whereas it is to our case, convenience and interest to keep them separate. The expences of the United States for carrying on the war, and the expences of each State for its own domestic government, are distinct things, and to involve them is a source of perplexity and a cloak for fraud. I love method, because I see and am convinced of its beauty and advantage. It is that which makes all business easy and understood, and without which every thing becomes embarrassed and difficult.

There are certain powers which the people of each State have delegated to their legislative and executive bodies, and there are other powers which the people of every State have delegated to Congress, among which is that of conducting the war, and, consequently, of managing the expences attending it; for how else can that be managed, which concerns every State, but by a delegation from each. When a State has furnished its quota, it has an undoubted right to know how it has been applied, and it is as much the duty of Congress to inform the State of the one, as it is the duty of the State to provide the other.

In the resolution of Congress already recited, it is recommended to the several States *to lay taxes for raising their quotas of money for the United States, separate from those laid for their own particular use.*

This is a most necessary point to be observed, and the distinction should follow all the way through. They should be levied, paid and collected separately, and kept separate in every instance. Neither have the civil officers of any State, or the government of that State, the least right to touch that money which the people pay for the support of their army and the war, any more than Congress has to touch that which each State raises for its own use.

This distinction will naturally be followed by another. It will occasion every State to examine nicely into the expences of its civil list, and to regulate, reduce and bring it into better order than it has hitherto been; because the money for that purpose must be raised apart, and accounted for to the public separately. But while the monies of both were blended, the necessary nicety was not observed, and the poor soldier, who ought to have been the first, was the last who was thought of.

Another convenience will be, that the people, by paying the taxes separately, will know what they are for; and will likewise know that those which are for the defence of the country will cease with the war, or soon after. For although, as I have before observed, the war is their own, and for the support of their own rights and the protection of their own property, yet they have the same right to know that they have to pay, and it is the want of not knowing that is often the cause of dissatisfaction.

This regulation of keeping the taxes separate has given rise to a regulation in the office of finance, by which it is directed,

"That the receivers shall, at the end of every month, make out an exact account of the monies received by them respectively, during such month, specifying therein the names of the persons from whom the same shall have been received, the dates and the sums; which account they shall respectively cause to be published in one of the newspapers of the State; to the end that every citizen may know how much of the monies collected from him, in taxes, is transmitted to the treasury of the United States for the support of the war; and also, that it may be known what monies have been at the order of the Superintendant of Finance. It being proper and necessary, that in a free country the people should be as fully informed of the administration of their affairs as the nature of things will admit."

It is an agreeable thing to see a spirit of order and œconomy taking place, after such a series of errors and difficulties. A government or an administration, who means and acts honestly, has nothing to fear, and consequently has nothing to conceal; and it would be of use if a monthly or quarterly account was to be published, as well of the expenditures as of the receipts. Eight millions of dollars must be husbanded with an exceeding deal of care to make it do, and therefore, as the management must be reputable, the publication would be serviceable.

I have heard of petitions which have been presented to the Assembly of this State (and probably the same may have happened in other States) praying to have the taxes lowered. Now the only way to keep taxes low is, for the United States to have ready money to go to market with; and tho' the taxes to be raised for the present year will fall heavy, and there will naturally be some difficulty in paying them, yet the difficulty, in proportion as money spreads about the country, will every day grow less, and in the end we shall save some millions of dollars by it. We see what a bitter, revengeful enemy we have to deal with, and any expence is cheap compared to their merciless paw. We have seen the unfortunate Carolineans hunted like partridges on the mountains, and it is only by providing means for our defence that we shall not be in the same condition. When we think or talk about taxes, we ought to recollect that we lie down in peace, and sleep in safety; that we can follow our farms or stores, or other occupations, in prosperous tranquility; and that these inestimable blessings are procured to us by the taxes that we pay. In this view, our taxes are properly our insurance-money; they are what we pay to be made safe, and in strict policy are the best money we can lay out.

It was my intention to offer some remarks on the impost law of *five per cent.* recommended by Congress, and to be established as a fund for the payment of the loan-office certificates and other debts of the United States; but I have already extended my piece beyond my intention. And as this fund will make our system of finance compleat, and is strictly just, and consequently requires nothing but honesty to do it, there needs but little to be said upon it.

C. S.

Philad. March 5, 1782.

[As this is on an interesting subject, the author requests the several printers throughout the United States to give it a place in their papers, without dividing it.]

The Necessity of Taxation

April 4, 1782

TO THE PEOPLE OF AMERICA.

CASTING my eye over a former publication (the Crisis, No. 9) on the loss of Charlestown, I was tempted to introduce this address by a quotation from the first paragraph of that number, as it appeared to me exceedingly applicable to the present circumstances of the country.

"Had America pursued her advantages with half the spirit she resisted her misfortunes, she would before now have been a conquering and a peaceful people; but lulled in the lap of soft tranquility, she rested on her hopes, and adversity only could convulse her into action."

This hath been the character of America in every part, and in every state and stage of the contest. Warmed by a love of liberty, and provoked by a sense of injuries, she encountered danger without fear, and misfortune without despondency: But no sooner was the point accomplished, than she returned with folded arms to rest, and seemed to wait with patience for new disasters.—Yet there is one reflection to be drawn from this character and conduct that is worth attending to, which is, that it is the sign and the natural effect of right principles, but not of right policy. Misfortune ever separates men in a bad cause, and unites them in a good one. The former are industrious only while they are prosperous, the latter while they are distressed. The one acts from impulse, the other from contrivance; and the whole mode and progress of their conduct, and their times of rest and action, are the reverse of each other.

But as we have learned knowledge from misfortune, let us likewise learn it from mistake; and wisely add for once, if we never do it again, the ardour of adversity to the strength of victory. Let us combine the glowing powers of resolute resistance with the tranquil advantages which conquest bestows; and render the present year as superior in system, as the latter was splendid in success.

The progress and revolution of our domestic circumstances are as extraordinary as the revolution itself. We began with paper, and we end with gold and silver. We sat out with parties, and we are approaching to unity. The strength, the property, and even the fashion of the country, are confederated in her support. Like robust and healthy youth, she hath shook off the agues of the winter, and steps forward with constitutional bloom and vigour. By suffering distresses, she hath learned both to bear and to prevent them; and the experience of every day, whether drawn from good fortune or from bad, whether from wisdom or mistake, hath added something to her cause, and much to her judgment.

From this general state of circumstances I shall proceed to more particular matters.

In my last publication I stated the yearly expence of the war, namely, eight millions of dollars; the nature of the union by which the States are bound together; and the propriety of keeping the taxes for the defence of the country separate from the expences of government; the right of the people to be regularly informed of the monies received and expended; and the duty of the country to provide its several quotas. — Government and the people do not in America constitute distinct bodies. They are one, and their interest the same. Members of Congress, members of Assembly, or Council, or by any other name they may be called, are only a selected part of the people. They are the representatives of majesty, but not majesty itself. That dignity exists inherently in the universal multitude, and, though it may be delegated, cannot be alienated. Their estates and property are subject to the same taxation with those they represent, and there is nothing they can do, that will not equally affect themselves as well as others. If they call for supplies, they call on themselves in common with the country. Their situation enables them to know the more secret circumstances of things, and that such or such revenues are necessary for the security and defence of their constituents, and the accomplishment of the great object for which they are chosen. And here the distinction ends.

The furnishing ourselves with right ideas, and the accustoming ourselves to right habits of thinking, have a powerful effect in strengthening and cementing the mind of the country and freeing it from the danger of partial or mistaken notions. It is not all the ardour which the love of liberty can inspire, nor the utmost fortitude which the most heroic virtue can create, that will of themselves make us successful conquerors. We must come down to order, system and method, and go through the cool and judicious, as well as the animating and elevated parts of patriotism. Method is to natural power, what slight is to human strength, without which a giant would lose his labour, and a country waste its force.

At the commencement of the war much political wisdom was not absolutely necessary. The high spirit of the country in a great measure supplied its place, and the printing-presses furnished the means. They became our Peru and Mexico, and as we wanted we drew them forth. Any body of men might at that time have carried on the war, who had resolution enough to proceed; because the difficulties of finance were then unknown, and the money came created to their hands. But those times are changed, and there is now a call on the wisdom and judgment, as well as on the firmness and patriotism of the country. Our situation is such, that the more it is understood the better it will appear; and with the means in our power, we want nothing but the united disposition to employ them.

When America resolved on independance, and determined to be free, she naturally included within that resolution all the means, whether of men or money, necessary to effect it. She had laid herself out for greater sufferings, and more expence and loss, than she has hitherto experienced, except in Carolina and Georgia. The idea of getting rich had not in those days an existance. All she expected was to live, and all she hoped for was to be free. She had resolved to abandon her habitations, to desert her towns, and to form new settlements in the wilderness, rather than submit. There was no condition to which her imagination could extend, that was not preferable to the oppressions that threatened her; and the experience of several years has shewn her opinion just, and proved her resolution firm.

Yet while the war was carried on by the mass of general opposition, the business of the country got deranged. Agriculture, trade and commerce became neglected, and something like poverty began to appear. Yet the resolution suffered no abatement, and their losses served to provoke them the higher. But experience has shewn that the way to enrich a country, and render it systematically formidable, is to give every possible rest to the inhabitants, that they may follow their various occupations undisturbed. A man who is harrassed about, either by the inroads of the enemy, or by marching to oppose them, soon suffers more by loss of time and the neglect of his affairs, than what a portion of taxes sufficient for his defence would amount to. And therefore it is to the good of the whole, as well as to the interest of the individual, that every one, who can, sets himself down to his business, and contributes his quota of taxes as one of the first duties he owes to his family, to himself, and to his country. Every amusement ought to be dispenced with, every indulgence curtailed, and every possible œconomy practiced, both public and private, until a revenue sufficient for the protection and good of the country is obtained, and the debt to public justice satisfied.

I have no idea of that kind of policy which ends in expence, disappointment and disgrace; and those have ever been and ever will be the consequence of deficient and unequal revenues. America has resolved to defend herself, and to support her independance at all hazards and events. Every man's portion of that charge becomes his debt of honour, interest and happiness; and to see any one indulging himself at home while that portion is unpaid, and the soldier who defends him suffering in the field, is the highest dishonour a man can undergo.

It is pity but some other word beside taxation had been devised for so noble and extraordinary an occasion, as the protection of liberty and the establishment of an independant world. We have given to a popular subject an unpopular name, and injured the service by a wrong assemblage of ideas. A man would be ashamed to be told that he signed a petition, praying that he might pay *less* than his share of the public expence, or that those who had trusted the public might never receive their money; yet he does the same thing when he petitions against taxation, and the only difference is, that by taking shelter under the name, he seems to conceal the meanness he would otherwise blush at. Is it popular to pay our debts, to do justice, to defend an injured and insulted country, to protect the aged and the infant, and to give to Liberty a land to live in? then must taxation, as the means by which those things are to be done, be popular likewise.

But to take a more local view of matters. Why has the back country been ravaged by the repeated incursions of the enemy and the Indians, but from the inability of the revenue to provide means for their protection? And yet the inhabitants of those countries were among the first to petition against taxation. In so doing, they eventually prayed for their own destruction, and, unhappily for them, their prayer was answered. Their quota of taxes would have been trifling, compared with their losses, and, what is still worse, their domestic sorrows. Alas! how unwisely, how unfeelingly, does a man argue, when he puts the safety of his family in competition with his tax.

There is so much of the honour, interest and independance of America staked upon taxation, that the subject must to every reflective mind make a strong impression. As we are now circumstanced, it is the criterion of public spirit; the touchstone of our good affections; and he who pays it the instant it is called for, does more for his country's good than the loudest talker in America. In vain are all our huzzas for liberty, without accompanying them with solid support. They will neither fill the soldier's belly, nor cloathe his back, they will neither pay the public creditors, nor purchase our supplies. They are well enough in their places, and though they are the effusion of our hearts, they are no part of our substance.

The Assembly of this State, Pennsylvania, have unanimously gone through the bill for raising the sum of 1,120,000 Dollars, being their quota for the year: And, as an example worthy both of notice and imitation, the oppressed and distressed State of South-Carolina, notwithstanding the severity of its fate, has already done the same. Those people know, by woeful experience, the value of defence, and that the inconvenience of struggling with a tax for the protection of the country is not to be named, in competition with the losses they have borne, and the sorrows and sufferings they have undergone.

However inconvenient the tax may be, we know it can last but for a time. Our expences will cease with the war, and our taxation in consequence. But while the war continues, and so great a part of every thing that is near and valuable to a country depends upon her revenue, I shall consider and treat taxation as a popular good. When the war shall be over, the case will be totally altered, and my language, if I then speak at all, will be entirely different. Besides, America is a new character in the universe. She started with a cause divinely right, and struck at an object vast and valuable. Her reputation for political integrity, perseverance, fortitude, and all the manly excellencies, stands high in the world, and it would be a thousand pities that, with those happy introductions into life, she suffered the least spot or blot to fall upon her *moral* fame. Never let it be said, that the country who could do what America has done, defrauded the widow and the orphan of their property, and the soldier of his pay.

The tax will be attended with some inconvenience; but what is inconvenience, when compared with distress and the ruin and plunderings of an enemy. How many things of far greater inconvenience has America already undergone, nay, even flourished in the midst of, which she once thought impossible to be borne. I hold taxation, which is to be applied to her own defence and her own good, one of the lightest of her difficulties, when considered with those which were occasioned by the want of it. We have several times been on the crisis of destruction by the insufficiency of our public revenues, and the heart of America would have ached with concern and sorrow, could she at all times have known what her exact situation has been. It is now the only point we have to attend to, nay it is the only one that is worth attending to; for let us accomplish this, and the rest will follow; and that consolation which every man's mind will feel, at knowing that the public Treasury is furnished with an ability of providing for the defence of the country, will amply recompence the difficulties he may go through, and the endeavours he may make, in paying in his allotted share. We shall be freed from the just murmurs of the suffering soldier; our eyes and ears will be no longer shocked with tales of slighted faith and suspected credit; and the face of our public, and of consequence of our private affairs, will wear a new and satisfied countenance. The idea, *that the country cannot bear it*, is a reproach upon her honour and firmness. She has borne ten times as much. Her fortitude and her principles have been tried in a thousand instances of severer fortune; and it is a paradox not to be explained, and which ought to be exploded, that the people whom no force or misfortune could conquer, no temptation seduce, should, at the summit of success, trepan themselves into destruction by an ignoble and impolitic covetousness.

Let us be, in every respect, such a nation as we ought to be, and shew to the enemy that it is no more in her power to conquer us by system than by arms. The purse of America, with œconomy, is longer than that of Britain, managed as it is by corruption and extravagance. The people of America are not a poor people, why should they appear so. We hurt our credit, our honour, our reputation in the world, by proclaiming ourselves what we are not, and give encouragement to the enemy to prolong the war, by holding out an idea of our want of money to carry it on. It is easy to see by the complexion of the New-York papers, that the present spirited exertions of the country to keep her public treasury supplied have wounded the last hopes of the enemy. It is a blow they never expected America to give, and their astonishment is as great as their despair.

It is a remark, worth making, that the people have always been a step forwarder than their representatives. There never was a backwardness in the country to do its part, when the part to be done became known and understood. National money matters are naturally attended with a degree of intricacy, which renders them not so easily comprehended as those which are more simple and obvious. Those of America have, from the fluctuating state of the former currency, been involved in new and original difficulties, and it required much judicious management to bring them right, and a vigorous exertion in the country afterwards to keep them so.

The present condition of our money matters, as concisely as they can be stated, is as follows:

There is a large sum due to persons who have lent their money to the Loan-Office, and to those who have otherwise trusted the public. Those debts are to be ascertained and proved, and the money arising from the impost duty of five per cent. on all imported goods is to be applied as a fund for the payment of the interest and principal, until the whole of them shall be discharged. This is the provision made for our debts already contracted, and when once the interest on them shall be regularly drawn, and the principal put into a train for payment, they will become as valuable as bond debts.

The sum of eight millions of dollars, which is apportioned out to be raised by the United States, is for the maintenance and other expences of the army, and to defray the government charges of the continent. If this sum is compared with the immense expence which Britain is at, the difference will appear exceedingly striking. She is obliged to raise upwards of ninety millions of dollars in taxes and loans every year, to do what we can accomplish, with ready money and frugality, for eight millions. So great is the contrast between a country sunk in corruption and extravagance, and one whose object is founded in just principles, and her plans regulated by good management.

But the difference may be carried still further. When the war shall cease with us, our taxes for that purpose will cease with it. We know they cannot now last for any long time; whereas the taxes of Britain being laid on only for the purpose of paying the interest, and never the principal of her debts, must continue for ever.

The publishing the sums of money received from each State, and expended on their united account, will be attended with several good effects. It will give satisfaction, which is a necessary object in national concerns. It will create emulation, and detect delinquency. The opener and fairer public business is transacted, the better it succeeds. Where no fraud is intended, there can be no occasion for concealment, and it is not only necessary that measures should be just, but that every body should know them to be so.

A few days will now carry us to the period of seven years war, and so extraordinary is the case, that instead of the country becoming poor and exhausted, she is grown rich and plentiful. There has been a singular fate attended all our wants, for whenever we imagined we should be ruined, by not having something which could not be done without, it arrived, as if of itself, just time enough to prevent the mischief. The last remarkable instance was in the influx of hard money, almost at the very moment when the paper currency failed, by which the circumstances of public and private business are so materially improved, that matters cannot go wrong, if we set heartily about what is right.

COMMON SENSE.

Response to an Accusation of Bribery

May 1, 1782

FOR THE FREEMAN'S JOURNAL.

THO' I do not think it worth while altogether on my own account, to take notice of a piece in the last Freeman's Journal, in which a very unwise and unkind allusion is made to a publication of mine in the latter end of the year 1780, entitled, PUBLIC GOOD, yet as that allusion is connected with a public measure, I shall for that reason, more than for myself, give it an answer.

The piece I refer to in the Freeman's Journal is signed *"Caractacus"* and the writer introduces it with the following paragraphs, viz.

"The public may be imposed on, when the condition and intention of the author is concealed, but when this is discovered, we may easily see the influence of twelve thousand acres of land, in causing a man to use all his talents to defraud the United States of their landed property, and at the same time unjustly incense them against a sister state.

"Few knew that the design of publishing a pamphlet, intitled Public Good, was to wrest out of the hands of the United States, a tract of land called Indiana, and appropriate it to the use of a sett of men, who can scarcely be called friends to the United States, excepting a few characters: but the design was evident to some, before the bribe was incautiously published. Through a prospect of receiving no opposition, the company committed a little blunder in being rather premature in the publication of their present."

If Caractacus is really an honest man and sincerely means to support the right of the United States, to the vacant western territory, against all encroachments either from Virginia or else where, he will gladly make himself known to me, because I can and will assist him; but if he is privately interested in the encroachments which Virginia has made, and is only making use of the name of the *United States* as a cover, he will conceal himself from me.

It certainly can be nothing to Caractacus, or even to the public (only as a matter of curiosity) how I came by the facts and materials which enabled me to write the pamphlet *Public Good*. It is sufficient to the public that I obtained them, and made use of them to prove their right to the western lands by, and that without putting them to any expence. But as I never do any thing that I wish to conceal, I shall relate the whole transaction, and all the material circumstances belonging to it.

In the pamphlet *Common Sense* published in January 1776, I mentioned the vacant western lands, as a fund which at the end of the war would redeem the expences of it. And in the arguments used in Congress in favour of independence, those very lands were pointed out for the same purpose. But to the astonishment of every reasonable man the state of Virginia set up a wild unfounded claim to the best part, and opened an office for the sale of them. By which means she has exhausted and weakened herself, and done much injustice to all her sister states, without even performing her quota of duty.

But it was impossible for me to pursue the subject, from the want of materials and information. I was struck with the general magnitude of the wrong done to the states, but could not enter as an advocate on their behalf, because, as I have already stated, the papers and proofs necessary to proceed upon were not in my possession, neither did I know where to obtain them. Another difficulty I found, or rather felt, was, the disagreeableness of taking up a subject of controversy against any state in the union, and particularly against Virginia, whose character I had, on every former occasion accustomed myself to esteem, and with many of whose principal citizens I continued on terms of intimacy, and friendship. And this nicety carried me so far as to decline a proposal, from the executive council of Pennsylvania, or some of them, in the year 1779 to attend on the commission for settling the boundary line between this state and Virginia; *because I would not interfere between two states. But the interest of the United States makes another question.*

Some time in the summer 1779, major Trent and other gentlemen of the Indiana Company came to me and stated the exceeding injuries they were likely to sustain, and the distress which several families were exposed to by the unkind conduct of Virginia, in endeavouring to wrest from them a tract of land which had been ceded to them by the Indians as a compensation for injuries which they, or some of their tribes, had committed, and to obtain a ratification of which, the company had been put to very great expences. They asked me for my assistance in behalf of the sufferers, and offered me any compensation I would require. Private justice is undoubtedly due to all men, and where that fails, public justice can have but a slender foundation.

However I might be inclined to wish them redress, my answer was short and decisive, which was, *that I never had nor ever would have any thing to do in private affairs.* And here the conference ended.

In the latter end of the year 1780, col. George Morgan and other gentlemen came again to me and endeavoured to make me understand, that whatever might be the event of the company's affairs, they were in possession of certain papers, which might be rendered exceedingly useful to the public, and proposed leaving them in my hands for perusal, which they did.

Here I got the very materials I had long wished for. The industry of the company, in prosecuting their own affairs, had collected together papers and documents in which the public, or in other words the United States, were exceedingly interested. I saw by those papers that the claim of Virginia to the western territory was ill founded either in right or reason, and that I could render a very essential service to the country by disentangling the matter from the obscurity in which it was then involved.

On a second interview I informed the gentlemen of my opinion respecting the papers they had left with me, and that I could make a very good use of them for the public interest; but that I would on *no account* mix the matter with any thing relative to the private affairs of the company, which as they were then before Congress would likewise be improper. They agreed to my proposition, and left them in my hands to do as I pleased with. From these papers and materials I compiled and finished the pamphlet PUBLIC GOOD, in which there is not a line or syllable respecting the company and every argument in it is in support of the public right of the United

States. I was glad to get at the papers, and I made the same use of them as if there had been no such body as the Indiana Company. But if the public have derived any service from the publication, and have acquired by it a better knowledge of their rights than they had before, they undoubtedly are under some obligation to the company for lending the materials, as well as to me for making use of them. And altho' the pamphlet has been published above a year and a half, it has never yet been answered by the advocates for the Virginia claims. I know it cannot be answered with success. I have ever kept a clear head and an upright heart, and am not afraid of being replied to. I never took up a matter without fully believing it to be right, and never yet failed in proving it so. But in this case I am the friend of Virginia as well as of the United States; because it is evident from her present circumstances, that her claims and her conduct have tended to impoverish her.

That the pamphlet was of service to the company is certain; but this is a natural consequence. The encroachment of Virginia extended over the company's lands as well as over those of the United States; and the company and the public standing thus in the same predicament with respect to Virginia, were reciprocally benefited by the endeavours of either to detect and eject her encroachments; and it was because the interest of the company was thus bound up with that of the United states, that made the acceptance of their present agreeable to me.

Caractacus says that "The design of publishing the pamphlet entitled PUBLIC GOOD was to wrest out of the hands of the *United States* a tract of land called Indiana."

Let the pamphlet speak for itself. There are yet some remaining copies which may be had at Mr. Claypoole's Printing office in Market street. The design of the pamphlet was to wrest, if I may copy the expression, the whole western territory from the unjust and enormous claims of Virginia. But Caractacus has I believe confessed more than he was aware of, for when he says that it was to wrest Indiana out of the *hands of the United States*, the declaration goes to prove that Indiana *is within* the *dominion of the United States and not within that of Virginia*. And consequently all the other western territory must be in the same situation. This is the very fact which the company are labouring to establish, and they certainly must be right, because their opposers cannot avoid occasionally declaring the same thing.

Thus much for the pamphlet. Now for the twelve thousand acres of land.

As soon as the pamphlet was published I returned the materials which the company had put into my hands, and they unanimously ordered a deed to be made out to me for what they call a voters share, which is, I suppose about the quantity mentioned. But so little effect or influence had this upon me, that I set off for France without ever applying for the deed, and returned again, without ever thinking about it, or taking the least notice of it, and it was not until the matter was mentioned to me again about three weeks or a month ago, that I gave myself any concern respecting it. And as to the paragraph in the newspapers which Caractacus refers to, of the company presenting me with a quantity of land, it was my own proposition that it should be made known, and I think it a reputation to the company that they have done that which those who were infinitely more obliged and indebted to me have neglected to do. From me the states have received the unremitted service of seven years, and to them I have not been the expence of a private soldier. I have done every thing *of* myself and *from* myself. The interest of the heart alone has carried me through a thousand things which others would have failed in or staggered at; and therefore the less Caractacus says upon this matter the less dishonor he will bring to light.

But as it ever was my disposition to acknowledge any return of kindness or friendship, from whatever quarter it came, I shall, in this place take the opportunity of mentioning a circumstance respecting the disposition of the present house of assembly of this state.

When the office of register of wills (a place worth six or seven hundred pounds a year) was likely to be vacant, and which has since happened, the speaker of the house, the hon F. A. Muhlenberg, informed me, that, from the knowledge he had of the house, the members had often expressed a wish of shewing me some instance of their respect, and that if I thought the office of register would be convenient to me, he would mention it in the house and he believed they would present me with it, without any application on my part.

I expressed to the speaker my sense of his friendship and of the good intentions of the house, and at the same time signified to him, that the necessary attendance on an office, or being any way charged with the duties of one, would unavoidably ingross my attention and take me out of the only line of service in which I could be generally useful, and therefore declined giving him the trouble of mentioning me on the occasion. I at the same time acquainted him with the present the Indiana company had made me.

Yet after this and several other instances I could mention, comes some unknown person sheltered under the machinery of a printer, and tells the public, that because the Indiana company, of their own accord had presented me with a quantity of land, and which I desired might be made known, and which was made known by all the papers of this city, about a week before the deed was made out, that I had accepted a *bribe*; when if there is any one circumstance in my character which distinguishes itself from the rest, it is *personal disinterestedness*, and an anxiety to serve a public cause in preference to myself. I never sought place, office, nor reward, since I have been in America; nor ever suffered resentment or disgust, nor the ins and outs of parties to warp me from the line of public good. And I have the pleasure of seeing, by the experience of every day, that the consistency of my character and the disinterestedness of my conduct have made almost every man my friend.

As to Caractacus I ought to be obliged to him for forcing me into the opportunity of saying what otherwise would not have been known, and I am persuaded that a thousand such little and unjustifiable insinuations will answer no other purpose than to procure me as many new friends. I have stood through too many tryals to be affected now either in fame or feeling by anonymous hints and insignificant falshoods; and perfectly satisfied that the public are satisfied with me, nay even that they conceive themselves obliged to me, and that among other things for the pamphlet in question, I shall take my farewel of Caractacus, and leave him to pursue at pleasure or at random whatever he likes best, for I have something of more consequence to attend to than minding either him or his squibs. I would not give a farthing to know who he is, nor care whether he writes or holds his tongue. And I farther assure him, that so far as justice goes, I shall endeavour to assist the company in any thing which I conceive to be right, and no farther. For it would be very extraordinary, that I should serve a whole country seven years for nothing, and refuse it to those who have served me.

COMMON SENSE.

The Crisis

NUMBER XI

May 11, 1782

ON THE PRESENT STATE OF NEWS.

SINCE the arrival of two, if not three packets, in quick succession, at New York from England, a variety of unconnected news has circulated through the country, and afforded as great a variety of speculation.

That something is the matter in the cabinet and councils of our enemies on the other side the water is certain; that they have run their length of madness, and are under a necessity of changing their measures may easily be seen into; but to what this change of measures may amount, or how far it may correspond with our interest, happiness and duty, is yet uncertain; and from what we have hitherto experienced, we have too much reason to suspect them in every thing.

I do not address this publication so much to the people of America as to the British ministry, whoever they may be, for if it is their intention to promote any kind of negociation, it is proper they should know before hand, that the United States have as much honour as bravery; that they are no more to be seduced from their alliance than their allegiance; that their line of politics is formed, and not dependant, like that of their enemy, on chance and accident.

On our part, in order to know, at any time, what the British government will do, we have only to find out what they ought NOT to do, and this last will be their conduct. For ever changing and for ever wrong; too distant from America to improve circumstances, and too unwise to foresee them; scheming without principle, and executing without probability, their whole line of management has hitherto been blunder and baseness. Every campaign has added to their loss, and every year to their disgrace; till unable to go on, and ashamed to go back, their politics have come to a halt, and all their fine prospects to the halter.

Could our affections forgive or humanity forget the

wounds of an infant country, we might, under the influence of a momentary oblivion, stand still and laugh. But they are engraven where no amusement can conceal them, and of a kind for which there is no recompence. Can ye restore to us the beloved dead? Can ye say to the grave give up the murdered? Can ye obliterate from our memories those who are no more? Think not then to tamper with our feelings by insidious contrivance, nor to suffocate our humanity by seducing us to dishonour.

In January 1780 I published part of the Crisis No. VIII in the Philadelphia news-papers, but did not conclude it in the following papers, and the remainder has lain by me to the present day.

There appeared about that time some disposition in the British cabinet to cease the further prosecution of the war, and as I had formed my opinion, that whenever such a design should take place, it would be accompanied with a dishonourable proposition to America respecting France; I had addressed the remainder of that number to expose the baseness of any such proposition. But the arrival of the next news from England declared her determination to go on with the war, and consequently as the political object I had then in view was not become a subject, it was unnecessary in me to bring it forward, which is the reason it was never published.

The matter which I allude to in the unpublished part I shall now make a quotation of, and apply it as the more enlarged state of things at this day shall make convenient or necessary. It is as follows.

"By the speeches which have appeared from the British parliament it is easy to perceive to what impolitic and imprudent excesses their passions and prejudices have in every instance carried them during the present war. Provoked at the upright and honourable treaty between America and France, they imagined nothing more was necessary to be done to prevent its final ratification, than to promise, through the agency of their commissioners (Carlisle, Eden and Johnstone) a repeal of their once offensive acts of parliament. The vanity of the conceit was as unpardonable as the experiment was impolitic. And so convinced am I of their wrong Ideas of America, that I shall not wonder, if in the last stage of political phrenzy, they propose to her to break her alliance with France and enter into one with them. Such a proposition, should it ever be made, and it has already been more than once hinted in parliament, would discover such a disposition to perfidiousness, and such disregard of honour and morals, as would add the finishing vice to national corruption.—I do not mention this to put America on the watch, but to put England on her guard, that she do not, in the looseness of her heart, envelop in disgrace every fragment of reputation."—Thus for the quotation.

By the complexion of some part of the news which have transpired through the New-York papers, it seems probable that this insidious era in the British politics is beginning to make its appearance. I wish it may not; for that which is a disgrace to human nature, throws something of a shade over all the human character, and the individual feels his share of the wound that is given to the whole.

The policy of Britain has ever been to divide America in some way or other. In the beginning of the dispute, she practised every art to prevent or destroy the union of the states, well knowing that could she once get them to stand singly she could conquer them unconditionally. Failing in this project in America she renewed it in Europe; and after the alliance had taken place, she made secret offers to France to induce her to give up America, and what is still more extraordinary, she at the same time made propositions to doctor Franklin then in Paris, the very court to which she was secretly applying, to draw off America from France. But this is not all.

On the 14th of September, 1778, the British court, through their secretary, lord Weymouth, made application to the marquis D'Almadovar the Spanish ambassador at London, to "ask the MEDIATION" for these were the words of the court of Spain for the purpose of negociating a peace with France, leaving America (as I shall hereafter show) out of the question. Spain readily offered her mediation, and likewise the city of Madrid as the place of conference, but withall, proposed that the United States of America should be invited to the treaty, and considered as independent during the time the business was negociating. But this was not the view of England. She wanted to draw France from the war, that she might uninterruptedly pour out all her force and fury upon America; and being disappointed in this plan, as well through the open and generous conduct of Spain, as the determination of France, she refused the mediation she had solicited.

I shall now give some extracts from the justifying memorial of the Spanish court, in which she has set the conduct and character of Britain, with respect to America, in a clear and striking point of light.

The memorial, speaking of the refusal of the British court to meet in conference with commissioners from the United States, who were to be considered as independent during the time of the conference, says,

"It is a thing very extraordinary and even ridiculous, that the court of London, who treats the colonies as independent, not only in acting, but of right, during the war, should have a repugnance to treat them as such, only in acting during a truce or suspension of hostilities. The convention of Saratoga; the reputing general Burgoyne as a lawful prisoner, in order to suspend his trial; the exchange and liberating other prisoners made from the colonies; the having named commissioners to go and supplicate the Americans, at their own doors, request peace of them, and treat with them and the Congress; and finally, by a thousand other acts of this sort, authorised by the court of London, which have been, and are true signs of the acknowledgment of their independence.

"In aggravation to all the foregoing, at the same time the British cabinet answered the King of Spain in the terms already mentioned; they were insinuating themselves at the court of France by means of secret emissaries, and making very great offers to her to abandon the colonies and make peace with England. But there is yet more: for at this same time the English ministry were treating by means of another certain emissary, with doctor Franklin, minister plenepotentiary from the colonies, residing at Paris, to whom they made various proposals to disunite them from France, and accommodate matters with England.

"From what has been observed it evidently follows, that the whole of the English politics was, to disunite the two courts of Paris and Madrid, by means of the suggestions and offers she separately made to them; and also to separate the colonies from their treaties and engagements entered into with France, and induce them to arm against the house of Bourbon, or MORE PROBABLY TO OPPRESS THEM WHEN THEY FOUND, FROM BREAKING THEIR ENGAGEMENTS, THEY STOOD ALONE AND WITHOUT PROTECTORS.

"This, therefore, is the net they laid for the American states; that is to say, to tempt them with flattering and very magnificent promises to come to an accommodation with them, exclusive of any intervention of Spain or France, that the British ministry might always remain the arbiters of the fate of the colonies.

"But the Catholic king, (the king of Spain) faithful on the one part to the engagements which bind him to the most Christian king, (the king of France) his nephew; just and upright on the other, to his own subjects whom he ought to protect and guard against so many insults; and finally, full of humanity and compassion for the Americans and other individuals who suffer in the present war; he is determined to pursue and prosecute it, and to make all the efforts in his power, until he can obtain a solid and permanent peace, with full and satisfactory securities that it shall be observed."

Thus far the memorial; a translation of which, into English, may be seen in full, under the head of STATE PAPERS, in the Annual Register for 1779, page 367.

The extracts I have here given, serve to shew the various endeavours and contrivances of the enemy to draw France from her connection with America, and to prevail on her to make a separate peace with England, leaving America totally out of the question and at the mercy of a merciless, unprincipled enemy. The opinion, likewise, which Spain has formed of the British cabinet character for meanness and perfidiousness, is so exactly the opinion of America, respecting it, that the memorial, in this instance, contains our own sentiments and language: for people, however remote, who think alike will unavoidably speak alike.

Thus we see the insidious use which Britain endeavoured to make of the propositions for a peace under the mediation of Spain. — I shall now proceed to the second propositions under the mediation of the emperor of Germany and the empress of Russia; the general outline of which was, that a congress of the several powers at war should meet at Vienna, in 1781, to settle preliminaries of peace.

I could wish myself at liberty to make use of all the information I am possessed of on this subject, but as there is a delicacy in the matter, I do not conceive it prudent, at least at present, to make references and quotations in the same manner as I have done with respect to the mediation of Spain, who published the whole proceedings herself; and, therefore, what comes from me, on this part of the business, must rest on my own credit with the public, assuring them, that when the whole proceedings, relating to the proposed congress at Vienna, shall appear, they will find my account not only true but studiously moderate.

We know that at the time this mediation was on the carpet, the expectations of the British king and ministry ran high with respect to the conquest of America. The English packet which was taken with the mail on board, and carried into l'Orient in France, contained letters from lord G. Germaine to sir Henry Clinton, which expressed in the fullest terms the ministerial idea of a total conquest. Copies of those letters were sent to congress and published in the News-papers of last year. Colonel Laurens brought over the originals, some of which, signed in the hand writing of the then secretary, Germaine, are now in my possession.

Filled with these high ideas, nothing could be more insolent towards America than the language of the British court on the proposed mediation. A peace with France and Spain she anxiously solicited; but America, as before, should be left to her mercy, neither would she hear any proposition for admitting an agent from the United States into the congress of Vienna.

On the other hand, France with an open, noble and manly determination, and the fidelity of a good ally, would hear no proposition for a separate peace, nor even meet in congress at Vienna, without an agent from America: and likewise that the independant character of the United States, represented by the agent, should be fully and unequivocally defined and settled before any conference should be entered on. The reasoning of the court of France on the several propositions of the two Imperial courts, which relate to us, is rather in the stile of an American than an ally; and she advocated the cause of America as if she had been America herself.—Thus the second mediation, like the first, proved ineffectual.

But since that time a reverse of fortune has overtaken the British arms, and all their high expectations are dashed to the ground. The noble exertions to the southward, under general Greene, the successful operations of the allied arms in the Chesepeak; the loss of most of their islands in the West-Indies and Minorca in the Mediterranean; the persevering spirit of Spain against Gibraltar; the expected capture of Jamaica; the failure of making a separate peace with Holland, and the expence of an hundred millions sterling, by which all these fine losses were obtained, have read them a loud lesson of disgraceful misfortune, and necessity has called on them to change their ground.

In this situation of confusion and despair their present councils have no fixt character. It is now the hurricane months of British politics. Every day seems to have a storm of its own, and they are scudding under the bare poles of hope. Beaten, but not humbled; condemned, but not penitent, they act like men trembling at fate and catching at a straw.—From this convulsion in the entrails of their politics, it is more than probable that the mountain groaning in labour, will bring forth a mouse as to its size, and a monster in its make. They will try on America the same insidious arts they tried on France and Spain.

We sometimes experience sensations to which language is not equal. The conception is too bulky to be born alive, and in the torture of thinking we stand dumb. Our feelings imprisoned by their magnitude, find no way out, and, in the struggle of expression, every finger tries to be a tongue. The machinery of the body seems too little for the mind and we look about for helps to shew our thoughts by.—Such must be the sensation of America, whenever Britain steaming with corruption, shall propose to her to sacrifice her faith.

But exclusive of the wickedness, there is a personal offence contained in every such attempt. It is calling us villains; for no man asks another to act the villain unless he believes him to be inclined to be one. No man attempts to seduce a truly modest woman. It is the supposed loseness of her mind that starts the thought of seduction, and he who offers it calls her a prostitute. Our pride is always hurt by the same propositions which offend our principles: for when we are shocked at the crime we are wounded by the supposition of our compliance.

Could I convey a thought that might serve to regulate the public mind, I would not make the interest of the alliance the basis of defending it. All the world are moved by interest, and it affords them nothing to boast of. But I would go a step higher and defend it on the ground of honour and principle. That our public affairs have flourished under the alliance, that it was wisely made and has been nobly executed, that by its assistance we are enabled to preserve our country from conquest and expel those who sought our destruction, that it is our true interest to maintain it unimpaired, and that while we do so no enemy can conquer us; are matters which experience has taught us, and the common good of ourselves, abstracted from principles of faith and honour, would lead us to maintain the connection.

But over and above the mere letter of the alliance, we have been nobly and generously treated, and have had the same respect and attention paid us, as if we had been an old established country. To oblige and be obliged is fair work among mankind, and we want an opportunity of showing to the world that we are a people sensible of kindness and worthy of confidence. Character is to us, in our present circumstances, of more importance than interest. We are a young nation just stepping upon the stage of public life, and the eye of the world is upon us to see how we act. We have an enemy that is watching to destroy our reputation, and who will go any length to gain some evidence against us, that may serve to render our conduct suspected and our character odious; because, could she accomplish this, wicked as it is, the world would withdraw from us, as from a people not to be trusted, and our task then would become difficult.

There is nothing sets the character of a nation in a higher or lower light with others, than the faithfully fulfilling, or perfidiously breaking of treaties. They are things not to be tampered with; and should Britain, which seems very probable, propose to seduce America into such an act of baseness, it would merit from her some mark of unusual detestation. It is one of these extraordinary instances in which we ought not to be contented with the bare negative of Congress, because it is an affront on the multitude as well as on the government. It goes on the supposition that the public are not honest men, and that they may be managed by contrivance tho' they cannot be conquered by arms. But, let the world and Britain know that we are neither to be bought nor sold. That our mind is great and fixt; our prospect clear: and that we will support our character as firmly as our independence.

But I will go still farther. General Conway who made the motion in the British parliament for discontinuing OFFENSIVE war in America, is a gentleman of an amiable character. We have no personal quarrel with him. But he feels not as we feel; he is not in our situation, and that alone, without any other explanation, is enough.

The British parliament supposes they have many friends in America, and that when all chance of conquest is over, they will be able to draw her from her alliance with France. Now, if I have any conception of the human heart, they will fail in this more than in any thing they have yet tried.

This part of the business is not a question of politics only but of honour and honesty; and the proposition will have in it something so visibly low and base that their partizans, if they have any, will be ashamed of it. Men are often hurt by a mean action who are not started at a wicked one, and this will be such a confession of inability, such a declaration of servile thinking, that the scandal of it will ruin all their hopes.

In short, we have nothing to do but to go on with vigour and determination. The enemy is yet in our country. They hold New York, Charlestown and Savannah, and the very being in those places is an offence, and a part of offensive war, and until they can be driven from them or captured in them, it would be folly in us to listen to an idle tale.—I take it for granted that the British ministry are sinking under the impossibility of carrying on the war. Let them then come to a fair and open peace with France, Spain, Holland and America in the manner they ought to do; but until then we can have nothing to say to them.

COMMON SENSE.

To Sir Guy Carleton

I⊤ is the nature of compassion to associate with misfortune; and I address this to you in behalf even of an enemy, a captain in the British service now on his way to the Head Quarters of the American army, and unfortunately doomed to death for a crime not his own.—A sentence so extraordinary, an execution so repugnant to every human sensation, ought never to be told without the circumstances which produced it: and as the destined victim is yet in existence, and in your hands rest his life or death, I shall briefly state the case and the melancholy consequence.

Captain Huddy, of the Jersey militia, was attacked in a small fort on Tom's river, by a party of refugees in the British pay and service, was made prisoner together with his company, carried to New-York and lodged in the provost of that city; about three weeks after which, he was taken out of the provost down to the water side, put into a boat and brought again upon the Jersey shore, and there, contrary to the practice of all nations but savages, was hung up on a tree, and left hanging until found by our people, who took him down and buried him.

The inhabitants of that part of the country where the murder was committed, sent a deputation to general Washington with a full and certified state of the fact. Struck, as every human breast must be, with such brutish outrage, and determined both to punish and prevent it for the future, the general represented the case to general Clinton, who then commanded, and demanded that the refugee officer who ordered and attended the execution, and whose name is Lippencut, should be delivered up as a murderer: and in case of refusal, that the person of some British officer should suffer in his stead. The demand, though not refused, has not been complied with; and the melancholy lot (not by selection, but by casting lots) has fallen upon captain Asgil, of the guards, who, as I have already mentioned, is on his way from Lancaster to camp, a martyr to the general wickedness of the cause he engaged in, and the ingratitude of those he has served.

The first reflection which arises on this black business is, what sort of men must Englishmen be, and what sort of order and discipline do they preserve in their army, when, in the immediate place of their Head-Quarters, and under the eye and nose of their commander in chief, a prisoner can be taken at pleasure from his confinement and his death made a matter of sport.

The history of the most savage Indians does not produce instances exactly of this kind. They, at least, have a formality in their punishments. With them it is the horridness of revenge, but with your army it is the still greater crime, the horridness of diversion.

The British generals who have succeeded each other, from the time of general Gage to yourself, have all affected to speak in language they have no right to. In their proclamations, their addresses, their letters to general Washington and their supplications to congress (for they deserve no other name) they talk of British honour, British generosity and British clemency, as if those things were matters of fact; whereas, we whose eyes are open, who speak the same language with yourselves, many of whom were born on the same spot with you, and who can no more be mistaken in your words than in your actions, can declare to all the world, that so far as our knowledge goes, there is not a more detestable character, nor a meaner or more barbarous enemy than the present British one. With us you have forfeited all pretention to reputation, and it is only by holding you like a wild beast, afraid of your keepers, that you can be made manageable.—But to return to the point in question.

Tho' I can think no man innocent who has lent his hand to destroy the country which he did not plant, and to ruin those he could not inslave, yet abstracted from all Ideas of right or wrong on the original question, captain Asgil, in the present case, is not the guilty man. The villain and the victim are here separated characters. You hold the one and we the other. You disown or affect to disown and reprobate the conduct of Lippencut, yet you give him sanctuary; and by so doing you as effectually become the executioner of Asgil, as if you put the rope on his neck and dismissed him from the world.

Whatever your feelings on this extraordinary case may be

are best known to yourself. Within the grave of your own mind lies burried the fate of Asgil. He becomes the corpse of your will, or the survivor of your justice. Deliver up the one and you save the other; withhold the one and the other dies by your choice.

On our part the case is exceedingly plain; AN OFFICER HAS BEEN TAKEN FROM HIS CONFINEMENT AND MURDERED, AND THE MURDERER IS WITHIN YOUR LINES. Your army have been guilty of a thousand instances of equal cruelty, but they have been rendered equivocal and sheltered from personal detection. Here the crime is fixt; and is one of those extraordinary cases which can neither be denied nor paliated, and to which the custom of war does not apply; for it never could be supposed that such a brutal outrage would ever be committed. It is an original in the history of civilized barbarians, and is truly British.

On your part, you are accountable to us for the personal safety of the prisoners within your walls. Here can be no mistake; they can neither be spies nor suspected as such; your security is not endangered, nor your operations subjected to miscarriage, by men immurred within a dangeon. They differ in every circumstance from men in the field and leave no pretence for severity or punishment. But if to the dismal condition of captivity with you, must be added the constant apprehensions of death; if to be imprisoned is so nearly to be entombed; and, if after all, the murderers are to be protected and thereby the crime encouraged, wherein do you differ from Indians either in character or conduct.

We can have no idea of your honour or your justice in any future transaction, of what nature it may be, while you shelter within your lines an outrageous murderer and sacrifice in his stead an officer of your own. If you have no regard to us, at least spare the blood which it is your duty to save. Whether the punishment will be greater on he, who, in this case, innocently dies, or on he whom sad necessity forces to retaliate, is, in the nicety of sensation an undecided question? It rests with you to prevent the sufferings of both. You have nothing to do but to give up the murderer and the matter end.

But to protect him, be he who he may, is to patronize his crime, and to trifle it off by frivolous and unmeaning enquiries is to promote it. There is no declaration you can make, no promise you can give, that will obtain credit. It is the man and not the apology that is demanded.

You see yourself pressed on all sides to spare the life of your own officer, for die he will if you withhold justice. The murder of captain Huddy is an offence not to be borne with, and there is no security we can have that such actions or similar ones shall not be repeated, but by making the punishment fall upon yourselves. To destroy the last security of captivity, and to take the unarmed, the unresisting prisoner to private and sportive execution, is carrying barbarity too high for silence. The evil MUST be put an end to; and the choice of persons rests with you. But if your attachment to the guilty is stronger than to the innocent, you invent a crime that must destroy your character, and if the cause of your king needs to be so supported, forever cease, sir, to torture our remembrance with the wretched phrases of British honour, British generosity, and British clemency.

From this melancholy circumstance, learn, sir, a lesson of morality. The refugees are men whom your predecessors have instructed in wickedness the better to fit them to their master's purpose. To make them useful they have made them vile, and the consequence of their tutored villainy is now descending on the heads of their encouragers. They have been trained like hounds to the scent of blood and cherished in every species of dissolute barbarity. Their ideas of right and wrong are worn away in the constant habitude of repeated infamy, till like men practised in executions they feel not the value of another's life.

The task before you, tho' painful, is not difficult; give up the murderer, and save your officer, as the first outset of a necessary reformation.

COMMON SENSE.

Philadelphia, May 31, 1782.

To the Earl of Shelburne

October 29, 1782

A SPEECH which has been printed in several of the British and New-York News-papers, as coming from your Lordship, in answer to one from the Duke of Richmond of the 10th of July last, contains expressions and opinions so new and singular, and so enveloped in mysterious reasoning, that I address this publication to you, for the purpose of giving them a free and candid examination. The speech I allude to is in these words:

"His Lordship said it had been mentioned in another place, that he had been guilty of inconsistence. To clear himself of this, he asserted that he still held the same principles in respect to American independence, which he at first imbibed. He had been, and yet was of opinion, whenever the Parliament of Great-Britain acknowledges that point, the sun of England's glory is set for ever. Such were the sentiments he possessed on a former day, and such the sentiments he continued to hold at this hour. It was the opinion of Lord Chatham, and the opinion of many able statesmen. Other noble Lords, however, think differently; and as the majority of the cabinet support them, he acquiesced in the measure; dissenting from the idea, and the point is settled for bringing the matter into the full discussion of Parliament, where it will be candidly, fairly, and impartially debated. The independence of America would end in the ruin of England; and that a peace patched up with France would give that proud enemy the means of yet trampling on this country. The sun of England's glory he wished not to see set for ever; he looked for a spark at least to be left, which might in time light us up to a new day. But if independence was to be granted, if Parliament deemed that measure prudent, he foresaw in his own mind that England was undone. He wished to God that he had been deputed to Congress, that he might plead the cause of that country as well as of this, and that he might exercise whatever powers he possessed, as an orator, to save both from ruin, in a conviction to Congress, that, if their independence was signed, their liberties were gone for ever.

"Peace, his Lordship added, was a desirable object, but it must be an honourable peace, and not an humiliating one, dictated by France, or insisted on by America. It was very true this kingdom was not in a flourishing state, it was impover-ished by war. But if we were not rich, it was evident that France was poor. If we were straitened in our finances, the enemy were exhausted in their resources. This was a great empire; it abounded with brave men, who were able and will-ing to fight in a common cause; the language of humiliation should not therefore be the language of Great-Britain. His Lordship said that he was not ashamed nor afraid of those expressions going to America. There were numbers, great numbers there, who were of the same way of thinking, in respect to that country being dependent on this, and who, with his Lordship, perceived ruin and independence linked together."

Thus far the speech, on which I remark,—That his Lord-ship is a total stranger to the mind and sentiments of America; that he has wrapped himself up in fond delusion that some-thing less than independence may, under his administration, be accepted; and he wishes himself sent to Congress, to prove, the most extraordinary of all doctrines, which is, that independence, the sublimest of all human conditions, is loss of liberty.

In answer to which we may say, that in order to know what the contrary word DEPENDENCE means, we have only to look back to those years of severe humiliation, when the mildest of all petitions could obtain no other notice than the haughtiest of all insults; and when the base terms of unconditional submission were demanded, or undistinguishable destruction threatened. It is nothing to us that the Ministry have been changed, for they may be changed again. The guilt of govern-ment is the crime of a whole country; and the nation that can, though but for a moment, think and act as England has done, can never afterwards be believed or trusted. There are cases in which it is as impossible to restore character to life, as it is to recover the dead. It is a phœnix that can expire but once, and from whose ashes there is no resurrection. Some offences are of such a slight composition, that they reach no further than the temper, and are created or cured by a thought. But the sin of England has struck the heart of America, and nature has not left it in our power to say we can forgive.

Your Lordship wishes for an opportunity to plead before Congress *the cause of England and America, and to save, as you say, both from ruin.*

That the country, which, for more than seven years, has sought our destruction, should now cringe to solicit our protection, is adding the wretchedness of disgrace to the misery of disappointment; and if England has the least spark of supposed honor left, that spark must be darkened by asking, and extinguished by receiving, the smallest favor from America: For the criminal, who owes his life to the grace and mercy of the injured, is more executed by living than he who dies.

But a thousand pleadings, even from your Lordship, can have no effect. Honor, interest, and every sensation of the heart would plead against you. We are a people who think not as you think; and what is equally true, you cannot feel as we feel. The situation of the two countries are exceedingly different. We have been the seat of war. You have seen nothing of it. The most wanton destruction has been committed in our sight. The most insolent barbarity has been acted on our feelings. We can look round and see the remains of burnt and destroyed houses, once the fair fruit of hard industry, and now the striking monuments of British brutality. We walk over the dead whom we loved, in every part of America, and remember by whom they fell. There is scarcely a village but brings to life some melancholy thought, and reminds us of what we have suffered, and of those we have lost by the brutishness of Britain. A thousand images arise to us, which, from situation, you cannot see, and are accompanied by as many ideas which you cannot know, and therefore your supposed system of reasoning would apply to nothing, and all your expectations die of themselves.

The question whether England shall accede to the independence of America, and which your Lordship says is to undergo a parliamentary discussion, is so very simple, and composed of so few cases, that it scarcely needs a debate.

It is the only way out of an expensive and ruinous war,

which has now no object, and without which acknowledgment there can be no peace.

But your Lordship says, *"The sun of Great-Britain will be set whenever she acknowledge the independence of America."* Whereas the metaphor would have been strictly just to have left the sun wholly out of the figure, and have ascribed her not acknowledging it to the influence of the moon.

But the expression, if true, is the greatest confession of disgrace that could be made, and furnishes America with the highest notions of sovereign independent importance. Mr. Wedderburne, about the year 1776, made use of an idea of much the same kind,— *"Relinquish America!* says he. *What is it but to desire a Giant to shrink spontaneously into a dwarf."*

Alas! Are those people who call themselves Englishmen, of so little internal consequence, that when America is gone, or shuts her eyes upon them, their sun is set, they can shine no more, but grope about in obscurity and contract into insignificant animals. Was America, then, the giant of the empire, and England only her dwarf in waiting? Is the case so strangely altered, that those who once thought we could not live without them, now declare they cannot exist without us? Will they tell to the world, and that from their first Minister of State, that America is their all in all, that it is by her importance only they can live and breathe and have a being? Will they, who threatened to bring us at their feet, now cast themselves at ours, and own that without us they are not a nation? Are they become so unqualified to debate on independence, that they have lost all idea of it themselves, and are calling to the rocks and mountains of America to cover their insignificance? Or, if America is lost, is it manly to sob over it like a child for its rattle, and invite the laughter of the world, by declarations of disgrace. Surely the more consistent conduct would be to bear it without complaint, and to shew that England, without America, can preserve her independence and a suitable rank with other European powers. You were not contented while you had her, and to weep for her now is childish.

But Lord Shelburne thinks that something may yet be done. What that something is, or how it is to be accomplished, is a matter in obscurity. By arms there is no hope.

The experience of nearly eight years, with the expence of an hundred million pounds sterling, and the loss of two armies, must positively decide that point. Besides the British have lost their interest in America with the disaffected. Every part of it has been tried. There is no new scene left for delusion: And the thousands who have been ruined by adhering to them, and have now to quit the settlements they had acquired, and be conveyed like transports to cultivate the deserts of Augustine and Nova Scotia, has put an end to all further expectations of aid.

If you cast your eyes on the people of England, what have they to console themselves with for the millions expended, or what encouragement is there left to continue throwing good money after bad? America can carry on the war for ten years longer, and all the charges of government included, for less than you can defray the charges of war and government for one year. And I, who know both countries, know well that the people of America can afford to pay their share of the expence much better than the people of England can. Besides, it is their own estates and property, their own rights, liberties and government, they are defending, and were they not to do it, they would deserve to lose all, and none would pity them. The fault would be their own, and their punishment just.

The British army in America care not how long the war lasts. They enjoy an easy and indolent life. They fatten on the folly of one country and the spoils of another; and, between their plunder and their pay, may go home rich. But the case is very different with the labouring farmer, the working tradesman, and the necessitous poor in England, the sweat of whose brow goes day after day to feed, in prodigality and sloth, the army that is robbing both them and us. Removed from the eye of the country that supports them, and distant from the government that employs them, they cut and carve for themselves and there is none to call them to account.

But England will be ruined, says Lord Shelburne, if America is independent.

Then, I say, is England already ruined, for America is already independent: And if Lord Shelburne will not allow this, he immediately denies the fact which he infers. Besides, to make England the meer creature of America, is paying too great a compliment to us, and too little to himself.

But the declaration is a rhapsody of inconsistence. For to say, as Lord Shelburne has numberless times said, that the war against America is ruinous, and yet to continue the prosecution of that ruinous war for the purpose of avoiding ruin, is a language which cannot be understood. Neither is it possible to see how the independence of America is to accomplish the ruin of England after the war is over, and yet not effect it before. America cannot be more independent of her, nor a greater enemy to her, hereafter than she is now; nor England derive less advantages from her than at present: Why then is ruin to follow in the best state of the case, and not in the worst; and if not in the worst, why is it to follow at all.

That a nation is to be ruined by peace and commerce, and fourteen or fifteen millions a year less expences than before, is a new doctrine in politics. We have heard much clamour of national savings and œconomy, but surely the true œconomy would be to save the whole charge of a silly, foolish and headstrong war; because, compared with this, all other retrenchments are baubles and trifles.

But is it possible that Lord Shelburne can be serious in supposing the least advantage can be obtained by arms, or that any advantage can be equal to the expence, or the danger of attempting it. Will not the capture of one army after another satisfy him, but all must become prisoners? Must England ever be the sport of hope, and the dupe of delusion? Sometimes our currency was to fail; another time our army was to disband; then whole provinces were to revolt; such a General said this and that; another wrote so and so; Lord Chatham was of this opinion; and Lord somebody else of another: To-day 20,000 Russians and 20 Russian ships of the line were to come; to-morrow the Empress was abused without mercy or decency. Then the Emperor of Germany was to be bribed with a million of money, and the King of Prussia was to do wonderful things; at one time it was Lo here! and then it was Lo there! Sometimes this power, and sometimes that power, was to engage in the war, just as if the whole world was as mad and foolish as Britain. And thus, from year to year, has every straw been catched at, and every will-with-a-whisp led them a new dance.

This year a still newer folly is to take place. Lord Shelburne wishes to be sent to Congress, and he thinks that something may be done.

Are not the repeated answers which Congress has given and which all America supports, that they will not even hear any proposals whatever, until the unconditional and unequivocal independence of America is recognised, are not, I say, these declarations answer enough?

But for England to receive any thing from America now, after so many insults, injuries and outrages, acted towards us, would shew such a spirit of meanness in her, that we could not but despise her for accepting it. And so far from Lord Shelburne coming here to solicit it, it would be the greatest disgrace we could do them to offer it. England would appear a wretch indeed, at this time of day, to ask or owe any thing to the bounty of America. Has not the name of Englishman blots enough upon it, without inventing more. Even Lucifer would scorn to reign in Heaven by permission, and yet an Englishman can creep for only an entrance into America. Or has a land of liberty so many charms, that to be a door-keeper in it is better than to be an English Minister of State?

But what can this expected something be? or, if obtained, what can it amount to but new disgraces, contentions and quarrels. The people of America have for years accustomed themselves to think and speak so freely and contemptuously of English authority, and the inveteracy is so deeply rooted, that a person invested with any authority from that country, and attempting to exercise it here, would have the life of a toad under a harrow. They would look on him as an interloper, to whom their compassion permitted a residence. He would be no more than the Mungo of the farce, and if he disliked that, he must set off. It would be a station of degradation, debased by our pity, and despised by our pride, and would place England in a more contemptible situation than any she has yet suffered by the war. We have too high an opinion of ourselves, ever to think of yielding again the least obedience to outlandish authority; and for a thousand reasons, England would be the last country in the world to yield it to. She has been treacherous, and we know it. Her character is gone, and we have seen the funeral.

Surely she loves to fish in troubled waters, and drink the cup of contention, or she would not now think of mingling her affairs with those of America. It would be like a foolish dotard taking to his arms the bride that despises him, or who has placed on his head the ensigns of her disgust. It is kissing the hand that boxes his ears, and proposing to renew the exchange. The thought is as servile as the war was wicked, and shews the last scene of the drama as inconsistent as the first.

As America is gone, the only act of manhood is to *let her go*. Your Lordship had no hand in the separation, and you will gain no honor by temporising politics. Besides, there is something so exceedingly whimsical, unsteady, and even insincere in the present conduct of England, that she exhibits herself in most dishonorable colours.

On the second of August last General Carleton and Admiral Digby wrote to General Washington in these words:

"The resolutions of the House of Commons of the 27th of February last have been placed in your Excellency's hands, and intimations given at the same time, that further pacific measures were likely to follow. Since which, until the present time, we have had no direct communications from England; but a mail is now arrived, which brings us very important information. We are acquainted, Sir, *by authority*, that negotiations for a general peace have already commenced at Paris, and that Mr. Grenville is invested with full powers to treat with all the parties at war, and is now at Paris in the execution of his commission. And we are farther, Sir, made acquainted, *that his Majesty, in order to remove all obstacles to that peace which he so ardently wishes to restore, has commanded his Ministers to direct Mr. Grenville, that the Independence of the Thirteen Provinces should be proposed by him in the first instance, instead of making it a condition of a general treaty.*"

Now, taking your present measures into view, and comparing them with the declarations in this letter, pray what is the word of your King, or his Ministers, or the Parliament, good for? Must we not look upon you as a confederated body of faithless, treacherous men, whose assurances are fraud, and their language deceit? What opinion can we possibly form of you, but that you are a lost, abandoned, profligate nation, who sport even with your own character, and are to be held by nothing but the bayonet or the halter.

To say, after this, *that the sun of Great Britain will be set, whenever she acknowledges the independence of America*, when the not doing it is the unqualified lie of government, can be no other than the language of ridicule, the jargon of inconsistency. There were thousands in America who predicted the delusion, and looked upon it as a trick of treachery, to take us from our guard, and draw off our attention from the only system of finance, by which we can be called, or deserve to be called, a sovereign, independent people. The fraud, on your part, might be worth attempting, but the sacrifice to obtain it is too high.

There were others who credited the assurances, because they thought it impossible that men who had their characters to establish should begin it with a lie. The prosecution of the war by the former Ministry was savage and horrid, since which it has been mean, trickish and delusive. The one went greedily into the passion of revenge, the other into the subtilties of low contrivance, till, between the crimes of both, there is scarcely left a man in America, be he whig or tory, who does not despise or detest the conduct of Britain.

The management of Lord Shelburne, whatever may be his views, is a caution to us, and must be to the world, never to regard British assurances. A perfidy so notorious cannot be hid. It stands even in the public papers of New-York, with the names of Carleton and Digby affixed to it. It is a proclamation that the King of England is not to be believed: That the spirit of lying is the governing principle of the Ministry. It is holding up the character of the House of Commons to public infamy, and warning all men not to credit them. Such is the consequence which Lord Shelburne's management has brought upon his country.

After the authorised declarations contained in Carleton and Digby's letter, you ought, from every motive of honor, policy and prudence, to have fulfilled them, whatever might have been the event. It was the least attonement you could possibly make to America, and the greatest kindness you could do to yourselves; for you will save millions by a general peace, and you will lose as many by continuing the war.

COMMON SENSE.

Philadelphia, October 29, 1782.

P. S. The manuscript copy of this letter is sent your Lordship, by the way of our Head-Quarters, to New-York, inclosing a late pamphlet of mine, addressed to the Abbe Reynal, which will serve to give your Lordship some idea of the principles and sentiments of America.

C. S.

The Last Crisis

NUMBER XIII

April 19, 1783

"The times that tried mens souls," * are over—and the greatest and compleatest revolution the world ever knew is gloriously and happily accomplished.

But to pass from the extremes of danger to safety—from the tumult of war to the tranquility of peace, though sweet in contemplation, requires a gradual composure of the senses to receive it. Even calmness has the power of stunning when it opens too instantly upon us. The long and raging hurricane that should cease in a moment, would leave us in a state rather of wonder than enjoyment; and some moments of recollection must pass before we could be capable of tasting the full felicity of repose. There are but few instances, in which the mind is fitted for sudden transitions: it takes in its pleasures by reflection and comparison, and those must have time to act, before the relish for new scenes is compleat.

In the present case—the mighty magnitude of the object—the various uncertainties of fate it has undergone—the numerous and complicated dangers we have suffered or escaped—the eminence we now stand on, and the vast prospect before us, must all conspire to impress us with contemplation.

To see it in our power to make a world happy—to teach mankind the art of being so—to exhibit on the theatre of the universe a character hitherto unknown—and to have, as it were, a new creation entrusted to our hands, are honors that command reflection, and can neither be too highly estimated, nor too gratefully received.

In this pause then of recollection—while the storm is ceasing, and the long agitated mind vibrating to a rest, let us look back on the scenes we have passed, and learn from experience what is yet to be done.

Never, I say, had a country so many openings to happiness

* "These are the times that try mens souls." Crisis No. I. published December 19, 1776.

348

as this. Her sitting out into life, like the rising of a fair morning, was unclouded and promising. Her cause was good. Her principles just and liberal. Her temper serene and firm. Her conduct regulated by the nicest steps of order, and every thing about her wore the mark of honor.

It is not every country (perhaps there is not another in the world) that can boast so fair an origin. Even the first settlement of America corresponds with the character of the revolution. Rome, once the proud mistress of the universe, was originally a band of ruffians. Plunder and rapine made her rich, and her oppression of millions made her great. But America needs never be ashamed to tell her birth, nor relate the stages by which she rose to empire.

The remembrance, then, of what is past, if it operates rightly, must inspire her with the most laudable of all ambition, that of adding to the fair fame she began with. The world has seen her great in adversity. Struggling, without a thought of yielding, beneath accumulated difficulties. Bravely, nay proudly, encountering distress, and rising in resolution as the storm encreased. All this is justly due to her, for her fortitude has merited the character.—Let, then, the world see that she can bear prosperity; and that her honest virtue in time of peace, is equal to the bravest virtue in time of war.

She is now descending to the scenes of quiet and domestic life. Not beneath the cypress shade of disappointment, but to enjoy in her own land, and under her own vine, the sweets of her labours, and the reward of her toil.—In this situation, may she never forget, that a fair national reputation is of as much importance as independence. That it possesses a charm which wins upon the world, and makes even enemies civil. That it gives a dignity which is often superior to power, and commands a reverence where pomp and splendor fail.

It would be a circumstance ever to be lamented and never to be forgotten, were a single blot, from any cause whatever, suffered to fall on a revolution, which to the end of time must be an honor to the age that accomplished it: and which has contributed more to enlighten the world, and diffuse a spirit of freedom and liberality among mankind, than any human event (if this may be called one) that ever preceded it.

It is not among the least of the calamities of a long continued war, that it unhinges the mind from those nice sensations which at other times appear so amiable. The continual spectacle of woe blunts the finer feelings, and the necessity of bearing with the sight renders it familiar. In like manner, are many of the moral obligations of society weakened, till the custom of acting by necessity, becomes an apology where it is truly a crime. Yet let but a nation conceive rightly of its character, and it will be chastely just in protecting it. None ever began with a fairer than America, and none can be under a greater obligation to preserve it.

The debt which America has contracted, compared with the cause she has gained, and the advantages to flow from it, ought scarcely to be mentioned. She has it in her choice to do, and to live, as happily, as she pleases. The world is in her hands. She has now no foreign power to monopolize her commerce, perplex her legislation, or controul her prosperity. The struggle is over, which must one day have happened, and, perhaps, never could have happened at a better time*.

---

*That the revolution began at the exact period of time best fitted to the purpose, is sufficiently proved by the event.—But the great hinge on which the whole machine turned is the UNION OF THE STATES: and this union was naturally produced by the inability of any one state to support itself against a foreign enemy without the assistance of the rest.

Had the states severally been less able than they were when the war began, their united strength would not have been equal to the undertaking, and they must, in all human probability, have failed—And on the other hand, had they severally been more able, they might not have seen, or, what is more, might not have felt, the necessity of uniting; and either by attempting to stand alone, or in small confederacies, would have been separately conquered.

Now, as we cannot see a time (and many years must pass away before it can arrive) when the strength of any one state, or of several united, can be equal to the whole of the present united states, and as we have seen the extreme difficulty of collectively prosecuting the war to a successful issue, and preserving our national importance in the world, therefore, from the experience we have had, and the knowledge we have gained, we must, unless we make a waste of wisdom, be strongly impressed with the advantage, as well as the necessity, of strengthening that happy union which has been our salvation, and without which we should have been a ruined people.

While I was writing this note, I cast my eye on the pamphlet COMMON SENSE, from which I shall make an extract, as it applies exactly to the case. It is as follows.

'I have never met with a man, either in England or America, who hath not confessed his opinion that a separation between the countries would take

And instead of a domineering master, she has gained an Ally, whose exemplary greatness, and universal liberality, have extorted a confession even from her enemies.

With the blessings of peace, independence, and an universal commerce, the states, individually and collectively, will have leisure and opportunity to regulate and establish their domestic concerns, and to put it beyond the power of calumny to throw the least reflection on their honor. Character is much easier kept than recovered, and that man, if any such there be, who, from any sinister views, or littleness of soul, lends unseen his hand to injure it, contrives a wound it will never be in his power to heal.

As we have established an inheritance for posterity, let that inheritance descend with every mark of an honorable conveyance. The little it will cost, compared with the worth of the states, the greatness of the object, and the value of national character, will be a profitable exchange.

But that which must more forcibly strike a thoughtful penetrating mind, and which includes and renders easy all inferior concerns, is the UNION OF THE STATES. On this, our great national character depends. It is this which must give us importance abroad and security at home. It is through this only that we are, or can be nationally known in the world. It is the flag of the united states which renders our ships and commerce safe on the seas, or in a foreign port. Our Mediterranean passes must be obtained under the same stile. All our treaties, whether of alliance, peace, or commerce, are formed

---

place one time or other: And there is no instance in which we have shewn less judgment, than in endeavouring to describe, what we call, the ripeness or fitness of the continent for independence.

'As all men allow the measure, and differ only in their opinion of the time, let us, in order to remove mistakes, take a general survey of things, and endeavour, if possible, to find out the VERY TIME. But we need not go far, the enquiry ceases at once, for, THE TIME HATH FOUND US. The general concurrence, the glorious union of all things prove the fact.

'It is not in numbers, but in a union, that our great strength lies. The continent is just arrived at that pitch of strength, in which no single colony is able to support itself, and the whole, when united, can accomplish the matter; and either more or less than this, might be fatal in its effects.'

PAMPHLET COMMON SENSE.

under the sovereignty of the united states, and Europe knows us by no other name or title.

The division of the empire into states is for our own convenience, but abroad this distinction ceases. The affairs of each state are local. They can go no farther than to itself. And were the whole worth of even the richest of them expended in revenue, it would not be sufficient to support sovereignty against a foreign attack. In short, we have no other national sovereignty than as united states. It would even be fatal for us if we had—too expensive to be maintained, and impossible to be supported. Individuals or individual states may call themselves what they please; but the world, and especially the world of enemies, is not to be held in awe by the whistling of a name. Sovereignty must have power to protect all the parts that compose and constitute it: and as UNITED STATES we are equal to the importance of the title, but otherwise we are not. Our union well and wisely regulated and cemented, is the cheapest way of being great—the easiest way of being powerful, and the happiest invention in government which the circumstances of America can admit of.—Because it collects from each state, that, which, by being inadequate, can be of no use to it, and forms an aggregate that serves for all.

The states of Holland are an unfortunate instance of the effects of individual sovereignty. Their disjointed condition exposes them to numerous intrigues, losses, calamities, and enemies; and the almost impossibility of bringing their measures to a decision, and that decision into execution, is to them, and would be to us, a source of endless misfortune.

It is with confederate states as with individuals in society; something must be yielded up to make the whole secure. In this view of things we gain by what we give, and draw an annual interest greater than the capital.—I ever feel myself hurt when I hear the union, that great palladium of our liberty and safety, the least irreverently spoken of. It is the most sacred thing in the constitution of America, and that which every man should be the most proud and tender of. Our citizenship in the united states is our national character. Our citizenship in any particular state is only our local distinction. By the latter we are known at home, by the former to the world. Our great title is, AMERICANS; our inferior one varies with the place.

So far as my endeavours could go, they have all been directed to conciliate the affections, unite the interests, and draw and keep the mind of the country together; and the better to assist in this foundation work of the revolution, I have avoided all places of profit or office, either in the state I live in, or in the united states; kept myself at a distance from all parties and party connections, and even disregarded all private and inferior concerns: and when we take into view the great work we have gone through, and feel, as we ought to feel, the just importance of it, we shall then see, that the little wranglings and indecent contentions of personal party, are as dishonorable to our characters, as they are injurious to our repose.

It was the cause of America that made me an author. The force with which it struck my mind, and the dangerous condition the country appeared to me in, by courting an impossible and unnatural reconciliation with those who were determined to reduce her, instead of striking out into the only line that could cement and save her, A DECLARATION OF INDEPENDENCE, made it impossible for me, feeling as I did, to be silent: and if, in the course of more than seven years, I have rendered her any service, I have likewise added something to the reputation of literature, by freely and disinterestedly employing it in the great cause of mankind, and shewing there may be genius without prostitution.

Independence always appeared to me practicable and probable; provided the sentiment of the country could be formed and held to the object: and there is no instance in the world, where a people so extended, and wedded to former habits of thinking, and under such a variety of circumstances, were so instantly and effectually pervaded, by a turn in politics, as in the case of independence, and who supported their opinion, undiminished, through such a succession of good and ill fortune, till they crowned it with success.

But as the scenes of war are closed, and every man preparing for home and happier times, I therefore take my leave of the subject. I have most sincerely followed it from beginning to end, and through all its turns and windings: and whatever country I may hereafter be in, I shall always feel an honest pride at the part I have taken and acted, and a gratitude to Nature and Providence for putting it in my power to be of some use to mankind.

COMMON SENSE.

Philadelphia, April 19, 1783.

Commerce with Britain and the Necessity of Union

December 9, 1783

TO THE PEOPLE OF AMERICA.

IN *"Rivington's New-York Gazette,"* of Dec. 6th, is a publication, under the appearance of a letter from London, dated Sept. 30th; and is on a subject which demands the attention of the United States.

The Public will remember, that a Treaty of Commerce between the United States and England was set on foot last Spring, and that until the said Treaty could be compleated, a Bill was brought into the British Parliament, by the then Chancellor of the Exchequer, Mr. Pitt, to admit and legalize (as the case then required) the Commerce of the United States into the British ports and dominions. But neither the one nor the other has been compleated. The Commercial Treaty is either broken off, or remains as it began; and the Bill in Parliament has been thrown aside. And in lieu thereof, a selfish system of English politics has started up, calculated to fetter the Commerce of America, by engrossing to England the carrying trade of the American produce to the West India Islands.

Among the advocates for this last measure, is Lord Sheffield, a member of the British Parliament, who has published a Pamphlet, entitled, *"Observations on the Commerce of the American States."* The pamphlet has two objects; the one is, to allure the Americans to purchase British manufactures; and the other, to spirit up the British Parliament to prohibit the Citizens of the United States from trading to the West-India Islands.

Viewed in this light, the pamphlet, though in some parts dextrously written, is an absurdity. It offends, in the very act of endeavouring to ingratiate; and his Lordship, as a politician, ought not to have suffered the two objects to have appeared together. The letter alluded to contains extracts from the pamphlet, with high encomiums on Lord Sheffield, for laboriously endeavouring (as the letter stiles it) "to shew the mighty advantages of retaining the carrying trade."

Since the publication of this pamphlet in England, the Commerce of the United States to the West-Indies, in American vessels, has been prohibited; and all intercourse, except in British bottoms, the property of, and navigated by British subjects, cut off.

That a country has a right to be as foolish as it pleases, has been proved by the practice of England for many years past: In her island-situation, sequestered from the world, she forgets that her whispers are heard by other nations; and in her plans of politics and commerce, she seems not to know, that other votes are necessary besides her own. America would be equally as foolish as Britain, were she to suffer so great a degradation on her flag, and such a stroke on the freedom of her Commerce, to pass without a balance.

We admit the right of any nation to prohibit the Commerce of another into its own dominions, where there are no treaties to the contrary; but as this right belongs to one side, as well as to the other, there is always a way left to bring avarice and insolence to reason.

But the ground of security which Lord Sheffield has chosen to erect his policy upon, is of a nature which ought, and I think must awaken, in every American, a just and strong sense of national dignity. Lord Sheffield appears to be sensible that in advising the British Nation and Parliament to engross to themselves so great a part of the Carrying Trade of America, he is attempting a measure which cannot succeed, if the Politics of the United States be properly directed to counteract the assumption.

But, says he, in his Pamphlet, *"It will be a long time before the American States can be brought to act as a Nation, neither are they to be feared as such by us."*

What is this more or less than to tell us, that while we have no National System of Commerce, the British will govern our trade by their own Laws and Proclamations as they please. The quotation discloses a truth too serious to be overlooked, and too mischievous not to be remedied.

Among other circumstances which led them to this discovery, none could operate so effectually, as, the injudicious, uncandid, and indecent opposition made by sundry persons in a certain State, to the recommendations of Congress last Winter, for an import duty of five per cent. It could not but explain to the British a weakness in the National Power of America, and encourage them to attempt restrictions on her trade, which otherwise they would not have dared to hazard. Neither is there any State in the Union, whose policy was more mis-directed to its interest than the State I allude to, because her principal support is the Carrying Trade, which Britain, induced by the want of a well-centered Power in the United States to protect and secure, is now attempting to take away. It fortunately happened (and to no state in the Union more than the State in question) that the Terms of peace were agreed on before the Opposition appeared, otherwise, there needs not a doubt, that if the same idea of the diminished authority of America, had occurred to them at that time as has occurred to them since, but they would have made the same grasp at the Fisheries, as they have done at the Carrying Trade.

It is surprising that an authority which can be supported with so much ease, and so little expence, and capable of such extensive advantages to the country, should be cavelled at by those whose duty it is to watch over it, and whose existance, as a people depends upon it. But this, perhaps, will ever be the case, till some misfortune awaken us into reason, and the instance now before us is but a gentle beginning of what America must expect, unless she guards her Union with nicer care and stricter honour. United, she is formidable, and that with the least possible charge, a Nation can be so: Separated, she is a medley of individual nothings, subject to the sport of foreign Nations.

It is very probable that the ingenuity of Commerce may have found out a method to evade and supercede the intentions of the British in interdicting the Trade with the West-India Islands. The language of both being the same, and their customs well understood, the vessels of one country may, by deception, pass for those of another. But this would be a practice too debasing for a Sovereign people to stoop to, and too profligate not to be discountenanced. An illicit Trade, under any shape it can be placed, cannot be carried on without a violation of truth. America is now Sovereign and Independent, and ought to act all her affairs in a regular stile of character. She has the same right to say that no British vessel shall enter her ports, or that no British manufactures shall be imported but in American bottoms, the property of, and navigated by American subjects, as Britain has to say the same thing respecting the West-Indies. Or she may lay a duty of ten, fifteen, or twenty shillings per ton, (exclusive of other duties) on every British vessel coming from any port of the West-Indies where she is not admitted to trade, the said tonnage to continue as long on her side as the prohibition continues on the other.

But it is only by acting in Union, that the usurpations of foreign Nations on the freedom of trade, can be counteracted, and security extended to the Commerce of America. And when we view a Flag, which to the eye is beautiful, and to contemplate its rise and origin, inspires a sensation of sublime delight, our National Honour must unite with our Interest to prevent injury to the one, or insult to the other.

COMMON SENSE.

New-York, Dec. 9, 1783.

On the Affairs of Pennsylvania

September 15, 1786

AT the commencement of the present constitution, it was strongly opposed, and as strongly contended for. This gave existence to two parties, which have since maintained nearly an equal contest, sometimes the one, and sometimes the other, prevailing at elections.

Among those who at that time opposed the alteration of the constitution, I bore my share, in a number of publications, entitled "A serious address to the people of Pennsylvania on the present state of their affairs."

Whether a single legislative Assembly, or a legislature composed of two branches, is best suited to support the just principles of equal liberty, is a point I never touched upon in any of those publications. My aim was to quiet the dispute, and prevent it from entangling the country, at a time when the utmost harmony of its powers was necessary to its safety. The constitution was upon experiment, and the manner in which a single House would use such an abundance of power would best determine whether it ought to be trusted with it. — Besides this, the constitution very prudently held out, in the forty-seventh section, the probability of its own defects, by appointing the means (by a convention) at the period of every seven years, of adding new articles or amending defective ones. The words in the said section are: — "The Council of Censors shall also have power to call a convention, to meet within two years after their sitting, if there appears to them an absolute necessity of amending any article of the constitution which may be defective, explaining such as may be thought not clearly expressed, and the adding such as are necessary for the preservation of the rights and happiness of the people." Therefore, any alteration which experience or circumstances shall prove necessary or proper is consistent with the constitution itself.

But the causes or reasons which then operated for not altering the constitution, could not be conclusively taken as causes or reasons for confirming it. When many people, those reasons went no further than to give the constitution a fair trial, or, rather, to give a single legislature a sufficient opportunity to shew with what degree of wisdom and prudence, impartiality and moderation, it would act. With others, the attempt to alter appeared to be ill-timed. And there were many who held an opinion, that has always prevailed among the political part of mankind, which is, that the form of government best calculated for preserving liberty in time of peace, is not the best form for conducting the operations of war; and that as the government of a single house had a considerable resemblance to the government of a single person, the present form, on account of the quickness of its execution, was preferable during the war to the proposed alterations.

There is, however, one fact very clearly deduced from the experience had, which is, that a single legislature, into the hands of whatever party it may fall, is capable of being made a compleat aristocracy for the time it exists: And that when the majority of a single house is made upon the ground of party prejudice, or fitted to be the dupes thereof, that its government, instead of comprehending the good of the whole dispassionately and impartially, will be that of party favor and oppression. To have established the present form as the best, it was absolutely necessary that the prejudices of party should have no operation within the walls of the legislature; for when it descends to this, a single legislature, on account of the superabundance of its power, and the uncontrouled rapidity of its execution, becomes as dangerous to the principles of liberty as that of a despotic monarchy. The present form was well intended, but the abuse of its power operates to its destruction. It withstood the opposition of its enemies, and will fall through the misconduct of its friends.

At the commencement of the revolution, it was supposed that what is called the executive part of a government was the only dangerous part; but we now see that quite as much mischief, if not more, may be done, and as much arbitrary conduct acted, by a legislature. In establishing the Executive Council, the constitution took care to prevent its being subject to inconsistent and contradictory conduct, and sudden convulsions. This is done by providing, that the periods of their elections shall not all expire at once. By this means, says the nineteenth section of the constitution, "there will in every subsequent year be found in the council a number of persons acquainted with the proceedings of the foregoing years, whereby the business will be more consistently conducted, and, moreover, the danger of establishing an inconvenient aristocracy be effectually prevented."

The council are as much the choice and representatives of the people as the assembly are, and have the same common interest in the community; and if it is necessary to guard against such events in the council, it is equally so in the legislature; and this would undoubtedly have been the case, could the convention have foreseen the capricious and inconsistent conduct of assemblies.

By the whole legislative power being entrusted to a single body of men, and that body expiring all at once, the state is subject to the perpetual convulsions of imperfect measures and rash proceedings; as by this means it may happen (as it has happened already) that a number of men, suddenly collected, unexperienced in business, and unacquainted with the grounds, reasons and principles, which former assemblies proceeded on in passing certain acts, and without seeking to inform themselves thereof, may precipitate the state into disorder by a confused medley of doing and undoing, and make the grievances they pretend to remove.

Of this kind was the attack made by a late assembly on that most useful and beneficial institution, incorporated by a former assembly, *The Bank of North-America*. The proceedings on this business are a stain to the national reputation of the state. They exhibit a train of little and envious thinking, a scene of passion of arbitrary principles and unconstitutional conduct; and the disgrace is filled up by assigning an untruth (which themselves have since acknowledged to) in the preamble to the act for annulling the charter of the Bank, as a cause for doing it. Such a disreputable circumstance in government could scarcely have happened, but from the cause I have already stated. For the Assembly which did it was newly formed, and elected on one of those sudden caprices which often happens in a free country, and there was not one man amongst them fully acquainted with the nature of the business they were going upon.

Public Banks are reckoned among the honors, privileges and advantages of a free people, and are never found among those under a despotic government. It is the confidence which people have in the measures and principles of government, and the strict observance of faith and honor on the part of government, which encourage people to put their money into circulation by means of a public Bank. A faithless or arbitrary government cannot be trusted, and therefore in free countries only are Banks established. In this state it has been the means of restoring that credit and confidence among individuals, which for many years was lost, and without which, agriculture, commerce, and every species of business, must decline and languish.

As gold and silver are not the natural products of Pennsylvania, we have no other hard money than what the produce of the country exported to foreign parts brings in. This being the case, the interest of the farmer and the merchant, the one being employed to raise the produce and the other to export it, are as naturally connected, as that of sowing the grain is connected with reaping the harvest; and any man must be held an enemy to the public prosperity, who endeavours to create a difference, or dissolve the mutual interest existing between them. The Plough and the Sail are the Arms of the state of Pennsylvania, and their connection should be held in remembrance by all good citizens.

As blood, tho' taken from the arm, is nevertheless taken from the whole body, so the attempt to destroy the Bank eventually operated to distress the farmer as well as the merchant; for if the one is prevented in the means of buying the produce of the country, the other, of consequence, is deprived of the opportunities of selling.

I shall conclude this paper with remarking, that so long as it shall be the choice of the people to continue the legislature in a single house, the circumstances of the country and the importance of the trust (being greater than that committed to any single body of men in any state in the union) evidently require, that the persons to be elected thereto be men freed from the bigotry and shackles of party, of liberal minds, and conversant in the means of increasing the riches of the state, and cultivating and extending the prosperity thereof.

COMMON SENSE.

Philad. Sept. 15, 1786.

Attack on Paper Money Laws

November 3, 1786

PAPER Money, Paper Money, and Paper Money! is now, in several of the states, both the bubble and the iniquity of the day. That there are some bad people concerned in schemes of this kind cannot be doubted, but the far greater part are misled. People are got so bewildered upon the subject that they put and mistake one thing for another. They say Paper Money has improved the country—Paper Money carried on the war, and Paper Money did a great many other fine things.

Not one syllable of this is truth; it is all error from beginning to end. It was CREDIT which did these things, and that credit has failed, by non-performance, and by the country being involved in debt and the levity and instability of government measures.

We have so far mistaken the matter that we have even mistaken the name. The name is not Paper Money, but Bills of Credit: But it seems as if we were ashamed to use the name, knowing how much we have abused the thing. All emissions of paper for government purposes is not making of money, but making use of credit to run into debt by. It is anticipating or forestalling the revenue of future years, and throwing the burden of redemption on future assemblies. It is like a man mortgaging his estate and leaving his successors to pay it off. But this is not the worst of it, it leaves us at last in the lurch by banishing the hard money, diminishing the value of the revenue, and filling up its place with paper, that may be like something to-day and to-morrow nothing.

So far as regards Pennsylvania, she cannot emit bills of credit, because the assembly which makes such an emission cannot bind future assemblies either to redeem them or receive them in taxes. The precedent of revoking the charter of the bank, established by a former assembly, is a precedent for any assembly to undo what another has done. It circumscribes the power of any assembly to the year in which it sits; that is, it cannot engage for the performance of any thing beyond that time. And as an assembly cannot issue bills of credit and redeem them within the year, and as it cannot by that precedent bind a future assembly so to do, it therefore cannot with the necessary security do it at all; because people will not put confidence in the paper promises or paper emissions of those who can neither perform the engagement within the time their own power exist nor compel the performance after that time is past. The politicians of the project for revoking the bank charter (and it was besides most wantonly done), to use a trite saying, aimed at the pidgeon and shot the crew—they fired at the bank and hit their own paper.

As to making those bills what is called legal tenders, we have no such thing in this state, which is one reason they have not depreciated more: But as it is a matter which engrosses the attention of some other states, I shall offer a few remarks on it.

The abuse of any power always operates to call the right of that power in question. To judge of the right or power of any assembly in America to make those bills a legal tender, we must have recourse to the principles on which civil government is founded; for if such an act is not compatible with those principles, the assembly which assumes such a power, assumes a power unknown in civil government, and commits treason against its principles.

The fundamental principles of civil government are security of our rights and persons as freeman, and security of property. A tender law, therefore, cannot stand on the principles of civil government, because it operates to take away a man's share of civil and natural freedom, and to render property insecure.

If a man had a hundred silver dollars in his possession, as his own property, it would be a strange law that should oblige him to deliver them up to any one who could discover that he possessed them, and take a hundred paper dollars in exchange. Now the case, in effect, is exactly the same; if he has lent a hundred hard dollars to his friend, and is compelled to take a hundred paper ones for them. The exchange is against his consent, and to his injury, and the principles of civil government provides for the protection, and not for the violation of his rights and property. The state, therefore, that is under the operation of such an act, is not in a state of civil government, and consequently the people cannot be bound to obey a law which abets and encourages treason against the first principles on which civil government is founded.

The principles of civil government extend in their operation to compel the exact performance of engagements entered into between man and man. The only kind of legal tenders that can exist in a country under a civil government is the particular thing expressed and specified in those engagements or contracts. That particular thing constitutes the legal tender. If a man engages to sell and deliver a quantity of wheat, he is not to deliver rye, any more than he who contracts to pay in hard money is at liberty to pay in paper or in any thing else. Those contracts or bargains have expressed the legal tender on both sides, and no assumed or presumptuous authority of any assembly can dissolve or alter them.

Another branch of this principle of civil government is, that it disowns the practice of retrospective laws. An assembly or legislature cannot punish a man by any new law made after the crime is committed; he can only be punished by the law which existed at the time he committed the crime. This principle of civil government extends to property as well as to life; for a law made after the time that any bargain or contract was entered into between individuals can no more become the law for deciding that contract, than, in the other case, it can become the law for punishing the crime; both of those cases must be referred to the laws existing at the time the crime was done or the bargain made. Each party then knew the relative situation they stood in with each other, and on that law and on that knowledge they acted, and by no other can they be adjudged—Therefore all tender laws which apply to the alteration of past contracts, by making them dischargable on either side, different to what was the law at the time they were made, is of the same nature as that law which inflicts a punishment different to what was the law at the time the crime was committed: For in all cases of civil government the law must be before the fact.

But was there no illegality in tender laws, they are naturally defective on another consideration. They cannot bind all and every interest in the state, because they cannot bind the state itself. They are, therefore, compulsive where they ought to be free; that is, between man and man, and are naturally free where, if at all, they ought to be compulsive: for in all cases where the state reserves to itself the right of freeing itself, it cannot bind the individual, because the right of the one stands on as good ground as that of the other.

COMMON SENSE.

Philadelphia, Nov. 3, 1786.

To Thomas Jefferson

February? 1788

AFTER I got home, being alone and wanting amusement I sat down to explain to myself (for there is such a thing) my Ideas of natural and civil rights and the distinction between them. I send them to you to see how nearly we agree.

Suppose 20 persons, strangers to each other, to meet in a Country not before inhabited. Each would be a sovereign in his own natural right. His will would be his Law, but his power, in many cases, inadequate to his right, and the consequence would be that each might be exposed, not only to each other, but to the other nineteen.

It would then occur to them that their condition would be much improved, if a way could be devised to exchange that quantity of danger into so much protection, so that each individual should possess the strength of the whole number.

As all their rights, in the first case, are natural rights, and the exercise of those rights supported only by their own natural individual power, they would begin by distinguishing between these rights they could individually exercise fully and perfectly and those they could not.

Of the first kind are the rights of thinking, speaking, forming and giving opinions, and perhaps all those which can be fully exercised by the individual without the aid of exterior assistance, or in other words, rights of personal competency. Of the second kind are those of personal protection of acquiring and possessing property, in the exercise of which the individual natural power is less than the natural right.

Having drawn this line they agree to retain individually the first Class of Rights or those of personal Competency; and to detach from their personal possession the second Class, or those of defective power and to accept in lieu thereof a right to the whole power produced by a condensation of all the parts. These I conceive to be civil rights or rights of Compact, and are distinguishable from Natural rights, because in the one we act wholly in our own person, in the other we agree not to do so, but act under the guarantee of society.

It therefore follows that the more of those imperfect natural rights, or rights of imperfect power we give up and thus exchange the more security we possess, and as the word liberty is often mistakenly put for security Mr. Wilson has confused his Argument by confounding the terms.

But it does not follow that the more natural rights of *every kind* we resign the more security we possess, because if we resign those of the first class we may suffer much by the exchange, for where the right and the power are equal with each other in the individual naturally they ought to rest there.

Mr. Wilson must have some allusion to this distinction or his position would be subject to the inference you draw from it.

I consider the individual sovereignty of the states retained under the Act of Confederation to be of the second class of rights. It becomes dangerous because it is defective in the power necessary to support it. It answers the pride and purpose of a few Men in each State, but the State collectively is injured by it.

To George Washington

My Dear Sir   London Octr 16th 1789

I need not tell you how much I rejoice at the prosperous accounts from America, or how happy I feel that you have relinquished the temptations of quiet retirement for the busy scenes of Public Good. Had the opportunity of your coming once more forward not have offered itself you might have injoyed retirement with serenity; but retirement would have lost its felicity, had it been haunted, as would have been the case, with the impression of having declined, for the sake of ease, a station in which you could be so publicly useful. I am certain you will feel the happier for this sacrifice, because to be perfectly so the mind must justify itself in every thing.

Mr Mappa the Gentleman who will present you this is an exiled Hollander, and, as I am informed, very capital in his line which is that of a letter-founder—I have given him a letter to Dr Franklin, the proper Patron of his Art, and as it is a branch in which improvement is wanted in America, I hope his coming will benifit both the Country and himself.

Mr Jefferson who, I expect, will arrive as soon as this letter, will inform you of my proceedings here—I am constructing a Bridge of one Arch in Partnership with the Walkers of Rotherham Yorkshire—The Arch is 110 feet Span and five feet high from the Cord line—We began it in July and I expect it in London about the Middle of Novr—In the mean time I am going over to France—A Share in two revolutions is living to some purpose—I shall be exceedingly happy to see a line from you, which if addressed to the Care of Benjn Vaughn Esqr.—Jeffries Square London will find me any where. With every Wish for your happiness and Mrs Washington's—I am—my Dear Sir your most affectiona. obedient Humble Servant

THOMAS PAINE

Please to remember me among the Circle of my friends.

To Benjamin Rush

Dear Friend   Paris March 16th 1790

As I do not expect this letter will come to hand of a considerable time I shall not enter into any details of news or circumstances. — My principal intention in writing it is to introduce a friend of mine and yourself, to the corresponding acquaintance of each other — Among the few intimates I have made on this side the water, I have met with none more congenial than the Gentleman I am writing of, M. Christie, and it is by his desire that I undertake this office — As it is probable your future acquaintance, with the Atlantic between you, may continue a long time, I will leave you, in the outset, nothing to guess at that may be convenient to know in an acquaintance of this kind — M. Christie's Father is a Banker at Montrose, Scotland, he has studied Physic as if he were to practice it, but his intention is to settle in London in the Banking line — He is passing some at Paris as a Man of observation before he undertakes, Atlas-like, the world on his own shoulders — He has made himself acquainted with as many subjects, and as many literary characters ancient and Modern as any one I have met with of his age — and is in confidence with several of our friends Dr. Price, Priestly and your friend Dr. Purcival of Manchester — by whom he was introduced a few days ago, by letter, to Mrs. Neckar and I have taken him with me to the Duke de la Rochefoucaut — the Marquis de la Fayette and others of my friends here.

I leave this Place in company with M. Rutlege tomorrow for London — I go expressly for the purpose of erecting an Iron Bridge which Mss. Walker's of Rotherham, Yorkshire, and I have already constructed, and is now ready for putting together. It is an Arch of 110 feet span, and five feet high, from the Cord line — It is as portable as common Bars of Iron, and can be put up and taken down at pleasure and is in fact rendering Bridges a portable manufacture — Sir Joseph Banks, after paying me some compliments by letter on this novel construction says — "I expect many similar improvements from your Countrymen, who think with vigour, and are in a great measure free from those Shackles of Theory which are imposed on the Minds of our people even before they are capable of exerting their mental faculties to advantage."

With respect to the French Revolution be assured that every thing is going on right—little inconveniences, the necessary consequence of pulling down and building up, may arise, but even those are much less than ought to have been expected. Our friend the Marquis is, like his Great Patron and Master, General Washington acting a great Part—I take over with me to London the Key of the Bastile which the Marquis entrusts to my Care as his present to General Washington and which I shall send by the first American Vessel to N. York—It will be yet some months before the New Constitution will be completed at which time there is to be procession, and I am engaged to return to Paris to carry the American flag—

In England, the Ministerial party oppose every Iota of Reformation—the high Benificed Clergy and Bishops, cry out that the Church is in danger and all those who are interested in the remains of the feudal System join the Clamour—I see very clearly that the conduct of the British Government by opposing reformations will detach great Numbers from the Political interest of that Country, and that France thro the influence of principles and the divine Right of Men to freedom will have a stronger party in England than she ever had thro the Jacobite bug-bear of the divine Right of Kings in the Stuart line—

I see by the papers that you have had a Convention to re-Model the Constitution—I very soon saw that the Constitutionalists would overthrow the Constitution by rashly using that power which was entrusted to their moderation—The spirit of the Constitution required prudence, and the Actors substituted temper and party in the room of it and thereby subjected the legislation of every year to the caprice of an election day—

I wish most anxiously to see my much loved America—it is the Country from whence all reformations must originally spring—I despair of seeing an Abolition of the infernal trafic in Negroes—we must push that matter further on your side the water—I wish that a few well instructed Negroes could be sent among their Brethren in Bondage, for until they are enabled to take their own part nothing will be done—

I hope this Summer will terminate all my prospects in Europe—but at any rate I will not exceed the spring Vessels of next year—Present me with much affection to all my friend—as I pride myself on having many I particularize none—

I am with many wishes for your happiness and your family & connections

Your affectionate friend,
THOMAS PAINE.

To George Washington

Sir   London May 1st 1790

Our very good Friend the Marquis de la Fayette has entrusted to my care the Key of the Bastile and a drawing, handsomely framed, representing the demolition of that detestible prison, as a present to your Excellency, of which his letter will more particularly inform. I feel myself happy in being the person thro' whom the Marquis has conveyed this early trophy of the Spoils of Despotism and the first ripe fruits of American principles transplanted into Europe to his great Master and Patron. When he mentioned to me the present he intended you my heart leaped with Joy—It is something so truly in character that no remarks can illustrate it, and is more happily expressive of his remembrance of his American friends than any letters can convey. That the principles of America opened the Bastile is not to be doubted, and therefore the Key comes to the right place.

I beg leave to suggest to your Excellency the propriety of congratulating the King and Queen of France (for they have been our friends) and the National assembly on the happy example they are giving to Europe. You will see by the King's Speech, which I inclose that he prides himself on being at the head of the Revolution, and I am certain that such a congratulation will be well received and have a good effect.

I should rejoice to be the direct bearer of the Marquis's present to your Excellency but I doubt I shall not be able to see my much loved America till next spring. I shall therefore send it by some *American* Vessel to New York. I have permitted no drawing to be taken here, tho' it has been often requested, as I think there is a propriety that it should first be presented. But Mr West wishes Mr Trumbull to make a painting of the presentation of the Key to you.

I returned from France to London about five Weeks ago—and I am engaged to return to Paris when the Constitution shall be proclaimed and to carry the American Flag in the procession—I have not the least doubt of the final and compleat success of the French Revolution—Little Ebbings and flowings, for and against, the natural companions of revolutions, sometimes appear, but the full current of it, is, in my opinion, as fixed as the Gulph Stream.

I have manufactured a Bridge (a Single arch) of one hundred & ten feet Span, and five feet high from the Cord of the Arch—It is now on board a vessel coming from Yorkshire to London, where it is to be erected—I see nothing yet to dissappoint my hopes of its being advantageous to me—it is this only which keeps me Europe—and happy shall I be when I shall have it in my power to return to America. I have not heard of Mr Jefferson since he sailed except of his arrival. As I have always indulged the belief of having many friends in America, or rather no Enemies, I have nothing else particularly to mention—but my affectionate remembrances to all—and am, Sir, with the greatest Respect your much obliged and Obedient Humble servant

THOMAS PAINE

If any of my Friends are disposed to favour me with a letter, it will come to hand by addressing it to the care of Benjn Vaughn Esqr. Jeffries Square London.

To the Authors of The Republican

July 2, 1791

GENTLEMEN,

M. *Duchastelet* has mentioned to me the intention of some persons to commence a Work under the title of the *Republican*.

As I am a Citizen of a Country which knows no other Majesty than that of the People—no other Government than that of the Representative body—no other Sovereignty than that of the Laws, and which is attached to *France* both by Alliance and by Gratitude, I voluntarily offer you my services in support of Principles as honourable to a Nation as they are adapted to promote the happiness of mankind. I offer them to you with the more zeal, as I know the moral, literary, and political Character of those who are engaged in the undertaking, and find myself honoured in their good opinion.

But I must at the same time observe, that from my ignorance of the French Language, my works must necessarily undergo a Translation. They can of course be but of little utility, and my offering must consist more of wishes than services—I must add, that I am obliged to pass a part of this summer in England and Ireland.

As the Public has done me the unmerited favour of recognizing me under the Appellation of "Common Sense," which is my usual signature, I shall continue it in this publication to avoid mistakes, and to prevent my being supposed the Author of works not my own. As to my Political Principles, I shall endeavour, in this letter, to trace their general features in such a manner as that they cannot be misunderstood.

It is desirable in most instances to avoid that, which may give even the least suspicion with respect to the part meant to be adopted; and particularly on the present occasion, where a perfect clearness of expression is necessary to the avoidance of any possible misinterpretation. I am happy, therefore, to find that the work in question is entitled "The *Republican*." This Word expresses perfectly the idea which we ought to have of

Government in general—*Res Publica*—the public affairs of a Nation.

As to the word *Monarchy*, though the address and intrigue of Courts have rendered it familiar, it does not contain the less of reproach or of insult to a nation. The word, in its immediate and original sense, signifies *the absolute Power of a single Individual*, who may prove a fool, an hypocrite, or a tyrant. The appellation admits of no other interpretation than that which is here given. *France* is therefore not a *Monarchy*; it is insulted when called by that name. The servile spirit which characterizes this species of Government is banished from FRANCE, and this Country, like AMERICA, can now afford to Monarchy no more than a glance of disdain.

Of the Errors which Monarchic Ignorance or knavery has spread through, the World, the one which bears the marks of the most dexterous invention is the opinion that the system of *Republicanism* is only adapted to a small Country, and that a *Monarchy* is suited on the contrary to those of greater extent. Such is the language of Courts, and such the sentiments which they have caused to be adopted in Monarchic Countries; but the opinion is contrary at the same time to principle and to experience.

The GOVERNMENT, to be of real use, should possess a complete knowledge of all the parties—all the circumstances—and all the interests of a Nation. The Monarchic System, in consequence, instead of being suited to a Country of great extent, would be more admissible in a small territory, where an Individual may be supposed to know the affairs and the interests of the whole.—But when it is attempted to extend this individual knowledge to the affairs of a great Country, the capacity of knowing bears no longer any proportion to the extent or multiplicity of the objects which ought to be known, and the Government inevitably falls from Ignorance into Tyranny. For the proof of this position we need only look to SPAIN, RUSSIA, GERMANY, TURKEY, and the whole of the Eastern Continent—Countries for the Deliverance of which I offer my most sincere wishes.

On the contrary, the true *Republican* System, by Election and Representation, offers the only means which are known, and in my opinion the only means which are possible of proportioning the Wisdom and the Information of a Government to the extent of a Country.

The system of *Representation* is the strongest and most powerful Center that can be devised for a Nation. Its Attraction acts so powerfully, that Men give it their Approbation even without reasoning on the Cause, and FRANCE, however distant its several parts, finds itself at this moment *an Whole* in its *central* Representation. The Citizen is assured that his rights are protected, and the Soldier feels that he is no longer the Slave of a Despot, but that he is become one of the Nation, and interested of course in its defence.

The States at present styled *Republican*, as HOLLAND, GENOA, VENICE, BERNE, &c. are not only unworthy of the name, but are actually in opposition to every Principle of a *Republican* Government, and the Countries submitted to their Power are, truly speaking, subjected to an *Aristocratic* Slavery!

It is perhaps impossible in the first steps which are made in a Revolution, to avoid all kind of error, in Principle or in Practice, or in some instances to prevent the Combination of both. Before the sense of a Nation is sufficiently enlightened, and before Men have entered into the habits of a free Communication with each other of their natural thoughts, a certain reserve—a timid prudence seizes on the human Mind, and prevents it from attaining its level, with that vigour and promptitude which belongs to *Right*.—An Example of this influence discovers itself in the commencement of the present Revolution. But happily this Discovery has been made before the Constitution was completed, and in time to provide a remedy.

The *Hereditary Succession* can never exist as a matter of right; it is a nullity—a *nothing*. To admit the idea is to regard men as a species of property belonging to some individuals, either born or to be born! It is to consider our descendants, and all posterity as mere Animals without a Right or a Will! It is, in fine, the most base, and humiliating idea, that ever degraded the human species, and which, for the honour of Humanity should be destroyed for ever.

The idea of Hereditary succession is so contrary to the Rights of Man, that if we were ourselves to be recalled to existence, instead of being replaced by our Posterity, we should not have the right of depriving ourselves before-hand, of those *Rights* which would then properly belong to us. On what ground then, or by what authority do we dare to deprive of their Rights those Children who will soon be Men? Why are we not struck with the injustice which we perpetrate on our descendants, by endeavouring to transmit them as a vile herd to Masters, whose vices are all that can be foreseen.

Whenever the *French* Constitution shall be rendered conformable to its *Declaration* of *Rights*, we shall then be enabled to give to FRANCE, and with justice, the appeliation of a *Civic Empire*; for its Government will be the Empire of Laws, founded on the great Republican Principles of *Elective Representation*, and the *Rights* of *Man*.—But Monarchy and Hereditary Succession are incompatible with the *Basis* of its Constitution.

I hope that I have at present sufficiently proved to you that I am a good Republican—and I have such a Confidence in the Truth of these Principles, that I doubt not they will soon be as universal in *France* as in *America*. The pride of human nature will assist their Evidence, will contribute to their Establishment, and Men will be ashamed of Monarchy.

I am, with respect,

Gentlemen,

Your Friend,

THOMAS PAINE.

To the Abbé Sieyès

Sir,   Paris, 8th July, 1791.

At the moment of my departure for England, I read, in the *Moniteur* of Tuesday last, your letter, in which you give the challenge, on the subject of Government, and offer to defend what is called the *Monarchical opinion* against the Republican system.

I accept of your challenge with pleasure; and I place such a confidence in the superiority of the Republican system over that nullity of a system, called *Monarchy*, that I engage not to exceed the extent of fifty pages, and to leave you the liberty of taking as much latitude as you may think proper.

The respect which I bear your moral and literary reputation, will be your security for my candour in the course of this discussion; but, notwithstanding that I shall treat the subject seriously and sincerely, let me promise, that I consider myself at liberty to ridicule, as they deserve, Monarchical absurdities, whensoever the occasion shall present itself.

By Republicanism, I do not understand what the name signifies in Holland, and in some parts of Italy. I understand simply a government by representation—a government founded upon the principles of the Declaration of Rights; principles to which several parts of the French Constitution arise in contradiction. The Declaration of Rights of France and America are but one and the same thing in principles, and almost in expressions; and this is the Republicanism which I undertake to defend against what is called *Monarchy* and *Aristocracy.*

I see with pleasure, that in respect to one point we are already agreed; and *that is, the extreme danger of a civil list of thirty millions.* I can discover no reason why one of the parts of the government should be supported with so extravagant a profusion, whilst the other scarcely receives what is sufficient for its common wants.

This dangerous and dishonourable disproportion at once supplies the one with the means of corrupting, and throws the other into the predicament of being corrupted. In America there is but little difference, with regard to this point, between the legislative and the executive part of our government; but the first is much better attended to than it is in France.

In whatsoever manner, Sir, I may treat the subject of which you have proposed the investigation, I hope that you will not doubt my entertaining for you the highest esteem. I must also add, that I am not the personal enemy of Kings. Quite the contrary. No man more heartily wishes than myself to see them all in the happy and honourable state of private individuals; but I am the avowed, open, and intrepid enemy of what is called Monarchy; and I am such by principles which nothing can either alter or corrupt—by my attachment to humanity; by the anxiety which I feel within myself, for the dignity and the honour of the human race; by the disgust which I experience, when I observe men directed by children, and governed by brutes; by the horror which all the evils that Monarchy has spread over the earth excite within my breast; and by those sentiments which make me shudder at the calamities, the exactions, the wars, and the massacres with which Monarchy has crushed mankind: in short, it is against all the hell of monarchy that I have declared war.

THOMAS PAINE.

Reasons for Wishing to Preserve the Life of Louis Capet

as Delivered to the National Convention

January 15, 1793

Citizen President,

MY hatred and abhorrence of monarchy are sufficiently known; they originate in principles of Reason and Conviction, nor, except with life, can they ever be extirpated; but my compassion for the unfortunate, whether friend or enemy, is equally lively and sincere.

I voted that Louis should be tried, because it was necessary to afford proofs to the world of the perfidy, corruption, and abomination of the monarchical system. The infinity of evidence that has been produced, exposes them in the most glaring and hideous colours. Thence it results, that monarchy, whatever form it may assume, arbitrary or otherwise, becomes necessarily a centre, round which are united every species of corruption, and that the *kingly trade* is no less destructive of all morality in the human breast, than the trade of an executioner is destructive of its sensibility.

I remember, during my residence in another country, that I was exceedingly struck with a sentence of M. Autheine, at the Jacobines, which corresponds exactly with my own idea, "Make me a king to-day," said he, "and I shall be a robber to-morrow."

Nevertheless, I am inclined to believe, that if Louis Capet had been born in an obscure condition, had he lived within the circle of an amiable and respectable neighbourhood, at liberty to practise the duties of domestic life, had he been thus situated, I cannot believe that he would have shewn himself destitute of social virtues; we are in a moment of fermentation like this, naturally little indulgent of his vices, or rather to those of monarchical governments, we regard them with additional horror and indignation; not that they are more heinous than those of his predecessors, but because our eyes are now open, and the veil of delusion at length withdrawn, yet the lamentable, degraded state to which he is actually reduced, is surely far less imputable to him, than to the Constituent Assembly, which, of its own authority, without consent or advice of the people, restored him to the throne.

I was in Paris at the time of the flight, or abdication of Louis XVI. and when he was taken and brought back. The proposal of restoring to him the supreme power struck me with amazement; and although at that time, I was not a French Citizen, yet as a Citizen of the World, I employed all the efforts that depended on me to prevent it.

A small society, composed only of five persons, two of whom are now members of the Convention, took, at that time, the name of the Republican Club, (Societé Republicaine). This society opposed the restoration of Louis, not so much on account of his own personal offences, as in order to overthrow the monarchy, and to erect on its ruins the Republican System, and an equal representation.

With this design, I traced out in the English language certain propositions, which were translated, with some trifling alterations, and signed by Achilles Duchastelet, actually Lieutenant-General in the army of the French Republic, and at that time one of the five members which composed our little party; the law requiring the signature of a citizen at bottom of each printed paper.

The paper was indignantly torn by Malouet and brought forth in this very room as an article of accusation against the Person who had signed it, the Author, and their adherents, but such is the revolution of events, that this paper is now revived, and brought forth for a very opposite purpose;—To remind the Nation of the error of that unfortunate day, that fatal error of having not then banished Louis XVI. from its bosom, and to plead this day in favour of his Exile, preferably to his death.

The paper in question was conceived in the following terms:

Brethren and Fellow Citizens,
The serene tranquillity, the mutual confidence which prevailed amongst us during the time of the late King's escape, the indifference with which we beheld him return, are unequivocal proofs that the absence of a King is more desirable than his presence, and that

he is not only a Political superfluity, but a grievous burthen pressing hard on the whole Nation.

Let us not be imposed on by sophisms: All that concerns this man, is reduced to four points.

He has abdicated the Throne in having fled from his post. Abdication and desertion are not characterized by the length of absence; but by the single act of flight. In the present instance, the act is every thing, and the time nothing.

The Nation can never give back its confidence to a Man who false to his trust, perjured to his oath, conspires a clandestine flight, obtains a fraudulent Passport, conceals a King of France under the disguise of a Valet, directs his course towards a frontier covered with traitors and deserters, and evidently meditates a return into our country, with a force capable of imposing his own despotic Laws.

Whether his flight ought to be considered as his own act, or the act of those who fled with him. Was it a spontaneous resolution of his own, or was it inspired into him by others? The alternative is immaterial: Whether Fool or Hypocrite, Idiot or Traitor, he has proved himself equally unworthy of the vast important functions that had been delegated to him.

In every sense that the question can be considered, the reciprocal obligation which subsisted between us is dissolved. He holds no longer authority: We owe him no longer obedience; We see in him now no more than an indifferent Person; we can regard him only as Louis Capet.

The history of France presents little else than a long series of public calamity, which takes its source from the vices of her Kings: We have been the wretched victims that have never ceased to suffer either for them or by them. The Catalogue of their oppressions was complete, but to complete the sum of their crimes, treason yet was wanting: Now, the only vacancy is filled up, the dreadful list is full; The system is exhausted; There are no remaining errors for them to commit, their reign is consequently at an end.

What kind of office must that be in a Government which requires neither experience or ability to execute? that may be abandoned to the desperate chance of birth, that may be filled by an Idiot, a Madman, a Tyrant, with equal effect, as by the good, the virtuous and the wise. An office of this nature is a mere nonentity; It is a place of Shew, not of Use. Let France then, arrived at the age of Reason, no longer be deluded by the sound of words, and let her deliberately examine, if a King, however insignificant and contemptible in himself, may not at the same time be extremely dangerous.

The thirty millions which it costs to support a King in the eclat of stupid brutal Luxury, present us with an easy method of reducing taxes, which reduction would at once release the people, and stop the progress of political corruption. The grandeur of nations consists not, as Kings pretend in the splendor of Thrones, but in a conscious sense of their own dignity, and in a Just disdain of those barbarous follies, and crimes, which under the sanction of Royalty, have hitherto desolated Europe.

As to the Personal Safety of Mr. Louis Capet, it is so much the more confirmed as France will not stop to degrade herself by a spirit of Revenge against a Wretch, who has dishonoured himself. In defending a just and glorious cause, it is not possible to degrade it, and the universal tranquillity which prevails, is an undeniable proof that a free People know how to respect themselves.

Having thus explained the principles and exertions of the Republicans at that fatal period when Louis was reinstated in full Possession of the executive Power which by his flight had been suspended, I return to the subject, and to the deplorable condition in which the Man is now actually involved.

What was neglected at the time of which I have been speaking, has been since brought about by the force of necessity; The wilful treacherous defects in the former constitution have been brought to light, the continual alarm of Treason and Conspiracy rouzed the Nation and produced eventually a second revolution. The People have beat down Royalty, never, never to rise again; They have brought Louis Capet to the bar, and demonstrated in the face of the whole World, the Intrigues, the Cabals, the falsehood, corruption, and rooted depravity, the inevitable effects of monarchical Governments. There remains then only one question to be considered, what is to be done with this Man?

For myself I freely confess that when I reflect on the unaccountable folly, that restored the executive Power to his hands, all covered as he was with Perjuries and Treason, I am far more ready to condemn the Constituent Assembly than the unfortunate Prisoner Louis Capet.

But abstracted from every other consideration, there is one circumstance in his Life which ought to cover, or at least to palliate a great number of his transgressions, and this very circumstance affords the French Nation a blessed occasion of extricating itself from the yoke of Kings, without defiling itself in the impurities of their blood.

It is to France alone I know, that the United States of America owe that support which enabled them to shake off the unjust and tyrannical yoke of *****. The ardour and zeal which she displayed to provide both men and money, were the natural consequences of a thirst for Liberty. But as the Nation at that time, restrained by the shackles of her own Government, could only act by means of a Monarchial organ, this organ — whatever in other respects the object might be — certainly performed a good, a great action. Let then these United States be the safeguard and asylum of Louis Capet. There, hereafter, far removed from the miseries and crimes of Royalty, he may learn, from the constant aspect of Public prosperity, that the true system of Government consists, not in Kings, but in fair, equal and honourable Representation.

In relating this circumstance, and in submitting this proposition, I consider myself as a citizen of both countries. I submit it as a citizen of America, who feels the debt of gratitude which he owes to every Frenchman. I submit it also as a Man, who, although the enemy of Kings, cannot forget that they are subject to human frailties. I support my proposition as a Citizen of the French Republic, because it appears to me the best, the most politic measure, that can be adopted.

As far as my experience in public life extends, I have ever observed, that the great mass of the People are invariably just, both in their intentions, and in their object; but the true method of accomplishing that effect, does not always shew itself in the first instance.

For example, the English Nation had groaned under the despotism of the Stuarts. Hence Charles the First lost his life; yet Charles the Second was restored to all the plentitude of power, which his father had lost.

Forty years had not expired, when the same family strove to re-establish their ancient oppressions; so the nation then banished from its territories the whole race. The remedy was effectual. The Stuart family sunk into obscurity, confounded itself with the multitude, and is at length extinct.

The French nation, more enlightened than England was at that time, has carried her measures of Government to a greater length. France is not satisfied with exposing the guilt of the Monarch, she has penetrated into the vices and horrors of the Monarchy. She has shewn them clear as daylight, and for ever crushed that infernal system; and he, whoever he may be, that should ever dare to reclaim those rights, he would be regarded not as a Pretender, but punished as a Traitor.

Two brothers of Louis Capet have banished themselves from the Country; but they are obliged to comply with the spirit and etiquette of the Courts where they reside. They can advance no pretensions on their own account, so long as Louis shall live.

The history of Monarchy, in France, was a system pregnant with crimes and murders, cancelling all natural ties, even those by which brothers are united. We know how often they have assassinated each other, to pave a way to Power. As those hopes which the Emigrants had reposed in Louis XVI. are fled; the last which remains rests upon his death, and their situation inclines them to desire this catastrophe, that they may once again rally round a more active chief, and try one further effort under the fortune of the Ci-devant Monsieur and d'Artois.

That such an enterprise would precipitate them into a new abyss of calamity and disgrace, it is not difficult to foresee; but yet it might be attended with mutual loss, and it is our duty as Legislators, not to spill a drop of blood, when our purpose may be effectually accomplished without it.

It has been already proposed to abolish the punishment of death; and it is with infinite satisfaction, that I recollect the humane and excellent oration pronounced by Robespierre, on that subject, in the Constituent Assembly. This cause must find its advocates in every corner, where enlightened Politicians, and lovers of Humanity exist; and it ought, above all, to find them in this Assembly.

Monarchical Governments have trained the Human race, and inured it to the sanguinary arts and refinements of punishment; and it is exactly the same punishment, which has so long shocked the sight, and tormented the patience of the People, that now, in their turn, they practise in revenge on their oppressors. But it becomes us to be strictly on our guard against the abomination and perversity of Monarchial examples: as France has been the first of European Nations to abolish Royalty, let her also be the first to abolish the Punishment of Death, and to find out a milder and more effectual substitute.

In the particular case now under consideration, I submit the following propositions: — 1st. That the National Convention shall pronounce sentence of Banishment on Louis and his Family. 2. That Louis Capet shall be detained in prison till the end of the War; and at that epoch for the sentence of banishment to be executed.

Shall Louis XVI. Have Respite?

SPEECH IN THE CONVENTION,
JANUARY 19, 1793

(Read in French by Deputy Bancal.)

VERY sincerely do I regret the Convention's vote of yesterday for death.

MARAT [*interrupting*]: I submit that Thomas Paine is incompetent to vote on this question; being a Quaker his religious principles are opposed to capital punishment. [*Much confusion, quieted by cries for "freedom of speech," on which Bancal proceeds with Paine's speech.*]

I have the advantage of some experience; it is near twenty years that I have been engaged in the cause of liberty, having contributed something to it in the revolution of the United States of America. My language has always been that of liberty *and* humanity, and I know that nothing so exalts a nation as the union of these two principles, under all circumstances. I know that the public mind of France, and particularly that of Paris, has been heated and irritated by the dangers to which they have been exposed; but could we carry our thoughts into the future, when the dangers are ended and the irritations forgotten, what to-day seems an act of justice may then appear an act of vengeance. [*Murmurs.*] My anxiety for the cause of France has become for the moment concern for her honor. If, on my return to America, I should employ myself on a history of the French Revolution, I had rather record a thousand errors on the side of mercy, than be obliged to tell one act of severe justice. I voted against an appeal to the people, because it appeared to me that the Convention was needlessly wearied on that point; but I so voted in the hope that this Assembly would pronounce against death, and for the same punishment that the nation would have voted, at least in my opinion, that is for reclusion during the war, and banishment thereafter. That is the punishment most efficacious, because it includes the whole family at once, and none other can so operate. I am still against the appeal to the primary assemblies, because there is a better method. This Convention has been elected to form a Constitution, which will be submitted to the primary assemblies. After its acceptance a necessary consequence will be an election and another assembly. We cannot suppose that the present Convention will last more than five or six months. The choice of new deputies will express the national opinion, on the propriety or impropriety of your sentence, with as much efficacy as if those primary assemblies had been consulted on it. As the duration of our functions here cannot be long, it is a part of our duty to consider the interests of those who shall replace us. If by any act of ours the number of the nation's enemies shall be needlessly increased, and that of its friends diminished, — at a time when the finances may be more strained than to-day, — we should not be justifiable for having thus unnecessarily heaped obstacles in the path of our successors. Let us therefore not be precipitate in our decisions.

France has but one ally — the United States of America. That is the only nation that can furnish France with naval provisions, for the kingdoms of northern Europe are, or soon will be, at war with her. It unfortunately happens that the person now under discussion is considered by the Americans as having been the friend of their revolution. His execution will be an affliction to them, and it is in your power not to wound the feelings of your ally. Could I speak the French language I would descend to your bar, and in their name become your petitioner to respite the execution of the sentence on Louis.

THURIOT: This is not the language of Thomas Paine.

MARAT: I denounce the interpreter. I maintain that it is not Thomas Paine's opinion. It is an untrue translation.

GARRAN: I have read the original, and the translation is correct.

[*Prolonged uproar. Paine, still standing in the tribune beside his interpreter, Deputy Bancal, declared the sentiments to be his.*]

Your Executive Committee will nominate an ambassador to Philadelphia; my sincere wish is that he may announce to America that the National Convention of France, out of pure friendship to America, has consented to respite Louis. That people, by my vote, ask you to delay the execution.

Ah, citizens, give not the tyrant of England the triumph of seeing the man perish on the scaffold who had aided my much-loved America to break his chains!

MARAT [*"launching himself into the middle of the hall"*]: Paine voted against the punishment of death because he is a Quaker.

PAINE: I voted against it from both moral motives and motives of public policy.

To Danton

Paris, May 6, 2d year of the Republic (1793).
Citoyen Danton:

As you read English I write this letter to you without passing it through the hands of a translator.

I am exceedingly distressed at the distractions, jealousies, discontents and uneasiness that reign among us and which, if they continue, will bring ruin and disgrace on the Republic. When I left America in the year 1787 it was my intention to return the year following, but the French revolution and the prospect it afforded of extending the principles of liberty and fraternity through the greater part of Europe have induced me to prolong my stay upwards of six years. I now despair of seeing the great object of European liberty accomplished, and my despair arises not from the combined foreign powers, not from the intrigues of aristocracy and priestcraft, but from the tumultuous misconduct with which the internal affairs of the present revolution is conducted.

All that now can be hoped for is limited to France only, and I agree with your motion of not interfering in the government of any foreign country, nor permitting any foreign country to interfere in the government of France. This decree was necessary as a preliminary toward terminating the war. But while these internal contentions continue, while the hope remains to the enemy of seeing the republic fall to pieces, while not only the representatives of the departments but representation itself is publicly insulted, as it has lately been and now is by the people of Paris, or at least by the tribunes, the enemy will be encouraged to hang about the frontiers and await the issue of circumstances.

I observe that the confederated powers have not yet recognised Monsieur, or D'Artois, as regent, nor made any Proclamation in favour of any of the Bourbons, but this negative conduct admits of two different conclusions. The one is that of abandoning the Bourbons and the war together, the other is that of changing the object of the war and substituting a partition scheme in the place of their first object as they have done by Poland. If this should be their object, the internal contentions that now rage will favour that object far more than it favoured their former object. The danger every day increases of a rupture between Paris and the departments. The departments did not send their deputies to Paris to be insulted, and every insult shown to them is an insult to the departments that elected and sent them. I see but one effectual plan to prevent this rupture taking place, and that is to fix the residence of the Convention and of the future assemblies at a distance from Paris.

I saw, during the American Revolution, the exceeding inconvenience that arose by having the government of Congress within the limits of any Municipal Jurisdiction. Congress first resided in Philadelphia, and after a residence of four years, it found it necessary to leave it. It then adjourned to the state of Jersey. It afterwards removed to New York; it again removed from New York to Philadelphia and, after experiencing in every one of these places the great inconvenience of a government within a government it formed the project of building a Town not within the limits of any municipal jurisdiction for the future residence of Congress. In any one of the places where Congress resided, the municipal authority privately or openly opposed itself to the authority of Congress and the people of each of those places expected more attention from Congress than their equal share with the other states amounted to. The same things now take place in France but in a far greater excess.

I see also another embarrassing circumstance arising in Paris of which we have had full experience in America. I mean that of fixing the price of provisions. But if this measure is to be attempted it ought to be done by the Municipality. The Convention has nothing to do with regulations of this kind; neither can they be carried into practice. The People of Paris may say they will not give more than a certain price for provisions, but as they cannot compel the country people to bring provisions to market the consequence will be directly contrary to their expectations, and they will find dearness and famine instead of plenty and cheapness. They may force the price down upon the Stock in hand, but after that the market will be empty. I will give you an example—

In Philadelphia we undertook among other regulations of

this kind to regulate the price of Salt; the consequence was that no Salt was brought to market, and the price rose to thirty-six shillings sterling per Bushel. The price before the war was only one shilling and six pence per Bushel; and we regulated the price of flour (*farine*) till there was none in the market and the people were glad to procure it at any price.

There is also a circumstance to be taken into the account which is not much attended to. The assignats are not of the same value they were a year ago and as the quantity encreases the value of them will diminish. This gives the appearance of things being dear when they are not so in fact, for in the same proportion that any kind of money falls in value articles rise in price. If it were not for this the quantity of assignats would be too great to be circulated. Paper money in America fell so much in value from this excessive quantity of it that in the year 1781 I gave three hundred Paper dollars for one pair of worsted stockings. What I write you upon this subject is experience and not merely opinion.

I have no personal interest in any of these matters nor in any party disputes. I attend only to general principles.

As soon as a constitution shall be established I shall return to America; and be the future prosperity of France ever so great I shall enjoy no other part of it than the happiness of knowing it. In the mean time I am distressed to see matters so badly conducted and so little attention paid to moral principles. It is these things that injure the character of the Revolution and discourages the progress of liberty all over the world.

When I began this letter I did not intend making it so lengthy, but since I have gone thus far I will fill up the remainder of the sheet with such matters as shall occur to me.

There ought to be some regulation with respect to the spirit of denunciation that now prevails. If every individual is to indulge his private malignancy, or his private ambition, to denounce at random and without any kind of proof, all confidence will be undermined and all authority be destroyed. Calumny is a species of Treachery that ought to be punished as well as any other kind of Treachery. It is a private vice productive of a public evil, because it is possible to irritate men into disaffection by continual calumny who never intended to be disaffected. It is therefore, equally as necessary to guard against the evils of unfounded or malignant suspicion as against the evils of blind confidence. It is equally as necessary to protect the characters of public officers from calumny as it is to punish them for treachery or misconduct. For my own part I shall hold it a matter of doubt, until better evidence arises than is known at present, whether Dumourier has been a traitor from policy or from resentment. There was certainly a time when he acted well, but it is not every man whose mind is strong enough to bear up against ingratitude and I think he experienced a great deal of this before he revolted.

Calumny becomes harmless and defeats itself when it attempts to act upon too large a scale. Thus the denunciation of the sections against the twenty-two deputies falls to the ground. The departments that elected them are better judges of their moral and political characters than those who have denounced them. This denunciation will injure Paris in the opinion of the departments because it has the appearance of dictating to them what sort of deputies they shall elect. Most of the acquaintances that I have in the Convention are among those who are in that list, and I know there are not better men nor better patriots than what they are.

I have written a letter to Marat of the same date as this but not on the same subject. He may show it to you if he chuse.

Votre ami,
THOMAS PAINE.

CITOYEN DANTON.

Agrarian Justice

OPPOSED TO AGRARIAN LAW, AND TO AGRARIAN MONOPOLY, BEING A PLAN FOR MELIORATING THE CONDITION OF MAN, &c.

Spring 1797

PREFACE.

THE following little Piece was written in the winter of 1795 and 96; and, as I had not determined whether to publish it during the present war, or to wait till the commencement of a peace, it has lain by me, without alteration or addition, from the time it was written.

What has determined me to publish it now is, a Sermon, preached by WATSON, *Bishop of Landaff.* Some of my Readers will recollect, that this Bishop wrote a Book, entitled *An Apology for the Bible*, in answer to my *Second Part of the Age of Reason*. I procured a copy of his book, and he may depend upon hearing from me on that subject.

At the end of the Bishop's book is a List of the Works he has written, among which is the Sermon alluded to; it is entitled,

"THE WISDOM AND GOODNESS OF GOD, IN HAVING MADE BOTH RICH AND POOR; with an Appendix, containing REFLECTIONS ON THE PRESENT STATE OF ENGLAND AND FRANCE."

The error contained in the title of this Sermon, determined me to publish my AGRARIAN JUSTICE. It is wrong to say that God made *Rich* and *Poor*; he made only *Male* and *Female*; and he gave them the earth for their inheritance.

       *   *   *   *
       *   *   *   *
       *   *   *   *

Instead of preaching to encourage one part of mankind in insolence   *   *   *   *
       *   *   *   *
       *   *   *   *

it would be better that Priests employed their time to render the general condition of man less miserable than it is. Practical religion consists in doing good; and the only way of serving God is, that of endeavouring to make his creation happy. All preaching that has not this for its object is nonsense and hypocrisy.

THOMAS PAINE.

AGRARIAN JUSTICE

To preserve the benefits of what is called civilized life, and to remedy, at the same time, the evils it has produced, ought to be considered as one of the first objects of reformed legislation.

Whether the state that is proudly, perhaps erroneously, called civilization, has most promoted or most injured the general happiness of man, is a question that may be strongly contested. — On one side, the spectator is dazzled by splendid appearances; on the other he is shocked by extremes of wretchedness; both of which he has erected. The most affluent and the most miserable of the human race are to be found in the countries that are called civilized.

To understand what the state of society ought to be, it is necessary to have some idea of the natural and primitive state of man; such as it is at this day among the Indians of North America. There is not, in that state, any of those spectacles of human misery which poverty and want present to our eyes, in all the towns and streets of Europe. Poverty, therefore, is a thing created by that which is called civilized life. It exists not in the natural state. On the other hand, the natural state is without those advantages which flow from Agriculture, Arts, Science, and Manufactures.

The life of an Indian is a continual holiday, compared with the poor of Europe; and, on the other hand, it appears to be abject when compared to the rich. Civilization, therefore, or that which is so called, has operated, two ways, to make one part of society more affluent, and the other part more wretched, than would have been the lot of either in a natural state.

It is always possible to go from the natural to the civilized state, but it is never possible to go from the civilized to the natural state. The reason is, that man, in a natural state, subsisting by hunting, requires ten times the quantity of land to range over, to procure himself sustenance, than would support him in a civilized state, where the earth is cultivated. When therefore a country becomes populous by the additional aids of cultivation, arts, and science, there is a necessity of preserving things in that state; because, without it, there cannot be sustenance for more, perhaps, than a tenth part of its inhabitants. The thing therefore now to be done, is, to remedy the evils, and preserve the benefits, that have arisen to society, by passing from the natural to that which is called the civilized state.

Taking then the matter up on this ground, the first principle of civilization ought to have been, and ought still to be, that the condition of every person born into the world, after a state of civilization commences, ought not to be worse than if he had been born before that period. But the fact is, that the condition of millions, in every country in Europe, is far worse than if they had been born before civilization began, or had been born among the Indians of North America of the present day. I will shew how this fact has happened.

It is a position not to be controverted, that the earth, in its natural uncultivated state, was, and ever would have continued to be, the COMMON PROPERTY OF THE HUMAN RACE. In that state every man would have been born to property. He would have been a joint life-proprietor with the rest in the property of the soil, and in all its natural productions, vegetable and animal.

But the earth, in its natural state, as before said, is capable of supporting but a small number of inhabitants compared with what it is capable of doing in a cultivated state. And as it is impossible to separate the improvement made by cultivation, from the earth itself, upon which that improvement is made, the idea of landed property arose from that inseparable connection; but it is nevertheless true, that it is the value of the improvement only, and not the earth itself, that is individual property. Every proprietor therefore of cultivated land, owes to the community a *ground-rent*; for I know no better term to express the idea by, for the land which he holds: and it is from this ground-rent that the fund proposed in this plan is to issue.

It is deducible, as well from the nature of the thing, as from all the histories transmitted to us, that the idea of landed property commenced with cultivation, and that there was no such thing as landed property before that time. It could not exist in the first state of man, that of hunters. It did not exist in the second state, that of shepherds: Neither Abraham, Isaac, Jacob, or Job, so far as the history of the Bible may be credited in probable things, were owners of land. Their property consisted, as is always enumerated, in flocks and herds, and they travelled with them from place to place. The frequent contentions at that time about the use of a well in the dry country of Arabia, where those people lived, shew also there was no landed property. It was not admitted that land could be located as property.

There could be no such thing as landed property originally. Man did not make the earth, and, though he had a natural right to *occupy* it, he had no right to *locate* as *his property* in perpetuity any part of it: neither did the Creator of the earth open a land-office, from whence the first title-deeds should issue. From whence then arose the idea of landed property? I answer as before, that when cultivation began, the idea of landed property began with it, from the impossibility of separating the improvement made by cultivation from the earth itself upon which that improvement was made. The value of the improvement so far exceeded the value of the natural earth, at that time, as to absorb it; till, in the end, the common right of all became confounded into the cultivated right of the individual. But they are nevertheless distinct species of rights, and will continue to be so as long as the earth endures.

It is only by tracing things to their origin, that we can gain rightful ideas of them, and it is by gaining such ideas that we discover the boundary that divides right from wrong, and which teaches every man to know his own. I have entitled this tract *Agrarian Justice*, to distinguish it from *Agrarian Law*. Nothing could be more unjust than Agrarian Law in a country improved by cultivation; for though every man, as an inhabitant of the earth, is a joint proprietor of it in its natural

state, it does not follow that he is a joint proprietor of cultivated earth. The additional value made by cultivation, after
the system was admitted, became the property of those who
did it, or who inherited it from them, or who purchased it. It
had originally an owner. Whilst, therefore, I advocate the
right, and interest myself in the hard case of all those who
have been thrown out of their natural inheritance by the introduction of the system of landed property, I equally defend
the right of the possessor to the part which is his.

Cultivation is, at least, one of the greatest natural improvements ever made by human invention. It has given to created
earth a ten-fold value. But the landed monopoly, that began
with it, has produced the greatest evil. It has dispossessed
more than half the inhabitants of every nation of their natural
inheritance, without providing for them, as ought to have
been done, as an indemnification for that loss, and has
thereby created a species of poverty and wretchedness, that
did not exist before.

In advocating the case of the persons thus dispossessed, it is
a right and not a charity that I am pleading for. But it is that
kind of right which, being neglected at first, could not be
brought forward afterwards, till heaven had opened the way
by a revolution in the system of government. Let us then do
honour to revolutions by justice, and give currency to their
principles by blessings.

Having thus, in a few words, opened the merits of the case,
I proceed to the plan I have to propose, which is,

*To create a National Fund, out of which there shall be paid to
every person, when arrived at the age of twenty-one years, the
sum of* Fifteen Pounds sterling, *as a compensation in part for
the loss of his or her natural inheritance by the introduction of
the system of landed property.*

AND ALSO,

The sum of Ten Pounds per annum, *during life, to every
person now living of the age of fifty years, and to all others as
they shall arrive at that age.*

MEANS BY WHICH THE FUND IS TO BE CREATED.

I have already established the principle, namely, that the
earth, in its natural uncultivated state, was, and ever would

have continued to be, the COMMON PROPERTY OF THE HU-MAN RACE—that in that state every person would have been born to property—and that the system of landed property, by its inseparable connection with cultivation, and with what is called civilized life, has absorbed the property of all those whom it dispossessed, without providing, as ought to have been done, an indemnification for that loss.

The fault, however, is not in the present possessors. No complaint is intended, or ought to be alledged against them, unless they adopt the crime by opposing justice. The fault is in the system, and it has stolen imperceptibly upon the world, aided afterwards by the Agrarian law of the sword. But the fault can be made to reform itself by successive generations, without diminishing or deranging the property of any of the present possessors, and yet the operation of the fund can commence, and be in full activity the first year of its establishment, or soon after, as I shall shew.

It is proposed that the payments, as already stated, be made to every person, rich or poor. It is best to make it so, to prevent invidious distinctions. It is also right it should be so, because it is in lieu of the natural inheritance, which, as a right, belongs to every man, over and above the property he may have created or inherited from those who did. Such persons as do not chuse to receive it, can throw it into the common fund.

Taking it then for granted, that no person ought to be in a worse condition when born under what is called a state of civilization, than he would have been, had he been born in a state of nature, and that civilization ought to have made, and ought still to make, provision for that purpose, it can only be done by subtracting from property a portion equal in value to the natural inheritance it has absorbed.

Various methods may be proposed for this purpose, but that which appears to be the best, not only because it will operate without deranging any present possessors, or without interfering with the collection of taxes, or emprunts necessary for the purpose of government and the revolution, but because it will be the least troublesome and the most effectual, and also because the subtraction will be made at a time that best admits it, which is, at the moment that property is passing by the death of one person to the possession of another. In this case, the bequeather gives nothing; the receiver pays nothing. The only matter to him is, that the monopoly of natural inheritance, to which there never was a right, begins to cease in his person. A generous man would not wish it to continue, and a just man will rejoice to see it abolished.

My state of health prevents my making sufficient enquiries with respect to the doctrine of probabilities, whereon to found calculations with such degrees of certainty as they are capable of. What, therefore, I offer on this head is more the result of observation and reflection, than of received information; but I believe it will be found to agree sufficiently enough with fact.

In the first place, taking twenty-one years as the epoch of maturity, all the property of a nation, real and personal, is always in the possession of persons above that age. It is then necessary to know as a datum of calculation, the average of years which persons above that age will live. I take this average to be about thirty years, for though many persons will live forty, fifty, or sixty years after the age of twenty-one years, others will die much sooner, and some in every year of that time.

Taking then thirty years as the average of time, it will give, without any material variation, one way or other, the average of time in which the whole property or capital of a nation, or a sum equal thereto, will have passed through one entire revolution in descent, that is, will have gone by deaths to new possessors; for though, in many instances, some parts of this capital will remain forty, fifty, or sixty years in the possession of one person, other parts will have revolved two or three times before that thirty years expire, which will bring it to that average; for were one half the capital of a nation to revolve twice in thirty years, it would produce the same fund as if the whole revolved once.

Taking then thirty years as the average of time in which the whole capital of a nation, or a sum equal thereto, will revolve once, the thirtieth part thereof will be the sum that will revolve every year, that is, will go by deaths to new possessors; and this last sum being thus known, and the ratio per cent. to be subtracted from it being determined, will give the annual amount or income of the proposed fund, to be applied as already mentioned.

In looking over the discourse of the English Minister, Pitt, in his opening of what is called in England the budget, (the scheme of finance for the year 1796,) I find an estimate of the national capital of that country. As this estimate of a national capital is prepared ready to my hand, I take it as a datum to act upon. When a calculation is made upon the known capital of any nation, combined with its population, it will serve as a scale for any other nation, in proportion as its capital and population be more or less. I am the more disposed to take this estimate of Mr. Pitt, for the purpose of shewing to that Minister, upon his own calculation, how much better money may be employed, than in wasting it, as he has done, on the wild project of setting up Bourbon kings. What, in the name of Heaven, are Bourbon kings to the people of England? It is better that the people have bread.

Mr. Pitt states the national capital of England, real and personal, to be one thousand three hundred millions sterling, which is about one-fourth part of the national capital of France, including Belgia. The event of the last harvest in each country proves that the soil of France is more productive than that of England, and that it can better support twenty-four or twenty-five millions of inhabitants than that of England can seven, or seven and an half.

The 30th part of this capital of £.1,300,000,000 is £.43,333,333, which is the part that will revolve every year by deaths in that country to new possessors; and the sum that will annually revolve in France in the proportion of four to one, will be about one hundred and seventy-three millions sterling. From this sum of £.43,333,333 annually revolving, is to be subtracted the value of the natural inheritance absorbed in it, which perhaps, in fair justice, cannot be taken at less, and ought not to be taken at more, than a tenth part.

It will always happen, that of the property thus revolving by deaths every year, part will descend in a direct line to sons and daughters, and the other part collaterally, and the proportion will be found to be about three to one; that is, about 30 millions of the above sum will descend to direct heirs, and the remaining sum of £.13,333,333 to more distant relations, and part to strangers.

Considering then that man is always related to society, that relationship will become comparatively greater in proportion as the next of kin is more distant. It is therefore consistent with civilization to say that where there are no direct heirs, society shall be heir to a part over and above the tenth part *due* to society. If this additional part be from five to ten or twelve per cent. in proportion as the next of kin be nearer or more remote, so as to average with the escheats that may fall, which ought always to go to society and not to the government, an addition of ten per cent. more, the produce from the annual sum of £.43,333,333 will be,

From 30,000,000 at ten per cent 3,000,000
From 13,333,333   at 10 per cent. with⎫
                   the addition of 10 ⎬   2,666,666
                   per cent. more   ⎭
    _____   _____
    £.43,333,333 . . . . £.5,666,666

Having thus arrived at the annual amount of the proposed fund, I come, in the next place, to speak of the population proportioned to this fund, and to compare it with uses to which the fund is to be applied.

The population (I mean that of England) does not exceed seven millions and a half, and the number of persons above the age of fifty will in that case be about four hundred thousand. There would not however be more than that number that would accept the proposed ten pounds sterling per annum, though they would be entitled to it. I have no idea it would be accepted by many persons who had a yearly income of two or three hundred pounds sterling. But as we often see instances of rich people falling into sudden poverty, even at the age of sixty, they would always have the right of drawing all the arrears due to them.—Four millions, therefore, of the above annual sum of £.5,666,666, will be required for four hundred thousand aged persons, at ten pounds sterling each.

I come now to speak of the persons annually arriving at twenty-one years of age. If all the persons who died were above the age of twenty-one years, the number of persons annually arriving at that age, must be equal to the annual number of deaths to keep the population stationary. But the greater part die under the age of twenty-one, and therefore the number of persons annually arriving at twenty-one, will be less than half the number of deaths. The whole number of deaths upon a population of seven millions and a half, will be about 220,000 annually. The number arriving at 21 years of age will be about 100,000. The whole number of these will not receive the proposed fifteen pounds for the reasons already mentioned, though, as in the former case, they would be intitled to it. Admitting then that a tenth part declined receiving it, the amount would stand thus:

Fund annually. . . . . £.5,666,666
To 400,000 aged persons
   at £. 10 each . . . . £.4,000,000 ⎫
To 90,000 persons of 21   ⎬ 5,350,000
   years, £. 15 sterling each . . . . 1,350,000 ⎭ _____

                                   remains £.316,666

There are in every country a number of blind and lame persons, totally incapable of earning a livelihood. But as it will always happen that the greater number of blind persons will be among those who are above the age of fifty years, they will be provided for in that class. The remaining sum of £.316,666, will provide for the lame and blind under that age, at the same rate of £.10 annually for each person.

Having now gone through all the necessary calculations, and stated the particulars of the plan, I shall conclude with some observations.

It is not charity but a right—not bounty but justice, that I am pleading for. The present state of what is called civilization, is   *   *   *   *   It is the reverse of what it ought to be, and   *   *   *   *   The contrast of affluence and wretchedness continually meeting and offending the eye, is like dead and living bodies chained together. Though I care as little about riches as any man, I am a friend to riches because they are capable of good. I care not how affluent some may be, provided that none be miserable in consequence of it. But it is impossible to enjoy affluence with the felicity it is capable of being enjoyed, whilst so much misery is mingled in the scene. The sight of the misery, and the unpleasant sensations it suggests, which though they may be suffocated cannot be extinguished, are a greater draw-back upon the felicity of affluence than the proposed 10 per cent. upon property is worth. He that would not give the one to get rid of the other, has no charity, even for himself.

There are in every country some magnificent charities established by individuals. It is however but little that any individual can do when the whole extent of the misery to be relieved be considered. He may satisfy his conscience, but not his heart. He may give all that he has, and that all will relieve but little. It is only by organizing civilization upon such principles as to act like a system of pullies, that the whole weight of misery can be removed.

The plan here proposed will reach the whole. It will immediately relieve and take out of view three classes of wretchedness. The blind, the lame, and the aged poor; and it will furnish the rising generation with means to prevent their becoming poor; and it will do this, without deranging or interfering with any national measures. To shew that this will be the case, it is sufficient to observe, that the operation and effect of the plan will, in all cases, be the same, as if every individual were *voluntarily* to make his will, and dispose of his property, in the manner here proposed.

But it is justice and not charity, that is the principle of the plan. In all great cases it is necessary to have a principle more universally active than charity; and with respect to justice, it ought not to be left to the choice of detached individuals, whether they will do justice or not. Considering then the plan on the ground of justice, it ought to be the act of the whole, growing spontaneously out of the principles of the revolution, and the reputation of it to be national and not individual.

A plan upon this principle would benefit the revolution by the energy that springs from the consciousness of justice. It would multiply also the national resources; for property, like vegetation, encreases by off-sets. When a young couple begins the world, the difference is exceedingly great whether they begin with nothing or with fifteen pounds apiece. With this aid they could buy a cow, and implements to cultivate a few acres of land; and instead of becoming burthens upon society, which is always the case, where children are produced faster than they can be fed, would be put in the way of becoming useful and profitable citizens. The national domains also would sell the better, if pecuniary aids were provided to cultivate them in small lots.

It is the practice of what has unjustly obtained the name of civilization (and the practice merits not to be called either charity or policy) to make some provision for persons becoming poor and wretched, only at the time they become so. Would it not, even as a matter of economy, be far better, to devise means to prevent their becoming poor. This can best be done by making every person, when arrived at the age of twenty-one years, an inheritor of something to begin with. The rugged face of society, chequered with the extremes of affluence and of want, proves that some extraordinary violence has been committed upon it, and calls on justice for redress. The great mass of the poor, in all countries, are become an hereditary race, and it is next to impossible for them to get out of that state of themselves. It ought also to be observed, that this mass increases in all the countries that are called civilized. More persons fall annually into it, than get out of it.

Though in a plan, in which justice and humanity are the foundation-principles, interest ought not to be admitted into the calculation, yet it is always of advantage to the establishment of any plan, to shew that it is beneficial as a matter of interest. The success of any proposed plan, submitted to public consideration, must finally depend on the numbers interested in supporting it, united with the justice of its principles.

The plan here proposed will benefit all, without injuring any. It will consolidate the interest of the republic with that of the individual. To the numerous class dispossessed of their natural inheritance by the system of landed property, it will be an act of national justice. To persons dying possessed of moderate fortunes, it will operate as a tontine to their children, more beneficial than the sum of money paid into the fund: and it will give to the accumulation of riches a degree of security that none of the old governments of Europe, now tottering on their foundations, can give.

I do not suppose that more than one family in ten, in any of the countries of Europe, has, when the head of the family dies, a clear property left of five hundred pounds sterling. To all such the plan is advantageous. That property would pay fifty pounds into the fund, and if there were only two children under age, they would receive fifteen pounds each (thirty pounds) on coming of age, and be entitled to ten pounds a year after fifty. It is from the overgrown acquisition of property that the fund will support itself; and I know that the possessors of such property in England, though they would eventually be benefited by the protection of nine tenths of it, will exclaim against the plan. But, without entering into any enquiry how they came by that property, let them recollect, that they have been the advocates of this war, and that Mr. Pitt has already laid on more new taxes to be raised annually upon the people of England, and that for supporting the despotism of Austria and the Bourbons, against the liberties of France, than would annually pay all the sums proposed in this plan.

I have made the calculations, stated in this plan, upon what is called personal, as well as upon landed property. The reason for making it upon land is already explained; and the reason for taking personal property into the calculation, is equally well founded, though on a different principle. Land, as before said, is the free gift of the Creator in common to the human race. Personal property is the *effect of Society*; and it is as impossible for an individual to acquire personal property without the aid of Society, as it is for him to make land originally. Separate an individual from society, and give him an island or a continent to possess, and he cannot acquire personal property. He cannot become rich. So inseparably are the means connected with the end, in all cases, that where the former do not exist, the latter cannot be obtained. All accumulation therefore of personal property, beyond what a man's own hands produce, is derived to him by living in society; and he owes, on every principle of justice, of gratitude, and of civilization, a part of that accumulation back again to society from whence the whole came. This is putting the matter on a general principle, and perhaps it is best to do so; for if we examine the case minutely, it will be found, that the accumulation of personal property is, in many instances, the effect of paying too little for the labour that produced it; the consequence of which is, that the working hand perishes in old age, and the employer abounds in affluence. It is perhaps impossible to proportion exactly the price of labour to the profits it produces; and it will also be said, as an apology for injustice, that were a workman to receive an increase of wages daily, he would not save it against old age nor be much the better for it in the interim. Make then Society the treasurer to guard it for him in a common fund, for it is no reason that because he might not make a good use of it for himself that another shall take it.

The state of civilization that has prevailed throughout Europe, is as unjust in its principle, as it is horrid in its effects; and it is the consciousness of this, and the apprehension that such a state cannot continue when once investigation begins in any country, that makes the possessors of property dread every idea of a revolution. It is the *hazard* and not the principles of a revolution that retards their progress. This being the case, it is necessary, as well for the protection of property, as for the sake of justice and humanity, to form a system, that whilst it preserves one part of society from wretchedness, shall secure the other from depredation.

The superstitious awe, the enslaving reverence, that formerly surrounded affluence, is passing away in all countries, and leaving the possessor of property to the convulsion of accidents. When wealth and splendour, instead of fascinating the multitude, excite emotions of disgust; when, instead of drawing forth admiration, it is beheld as an insult upon wretchedness: when the ostentatious appearance it makes serves to call the right of it in question, the case of property becomes critical, and it is only in a system of justice that the possessor can contemplate security.

To remove the danger, it is necessary to remove the antipathies, and this can only be done by making property productive of a national blessing, extending to every individual. When the riches of one man above another shall increase the national fund in the same proportion; when it shall be seen that the prosperity of that fund depends on the prosperity of individuals; when the more riches a man acquires, the better it shall be for the general mass; it is then that antipathies will cease, and property be placed on the permanent basis of national interest and protection.

I have no property in France to become subject to the plan I propose. What I have, which is not much, is in the United States of America. But I will pay one hundred pounds sterling towards this fund in France, the instant it shall be established; and I will pay the same sum in England, whenever a similar establishment shall take place in that country.

A revolution in the state of civilization, is the necessary companion of revolutions in the system of government. If a revolution in any country be from bad to good, or from good to bad, the state of what is called civilization in that country, must be made conformable thereto, to give that revolution effects. Despotic government supports itself by abject civilization, in which debasement of the human mind, and wretchedness in the mass of the people, are the chief criterians. Such governments consider man merely as an animal; that the exercise of intellectual faculty is not his privilege; *that he has nothing to do with the laws, but to obey them;* * and they politically depend more upon breaking the spirit of the people by poverty, than they fear enraging it by desperation.

It is a revolution in the state of civilization, that will give perfection to the revolution of France. Already the conviction that government, by representation, is the true system of government, is spreading itself fast in the world. The reasonableness of it can be seen by all. The justness of it makes itself felt even by its opposers. But when a system of civilization, growing out of that system of government, shall be so organized, that not a man or woman born in the republic, but shall inherit some means of beginning the world, and see before them the certainty of escaping the miseries, that under other governments accompany old age, the revolution of France will have an advocate and an ally in the heart of all nations.

*Expression of Horsley, an English Bishop, in the English parliament.

An army of principles will penetrate where an army of soldiers cannot—It will succeed where diplomatic management would fail—It is neither the Rhine, the Channel, nor the Ocean, that can arrest its progress—It will march on the horizon of the world, and it will conquer.

THOMAS PAINE.

Means for carrying the proposed Plan into execution, and to render it at the same time conducive to the public Interest.

I.

Each canton shall elect in its primary assemblies, three persons, as commissioners for the canton, who shall take cognizance, and keep a register of all matters happening in that canton, conformable to the charter that shall be established by law, for carrying this plan into execution.

II.

The law shall fix the manner in which the property of deceased persons shall be ascertained.

III.

When the amount of the property of any deceased person shall be ascertained, the principal heir to that property, or the eldest of the co-heirs, if of lawful age, or if under age, the person authorized by the will of the deceased to represent him, or them, shall give bond to the commissioners of the canton, to pay the said tenth part thereof, within the space of one year, in four equal quarterly payments, or sooner, at the choice of the payers. One half of the whole property shall remain as security until the bond be paid off.

IV.

The bonds shall be registered in the office of the commissioners of the canton, and the original bonds shall be deposited in the national bank at Paris. The bank shall publish every quarter of a year the amount of the bonds in its possession, and also the bonds that shall have been paid off, or what parts thereof, since the last quarterly publication.

V.

The national bank shall issue bank notes upon the security of the bonds in its possession. The notes so issued, shall be applied to pay the pensions of aged persons, and the compensations to persons arriving at twenty-one years of age. —It is both reasonable and generous to suppose, that persons not under immediate necessity, will suspend their right of drawing on the fund, until it acquire, as it will do, a greater degree of ability. In this case, it is proposed, that an honorary register be kept in each canton, of the names of the persons thus suspending that right, at least during the present war.

VI.

As the inheritors of property must always take up their bonds in four quarterly payments, or sooner if they chuse, there will always be numeraire arriving at the bank after the expiration of the first quarter, to exchange for the bank notes that shall be brought in.

VII.

The bank notes being thus got into circulation, upon the best of all possible security, that of actual property to more than four times the amount of the bonds upon which the notes are issued, and with numeraire continually arriving at the bank to exchange or pay them off whenever they shall be presented for that purpose, they will acquire a permanent value in all parts of the republic. They can therefore be received in payment of taxes or emprunts, equal to numeraire, because the government can always receive numeraire for them at the bank.

VIII.

It will be necessary that the payments of the ten *per cent.* be made in numeraire for the first year, from the establishment of the plan. But after the expiration of the first year, the inheritors of property may pay the ten *per cent.* either in bank notes issued upon the fund, or in numeraire. If the payments be in numeraire, it will lie as a deposit at the bank, to be exchanged for a quantity of notes equal to that amount; and if in notes issued upon the fund, it will cause a demand upon the fund equal thereto; and thus the operation of the plan will create means to carry itself into execution.

To Samuel Adams

————

January 1, 1803

————

FOR THE NATIONAL INTELLIGENCER.

TOWARDS the latter end of last December I received a letter from a venerable patriot, Samuel Adams, dated Boston, Nov. 30. It came by a private hand, which I suppose was the cause of the delay. I wrote Mr. Adams an answer dated Jan. 1st, and that I might be certain of his receiving it, and also that I might know of that reception, I desired a friend of mine at Washington to put it under cover to some friend of his at Boston, and desire him to present it to Mr. Adams. The letter was accordingly put under cover while I was present and given to one of the clerks of the Post-Office to seal and put in the mail. The clerk put it in his pocket-book, and either forgot to put it in the mail, or supposed he had done so among other letters. The Post-master General, on learning this mistake, informed me of it last Saturday, and as the cover was then out of date, the letter was put under a new cover with the same request and forwarded by the post. I felt concern at this accident, lest Mr. Adams should conclude I was unmindful of his attention to me; and therefore, lest any further accident should prevent or delay his receiving it, as well as to relieve myself from that concern, I give the letter the opportunity of reaching him by the news-papers. I am the more induced to do this, because some manuscript copies have been taken of both letters, and therefore, there is a possibility of imperfect copies getting into print; and besides this, if some of the federal printers, (for I hope they are not all base alike) could get hold of a copy they would make no scruple of altering it and publishing it as mine. I therefore send you the original letter of Mr. Adams and my own copy of the answer.

THOMAS PAINE.

Federal City, Jan. 22, 1803.

Boston, Nov. 30th, 1802.

SIR,

I have frequently with pleasure reflected on your services to my native, and your adopted country. Your Common Sense, and your Crisis unquestionably awakened the public mind, and led the people loudly to call for a declaration of our national independence. I therefore esteemed you as a warm friend to the liberty, & lasting welfare of the human race. But when I heard, that you had turned your mind to a defence of infidelity, I felt myself much astonished, and more grieved, that you had attempted a measure so injurious to the feelings, and so repugnant to the true interest of so great a part of the citizens of the United States. The people of New-England, if you will allow me to use a Scripture phrase, are fast returning to their first love. Will you excite among them the spirit of angry controversy, at a time, when they are hastning to unity and peace? I am told that some of our news-papers have announced your intention to publish an additional pamphlet upon the principles of your Age of Reason. Do you think, that *your pen*, or the pen of any other man can unchristianize the mass of our citizens, or have you hopes of converting a few of them to assist you in so bad a cause? We ought to think ourselves happy in the enjoyment of opinion without the danger of persecution by civil or ecclesiastical law.

Our friend, the present President of the United States, has been calumniated for his liberal sentiments by men, who have attributed that liberality to a latent design to promote the cause of infidelity. This, and all other slanders have been made without a shadow of proof. Neither religion, nor liberty can long subsist in the tumult of altercation, and amidst the noise and violence of faction.

Felix qui cautus.
Adieu.
Samuel Adams.

Mr. Thomas Paine.

TO SAMUEL ADAMS

My dear and venerable friend,

I received with great pleasure your friendly and affectionate letter of Nov. 30th and I thank you also for the frankness of it. Between men in pursuit of truth, and whose object is the happiness of man both here and hereafter, there ought to be no reserve. Even error has a claim to indulgence, if not to respect, when it is believed to be truth. I am obliged to you for your affectionate remembrance of what you stile my services in awakening the public mind to a declaration of independence and supporting it after it was declared. I also, like you, have often looked back on those times, and have thought that if independence had not been declared at the time it was the public mind could not have been brought up to it afterwards. It will immediately occur to you, who were so intimately acquainted with the situation of things at that time, that I allude to the black times of *Seventy six*; for though I know, and you my friend also know, they were no other than the natural consequences of the military blunders of that campaign, the country might have viewed them as proceeding from a natural inability to support its cause against the enemy, and have sunk under the despondency of that misconceived idea. This was the impression against which it was necessary the country should be strongly animated.

I now come to the second part of your letter, on which I shall be as frank with you as you are with me. "But, (say you) when I *heard* you had turned your mind to a defence of *infidelity,* I felt myself much astonished, &c." What, my good friend, do you call believing in God *infidelity?* for that is the great point maintained in the *Age of Reason* against all divided beliefs and *allegorical* divinities. The bishop of Landaff (Doctor Watson) not only acknowleges this, but pays me some compliments upon it in his answer to the second part of that work. *"There is,* (says he) *a philosophical sublimity in some of your ideas when speaking of the Creator of the Universe."*

What then, (my much esteemed friend for I do not respect

you the less because we differ, and that perhaps not much, in religious sentiments) what I ask is this thing called *infidelity?* If we go back to your ancestors and mine, three or four hundred years ago, for we must have had fathers and grandfathers or we should not be here, we shall find them praying to saints and virgins, and believing in purgatory and transubstantiation, and therefore all of us are infidels according to our forefathers belief. If we go back to times more ancient we shall again be infidels according to the belief of some other fore fathers.

The case, my friend, is, that the world has been over-run with fable and creeds of human invention, with Sectaries of whole nations, against other nations, and sectaries of those sectaries in each of them against each other. Every sectary, except the quakers, has been a persecutor. Those who fled from persecution persecuted in their turn, and it is this confusion of creeds that has filled the world with persecution and deluged it with blood. Even the depredation on your commerce by the Barbary powers, sprang from the crusades of the church against those powers. It was a war of creed against creed, each boasting of God for its author, and reviling each other with the name of infidel. If I do not believe as you believe, it proves that you do not believe as I believe, and this is all that it proves.

There is however one point of union wherein all religions meet, and that is in the first article of every man's creed, and of every nation's creed, that has any creed at all. *I believe in God.* Those who rest here, and there are millions who do, cannot be wrong as far as their creed goes. Those who chuse to go further *may be wrong,* for it is impossible that all can be right since there is so much contradiction among them. The first, therefore, are in my opinion on the safest side.

I presume you are so far acquainted with ecclesiastical history as to know, and the bishop who has answered me has been obliged to acknowlege the fact, that the books that compose the New Testament were voted by *yeas* and *nays* to be the word of God as you now vote a law, by the popish councils of Nice and Laodocia, about 1450 years ago. With respect to the fact there is no dispute, neither do I mention it for the sake of controversy. This vote may appear authority enough to some, and not authority enough to others. It is proper however that every body should know the fact.

With respect to the *Age of Reason* which you so much condemn, and that I believe without having read it, for you say only that you *heard* of it, I will inform you of a circumstance because you cannot know it by other means.

I have said in the first page of the first part of that work, that it had long been my intention to publish my thoughts upon religion, but that I had reserved it to a later time of life. I have now to inform you why I wrote it and published it at the time I did.

In the first place, I saw my life in continual danger. My friends were falling as fast the guilliotine could cut their heads off, and as I every day expected the same fate, I resolved to begin my work. I appeared to myself to be on my death bed, for death was on every side of me, and I had no time to lose. This accounts for my writing at the time I did; and so nicely did the time and the intention meet, that I had not finished the first part of that work more than six hours before I was arrested and taken to prison. Joel Barlow was with me, and knows the fact.

In the second place, the people of France were running headlong into Atheism, and I had the work translated and published in their own language, to stop them in that career, and fix them to the first article (as I have before said) of every man's creed who has any creed at all, *I believe in God*. I endangered my own life, in the first place, by opposing in the convention the execution of the king, and labouring to shew they were trying the monarchy, and not the man, and that the crimes imputed to him were the crimes of the monarchical system; and I endangered it a second time by opposing Atheism, and yet *some* of your priests, for I do not believe that all are perverse, cry out, in the *war whoop* of monarchical priestcraft, What an infidel! What a wicked man is Thomas Paine! They might as well add, for he believes in God, and is against shedding blood.

But all this *war whoop* of the pulpit has some concealed object. Religion is not the cause, but is the stalking horse. They put it forward to conceal themselves behind it. It is not a secret that there has been a party composed of the leaders of the Federalists, for I do not include all Federalists with their leaders, who have been working by various means for several years past, to overturn the Federal constitution established on the representative system, and place government in the new world on the corrupt system of the old. To accomplish this a large standing army was necessary, and as a pretence for such an army, the danger of a foreign invasion must be bellowed forth, from the pulpit, from the press, and by their public orators.

I am not of a disposition inclined to suspicion. It is in its nature a mean and cowardly passion, and upon the whole, even admitting error into the case, it is better, I am sure it is more generous, to be wrong on the side of confidence, than on the side of suspicion. But I know as a fact, that the English government distributes annually fifteen hundred pounds sterling among the Presbyterian ministers in England, and one thousand among those of Ireland, and when I hear of the strange discourses of some of your ministers and professors of colleges, I cannot, as the quakers say, find freedom in my mind to acquit them. Their anti-revolutionary doctrines invite suspicion even against one's will, and in spite of one's charity to believe well of them.

As you have given me one scripture phrase I will give you another for those ministers. It is said in Exodus, chapter 22, verse 28, *"Thou shalt not revile the gods nor curse the ruler of thy people."* But those ministers, such I mean as Dr. Emmons, curse ruler and people both, for the majority are, politically, the people, and it is those who have chosen the ruler whom they curse. As to the first part of the verse, that of *not reviling the gods*, it makes no part of my scripture. I have but one God.

Since I began this letter, for I write it by piece-meals, as I have leisure, I have seen the four letters that passed between you and John Adams. In your first letter you say, "let divines and philosophers, statesmen and patriots, unite their endeavours to *renovate the age* by inculcating in the minds of youth *the fear and love of the Deity, and universal philanthropy.*" Why, my dear friend, this is exactly *my* religion, and is the whole of it. That you may have an idea that the *Age of Reason* (for I believe you have not read it) inculcates this reverential fear and love of the Deity, I will give you a paragraph from it:

"Do we want to contemplate his power? We see it in the immensity of the creation. Do we want to contemplate his wisdom? We see it in the unchangeable order by which the incomprehensible whole is governed. Do we want to contemplate his munificence? We see it in the abundance with which he fills the earth. Do we want to contemplate his mercy? We see it in his not withholding that abundance even from the unthankful."

As I am fully with you in your first part, that respecting the deity, so am I in your second, that of *universal philanthropy;* by which I do not mean merely the sentimental benevolence of wishing well, but the practical benevolence of doing good. We cannot serve the Deity in the manner we serve those who cannot do without that service. He needs no service from us. We can add nothing to eternity. But it is in our power to render a service *acceptable* to him, and that is not by praying, but by endeavouring to make his creatures happy. A man does not serve God when he prays, for it is himself he is trying to serve, and as to hiring or paying men to pray, as if the Deity needed instruction, it is in my opinion an abomination. One good School Master is of more use and of more value than a load of such persons as Dr. Emmons and some others.

You, my dear and much respected friend, are now far in the vale of years; I have yet, I believe, some years in store, for I have a good state of health and a happy mind, and I take care of both, by nourishing the first with temperance and the latter with abundance.

This, I believe, you will allow to be the true philosophy of life. You will see by my third letter to the citizens of the United States, that I have been exposed to, and preserved through, many dangers, but instead of buffetting the Deity with prayers as if I distrusted him or must dictate to him, I reposed myself on his protection; and you, my friend, will find, even in your last moments, more consolation in the silence of resignation than in the murmuring wish of prayer.

In every thing which you say in your second letter to John Adams respecting our rights as men and citizens in this world I am perfectly with you. On other points we have to answer to our creator and not to each other. The key of heaven is not in the keeping of any sect, nor ought the road to it to be obstructed by any. Our relation to each other in this world is as men, and the man who is a friend to man and to his rights, let his religious opinions be what they may, is a good citizen, to whom I can give, as I ought to do, and as every other ought, the right hand of fellowship, and to none with more hearty good will, my dear friend, than to you.

THOMAS PAINE.

Federal City, Jan^{ry} 1, 1803.

The Construction of Iron Bridges

June 13, 1803

As bridges, and the method of constructing them, are becoming objects of great importance throughout the United States, and as there are at this time proposals for a bridge over the Delaware, and also a bridge beginning to be erected over the Schuylkill at Philadelphia, I present the public with some account of the construction of Iron bridges.

The following memoir on that subject, written last winter at the federal city, was intended to be presented to congress. But as the session would necessarily be short, and as several of its members would be replaced by new elections on the ensuing session, it was judged better to let it lie over. In the mean time, on account of the bridges now in contemplation, or began, I give the memoir the opportunity of appearing before the public and the persons concerned in those works.

THOMAS PAINE.

Bordentown on the Delaware,
    New Jersey, June 13, 1803.

TO THE CONGRESS OF THE UNITED STATES.

I have deposited in the office of the secretary of state, and under the care of the patent office, two models of iron bridges; the one in paste board, the other cast in metal. As they will shew by inspection the manner of constructing iron bridges, I shall not take up the time of congress with a description by words.

My intention in presenting this memoir to congress is to put the country in possession of the means and of the right of making use of the construction freely; As I do not intend to take any patent right for it.

As America abounds in rivers that interrupt the land communication, and as by the violence of floods, and the breaking up of the ice in the spring, the bridges, depending for support from the bottom of the river, are frequently carried away. I turned my attention, after the revolutionary war was over, to find a method of constructing an arch, that might, without rendering the height inconvenient or the ascent difficult, extend at once from shore to shore, over rivers of three, four, or five hundred feet and probably more.

The principle I took to begin with, and work upon, was that the small segment of a large circle was preferable to the great segment of a small circle. The appearance of such arches and the manner of forging and putting the parts together admit of many varieties, but the principle will be the same in all. The bridge architects I conversed with in England denied the principle, but it was generally supported by mathematicians, and experiment has now established the fact.

In 1786 I made three models, partly at Philadelphia, but mostly at Bordentown in the state of Jersey. One model was in wood, one in cast iron, and one in wrought iron connected with blocks of wood, representing cast iron blocks, but all on the same principle that of the small segment of a large circle.

I took the last mentioned one with me to France in 1787, and presented it to the academy of sciences at Paris for their opinion of it. The academy appointed a committee of three of their own body—Mons. Le Roy, and Abbe Bossou, and Mons. Borda. The first was an acquaintance of Dr. Franklin, and of Mr. Jefferson, then minister at Paris. The two others were celebrated as mathematicians. I presented it as a model for a bridge of a single arch of 400 feet span over the river Schuylkill at Philadelphia. The committee brought in a report which the academy adopted—that an arch on the principle and construction of the model, might, in their opinion, be extended 400 feet, the extent proposed.

In September of the same year, I sent the model to Sir Joseph Banks, President of the Royal Society in England, and soon after went there myself.

In order to ascertain the truth of the principle on a larger scale than could be shewn by a portable model of five or six feet in length, I went to the iron foundery of Messrs. Walkers, at Rotherham in the county of Yorkshire in England, and had a compleat Rib of 90 feet span, and 5 feet of height from the cord-line to the centre of the arch, manufactured and erected.

It was a segment of a circle of 410 feet diameter; and until this was done, no experiment on a circle of such an extensive diameter had ever been made in architecture, or the practicability of it supposed.

The Rib was erected between a wall of a furnace belonging to the iron-works, and the gable end of a brick building, which served as butments. The weight of iron in the Rib was three tons, and we loaded it with double its weight in pig iron. I wrote to Mr. Jefferson, who was then at Paris, an account of this experiment; and also Sir Joseph Banks in London, who in his answer to me says—"I look for many other bold improvements from your countrymen, the Americans, who think with vigour, and are not fettered with the trammels of science, before they are capable of exerting their mental faculties to advantage."

On the success of this experiment, I entered into an agreement with the iron founders at Rotherham to cast and manufacture a compleat bridge, to be composed of five ribs of 110 feet span, and 5 feet of height from the cord-line, being a segment of a circle of 610 feet diameter, and to send it to London to be erected as a specimen for establishing a manufactory of iron bridges to be sent to any part of the world.

The bridge was erected at the village of Paddington near London, but being in a plain field where no advantage could be taken of butments without the expence of building them, as in the former case, it served only as a specimen of the practicability of a manufactory of iron bridges. It was brought by sea, packed in the hold of a vessel, from the place where it was made; and after standing a year was taken down without injury to any of its parts, and might be erected any where else.

At this time my bridge operations became suspended. Mr. Edmund Burke published his attack on the French revolution and the system of representative government, and in defence of government by hereditary sucession, a thing which is in its nature an absurdity because it is impossible to make wisdom hereditary; and therefore, so far as wisdom is necessary in a government, it must be looked for where it can be found. Sometimes in one family; sometimes in another. History informs us that the son of Solomon was a fool. He lost ten tribes out of twelve.* There are those in later times who lost thirteen.

The publication of this work of Mr. Burke, absurd in its principles and outrageous in its manner, drew me, as I have said, from my bridge operations, and my time became employed in defending a system then established and operating in America and which I wished to see peaceably adopted in Europe—I therefore ceased my work on the bridge to employ myself on the more necessary work, *Rights of Man*, in answer to Mr. Burke.

In 1792 a convention was elected in France for the express purpose of forming a constitution on the authority of the people, as had been done in America, of which convention I was elected a member. I was at that time in England, and knew nothing of my being elected till the arrival of the person who was sent officially to inform me of it.

During my residence in France, which was from 1792 to 1802, an iron bridge of 236 feet span and 34 of height from the cord line was erected over the river Wear at the town of Sunderland in the county of Durham in England. It was done chiefly at the expence of the two members in parliament for that county, Milbanke and Burdon.

It happened that a very intimate friend of mine sir Robert Smyth (who was also an acquaintance of Mr. Monroe the American minister and since of Mr. Livingston) was then at Paris. He had been colleague in parliament with Milbanke, and supposing that the persons who constructed the iron bridge at Sunderland had made free with my model, which was at the iron works where the Sunderland bridge was cast, he wrote to Milbanke on the subject, and the following is that gentleman's answer.

With respect to the bridge over the river Wear at Sunderland, it certainly is a work well deserving admiration both for its structure and utility, and I have good grounds for saying, that the first idea was suggested by Mr. Paine's bridge exhibited at Paddington. What difference there may be in some part of the structure, or in the proportion of wrought and cast iron, I cannot pretend to say, Burdon

*2 Chron. Chap. 10.

having undertaken to build the bridge, in consequence of his having taken upon himself whatever the expence might be beyond between three and four thousand pounds (sterling) subscribed by myself and some other gentlemen. But whatever the mechanism might be it did not supercede the necessity of a center* [The writer has here confounded a center with a scaffolding] which center [continues the writer] was esteemed a very ingenious piece of workmanship, and taken from a plan sketched out by Mr. Nash an architect of great merit who had been consulted in the outset of the business, when a bridge of stone was in contemplation.

With respect therefore to any gratuity to Mr. Paine, though ever so desirous of rewarding the labours of an ingenious man, I do not feel, how, under the circumstances already described I have it in my power, having had nothing to do with the bridge after the payment of my subscription, Mr. Burdon then becoming accountable for the whole.—But if you can point out any mode, according to which it should be in my power to be instrumental in procuring him any compensation for the advantages the public may have derived from his ingenious model, from which certainly the outline of the bridge at Sunderland was taken, be assured it will afford me very great satisfaction†.   RA. MILBANKE.

The year before I left France the government of that country had it in contemplation to erect an iron bridge over the river Seine at Paris. As all edifices of public construction came under the cognizance of the minister of the interior, (and as their plan was to erect a bridge of five iron arches of one hundred feet span each, instead of passing the river with a single arch, and which was going backward in practice, instead of forward, as there was already an iron arch of 236 feet in existence) I wrote the minister of the interior, the citizen Chaptal, a memoir on the construction of iron bridges. The following is his answer.

The minister of the interior to the citizen Thomas Paine.

I have received, citizen, the observations that you have been so good as to address to me upon the construction of iron bridges. They will be of the greatest utility to us in a moment when this new

*It is the technical term, meaning the boards and timbers which form the arch upon which the permanent materials are laid: when a bridge is finished, the workmen they say are ready to strike centre, that is to take down the scaffolding.

†The original is in my possession.

kind of construction goes to be executed for the first time. I see with pleasure, citizen, that you have rights of more than of one kind to the thankfulness of nations, and I give you, cordially, the particular expression of my esteem*. CHAPTAL.

A short time before I left France a person came to me from London with plans and drawings for an iron bridge of one arch over the river Thames at London, of 600 feet span, and sixty feet of height from the cord line. The subject was then before a committee of the house of commons, but I know not the proceedings thereon.

As this new construction of an arch for bridges, and the principles on which it is founded, originated in America, as the documents I have produced sufficiently prove, and is becoming an object of importance to the world, and to no part of it more than our own, on account of its numerous rivers, and as no experiment has been made in America to bring it into practice, further than on the models I have executed myself, and at my own expence, I beg leave to submit a proposal to Congress on the subject, which is,

To erect an experiment rib of about 400 feet span, to be the segment of a circle of at least 1000 feet diameter, and to let it remain exposed to public view, that the method of constructing such arches may be generally known.

It is an advantage peculiar to the construction of iron bridges, that the success of an arch of given extent and height, can be ascertained without being at the expence of building the bridge; which is, by the method I propose, that of erecting an experiment rib on the ground where advantage can be taken of two hills for butments.

I began in this manner with the rib of 90 feet span, and five feet of height, being a segment of a circle of 410 feet diameter. The undertakers of the Sunderland bridge began in the same manner. They contracted with the iron founders for a single rib, and finding it to answer, had five more manufactured like it, and erected into a bridge consisting of six ribs, the experiment rib being one. But the Sunderland bridge does not carry the principle much further into practice than had been done by the rib of 90 feet span and five feet in

*The original in French is in my possession.

height, being, as before said, a segment of a circle of 410 feet diameter. The Sunderland bridge being 206 feet span and 34 feet of height, gives the diameter of the circle of which it is a segment, to be 444 feet, within a few inches, which is but a larger segment of a circle of 34 feet more diameter.

The construction of those bridges does not come within the line of any established practice of business. The stone architect can derive but little from the theory or practice of his art that enters into the construction of an iron bridge; and the iron founder, though he may be expert in moulding and casting the parts, when the models are given him, would be at a loss to proportion them unless he was acquainted with all the lines and properties belonging to a circle.

If it should appear to Congress that the construction of iron bridges will be of utility to the country, and they should direct that an experiment rib be made for that purpose, I will furnish the proportions for the several parts of the work, and give my attendance to superintend the erection of it freely.

But, in any case, I have to request that this memoir may be put on the Journals of Congress, as an evidence hereafter, that this new construction of bridges originated in America.

THOMAS PAINE.

Federal City, Jan. 3, 1803.

N. B. The two models mentioned in the memoire, will, I expect, arrive at Philadelphia by the next packet from the federal city, and will remain for some time in Mr. Peale's Museum.

Of the Term
"Liberty of the Press"

October 20, 1806

THE writer of this remembers a remark made to him by Mr. Jefferson concerning the English Newspapers which at that time, 1787, while Mr. Jefferson was Minister at Paris, were most vulgarly abusive. The remark applies with equal force to the Federal papers of America. The remark was, that "the licentiousness of the press produces the same effect as the restraint of the press was intended to do. The restraint, said he, was to prevent things being told, and the licentiousness of the press prevents things being believed when they are told." We have in this state an evidence of the truth of this remark. The number of federal papers in the city and state of New-York are more than five to one to the number of republican papers, yet the majority of the elections go always against the federal papers, which is demonstrative evidence that the licentiousness of those papers are destitute of credit.

Whoever has made observation on the characters of nations will find it generally true, that the manners of a nation, or of a party, can be better ascertained from the character of its press than from any other public circumstance. If its press is licentious, its manners are not good. Nobody believes a common liar, or a common defamer.

Nothing is more common with printers, especially of Newspapers, than the continual cry of the *liberty of the press*, as if because they are Printers they are to have more privileges than other people. As the term *"liberty of the press"* is adopted in this country without being understood I will state the origin of it and shew what it means. The term comes from England, and the case was as follows.

Prior to what is called in England *the revolution*, which was in 1688, no work could be published in that country without first obtaining the permission of an officer appointed by the government for inspecting works intended for publication. The same was the case in France, except that in France there were forty who were called *censors*, and in England there was but one, called Impremateur.

At the revolution the office of Impremateur was abolished and as works could then be published without first obtaining the permission of the government officer, the press was, in consequence of that abolition, said to be free, and it was from this circumstance that the term *liberty of the press* arose. The press, which is a tongue to the eye, was then put exactly in the case of the human tongue. A man does not ask liberty before hand to say something he has a mind to say, but he becomes answerable afterwards for the atrocities he may utter. In like manner, if a man makes the press utter attrocious things he becomes as answerable for them as if he had uttered them by word of mouth. Mr. Jefferson has said in his inaugural speech, that *"error of opinion might be tolerated when reason was left free to combat it."* This is sound philosophy in cases of error. But there is a difference between error and licentiousness.

Some lawyers in defending their clients, (for the generality of lawyers like Swiss soldiers will fight on either side) have often given their opinion of what they defined the liberty of the press to be. One said it was this; another said it was that, and so on, according the case they were pleading. Now these men ought to have known that the term, *liberty of the press,* arose from a FACT, the abolition of the office of Imprimateur, and that opinion has nothing to do in the case. The term refers to the fact of Printing *free from prior restraint*, and not at all to the matter Printed whether good or bad. The public at large, or in case of prosecution, a jury of the country will be the judges of the matter.

COMMON SENSE.

RIGHTS OF MAN

Rights of Man

Being an
Answer to Mr. Burke's Attack
on the French Revolution

———
1791
———

TO GEORGE WASHINGTON,
PRESIDENT OF THE UNITED STATES
OF AMERICA.

SIR,

I present you a small Treatise in defence of those Principles of Freedom which your exemplary Virtue hath so eminently contributed to establish.—That the Rights of Man may become as universal as your Benevolence can wish, and that you may enjoy the Happiness of seeing the New World regenerate the Old, is the Prayer of

SIR,

Your much obliged, and

Obedient humble Servant,

THOMAS PAINE.

PREFACE TO THE ENGLISH EDITION.

FROM the part Mr. Burke took in the American Revolution, it was natural that I should consider him a friend to mankind; and as our acquaintance commenced on that ground, it would have been more agreeable to me to have had cause to continue in that opinion, than to change it.

At the time Mr. Burke made his violent speech last winter in the English Parliament against the French Revolution and the National Assembly, I was in Paris, and had written him, but a short time before, to inform him how prosperously matters were going on. Soon after this, I saw his advertisement of the Pamphlet he intended to publish: As the attack was to be made in a language but little studied, and less understood, in France, and as every thing suffers by translation, I promised some of the friends of the Revolution in that country, that whenever Mr. Burke's Pamphlet came forth, I would answer it. This appeared to me the more necessary to be done, when I saw the flagrant misrepresentations which Mr. Burke's Pamphlet contains; and that while it is an outrageous abuse on the French Revolution, and the principles of Liberty, it is an imposition on the rest of the world.

I am the more astonished and disappointed at this conduct in Mr. Burke, as (from the circumstance I am going to mention), I had formed other expectations.

I had seen enough of the miseries of war, to wish it might never more have existence in the world, and that some other mode might be found out to settle the differences that should occasionally arise in the neighbourhood of nations. This certainly might be done if Courts were disposed to set honestly about it, or if countries were enlightened enough not to be made the dupes of Courts. The people of America had been bred up in the same prejudices against France, which at that time characterized the people of England; but experience and an acquaintance with the French Nation have most effectually shown to the Americans the falsehood of those prejudices; and I do not believe that a more cordial and confidential intercourse exists between any two countries than between America and France.

When I came to France in the Spring of 1787, the Archbishop of Thoulouse was then Minister, and at that time highly esteemed. I became much acquainted with the private Secretary of that Minister, a man of an enlarged benevolent heart; and found, that his sentiments and my own perfectly agreed with respect to the madness of war, and the wretched impolicy of two nations, like England and France, continually worrying each other, to no other end than that of a mutual increase of burdens and taxes. That I might be assured I had not misunderstood him, nor he me, I put the substance of our opinions into writing, and sent it to him; subjoining a request, that if I should see among the people of England, any disposition to cultivate a better understanding between the two nations than had hitherto prevailed, how far I might be authorized to say that the same disposition prevailed on the part of France? He answered me by letter in the most unreserved manner, and that not for himself only, but for the

Minister, with whose knowledge the letter was declared to be written.

I put this letter into the hands of Mr. Burke almost three years ago, and left it with him, where it still remains; hoping, and at the same time naturally expecting, from the opinion I had conceived of him, that he would find some opportunity of making a good use of it, for the purpose of removing those errors and prejudices, which two neighbouring nations, from the want of knowing each other, had entertained, to the injury of both.

When the French Revolution broke out, it certainly afforded to Mr. Burke an opportunity of doing some good, had he been disposed to it; instead of which, no sooner did he see the old prejudices wearing away, than he immediately began sowing the seeds of a new inveteracy, as if he were afraid that England and France would cease to be enemies. That there are men in all countries who get their living by war, and by keeping up the quarrels of Nations, is as shocking as it is true; but when those who are concerned in the government of a country, make it their study to sow discord, and cultivate prejudices between Nations, it becomes the more unpardonable.

With respect to a paragraph in this Work alluding to Mr. Burke's having a pension, the report has been some time in circulation, at least two months; and as a person is often the last to hear what concerns him the most to know, I have mentioned it, that Mr. Burke may have an opportunity of contradicting the rumour, if he thinks proper.

THOMAS PAINE.

RIGHTS OF MAN, &c.

AMONG the incivilities by which nations or individuals provoke and irritate each other, Mr. Burke's pamphlet on the French Revolution is an extraordinary instance. Neither the people of France, nor the National Assembly, were troubling themselves about the affairs of England, or the English Parliament; and why Mr. Burke should commence an unprovoked attack upon them, both in parliament and in public, is a conduct that cannot be pardoned on the score of manners, nor justified on that of policy.

There is scarcely an epithet of abuse to be found in the English language, with which Mr. Burke has not loaded the French nation and the National Assembly. Every thing which rancour, prejudice, ignorance or knowledge could suggest, are poured forth in the copious fury of near four hundred pages. In the strain and on the plan Mr. Burke was writing, he might have wrote on to as many thousands. When the tongue or the pen is let loose in a phrenzy of passion, it is the man, and not the subject, that becomes exhausted.

Hitherto Mr. Burke has been mistaken and disappointed in the opinions he had formed of the affairs of France; but such is the ingenuity of his hope, or the malignancy of his despair, that it furnishes him with new pretences to go on. There was a time when it was impossible to make Mr. Burke believe there would be any revolution in France. His opinion then was, that the French had neither spirit to undertake it, nor fortitude to support it; and now that there is one, he seeks an escape by condemning it.

Not sufficiently content with abusing the National Assembly, a great part of his work is taken up with abusing Dr. Price (one of the best-hearted men that lives), and the two societies in England known by the name of the Revolution and the Constitutional Societies.

Dr. Price had preached a sermon on the 4th of November, 1789, being the anniversary of what is called in England the Revolution which took place 1688. Mr. Burke, speaking of this sermon, says, "The political Divine proceeds dogmatically to assert, that, by the principles of the Revolution, the people of England have acquired three fundamental rights:

"1. To chuse our own governors.

"2. To cashier them for misconduct.

"3. To frame a government for ourselves."

Dr. Price does not say that the right to do these things exists in this or in that person, or in this or in that description of persons, but that it exists in the *whole*; that it is a right resident in the nation. — Mr. Burke, on the contrary, denies that such a right exists in the nation, either in whole or in part, or that it exists any where; and what is still more strange

and marvellous, he says, "that the people of England utterly
disclaim such a right, and that they will resist the practical
assertion of it with their lives and fortunes." That men should
take up arms, and spend their lives and fortunes, *not* to maintain their rights, but to maintain they have *not* rights, is an
entire new species of discovery, and suited to the paradoxial
genius of Mr. Burke.

The method which Mr. Burke takes to prove that the
people of England have no such rights, and that such rights
do not now exist in the nation, either in whole or in part, or
any where at all, is of the same marvellous and monstrous
kind with what he has already said; for his arguments are, that
the persons, or the generation of persons, in whom they did
exist, are dead, and with them the right is dead also. To prove
this, he quotes a declaration made by parliament about a hundred years ago, to William and Mary, in these words:—"The
Lords spiritual and temporal, and Commons, do, in the name
of the people aforesaid—(meaning the people of England
then living)—most humbly and faithfully *submit* themselves,
their *heirs* and *posterities*, for EVER." He also quotes a clause
of another act of parliament made in the same reign, the
terms of which, he says, "binds us—(meaning the people of
that day)—"our *heirs* and our *posterity*, to *them*, their *heirs*
and *posterity*, to the end of time."

Mr. Burke conceives his point sufficiently established by
producing those clauses, which he enforces by saying that
they exclude the right of the nation for *ever* : and not yet
content with making such declarations, repeated over and
over again, he further says, "that if the people of England
possessed such a right before the Revolution, (which he acknowledges to have been the case, not only in England, but
throughout Europe, at an early period) yet that the *English
nation* did, at the time of the Revolution, most solemnly renounce and abdicate it, for themselves, and for *all their posterity for ever*."

As Mr. Burke occasionally applies the poison drawn from
his horrid principles (if it is not a prophanation to call them
by the name of principles) not only to the English nation, but
to the French Revolution and the National Assembly, and
charges that august, illuminated and illuminating body of

men with the epithet of *usurpers*, I shall, *sans ceremonie*, place
another system of principles in opposition to his.

The English Parliament of 1688 did a certain thing, which,
for themselves and their constituents, they had a right to do,
and which it appeared right should be done: but, in addition
to this right, which they possessed by delegation, *they set up
another right by assumption*, that of binding and controuling
posterity to the end of time. The case, therefore, divides itself
into two parts; the right which they possessed by delegation,
and the right which they set up by assumption. The first is
admitted; but, with respect to the second, I reply—

There never did, there never will, and there never can exist
a parliament, or any description of men, or any generation of
men, in any country, possessed of the right or the power of
binding and controuling posterity to the *"end of time,"* or of
commanding for ever how the world shall be governed, or
who shall govern it: and therefore all such clauses, acts or
declarations, by which the makers of them attempt to do what
they have neither the right nor the power to do, nor the
power to execute, are in themselves null and void. Every age
and generation must be as free to act for itself, *in all cases*, as
the ages and generations which preceded it. The vanity and
presumption of governing beyond the grave, is the most ridiculous and insolent of all tyrannies. Man has no property in
man; neither has any generation a property in the generations
which are to follow. The parliament or the people of 1688, or
of any other period, had no more right to dispose of the
people of the present day, or to bind or to controul them *in
any shape whatever*, than the parliament or the people of the
present day have to dispose of, bind or controul those who
are to live a hundred or a thousand years hence. Every generation is and must be competent to all the purposes which its
occasions require. It is the living, and not the dead, that are
to be accommodated. When man ceases to be, his power and
his wants cease with him; and having no longer any participation in the concerns of this world, he has no longer any
authority in directing who shall be its governors, or how its
government shall be organized, or how administered.

I am not contending for, nor against, any form of government, nor for, nor against, any party here or elsewhere. That

which a whole nation chooses to do, it has a right to do. Mr. Burke says, No. Where then *does* the right exist? I am contending for the right of the *living*, and against their being willed away, and controuled and contracted for, by the manuscript assumed authority of the dead; and Mr. Burke is contending for the authority of the dead over the rights and freedom of the living. There was a time when kings disposed of their crowns by will upon their death-beds, and consigned the people, like beasts of the field, to whatever successor they appointed. This is now so exploded as scarcely to be remembered, and so monstrous as hardly to be believed: But the parliamentary clauses upon which Mr. Burke builds his political church, are of the same nature.

The laws of every country must be analogous to some common principle. In England, no parent or master, nor all the authority of parliament, omnipotent as it has called itself, can bind or controul the personal freedom even of an individual beyond the age of twenty-one years: On what ground of right then could the parliament of 1688, or any other parliament, bind all posterity for ever?

Those who have quitted the world, and those who are not yet arrived at it, are as remote from each other as the utmost stretch of mortal imagination can conceive: What possible obligation then can exist between them, what rule or principle can be laid down, that two non-entities, the one out of existence, and the other not in, and who never can meet in this world, that the one should controul the other to the end of time?

In England, it is said that money cannot be taken out of the pockets of the people without their consent: But who authorized, and who could authorize the parliament of 1688 to controul and take away the freedom of posterity, and limit and confine their rights of acting in certain cases for ever, who were not in existence to give or to with-hold their consent?

A greater absurdity cannot present itself to the understanding of man, than what Mr. Burke offers to his readers. He tells them, and he tells the world to come, that a certain body of men, who existed a hundred years ago, made a law, and that there does not now exist in the nation, nor ever will, nor ever can, a power to alter it. Under how many subtilties, or absurdities, has the divine right to govern been imposed on the credulity of mankind! Mr. Burke has discovered a new one, and he has shortened his journey to Rome, by appealing to the power of this infallible parliament of former days; and he produces what it has done, as of divine authority: for that power must certainly be more than human, which no human power to the end of time can alter.

But Mr. Burke has done some service, not to his cause, but to his country, by bringing those clauses into public view. They serve to demonstrate how necessary it is at all times to watch against the attempted encroachment of power, and to prevent its running to excess. It is somewhat extraordinary, that the offence for which James II. was expelled, that of setting up power by *assumption*, should be re-acted, under another shape and form, by the parliament that expelled him. It shews, that the rights of man were but imperfectly understood at the Revolution; for certain it is, that the right which that parliament set up by *assumption* (for by delegation it had it not, and could not have it, because none could give it) over the persons and freedom of posterity for ever, was of the same tyrannical unfounded kind which James attempted to set up over the parliament and the nation, and for which he was expelled. The only difference is, (for in principle they differ not) that the one was an usurper over the living, and the other over the unborn; and as the one has no better authority to stand upon than the other, both of them must be equally null and void, and of no effect.

From what, or from whence, does Mr. Burke prove the right of any human power to bind posterity for ever? He has produced his clauses; but he must produce also his proofs, that such a right existed, and shew how it existed. If it ever existed, it must now exist; for whatever appertains to the nature of man, cannot be annihilated by man. It is the nature of man to die, and he will continue to die as long as he continues to be born. But Mr. Burke has set up a sort of political Adam, in whom all posterity are bound for ever; he must therefore prove that his Adam possessed such a power, or such a right.

The weaker any cord is, the less will it bear to be stretched, and the worse is the policy to stretch it, unless it is intended to break it. Had a person contemplated the overthrow of Mr. Burke's positions, he would have proceeded as Mr. Burke has done. He would have magnified the authorities, on purpose to have called the *right* of them into question; and the instant the question of right was started, the authorities must have been given up.

It requires but a very small glance of thought to perceive, that altho' laws made in one generation often continue in force through succeeding generations, yet that they continue to derive their force from the consent of the living. A law not repealed continues in force, not because it *cannot* be repealed, but because it *is not* repealed; and the non-repealing passes for consent.

But Mr. Burke's clauses have not even this qualification in their favour. They become null, by attempting to become immortal. The nature of them precludes consent. They destroy the right which they *might* have, by grounding it on a right which they *cannot* have. Immortal power is not a human right, and therefore cannot be a right of parliament. The parliament of 1688 might as well have passed an act to have authorised themselves to live for ever, as to make their authority live for ever. All therefore that can be said of them is, that they are a formality of words, of as much import, as if those who used them had addressed a congratulation to themselves, and, in the oriental stile of antiquity, had said, O Parliament, live for ever!

The circumstances of the world are continually changing, and the opinions of men change also; and as government is for the living, and not for the dead, it is the living only that has any right in it. That which may be thought right and found convenient in one age, may be thought wrong and found inconvenient in another. In such cases, Who is to decide, the living, or the dead?

As almost one hundred pages of Mr. Burke's book are employed upon these clauses, it will consequently follow, that if the clauses themselves, so far as they set up an *assumed*, *usurped* dominion over posterity for ever, are unauthoritative, and in their nature null and void, that all his voluminous inferences and declamation drawn therefrom, or founded thereon, are null and void also: and on this ground I rest the matter.

We now come more particularly to the affairs of France. Mr. Burke's book has the appearance of being written as instruction to the French nation; but if I may permit myself the use of an extravagant metaphor, suited to the extravagance of the case, It is darkness attempting to illuminate light.

While I am writing this, there is accidentally before me some proposals for a declaration of rights by the Marquis de la Fayette (I ask his pardon for using his former address, and do it only for distinction's sake) to the National Assembly on the 11th of July 1789, three days before the taking of the Bastille; and I cannot but be struck how opposite the sources are from which that Gentleman and Mr. Burke draw their principles. Instead of referring to musty records and mouldy parchments to prove that the rights of the living are lost, "renounced and abdicated for ever," by those who are now no more, as Mr. Burke has done, M. de la Fayette applies to the living world, and emphatically says, "Call to mind the sentiments which Nature has engraved in the heart of every citizen, and which take a new force when they are solemnly recognized by all:—For a nation to love liberty, it is sufficient that she knows it; and to be free, it is sufficient that she wills it." How dry, barren, and obscure, is the source from which Mr. Burke labours; and how ineffectual, though gay with flowers, are all his declamation and his argument, compared with these clear, concise, and soul-animating sentiments! Few and short as they are, they lead on to a vast field of generous and manly thinking, and do not finish, like Mr. Burke's periods, with music in the ear, and nothing in the heart.

As I have introduced the mention of M. de la Fayette, I will take the liberty of adding an anecdote respecting his farewel address to the Congress of America in 1783, and which occurred fresh to my mind when I saw Mr. Burke's thundering attack on the French Revolution.—M. de la Fayette went to America at an early period of the war, and continued a volunteer in her service to the end. His conduct through the whole of that enterprise is one of the most extraordinary that is to be found in the history of a young man, scarcely then twenty years of age. Situated in a country that was like the lap of sensual pleasure, and with the means of enjoying it, how few are there to be found who would exchange such a scene for the woods and wilderness of America, and pass the flowery years of youth in unprofitable danger and hardship! but such is the fact. When the war ended, and he was on the point of taking his final departure, he presented himself to Congress, and contemplating, in his affectionate farewel, the revolution he had seen, expressed himself in these words: *"May this great monument, raised to Liberty, serve as a lesson to the oppressor, and an example to the oppressed!"*—When this address came to the hands of Doctor Franklin, who was then in France, he applied to Count Vergennes to have it inserted in the French Gazette, but never could obtain his consent. The fact was, that Count Vergennes was an aristocratical despot at home, and dreaded the example of the American revolution in France, as certain other persons now dread the example of the French revolution in England; and Mr. Burke's tribute of fear (for in this light his book must be considered) runs parallel with Count Vergennes' refusal. But, to return more particularly to his work—

"We have seen (says Mr. Burke) the French rebel against a mild and lawful Monarch, with more fury, outrage, and insult, than any people has been known to rise against the most illegal usurper, or the most sanguinary tyrant."—This is one among a thousand other instances, in which Mr. Burke shews that he is ignorant of the springs and principles of the French revolution.

It was not against Louis the XVIth, but against the despotic principles of the government, that the nation revolted. These principles had not their origin in him, but in the original establishment, many centuries back; and they were become too deeply rooted to be removed, and the augean stable of parasites and plunderers too abominably filthy to be cleansed, by any thing short of a complete and universal revolution. When it becomes necessary to do a thing, the whole heart and soul should go into the measure, or not attempt it. That crisis was then arrived, and there remained no choice but to act with determined vigour, or not to act at all. The King was known to be the friend of the nation, and this circumstance was favourable to the enterprise. Perhaps no man bred up in the stile of an absolute King, ever possessed a heart so little disposed to the exercise of that species of power as the present King of France. But the principles of the government itself still remained the same. The Monarch and the Monarchy were distinct and separate things; and it was against the established despotism of the latter, and not against the person or principles of the former, that the revolt commenced, and the revolution has been carried.

Mr. Burke does not attend to the distinction between *men* and *principles*, and therefore he does not see that a revolt may take place against the despotism of the latter, while there lies no charge of despotism against the former.

The natural moderation of Louis XVI. contributed nothing to alter the hereditary despotism of the monarchy. All the tyrannies of former reigns, acted under that hereditary despotism, were still liable to be revived in the hands of a successor. It was not the respite of a reign that would satisfy France, enlightened as she was then become. A casual discontinuance of the *practice* of despotism, is not a discontinuance of its *principles*; the former depends on the virtue of the individual who is in immediate possession of the power; the latter, on the virtue and fortitude of the nation. In the case of Charles I. and James II. of England, the revolt was against the personal despotism of the men; whereas in France, it was against the hereditary despotism of the established government. But men who can consign over the rights of posterity for ever on the authority of a mouldy parchment, like Mr. Burke, are not qualified to judge of this revolution. It takes in a field too vast for their views to explore, and proceeds with a mightiness of reason they cannot keep pace with.

But there are many points of view in which this revolution may be considered. When despotism has established itself for ages in a country, as in France, it is not in the person of the King only that it resides. It has the appearance of being so in show, and in nominal authority; but it is not so in practice, and in fact. It has its standard every where. Every office and department has its despotism, founded upon custom and usage. Every place has its Bastille, and every Bastille its despot. The original hereditary despotism resident in the person of

the King, divides and subdivides itself into a thousand shapes
and forms, till at last the whole of it is acted by deputation.
This was the case in France; and against this species of despotism, proceeding on through an endless labyrinth of office till
the source of it is scarcely perceptible, there is no mode of
redress. It strengthens itself by assuming the appearance of
duty, and tyrannises under the pretence of obeying.

When a man reflects on the condition which France was in
from the nature of her government, he will see other causes
for revolt than those which immediately connect themselves
with the person or character of Louis XVI. There were, if I
may so express it, a thousand despotisms to be reformed in
France, which had grown up under the hereditary despotism
of the monarchy, and became so rooted as to be in a great
measure independent of it. Between the monarchy, the parliament, and the church, there was a *rivalship* of despotism;
besides the feudal despotism operating locally, and the ministerial despotism operating every-where. But Mr. Burke, by
considering the King as the only possible object of a revolt,
speaks as if France was a village, in which every thing that
passed must be known to its commanding officer, and no oppression could be acted but what he could immediately controul. Mr. Burke might have been in the Bastille his whole
life, as well under Louis XVI. as Louis XIV. and neither the
one nor the other have known that such a man as Mr. Burke
existed. The despotic principles of the government were the
same in both reigns, though the dispositions of the men were
as remote as tyranny and benevolence.

What Mr. Burke considers as a reproach to the French
Revolution (that of bringing it forward under a reign more
mild than the preceding ones), is one of its highest honours.
The revolutions that have taken place in other European
countries, have been excited by personal hatred. The rage was
against the man, and he became the victim. But, in the instance of France, we see a revolution generated in the rational
contemplation of the rights of man, and distinguishing from
the beginning between persons and principles.

But Mr. Burke appears to have no idea of principles, when
he is contemplating governments. "Ten years ago (says he) I
could have felicitated France on her having a government,

without enquiring what the nature of that government was, or how it was administered." Is this the language of a rational man? Is it the language of a heart feeling as it ought to feel for the rights and happiness of the human race? On this ground Mr. Burke must compliment every government in the world, while the victims who suffer under them, whether sold into slavery, or tortured out of existence, are wholly forgotten. It is power, and not principles, that Mr. Burke venerates; and under this abominable depravity, he is disqualified to judge between them.—Thus much for his opinion as to the occasions of the French Revolution. I now proceed to other considerations.

I know a place in America called Point-no-Point; because as you proceed along the shore, gay and flowery as Mr. Burke's language, it continually recedes and presents itself at a distance a head; and when you have got as far as you can go, there is no point at all. Just thus it is with Mr. Burke's three hundred and fifty-six pages. It is therefore difficult to reply to him. But as the points he wishes to establish may be inferred from what he abuses, it is in his paradoxes that we must look for his arguments.

As to the tragic paintings by which Mr. Burke has outraged his own imagination, and seeks to work upon that of his readers, they are very well calculated for theatrical representation, where facts are manufactured for the sake of show, and accommodated to produce, through the weakness of sympathy, a weeping effect. But Mr. Burke should recollect that he is writing History, and not *Plays*; and that his readers will expect truth, and not the spouting rant of high-toned exclamation.

When we see a man dramatically lamenting in a publication intended to be believed, that, *"The age of chivalry is gone!* that *The glory of Europe is extinguished for ever!* that *The unbought grace of life,* (if any one knows what it is), *the cheap defence of nations, the nurse of manly sentiment and heroic enterprize, is gone!"* and all this because the Quixote age of chivalry nonsense is gone, What opinion can we form of his judgment, or what regard can we pay to his facts? In the rhapsody of his imagination, he has discovered a world of wind-mills, and his sorrows are, that there are no Quixotes to attack them. But if the age of aristocracy, like that of chivalry, should fall, and they had originally some connection, Mr. Burke, the trumpeter of the Order, may continue his parody to the end, and finish with exclaiming— *"Othello's occupation's gone!"*

Notwithstanding Mr. Burke's horrid paintings, when the French Revolution is compared with that of other countries, the astonishment will be, that it is marked with so few sacrifices; but this astonishment will cease when we reflect that it was *principles*, and not *persons*, that were the meditated objects of destruction. The mind of the nation was acted upon by a higher stimulus than what the consideration of persons could inspire, and sought a higher conquest than could be produced by the downfal of an enemy. Among the few who fell, there do not appear to be any that were intentionally singled out. They all of them had their fate in the circumstances of the moment, and were not pursued with that long, cold-blooded, unabated revenge which pursued the unfortunate Scotch in the affair of 1745.

Through the whole of Mr. Burke's book I do not observe that the Bastille is mentioned more than once, and that with a kind of implication as if he were sorry it is pulled down, and wished it were built up again. "We have rebuilt Newgate (says he), and tenanted the mansion; and we have prisons almost as strong as the Bastille for those who dare to libel the Queens of France*." As to what a madman, like the person called Lord George Gordon, might say, and to whom Newgate is rather a bedlam than a prison, it is unworthy a rational consideration. It was a madman that libelled—and that is sufficient apology; and it afforded an opportunity for confining him, which was the thing that was wished for: But certain it is that Mr. Burke, who does not call himself a madman, whatever other people may do, has libelled, in the most un-

---

*Since writing the above, two other places occur in Mr. Burke's pamphlet, in which the name of the Bastille is mentioned, but in the same manner. In the one, he introduces it in a sort of obscure question, and asks—"Will any ministers who now serve such a king, with but a decent appearance of respect, cordially obey the orders of those whom but the other day, *in his name*, they had committed to the Bastille?" In the other, the taking it is mentioned as implying criminality in the French guards who assisted in demolishing it.—"They have not (says he) forgot the taking the king's castles at Paris."—This is Mr. Burke, who pretends to write on constitutional freedom.

provoked manner, and in the grossest stile of the most vulgar abuse, the whole representative authority of France; and yet Mr. Burke takes his seat in the British House of Commons! From his violence and his grief, his silence on some points, and his excess on others, it is difficult not to believe that Mr. Burke is sorry, extremely sorry, that arbitrary power, the power of the Pope, and the Bastille, are pulled down.

Not one glance of compassion, not one commiserating reflection, that I can find throughout his book, has he bestowed on those who lingered out the most wretched of lives, a life without hope, in the most miserable of prisons. It is painful to behold a man employing his talents to corrupt himself. Nature has been kinder to Mr. Burke than he is to her. He is not affected by the reality of distress touching upon his heart, but by the showy resemblance of it striking his imagination. He pities the plumage, but forgets the dying bird. Accustomed to kiss the aristocratical hand that hath purloined him from himself, he degenerates into a composition of art, and the genuine soul of nature forsakes him. His hero or his heroine must be a tragedy-victim expiring in show, and not the real prisoner of misery, sliding into death in the silence of a dungeon.

As Mr. Burke has passed over the whole transaction of the Bastille (and his silence is nothing in his favour), and has entertained his readers with reflections on supposed facts distorted into real falsehoods, I will give, since he has not, some account of the circumstances which preceded that transaction. They will serve to shew, that less mischief could scarcely have accompanied such an event, when considered with the treacherous and hostile aggravations of the enemies of the Revolution.

The mind can hardly picture to itself a more tremendous scene than what the city of Paris exhibited at the time of taking the Bastille, and for two days before and after, nor conceive the possibility of its quieting so soon. At a distance, this transaction has appeared only as an act of heroism, standing on itself; and the close political connection it had with the Revolution is lost in the brilliancy of the atchievement. But we are to consider it as the strength of the parties, brought man to man, and contending for the issue. The Bastille was to be either the prize or the prison of the assailants. The downfal of it included the idea of the downfal of Despotism; and this compounded image was become as figuratively united as Bunyan's Doubting Castle and giant Despair.

The National Assembly, before and at the time of taking the Bastille, was sitting at Versailles, twelve miles distant from Paris. About a week before the rising of the Parisians, and their taking the Bastille, it was discovered that a plot was forming, at the head of which was the Count d'Artois, the King's youngest brother, for demolishing the National Assembly, seizing its members, and thereby crushing, by a *coup de main*, all hopes and prospects of forming a free government. For the sake of humanity, as well as of freedom, it is well this plan did not succeed. Examples are not wanting to shew how dreadfully vindictive and cruel are all old governments, when they are successful against what they call a revolt.

This plan must have been some time in contemplation; because, in order to carry it into execution, it was necessary to collect a large military force round Paris, and to cut off the communication between that city and the National Assembly at Versailles. The troops destined for this service were chiefly the foreign troops in the pay of France, and who, for this particular purpose, were drawn from the distant provinces where they were then stationed. When they were collected, to the amount of between twenty-five and thirty thousand, it was judged time to put the plan into execution. The ministry who were then in office, and who were friendly to the Revolution, were instantly dismissed, and a new ministry formed of those who had concerted the project;—among whom was Count de Broglio, and to his share was given the command of those troops. The character of this man, as described to me in a letter which I communicated to Mr. Burke before he began to write his book, and from an authority which Mr. Burke well knows was good, was that of "an high-flying aristocrat, cool, and capable of every mischief."

While these matters were agitating, the National Assembly stood in the most perilous and critical situation that a body of men can be supposed to act in. They were the devoted victims, and they knew it. They had the hearts and wishes of their country on their side, but military authority they had none. The guards of Broglio surrounded the hall where the assembly sat, ready, at the word of command, to seize their persons, as had been done the year before to the parliament of Paris. Had the National Assembly deserted their trust, or had they exhibited signs of weakness or fear, their enemies had been encouraged, and the country depressed. When the situation they stood in, the cause they were engaged in, and the crisis then ready to burst which should determine their personal and political fate, and that of their country, and probably of Europe, are taken into one view, none but a heart callous with prejudice, or corrupted by dependance, can avoid interesting itself in their success.

The archbishop of Vienne was at this time president of the National Assembly; a person too old to undergo the scene that a few days, or a few hours, might bring forth. A man of more activity, and bolder fortitude, was necessary; and the National Assembly chose (under the form of a vice-president, for the presidency still resided in the archbishop) M. de la Fayette; and this is the only instance of a vice-president being chosen. It was at the moment that this storm was pending (July 11.) that a declaration of rights was brought forward by M. de la Fayette, and is the same which is alluded to in page 442. It was hastily drawn up, and makes only a part of a more extensive declaration of rights, agreed upon and adopted afterwards by the National Assembly. The particular reason for bringing it forward at this moment, (M. de la Fayette has since informed me) was, that if the National Assembly should fall in the threatened destruction that then surrounded it, some traces of its principles might have the chance of surviving the wreck.

Every thing now was drawing to a crisis. The event was freedom or slavery. On one side, an army of nearly thirty thousand men; on the other, an unarmed body of citizens; for the citizens of Paris, on whom the National Assembly must then immediately depend, were as unarmed and as undisciplined as the citizens of London are now.—The French guards had given strong symptoms of their being attached to the national cause; but their numbers were small, not a tenth part of the force that Broglio commanded, and their officers were in the interest of Broglio.

Matters being now ripe for execution, the new ministry made their appearance in office. The reader will carry in his mind, that the Bastille was taken the 14th of July: the point of time I am now speaking to, is the 12th. Immediately on the news of the change of ministry reaching Paris in the after-noon, all the play-houses and places of entertainment, shops and houses, were shut up. The change of ministry was consid-ered as the prelude of hostilities, and the opinion was rightly founded.

The foreign troops began to advance towards the city. The Prince de Lambesc, who commanded a body of German cav-alry, approached by the Place of Louis XV. which connects itself with some of the streets. In his march, he insulted and struck an old man with his sword. The French are remarkable for their respect to old age, and the insolence with which it appeared to be done, uniting with the general fermentation they were in, produced a powerful effect, and a cry of *To arms! to arms!* spread itself in a moment over the city.

Arms they had none, nor scarcely any who knew the use of them: but desperate resolution, when every hope is at stake, supplies, for a while, the want of arms. Near where the Prince de Lambesc was drawn up, were large piles of stones collected for building the new bridge, and with these the people at-tacked the cavalry. A party of the French guards, upon hear-ing the firing, rushed from their quarters and joined the people; and night coming on the cavalry retreated.

The streets of Paris, being narrow, are favourable for de-fence; and the loftiness of the houses, consisting of many stories, from which great annoyance might be given, secured them against nocturnal enterprises; and the night was spent in providing themselves with every sort of weapon they could make or procure: Guns, swords, blacksmiths hammers, carpenters axes, iron crows, pikes, halberts, pitchforks, spits, clubs, &c. &c.

The incredible numbers with which they assembled the next morning, and the still more incredible resolution they exhibited, embarrassed and astonished their enemies. Little did the new ministry expect such a salute. Accustomed to slavery themselves, they had no idea that Liberty was capable of such inspiration, or that a body of unarmed citizens would dare to face the military force of thirty thousand men. Every moment of this day was employed in collecting arms, concerting plans, and arranging themselves into the best order which such an instantaneous movement could afford. Broglio continued lying round the city, but made no further advances this day, and the succeeding night passed with as much tranquillity as such a scene could possibly produce.

But defence only was not the object of the citizens. They had a cause at stake, on which depended their freedom or their slavery. They every moment expected an attack, or to hear of one made on the National Assembly; and in such a situation, the most prompt measures are sometimes the best. The object that now presented itself, was the Bastille; and the eclat of carrying such a fortress in the face of such an army, could not fail to strike a terror into the new ministry, who had scarcely yet had time to meet. By some intercepted correspondence this morning, it was discovered, that the Mayor of Paris, M. Defflesselles, who appeared to be in their interest, was betraying them; and from this discovery, there remained no doubt that Broglio would reinforce the Bastille the ensuing evening. It was therefore necessary to attack it that day; but before this could be done, it was first necessary to procure a better supply of arms than they were then possessed of.

There was adjoining to the city, a large magazine of arms deposited at the Hospital of the Invalids, which the citizens summonsed to surrender; and as the place was not defensible, nor attempted much defence, they soon succeeded. Thus supplied, they marched to attack the Bastille; a vast mixed multitude of all ages, and of all degrees, and armed with all sorts of weapons. Imagination would fail in describing to itself the appearance of such a procession, and of the anxiety for the events which a few hours or a few minutes might produce. What plans the ministry was forming, were as unknown to the people within the city, as what the citizens were doing was unknown to them; and what movements Broglio might make for the support or relief of the place, were to the citizens equally as unknown. All was mystery and hazard.

That the Bastille was attacked with an enthusiasm of heroism, such only as the highest animation of liberty could inspire, and carried in the space of a few hours, is an event which the world is fully possessed of. I am not undertaking a detail of the attack, but bringing into view the conspiracy against the nation which provoked it, and which fell with the Bastille. The prison to which the new ministry were dooming the National Assembly, in addition to its being the high altar and castle of despotism, became the proper object to begin with. This enterprise broke up the new ministry, who began now to fly from the ruin they had prepared for others. The troops of Broglio dispersed, and himself fled also.

Mr. Burke has spoken a great deal about plots, but he has never once spoken of this plot against the National Assembly, and the liberties of the nation; and that he might not, he has passed over all the circumstances that might throw it in his way. The exiles who have fled from France, whose case he so much interests himself in, and from whom he has had his lesson, fled in consequence of the miscarriage of this plot. No plot was formed against them: it were they who were plotting against others; and those who fell, met, not unjustly, the punishment they were preparing to execute. But will Mr. Burke say, that if this plot, contrived with the subtlety of an ambuscade, had succeeded, the successful party would have restrained their wrath so soon? Let the history of all old governments answer the question.

Whom has the National Assembly brought to the scaffold? None. They were themselves the devoted victims of this plot, and they have not retaliated; why then are they charged with revenge they have not acted? In the tremendous breaking forth of a whole people, in which all degrees, tempers and characters are confounded, and delivering themselves, by a miracle of exertion, from the destruction meditated against them, is it to be expected that nothing will happen? When men are sore with the sense of oppressions, and menaced with the prospect of new ones, is the calmness of philosophy, or the palsy of insensibility, to be looked for? Mr. Burke exclaims against outrage; yet the greatest is that which himself has committed. His book is a volume of outrage, not apologized for by the impulse of a moment, but cherished through a space of ten months; yet Mr. Burke had no provocation, no life, no interest at stake.

More citizens fell in this struggle than of their opponents:

but four or five persons were seized by the populace, and instantly put to death; the Governor of the Bastille, and the Mayor of Paris, who was detected in the act of betraying them; and afterwards Foulon, one of the new ministry, and Berthier his son-in-law, who had accepted the office of intendant of Paris. Their heads were stuck upon spikes, and carried about the city; and it is upon this mode of punishment that Mr. Burke builds a great part of his tragic scenes. Let us therefore examine how men came by the idea of punishing in this manner.

They learn it from the governments they live under, and retaliate the punishments they have been accustomed to behold. The heads stuck upon spikes, which remained for years upon Temple-bar, differed nothing in the horror of the scene from those carried about upon spikes at Paris: yet this was done by the English government. It may perhaps be said, that it signifies nothing to a man what is done to him after he is dead; but it signifies much to the living: it either tortures their feelings, or hardens their hearts; and in either case, it instructs them how to punish when power falls into their hands.

Lay then the axe to the root, and teach governments humanity. It is their sanguinary punishments which corrupt mankind. In England, the punishment in certain cases, is by *hanging*, *drawing*, and *quartering*; the heart of the sufferer is cut out, and held up to the view of the populace. In France, under the former government, the punishments were not less barbarous. Who does not remember the execution of Damien, torn to pieces by horses? The effect of those cruel spectacles exhibited to the populace, is to destroy tenderness, or excite revenge; and by the base and false idea of governing men by terror, instead of reason, they become precedents. It is over the lowest class of mankind that government by terror is intended to operate, and it is on them that it operates to the worst effect. They have sense enough to feel they are the objects aimed at; and they inflict in their turn the examples of terror they have been instructed to practise.

There are in all European countries, a large class of people of that description which in England are called the *"mob."* Of this class were those who committed the burnings and devastations in London in 1780, and of this class were those who carried the heads upon spikes in Paris. Foulon and Berthier were taken up in the country, and sent to Paris, to undergo their examination at the Hotel de Ville; for the National Assembly, immediately on the new ministry coming into office, passed a decree, which they communicated to the King and Cabinet, that they (the National Assembly) would hold the ministry, of which Foulon was one, responsible for the measures they were advising and pursuing; but the mob, incensed at the appearance of Foulon and Berthier, tore them from their conductors before they were carried to the Hotel de Ville, and executed them on the spot. Why then does Mr. Burke charge outrages of this kind on a whole people? As well may he charge the riots and outrages of 1780 on all the people of London, or those in Ireland on all his country.

But every thing we see or hear offensive to our feelings, and derogatory to the human character, should lead to other reflections than those of reproach. Even the beings who commit them have some claim to our consideration. How then is it that such vast classes of mankind as are distinguished by the appellation of the vulgar, or the ignorant mob, are so numerous in all old countries? The instant we ask ourselves this question, reflection feels an answer. They arise, as an unavoidable consequence, out of the ill construction of all the old governments in Europe, England included with the rest. It is by distortedly exalting some men, that others are distortedly debased, till the whole is out of nature. A vast mass of mankind are degradedly thrown into the back-ground of the human picture, to bring forward, with greater glare, the puppet-show of state and aristocracy. In the commencement of a Revolution, those men are rather the followers of the *camp* than of the *standard* of liberty, and have yet to be instructed how to reverence it.

I give to Mr. Burke all his theatrical exaggerations for facts, and I then ask him, if they do not establish the certainty of what I here lay down? Admitting them to be true, they shew the necessity of the French Revolution, as much as any one thing he could have asserted. These outrages were not the effect of the principles of the Revolution, but of the degraded mind that existed before the Revolution, and which the Revolution is calculated to reform. Place them then to their proper cause, and take the reproach of them to your own side.

It is to the honour of the National Assembly, and the city of Paris, that during such a tremendous scene of arms and confusion, beyond the controul of all authority, that they have been able, by the influence of example and exhortation, to restrain so much. Never were more pains taken to instruct and enlighten mankind, and to make them see that their interest consisted in their virtue, and not in their revenge, than what have been displayed in the Revolution of France.—I now proceed to make some remarks on Mr. Burke's account of the expedition to Versailles, October 5th and 6th.

I cannot consider Mr. Burke's book in scarcely any other light than a dramatic performance; and he must, I think, have considered it in the same light himself, by the poetical liberties he has taken of omitting some facts, distorting others, and making the whole machinery bend to produce a stage effect. Of this kind is his account of the expedition to Versailles. He begins this account by omitting the only facts which as causes are known to be true; every thing beyond these is conjecture even in Paris; and he then works up a tale accommodated to his own passions and prejudices.

It is to be observed throughout Mr. Burke's book, that he never speaks of plots *against* the Revolution; and it is from those plots that all the mischiefs have arisen. It suits his purpose to exhibit the consequences without their causes. It is one of the arts of the drama to do so. If the crimes of men were exhibited with their sufferings, the stage effect would sometimes be lost, and the audience would be inclined to approve where it was intended they should commiserate.

After all the investigations that have been made into this intricate affair, (the expedition to Versailles) it still remains enveloped in all that kind of mystery which ever accompanies events produced more from a concurrence of awkward circumstances, than from fixed design. While the characters of men are forming, as is always the case in revolutions, there is a reciprocal suspicion, and a disposition to misinterpret each other; and even parties directly opposite in principle, will sometimes concur in pushing forward the same movement with very different views, and with the hopes of its producing very different consequences. A great deal of this may be discovered in this embarrassed affair, and yet the issue of the whole was what nobody had in view.

The only things certainly known, are, that considerable uneasiness was at this time excited at Paris, by the delay of the King in not sanctioning and forwarding the decrees of the National Assembly, particularly that of the *Declaration of the rights of Man*, and the decrees of the *fourth of August*, which contained the foundation principles on which the constitution was to be erected. The kindest, and perhaps the fairest conjecture upon this matter is, that some of the ministers intended to make remarks and observations upon certain parts of them, before they were finally sanctioned and sent to the provinces; but be this as it may, the enemies of the revolution derived hopes from the delay, and the friends of the revolution, uneasiness.

During this state of suspense, the *Garde du Corps*, which was composed, as such regiments generally are, of persons much connected with the Court, gave an entertainment at Versailles (Oct. 1,) to some foreign regiments then arrived; and when the entertainment was at the height, on a signal given, the *Garde du Corps* tore the national cockade from their hats, trampled it under foot, and replaced it with a counter cockade prepared for the purpose. An indignity of this kind amounted to defiance. It was like declaring war; and if men will give challenges, they must expect consequences. But all this Mr. Burke has carefully kept out of sight. He begins his account by saying, "History will record, that on the morning of the 6th of October 1789, the King and Queen of France, after a day of confusion, alarm, dismay, and slaughter, lay down under the pledged security of public faith, to indulge nature in a few hours of respite, and troubled melancholy repose." This is neither the sober stile of history, nor the intention of it. It leaves every thing to be guessed at, and mistaken. One would at least think there had been a battle; and a battle there probably would have been, had it not been for the moderating prudence of those whom Mr. Burke involves in his censures. By his keeping the *Garde du Corps* out of sight, Mr. Burke has afforded himself the dramatic licence of putting the King and Queen in their places, as if the object of the expedition was against them.—But, to return to my account—

This conduct of the *Garde du Corps*, as might well be expected, alarmed and enraged the Parisians. The colours of the cause, and the cause itself, were become too united to mistake the intention of the insult, and the Parisians were determined to call the *Garde du Corps* to an account. There was certainly nothing of the cowardice of assassination in marching in the face of day to demand satisfaction, if such a phrase may be used, of a body of armed men who had voluntarily given defiance. But the circumstance which serves to throw this affair into embarrassment is, that the enemies of the revolution appear to have encouraged it, as well as its friends. The one hoped to prevent a civil war by checking it in time, and the other to make one. The hopes of those opposed to the revolution, rested in making the King of their party, and getting him from Versailles to Metz, where they expected to collect a force, and set up a standard. We have therefore two different objects presenting themselves at the same time, and to be accomplished by the same means: the one, to chastise the *Garde du Corps*, which was the object of the Parisians; the other, to render the confusion of such a scene an inducement to the King to set off for Metz.

On the 5th of October, a very numerous body of women, and men in the disguise of women, collected round the Hotel de Ville or town-hall at Paris, and set off for Versailles. Their professed object was the *Garde du Corps*; but prudent men readily recollect that mischief is easier begun than ended; and this impressed itself with the more force, from the suspicions already stated, and the irregularity of such a cavalcade. As soon therefore as a sufficient force could be collected, M. de la Fayette, by orders from the civil authority of Paris, set off after them at the head of twenty thousand of the Paris militia. The revolution could derive no benefit from confusion, and its opposers might. By an amiable and spirited manner of address, he had hitherto been fortunate in calming disquietudes, and in this he was extraordinarily successful; to frustrate, therefore, the hopes of those who might seek to improve this scene into a sort of justifiable necessity for the King's quitting Versailles and withdrawing to Metz, and to prevent at the same time the consequences that might ensue between the *Garde du Corps* and this phalanx of men and women, he forwarded expresses to the King, that he was on his march to Versailles, at the orders of the civil authority of Paris, for the purpose of peace and protection, expressing at the same time the necessity of restraining the *Garde du Corps* from firing upon the people*.

He arrived at Versailles between ten and eleven at night. The *Garde du Corps* was drawn up, and the people had arrived some time before, but every thing had remained suspended. Wisdom and policy now consisted in changing a scene of danger into a happy event. M. de la Fayette became the mediator between the enraged parties; and the King, to remove the uneasiness which had arisen from the delay already stated, sent for the President of the National Assembly, and signed the *Declaration of the rights of Man*, and such other parts of the constitution as were in readiness.

It was now about one in the morning. Every thing appeared to be composed, and a general congratulation took place. At the beat of drum a proclamation was made, that the citizens of Versailles would give the hospitality of their houses to their fellow-citizens of Paris. Those who could not be accommodated in this manner, remained in the streets, or took up their quarters in the churches; and at two o'clock the King and Queen retired.

In this state matters passed till the break of day, when a fresh disturbance arose from the censurable conduct of some of both parties, for such characters there will be in all such scenes. One of the *Garde du Corps* appeared at one of the windows of the palace, and the people who had remained during the night in the streets accosted him with reviling and provocative language. Instead of retiring, as in such a case prudence would have dictated, he presented his musket, fired, and killed one of the Paris militia. The peace being thus broken, the people rushed into the palace in quest of the

*I am warranted in asserting this, as I had it personally from M. de la Fayette, with whom I have lived in habits of friendship for fourteen years.

offender. They attacked the quarters of the *Garde du Corps* within the palace, and pursued them throughout the avenues of it, and to the apartments of the King. On this tumult, not the Queen only, as Mr. Burke has represented it, but every person in the palace, was awakened and alarmed; and M. de la Fayette had a second time to interpose between the parties, the event of which was, that the *Garde du Corps* put on the national cockade, and the matter ended as by oblivion, after the loss of two or three lives.

During the latter part of the time in which this confusion was acting, the King and Queen were in public at the balcony, and neither of them concealed for safety's sake, as Mr. Burke insinuates. Matters being thus appeased, and tranquillity restored, a general acclamation broke forth, of *Le Roi à Paris*— *Le Roi à Paris*—The King to Paris. It was the shout of peace, and immediately accepted on the part of the King. By this measure, all future projects of trapanning the King to Metz, and setting up the standard of opposition to the constitution, were prevented, and the suspicions extinguished. The King and his family reached Paris in the evening, and were congratulated on their arrival by M. Bailley the Mayor of Paris, in the name of the citizens. Mr. Burke, who throughout his book confounds things, persons, and principles, has in his remarks on M. Bailley's address, confounded time also. He censures M. Bailley for calling it, *"un bon jour,"* a good day. Mr. Burke should have informed himself, that this scene took up the space of two days, the day on which it began with every appearance of danger and mischief, and the day on which it terminated without the mischiefs that threatened; and that it is to this peaceful termination that M. Bailley alludes, and to the arrival of the King at Paris. Not less than three hundred thousand persons arranged themselves in the procession from Versailles to Paris, and not an act of molestation was committed during the whole march.

Mr. Burke, on the authority of M. Lally Tollendal, a deserter from the National Assembly, says, that on entering Paris, the people shouted, *"Tous les eveques à la lanterne."* All Bishops to be hanged at the lanthorn or lamp-posts.—It is surprising that nobody should hear this but Lally Tollendal, and that nobody should believe it but Mr. Burke. It has not the least connection with any part of the transaction, and is totally foreign to every circumstance of it. The bishops have never been introduced before into any scene of Mr. Burke's drama; Why then are they, all at once, and altogether, *tout à coup et tous ensemble*, introduced now? Mr. Burke brings forward his bishops and his lanthorn like figures in a magic lanthorn, and raises his scenes by contrast instead of connection. But it serves to shew, with the rest of his book, what little credit ought to be given, where even probability is set at defiance, for the purpose of defaming; and with this reflection, instead of a soliloquy in praise of chivalry, as Mr. Burke has done, I close the account of the expedition to Versailles*.

I have now to follow Mr. Burke through a pathless wilderness of rhapsodies, and a sort of descant upon governments, in which he asserts whatever he pleases, on the presumption of its being believed, without offering either evidence or reasons for so doing.

Before any thing can be reasoned upon to a conclusion, certain facts, principles, or data, to reason from, must be established, admitted, or denied. Mr. Burke, with his usual outrage, abuses the *Declaration of the rights of Man*, published by the National Assembly of France as the basis on which the constitution of France is built. This he calls "paltry and blurred sheets of paper about the rights of man."—Does Mr. Burke mean to deny that *man* has any rights? If he does, then he must mean that there are no such things as rights any where, and that he has none himself; for who is there in the world but man? But if Mr. Burke means to admit that man has rights, the question then will be, What are those rights, and how came man by them originally?

The error of those who reason by precedents drawn from antiquity, respecting the rights of man, is, that they do not go far enough into antiquity. They do not go the whole way. They stop in some of the intermediate stages of an hundred or a thousand years, and produce what was then done as a rule for the present day. This is no authority at all. If we travel still farther into antiquity, we shall find a direct contrary

*An account of the expedition to Versailles may be seen in No. 13. of the *Revolution de Paris*, containing the events from the 3d to the 10th of October 1789.

opinion and practice prevailing; and if antiquity is to be authority, a thousand such authorities may be produced,
successively contradicting each other: But if we proceed on,
we shall at last come out right; we shall come to the time
when man came from the hand of his Maker. What was he
then? Man. Man was his high and only title, and a higher
cannot be given him.—But of titles I shall speak hereafter.

We are now got at the origin of man, and at the origin of
his rights. As to the manner in which the world has been
governed from that day to this, it is no farther any concern of
ours than to make a proper use of the errors or the improvements which the history of it presents. Those who lived a
hundred or a thousand years ago, were then moderns as we
are now. They had *their* ancients, and those ancients had
others, and we also shall be ancients in our turn. If the mere
name of antiquity is to govern in the affairs of life, the people
who are to live an hundred or a thousand years hence, may as
well take us for a precedent, as we make a precedent of those
who lived an hundred or a thousand years ago. The fact is,
that portions of antiquity, by proving every thing, establish
nothing. It is authority against authority all the way, till we
come to the divine origin of the rights of man at the creation.
Here our enquiries find a resting-place, and our reason finds a
home. If a dispute about the rights of man had arose at the
distance of an hundred years from the creation, it is to this
source of authority they must have referred, and it is to the
same source of authority that we must now refer.

Though I mean not to touch upon any sectarian principle
of religion, yet it may be worth observing, that the genealogy
of Christ is traced to Adam. Why then not trace the rights of
man to the creation of man? I will answer the question. Because there have been an upstart of governments, thrusting
themselves between, and presumptuously working to *unmake* man.

If any generation of men ever possessed the right of dictating the mode by which the world should be governed for
ever, it was the first generation that existed; and if that generation did not do it, no succeeding generation can shew any
authority for doing it, nor set any up. The illuminating and
divine principle of the equal rights of man, (for it has its

origin from the Maker of man) relates, not only to the living individuals, but to generations of men succeeding each other. Every generation is equal in rights to the generations which preceded it, by the same rule that every individual is born equal in rights with his cotemporary.

Every history of the creation, and every traditionary account, whether from the lettered or unlettered world, however they may vary in their opinion or belief of certain particulars, all agree in establishing one point, *the unity of man*; by which I mean that man is all of *one degree*, and consequently that all men are born equal, and with equal natural rights, in the same manner as if posterity had been continued by *creation* instead of *generation*, the latter being only the mode by which the former is carried forward; and consequently, every child born into the world must be considered as deriving its existence from God. The world is as new to him as it was to the first man that existed, and his natural right in it is of the same kind.

The Mosaic account of the creation, whether taken as divine authority, or merely historical, is fully up to this point, *the unity or equality of man*. The expressions admit of no controversy. "And God said, Let us make man in our own image. In the image of God created he him; male and female created he them." The distinction of sexes is pointed out, but no other distinction is even implied. If this be not divine authority, it is at least historical authority, and shews that the equality of man, so far from being a modern doctrine, is the oldest upon record.

It is also to be observed, that all the religions known in the world are founded, so far as they relate to man, on the *unity of man*, as being all of one degree. Whether in heaven or in hell, or in whatever state man may be supposed to exist hereafter, the good and the bad are the only distinctions. Nay, even the laws of governments are obliged to slide into this principle, by making degrees to consist in crimes, and not in persons.

It is one of the greatest of all truths, and of the highest advantage to cultivate. By considering man in this light, and by instructing him to consider himself in this light, it places him in a close connection with all his duties, whether to his

Creator, or to the creation, of which he is a part; and it is only when he forgets his origin, or, to use a more fashionable phrase, his *birth and family*, that he becomes dissolute. It is not among the least of the evils of the present existing governments in all parts of Europe, that man, considered as man, is thrown back to a vast distance from his Maker, and the artificial chasm filled up by a succession of barriers, or a sort of turnpike gates, through which he has to pass. I will quote Mr. Burke's catalogue of barriers that he has set up between man and his Maker. Putting himself in the character of a herald, he says— "We fear God—we look with *awe* to kings—with affection to parliaments—with duty to magistrates—with reverence to priests, and with respect to nobility." Mr. Burke has forgot to put in *"chivalry."* He has also forgot to put in Peter.

The duty of man is not a wilderness of turnpike gates, through which he is to pass by tickets from one to the other. It is plain and simple, and consists but of two points. His duty to God, which every man must feel; and with respect to his neighbour, to do as he would be done by. If those to whom power is delegated do well, they will be respected; if not, they will be despised: and with regard to those to whom no power is delegated, but who assume it, the rational world can know nothing of them.

Hitherto we have spoken only (and that but in part) of the natural rights of man. We have now to consider the civil rights of man, and to shew how the one originates out of the other. Man did not enter into society to become *worse* than he was before, nor to have less rights than he had before, but to have those rights better secured. His natural rights are the foundation of all his civil rights. But in order to pursue this distinction with more precision, it will be necessary to mark the different qualities of natural and civil rights.

A few words will explain this. Natural rights are those which appertain to man in right of his existence. Of this kind are all the intellectual rights, or rights of the mind, and also all those rights of acting as an individual for his own comfort and happiness, which are not injurious to the natural rights of others.—Civil rights are those which appertain to man in right of his being a member of society. Every civil right has for its foundation some natural right pre-existing in the individual, but to which his individual power is not, in all cases, sufficiently competent. Of this kind are all those which relate to security and protection.

From this short review, it will be easy to distinguish between that class of natural rights which man retains after entering into society, and those which he throws into common stock as a member of society.

The natural rights which he retains, are all those in which the *power* to execute is as perfect in the individual as the right itself. Among this class, as is before mentioned, are all the intellectual rights, or rights of the mind: consequently, religion is one of those rights. The natural rights which are not retained, are all those in which, though the right is perfect in the individual, the power to execute them is defective. They answer not his purpose. A man, by natural right, has a right to judge in his own cause; and so far as the right of the mind is concerned, he never surrenders it: But what availeth it him to judge, if he has not power to redress? He therefore deposits this right in the common stock of society, and takes the arm of society, of which he is a part, in preference and in addition to his own. Society *grants* him nothing. Every man is a proprietor in society, and draws on the capital as a matter of right.

From those premises, two or three certain conclusions will follow.

First: That every civil right grows out of a natural right; or, in other words, is a natural right exchanged.

Secondly, That civil power, properly considered as such, is made up of the aggregate of that class of the natural rights of man, which becomes defective in the individual in point of power, and answers not his purpose; but when collected to a focus, becomes competent to the purpose of every one.

Thirdly, That the power produced from the aggregate of natural rights, imperfect in power in the individual, cannot be applied to invade the natural rights which are retained in the individual, and in which the power to execute is as perfect as the right itself.

We have now, in a few words, traced man from a natural

individual to a member of society, and shewn, or endeavoured to shew, the quality of the natural rights retained, and of those which are exchanged for civil rights. Let us now apply those principles to governments.

In casting our eyes over the world, it is extremely easy to distinguish the governments which have arisen out of society, or out of the social compact, from those which have not: but to place this in a clearer light than what a single glance may afford, it will be proper to take a review of the several sources from which governments have arisen, and on which they have been founded.

They may be all comprehended under three heads. First, Superstition. Secondly, Power. Thirdly, the common interest of society, and the common rights of man.

The first was a government of priestcraft, the second of conquerors, and the third of reason.

When a set of artful men pretended, through the medium of oracles, to hold intercourse with the Deity, as familiarly as they now march up the back-stairs in European courts, the world was completely under the government of superstition. The oracles were consulted, and whatever they were made to say, became the law; and this sort of government lasted as long as this sort of superstition lasted.

After these a race of conquerors arose, whose government, like that of William the Conqueror, was founded in power, and the sword assumed the name of a scepter. Governments thus established, last as long as the power to support them lasts; but that they might avail themselves of every engine in their favour, they united fraud to force, and set up an idol which they called *Divine Right*, and which, in imitation of the Pope, who affects to be spiritual and temporal, and in contradiction to the Founder of the Christian religion, twisted itself afterwards into an idol of another shape, called *Church and State*. The key of St. Peter, and the key of the Treasury, became quartered on one another, and the wondering cheated multitude worshipped the invention.

When I contemplate the natural dignity of man; when I feel (for Nature has not been kind enough to me to blunt my feelings) for the honour and happiness of its character, I become irritated at the attempt to govern mankind by force and fraud, as if they were all knaves and fools, and can scarcely avoid disgust at those who are thus imposed upon.

We have now to review the governments which arise out of society, in contradistinction to those which arose out of superstition and conquest.

It has been thought a considerable advance towards establishing the principles of Freedom, to say, that government is a compact between those who govern and those who are governed: but this cannot be true, because it is putting the effect before the cause; for as man must have existed before governments existed, there necessarily was a time when governments did not exist, and consequently there could originally exist no governors to form such a compact with. The fact therefore must be, that the *individuals themselves*, each in his own personal and sovereign right, *entered into a compact with each other* to produce a government: and this is the only mode in which governments have a right to arise, and the only principle on which they have a right to exist.

To possess ourselves of a clear idea of what government is, or ought to be, we must trace it to its origin. In doing this, we shall easily discover that governments must have arisen, either *out* of the people, or *over* the people. Mr. Burke has made no distinction. He investigates nothing to its source, and therefore he confounds every thing: but he has signified his intention of undertaking at some future opportunity, a comparison between the constitutions of England and France. As he thus renders it a subject of controversy by throwing the gauntlet, I take him up on his own ground. It is in high challenges that high truths have the right of appearing; and I accept it with the more readiness, because it affords me, at the same time, an opportunity of pursuing the subject with respect to governments arising out of society.

But it will be first necessary to define what is meant by a *constitution*. It is not sufficient that we adopt the word; we must fix also a standard signification to it.

A constitution is not a thing in name only, but in fact. It has not an ideal, but a real existence; and wherever it cannot be produced in a visible form, there is none. A constitution is a thing *antecedent* to a government, and a government is only the creature of a constitution. The constitution of a country is not the act of its government, but of the people constituting a government. It is the body of elements, to which you can refer, and quote article by article; and which contains the principles on which the government shall be established, the manner in which it shall be organized, the powers it shall have, the mode of elections, the duration of parliaments, or by what other name such bodies may be called; the powers which the executive part of the government shall have; and, in fine, every thing that relates to the compleat organization of a civil government, and the principles on which it shall act, and by which it shall be bound. A constitution, therefore, is to a government, what the laws made afterwards by that government are to a court of judicature. The court of judicature does not make the laws, neither can it alter them; it only acts in conformity to the laws made; and the government is in like manner governed by the constitution.

Can then Mr. Burke produce the English Constitution? If he cannot, we may fairly conclude, that though it has been so much talked about, no such thing as a constitution exists, or ever did exist, and consequently that the people have yet a constitution to form.

Mr. Burke will not, I presume, deny the position I have already advanced; namely, that governments arise either *out* of the people, or *over* the people. The English government is one of those which arose out of a conquest, and not out of society, and consequently it arose over the people; and though it has been much modified from the opportunity of circumstances since the time of William the Conqueror, the country has never yet regenerated itself, and is therefore without a constitution.

I readily perceive the reason why Mr. Burke declined going into the comparison between the English and French constitutions, because he could not but perceive, when he sat down to the task, that no such thing as a constitution existed on his side the question. His book is certainly bulky enough to have contained all he could say on this subject, and it would have been the best manner in which people could have judged of their separate merits. Why then has he declined the only thing that was worth while to write upon? It was the strongest ground he could take, if the advantages were on his side; but the weakest, if they were not; and his declining to take it, is either a sign that he could not possess it, or could not maintain it.

Mr. Burke has said in a speech last winter in parliament, that when the National Assembly first met in three Orders, (the Tiers Etats, the Clergy, and the Noblesse), that France had then a good constitution. This shews, among numerous other instances, that Mr. Burke does not understand what a constitution is. The persons so met, were not a *constitution*, but a *convention* to make a constitution.

The present National Assembly of France is, strictly speaking, the personal social compact.—The members of it are the delegates of the nation in its *original* character; future assemblies will be the delegates of the nation in its *organized* character. The authority of the present Assembly is different to what the authority of future Assemblies will be. The authority of the present one is to form a constitution; the authority of future Assemblies will be to legislate according to the principles and forms prescribed in that constitution; and if experience should hereafter shew that alterations, amendments, or additions are necessary, the constitution will point out the mode by which such things shall be done, and not leave it to the discretionary power of the future government.

A government on the principles on which constitutional governments arising out of society are established, cannot have the right of altering itself. If it had, it would be arbitrary. It might make itself what it pleased; and wherever such a right is set up, it shews there is no constitution. The act by which the English Parliament empowered itself to sit seven years, shews there is no constitution in England. It might, by the same self-authority, have sit any greater number of years, or for life. The Bill which the present Mr. Pitt brought into parliament some years ago, to reform parliament, was on the same erroneous principle. The right of reform is in the nation in its original character, and the constitutional method would be by a general convention elected for the purpose. There is moreover a paradox in the idea of vitiated bodies reforming themselves.

From these preliminaries I proceed to draw some comparisons. I have already spoken of the declaration of rights; and as I mean to be as concise as possible, I shall proceed to other parts of the French constitution.

The constitution of France says, that every man who pays a tax of sixty sous *per annum*, (2s. and 6d. English), is an elector. — What article will Mr. Burke place against this? Can any thing be more limited, and at the same time more capricious, than what the qualifications of electors are in England? Limited — because not one man in an hundred (I speak much within compass) is admitted to vote: Capricious — because the lowest character that can be supposed to exist, and who has not so much as the visible means of an honest livelihood, is an elector in some places; while, in other places, the man who pays very large taxes, and with a fair known character, and the farmer who rents to the amount of three or four hundred pounds a year, and with a property on that farm to three or four times that amount, is not admitted to be an elector. Every thing is out of nature, as Mr. Burke says on another occasion, in this strange chaos, and all sorts of follies are blended with all sorts of crimes. William the Conqueror and his descendants parcelled out the country in this manner, and bribed one part of it by what they called Charters, to hold the other parts of it the better subjected to their will. This is the reason why so many of those Charters abound in Cornwall. The people were averse to the government established at the conquest, and the towns were garrisoned and bribed to enslave the country. All the old Charters are the badges of this conquest, and it is from this source that the capriciousness of elections arise.

The French constitution says, that the number of representatives for any place shall be in a ratio to the number of taxable inhabitants or electors. What article will Mr. Burke place against this? The county of Yorkshire, which contains near a million of souls, sends two county members; and so does the county of Rutland, which contains not an hundredth part of that number. The town of old Sarum, which contains not three houses, sends two members; and the town of Manchester, which contains upwards of sixty thousand souls, is not admitted to send any. Is there any principle in these things? Is there any thing by which you can trace the marks of freedom, or discover those of wisdom? No wonder then Mr. Burke has declined the comparison, and endeavoured to lead his readers from the point by a wild unsystematical display of paradoxial rhapsodies.

The French constitution says, that the National Assembly shall be elected every two years.—What article will Mr. Burke place against this? Why, that the nation has no right at all in the case: that the government is perfectly arbitrary with respect to this point; and he can quote for his authority, the precedent of a former parliament.

The French constitution says, there shall be no game laws; that the farmer on whose lands wild game shall be found (for it is by the produce of those lands they are fed) shall have a right to what he can take. That there shall be no monopolies of any kind—that all trade shall be free, and every man free to follow any occupation by which he can procure an honest livelihood, and in any place, town or city throughout the nation.—What will Mr. Burke say to this? In England, game is made the property of those at whose expence it is not fed; and with respect to monopolies, the country is cut up into monopolies. Every chartered town is an aristocratical monopoly in itself, and the qualification of electors proceeds out of those chartered monopolies. Is this freedom? Is this what Mr. Burke means by a constitution?

In these chartered monopolies, a man coming from another part of the country, is hunted from them as if he were a foreign enemy. An Englishman is not free of his own country: every one of those places presents a barrier in his way, and tells him he is not a freeman—that he has no rights. Within these monopolies, are other monopolies. A city, such for instance as Bath, which contains between twenty and thirty thousand inhabitants, the right of electing representatives to parliament is monopolised into about thirty-one persons. And within these monopolies are still others. A man even of the same town, whose parents were not in circumstances to give him an occupation, is debarred, in many cases, from the natural right of acquiring one, be his genius or industry what it may.

Are these things examples to hold out to a country regenerating itself from slavery, like France?—Certainly they are not; and certain am I, that when the people of England come to reflect upon them, they will, like France, annihilate those badges of ancient oppression, those traces of a conquered nation.—Had Mr. Burke possessed talents similar to the author of "On the Wealth of Nations," he would have comprehended all the parts which enter into, and, by assemblage, form a constitution. He would have reasoned from minutiæ to magnitude. It is not from his prejudices only, but from the disorderly cast of his genius, that he is unfitted for the subject he writes upon. Even his genius is without a constitution. It is a genius at random, and not a genius constituted. But he must say something—He has therefore mounted in the air like a balloon, to draw the eyes of the multitude from the ground they stand upon.

Much is to be learned from the French constitution. Conquest and tyranny transplanted themselves with William the Conqueror from Normandy into England, and the country is yet disfigured with the marks. May then the example of all France contribute to regenerate the freedom which a province of it destroyed!

The French constitution says, That to preserve the national representation from being corrupt, no member of the National Assembly shall be an officer of the government, a placeman, or a pensioner.—What will Mr. Burke place against this? I will whisper his answer: *Loaves* and *fishes*. Ah! this government of loaves and fishes has more mischief in it than people have yet reflected on. The National Assembly has made the discovery, and it holds out the example to the world. Had governments agreed to quarrel on purpose to fleece their countries by taxes, they could not have succeeded better than they have done.

Every thing in the English government appears to me the reverse of what it ought to be, and of what it is said to be. The parliament, imperfectly and capriciously elected as it is, is nevertheless *supposed* to hold the national purse in *trust* for the nation: but in the manner in which an English parliament is constructed, it is like a man being both mortgager and mortgagee; and in the case of misapplication of trust, it is the criminal sitting in judgment upon himself. If those who vote the supplies are the same persons who receive the supplies when voted, and are to account for the expenditure of those supplies to those who voted them, it is *themselves accountable to themselves*, and the Comedy of Errors concludes with the Pantomime of HUSH. Neither the ministerial party, nor the opposition, will touch upon this case. The national purse is the common hack which each mounts upon. It is like what the country people call, "Ride and tie—You ride a little way, and then I*."—They order these things better in France.

The French constitution says, that the right of war and peace is in the nation. Where else should it reside, but in those who are to pay the expence?

In England, this right is said to reside in a *metaphor*, shewn at the Tower for sixpence or a shilling a-piece: so are the lions; and it would be a step nearer to reason to say it resided in them, for any inanimate metaphor is no more than a hat or a cap. We can all see the absurdity of worshipping Aaron's molton calf, or Nebuchadnezzar's golden image; but why do men continue to practise in themselves, the absurdities they despise in others?

It may with reason be said, that in the manner the English nation is represented, it signifies not where this right resides, whether in the crown or in the parliament. War is the common harvest of all those who participate in the division and expenditure of public money, in all countries. It is the art of *conquering at home*: the object of it is an increase of revenue; and as revenue cannot be increased without taxes, a pretence must be made for expenditures. In reviewing the history of the English government, its wars and its taxes, a stander-by, not blinded by prejudice, nor warped by interest, would declare, that taxes were not raised to carry on wars, but that wars were raised to carry on taxes.

Mr. Burke, as a Member of the House of Commons, is a part of the English Government; and though he professes himself an enemy to war, he abuses the French Constitution,

---

*It is a practice in some parts of the country, when two travellers have but one horse, which like the national purse will not carry double, that the one mounts and rides two or three miles a-head, and then ties the horse to a gate, and walks on. When the second traveller arrives, he takes the horse, rides on, and passes his companion a mile or two, and ties again; and so on— *Ride and tie.*

which seeks to explode it. He holds up the English Government as a model in all its parts, to France; but he should first know the remarks which the French make upon it. They contend, in favour of their own, that the portion of liberty enjoyed in England, is just enough to enslave a country by, more productively than by despotism; and that as the real object of all despotism is revenue, that a government so formed obtains more than it could either by direct despotism, or in a full state of freedom, and is, therefore, on the ground of interest, opposed to both. They account also for the readiness which always appears in such governments for engaging in wars, by remarking on the different motives which produce them. In despotic governments, wars are the effect of pride; but in those governments in which they become the means of taxation, they acquire thereby a more permanent promptitude.

The French Constitution, therefore, to provide against both those evils, have taken away the power of declaring war from kings and ministers, and placed the right where the expence must fall.

When the question on the right of war and peace was agitating in the National Assembly, the people of England appeared to be much interested in the event, and highly to applaud the decision.—As a principle, it applies as much to one country as to another. William the Conqueror, *as a conqueror*, held this power of war and peace in himself, and his descendants have ever since claimed it under him as a right.

Although Mr. Burke has asserted the right of the parliament at the Revolution to bind and controul the nation and posterity for *ever*, he denies, at the same time, that the parliament or the nation had any right to alter what he calls the succession of the crown, in any thing but in part, or by a sort of modification. By his taking this ground, he throws the case back to the *Norman Conquest*; and by thus running a line of succession springing from William the Conqueror to the present day, he makes it necessary to enquire who and what William the Conqueror was, and where he came from; and into the origin, history, and nature of what are called prerogatives. Every thing must have had a beginning, and the fog of time and antiquity should be penetrated to discover it. Let then Mr. Burke bring forward his William of Normandy, for it is to this origin that his argument goes. It also unfortunately happens, in running this line of succession, that another line, parallel thereto, presents itself, which is, that if the succession runs in the line of the conquest, the nation runs in the line of being conquered, and it ought to rescue itself from this reproach.

But it will perhaps be said, that tho' the power of declaring war descends in the heritage of the conquest, it is held in check by the right of the parliament to with-hold the supplies. It will always happen, when a thing is originally wrong, that amendments do not make it right, and it often happens that they do as much mischief one way as good the other: and such is the case here; for if the one rashly declares war as a matter of right, and the other peremptorily with-holds the supplies as a matter of right, the remedy becomes as bad or worse than the disease. The one forces the nation to a combat, and the other ties its hands: But the more probable issue is, that the contrast will end in a collusion between the parties, and be made a screen to both.

On this question of war, three things are to be considered. First, the right of declaring it: Secondly, the expence of supporting it: Thirdly, the mode of conducting it after it is declared. The French constitution places the *right* where the *expence* must fall, and this union can be only in the nation. The mode of conducting it after it is declared, it consigns to the executive department.—Were this the case in all countries, we should hear but little more of wars.

Before I proceed to consider other parts of the French constitution, and by way of relieving the fatigue of argument, I will introduce an anecdote which I had from Dr. Franklin.—

While the Doctor resided in France as minister from America during the war, he had numerous proposals made to him by projectors of every country and of every kind, who wished to go to the land that floweth with milk and honey, America; and among the rest, there was one who offered himself to be King. He introduced his proposal to the Doctor by letter, which is now in the hands of M. Beaumarchais, of Paris—stating, first, that as the Americans had dismissed or sent away* their King, that they would want another. Secondly, that himself was a Norman. Thirdly, that he was of a more ancient family than the Dukes of Normandy, and of a more honourable descent, his line having never been bastardized. Fourthly, that there was already a precedent in England, of Kings coming out of Normandy: and on these grounds he rested his offer, *enjoining* that the Doctor would forward it to America. But as the Doctor did not do this, nor yet send him an answer, the projector wrote a second letter; in which he did not, it is true, threaten to go over and conquer America, but only, with great dignity, proposed, that if his offer was not accepted, that an acknowledgment of about £ 30,000 might be made to him for his generosity! — Now, as all arguments respecting succession must necessarily connect that succession with some beginning, Mr. Burke's arguments on this subject go to shew, that there is no English origin of kings, and that they are descendants of the Norman line in right of the Conquest. It may, therefore, be of service to his doctrine to make this story known, and to inform him, that in case of that natural extinction to which all mortality is subject, that kings may again be had from Normandy, on more reasonable terms than William the Conqueror; and consequently that the good people of England, at the Revolution of 1688, might have done much better, had such a generous Norman as *this* known *their* wants, and they had known *his*. The chivalry character which Mr. Burke so much admires, is certainly much easier to make a bargain with than a hard-dealing Dutchman. — But, to return to the matters of the constitution —

The French constitution says, *There shall be no titles*; and of consequence, all that class of equivocal generation, which in some countries is called *"aristocracy,"* and in others *"nobility,"* is done away, and the *peer* is exalted into MAN.

Titles are but nick-names, and every nick-name is a title. The thing is perfectly harmless in itself, but it marks a sort of foppery in the human character which degrades it. It renders man into the diminutive of man in things which are great, and the counterfeit of woman in things which are little. It

---

*The word he used was *renvoyé*, dismissed or sent away.

talks about its fine *blue ribbon* like a girl, and shews its new *garter* like a child. A certain writer of some antiquity, says, "When I was a child, I thought as a child; but when I became a man, I put away childish things."

It is, properly, from the elevated mind of France, that the folly of titles have fallen. It has outgrown the baby-cloaths of *Count* and *Duke*, and breeched itself in manhood. France has not levelled; it has exalted. It has put down the dwarf, to set up the man. The punyism of a senseless word like *Duke*, or *Count*, or *Earl*, has ceased to please. Even those who possessed them have disowned the gibberish, and, as they outgrew the rickets, have despised the rattle. The genuine mind of man, thirsting for its native home, society, contemns the gewgaws that separate him from it. Titles are like circles drawn by the magician's wand, to contract the sphere of man's felicity. He lives immured within the Bastille of a word, and surveys at a distance the envied life of man.

Is it then any wonder that titles should fall in France? Is it not a greater wonder they should be kept up any where? What are they? What is their worth, and "what is their amount?" When we think or speak of a *Judge* or a *General*, we associate with it the ideas of office and character; we think of gravity in the one, and bravery in the other: but when we use a word merely as a *title*, no ideas associate with it. Through all the vocabulary of Adam, there is not such an animal as a Duke or a Count; neither can we connect any certain idea to the words. Whether they mean strength or weakness, wisdom or folly, a child or a man, or the rider or the horse, is all equivocal. What respect then can be paid to that which describes nothing, and which means nothing? Imagination has given figure and character to centaurs, satyrs, and down to all the fairy tribe; but titles baffle even the powers of fancy, and are a chimerical non-descript.

But this is not all.—If a whole country is disposed to hold them in contempt, all their value is gone, and none will own them. It is common opinion only that makes them any thing, or nothing, or worse than nothing. There is no occasion to take titles away, for they take themselves away when society concurs to ridicule them. This species of imaginary consequence has visibly declined in every part of Europe, and it hastens to its exit as the world of reason continues to rise. There was a time when the lowest class of what are called nobility was more thought of than the highest is now, and when a man in armour riding throughout Christendom in quest of adventures was more stared at than a modern Duke. The world has seen this folly fall, and it has fallen by being laughed at, and the farce of titles will follow its fate.—The patriots of France have discovered in good time, that rank and dignity in society must take a new ground. The old one has fallen through.—It must now take the substantial ground of character, instead of the chimerical ground of titles; and they have brought their titles to the altar, and made of them a burnt-offering to reason.

If no mischief had annexed itself to the folly of titles, they would not have been worth a serious and formal destruction, such as the National Assembly have decreed them: and this makes it necessary to enquire further into the nature and character of aristocracy.

That, then, which is called aristocracy in some countries, and nobility in others, arose out of the governments founded upon conquest. It was originally a military order for the purpose of supporting military government, (for such were all governments founded in conquest); and to keep up a succession of this order for the purpose for which it was established, all the younger branches of those families were disinherited, and the law of *primogenitureship* set up.

The nature and character of aristocracy shews itself to us in this law. It is a law against every law of nature, and Nature herself calls for its destruction. Establish family justice, and aristocracy falls. By the aristocratical law of primogenitureship, in a family of six children, five are exposed. Aristocracy has never but *one* child. The rest are begotten to be devoured. They are thrown to the canibal for prey, and the natural parent prepares the unnatural repast.

As every thing which is out of nature in man, affects, more or less, the interest of society, so does this. All the children which the aristocracy disowns (which are all, except the eldest) are, in general, cast like orphans on a parish, to be provided for by the public, but at a greater charge.—

Unnecessary offices and places in governments and courts are created at the expence of the public, to maintain them.

With what kind of parental reflections can the father or mother contemplate their younger offspring. By nature they are children, and by marriage they are heirs; but by aristocracy they are bastards and orphans. They are the flesh and blood of their parents in one line, and nothing akin to them in the other. To restore, therefore, parents to their children, and children to their parents—relations to each other, and man to society—and to exterminate the monster Aristocracy, root and branch—the French constitution has destroyed the law of PRIMOGENITURESHIP. Here then lies the monster; and Mr. Burke, if he pleases, may write its epitaph.

Hitherto we have considered aristocracy chiefly in one point of view. We have now to consider it in another. But whether we view it before or behind, or side-ways, or any way else, domestically or publicly, it is still a monster.

In France, aristocracy had one feature less in its countenance than what it has in some other countries. It did not compose a body of hereditary legislators. It was not *"a corporation of aristocracy,"* for such I have heard M. de la Fayette describe an English House of Peers. Let us then examine the grounds upon which the French constitution has resolved against having such an House in France.

Because, in the first place, as is already mentioned, aristocracy is kept up by family tyranny and injustice.

Secondly, Because there is an unnatural unfitness in an aristocracy to be legislators for a nation. Their ideas of *distributive justice* are corrupted at the very source. They begin life by trampling on all their younger brothers and sisters, and relations of every kind, and are taught and educated so to do. With what ideas of justice or honour can that man enter an house of legislation, who absorbs in his own person the inheritance of a whole family of children, or doles out to them some pitiful portion with the insolence of a gift?

Thirdly, Because the idea of hereditary legislators is as inconsistent as that of hereditary judges, or hereditary juries; and as absurd as an hereditary mathematician, or an hereditary wise man; and as ridiculous as an hereditary poet-laureat.

Fourthly, Because a body of men holding themselves accountable to nobody, ought not to be trusted by any body.

Fifthly, Because it is continuing the uncivilized principle of governments founded in conquest, and the base idea of man having property in man, and governing him by personal right.

Sixthly, Because aristocracy has a tendency to degenerate the human species.—By the universal œconomy of nature it is known, and by the instance of the Jews it is proved, that the human species has a tendency to degenerate, in any small number of persons, when separated from the general stock of society, and intermarrying constantly with each other. It defeats even its pretended end, and becomes in time the opposite of what is noble in man. Mr. Burke talks of nobility; let him shew what it is. The greatest characters the world have known, have rose on the democratic floor. Aristocracy has not been able to keep a proportionate pace with democracy. The artificial NOBLE shrinks into a dwarf before the NOBLE of Nature; and in the few instances (for there are some in all countries) in whom nature, as by a miracle, has survived in aristocracy, THOSE MEN DESPISE IT.—But it is time to proceed to a new subject.

The French constitution has reformed the condition of the clergy. It has raised the income of the lower and middle classes, and taken from the higher. None are now less than twelve hundred livres (fifty pounds sterling) nor any higher than about two or three thousand pounds. What will Mr. Burke place against this? Hear what he says.

He says, "that the people of England can see without pain or grudging, an archbishop precede a duke; they can see a bishop of Durham, or a bishop of Winchester, in possession of £.10,000 a-year; and cannot see why it is in worse hands than estates to the like amount in the hands of this earl or that 'squire." And Mr. Burke offers this as an example to France.

As to the first part, whether the archbishop precedes the duke, or the duke the bishop, it is, I believe, to the people in general, somewhat like *Sternhold* and *Hopkins*, or *Hopkins* and *Sternhold*; you may put which you please first; and as I confess that I do not understand the merits of this case, I will not contend it with Mr. Burke.

But with respect to the latter, I have something to say.— Mr. Burke has not put the case right.—The comparison is out of order by being put between the bishop and the earl or the 'squire. It ought to be put between the bishop and the curate, and then it will stand thus:— *The people of England can see without pain or grudging, a bishop of Durham, or a bishop of Winchester, in possession of ten thousand pounds a-year, and a curate on thirty or forty pounds a-year, or less.*— No, Sir, they certainly do not see those things without great pain or grudging. It is a case that applies itself to every man's sense of justice, and is one among many that calls aloud for a constitution.

In France, the cry of *"the church! the church!"* was repeated as often as in Mr. Burke's book, and as loudly as when the dissenters' bill was before the English parliament; but the generality of the French clergy were not to be deceived by this cry any longer. They knew, that whatever the pretence might be, it was themselves who were one of the principal objects of it. It was the cry of the high-beneficed clergy, to prevent any regulation of income taking place between those of ten thousand pounds a-year and the parish priest. They, therefore, joined their case to those of every other oppressed class of men, and by this union obtained redress.

The French constitution has abolished tythes, that source of perpetual discontent between the tythe-holder and the parishioner. When land is held on tythe, it is in the condition of an estate held between two parties; the one receiving one-tenth, and the other nine-tenths of the produce: and, consequently, on principles of equity, if the estate can be improved, and made to produce by that improvement double or treble what it did before, or in any other ratio, the expence of such improvement ought to be borne in like proportion between the parties who are to share the produce. But this is not the case in tythes; the farmer bears the whole expence, and the tythe-holder takes a tenth of the improvement, in addition to the original tenth, and by this means gets the value of two-tenths instead of one. This is another case that calls for a constitution.

The French constitution hath abolished or renounced *Toleration*, and *Intoleration* also, and hath established UNIVERSAL RIGHT OF CONSCIENCE.

Toleration is not the *opposite* of Intoleration, but is the *counterfeit* of it. Both are despotisms. The one assumes to itself the right of with-holding Liberty of Conscience, and the other of granting it. The one is the pope, armed with fire and faggot, and the other is the pope selling or granting indulgences. The former is church and state, and the latter is church and traffic.

But Toleration may be viewed in a much stronger light. Man worships not himself, but his Maker; and the liberty of conscience which he claims, is not for the service of himself, but of his God. In this case, therefore, we must necessarily have the associated idea of two beings; the *mortal* who renders the worship, and the IMMORTAL BEING who is worshipped. Toleration, therefore, places itself, not between man and man, nor between church and church, nor between one denomination of religion and another, but between God and man; between the being who worships, and the BEING who is worshipped; and by the same act of assumed authority by which it tolerates man to pay his worship, it presumptuously and blasphemously sets itself up to tolerate the Almighty to receive it.

Were a Bill brought into any parliament, entitled "AN ACT to tolerate or grant liberty to the Almighty to receive the worship of a Jew or a Turk," or "to prohibit the Almighty from receiving it," all men would startle, and call it blasphemy. There would be an uproar. The presumption of toleration in religious matters would then present itself unmasked: but the presumption is not the less because the name of "Man" only appears to those laws, for the associated idea of the *worshipper* and the *worshipped* cannot be separated.—Who, then, art thou, vain dust and ashes! by whatever name thou art called, whether a King, a Bishop, a Church or a State, a Parliament, or any thing else, that obtruded thine insignificance between the soul of man and its Maker? Mind thine own concerns. If he believes not as thou believest, it is a proof that thou believest not as he believeth, and there is no earthly power can determine between you.

With respect to what are called denominations of religion, if every one is left to judge of its own religion, there is no such thing as a religion that is wrong; but if they are to judge of each others religion, there is no such thing as a religion that is right; and therefore, all the world are right, or all the world are wrong. But with respect to religion itself, without regard to names, and as directing itself from the universal family of mankind to the Divine object of all adoration, *it is man bringing to his Maker the fruits of his heart*; and though those fruits may differ from each other like the fruits of the earth, the grateful tribute of every one is accepted.

A Bishop of Durham, or a Bishop of Winchester, or the Archbishop who heads the Dukes, will not refuse a tythe-sheaf of wheat, because it is not a cock of hay; nor a cock of hay, because it is not a sheaf of wheat; nor a pig, because it is neither the one nor the other: but these same persons, under the figure of an established church, will not permit their Maker to receive the varied tythes of man's devotion.

One of the continual choruses of Mr. Burke's book is, "Church and State:" he does not mean some one particular church, or some one particular state, but any church and state; and he uses the term as a general figure to hold forth the political doctrine of always uniting the church with the state in every country, and he censures the National Assembly for not having done this in France.—Let us bestow a few thoughts on this subject.

All religions are in their nature mild and benign, and united with principles of morality. They could not have made proselites at first, by professing any thing that was vicious, cruel, persecuting, or immoral. Like every thing else, they had their beginning; and they proceeded by persuasion, exhortation, and example. How then is it that they lose their native mildness, and become morose and intolerent?

It proceeds from the connection which Mr. Burke recommends. By engendering the church with the state, a sort of mule animal, capable only of destroying, and not of breeding up, is produced, called *The Church established by Law*. It is a stranger, even from its birth, to any parent mother on which it is begotten, and whom in time it kicks out and destroys.

The inquisition in Spain does not proceed from the religion originally professed, but from this mule-animal, engendered between the church and the state. The burnings in Smithfield proceeded from the same heterogeneous production; and it was the regeneration of this strange animal in England afterwards, that renewed rancour and irreligion among the inhabitants, and that drove the people called Quakers and Dissenters to America. Persecution is not an original feature in *any* religion; but it is always the strongly-marked feature of all law-religions, or religions established by law. Take away the law-establishment, and every religion reassumes its original benignity. In America, a Catholic Priest is a good citizen, a good character, and a good neighbour; an Episcopalian Minister is of the same description: and this proceeds, independent of the men, from there being no law establishment in America.

If also we view this matter in a temporal sense, we shall see the ill effects it has had on the prosperity of nations. The union of church and state has impoverished Spain. The revoking the edict of Nantz drove the silk manufacture from that country into England; and church and state are now driving the cotton manufacture from England to America and France. Let then Mr. Burke continue to preach his anti-political doctrine of Church and State. It will do some good. The National Assembly will not follow his advice, but will benefit by his folly. It was by observing the ill effects of it in England, that America has been warned against it; and it is by experiencing them in France, that the National Assembly have abolished it, and, like America, has established UNIVERSAL RIGHT OF CONSCIENCE, AND UNIVERSAL RIGHT OF CITIZENSHIP*.

---

*When in any country we see extraordinary circumstances taking place, they naturally lead any man who has a talent for observation and investigation, to enquire into the causes. The manufactures of Manchester, Birmingham, and Sheffield, are the most principal manufactures in England. From whence did this arise? A little observation will explain the case. The principal, and the generality of the inhabitants of those places, are not of what is called in England, *the church established by law*; and they, or their fathers, (for it is within but a few years), withdrew from the persecution of the chartered

I will here cease the comparison with respect to the principles of the French constitution, and conclude this part of the subject with a few observations on the organization of the formal parts of the French and English governments.

The executive power in each country is in the hands of a person stiled, the King; but the French constitution distinguishes between the King and the Sovereign: It considers the station of King as official, and places Sovereignty in the nation.

The representatives of the nation, which compose the National Assembly, and who are the legislative power, originate in and from the people by election, as an inherent right in the people.—In England it is otherwise; and this arises from the original establishment of what is called its monarchy; for, as by the conquest all the rights of the people or the nation were absorbed into the hands of the Conqueror, and who added the title of King to that of Conqueror, those same matters

---

towns, where Test-laws more particularly operate, and established a sort of asylum for themselves in those places. It was the only asylum that then offered, for the rest of Europe was worse.—But the case is now changing. France and America bid all comers welcome, and initiate them into all the rights of citizenship. Policy and interest, therefore, will, but perhaps too late, dictate in England, what reason and justice could not. Those manufactures are withdrawing, and are arising in other places. There is now erecting at Passey, three miles from Paris, a large cotton mill, and several are already erected in America. Soon after the rejecting the Bill for repealing the Test-law, one of the richest manufacturers in England said in my hearing, "England, Sir, is not a country for a dissenter to live in—we must go to France." These are truths, and it is doing justice to both parties to tell them. It is chiefly the dissenters that have carried English manufactures to the height they are now at, and the same men have it in their power to carry them away; and though those manufactures will afterwards continue to be made in those places, the foreign market will be lost. There are frequently appearing in the London Gazette, extracts from certain acts to prevent machines, as far as it can extend to persons, from going out of the country. It appears from these, that the ill effects of the test-laws and church-establishment begin to be much suspected; but the remedy of force can never supply the remedy of reason. In the progress of less than a century, all the unrepresented part of England, of all denominations, which is at least a hundred times the most numerous, may begin to feel the necessity of a constitution, and then all those matters will come regularly before them.

which in France are now held as rights in the people, or in the nation, are held in England as grants from what is called the Crown. The Parliament in England, in both its branches, were erected by patents from the descendants of the Conqueror. The House of Commons did not originate as a matter of right in the people to delegate or elect, but as a grant or boon.

By the French constitution, the Nation is always named before the King. The third article of the Declaration of rights says, *"The nation is essentially the source* (or fountain) *of all sovereignty."* Mr. Burke argues, that, in England, a King is the fountain—that he is the fountain of all honour. But as this idea is evidently descended from the conquest, I shall make no other remark upon it than that it is the nature of conquest to turn every thing upside down; and as Mr. Burke will not be refused the privilege of speaking twice, and as there are but two parts in the figure, the *fountain* and the *spout*, he will be right the second time.

The French constitution puts the legislative before the executive; the Law before the King; *La Loi, Le Roi.* This also is in the natural order of things; because laws must have existence, before they can have execution.

A King in France does not, in addressing himself to the National Assembly, say, "My assembly," similar to the phrase used in England of "*my* Parliament;" neither can he use it consistent with the constitution, nor could it be admitted. There may be propriety in the use of it in England, because, as is before mentioned, both Houses of Parliament originated out of what is called the Crown, by patent or boon—and not out of the inherent rights of the people, as the National Assembly does in France, and whose name designates its origin.

The President of the National Assembly does not ask the King *to grant to the Assembly liberty of speech*, as is the case with the English House of Commons. The constitutional dignity of the National Assembly cannot debase itself. Speech is, in the first place, one of the natural rights of man always retained; and with respect to the National Assembly, the use of it is their *duty*, and the nation is their *authority*. They were elected by the greatest body of men exercising the right of election the European world ever saw. They sprung not from the filth of rotten boroughs, nor are they the vassal representatives of aristocratical ones. Feeling the proper dignity of their character, they support it. Their parliamentary language, whether for or against a question, is free, bold, and manly, and extend to all the parts and circumstances of the case. If any matter or subject respecting the executive department, or the person who presides in it, (the King), comes before them, it is debated on with the spirit of men, and the language of gentlemen; and their answer, or their address, is returned in the same stile. They stand not aloof with the gaping vacuity of vulgar ignorance, nor bend with the cringe of sycophantic insignificance. The graceful pride of truth knows no extremes, and preserves, in every latitude of life, the right-angled character of man.

Let us now look to the other side of the question.—In the addresses of the English Parliaments to their Kings, we see neither the intrepid spirit of the old Parliaments of France, nor the serene dignity of the present National Assembly; neither do we see in them any thing of the stile of English manners, which borders somewhat on bluntness. Since then they are neither of foreign extraction, nor naturally of English production, their origin must be sought for elsewhere, and that origin is the Norman Conquest. They are evidently of the vassalage class of manners, and emphatically mark the prostrate distance that exists in no other condition of men than between the conqueror and the conquered. That this vassalage idea and stile of speaking was not got rid of even at the Revolution of 1688, is evident from the declaration of Parliament to William and Mary, in these words: "We do most humbly and faithfully submit ourselves, our heirs and posterities, for ever." Submission is wholly a vassalage term, repugnant to the dignity of Freedom, and an echo of the language used at the Conquest.

As the estimation of all things is by comparison, the Revolution of 1688, however from circumstances it may have been exalted beyond its value, will find its level. It is already on the wane, eclipsed by the enlarging orb of reason, and the luminous revolutions of America and France. In less than another century, it will go, as well as Mr. Burke's labours, "to the family vault of all the Capulets." Mankind will then scarcely believe that a country calling itself free, would send to Holland for a man, and clothe him with power on purpose to put themselves in fear of him, and give him almost a million sterling a-year for leave to *submit* themselves and their posterity, like bond-men and bond-women, for ever.

But there is a truth that ought to be made known: I have had the opportunity of seeing it; which is, *that notwithstanding appearances, there is not any description of men that despise monarchy so much as courtiers.* But they well know, that if it were seen by others, as it is seen by them, the juggle could not be kept up. They are in the condition of men who get their living by a show, and to whom the folly of that show is so familiar that they ridicule it; but were the audience to be made as wise, in this respect, as themselves, there would be an end to the show and the profits with it. The difference between a republican and a courtier with respect to monarchy is, that the one opposes monarchy believing it to be something, and the other laughs at it knowing it to be nothing.

As I used sometimes to correspond with Mr. Burke, believing him then to be a man of sounder principles than his book shews him to be, I wrote to him last winter from Paris, and gave him an account how prosperously matters were going on. Among other subjects in that letter, I referred to the happy situation the National Assembly were placed in; that they had taken a ground on which their moral duty and their political interest were united. They have not to hold out a language which they do not believe, for the fraudulent purpose of making others believe it. Their station requires no artifice to support it, and can only be maintained by enlightening mankind. It is not their interest to cherish ignorance, but to dispel it. They are not in the case of a ministerial or an opposition party in England, who, though they are opposed, are still united to keep up the common mystery. The National Assembly must throw open a magazine of light. It must shew man the proper character of man; and the nearer it can bring him to that standard, the stronger the National Assembly becomes.

In contemplating the French constitution, we see in it a rational order of things. The principles harmonise with the forms, and both with their origin. It may perhaps be said as an excuse for bad forms, that they are nothing more than forms; but this is a mistake. Forms grow out of principles, and operate to continue the principles they grow from. It is impossible to practise a bad form on any thing but a bad principle. It cannot be ingrafted on a good one; and wherever the forms in any government are bad, it is a certain indication that the principles are bad also.

I will here finally close this subject. I began it by remarking that Mr. Burke had *voluntarily* declined going into a comparison of the English and French constitutions. He apologises (in page 241) for not doing it, by saying that he had not time. Mr. Burke's book was upwards of eight months in hand, and is extended to a volume of three hundred and fifty-six pages. As his omission does injury to his cause, his apology makes it worse; and men on the English side the water will begin to consider, whether there is not some radical defect in what is called the English constitution, that made it necessary in Mr. Burke to suppress the comparison, to avoid bringing it into view.

As Mr. Burke has not written on constitutions, so neither has he written on the French revolution. He gives no account of its commencement or its progress. He only expresses his wonder. "It looks," says he, "to me, as if I were in a great crisis, not of the affairs of France alone, but of all Europe, perhaps of more than Europe. All circumstances taken together, the French revolution is the most astonishing that has hitherto happened in the world."

As wise men are astonished at foolish things, and other people at wise ones, I know not on which ground to account for Mr. Burke's astonishment; but certain it is, that he does not understand the French revolution. It has apparently burst forth like a creation from a chaos, but it is no more than the consequence of a mental revolution priorily existing in France. The mind of the nation had changed before hand, and the new order of things has naturally followed the new order of thoughts.—I will here, as concisely as I can, trace out the growth of the French revolution, and mark the circumstances that have contributed to produce it.

The despotism of Louis XIV. united with the gaiety of his

Court, and the gaudy ostentation of his character, had so humbled, and at the same time so fascinated the mind of France, that the people appear to have lost all sense of their own dignity in contemplating that of their grand Monarch: and the whole reign of Louis XV. remarkable only for weakness and effeminacy, made no other alteration than that of spreading a sort of lethargy over the nation, from which it shewed no disposition to rise.

The only signs which appeared of the spirit of liberty during those periods, are to be found in the writings of the French philosophers. Montesquieu, president of the Parliament of Bourdeaux, went as far as a writer under a despotic government could well proceed; and being obliged to divide himself between principle and prudence, his mind often appears under a veil, and we ought to give him credit for more than he has expressed.

Voltaire, who was both the flatterer and the satyrist of despotism, took another line. His forte lay in exposing and ridiculing the superstitions which priest-craft united with state-craft had interwoven with governments. It was not from the purity of his principles, or his love of mankind, (for satire and philanthropy are not naturally concordant), but from his strong capacity of seeing folly in its true shape, and his irresistible propensity to expose it, that he made those attacks. They were however as formidable as if the motives had been virtuous; and he merits the thanks rather than the esteem of mankind.

On the contrary, we find in the writings of Rousseau, and the Abbé Raynal, a loveliness of sentiment in favour of Liberty, that excites respect, and elevates the human faculties; but having raised this animation, they do not direct its operations and leave the mind in love with an object, without describing the means of possessing it.

The writings of Quesnay, Turgot, and the friends of those authors, are of the serious kind; but they laboured under the same disadvantage with Montesquieu: their writings abound with moral maxims of government, but are rather directed to œconomise and reform the administration of the government, than the government itself.

But all those writings and many others had their weight; and by the different manner in which they treated the subject of government, Montesquieu by his judgment and knowledge of laws, Voltaire by his wit, Rousseau and Raynal by their animation, and Quesnay and Turgot by their moral maxims and systems of œconomy, readers of every class met with something to their taste, and a spirit of political enquiry began to diffuse itself through the nation at the time the dispute between England and the then colonies of America broke out.

In the war which France afterwards engaged in, it is very well known that the nation appeared to be before hand with the French ministry. Each of them had its view: but those views were directed to different objects; the one sought liberty, and the other retaliation on England. The French officers and soldiers who after this went to America, were eventually placed in the school of Freedom, and learned the practice as well as the principles of it by heart.

As it was impossible to separate the military events which took place in America from the principles of the American revolution, the publication of those events in France necessarily connected themselves with the principles that produced them. Many of the facts were in themselves principles; such as the declaration of American independence, and the treaty of alliance between France and America, which recognised the natural right of man, and justified resistance to oppression.

The then Minister of France, Count Vergennes, was not the friend of America; and it is both justice and gratitude to say, that it was the Queen of France who gave the cause of America a fashion at the French Court. Count Vergennes was the personal and social friend of Dr. Franklin; and the Doctor had obtained, by his sensible gracefulness, a sort of influence over him; but with respect to principles, Count Vergennes was a despot.

The situation of Dr. Franklin as Minister from America to France, should be taken into the chain of circumstances. The deplomatic character is of itself the narrowest sphere of society that man can act in. It forbids intercourse by a reciprocity of suspicion; and a Deplomatic is a sort of unconnected atom, continually repelling and repelled. But this was not the case with Dr. Franklin. He was not the deplomatic of a Court, but of MAN. His character as a philosopher had been long established, and his circle of society in France was universal.

Count Vergennes resisted for a considerable time the publication of the American constitutions in France, translated into the French language; but even in this he was obliged to give way to public opinion, and a sort of propriety in admitting to appear what he had undertaken to defend. The American constitutions were to liberty, what a grammar is to language: they define its parts of speech, and practically construct them into syntax.

The peculiar situation of the then Marquis de la Fayette is another link in the great chain. He served in America as an American officer under a commission of Congress, and by the universality of his acquaintance, was in close friendship with the civil government of America, as well as with the military line. He spoke the language of the country, entered into the discussions on the principles of government, and was always a welcome friend at any election.

When the war closed, a vast reinforcement to the cause of Liberty spread itself over France, by the return of the French officers and soldiers. A knowledge of the practice was then joined to the theory; and all that was wanting to give it real existence, was opportunity. Man cannot, properly speaking, make circumstances for his purpose, but he always has it in his power to improve them when they occur; and this was the case in France.

M. Neckar was displaced in May 1781; and by the ill management of the finances afterwards, and particularly during the extravagant administration of M. Calonne, the revenue of France, which was nearly twenty-four millions sterling *per* year, was become unequal to the expenditures, not because the revenue had decreased, but because the expences had increased; and this was the circumstance which the nation laid hold of to bring forward a revolution. The English Minister, Mr. Pitt, has frequently alluded to the state of the French finances in his budgets, without understanding the subject. Had the French Parliaments been as ready to register edicts for new taxes, as an English Parliament is to grant them, there had been no derangement in the finances, nor yet any revolution; but this will better explain itself as I proceed.

It will be necessary here to shew how taxes were formerly raised in France. The King, or rather the Court or Ministry acting under the use of that name, framed the edicts for taxes at their own discretion, and sent them to the Parliaments to be registered; for until they were registered by the Parliaments, they were not operative. Disputes had long existed between the Court and the Parliament with respect to the extent of the Parliament's authority on this head. The Court insisted that the authority of Parliament went no further than to remonstrate or shew reasons against the tax, reserving to itself the right of determining whether the reasons were well or ill-founded; and in consequence thereof, either to withdraw the edict as a matter of choice, or to *order* it to be enregistered as a matter of authority. The Parliaments on their part insisted, that they had not only a right to remonstrate, but to reject; and on this ground they were always supported by the nation.

But, to return to the order of my narrative—M. Calonne wanted money; and as he knew the sturdy disposition of the Parliaments with respect to new taxes, he ingeniously sought either to approach them by a more gentle means than that of direct authority, or to get over their heads by a manoeuvre: and, for this purpose, he revived the project of assembling a body of men from the several provinces, under the stile of an "Assembly of the Notables," or Men of Note, who met in 1787, and who were either to recommend taxes to the Parliaments, or to act as a Parliament themselves. An Assembly under this name had been called in 1617.

As we are to view this as the first practical step towards the revolution, it will be proper to enter into some particulars respecting it. The Assembly of the Notables has in some places been mistaken for the States-General, but was wholly a different body; the States-General being always by election. The persons who composed the Assembly of the Notables were all nominated by the King, and consisted of one hundred and forty members. But as M. Calonne could not depend upon a majority of this Assembly in his favour, he very ingeniously arranged them in such a manner as to make forty-four a majority of one hundred and forty: to effect this, he disposed of them into seven separate committees, of twenty members each. Every general question was to be decided, not by a majority of persons, but by a majority of committees; and as eleven votes would make a majority in a committee, and four committees a majority of seven, M. Calonne had good reason to conclude, that as forty-four would determine any general question, he could not be out-voted. But all his plans deceived him, and in the event became his overthrow.

The then Marquis de la Fayette was placed in the second Committee, of which Count D'Artois was president: and as money-matters was the object, it naturally brought into view every circumstance connected with it. M. de la Fayette made a verbal charge against Calonne, for selling crown lands to the amount of two millions of livres, in a manner that appeared to be unknown to the King. The Count D'Artois (as if to intimidate, for the Bastille was then in being) asked the Marquis, if he would render the charge in writing? He replied, that he would.—The Count D'Artois did not demand it, but brought a message from the King to that purport. M. de la Fayette then delivered in his charge in writing, to be given to the King, undertaking to support it. No farther proceedings were had upon this affair; but M. Calonne was soon after dismissed by the King, and set off to England.

As M. de la Fayette, from the experience he had seen in America, was better acquainted with the science of civil government than the generality of the members who composed the Assembly of the Notables could then be, the brunt of the business fell considerably to his share. The plan of those who had a constitution in view, was to contend with the Court on the ground of taxes, and some of them openly professed their object. Disputes frequently arose between Count D'Artois and M. de la Fayette, upon various subjects. With respect to the arrears already incurred, the latter proposed to remedy them, by accommodating the expences to the revenue, instead of the revenue to the expences; and as objects of reform, he proposed to abolish the Bastille, and all the State-prisons throughout the nation, (the keeping of which were attended with great expence), and to suppress *Lettres de Cachet*: But those matters were not then much attended to; and with respect to *Lettres de Cachet, a majority of the Nobles appeared to be in favour of them.*

On the subject of supplying the Treasury by new taxes, the Assembly declined taking the matter on themselves, concurring in the opinion that they had not authority. In a debate on this subject, M. de la Fayette said, that raising money by taxes could only be done by a National Assembly, freely elected by the people, and acting as their representatives. Do you mean, said the Count D'Artois, the *States General*? M. de la Fayette replied, that he did. Will you, said the Count D'Artois, sign what you say, to be given to the King? The other replied, that he not only would do this, but that he would go farther, and say, that the effectual mode would be, for the King to agree to the establishment of a Constitution.

As one of the plans had thus failed, that of getting the Assembly to act as a Parliament, the other came into view, that of recommending. On this subject, the Assembly agreed to recommend two new taxes to be enregistered by the Parliament: the one a stamp-tax, and the other a territorial tax, or sort of land tax. The two have been estimated at about five millions Sterl. *per ann*. We have now to turn our attention to the Parliaments, on whom the business was again devolving.

The Archbishop of Thoulouse (since Archbishop of Sens, and now a Cardinal) was appointed to the administration of the finances, soon after the dismission of Calonne. He was also made Prime Minister, an office that did not always exist in France. When this office did not exist, the Chief of each of the principal departments transacted business immediately with the King; but when a Prime Minister was appointed, they did business only with him. The Archbishop arrived to more State-authority than any Minister since the Duke de Choiseuil, and the Nation was strongly disposed in his favour; but by a line of conduct scarcely to be accounted for, he perverted every opportunity, turned out a despot, and sunk into disgrace, and a Cardinal.

The Assembly of the Notables having broke up, the new Minister sent the edicts for the two new taxes recommended by the Assembly to the Parliaments, to be enregistered. They of course came first before the Parliament of Paris, who returned for answer, *That with such a revenue as the Nation then supported, the name of taxes ought not to be mentioned, but for the purpose of reducing them;* and threw both the edicts out*.

On this refusal, the Parliament was ordered to Versailles, where, in the usual form, the King held, what under the old government was called, a Bed of Justice; and the two edicts were enregistered in presence of the Parliament, by an order of State, in the manner mentioned in page 493. On this, the Parliament immediately returned to Paris, renewed their session in form, and ordered the enregistering to be struck out, declaring that every thing done at Versailles was illegal. All the members of the Parliament were then served with Lettres de Cachet, and exiled to Trois; but as they continued as inflexible in exile as before, and as vengeance did not supply the place of taxes, they were after a short time recalled to Paris.

The edicts were again tendered to them, and the Count D'Artois undertook to act as representative for the King. For this purpose, he came from Versailles to Paris, in a train of procession; and the Parliament were assembled to receive him. But show and parade had lost their influence in France; and whatever ideas of importance he might set off with, he had to return with those of mortification and disappointment. On alighting from his carriage to ascend the steps of the Parliament House, the crowd (which was numerously collected) threw out trite expressions, saying, "This is Monsieur D'Artois, who wants more of our money to spend." The marked disapprobation which he saw, impressed him with apprehensions; and the word *Aux armes* (*To arms*) was given out by the officer of the guard who attended him. It was so loudly vociferated, that it echoed through the avenues of the House, and produced a temporary confusion: I was then standing in one of the apartments through which he had to pass, and could not avoid reflecting how wretched was the condition of a disrespected man.

He endeavoured to impress the Parliament by great words, and opened his authority by saying, "The King, our Lord and

---

*When the English Minister, Mr. Pitt, mentions the French finances again in the English Parliament, it would be well that he noticed this as an example.

Master." The Parliament received him very coolly, and with their usual determination not to register the taxes: and in this manner the interview ended.

After this a new subject took place: In the various debates and contests that arose between the Court and the Parliaments on the subject of taxes, the Parliament of Paris at last declared, that although it had been customary for Parliaments to enregister edicts for taxes as a matter of convenience, the right belonged only to the *States-General*; and that, therefore, the Parliament could no longer with propriety continue to debate on what it had not authority to act. The King after this came to Paris, and held a meeting with the Parliament, in which he continued from ten in the morning till about six in the evening; and, in a manner that appeared to proceed from him, as if unconsulted upon with the cabinet or the ministry, gave his word to the Parliament, that the States-General should be convened.

But after this another scene arose, on a ground different from all the former. The minister and the cabinet were averse to calling the States-General: They well knew, that if the States-General were assembled, that themselves must fall; and as the King had not mentioned *any time*, they hit on a project calculated to elude, without appearing to oppose.

For this purpose, the Court set about making a sort of Constitution itself: It was principally the work of M. Lamoignon, Keeper of the Seals, who afterwards shot himself. This new arrangement consisted in establishing a body under the name of a *Cour pléniere*, or full Court, in which were invested all the powers that the government might have occasion to make use of. The persons composing this Court were to be nominated by the King; the contended right of taxation was given up on the part of the King, and a new criminal code of laws, and law proceedings, was substituted in room of the former. The thing, in many points, contained better principles than those upon which the government had hitherto been administered: but with respect to the *Cour pléniere*, it was no other than a medium through which despotism was to pass, without appearing to act directly from itself.

The Cabinet had high expectations from their new contrivance. The persons who were to compose the *Cour pléniere*, were already nominated; and as it was necessary to carry a fair appearance, many of the best characters in the nation were appointed among the number. It was to commence on the 8th of May 1788: But an opposition arose to it, on two grounds—the one as to Principle, the other as to Form.

On the ground of Principle it was contended, That government had not a right to alter itself; and that if the practice was once admitted, it would grow into a principle, and be made a precedent for any future alterations the government might wish to establish: That the right of altering the government was a national right, and not a right of government.—And on the ground of Form, it was contended, That the *Cour pléniere* was nothing more than a larger Cabinet.

The then Duke de la Rochefoucault, Luxembourg, De Noailles, and many others, refused to accept the nomination, and strenuously opposed the whole plan. When the edict for establishing this new Court was sent to the Parliaments to be enregistered, and put into execution, they resisted also. The Parliament of Paris not only refused, but denied the authority; and the contest renewed itself between the Parliament and the Cabinet more strongly than ever. While the Parliament were sitting in debate on this subject, the Ministry ordered a regiment of soldiers to surround the House, and form a blockade. The Members sent out for beds and provision, and lived as in a besieged citadel; and as this had no effect, the commanding officer was ordered to enter the Parliament House and seize them, which he did, and some of the principal members were shut up in different prisons. About the same time a deputation of persons arrived from the province of Brittany, to remonstrate against the establishment of the *Cour pléniere*; and those the Archbishop sent to the Bastille. But the spirit of the Nation was not to be overcome; and it was so fully sensible of the strong ground it had taken, that of withholding taxes, that it contented itself with keeping up a sort of quiet resistance, which effectually overthrew all the plans at that time formed against it. The project of the *Cour pléniere* was at last obliged to be given up, and the Prime Minister not long afterwards followed its fate; and M. Neckar was recalled into office.

The attempt to establish the *Cour pléniere* had an effect

upon the Nation, which itself did not perceive. It was a sort of new form of government, that insensibly served to put the old one out of sight, and to unhinge it from the superstitious authority of antiquity. It was government dethroning government; and the old one, by attempting to make a new one, made a chasm.

The failure of this scheme renewed the subject of convening the States-General; and this gave rise to a new series of politics. There was no settled form for convening the States-General: all that it positively meant, was a deputation from what was then called the Clergy, the Noblesse, and the Commons; but their numbers, or their proportions, had not been always the same. They had been convened only on extraordinary occasions, the last of which was in 1614; their numbers were then in equal proportions, and they voted by orders.

It could not well escape the sagacity of M. Neckar, that the mode of 1614 would answer neither the purpose of the then government, nor of the nation. As matters were at that time circumstanced, it would have been too contentious to agree upon any thing. The debates would have been endless upon privileges and exemptions, in which neither the wants of the government, nor the wishes of the nation for a constitution, would have been attended to. But as he did not chuse to take the decision upon himself, he summoned again the *Assembly of the Notables*, and referred it to them. This body was in general interested in the decision, being chiefly of the aristocracy and the high paid clergy; and they decided in favour of the mode of 1614. This decision was against the sense of the Nation, and also against the wishes of the Court; for the aristocracy opposed itself to both, and contended for privileges independent of either. The subject was then taken up by the Parliament, who recommended that the number of the Commons should be equal to the other two; and that they should all sit in one house, and vote in one body. The number finally determined on was twelve hundred: six hundred to be chosen by the Commons, (and this was less than their proportion ought to have been when their worth and consequence is considered on a national scale), three hundred by the clergy, and three hundred by the aristocracy; but with respect to the mode of assembling themselves, whether together or apart, or the manner in which they should vote, those matters were referred*.

The election that followed, was not a contested election, but an animated one. The candidates were not men, but principles. Societies were formed in Paris, and committees of correspondence and communication established throughout the nation, for the purpose of enlightening the people, and explaining to them the principles of civil government; and so orderly was the election conducted, that it did not give rise even to the rumour of tumult.

The States-General were to meet at Versailles in April 1789, but did not assemble till May. They situated themselves in three separate chambers, or rather the clergy and the aristocracy withdrew each into a separate chamber. The majority of the aristocracy claimed what they called the privilege of voting as a separate body, and of giving their consent or their negative in that manner; and many of the bishops and the high-beneficed clergy claimed the same privilege on the part of their Order.

---

*Mr. Burke (and I must take the liberty of telling him he is very unacquainted with French affairs), speaking upon this subject, says, "The first thing that struck me in the calling the States-General, was a great departure from the ancient course;"—and he soon after says, "From the moment I read the list, I saw distinctly, and very nearly as it has happened, all that was to follow."—Mr. Burke certainly did not see all that was to follow. I endeavoured to impress him, as well before as after the States-General met, that there would be a *revolution*; but was not able to make him see it, neither would he believe it. How then he could distinctly see all the parts, when the whole was out of sight, is beyond my comprehension. And with respect to the "departure from the ancient course," besides the natural weakness of the remark, it shews that he is unacquainted with circumstances. The departure was necessary, from the experience had upon it, that the ancient course was a bad one. The States-General of 1614 were called at the commencement of the civil war in the minority of Louis XIII; but by the clash of arranging them by orders, they increased the confusion they were called to compose. The author of *L'Intrigue du Cabinet* (Intrigue of the Cabinet), who wrote before any revolution was thought of in France, speaking of the States-General of 1614, says, "They held the public in suspense five months; and by the questions agitated therein, and the heat with which they were put, it appears that the Great (*les grands*) thought more to satisfy their *particular* passions, than to procure the good of the nation; and the whole time passed away in altercations, ceremonies, and parade." L'Intrigue du Cabinet, vol. i. p. 329.

The *Tiers Etat* (as they were then called) disowned any knowledge of artificial Orders and artificial privileges; and they were not only resolute on this point, but somewhat disdainful. They began to consider aristocracy as a kind of fungus growing out of the corruption of society, that could not be admitted even as a branch of it; and from the disposition the aristocracy had shewn by upholding Lettres de Cachet, and in sundry other instances, it was manifest that no constitution could be formed by admitting men in any other character than as National Men.

After various altercations on this head, the Tiers Etat or Commons (as they were then called) declared themselves (on a motion made for that purpose by the Abbé Sieyes) "THE REPRESENTATIVES OF THE NATION; *and that the two Orders could be considered but as deputies of corporations, and could only have a deliberative voice but when they assembled in a national character with the national representatives.*" This proceeding extinguished the stile of *Etats Généraux* or States-General, and erected it into the stile it now bears, that of L'Assemble Nationale, or National Assembly.

This motion was not made in a precipitate manner: It was the result of cool deliberation, and concerted between the national representatives and the patriotic members of the two chambers, who saw into the folly, mischief, and injustice of artificial privileged distinctions. It was become evident, that no constitution, worthy of being called by that name, could be established on any thing less than a national ground. The aristocracy had hitherto opposed the despotism of the Court, and affected the language of patriotism; but it opposed it as its rival, (as the English Barons opposed King John); and it now opposed the nation from the same motives.

On carrying this motion, the national representatives, as had been concerted, sent an invitation to the two chambers, to unite with them in a national character, and proceed to business. A majority of the clergy, chiefly of the parish priests, withdrew from the clerical chamber, and joined the nation; and forty-five from the other chamber joined in like manner. There is a sort of secret history belonging to this last circumstance, which is necessary to its explanation: It was not judged prudent that all the patriotic members of the chamber, stiling itself the Nobles, should quit it at once; and in consequence of this arrangement, they drew off by degrees, always leaving some, as well to reason the case, as to watch the suspected. In a little time, the numbers increased from forty-five to eighty, and soon after to a greater number; which, with a majority of the clergy, and the whole of the national representatives, put the mal-contents in a very diminutive condition.

The King, who, very different to the general class called by that name, is a man of a good heart, shewed himself disposed to recommend a union of the three chambers, on the ground the National Assembly had taken; but the mal-contents exerted themselves to prevent it, and began now to have another project in view. Their numbers consisted of a majority of the aristocratical chamber, and a minority of the clerical chamber, chiefly of bishops and high-benificed clergy; and these men were determined to put every thing to issue, as well by strength as by stratagem. They had no objection to a constitution; but it must be such an one as themselves should dictate, and suited to their own views and particular situations. On the other hand, the Nation disowned knowing any thing of them but as citizens, and was determined to shut out all such up-start pretensions. The more aristocracy appeared, the more it was despised; there was a visible imbecillity and want of intellects in the majority, a sort of *je ne sais quoi*, that while it affected to be more than citizen, was less than man. It lost ground from contempt more than from hatred; and was rather jeered at as an ass, than dreaded as a lion. This is the general character of aristocracy, or what are called Nobles or Nobility, or rather No-ability, in all countries.

The plan of the mal-contents consisted now of two things; either to deliberate and vote by chambers, (or orders), more especially on all questions respecting a constitution, (by which the aristocratical chamber would have had a negative on any article of the constitution); or, in case they could not accomplish this object, to overthrow the National Assembly entirely.

To effect one or other of these objects, they began now to cultivate a friendship with the despotism they had hitherto attempted to rival, and the Count D'Artois became their chief. The King (who has since declared himself deceived into their measures) held, according to the old form, *a Bed of*

Justice, in which he accorded to the deliberation and vote *par tete* (by head) upon several objects; but reserved the deliberation and vote upon all questions respecting a constitution to the three chambers separately. This declaration of the King was made against the advice of M. Neckar, who now began to perceive that he was growing out of fashion at Court, and that another minister was in contemplation.

As the form of sitting in separate chambers was yet apparently kept up, though essentially destroyed, the national representatives, immediately after this declaration of the King, resorted to their own chambers, to consult on a protest against it; and the minority of the chamber (calling itself the Nobles), who had joined the national cause, retired to a private house, to consult in like manner. The mal-contents had by this time concerted their measures with the Court, which Count D'Artois undertook to conduct; and as they saw, from the discontent which the declaration excited, and the opposition making against it, that they could not obtain a controul over the intended constitution by a separate vote, they prepared themselves for their final object—that of conspiring against the National Assembly, and overthrowing it.

The next morning, the door of the chamber of the National Assembly was shut against them, and guarded by troops; and the Members were refused admittance. On this, they withdrew to a tenis-ground in the neighbourhood of Versailles, as the most convenient place they could find, and, after renewing their session, took an oath never to separate from each other, under any circumstance whatever, death excepted, until they had established a constitution. As the experiment of shutting up the house had no other effect than that of producing a closer connection in the Members, it was opened again the next day, and the public business recommenced in the usual place.

We now are to have in view the forming of the new Ministry, which was to accomplish the overthrow of the National Assembly. But as force would be necessary, orders were issued to assemble thirty thousand troops, the command of which was given to Broglio, one of the new-intended Ministry, who was recalled from the country for this purpose. But as some management was necessary to keep this plan concealed till the moment it should be ready for execution, it is to this policy that a declaration made by Count D'Artois must be attributed, and which is here proper to be introduced.

It could not but occur, that while the mal-contents continued to resort to their chambers separate from the National Assembly, that more jealousy would be excited than if they were mixed with it, and that the plot might be suspected. But as they had taken their ground, and now wanted a pretence for quitting it, it was necessary that one should be devised. This was effectually accomplished by a declaration made by Count D'Artois, *"That if they took not a part in the National Assembly, the life of the King would be endangered:"* on which they quitted their chambers, and mixed with the Assembly in one body.

At the time this declaration was made, it was generally treated as a piece of absurdity in Count D'Artois, and calculated merely to relieve the outstanding Members of the two chambers from the diminutive situation they were put in; and if nothing more had followed, this conclusion would have been good. But as things best explain themselves by their events, this apparent union was only a cover to the machinations that were secretly going on; and the declaration accommodated itself to answer that purpose. In a little time the National Assembly found itself surrounded by troops, and thousands daily arriving. On this a very strong declaration was made by the National Assembly to the King, remonstrating on the impropriety of the measure, and demanding the reason. The King, who was not in the secret of this business, as himself afterwards declared, gave substantially for answer, that he had no other object in view than to preserve the public tranquillity, which appeared to be much disturbed.

But in a few days from this time, the plot unravelled itself. M. Neckar and the Ministry were displaced, and a new one formed, of the enemies of the Revolution; and Broglio, with between twenty-five and thirty thousand foreign troops, was arrived to support them. The mask was now thrown off, and matters were come to a crisis. The event was, that in the space of three days, the new Ministry and their abettors found it prudent to fly the nation; the Bastille was taken, and Broglio and his foreign troops dispersed; as is already related in the former part of this work.

There are some curious circumstances in the history of this short-lived ministry, and this short-lived attempt at a counter-revolution. The palace of Versailles, where the Court was sitting, was not more than four hundred yards distant from the hall where the National Assembly was sitting. The two places were at this moment like the separate head-quarters of two combatant armies; yet the Court was as per-fectly ignorant of the information which had arrived from Paris to the National Assembly, as if it had resided at an hundred miles distance. The then Marquis de la Fayette, who (as has been already mentioned) was chosen to preside in the National Assembly on this particular occasion, named, by order of the Assembly, three successive deputations to the King, on the day, and up to the evening on which the Bastille was taken, and to inform and confer with him on the state of affairs: but the ministry, who knew not so much as that it was attacked, precluded all communication, and were solacing themselves how dexterously they had succeeded; but in a few hours the accounts arrived so thick and fast, that they had to start from their desks and run. Some set off in one disguise, and some in another, and none in their own character. Their anxiety now was to outride the news lest they should be stopt, which, though it flew fast, flew not so fast as themselves.

It is worth remarking, that the National Assembly neither pursued those fugitive conspirators, nor took any notice of them, nor sought to retaliate in any shape whatever. Occu-pied with establishing a constitution founded on the Rights of Man and the Authority of the People, the only authority on which government has a right to exist in any country, the National Assembly felt none of those mean passions which mark the character of impertinent governments, founding themselves on their own authority, or on the absurdity of he-reditary succession. It is the faculty of the human mind to become what it contemplates, and to act in unison with its object.

The conspiracy being thus dispersed, one of the first works of the National Assembly, instead of vindictive proclamations, as has been the case with other governments, published a Declaration of the Rights of Man, as the basis on which the new constitution was to be built, and which is here subjoined.

DECLARATION OF THE RIGHTS OF MAN AND OF CITIZENS,

BY THE NATIONAL ASSEMBLY OF FRANCE.

"The Representatives of the people of FRANCE formed into a National Assembly, considering that ignorance, neglect, or contempt of human rights, are the sole causes of public misfortunes and corruptions of government, have resolved to set forth, in a solemn declaration, these natural, imprescriptible, and unalienable rights: that this declaration being constantly present to the minds of the members of the body social, they may be ever kept attentive to their rights and their duties: that the acts of the legislative and executive powers of government, being capable of being every moment compared with the end of political institutions, may be more respected; and also, that the future claims of the citizens, being directed by simple and incontestible principles, may always tend to the maintenance of the constitution, and the general happiness.

"For these reasons, the NATIONAL ASSEMBLY doth recognize and declare, in the presence of the Supreme Being, and with the hope of his blessing and favour, the following *sacred* rights of men and of citizens:

" 'I. *Men are born and always continue free, and equal in respect of their rights. Civil distinctions, therefore, can be founded only on public utility.*

" 'II. *The end of all political associations is the preservation of the natural and imprescriptible rights of man; and these rights are liberty, property, security, and resistance of oppression.*

" 'III. *The nation is essentially the source of all sovereignty; nor can any* INDIVIDUAL, *or* ANY BODY OF MEN, *be entitled to any authority which is not expressly derived from it.*

" 'IV. Political Liberty consists in the power of doing whatever does not injure another. The exercise of the natural rights of every man, has no other limits than those which are necessary to secure to every *other* man the free exercise of the same rights; and these limits are determinable only by the law.

" 'V. The law ought to prohibit only actions hurtful to society. What is not prohibited by the law, should not be hindered; nor should any one be compelled to that which the law does not require.

" 'VI. The law is an expression of the will of the community. All citizens have a right to concur, either personally, or by their representatives, in its formation. It should be the same to all, whether it protects or punishes; and *all being equal in its sight, are equally eligible to all honours, places, and employments, according to their different abilities, without any other distinction than that created by their virtues and talents.*

" 'VII. No man should be accused, arrested, or held in confinement, except in cases determined by the law, and according to the forms which it has prescribed. All who promote, solicit, execute, or cause to be executed, arbitrary orders, ought to be punished; and every citizen called upon or apprehended by virtue of the law, ought immediately to obey, and renders himself culpable by resistance.

" 'VIII. The law ought to impose no other penalties than such as are absolutely and evidently necessary: and no one ought to be punished, but in virtue of a law promulgated before the offence, and legally applied.

" 'IX. Every man being presumed innocent till he has been convicted, whenever his detention becomes indispensible, all rigour to him, more than is necessary to secure his person, ought to be provided against by the law.

" 'X. No man ought to be molested on account of his opinions, not even on account of his *religious* opinions, provided his avowal of them does not disturb the public order established by the law.

" 'XI. The unrestrained communication of thoughts and opinions being one of the most precious rights of man, every citizen may speak, write, and publish freely, provided he is responsible for the abuse of this liberty in cases determined by the law.

" 'XII. A public force being necessary to give security to the rights of men and of citizens, that force is instituted for the benefit of the community, and not for the particular benefit of the persons with whom it is entrusted.

" 'XIII. A common contribution being necessary for the support of the public force, and for defraying the other expences of government, it ought to be divided equally among the members of the community, according to their abilities.

" 'XIV. Every citizen has a right, either by himself or his representative, to a free voice in determining the necessity of public contributions, the appropriation of them, and their amount, mode of assessment, and duration.

" 'XV. Every community has a right to demand of all its agents, an account of their conduct.

" 'XVI. Every community in which a separation of powers and a security of rights is not provided for, wants a constitution.

" 'XVII. The right to property being inviolable and sacred, no one ought to be deprived of it, except in cases of evident public necessity legally ascertained, and on condition of a previous just indemnity.' "

OBSERVATIONS on the DECLARATION OF RIGHTS.

The three first articles comprehend in general terms, the whole of a Declaration of Rights: All the succeeding articles either originate out of them, or follow as elucidations. The 4th, 5th, and 6th, define more particularly what is only generally expressed in the 1st, 2d, and 3d.

The 7th, 8th, 9th, 10th, and 11th articles, are declaratory of *principles* upon which laws shall be constructed conformable to *rights* already declared. But it is questioned by some very good people in France, as well as in other countries, whether the 10th article sufficiently guarantees the right it is intended to accord with: besides which, it takes off from the divine dignity of religion, and weakens its operative force upon the mind to make it a subject of human laws. It then presents itself to Man, like light intercepted by a cloudy medium, in which the source of it is obscured from his sight, and he sees nothing to reverence in the dusky ray*.

---

*There is a single idea, which, if it strikes rightly upon the mind either in a legal or a religious sense, will prevent any man, or any body of men, or any government, from going wrong on the subject of Religion; which is, that

The remaining articles, beginning with the twelfth, are substantially contained in the principles of the preceding articles; but, in the particular situation which France then was, having to undo what was wrong, as well as to set up what was right, it was proper to be more particular than what in another condition of things would be necessary.

While the Declaration of Rights was before the National Assembly, some of its members remarked, that if a Declaration of Rights was published, it should be accompanied by a Declaration of Duties. The observation discovered a mind that reflected, and it only erred by not reflecting far enough. A Declaration of Rights is, by reciprocity, a Declaration of Duties also. Whatever is my right as a man, is also the right of another; and it becomes my duty to guarantee, as well as to possess.

The three first articles are the basis of Liberty, as well individual as national; nor can any country be called free, whose government does not take its beginning from the principles they contain, and continue to preserve them pure; and the whole of the Declaration of Rights is of more value to the world, and will do more good, than all the laws and statutes that have yet been promulgated.

In the declaratory exordium which prefaces the Declaration of Rights, we see the solemn and majestic spectacle of a Nation opening its commission, under the auspices of its Creator, to establish a Government; a scene so new, and so transcendently unequalled by any thing in the European world, that the name of a Revolution is diminutive of its char-

---

before any human institutions of government were known in the world, there existed, if I may so express it, a compact between God and Man, from the beginning of time; and that as the relation and condition which man in his *individual person* stands in towards his Maker cannot be changed, or any ways altered by any human laws or human authority, that religious devotion, which is a part of this compact, cannot so much as be made a subject of human laws; and that all laws must conform themselves to this prior existing compact, and not assume to make the compact conform to the laws, which, besides being human, are subsequent thereto. The first act of man, when he looked around and saw himself a creature which he did not make, and a world furnished for his reception, must have been devotion; and devotion must ever continue sacred to every individual man, *as it appears right to him*; and governments do mischief by interfering.

acter, and it rises into a Regeneration of man. What are the
present Governments of Europe, but a scene of iniquity and
oppression? What is that of England? Does not its own inhabitants say, It is a market where every man has his price, and
where corruption is common traffic, at the expence of a deluded people? No wonder, then, that the French Revolution
is traduced. Had it confined itself merely to the destruction of
flagrant despotism, perhaps Mr. Burke and some others had
been silent. Their cry now is, "It has gone too far:" that is, it
has gone too far for them. It stares corruption in the face, and
the venal tribe are all alarmed. Their fear discovers itself in
their outrage, and they are but publishing the groans of a
wounded vice. But from such opposition, the French Revolution, instead of suffering, receives an homage. The more it is
struck, the more sparks it will emit; and the fear is, it will not
be struck enough. It has nothing to dread from attacks: Truth
has given it an establishment; and Time will record it with a
name as lasting as his own.

Having now traced the progress of the French Revolution
through most of its principal stages, from its commencement
to the taking of the Bastille, and its establishment by the Declaration of Rights, I will close the subject with the energetic
apostrophe of M. de la Fayette — *May this great monument
raised to Liberty, serve as a lesson to the oppressor, and an example to the oppressed!**

MISCELLANEOUS CHAPTER

To prevent interrupting the argument in the preceding
part of this work, or the narrative that follows it, I reserved
some observations to be thrown together into a Miscellaneous Chapter; by which variety might not be censured for
confusion. Mr. Burke's Book is *all* Miscellany. His intention
was to make an attack on the French Revolution; but instead
of proceeding with an orderly arrangement, he has stormed

---

*See page 443 of this work. — N. B. Since the taking the Bastille, the oc-
currences have been published: but the matters recorded in this narrative, are
prior to that period; and some of them, as may easily be seen, can be but very
little known.

it with a Mob of ideas, tumbling over and destroying one another.

But this confusion and contradiction in Mr. Burke's Book, is easily accounted for.—When a man in a long cause attempts to steer his course by any thing else than some polar truth or principle, he is sure to be lost. It is beyond the compass of his capacity, to keep all the parts of an argument together, and make them unite in one issue, by any other means than having this guide always in view. Neither memory nor invention will supply the want of it. The former fails him, and the latter betrays him.

Notwithstanding the nonsense, for it deserves no better name, that Mr. Burke has asserted about hereditary rights, and hereditary succession, and that a Nation has not a right to form a Government for itself; it happened to fall in his way to give some account of what Government is. *"Government,* says he, *is a contrivance of human wisdom."*

Admitting that Government is a contrivance of human *wisdom*, it must necessarily follow, that hereditary succession, and hereditary rights, (as they are called), can make no part of it, because it is impossible to make wisdom hereditary; and on the other hand, *that* cannot be a wise contrivance, which in its operation may commit the government of a nation to the wisdom of an ideot. The ground which Mr. Burke now takes is fatal to every part of his cause. The argument changes from hereditary rights to hereditary wisdom; and the question is, Who is the wisest man? He must now shew that every one in the line of hereditary succession was a Solomon, or his title is not good to be a king.—What a stroke has Mr. Burke now made! To use a sailor's phrase, he has *swabbed the deck,* and scarcely left a name legible in the list of kings; and he has mowed down and thinned the House of Peers, with a scythe as formidable as Death and Time.

But, Mr. Burke appears to have been aware of this retort, and he has taken care to guard against it, by making government to be not only a *contrivance* of human wisdom, but a *monopoly* of wisdom. He puts the nation as fools on one side, and places his government of wisdom, all wise-men of Gotham, on the other side; and he then proclaims, and says, that *"Men have a* RIGHT *that their* WANTS *should be pro-*

vided for by this wisdom." Having thus made proclamation, he next proceeds to explain to them what their *wants* are, and also what their *rights* are. In this he has succeeded dextrously, for he makes their wants to be a *want* of wisdom; but as this is but cold comfort, he then informs them, that they have a *right* (not to any of the wisdom) but to be governed by it: and in order to impress them with a solemn reverence for this monopoly-government of wisdom, and of its vast capacity for all purposes, possible or impossible, right or wrong, he proceeds with astrological mysterious importance, to tell to them its powers, in these words—"The Rights of men in government are their advantages; and these are often in balances between differences of good; and in compromises sometimes between *good* and *evil*, and sometimes between *evil* and *evil*. Political reason is a *computing principle*; adding—subtracting—multiplying—and dividing, morally, and not metaphysically or mathematically, true moral demonstrations."

As the wondering audience whom Mr. Burke supposes himself talking to, may not understand all this learned jargon, I will undertake to be its interpreter. The meaning then, good people, of all this is, *That government is governed by no principle whatever; that it can make evil good, or good evil, just as it pleases. In short, that government is arbitrary power.*

But there are some things which Mr. Burke has forgotten. *First,* He has not shewn where the wisdom originally came from: and *secondly,* he has not shewn by what authority it first began to act. In the manner he introduces the matter, it is either government stealing wisdom, or wisdom stealing government. It is without an origin, and its powers without authority. In short, it is usurpation.

Whether it be from a sense of shame, or from a consciousness of some radical defect in a government necessary to be kept out of sight, or from both, or from any other cause, I undertake not to determine; but so it is, that a monarchical reasoner never traces government to its source, or from its source. It is one of the *shibboleths* by which he may be known. A thousand years hence, those who shall live in America or in France, will look back with contemplative pride on the origin of their governments, and say, *This was the work of our glorious ancestors!* But what can a monarchical talker say? What has he to exult in? Alas! he has nothing. A certain something forbids him to look back to a beginning, lest some robber or some Robin Hood should rise from the long obscurity of time, and say, *I am the origin*. Hard as Mr. Burke laboured the Regency Bill and hereditary succession two years ago, and much as he dived for precedents, he still had not boldness enough to bring up William of Normandy, and say, *There is the head of the list, there is the fountain of honour*, the son of a prostitute, and the plunderer of the English nation.

The opinions of men with respect to government, are changing fast in all countries. The revolutions of America and France have thrown a beam of light over the world, which reaches into man. The enormous expence of governments have provoked people to think, by making them feel: and when once the veil begins to rend, it admits not of repair. Ignorance is of a peculiar nature: once dispelled, and it is impossible to re-establish it. It is not originally a thing of itself, but is only the absence of knowlege; and though man may be *kept* ignorant, he cannot be *made* ignorant. The mind, in discovering truth, acts in the same manner as it acts through the eye in discovering objects; when once any object has been seen, it is impossible to put the mind back to the same condition it was in before it saw it. Those who talk of a counter revolution in France, shew how little they understand of man. There does not exist in the compass of language, an arrangement of words to express so much as the means of affecting a counter revolution. The means must be an obliteration of knowlege; and it has never yet been discovered, how to make man *unknow* his knowlege, or *unthink* his thoughts.

Mr. Burke is labouring in vain to stop the progress of knowlege; and it comes with the worse grace from him, as there is a certain transaction known in the city, which renders him suspected of being a pensioner in a fictitious name. This may account for some strange doctrine he has advanced in his book, which, though he points it at the Revolution Society, is effectually directed against the whole Nation.

"The King of England," says he, "holds *his* Crown (for it does not belong to the nation, according to Mr. Burke) in *contempt* of the choice of the Revolution Society, who have not a single vote for a King among them either *individually* or *collectively*, and his Majesty's heirs, each in their time and order, will come to the Crown *with the same contempt* of their choice, with which his Majesty has succeeded to that which he now wears."

As to who is king in England or elsewhere, or whether there is any king at all, or whether the people chuse a Cherokee Chief, or a Hessian Hussar for a King, is not a matter that I trouble myself about, be that to themselves; but with respect to the doctrine, so far as it relates to the Rights of Men and Nations, it is as abominable as any thing ever uttered in the most enslaved country under heaven. Whether it sounds worse to my ear, by not being accustomed to hear such despotism, than what it does to the ear of another person, I am not so well a judge of; but of its abominable principle, I am at no loss to judge.

It is not the Revolution Society that Mr. Burke means; it is the Nation, as well in its *original*, as in its *representative* character; and he has taken care to make himself understood, by saying that they have not a vote either *collectively* or *individually*. The Revolution Society is composed of citizens of all denominations, and of members of both the Houses of Parliament; and consequently, if there is not a right to a vote in any of the characters, there can be no right to any either in the nation or in its parliament. This ought to be a caution to every country, how it imports foreign families to be Kings. It is somewhat curious to observe, that although the people of England have been in the habit of talking about Kings, it is always a foreign house of Kings; hating foreigners, yet governed by them. It is now the House of Brunswick, one of the petty tribes of Germany.

It has hitherto been the practice of the English Parliaments, to regulate what was called the succession, (taking it for granted, that the nation then continued to accord to the form of annexing a monarchical branch to its government; for without this, the parliament could not have had authority to have sent either to Holland or to Hanover, or to impose a King upon the nation against its will.) And this must be the utmost limit to which Parliament can go upon the case; but the right of the nation goes to the *whole* case, because it has the right of changing its *whole* form of government. The right of a Parliament is only a right in trust, a right by delegation, and that but from a very small part of the nation; and one of its Houses has not even this. But the right of the nation is an original right, as universal as taxation. The nation is the pay-master of every thing, and every thing must conform to its general will.

I remember taking notice of a speech in what is called the English House of Peers, by the then Earl of Shelburne, and I think it was at the time he was Minister, which is applicable to this case. I do not directly charge my memory with every par-ticular; but the words and the purport, as nearly as I remem-ber, were these: *That the form of a Government was a matter wholly at the will of a Nation at all times: that if it chose a monarchical form, it had a right to have it so; and if it after-wards chose to be a Republic, it had a right to be a Republic, and to say to a King, we have no longer any occasion for you.*

When Mr. Burke says that "His Majesty's heirs and succes-sors, each in their time and order, will come to the crown with the *same contempt* of their choice with which His Maj-esty has succeeded to that he wears," it is saying too much even to the humblest individual in the country; part of whose daily labour goes towards making up the million sterling a year, which the country gives the person it stiles a King. Gov-ernment with insolence, is despotism; but when contempt is added, it becomes worse; and to pay for contempt, is the ex-cess of slavery. This species of Government comes from Ger-many; and reminds me of what one of the Brunswick soldiers told me, who was taken prisoner by the Americans in the late war: "Ah!" said he, "America is a fine free country, it is worth the people's fighting for; I know the difference by knowing my own; in my country, if the prince say, Eat straw, we eat straw." — God help that country, thought I, be it England or elsewhere, whose liberties are to be protected by German principles of government and princes of Brunswick.

As Mr. Burke sometimes speaks of England, sometimes of France, and sometimes of the world, and of government in general, it is difficult to answer his book without apparently meeting him on the same ground. Although principles of Government are general subjects, it is next to impossible in many cases to separate them from the idea of place and circumstance; and the more so when circumstances are put for arguments, which is frequently the case with Mr. Burke.

In the former part of his Book, addressing himself to the people of France, he says, "No experience has taught us, (meaning the English), that in any other course or method than that of an *hereditary crown*, can our liberties be regularly perpetuated and preserved sacred as our *hereditary right*." I ask Mr. Burke who is to take them away? M. de la Fayette, in speaking to France, says, *"For a Nation to be free, it is sufficient that she wills it."* But Mr. Burke represents England as wanting capacity to take care of itself; and that its liberties must be taken care of by a King, holding it in "contempt." If England is sunk to this, it is preparing itself to eat straw, as in Hanover or in Brunswick. But besides the folly of the declaration, it happens that the facts are all against Mr. Burke. It was by the Government *being hereditary*, that the liberties of the people were endangered. Charles the first, and James the second, are instances of this truth; yet neither of them went so far as to hold the Nation in contempt.

As it is sometimes of advantage to the people of one country, to hear what those of other countries have to say respecting it, it is possible that the people of France may learn something from Mr. Burke's Book, and that the people of England may also learn something from the answers it will occasion. When Nations fall out about freedom, a wide field of debate is opened. The argument commences with the rights of war, without its evils; and as knowledge is the object contended for, the party that sustains the defeat obtains the prize.

Mr. Burke talks about what he calls an hereditary crown, as if it were some production of nature; or as if, like time, it had a power to operate not only independent, but in spite of man; or as if it were a thing or a subject universally consented to. Alas! it has none of those properties, but is the reverse of them all. It is a thing in imagination, the propriety of which is more than doubted, and the legality of which in a few years will be denied.

But, to arrange this matter in a clearer view than what general expressions can convey, it will be necessary to state the distinct heads under which (what is called) an hereditary crown, or, more properly speaking, an hereditary succession to the Government of a Nation, can be considered; which are,

First, The right of a particular family to establish itself.

Secondly, The right of a Nation to establish a particular family.

With respect to the *first* of these heads, that of a family establishing itself with hereditary powers on its own authority, and independent of the consent of a Nation, all men will concur in calling it despotism; and it would be trespassing on their understanding to attempt to prove it.

But the *second* head, that of a Nation establishing a particular family with *hereditary powers*, it does not present itself as despotism on the first reflection; but if men will permit a second reflection to take place, and carry that reflection forward but one remove out of their own persons to that of their offspring, they will then see that hereditary succession becomes in its consequences the same despotism to others, which they reprobated for themselves. It operates to preclude the consent of the succeeding generation, and the preclusion of consent is despotism. When the person who at any time shall be in possession of a Government, or those who stand in succession to him, shall say to a Nation, I hold this power in "contempt" of you, it signifies not on what authority he pretends to say it. It is no relief, but an aggravation to a person in slavery, to reflect that he was sold by his parent; and as that which heightens the criminality of an act cannot be produced to prove the legality of it, hereditary succession cannot be established as a legal thing.

In order to arrive at a more perfect decision on this head, it will be proper to consider the generation which undertakes to establish a family with *hereditary powers*, a-part and separate from the generations which are to follow; and also to consider the character in which the *first* generation acts with respect to succeeding generations.

The generation which first selects a person, and puts him at the head of its Government, either with the title of King, or any other distinction, acts its *own choice*, be it wise or foolish, as a free agent for itself. The person so set up is not hereditary, but selected and appointed; and the generation who sets him up, does not live under an hereditary government, but under a government of its own choice and establishment. Were the generation who sets him up, and the person so set up, to live for ever, it never could become hereditary succession; and of consequence, hereditary succession can only follow on the death of the first parties.

As therefore hereditary succession is out of the question with respect to the *first* generation, we have now to consider the character in which *that* generation acts with respect to the commencing generation, and to all succeeding ones.

It assumes a character, to which it has neither right nor title. It changes itself from a *Legislator* to a *Testator*, and affects to make its Will, which is to have operation after the demise of the makers, to bequeath the Government; and it not only attempts to bequeath, but to establish on the succeeding generation, a new and different form of government under which itself lived. Itself, as is already observed, lived not under an hereditary Government, but under a Government of its own choice and establishment; and it now attempts, by virtue of a will and testament, (and which it has not authority to make), to take from the commencing generation, and all future ones, the rights and free agency by which itself acted.

But, exclusive of the right which any generation has to act collectively as a testator, the objects to which it applies itself in this case, are not within the compass of any law, or of any will or testament.

The rights of men in society, are neither deviseable, nor transferable, nor annihilable, but are descendable only; and it is not in the power of any generation to intercept finally, and cut off the descent. If the present generation, or any other, are disposed to be slaves, it does not lessen the right of the succeeding generation to be free: wrongs cannot have a legal descent. When Mr. Burke attempts to maintain, that the *English Nation did at the Revolution of 1688, most solemnly renounce and abdicate their rights for themselves, and for all their posterity for ever;* he speaks a language that merits not reply, and which can only excite contempt for his prostitute principles, or pity for his ignorance.

In whatever light hereditary succession, as growing out of the will and testament of some former generation, presents itself, it is an absurdity. A cannot make a will to take from B the property of B, and give it to C; yet this is the manner in which (what is called) hereditary succession by law operates. A certain former generation made a will to take away the rights of the commencing generation and all future ones, and convey those rights to a third person, who afterwards comes forward, and tells them in Mr. Burke's language, that they have *no rights*, that their rights are already bequeathed to him, and that he will govern in *contempt* of them. From such principles, and such ignorance, Good Lord deliver the world!

But, after all, what is this metaphor called a crown, or rather what is monarchy? Is it a thing, or is it a name, or is it a fraud? Is it "a contrivance of human wisdom," or of human craft to obtain money from a nation under specious pretences? Is it a thing necessary to a nation? If it is, in what does that necessity consist, what services does it perform, what is its business, and what are its merits? Doth the virtue consist in the metaphor, or in the man? Doth the goldsmith that makes the crown, make the virtue also? Doth it operate like Fortunatus's wishing-cap, or Harlequin's wooden sword? Doth it make a man a conjuror? In fine, what is it? It appears to be a something going much out of fashion, falling into ridicule, and rejected in some countries both as unnecessary and expensive. In America it is considered as an absurdity, and in France it has so far declined, that the goodness of the man, and the respect for his personal character, are the only things that preserve the appearance of its existence.

If Government be what Mr. Burke describes it, "a contrivance of human wisdom," I might ask him, if wisdom was at such a low ebb in England, that it was become necessary to import it from Holland and from Hanover? But I will do the country the justice to say, that was not the case; and even if it was, it mistook the cargo. The wisdom of every country, when properly exerted, is sufficient for all its purposes; and there could exist no more real occasion in England to have sent for a Dutch Stadtholder, or a German Elector, than there was in America to have done a similar thing. If a country does not understand its own affairs, how is a foreigner to understand them, who knows neither its laws, its manners, nor its language? If there existed a man so transcendently wise above all others, that his wisdom was necessary to instruct a nation, some reason might be offered for monarchy; but when we cast our eyes about a country, and observe how every part understands its own affairs; and when we look around the world, and see that of all men in it, the race of kings are the most insignificant in capacity, our reason cannot fail to ask us—What are those men kept for?

If there is any thing in monarchy which we people of America do not understand, I wish Mr. Burke would be so kind as to inform us. I see in America, a government extending over a country ten times as large as England, and conducted with regularity for a fortieth part of the expence which government cost in England. If I ask a man in America, if he wants a King? he retorts, and asks me if I take him for an ideot? How is it that this difference happens? are we more or less wise than others? I see in America, the generality of people living in a stile of plenty unknown in monarchical countries; and I see that the principle of its government, which is that of the *equal Rights of Man*, is making a rapid progress in the world.

If monarchy is a useless thing, why is it kept up any where? and if a necessary thing, how can it be dispensed with? That *civil government* is necessary, all civilized nations will agree in; but civil government is republican government. All that part of the government of England which begins with the office of constable, and proceeds through the department of magistrate, quarter-session, and general assize, including trial by jury, is republican government. Nothing of monarchy appears in any part of it, except the name which William the Conqueror imposed upon the English, that of obliging them to call him "Their Sovereign Lord the King."

It is easy to conceive, that a band of interested men, such as placemen, pensioners, Lords of the bed-chamber, Lords of the kitchen, Lords of the necessary-house, and the Lord knows what besides, can find as many reasons for monarchy as their salaries, paid at the expence of the country, amount to; but if I ask the farmer, the manufacturer, the merchant, the tradesman, and down through all the occupations of life to the common labourer, what service monarchy is to him? he can give me no answer. If I ask him what monarchy is, he believes it is something like a sinecure.

Notwithstanding the taxes of England amount to almost seventeen millions a-year, said to be for the expences of Government, it is still evident that the sense of the Nation is left to govern itself, and does govern itself by magistrates and juries, almost at its own charge, on republican principles, exclusive of the expence of taxes. The salaries of the Judges are almost the only charge that is paid out of the revenue. Considering that all the internal government is executed by the people, the taxes of England ought to be lightest of any nation in Europe; instead of which, they are the contrary. As this cannot be accounted for on the score of civil government, the subject necessarily extends itself to the monarchical part.

When the people of England sent for George the First, (and it would puzzle a wiser man than Mr. Burke to discover for what he could be wanted, or what service he could render), they ought at least to have conditioned for the abandonment of Hanover. Besides the endless German intrigues that must follow from a German Elector being King of England, there is a natural impossibility of uniting in the same person the principles of Freedom and the principles of Despotism, or, as it is usually called in England, Arbitrary Power. A German Elector is in his electorate a despot: How then could it be expected that he should be attached to principles of liberty in one country, while his interest in another was to be supported by despotism? The union cannot exist; and it might easily have been foreseen, that German Electors would make German Kings, or, in Mr. Burke's words, would assume government with 'contempt.' The English have been in the habit of considering a King of England only in the character in which he appears to them: whereas the same person, while the connection lasts, has a home-seat in another country, the interest of which is different to their own, and the principles of the governments in opposition to each other—To such a person England will appear as a town-residence, and the Electorate as the estate. The English may wish, as I believe they do, success to the principles of Liberty in France, or in Germany; but a German Elector trembles for the fate of despotism in his electorate: and the Duchy of Mecklenburgh, where the present

Queen's family governs, is under the same wretched state of arbitrary power, and the people in slavish vassalage.

There never was a time when it became the English to watch continental intrigues more circumspectly than at the present moment, and to distinguish the politics of the Electorate from the politics of the Nation. The revolution of France has entirely changed the ground with respect to England and France, as nations: but the German despots, with Prussia at their head, are combining against Liberty; and the fondness of Mr. Pitt for office, and the interest which all his family-connections have obtained, do not give sufficient security against this intrigue.

As every thing which passes in the world becomes matter for history, I will now quit this subject, and take a concise review of the state of parties and politics in England, as Mr. Burke has done in France.

Whether the present reign commenced with contempt, I leave to Mr. Burke: certain however it is, that it had strongly that appearance. The animosity of the English Nation, it is very well remembered, ran high; and, had the true principles of Liberty been as well understood then as they now promise to be, it is probable the Nation would not have patiently submitted to so much. George the First and Second were sensible of a rival in the remains of the Stuarts; and as they could not but consider themselves as standing on their good behaviour, they had prudence to keep their German principles of Government to themselves; but as the Stuart Family wore away, the prudence became less necessary.

The contest between rights, and what were called prerogatives, continued to heat the Nation till some time after the conclusion of the American War, when all at once it fell a calm—Execration exchanged itself for applause, and Court popularity sprung up like a mushroom in a night.

To account for this sudden transition, it is proper to observe, that there are two distinct species of popularity; the one excited by merit, the other by resentment. As the Nation had formed itself into two parties, and each was extolling the merits of its parliamentary champions for and against prerogative, nothing could operate to give a more general shock than an immediate coalition of the champions themselves. The parti-

sans of each being thus suddenly left in the lurch, and mutually heated with disgust at the measure, felt no other relief
than uniting in a common execration against both. A higher
stimulus of resentment being thus excited, than what the contest on prerogatives had occasioned, the Nation quitted all
former objects of rights and wrongs, and sought only that of
gratification. The indignation at the Coalition, so effectually
superseded the indignation against the Court, as to extinguish
it; and without any change of principles on the part of the
Court, the same people who had reprobated its despotism,
united with it, to revenge themselves on the Coalition Parliament. The case was not, which they liked best,—but, which
they hated most; and the least hated passed for love. The dissolution of the Coalition Parliament, as it afforded the means
of gratifying the resentment of the Nation, could not fail to
be popular; and from hence arose the popularity of the Court.

Transitions of this kind exhibit a Nation under the government of temper, instead of a fixed and steady principle;
and having once committed itself, however rashly, it feels
itself urged along to justify by continuance its first proceeding. Measures which at other times it would censure, it now
approves, and acts persuasion upon itself to suffocate its
judgment.

On the return of a new Parliament, the new Minister, Mr.
Pitt, found himself in a secure majority: and the Nation gave
him credit, not out of regard to himself, but because it had
resolved to do it out of resentment to another. He introduced
himself to public notice by a proposed reform of Parliament,
which in its operation would have amounted to a public jus-
tification of corruption. The Nation was to be at the expence
of buying up the rotten boroughs, whereas it ought to punish
the persons who deal in the traffic.

Passing over the two bubbles, of the Dutch business, and
the million a-year to sink the national debt, the matter which
most presents itself, is the affair of the Regency. Never, in the
course of my observation, was delusion more successfully
acted, nor a nation more completely deceived.—But, to make
this appear, it will be necessary to go over the circumstances.

Mr. Fox had stated in the House of Commons, that the
Prince of Wales, as heir in succession, had a right in himself to

assume the government. This was opposed by Mr. Pitt; and, so far as the opposition was confined to the doctrine, it was just. But the principles which Mr. Pitt maintained on the contrary side, were as bad, or worse in their extent, than those of Mr. Fox; because they went to establish an aristocracy over the Nation, and over the small representation it has in the House of Commons.

Whether the English form of Government be good or bad, is not in this case the question; but, taking it as it stands, without regard to its merits or demerits, Mr. Pitt was farther from the point than Mr. Fox.

It is supposed to consist of three parts:—while, therefore, the Nation is disposed to continue this form, the parts have a *national standing*, independent of each other, and are not the creatures of each other. Had Mr. Fox passed through Parliament, and said, that the person alluded to claimed on the ground of the Nation, Mr. Pitt must then have contended (what he called) the right of the Parliament, against the right of the Nation.

By the appearance which the contest made, Mr. Fox took the hereditary ground, and Mr. Pitt the parliamentary ground; but the fact is, they both took hereditary ground, and Mr. Pitt took the worst of the two.

What is called the Parliament, is made up of two Houses; one of which is more hereditary, and more beyond the controul of the Nation, than what the Crown (as it is called) is supposed to be. It is an hereditary aristocracy, assuming and asserting indefeasible, irrevocable rights and authority, wholly independent of the Nation. Where then was the merited popularity of exalting this hereditary power over another hereditary power less independent of the Nation than what itself assumed to be, and of absorbing the rights of the Nation into a House over which it has neither election nor controul?

The general impulse of the Nation was right; but it acted without reflection. It approved the opposition made to the right set up by Mr. Fox, without perceiving that Mr. Pitt was supporting another indefeasible right, more remote from the Nation, in opposition to it.

With respect to the House of Commons, it is elected but by a small part of the Nation; but were the election as universal as taxation, which it ought to be, it would still be only the organ of the Nation, and cannot possess inherent rights.—When the National Assembly of France resolves a matter, the resolve is made in right of the Nation; but Mr. Pitt, on all national questions, so far as they refer to the House of Commons, absorbs the rights of the Nation into the organ, and makes the organ into a Nation, and the Nation itself into a cypher.

In a few words, the question on the Regency was a question on a million a-year, which is appropriated to the executive department: and Mr. Pitt could not possess himself of any management of this sum, without setting up the supremacy of Parliament; and when this was accomplished, it was indifferent who should be Regent, as he must be Regent at his own cost. Among the curiosities which this contentious debate afforded, was that of making the Great Seal into a King; the affixing of which to an act, was to be royal authority. If, therefore, Royal Authority is a Great Seal, it consequently is in itself nothing; and a good Constitution would be of infinitely more value to the Nation, than what the three Nominal Powers, as they now stand, are worth.

The continual use of the word *Constitution* in the English Parliament shews there is none; and that the whole is merely a form of Government without a Constitution, and constituting itself with what powers it pleases. If there were a Constitution, it certainly could be referred to; and the debate on any constitutional point, would terminate by producing the Constitution. One member says, This is Constitution; another says, That is Constitution—To-day it is one thing; and to-morrow, it is something else—while the maintaining the debate proves there is none. Constitution is now the cant word of Parliament, tuning itself to the ear of the Nation. Formerly it was the *universal supremacy of Parliament*—the *omnipotence of Parliament*: But, since the progress of Liberty in France, those phrases have a despotic harshness in their note; and the English Parliament have catched the fashion from the National Assembly, but without the substance, of speaking of *Constitution*.

As the present generation of people in England did not make the Government, they are not accountable for any of its defects; but that sooner or later it must come into their hands to undergo a constitutional reformation, is as certain as that the same thing has happened in France. If France, with a revenue of nearly twenty-four millions sterling, with an extent of rich and fertile country above four times larger than England, with a population of twenty-four millions of inhabitants to support taxation, with upwards of ninety millions sterling of gold and silver circulating in the nation, and with a debt less than the present debt of England—still found it necessary, from whatever cause, to come to a settlement of its affairs, it solves the problem of funding for both countries.

It is out of the question to say how long, what is called, the English constitution has lasted, and to argue from thence how long it is to last; the question is, how long can the funding system last? It is a thing but of modern invention, and has not yet continued beyond the life of a man; yet in that short space it has so far accumulated, that, together with the current expences, it requires an amount of taxes at least equal to the whole landed rental of the nation in acres to defray the annual expenditures. That a Government could not always have gone on by the same system which has been followed for the last seventy years, must be evident to every man; and for the same reason it cannot always go on.

The funding system is not money; neither is it, properly speaking, credit. It in effect, creates upon paper the sum which it appears to borrow, and lays on a tax to keep the imaginary capital alive by the payment of interest, and sends the annuity to market, to be sold for paper already in circulation. If any credit is given, it is to the disposition of the people to pay the tax, and not to the Government which lays it on. When this disposition expires, what is supposed to be the credit of Government expires with it. The instance of France under the former Government, shews that it is impossible to compel the payment of taxes by force, when a whole nation is determined to take its stand upon that ground.

Mr. Burke, in his review of the finances of France, states the quantity of gold and silver in France, at about eighty-eight millions sterling. In doing this, he has, I presume, divided by the difference of exchange, instead of the standard of twenty-four livres to a pound sterling; for M. Neckar's statement, from which Mr. Burke's is taken, is *two thousand two hundred millions of livres*, which is upwards of ninety-one millions and an half sterling.

M. Neckar in France, and Mr. George Chalmers of the Office of Trade and Plantation in England, of which Lord Hawkesbury is president, published nearly about the same time (1786) an account of the quantity of money in each nation, from the returns of the Mint of each nation. Mr. Chalmers, from the returns of the English Mint at the Tower of London, states the quantity of money in England, including Scotland and Ireland, to be twenty millions sterling*.

M. Neckar† says, that the amount of money in France, re-coined from the old coin which was called in, was two thousand five hundred millions of livres, (upwards of one hundred and four millions sterling); and, after deducting for waste, and what may be in the West Indies, and other possible circumstances, states the circulating quantity at home, to be ninety-one millions and an half sterling; but, taking it as Mr. Burke has put it, it is sixty-eight millions more than the national quantity in England.

That the quantity of money in France cannot be under this sum, may at once be seen from the state of the French Revenue, without referring to the records of the French Mint for proofs. The revenue of France prior to the Revolution, was nearly twenty-four millions sterling; and as paper had then no existence in France, the whole revenue was collected upon gold and silver; and it would have been impossible to have collected such a quantity of revenue upon a less national quantity than M. Neckar has stated. Before the establishment of paper in England, the revenue was about a fourth part of the national amount of gold and silver, as may be known by referring to the revenue prior to King William, and the quantity of money stated to be in the nation at that time, which was nearly as much as it is now.

It can be of no real service to a Nation, to impose upon itself, or to permit itself to be imposed upon; but the prejudices of some, and the imposition of others, have always rep-

*See *Estimate of the Comparative Strength of Great Britain*, by G. Chalmers.

†See Administration of the Finances of France, Vol. III. by M. Neckar.

resented France as a nation possessing but little money—whereas the quantity is not only more than four times what the quantity is in England, but is considerably greater on a proportion of numbers. To account for this deficiency on the part of England, some reference should be had to the English system of funding. It operates to multiply paper, and to substitute it in the room of money, in various shapes; and the more paper is multiplied, the more opportunities are afforded to export the specie; and it admits of a possibility (by extending it to small notes) of increasing paper, till there is no money left.

I know this is not a pleasant subject to English readers; but the matters I am going to mention, are so important in themselves, as to require the attention of men interested in money-transactions of a public nature.—There is a circumstance stated by M. Neckar, in his treatise on the administration of the finances, which has never been attended to in England, but which forms the only basis whereon to estimate the quantity of money (gold and silver) which ought to be in every nation in Europe, to preserve a relative proportion with other nations.

Lisbon and Cadiz are the two ports into which (money) gold and silver from South America are imported, and which afterwards divides and spreads itself over Europe by means of commerce, and increases the quantity of money in all parts of Europe. If, therefore, the amount of the annual importation into Europe can be known, and the relative proportion of the foreign commerce of the several nations by which it is distributed can be ascertained, they give a rule, sufficiently true, to ascertain the quantity of money which ought to be found in any nation at any given time.

M. Neckar shews from the registers of Lisbon and Cadiz, that the importation of gold and silver into Europe, is five millions sterling annually. He has not taken it on a single year, but on an average of fifteen succeeding years, from 1763 to 1777, both inclusive; in which time, the amount was one thousand eight hundred million livres, which is seventy-five millions sterling*.

*Administration of the Finances of France, Vol. iii.

From the commencement of the Hanover succession in 1714, to the time Mr. Chalmers published, is seventy-two years; and the quantity imported into Europe, in that time, would be three hundred and sixty millions sterling.

If the foreign commerce of Great Britain be stated at a sixth part of what the whole foreign commerce of Europe amounts to, (which is probably an inferior estimation to what the gentlemen at the Exchange would allow), the proportion which Britain should draw by commerce of this sum, to keep herself on a proportion with the rest of Europe, would be also a sixth part, which is sixty millions sterling; and if the same allowance for waste and accident be made for England which M. Neckar makes for France, the quantity remaining after these deductions would be fifty-two millions; and this sum ought to have been in the nation (at the time Mr. Chalmers published) in addition to the sum which was in the nation at the commencement of the Hanover succession, and to have made in the whole at least sixty-six millions sterling; instead of which, there were but twenty millions, which is forty-six millions below its proportionate quantity.

As the quantity of gold and silver imported into Lisbon and Cadiz is more exactly ascertained than that of any commodity imported into England; and as the quantity of money coined at the Tower of London is still more positively known, the leading facts do not admit of controversy. Either, therefore, the commerce of England is unproductive of profit, or the gold and silver which it brings in leak continually away by unseen means, at the average rate of about three quarters of a million a-year, which, in the course of seventy-two years, accounts for the deficiency; and its absence is supplied by paper*.

---

*Whether the English commerce does not bring in money, or whether the Government sends it out after it is brought in, is a matter which the parties concerned can best explain; but that the deficiency exists, is not in the power of either to disprove. While Dr. Price, Mr. Eden (now Auckland), Mr. Chalmers, and others, were debating whether the quantity of money in England was greater or less than at the Revolution, the circumstance was not adverted to, that since the Revolution, there cannot have been less than four hundred millions sterling imported into Europe; and therefore, the quantity in England ought at least to have been four times greater than it was at the Revolution, to be on a proportion with Europe. What England is now doing by paper, is what she would have been able to have done by solid money, if

The Revolution of France is attended with many novel circumstances, not only in the political sphere, but in the circle of money transactions. Among others, it shews that a Government may be in a state of insolvency, and a Nation rich. So far as the fact is confined to the late Government of France, it was insolvent; because the Nation would no longer support its extravagance, and therefore it could no longer support itself—but with respect to the Nation, all the means existed. A Government may be said to be insolvent, every time it applies to a Nation to discharge its arrears. The insolvency of the late

---

gold and silver had come into the nation in the proportion it ought, or had not been sent out; and she is endeavouring to restore by paper, the balance she has lost by money. It is certain, that the gold and silver which arrive annually in the register-ships to Spain and Portugal, do not remain in those countries. Taking the value half in gold and half in silver, it is about four hundred tons annually; and from the number of ships and galloons employed in trade of bringing those metals from South America to Portugal and Spain, the quantity sufficiently proves itself, without referring to the registers.

In the situation England now is, it is impossible she can increase in money. High taxes not only lessen the property of the individuals, but they lessen also the money-capital of a nation, by inducing smuggling, which can only be carried on by gold and silver. By the politics which the British Government have carried on with the Inland Powers of Germany and the Continent, it has made an enemy of all the Maritime Powers, and is therefore obliged to keep up a large navy; but through the navy is built in England, the naval stores must be purchased from abroad, and that from countries where the greatest part must be paid for in gold and silver. Some fallacious rumours have been set afloat in England to induce a belief of money, and, among others, that of the French refugees bringing great quantities. The idea is ridiculous. The general part of the money in France is silver; and it would take upwards of twenty of the largest broad wheel waggons, with ten horses each, to remove one million sterling of silver. Is it then to be supposed, that a few people fleeing on horse-back, or in post chaises, in a secret manner, and having the French Custom-House to pass, and the sea to cross, could bring even a sufficiency for their own expences?

When millions of money are spoken of, it should be recollected, that such sums can only accumulate in a country by slow degrees, and a long procession of time. The most frugal system that England could now adopt, would not recover in a century the balance she has lost in money since the commencement of the Hanover succession. She is seventy millions behind France, and she must be in some considerable proportion behind every country in Europe, because the returns of the English Mint do not shew an increase of money, while the registers of Lisbon and Cadiz shew a European increase of between three and four hundred millions sterling.

Government of France, and the present Government of England, differed in no other respect than as the disposition of the people differ. The people of France refused their aid to the old Government; and the people of England submit to taxation without enquiry. What is called the Crown in England, has been insolvent several times; the last of which, publicly known, was in May 1777, when it applied to the Nation to discharge upwards of £600,000, private debts, which otherwise it could not pay.

It was the error of Mr. Pitt, Mr. Burke, and all those who were unacquainted with the affairs of France, to confound the French Nation with the French Government. The French Nation, in effect, endeavoured to render the late Government insolvent, for the purpose of taking government into its own hands; and it reserved its means for the support of the new Government. In a country of such vast extent and population as France, the natural means cannot be wanting; and the political means appear the instant the Nation is disposed to permit them. When Mr. Burke, in a speech last Winter in the British Parliament, *cast his eyes over the map of Europe, and saw a chasm that once was France*, he talked like a dreamer of dreams. The same natural France existed as before, and all the natural means existed with it. The only chasm was that which the extinction of despotism had left, and which was to be filled up with a constitution more formidable in resources than the power which had expired.

Although the French Nation rendered the late Government insolvent, it did not permit the insolvency to act towards the creditors; and the creditors considering the Nation as the real paymaster, and the Government only as the agent, rested themselves on the Nation, in preference to the Government. This appears greatly to disturb Mr. Burke, as the precedent is fatal to the policy by which Governments have supposed themselves secure. They have contracted debts, with a view of attaching what is called the monied interest of a Nation to their support; but the example in France shews, that the permanent security of the creditor is in the Nation, and not in the Government; and that in all possible revolutions that may happen in Governments, the means are always with the Nation, and the Nation always in existence. Mr. Burke argues, that the creditors ought to have abided the fate of the Government which they trusted; but the National Assembly considered them as the creditors of the Nation, and not of the Government—of the master, and not of the steward.

Notwithstanding the late Government could not discharge the current expences, the present Government has paid off a great part of the capital. This has been accomplished by two means; the one by lessening the expences of Government, and the other by the sale of the monastic and ecclesiastical landed estates. The devotees and penitent debauchees, extortioners and misers of former days, to ensure themselves a better world than that which they were about to leave, had bequeathed immense property in trust to the priesthood, for *pious uses*, and the priesthood kept it for themselves. The National Assembly has ordered it to be sold for the good of the whole Nation, and the priesthood to be decently provided for.

In consequence of the Revolution, the annual interest of the debt of France will be reduced at least six millions sterling, by paying off upwards of one hundred millions of the capital; which, with lessening the former expences of Government at least three millions, will place France in a situation worthy the imitation of Europe.

Upon a whole review of the subject, how vast is the contrast! While Mr. Burke has been talking of a general bankruptcy in France, the National Assembly has been paying off the capital of its debt; and while taxes have increased near a million a-year in England, they have lowered several millions a-year in France. Not a word has either Mr. Burke or Mr. Pitt said about French affairs, or the state of the French finances, in the present Session of Parliament. The subject begins to be too well understood, and imposition serves no longer.

There is a general enigma running through the whole of Mr. Burke's Book. He writes in a rage against the National Assembly; but what is he enraged about? If his assertions were as true as they are groundless, and that France by her Revolution had annihilated her power, and become what he calls a *chasm*, it might excite the grief of a Frenchman, (considering himself as a national man), and provoke his rage against the National

Assembly; but why should it excite the rage of Mr. Burke?—
Alas! it is not the Nation of France that Mr. Burke means, but
the COURT; and every Court in Europe, dreading the same
fate, is in mourning. He writes neither in the character of a
Frenchman nor an Englishman, but in the fawning character
of that creature known in all countries, and a friend to none, a
COURTIER. Whether it be the Court of Versailles, or the
Court of St. James or of Carlton-House, or the Court in expectation, signifies not; for the caterpillar principle of all
Courts and Courtiers are alike. They form a common policy
throughout Europe, detached and separate from the interest
of Nations: and while they appear to quarrel, they agree to
plunder. Nothing can be more terrible to a Court or a Courtier, than the Revolution of France. That which is a blessing to
Nations, is bitterness to them; and as their existence depends
on the duplicity of a country, they tremble at the approach of
principles, and dread the precedent that threatens their overthrow.

CONCLUSION.

Reason and Ignorance, the opposites of each other, influence the great bulk of mankind. If either of these can be
rendered sufficiently extensive in a country, the machinery of
Government goes easily on. Reason obeys itself; and Ignorance submits to whatever is dictated to it.

The two modes of Government which prevail in the world,
are, *first,* Government by election and representation: *Secondly,* Government by hereditary succession. The former is
generally known by the name of republic; the latter by that of
monarchy and aristocracy.

Those two distinct and opposite forms, erect themselves on
the two distinct and opposite basis of Reason and Ignorance.—As the exercise of Government requires talents and
abilities, and as talents and abilities cannot have hereditary
descent, it is evident that hereditary succession requires a
belief from man, to which his reason cannot subscribe, and
which can only be established upon his ignorance; and the
more ignorant any country is, the better it is fitted for this
species of Government.

On the contrary, Government in a well constituted republic, requires no belief from man beyond what his reason can give. He sees the *rationale* of the whole system, its origin and its operation; and as it is best supported when best understood, the human faculties act with boldness, and acquire, under this form of Government, a gigantic manliness.

As, therefore, each of those forms acts on a different base, the one moving freely by the aid of reason, the other by ignorance; we have next to consider, what it is that gives motion to that species of Government which is called mixed Government, or, as it is sometimes ludicrously stiled, a Government of *this, that*, and *t'other.*

The moving power in this species of Government, is of necessity, Corruption. However imperfect election and representation may be in mixed Governments, they still give exercise to a greater portion of reason than is convenient to the hereditary Part; and therefore it becomes necessary to buy the reason up. A mixed Government is an imperfect everything, cementing and soldering the discordant parts together by corruption, to act as a whole. Mr. Burke appears highly disgusted, that France, since she had resolved on a revolution, did not adopt what he calls *"A British Constitution;"* and the regretful manner in which he expresses himself on this occasion, implies a suspicion, that the British Constitution needed something to keep its defects in countenance.

In mixed Governments there is no responsibility: the parts cover each other till responsibility is lost; and the corruption which moves the machine, contrives at the same time its own escape. When it is laid down as a maxim, that *a King can do no wrong*, it places him in a state of similar security with that of ideots and persons insane, and responsibility is out of the question with respect to himself. It then descends upon the Minister, who shelters himself under a majority in Parliament, which, by places, pensions, and corruption, he can always command; and that majority justifies itself by the same authority with which it protects the Minister. In this rotatory motion, responsibility is thrown off from the parts, and from the whole.

When there is a Part in a Government which can do no wrong, it implies that it does nothing; and is only the machine of another power, by whose advice and direction it acts. What is supposed to be the King in mixed Governments, is the Cabinet; and as the Cabinet is always a part of the Parliament, and the members justifying in one character what they advise and act in another, a mixed Government becomes a continual enigma; entailing upon a country, by the quantity of corruption necessary to solder the parts, the expence of supporting all the forms of Government at once, and finally resolving itself into a Government by Committee; in which the advisers, the actors, the approvers, the justifiers, the persons responsible, and the persons not responsible, are the same persons.

By this pantomimical contrivance, and change of scene and character, the parts help each other out in matters, which, neither of them singly would assume to act. When money is to be obtained, the mass of variety apparently dissolves, and a profusion of parliamentary praises passes between the parts. Each admires with astonishment the wisdom, the liberality, the disinterestedness of the other; and all of them breathe a pitying sigh at the burthens of the Nation.

But in a well-constituted republic, nothing of this soldering, praising, and pitying, can take place; the representation being equal throughout the country, and compleat in itself, however it may be arranged into legislative and executive, they have all one and the same natural source. The parts are not foreigners to each other, like democracy, aristocracy, and monarchy. As there are no discordant distinctions, there is nothing to corrupt by compromise, nor confound by contrivance. Public measures appeal of themselves to the understanding of the Nation, and, resting on their own merits, disown any flattering application to vanity. The continual whine of lamenting the burden of taxes, however successfully it may be practised in mixed Governments, is inconsistent with the sense and spirit of a republic. If taxes are necessary, they are of course advantageous; but if they require an apology, the apology itself implies an impeachment. Why then is man thus imposed upon, or why does he impose upon himself?

When men are spoken of as kings and subjects, or when Government is mentioned under the distinct or combined heads of monarchy, aristocracy, and democracy, what is it that *reasoning* man is to understand by the terms? If there really existed in the world two or more distinct and separate *elements* of human power, we should then see the several origins to which those terms would descriptively apply: but as there is but one species of man, there can be but one element of human power; and that element is man himself. Monarchy, aristocracy, and democracy, are but creatures of imagination; and a thousand such may be contrived, as well as three.

———————

From the Revolutions of America and France, and the symptoms that have appeared in other countries, it is evident that the opinion of the world is changing with respect to systems of Government, and that revolutions are not within the compass of political calculations. The progress of time and circumstances, which men assign to the accomplishment of great changes, is too mechanical to measure the force of the mind, and the rapidity of reflection, by which revolutions are generated: All the old governments have received a shock from those that already appear, and which were once more improbable, and are a greater subject of wonder, than a general revolution in Europe would be now.

When we survey the wretched condition of man under the monarchical and hereditary systems of Government, dragged from his home by one power, or driven by another, and impoverished by taxes more than by enemies, it becomes evident that those systems are bad, and that a general revolution in the principle and construction of Governments is necessary.

What is government more than the management of the affairs of a Nation? It is not, and from its nature cannot be, the property of any particular man or family, but of the whole community, at whose expence it is supported; and though by force or contrivance it has been usurped into an inheritance, the usurpation cannot alter the right of things. Sovereignty, as a matter of right, appertains to the Nation only, and not to any individual; and a Nation has at all times an inherent indefeasible right to abolish any form of Government it finds inconvenient, and establish such as accords with its interest, disposition, and happiness. The romantic and barbarous distinction of men into Kings and subjects, though it may suit the condition of courtiers, cannot that of citizens; and is exploded by the principle upon which Governments are now founded. Every citizen is a member of the Sovereignty, and, as such, can acknowledge no personal subjection; and his obedience can be only to the laws.

When men think of what Government is, they must necessarily suppose it to possess a knowledge of all the objects and matters upon which its authority is to be exercised. In this view of Government, the republican system, as established by America and France, operates to embrace the whole of a Nation; and the knowledge necessary to the interest of all the parts, is to be found in the center, which the parts by representation form: But the old Governments are on a construction that excludes knowledge as well as happiness; Government by Monks, who know nothing of the world beyond the walls of a Convent, is as consistent as government by Kings.

What were formerly called Revolutions, were little more than a change of persons, or an alteration of local circumstances. They rose and fell like things of course, and had nothing in their existence or their fate that could influence beyond the spot that produced them. But what we now see in the world, from the Revolutions of America and France, are a renovation of the natural order of things, a system of principles as universal as truth and the existence of man, and combining moral with political happiness and national prosperity.

"I. *Men are born and always continue free, and equal in respect of their rights. Civil distinctions, therefore, can be founded only on public utility.*

"II. *The end of all political associations is the preservation of the natural and imprescriptible rights of man; and these rights are liberty, property, security, and resistance of oppression.*

"III. *The Nation is essentially the source of all Sovereignty; nor can any* INDIVIDUAL, *or* ANY BODY OF MEN, *be entitled to any authority which is not expressly derived from it.*"

In these principles, there is nothing to throw a Nation into confusion by inflaming ambition. They are calculated to call forth wisdom and abilities, and to exercise them for the public good, and not for the emolument or aggrandizement of particular descriptions of men or families. Monarchical sovereignty, the enemy of mankind, and the source of misery, is abolished; and sovereignty itself is restored to its natural and original place, the Nation. Were this the case throughout Europe, the cause of wars would be taken away.

It is attributed to Henry the Fourth of France, a man of an enlarged and benevolent heart, that he proposed, about the year 1610, a plan for abolishing war in Europe. The plan consisted in constituting a European Congress, or as the French Authors stile it, a Pacific Republic; by appointing delegates from the several Nations, who were to act as a Court of arbitration in any disputes that might arise between nation and nation.

Had such a plan been adopted at the time it was proposed, the taxes of England and France, as two of the parties, would have been at least ten millions sterling annually to each Nation less than they were at the commencement of the French Revolution.

To conceive a cause why such a plan has not been adopted, (and that instead of a Congress for the purpose of *preventing* war, it has been called only to *terminate* a war, after a fruitless expence of several years), it will be necessary to consider the interest of Governments as a distinct interest to that of Nations.

Whatever is the cause of taxes to a Nation, becomes also the means of revenue to a Government. Every war terminates with an addition of taxes, and consequently with an addition of revenue; and in any event of war, in the manner they are now commenced and concluded, the power and interest of Governments are increased. War, therefore, from its productiveness, as it easily furnishes the pretence of necessity for taxes and appointments to places and offices, becomes a principal part of the system of old Governments; and to establish any mode to abolish war, however advantageous it might be to Nations, would be to take from such Government the most lucrative of its branches. The frivolous matters upon which war is made, shew the disposition and avidity of Governments to uphold the system of war, and betray the motives upon which they act.

Why are not Republics plunged into war, but because the nature of their Government does not admit of an interest distinct to that of the Nation? Even Holland, though an ill-constructed Republic, and with a commerce extending over the world, existed nearly a century without war: and the instant the form of Government was changed in France, the republican principles of peace and domestic prosperity and œconomy arose with the new Government; and the same consequences would follow the same causes in other Nations.

As war is the system of Government on the old construction, the animosity which Nations reciprocally entertain, is nothing more than what the policy of their Governments excite, to keep up the spirit of the system. Each Government accuses the other of perfidy, intrigue, and ambition, as a means of heating the imagination of their respective Nations, and incensing them to hostilities. Man is not the enemy of man, but through the medium of a false system of Government. Instead, therefore, of exclaiming against the ambition of Kings, the exclamation should be directed against the principle of such Governments; and instead of seeking to reform the individual, the wisdom of a Nation should apply itself to reform the system.

Whether the forms and maxims of Governments which are still in practice, were adapted to the condition of the world at the period they were established, is not in this case the question. The older they are, the less correspondence can they have with the present state of things. Time, and change of circumstances and opinions, have the same progressive effect in rendering modes of Government obsolete, as they have upon customs and manners.—Agriculture, commerce, manufactures, and the tranquil arts, by which the prosperity of Nations is best promoted, require a different system of Government, and a different species of knowledge to direct its operations, to what might have been the former condition of the world.

As it is not difficult to perceive, from the enlightened state of mankind, that hereditary Governments are verging to their decline, and that Revolutions on the broad basis of national sovereignty, and Government by representation, are making their way in Europe, it would be an act of wisdom to anticipate their approach, and produce Revolutions by reason and accommodation, rather than commit them to the issue of convulsions.

From what we now see, nothing of reform in the political world ought to be held improbable. It is an age of Revolutions, in which every thing may be looked for. The intrigue of Courts, by which the system of war is kept up, may provoke a confederation of Nations to abolish it: and a European Congress, to patronize the progress of free Government, and promote the civilization of Nations with each other, is an event nearer in probability, than once were the revolutions and alliance of France and America.

Rights of Man
Part the Second

Combining Principle and Practice

1792

TO M. DE LA FAYETTE.

AFTER an acquaintance of nearly fifteen years, in difficult situations in America, and various consultations in Europe, I feel a pleasure in presenting to you this small treatise, in gratitude for your services to my beloved America, and as a testimony of my esteem for the virtues, public and private, which I know you to possess.

The only point upon which I could ever discover that we differed, was not as to principles of government, but as to time. For my own part, I think it equally as injurious to good principles to permit them to linger, as to push them on too fast. That which you suppose accomplishable in fourteen or fifteen years, I may believe practicable in a much shorter period. Mankind, as it appears to me, are always ripe enough to understand their true interest, provided it be presented clearly to their understanding, and that in a manner not to create suspicion by any thing like self-design, nor offend by assuming too much. Where we would wish to reform we must not reproach.

When the American revolution was established, I felt a disposition to sit serenely down and enjoy the calm. It did not appear to me that any object could afterwards arise great enough to make me quit tranquillity, and feel as I had felt before. But when principle, and not place, is the energetic cause of action, a man, I find, is every where the same.

I am now once more in the public world; and as I have not a right to contemplate on so many years of remaining life as you have, I am resolved to labour as fast as I can; and as I am anxious for your aid and your company, I wish you to hasten your principles, and overtake me.

If you make a campaign the ensuing spring, which it is most probable there will be no occasion for, I will come and

join you. Should the campaign commence, I hope it will terminate in the extinction of German despotism, and in establishing the freedom of all Germany. When France shall be
surrounded with revolutions, she will be in peace and safety,
and her taxes, as well as those of Germany, will consequently
become less.

Your sincere,

Affectionate Friend,

THOMAS PAINE.

London, Feb. 9, 1792.

PREFACE.

WHEN I began the chapter entitled the *"Conclusion"* in the
former part of the RIGHTS OF MAN, published last year, it
was my intention to have extended it to a greater length; but
in casting the whole matter in my mind which I wished to
add, I found that I must either make the work too bulky, or
contract my plan too much. I therefore brought it to a close
as soon as the subject would admit, and reserved what I had
further to say to another opportunity.

Several other reasons contributed to produce this determination. I wished to know the manner in which a work, written in a style of thinking and expression different to what had
been customary in England, would be received before I proceeded farther. A great field was opening to the view of
mankind by means of the French Revolution. Mr. Burke's
outrageous opposition thereto brought the controversy into
England. He attacked principles which he knew (from information) I would contest with him, because they are principles
I believe to be good, and which I have contributed to establish, and conceive myself bound to defend. Had he not urged
the controversy, I had most probably been a silent man.

Another reason for deferring the remainder of the work
was, that Mr. Burke promised in his first publication to renew
the subject at another opportunity, and to make a comparison
of what he called the English and French Constitutions. I
therefore held myself in reserve for him. He has published
two works since, without doing this; which he certainly would
not have omitted, had the comparison been in his favour.

In his last work, *"His appeal from the new to the old Whigs,"* he has quoted about ten pages from the *Rights of Man*, and having given himself the trouble of doing this, says, "he shall not attempt in the smallest degree to refute them," meaning the principles therein contained. I am enough acquainted with Mr. Burke to know, that he would if he could. But instead of contesting them, he immediately after consoles himself with saying, that "he has done his part."—He has not done his part. He has not performed his promise of a comparison of constitutions. He started the controversy, he gave the challenge, and has fled from it; and he is now a *case in point* with his own opinion, that, *"the age of chivalry is gone!"*

The title, as well as the substance of his last work, his *"Appeal,"* is his condemnation. Principles must stand on their own merits, and if they are good they certainly will. To put them under the shelter of other men's authority, as Mr. Burke has done, serves to bring them into suspicion. Mr. Burke is not very fond of dividing his honours, but in this case he is artfully dividing the disgrace.

But who are those to whom Mr. Burke has made his appeal? A set of childish thinkers and half-way politicians born in the last century; men who went no farther with any principle than as it suited their purpose as a party; the nation was always left out of the question; and this has been the character of every party from that day to this. The nation sees nothing in such works, or such politics worthy its attention. A little matter will move a party, but it must be something great that moves a nation.

Though I see nothing in Mr. Burke's Appeal worth taking much notice of, there is, however, one expression upon which I shall offer a few remarks.—After quoting largely from the *Rights of Man*, and declining to contest the principles contained in that work, he says, "This will most probably be done (*if such writings shall be thought to deserve any other refutation than that of criminal justice*) by others, who may think with Mr. Burke and with the same zeal."

In the first place, it has not yet been done by any body. Not less, I believe, than eight or ten pamphlets intended as answers to the former part of the "Rights of Man" have been published by different persons, and not one of them, to my knowledge, has extended to a second edition, nor are even the titles of them so much as generally remembered. As I am averse to unnecessarily multiplying publications, I have answered none of them. And as I believe that a man may write himself out of reputation when nobody else can do it, I am careful to avoid that rock.

But as I would decline unnecessary publications on the one hand, so would I avoid every thing that might appear like sullen pride on the other. If Mr. Burke, or any person on his side the question, will produce an answer to the "Rights of Man," that shall extend to an half, or even to a fourth part of the number of copies to which the Rights of Man extended, I will reply to his work. But until this be done, I shall so far take the sense of the public for my guide (and the world knows I am not a flatterer) that what they do not think worth while to read, is not worth mine to answer. I suppose the number of copies to which the first part of the *Rights of Man* extended, taking England, Scotland, and Ireland, is not less than between forty and fifty thousand.

I now come to remark on the remaining part of the quotation I have made from Mr. Burke.

"If," says he, "such writings shall be thought to deserve any other refutation than that of *criminal* justice."

Pardoning the pun, it must be *criminal* justice indeed that should condemn a work as a substitute for not being able to refute it. The greatest condemnation that could be passed upon it would be a refutation. But in proceeding by the method Mr. Burke alludes to, the condemnation would, in the final event, pass upon the criminality of the process and not upon the work, and in this case, I had rather be the author, than be either the judge, or the jury, that should condemn it.

But to come at once to the point. I have differed from some professional gentlemen on the subject of prosecutions, and I since find they are falling into my opinion, which I will here state as fully, but as concisely as I can.

I will first put a case with respect to any law, and then compare it with a government, or with what in England is, or has been, called a constitution.

It would be an act of despotism, or what in England is

called arbitrary power, to make a law to prohibit investigating the principles, good or bad, on which such a law, or any other is founded.

If a law be bad, it is one thing to oppose the practice of it, but it is quite a different thing to expose its errors, to reason on its defects, and to shew cause why it should be repealed, or why another ought to be substituted in its place. I have always held it an opinion (making it also my practice) that it is better to obey a bad law, making use at the same time of every argument to shew its errors and procure its repeal, than forcibly to violate it; because the precedent of breaking a bad law might weaken the force, and lead to a discretionary violation, of those which are good.

The case is the same with respect to principles and forms of government, or to what are called constitutions and the parts of which they are composed.

It is for the good of nations, and not for the emolument or aggrandizement of particular individuals, that government ought to be established, and that mankind are at the expence of supporting it. The defects of every government and constitution, both as to principle and form must, on a parity of reasoning, be as open to discussion as the defects of a law, and it is a duty which every man owes to society to point them out. When those defects, and the means of remedying them are generally seen by a nation, that nation will reform its government or its constitution in the one case, as the government repealed or reformed the law in the other. The operation of government is restricted to the making and the administering of laws; but it is to a nation that the right of forming or reforming, generating or regenerating constitutions and governments belong; and consequently those subjects, as subjects of investigation, are always before a country *as a matter of right*, and cannot, without invading the general rights of that country, be made subjects for prosecution. On this ground I will meet Mr. Burke whenever he please. It is better that the whole argument should come out, than to seek to stifle it. It was himself that opened the controversy, and he ought not to desert it.

I do not believe that monarchy and aristocracy will continue seven years longer in any of the enlightened countries in

Europe. If better reasons can be shewn for them than against them, they will stand; if the contrary, they will not. Mankind are not now to be told they shall not think, or they shall not read; and publications that go no farther than to investigate principles of government, to invite men to reason and to reflect, and to shew the errors and excellences of different systems, have a right to appear. If they do not excite attention, they are not worth the trouble of a prosecution; and if they do, the prosecution will amount to nothing, since it cannot amount to a prohibition of reading. This would be a sentence on the public, instead of the author, and would also be the most effectual mode of making or hastening revolutions.

On all cases that apply universally to a nation, with respect to systems of government, a jury of *twelve* men is not competent to decide. Where there are no witnesses to be examined, no facts to be proved, and where the whole matter is before the whole public, and the merits or demerits of it resting on their opinion; and where there is nothing to be known in a court, but what every body knows out of it, every twelve men is equally as good a jury as the other, and would most probably reverse each other's verdict; or from the variety of their opinions, not be able to form one. It is one case, whether a nation approve a work, or a plan; but it is quite another case, whether it will commit to any such jury the power of determining whether that nation have a right to, or shall reform its government, or not. I mention those cases, that Mr. Burke may see I have not written on Government without reflecting on what is Law, as well as on what are Rights.—The only effectual jury in such cases would be, a convention of the whole nation fairly elected; for in all such cases the whole nation is the vicinage. If Mr. Burke will propose such a jury, I will wave all privileges of being the citizen of another country, and, defending its principles, abide the issue, provided he will do the same; for my opinion is, that his work and his principles would be condemned instead of mine.

As to the prejudices which men have from education and habit, in favour of any particular form or system of government, those prejudices have yet to stand the test of reason and reflection. In fact, such prejudices are nothing. No man is prejudiced in favour of a thing, knowing it to be wrong. He is attached to it on the belief of its being right; and when he see it is not so, the prejudice will be gone. We have but a defective idea of what prejudice is. It might be said, that until men think for themselves the whole is prejudice, and *not opinion*; for that only is opinion which is the result of reason and reflection. I offer this remark, that Mr. Burke may not confide too much in what has been the customary prejudices of the country.

I do not believe that the people of England have ever been fairly and candidly dealt by. They have been imposed upon by parties, and by men assuming the character of leaders. It is time that the nation should rise above those trifles. It is time to dismiss that inattention which has so long been the encouraging cause of stretching taxation to excess. It is time to dismiss all those songs and toasts which are calculated to enslave, and operate to suffocate reflection. On all such subjects men have but to think, and they will neither act wrong nor be misled. To say that any people are not fit for freedom, is to make poverty their choice, and to say they had rather be loaded with taxes than not. If such a case could be proved, it would equally prove, that those who govern are not fit to govern them, for they are a part of the same national mass.

But admitting governments to be changed all over Europe; it certainly may be done without convulsion or revenge. It is not worth making changes or revolutions, unless it be for some great national benefit; and when this shall appear to a nation, the danger will be, as in America and France, to those who oppose; and with this reflection I close my Preface.

London, Feb. 9, 1792. THOMAS PAINE.

INTRODUCTION.

WHAT Archimedes said of the mechanical powers, may be applied to Reason and Liberty: *"Had we,"* said he, *"a place to stand upon, we might raise the world."*

The revolution of America presented in politics what was only theory in mechanics. So deeply rooted were all the governments of the old world, and so effectually had the tyranny and the antiquity of habit established itself over the mind, that no beginning could be made in Asia, Africa, or Europe, to reform the political condition of man. Freedom had been hunted round the globe; reason was considered as rebellion; and the slavery of fear had made men afraid to think.

But such is the irresistible nature of truth, that all it asks, and all it wants, is the liberty of appearing. The sun needs no inscription to distinguish him from darkness; and no sooner did the American governments display themselves to the world, than despotism felt a shock, and man began to contemplate redress.

The independence of America, considered merely as a separation from England, would have been a matter but of little importance, had it not been accompanied by a revolution in the principles and practice of governments. She made a stand, not for herself only, but for the world, and looked beyond the advantages herself could receive. Even the Hessian, though hired to fight against her, may live to bless his defeat; and England, condemning the viciousness of its government, rejoice in its miscarriage.

As America was the only spot in the political world, where the principles of universal reformation could begin, so also was it the best in the natural world. An assemblage of circumstances conspired, not only to give birth, but to add gigantic maturity to its principles. The scene which that country presents to the eye of a spectator, has something in it which generates and encourages great ideas. Nature appears to him in magnitude. The mighty objects he beholds, act upon his mind by enlarging it, and he partakes of the greatness he contemplates.—Its first settlers were emigrants from different European nations, and of diversified professions of religion, retiring from the governmental persecutions of the old world, and meeting in the new, not as enemies, but as brothers. The wants which necessarily accompany the cultivation of a wilderness produced among them a state of society, which countries, long harassed by the quarrels and intrigues of governments, had neglected to cherish. In such a situation man becomes what he ought. He sees his species, not with the inhuman idea of a natural enemy, but as kindred; and the example shews to the artificial world, that man must go back to Nature for information.

From the rapid progress which America makes in every species of improvement, it is rational to conclude, that if the governments of Asia, Africa, and Europe, had begun on a principle similar to that of America, or had not been very early corrupted therefrom, that those countries must by this time have been in a far superior condition to what they are. Age after age has passed away, for no other purpose than to behold their wretchedness. — Could we suppose a spectator who knew nothing of the world, and who was put into it merely to make his observations, he would take a great part of the old world to be new, just struggling with the difficulties and hardships of an infant settlement. He could not suppose that the hordes of miserable poor, with which old countries abound, could be any other than those who had not yet had time to provide for themselves. Little would he think they were the consequence of what in such countries is called government.

If, from the more wretched parts of the old world, we look at those which are in an advanced stage of improvement, we still find the greedy hand of government thrusting itself into every corner and crevice of industry, and grasping the spoil of the multitude. Invention is continually exercised, to furnish new pretences for revenue and taxation. It watches prosperity as its prey, and permits none to escape without a tribute.

As revolutions have begun, (and as the probability is always greater against a thing beginning, than of proceeding after it has begun), it is natural to expect that other revolutions will follow. The amazing and still increasing expences with which old governments are conducted, the numerous wars they engage in or provoke, the embarrassments they throw in the way of universal civilization and commerce, and the oppression and usurpation they act at home, have wearied out the patience, and exhausted the property of the world. In such a situation, and with the examples already existing, revolutions are to be looked for. They are become subjects of universal conversation, and may be considered as the *Order of the day*.

If systems of government can be introduced, less expensive, and more productive of general happiness, than those which have existed, all attempts to oppose their progress will in the end be fruitless. Reason, like time, will make its own way, and prejudice will fall in a combat with interest. If universal peace, civilization, and commerce, are ever to be the happy lot of man, it cannot be accomplished but by a revolution in the system of governments. All the monarchical governments are military. War is their trade, plunder and revenue their objects. While such governments continue, peace has not the absolute security of a day. What is the history of all monarchical governments, but a disgustful picture of human wretchedness, and the accidental respite of a few years repose? Wearied with war, and tired with human butchery, they sat down to rest and called it peace. This certainly is not the condition that Heaven intended for man; and if *this be monarchy*, well might monarchy be reckoned among the sins of the Jews.

The revolutions which formerly took place in the world, had nothing in them that interested the bulk of mankind. They extended only to a change of persons and measures but not of principles, and rose or fell among the common transactions of the moment. What we now behold, may not improperly be called a *"counter revolution."* Conquest and tyranny, at some early period, dispossessed man of his rights, and he is now recovering them. And as the tide of all human affairs has its ebb and flow in directions contrary to each other, so also is it in this. Government founded on a *moral theory, on a system of universal peace, on the indefeasible hereditary Rights of Man*, is now revolving from west to east, by a stronger impulse than the government of the sword revolved from east to west. It interests not particular individuals, but nations, in its progress, and promises a new æra to the human race.

The danger to which the success of revolutions is most exposed, is that of attempting them before the principles on which they proceed, and the advantages to result from them, are sufficiently seen and understood. Almost every thing appertaining to the circumstances of a nation, has been absorbed and confounded under the general and mysterious word *government*. Though it avoids taking to its account the errors it commits, and the mischiefs it occasions, it fails not to arrogate to itself whatever has the appearance of prosperity. It robs industry of its honours, by pedanticly making itself the cause of its effects; and purloins from the general character of man, the merits that appertain to him as a social being.

It may therefore be of use, in this day of revolutions, to discriminate between those things which are the effect of government, and those which are not. This will best be done by taking a review of society and civilization, and the consequences resulting therefrom, as things distinct from what are called governments. By beginning with this investigation, we shall be able to assign effects to their proper cause, and analize the mass of common errors.

CHAP. I.

OF SOCIETY AND CIVILIZATION.

GREAT part of that order which reigns among mankind is not the effect of government. It has its origin in the principles of society and the natural constitution of man. It existed prior to government, and would exist if the formality of government was abolished. The mutual dependance and reciprocal interest which man has upon man, and all the parts of a civilized community upon each other, create that great chain of connection which holds it together. The landholder, the farmer, the manufacturer, the merchant, the tradesman, and every occupation, prospers by the aid which each receives from the other, and from the whole. Common interest regulates their concerns, and forms their law; and the laws which common usage ordains, have a greater influence than the laws of government. In fine, society performs for itself almost every thing which is ascribed to government.

To understand the nature and quantity of government proper for man, it is necessary to attend to his character. As Nature created him for social life, she fitted him for the station she intended. In all cases she made his natural wants greater than his individual powers. No one man is capable, without the aid of society, of supplying his own wants; and those wants, acting upon every individual, impel the whole of them into society, as naturally as gravitation acts to a center.

But she has gone further. She has not only forced man into society, by a diversity of wants, which the reciprocal aid of each other can supply, but she has implanted in him a system of social affections, which, though not necessary to his existence, are essential to his happiness. There is no period in life when this love for society ceases to act. It begins and ends with our being.

If we examine, with attention, into the composition and constitution of man, the diversity of his wants, and the diversity of talents in different men for reciprocally accommodating the wants of each other, his propensity to society, and consequently to preserve the advantages resulting from it, we shall easily discover, that a great part of what is called government is mere imposition.

Government is no farther necessary than to supply the few cases to which society and civilization are not conveniently competent; and instances are not wanting to shew, that every thing which government can usefully add thereto, has been performed by the common consent of society, without government.

For upwards of two years from the commencement of the American war, and to a longer period in several of the American States, there were no established forms of government. The old governments had been abolished, and the country was too much occupied in defence, to employ its attention in establishing new governments; yet during this interval, order and harmony were preserved as inviolate as in any country in Europe. There is a natural aptness in man, and more so in society, because it embraces a greater variety of abilities and resource, to accommodate itself to whatever situation it is in. The instant formal government is abolished, society begins to act. A general association takes place, and common interest produces common security.

So far is it from being true, as has been pretended, that the abolition of any formal government is the dissolution of society, that it acts by a contrary impulse, and brings the latter the closer together. All that part of its organization which it had committed to its government, devolves again upon itself, and acts through its medium. When men, as well from natural instinct, as from reciprocal benefits, have habituated themselves to social and civilized life, there is always enough of its principles in practice to carry them through any changes they may find necessary or convenient to make in their government. In short, man is so naturally a creature of society, that it is almost impossible to put him out of it.

Formal government makes but a small part of civilized life; and when even the best that human wisdom can devise is established, it is a thing more in name and idea, than in fact. It is to the great and fundamental principles of society and civilization—to the common usage universally consented to, and mutually and reciprocally maintained—to the unceasing circulation of interest, which, passing through its million channels, invigorates the whole mass of civilized man—it is to these things, infinitely more than to any thing which even the best instituted government can perform, that the safety and prosperity of the individual and of the whole depends.

The more perfect civilization is, the less occasion has it for government, because the more does it regulate its own affairs, and govern itself; but so contrary is the practice of old governments to the reason of the case, that the expences of them increase in the proportion they ought to diminish. It is but few general laws that civilized life requires, and those of such common usefulness, that whether they are enforced by the forms of government or not, the effect will be nearly the same. If we consider what the principles are that first condense men into society, and what the motives that regulate their mutual intercourse afterwards, we shall find, by the time we arrive at what is called government, that nearly the whole of the business is performed by the natural operation of the parts upon each other.

Man, with respect to all those matters, is more a creature of consistency than he is aware, or that governments would wish him to believe. All the great laws of society are laws of nature. Those of trade and commerce, whether with respect to the intercourse of individuals, or of nations, are laws of mutual and reciprocal interest. They are followed and obeyed, because it is the interest of the parties so to do, and not on account of any formal laws their governments may impose or interpose.

But how often is the natural propensity to society disturbed or destroyed by the operations of government! When the latter, instead of being ingrafted on the principles of the former, assumes to exist for itself, and acts by partialities of favour and oppression, it becomes the cause of the mischiefs it ought to prevent.

If we look back to the riots and tumults, which at various times have happened in England, we shall find, that they did not proceed from the want of a government, but that government was itself the generating cause; instead of consolidating society it divided it; it deprived it of its natural cohesion, and engendered discontents and disorders, which otherwise would not have existed. In those associations which men promiscuously form for the purpose of trade, or of any concern, in which government is totally out of the question, and in which they act merely on the principles of society, we see how naturally the various parties unite; and this shews, by comparison, that governments, so far from being always the cause or means of order, are often the destruction of it. The riots of 1780 had no other source than the remains of those prejudices, which the government itself had encouraged. But with respect to England there are also other causes.

Excess and inequality of taxation, however disguised in the means, never fail to appear in their effects. As a great mass of the community are thrown thereby into poverty and discontent, they are constantly on the brink of commotion; and, deprived, as they unfortunately are, of the means of information, are easily heated to outrage. Whatever the apparent cause of any riots may be, the real one is always want of happiness. It shews that something is wrong in the system of government, that injures the felicity by which society is to be preserved.

But as fact is superior to reasoning, the instance of America presents itself to confirm these observations.—If there is a country in the world, where concord, according to common calculation, would be least expected, it is America. Made up, as it is, of people from different nations*, accustomed to dif-

*That part of America which is generally called New-England, including New-Hampshire, Massachusetts, Rhode-Island, and Connecticut, is peopled

ferent forms and habits of government, speaking different languages, and more different in their modes of worship, it would appear that the union of such a people was impracticable; but by the simple operation of constructing government on the principles of society and the rights of man, every difficulty retires, and all the parts are brought into cordial unison. There, the poor are not oppressed, the rich are not privileged. Industry is not mortified by the splendid extravagance of a court rioting at its expence. Their taxes are few, because their government is just; and as there is nothing to render them wretched, there is nothing to engender riots and tumults.

A metaphysical man, like Mr. Burke, would have tortured his invention to discover how such a people could be governed. He would have supposed that some must be managed by fraud, others by force, and all by some contrivance; that genius must be hired to impose upon ignorance, and shew and parade to fascinate the vulgar. Lost in the abundance of his researches, he would have resolved and re-resolved, and finally overlooked the plain and easy road that lay directly before him.

One of the great advantages of the American revolution has been, that it led to a discovery of the principles, and laid open the imposition of governments. All the revolutions till then had been worked within the atmosphere of a court, and never on the great floor of a nation. The parties were always of the class of courtiers; and whatever was their rage for reformation, they carefully preserved the fraud of the profession.

In all cases they took care to represent government as a thing made up of mysteries, which only themselves under-

---

chiefly by English descendants. In the state of New-York, about half are Dutch, the rest English, Scotch, and Irish. In New-Jersey, a mixture of English and Dutch, with some Scotch and Irish. In Pennsylvania, about one third are English, another Germans, and the remainder Scotch and Irish, with some Swedes. The States to the southward have a greater proportion of English than the middle States, but in all of them there is a mixture; and besides those enumerated, there are a considerable number of French, and some few of all the European nations lying on the coast. The most numerous religious denomination are the Presbyterians; but no one sect is established above another, and all men are equally citizens.

stood; and they hid from the understanding of the nation, the only thing that was beneficial to know, namely, *That government is nothing more than a national association acting on the principles of society.*

Having thus endeavoured to shew, that the social and civilized state of man is capable of performing within itself, almost every thing necessary to its protection and government, it will be proper, on the other hand, to take a review of the present old governments, and examine whether their principles and practice are correspondent thereto.

CHAP. II.

OF THE ORIGIN OF THE PRESENT OLD GOVERNMENTS.

It is impossible that such governments as have hitherto existed in the world, could have commenced by any other means than a total violation of every principle sacred and moral. The obscurity in which the origin of all the present old governments is buried, implies the iniquity and disgrace with which they began. The origin of the present government of America and France will ever be remembered, because it is honourable to record it; but with respect to the rest, even Flattery has consigned them to the tomb of time, without an inscription.

It could have been no difficult thing in the early and solitary ages of the world, while the chief employment of men was that of attending flocks and herds, for a banditti of ruffians to over-run a country, and lay it under contributions. Their power being thus established, the chief of the band contrived to lose the name of Robber in that of Monarch; and hence the origin of Monarchy and Kings.

The origin of the government of England, so far as relates to what is called its line of monarchy, being one of the latest, is perhaps the best recorded. The hatred which the Norman invasion and tyranny begat, must have been deeply rooted in the nation, to have outlived the contrivance to obliterate it. Though not a courtier will talk of the curfeu-bell, not a village in England has forgotten it.

Those bands of robbers having parcelled out the world, and divided it into dominions, began, as is naturally the case, to quarrel with each other. What at first was obtained by violence, was considered by others as lawful to be taken, and a second plunderer succeeded the first. They alternately invaded the dominions which each had assigned to himself, and the brutality with which they treated each other explains the original character of monarchy. It was ruffian torturing ruffian. The conqueror considered the conquered, not as his prisoner, but his property. He led him in triumph rattling in chains, and doomed him, at pleasure, to slavery or death. As time obliterated the history of their beginning, their successors assumed new appearances, to cut off the entail of their disgrace, but their principles and objects, remained the same. What at first was plunder, assumed the softer name of revenue; and the power originally usurped, they affected to inherit.

From such beginning of governments, what could be expected, but a continual system of war and extortion? It has established itself into a trade. The vice is not peculiar to one more than to another, but is the common principle of all. There does not exist within such governments, a stamina whereon to ingraft reformation; and the shortest and most effectual remedy is to begin anew.

What scenes of horror, what perfection of iniquity, present themselves in contemplating the character, and reviewing the history of such governments! If we would delineate human nature with a baseness of heart, and hypocrisy of countenance, that reflection would shudder at and humanity disown, it is kings, courts, and cabinets, that must sit for the portrait. Man, naturally as he is, with all his faults about him, is not up to the character.

Can we possibly suppose that if governments had originated in a right principle, and had not an interest in pursuing a wrong one, that the world could have been in the wretched and quarrelsome condition we have seen it? What inducement has the farmer, while following the plough, to lay aside his peaceful pursuits, and go to war with the farmer of another country? or what inducement has the manufacturer? What is dominion to them, or to any class of men in a nation? Does it

add an acre to any man's estate, or raise its value? Are not
conquest and defeat each of the same price, and taxes the
never-failing consequence?—Though this reasoning may be
good to a nation, it is not so to a government. War is the
Pharo table of governments, and nations the dupes of the
game.

If there is any thing to wonder at in this miserable scene of
governments, more than might be expected, it is the progress
which the peaceful arts of agriculture, manufacture and commerce have made, beneath such a long accumulating load of
discouragement and oppression. It serves to shew, that instinct in animals does not act with stronger impulse, than the
principles of society and civilization operate in man. Under all
discouragements, he pursues his object, and yields to nothing
but impossibilities.

CHAP. III.

OF THE OLD AND NEW SYSTEMS OF GOVERNMENT.

NOTHING can appear more contradictory than the principles
on which the old governments began, and the condition to
which society, civilization, and commerce, are capable of
carrying mankind. Government on the old system, is an assumption of power, for the aggrandisement of itself; on the
new, a delegation of power, for the common benefit of society. The former supports itself by keeping up a system of war;
the latter promotes a system of peace, as the true means of
enriching a nation. The one encourages national prejudices;
the other promotes universal society, as the means of universal commerce. The one measures its prosperity, by the quantity of revenue it extorts; the other proves its excellence, by
the small quantity of taxes it requires.

Mr. Burke has talked of old and new whigs. If he can
amuse himself with childish names and distinctions, I shall
not interrupt his pleasure. It is not to him, but to the Abbé
Sieyes, that I address this chapter. I am already engaged to
the latter gentleman, to discuss the subject of monarchical
government; and as it naturally occurs in comparing the old

and new systems, I make this the opportunity of presenting to him my observations. I shall occasionally take Mr. Burke in my way.

Though it might be proved that the system of government now called the NEW, is the most ancient in principle of all that have existed, being founded on the original inherent Rights of Man: yet, as tyranny and the sword have suspended the exercise of those rights for many centuries past, it serves better the purpose of distinction to call it the *new*, than to claim the right of calling it the old.

The first general distinction between those two systems, is, that the one now called the old is *hereditary*, either in whole or in part; and the new is entirely *representative*. It rejects all hereditary government:

First, As being an imposition on mankind.

Secondly, As inadequate to the purposes for which government is necessary.

With respect to the first of these heads—It cannot be proved by what right hereditary government could begin: neither does there exist within the compass of mortal power, a right to establish it. Man has no authority over posterity in matters of personal right; and therefore, no man, or body of men, had, or can have, a right to set up hereditary government. Were even ourselves to come again into existence, instead of being succeeded by posterity, we have not now the right of taking from ourselves the rights which would then be ours. On what ground, then, do we pretend to take them from others?

All hereditary government is in its nature tyranny. An heritable crown, or an heritable throne, or by what other fanciful name such things may be called, have no other significant explanation than that mankind are heritable property. To inherit a government, is to inherit the people, as if they were flocks and herds.

With respect to the second head, that of being inadequate to the purposes for which government is necessary, we have only to consider what government essentially is, and compare it with the circumstances to which hereditary succession is subject.

Government ought to be a thing always in full maturity. It

ought to be so constructed as to be superior to all the accidents to which individual man is subject; and therefore, hereditary succession, by being *subject to them all*, is the most irregular and imperfect of all the systems of government.

We have heard the *Rights of Man* called a *levelling* system; but the only system to which the word *levelling* is truly applicable, is the hereditary monarchical system. It is a system of *mental levelling*. It indiscriminately admits every species of character to the same authority. Vice and virtue, ignorance and wisdom, in short, every quality, good or bad, is put on the same level. Kings succeed each other, not as rationals, but as animals. It signifies not what their mental or moral characters are. Can we then be surprised at the abject state of the human mind in monarchical countries, when the government itself is formed on such an abject levelling system? — It has no fixed character. To-day it is one thing; to-morrow it is something else. It changes with the temper of every succeeding individual, and is subject to all the varieties of each. It is government through the medium of passions and accidents. It appears under all the various characters of childhood, decrepitude, dotage, a thing at nurse, in leading-strings, or in crutches. It reverses the wholesome order of nature. It occasionally puts children over men, and the conceits of non-age over wisdom and experience. In short, we cannot conceive a more ridiculous figure of government, than hereditary succession, in all its cases, presents.

Could it be made a decree in nature, or an edict registered in heaven, and man could know it, that virtue and wisdom should invariably appertain to hereditary succession, the objections to it would be removed; but when we see that nature acts as if she disowned and sported with the hereditary system; that the mental characters of successors, in all countries, are below the average of human understanding; that one is a tyrant, another an ideot, a third insane, and some all three together, it is impossible to attach confidence to it, when reason in man has power to act.

It is not to the Abbé Sieyes that I need apply this reasoning; he has already saved me that trouble, by giving his own opinion upon the case. "If it be asked," says he, "what is my opinion with respect to hereditary right, I answer, without hesitation, That, in good theory, an hereditary transmission of any power or office, can never accord with the laws of a true representation. Hereditaryship is, in this sense, as much an attaint upon principle, as an outrage upon society. But let us," continues he, "refer to the history of all elective monarchies and principalities: Is there one in which the elective mode is not worse than the hereditary succession?"

As to debating on which is the worst of the two, is admitting both to be bad; and herein we are agreed. The preference which the Abbé has given, is a condemnation of the thing that he prefers. Such a mode of reasoning on such a subject is inadmissible, because it finally amounts to an accusation upon Providence, as if she had left to man no other choice with respect to government than between two evils, the best of which he admits to be *an attaint upon principle, and an outrage upon society.*

Passing over, for the present, all the evils and mischiefs which monarchy has occasioned in the world, nothing can more effectually prove its uselessness in a state of *civil government*, than making it hereditary. Would we make any office hereditary that required wisdom and abilities to fill it? and where wisdom and abilities are not necessary, such an office, whatever it may be, is superfluous or insignificant.

Hereditary succession is a burlesque upon monarchy. It puts it in the most ridiculous light, by presenting it as an office which any child or ideot may fill. It requires some talents to be a common mechanic; but, to be a king, requires only the animal figure of man—a sort of breathing automaton. This sort of superstition may last a few years more, but it cannot long resist the awakened reason and interest of man.

As to Mr. Burke, he is a stickler for monarchy, not altogether as a pensioner, if he is one, which I believe, but as a political man. He has taken up a contemptible opinion of mankind, who, in their turn, are taking up the same of him. He considers them as a herd of beings that must be governed by fraud, effigy and shew; and an idol would be as good a figure of monarchy with him, as a man. I will, however, do him the justice to say, that, with respect to America, he has been very complimentary. He always contended, at least in my hearing, that the people of America were more enlightened than those of England, or of any country in Europe; and that therefore the imposition of shew was not necessary in their governments.

Though the comparison between hereditary and elective monarchy, which the Abbé has made, is unnecessary to the case, because the representative system rejects both; yet, were I to make the comparison, I should decide contrary to what he has done.

The civil wars which have originated from contested hereditary claims, are more numerous, and have been more dreadful, and of longer continuance, than those which have been occasioned by election. All the civil wars in France arose from the hereditary system; they were either produced by hereditary claims, or by the imperfection of the hereditary form, which admits of regencies, or monarchy at nurse. With respect to England, its history is full of the same misfortunes. The contests for succession between the Houses of York and Lancaster, lasted a whole century; and others of a similar nature, have renewed themselves since that period. Those of 1715 and 1745, were of the same kind. The succession war for the crown of Spain, embroiled almost half Europe. The disturbances in Holland are generated from the hereditaryship of the Stadtholder. A government calling itself free, with an hereditary office, is like a thorn in the flesh, that produces a fermentation which endeavours to discharge it.

But I might go further, and place also foreign wars, of whatever kind, to the same cause. It is by adding the evil of hereditary succession to that of monarchy, that a permanent family-interest is created, whose constant objects are dominion and revenue. Poland, though an elective monarchy, has had fewer wars than those which are hereditary; and it is the only government that has made a voluntary essay, though but a small one, to reform the condition of the country.

Having thus glanced at a few of the defects of the old, or hereditary systems of government, let us compare it with the new, or representative system.

The representative system takes society and civilization for its basis; nature, reason, and experience, for its guide.

Experience, in all ages, and in all countries, has demonstrated, that it is impossible to controul Nature in her distribution of mental powers. She gives them as she pleases. Whatever is the rule by which she, apparently to us, scatters them among mankind, that rule remains a secret to man. It would be as ridiculous to attempt to fix the hereditaryship of human beauty, as of wisdom. Whatever wisdom constituently is, it is like a seedless plant; it may be reared when it appears, but it cannot be voluntarily produced. There is always a sufficiency somewhere in the general mass of society for all purposes; but with respect to the parts of society, it is continually changing its place. It rises in one to-day, in another to-morrow, and has most probably visited in rotation every family of the earth, and again withdrawn.

As this is the order of nature, the order of government must necessarily follow it, or government will, as we see it does, degenerate into ignorance. The hereditary system, therefore, is as repugnant to human wisdom, as to human rights; and is as absurd, as it is unjust.

As the republic of letters brings forward the best literary productions, by giving to genius a fair and universal chance; so the representative system of government is calculated to produce the wisest laws, by collecting wisdom from where it can be found. I smile to myself when I contemplate the ridiculous insignificance into which literature and all the sciences would sink, were they made hereditary; and I carry the same idea into governments. An hereditary governor is as inconsistent as an hereditary author. I know not whether Homer or Euclid had sons: but I will venture an opinion, that if they had, and had left their works unfinished, those sons could not have completed them.

Do we need a stronger evidence of the absurdity of hereditary government, than is seen in the descendants of those men, in any line of life, who once were famous? Is there scarcely an instance in which there is not a total reverse of the character? It appears as if the tide of mental faculties flowed as far as it could in certain channels, and then forsook its course, and arose in others. How irrational then is the hereditary system which establishes channels of power, in company with which wisdom refuses to flow! By continuing this absurdity, man is perpetually in contradiction with himself; he accepts, for a king, or a chief magistrate, or a legislator, a person whom he would not elect for a constable.

It appears to general observation, that revolutions create genius and talents; but those events do no more than bring them forward. There is existing in man, a mass of sense lying in a dormant state, and which, unless something excites it to action, will descend with him, in that condition, to the grave. As it is to the advantage of society that the whole of its faculties should be employed, the construction of government ought to be such as to bring forward, by a quiet and regular operation, all that extent of capacity which never fails to appear in revolutions.

This cannot take place in the insipid state of hereditary government, not only because it prevents, but because it operates to benumb. When the mind of a nation is bowed down by any political superstition in its government, such as hereditary succession is, it loses a considerable portion of its powers on all other subjects and objects. Hereditary succession requires the same obedience to ignorance, as to wisdom; and when once the mind can bring itself to pay this indiscriminate reverence, it descends below the stature of mental manhood. It is fit to be great only in little things. It acts a treachery upon itself, and suffocates the sensations that urge to detection.

Though the ancient governments present to us a miserable picture of the condition of man, there is one which above all others exempts itself from the general description. I mean the democracy of the Athenians. We see more to admire, and less to condemn, in that great, extraordinary people, than in any thing which history affords.

Mr. Burke is so little acquainted with constituent principles of government, that he confounds democracy and representation together. Representation was a thing unknown in the ancient democracies. In those the mass of the people met and enacted laws (grammatically speaking) in the first person. Simple democracy was no other than the common-hall of the ancients. It signifies the *form*, as well as the public principle of the government. As these democracies increased in population, and the territory extended, the simple democratical form became unwieldy and impracticable; and as the system of representation was not known, the consequence was, they either degenerated convulsively into monarchies, or became absorbed into such as then existed. Had the system of representation been then understood, as it now is, there is no reason to believe that those forms of government, now called monarchical or aristocratical, would ever have taken place. It was the want of some method to consolidate the parts of society, after it became too populous, and too extensive for the simple democratical form, and also the lax and solitary condition of shepherds and herdsmen in other parts of the world, that afforded opportunities to those unnatural modes of government to begin.

As it is necessary to clear away the rubbish of errors, into which the subject of government has been thrown, I shall proceed to remark on some others.

It has always been the political craft of courtiers and court-governments, to abuse something which they called republicanism; but what republicanism was, or is, they never attempt to explain. Let us examine a little into this case.

The only forms of government are, the democratical, the aristocratical, the monarchical, and what is now called the representative.

What is called a *republic*, is not any *particular form* of government. It is wholly characteristical of the purport, matter, or object for which government ought to be instituted, and on which it is to be employed, RES-PUBLICA, the public affairs, or the public good; or, literally translated, the *public thing*. It is a word of a good original, referring to what ought to be the character and business of government; and in this sense it is naturally opposed to the word *monarchy*, which has a base original signification. It means arbitrary power in an individual person; in the exercise of which, *himself*, and not the *res-publica*, is the object.

Every government that does not act on the principle of a *Republic*, or in other words, that does not make the *res-publica* its whole and sole object, is not a good government. Republican government is no other than government established and conducted for the interest of the public, as well individually as collectively. It is not necessarily connected with any particular form, but it most naturally associates with the

representative form, as being best calculated to secure the end
for which a nation is at the expence of supporting it.

Various forms of government have affected to style themselves a republic. Poland calls itself a republic, which is an
hereditary aristocracy, with what is called an elective monarchy. Holland calls itself a republic, which is chiefly aristocratical, with an hereditary stadtholdership. But the government
of America, which is wholly on the system of representation,
is the only real republic in character and in practice, that now
exists. Its government has no other object than the public
business of the nation, and therefore it is properly a republic;
and the Americans have taken care that THIS, and no other,
shall always be the object of their government, by their rejecting every thing hereditary, and establishing government on
the system of representation only.

Those who have said that a republic is not a *form* of government calculated for countries of great extent, mistook, in
the first place, the *business* of a government, for a *form* of
government; for the *res-publica* equally appertains to every extent of territory and population. And, in the second place, if
they meant any thing with respect to *form*, it was the simple
democratical form, such as was the mode of government in
the ancient democracies, in which there was no representation. The case, therefore, is not, that a republic cannot be
extensive, but that it cannot be extensive on the simple democratical form; and the question naturally presents itself, *What
is the best form of government for conducting the* RES-PUBLICA,
or the PUBLIC BUSINESS *of a nation, after it becomes too extensive and populous for the simple democratical form?*

It cannot be monarchy, because monarchy is subject to an
objection of the same amount to which the simple democratical form was subject.

It is possible that an individual may lay down a system of
principles, on which government shall be constitutionally established to any extent of territory. This is no more than an
operation of the mind, acting by its own powers. But the
practice upon those principles, as applying to the various and
numerous circumstances of a nation, its agriculture, manufacture, trade, commerce, &c. &c. requires a knowledge of a dif-

ferent kind, and which can be had only from the various parts of society. It is an assemblage of practical knowledge, which no one individual can possess; and therefore the monarchical form is as much limited, in useful practice, from the incompetency of knowledge, as was the democratical form, from the multiplicity of population. The one degenerates, by extension, into confusion; the other, into ignorance and incapacity, of which all the great monarchies are an evidence. The monarchical form, therefore, could not be a substitute for the democratical, because it has equal inconveniences.

Much less could it when made hereditary. This is the most effectual of all forms to preclude knowledge. Neither could the high democratical mind have voluntarily yielded itself to be governed by children and idiots, and all the motley insignificance of character, which attends such a mere animal-system, the disgrace and the reproach of reason and of man.

As to the aristocratical form, it has the same vices and defects with the monarchical, except that the chance of abilities is better from the proportion of numbers, but there is still no security for the right use and application of them*.

Referring, then, to the original simple democracy, it affords the true data from which government on a large scale can begin. It is incapable of extension, not from its principle, but from the inconvenience of its form; and monarchy and aristocracy, from their incapacity. Retaining, then, democracy as the ground, and rejecting the corrupt systems of monarchy and aristocracy, the representative system naturally presents itself; remedying at once the defects of the simple democracy as to form, and the incapacity of the other two with respect to knowledge.

Simple democracy was society governing itself without the aid of secondary means. By ingrafting representation upon democracy, we arrive at a system of government capable of embracing and confederating all the various interests and every extent of territory and population; and that also with

*For a character of aristocracy, the reader is referred to *Rights of Man*, Part I. page 476.

advantages as much superior to hereditary government, as the republic of letters is to hereditary literature.

It is on this system that the American government is founded. It is representation ingrafted upon democracy. It has fixed the form by a scale parallel in all cases to the extent of the principle. What Athens was in miniature, America will be in magnitude. The one was the wonder of the ancient world; the other is becoming the admiration and model of the present. It is the easiest of all the forms of government to be understood, and the most eligible in practice; and excludes at once the ignorance and insecurity of the hereditary mode, and the inconvenience of the simple democracy.

It is impossible to conceive a system of government capable of acting over such an extent of territory, and such a circle of interests, as is immediately produced by the operation of representation. France, great and populous as it is, is but a spot in the capaciousness of the system. It adapts itself to all possible cases. It is preferable to simple democracy even in small territories. Athens, by representation, would have outrivalled her own democracy.

That which is called government, or rather that which we ought to conceive government to be, is no more than some common center, in which all the parts of society unite. This cannot be accomplished by any method so conducive to the various interests of the community, as by the representative system. It concentrates the knowledge necessary to the interest of the parts, and of the whole. It places government in a state of constant maturity. It is, as has been already observed, never young, never old. It is subject neither to nonage, nor dotage. It is never in the cradle, nor on crutches. It admits not of a separation between knowledge and power, and is superior, as government always ought to be, to all the accidents of individual man, and is therefore superior to what is called monarchy.

A nation is not a body, the figure of which is to be represented by the human body; but is like a body contained within a circle, having a common center, in which every radius meets; and that center is formed by representation. To connect representation with what is called monarchy, is eccentric government. Representation is of itself the delegated monarchy of a nation, and cannot debase itself by dividing it with another.

Mr. Burke has two or three times, in his parliamentary speeches, and in his publications, made use of a jingle of words that convey no ideas. Speaking of government, he says, "It is better to have monarchy for its basis, and republicanism for its corrective, than republicanism for its basis, and monarchy for its corrective."—If he means that it is better to correct folly with wisdom, than wisdom with folly, I will no otherwise contend with him, than that it would be much better to reject the folly entirely.

But what is this thing which Mr. Burke calls monarchy? Will he explain it? All men can understand what representation is; and that it must necesarily include a variety of knowledge and talents. But, what security is there for the same qualities on the part of monarchy? or, when this monarchy is a child, where then is the wisdom? What does it know about government? Who then is the monarch, or where is the monarchy? If it is to be performed by regency, it proves it to be a farce. A regency is a mock species of republic, and the whole of monarchy deserves no better description. It is a thing as various as imagination can paint. It has none of the stable character that government ought to possess. Every succession is a revolution, and every regency a counter-revolution. The whole of it is a scene of perpetual court cabal and intrigue, of which Mr. Burke is himself an instance. To render monarchy consistent with government, the next in succession should not be born a child, but a man at once, and that man a Solomon. It is ridiculous that nations are to wait, and government be interrupted, till boys grow to be men.

Whether I have too little sense to see, or too much to be imposed upon; whether I have too much or too little pride, or of any thing else, I leave out of the question; but certain it is, that what is called monarchy, always appears to me a silly, contemptible thing. I compare it to something kept behind a curtain, about which there is a great deal of bustle and fuss, and a wonderful air of seeming solemnity; but when, by any accident, the curtain happens to be open, and the company see what it is, they burst into laughter.

In the representative system of government, nothing of this

can happen. Like the nation itself, it possesses a perpetual stamina, as well of body as of mind, and presents itself on the open theatre of the world in a fair and manly manner. Whatever are its excellences or its defects, they are visible to all. It exists not by fraud and mystery; it deals not in cant and sophistry; but inspires a language, that, passing from heart to heart, is felt and understood.

We must shut our eyes against reason, we must basely degrade our understanding, not to see the folly of what is called monarchy. Nature is orderly in all her works; but this is a mode of government that counteracts nature. It turns the progress of the human faculties upside down. It subjects age to be governed by children, and wisdom by folly.

On the contrary, the representative system is always parallel with the order and immutable laws of nature, and meets the reason of man in every part. For example:

In the American federal government, more power is delegated to the President of the United States, than to any other individual member of congress. He cannot, therefore, be elected to this office under the age of thirty-five years. By this time the judgment of man becomes matured, and he has lived long enough to be acquainted with men and things, and the country with him. — But on the monarchical plan, (exclusive of the numerous chances there are against every man born into the world, of drawing a prize in the lottery of human faculties), the next in succession, whatever he may be, is put at the head of a nation, and of a government, at the age of eighteen years. Does this appear like an act of wisdom? Is it consistent with the proper dignity and the manly character of a nation? Where is the propriety of calling such a lad the father of the people? — In all other cases, a person is a minor until the age of twenty-one years. Before this period, he is not trusted with the management of an acre of land, or with the heritable property of a flock of sheep, or an herd of swine; but, wonderful to tell! he may, at the age of eighteen years, be trusted with a nation.

That monarchy is all a bubble, a mere court artifice to procure money, is evident, (at least to me), in every character in which it can be viewed. It would be impossible, on the rational system of representative government, to make out a bill of expences to such an enormous amount as this deception admits. Government is not of itself a very chargeable institution. The whole expence of the federal government of America, founded, as I have already said, on the system of representation, and extending over a country nearly ten times as large as England, is but six hundred thousand dollars, or one hundred and thirty-five thousand pounds sterling.

I presume, that no man in his sober senses, will compare the character of any of the kings of Europe with that of General Washington. Yet, in France, and also in England, the expence of the civil list only, for the support of one man, is eight times greater than the whole expence of the federal government in America. To assign a reason for this, appears almost impossible. The generality of people in America, especially the poor, are more able to pay taxes, than the generality of people either in France or England.

But the case is, that the representative system diffuses such a body of knowledge throughout a nation, on the subject of government, as to explode ignorance and preclude imposition. The craft of courts cannot be acted on that ground. There is no place for mystery; no where for it to begin. Those who are not in the representation, know as much of the nature of business as those who are. An affectation of mysterious importance would there be scouted. Nations can have no secrets; and the secrets of courts, like those of individuals, are always their defects.

In the representative system, the reason for every thing must publicly appear. Every man is a proprietor in government, and considers it a necessary part of his business to understand. It concerns his interest, because it affects his property. He examines the cost, and compares it with the advantages; and above all, he does not adopt the slavish custom of following what in other governments are called LEADERS.

It can only be by blinding the understanding of man, and making him believe that government is some wonderful mysterious thing, that excessive revenues are obtained. Monarchy is well calculated to ensure this end. It is the popery of government; a thing kept up to amuse the ignorant, and quiet them into taxes.

The government of a free country, properly speaking, is not

in the persons, but in the laws. The enacting of those requires no great expence; and when they are administered, the whole of civil government is performed—the rest is all court contrivance.

CHAP. IV.

OF CONSTITUTIONS.

THAT men mean distinct and separate things when they speak of constitutions and of governments, is evident; or, why are those terms distinctly and separately used? A constitution is not the act of a government, but of a people constituting a government; and government without a constitution, is power without a right.

All power exercised over a nation, must have some beginning. It must be either delegated, or assumed. There are no other sources. All delegated power is trust, and all assumed power is usurpation. Time does not alter the nature and quality of either.

In viewing this subject, the case and circumstances of America present themselves as in the beginning of a world; and our enquiry into the origin of government is shortened, by referring to the facts that have arisen in our own day. We have no occasion to roam for information into the obscure field of antiquity, nor hazard ourselves upon conjecture. We are brought at once to the point of seeing government begin, as if we had lived in the beginning of time. The real volume, not of history, but of facts, is directly before us, unmutilated by contrivance, or the errors of tradition.

I will here concisely state the commencement of the American constitutions; by which the difference between constitutions and governments will sufficiently appear.

It may not be improper to remind the reader, that the United States of America consist of thirteen separate states, each of which established a government for itself, after the declaration of independence, done the fourth of July 1776. Each state acted independently of the rest, in forming its government; but the same general principle pervades the whole. When the several state governments were formed, they proceeded to form the federal government, that acts over the whole in all matters which concern the interest of the whole, or which relate to the intercourse of the several states with each other, or with foreign nations. I will begin with giving an instance from one of the state governments, (that of Pennsylvania), and then proceed to the federal government.

The state of Pennsylvania, though nearly of the same extent of territory as England, was then divided into only twelve counties. Each of those counties had elected a committee at the commencement of the dispute with the English government; and as the city of Philadelphia, which also had its committee, was the most central for intelligence, it became the center of communication to the several county committees. When it became necessary to proceed to the formation of a government, the committee of Philadelphia proposed a conference of all the county committees, to be held in that city, and which met the latter end of July 1776.

Though these committees had been elected by the people, they were not elected expressly for the purpose, nor invested with the authority, of forming a constitution; and as they could not, consistently with the American idea of rights, assume such a power, they could only confer upon the matter, and put it into a train of operation. The conferees, therefore, did no more than state the case, and recommend to the several counties to elect six representatives for each county, to meet in convention at Philadelphia, with powers to form a constitution, and propose it for public consideration.

This convention, of which Benjamin Franklin was president, having met and deliberated, and agreed upon a constitution, they next ordered it to be published, not as a thing established, but for the consideration of the whole people, their approbation or rejection, and then adjourned to a stated time. When the time of adjournment was expired, the convention re-assembled; and as the general opinion of the people in approbation of it was then known, the constitution was signed, sealed, and proclaimed on the *authority of the people* and the original instrument deposited as a public record. The convention then appointed a day for the general election of the representatives who were to compose the government, and the time it should commence; and having done this, they dissolved, and returned to their several homes and occupations.

In this constitution were laid down, first, a declaration of rights. Then followed the form which the government should have, and the powers it should possess—the authority of the courts of judicature, and of juries—the manner in which elections should be conducted, and the proportion of representatives to the number of electors—the time which each succeeding assembly should continue, which was one year—the mode of levying, and of accounting for the expenditure, of public money—of appointing public officers, &c. &c. &c.

No article of this constitution could be altered or infringed at the discretion of the government that was to ensue. It was to that government a law. But as it would have been unwise to preclude the benefit of experience, and in order also to prevent the accumulation of errors, if any should be found, and to preserve an unison of government with the circumstances of the state at all times, the constitution provided, that, at the expiration of every seven years, a convention should be elected, for the express purpose of revising the constitution, and making alterations, additions, or abolitions therein, if any such should be found necessary.

Here we see a regular process—a government issuing out of a constitution, formed by the people in their original character; and that constitution serving, not only as an authority, but as a law of controul to the government. It was the political bible of the state. Scarcely a family was without it. Every member of the government had a copy; and nothing was more common, when any debate arose on the principle of a bill, or on the extent of any species of authority, than for the members to take the printed constitution out of their pocket, and read the chapter with which such matter in debate was connected.

Having thus given an instance from one of the states, I will shew the proceedings by which the federal constitution of the United States arose and was formed.

Congress, at its two first meetings, in September 1774, and May 1775, was nothing more than a deputation from the legislatures of the several provinces, afterwards states; and had no other authority than what arose from common consent, and the necessity of its acting as a public body. In every thing which related to the internal affairs of America, congress went no further than to issue recommendations to the several provincial assemblies, who at discretion adopted them or not. Nothing on the part of congress was compulsive; yet, in this situation, it was more faithfully and affectionately obeyed, than was any government in Europe. This instance, like that of the national assembly in France, sufficiently shews, that the strength of government does not consist in any thing *within* itself, but in the attachment of a nation, and the interest which the people feel in supporting it. When this is lost, government is but a child in power; and though, like the old government of France, it may harrass individuals for a while, it but facilitates its own fall.

After the declaration of independence, it became consistent with the principle on which representative government is founded, that the authority of congress should be defined and established. Whether that authority should be more or less than congress then discretionarily exercised, was not the question. It was merely the rectitude of the measure.

For this purpose, the act, called the act of confederation, (which was a sort of imperfect federal constitution), was proposed, and, after long deliberation, was concluded in the year 1781. It was not the act of congress, because it is repugnant to the principles of representative government that a body should give power to itself. Congress first informed the several states, of the powers which it conceived were necessary to be invested in the union, to enable it to perform the duties and services required from it; and the states severally agreed with each other, and concentrated in congress those powers.

It may not be improper to observe, that in both those instances, (the one of Pennsylvania, and the other of the United States), there is no such thing as the idea of a compact between the people on one side, and the government on the other. The compact was that of the people with each other, to produce and constitute a government. To suppose that any government can be a party in a compact with the whole people, is to suppose it to have existence before it can have a right to exist. The only instance in which a compact can take place between the people and those who exercise the government, is, that the people shall pay them, while they chuse to employ them.

Government is not a trade which any man or body of men has a right to set up and exercise for his own emolument, but is altogether a trust, in right of those by whom that trust is delegated, and by whom it is always resumeable. It has of itself no rights; they are altogether duties.

Having thus given two instances of the original formation of a constitution, I will shew the manner in which both have been changed since their first establishment.

The powers vested in the governments of the several states, by the state constitutions, were found, upon experience, to be too great; and those vested in the federal government, by the act of confederation, too little. The defect was not in the principle, but in the distribution of power.

Numerous publications, in pamphlets and in the newspapers, appeared, on the propriety and necessity of new modelling the federal government. After some time of public discussion, carried on through the channel of the press, and in conversations, the state of Virginia, experiencing some inconvenience with respect to commerce, proposed holding a continental conference; in consequence of which, a deputation from five or six of the state assemblies met at Anapolis in Maryland, in 1786. This meeting, not conceiving itself sufficiently authorised to go into the business of a reform, did no more than state their general opinions of the propriety of the measure, and recommend that a convention of all the states should be held the year following.

This convention met at Philadelphia in May 1787, of which General Washington was elected president. He was not at that time connected with any of the state governments, or with congress. He delivered up his commission when the war ended, and since then had lived a private citizen.

The convention went deeply into all the subjects; and having, after a variety of debate and investigation, agreed among themselves upon the several parts of a federal constitution, the next question was, the manner of giving it authority and practice.

For this purpose, they did not, like a cabal of courtiers, send for a Dutch Stadtholder, or a German Elector; but they referred the whole matter to the sense and interest of the country.

They first directed, that the proposed constitution should be published. Secondly, that each state should elect a convention, expressly for the purpose of taking it into consideration, and of ratifying or rejecting it; and that as soon as the approbation and ratification of any nine states should be given, that those states should proceed to the election of their proportion of members to the new federal government; and that the operation of it should then begin, and the former federal government cease.

The several states proceeded accordingly to elect their conventions. Some of those conventions ratified the constitution by very large majorities, and two or three unanimously. In others there were much debate and division of opinion. In the Massachusetts convention, which met at Boston, the majority was not above nineteen or twenty, in about three hundred members; but such is the nature of representative government, that it quietly decides all matters by majority. After the debate in the Massachusetts convention was closed, and the vote taken, the objecting members rose, and declared, *"That though they had argued and voted against it, because certain parts appeared to them in a different light to what they appeared to other members; yet, as the vote had decided in favour of the constitution as proposed, they should give it the same practical support as if they had voted for it."*

As soon as nine states had concurred, (and the rest followed in the order their conventions were elected), the old fabric of the federal government was taken down, and the new one erected, of which General Washington is president. —In this place I cannot help remarking, that the character and services of this gentleman are sufficient to put all those men called kings to shame. While they are receiving from the sweat and labours of mankind, a prodigality of pay, to which neither their abilities nor their services can entitle them, he is rendering every service in his power, and refusing every pecuniary reward. He accepted no pay as commander in chief; he accepts none as president of the United States.

After the new federal constitution was established, the state of Pennsylvania, conceiving that some parts of its own constitution required to be altered, elected a convention for that purpose. The proposed alterations were published, and the people concurring therein, they were established.

In forming those constitutions, or in altering them, little or no inconvenience took place. The ordinary course of things was not interrupted, and the advantages have been much. It is always the interest of a far greater number of people in a nation to have things right, than to let them remain wrong; and when public matters are open to debate, and the public judgment free, it will not decide wrong, unless it decides too hastily.

In the two instances of changing the constitutions, the governments then in being were not actors either way. Government has no right to make itself a party in any debate respecting the principles or modes of forming, or of changing, constitutions. It is not for the benefit of those who exercise the powers of government, that constitutions, and the governments issuing from them, are established. In all those matters, the right of judging and acting are in those who pay, and not in those who receive.

A constitution is the property of a nation, and not of those who exercise the government. All the constitutions of America are declared to be established on the authority of the people. In France, the word nation is used instead of the people; but in both cases, a constitution is a thing antecedent to the government, and always distinct therefrom.

In England, it is not difficult to perceive that every thing has a constitution, except the nation. Every society and association that is established, first agreed upon a number of original articles, digested into form, which are its constitution. It then appointed its officers, whose powers and authorities are described in that constitution, and the government of that society then commenced. Those officers, by whatever name they are called, have no authority to add to, alter, or abridge the original articles. It is only to the constituting power that this right belongs.

From the want of understanding the difference between a constitution and a government, Dr. Johnson, and all writers of his description, have always bewildered themselves. They could not but perceive, that there must necessarily be a *con-*

trouling power existing somewhere, and they placed this power in the discretion of the persons exercising the government, instead of placing it in a constitution formed by the nation. When it is in a constitution, it has the nation for its support, and the natural and the political controuling powers are together. The laws which are enacted by governments, controul men only as individuals, but the nation, through its constitution, controuls the whole government, and has a natural ability so to do. The final controuling power, therefore, and the original constituting power, are one and the same power.

Dr. Johnson could not have advanced such a position in any country where there was a constitution; and he is himself an evidence, that no such thing as a constitution exists in England.—But it may be put as a question, not improper to be investigated, That if a constitution does not exist, how came the idea of its existence so generally established?

In order to decide this question, it is necessary to consider a constitution in both its cases:—First, as creating a government and giving it powers. Secondly, as regulating and restraining the powers so given.

If we begin with William of Normandy, we find that the government of England was originally a tyranny, founded on an invasion and conquest of the country. This being admitted, it will then appear, that the exertion of the nation, at different periods, to abate that tyranny, and render it less intolerable, has been credited for a constitution.

Magna Charta, as it was called, (it is now like an almanack of the same date,) was no more than compelling the government to renounce a part of its assumptions. It did not create and give powers to government in the manner a constitution does; but was, as far as it went, of the nature of a re-conquest, and not of a constitution; for could the nation have totally expelled the usurpation, as France has done its despotism, it would then have had a constitution to form.

The history of the Edwards and the Henries, and up to the commencement of the Stuarts, exhibits as many instances of tyranny as could be acted within the limits to which the nation had restricted it. The Stuarts endeavoured to pass those limits, and their fate is well known. In all those instances we see nothing of a constitution, but only of restrictions on assumed power.

After this, another William, descended from the same stock, and claiming from the same origin, gained possession; and of the two evils, *James* and *William*, the nation preferred what it thought the least; since, from circumstances, it must take one. The act, called the Bill of Rights, comes here into view. What is it, but a bargain, which the parts of the government made with each other to divide powers, profits, and privileges? You shall have so much, and I will have the rest; and with respect to the nation, it said, for *your share,* YOU *shall have the right of petitioning.* This being the case, the bill of rights is more properly a bill of wrongs, and of insult. As to what is called the convention parliament, it was a thing that made itself, and then made the authority by which it acted. A few persons got together, and called themselves by that name. Several of them had never been elected, and none of them for the purpose.

From the time of William, a species of government arose, issuing out of this coalition bill of rights; and more so, since the corruption introduced at the Hanover succession, by the agency of Walpole; that can be described by no other name than a despotic legislation. Though the parts may embarrass each other, the whole has no bounds; and the only right it acknowledges out of itself, is the right of petitioning. Where then is the constitution either that gives or that restrains power?

It is not because a part of the government is elective, that makes it less a despotism, if the persons so elected, possess afterwards, as a parliament, unlimited powers. Election, in this case, becomes separated from representation, and the candidates are candidates for despotism.

I cannot believe that any nation, reasoning on its own rights, would have thought of calling those things *a constitution,* if the cry of constitution had not been set up by the government. It has got into circulation like the words *bore* and *quoz,* by being chalked up in the speeches of parliament, as those words were on window shutters and door posts; but whatever the constitution may be in other respects, it has un-

doubtedly been *the most productive machine of taxation that
was ever invented*. The taxes in France, under the new constitution, are not quite thirteen shillings per head*, and the
taxes in England, under what is called its present constitution,
are forty-eight shillings and sixpence per head, men, women,
and children, amounting to nearly seventeen millions sterling,
besides the expence of collection, which is upwards of a million more.

In a country like England, where the whole of the civil government is executed by the people of every town and county,
by means of parish officers, magistrates, quarterly sessions, juries, and assize; without any trouble to what is called the government, or any other expence to the revenue than the salary
of the judges, it is astonishing how such a mass of taxes can
be employed. Not even the internal defence of the country is
paid out of the revenue. On all occasions, whether real or
contrived, recourse is continually had to new loans and new
taxes. No wonder, then, that a machine of government so
advantageous to the advocates of a court, should be so tri-
umphantly extolled! No wonder, that St. James's or St.
Stephen's should echo with the continual cry of constitution! No wonder, that the French revolution should be reprobated, and the *res-publica* treated with reproach! The *red
book* of England, like the red book of France, will explain the
reason†.

I will now, by way of relaxation, turn a thought or two to
Mr. Burke. I ask his pardon for neglecting him so long.

*The whole amount of the assessed taxes of France, for the present year, is
three hundred millions of livres, which is twelve millions and a half sterling;
and the incidental taxes are estimated at three millions, making in the whole
fifteen millions and a half; which, among twenty-four millions of people, is
not quite thirteen shillings per head. France has lessened her taxes since the
revolution, nearly nine millions sterling annually. Before the revolution, the
city of Paris paid a duty of upwards of thirty per cent. on all articles brought
into the city. This tax was collected at the city gates. It was taken off on the
first of last May, and the gates taken down.

†What was called the *livre rouge*, or the red book, in France, was not
exactly similar to the court calendar in England; but it sufficiently shewed
how a great part of the taxes was lavished.

"America," says he, (in his speech on the Canada constitution bill) "never dreamed of such absurd doctrine as the *Rights of Man*."

Mr. Burke is such a bold presumer, and advances his assertions and his premises with such a deficiency of judgment, that, without troubling ourselves about principles of philosophy or politics, the mere logical conclusions they produce, are ridiculous. For instance,

If governments, as Mr. Burke asserts, are not founded on the Rights of MAN, and are founded on *any rights* at all, they consequently must be founded on the rights of *something* that is *not man*. What then is that something?

Generally speaking, we know of no other creatures that inhabit the earth than man and beast; and in all cases, where only two things offer themselves, and one must be admitted, a negation proved on any one, amounts to an affirmative on the other; and therefore, Mr. Burke, by proving against the Rights of *Man*, proves in behalf of the *beast*; and consequently, proves that government is a beast: and as difficult things sometimes explain each other, we now see the origin of keeping wild beasts in the Tower; for they certainly can be of no other use than to shew the origin of the government. They are in the place of a constitution. O John Bull, what honours thou hast lost by not being a wild beast. Thou mightest, on Mr. Burke's system, have been in the Tower for life.

If Mr. Burke's arguments have not weight enough to keep one serious, the fault is less mine than his; and as I am willing to make an apology to the reader for the liberty I have taken, I hope Mr. Burke will also make his for giving the cause.

Having thus paid Mr. Burke the compliment of remembering him, I return to the subject.

From the want of a constitution in England to restrain and regulate the wild impulse of power, many of the laws are irrational and tyrannical, and the administration of them vague and problematical.

The attention of the government of England, (for I rather chuse to call it by this name, than the English government) appears, since its political connection with Germany, to have been so compleatly engrossed and absorbed by foreign affairs, and the means of raising taxes, that it seems to exist for no other purposes. Domestic concerns are neglected; and, with respect to regular law, there is scarcely such a thing.

Almost every case now must be determined by some precedent, be that precedent good or bad, or whether it properly applies or not; and the practice is become so general, as to suggest a suspicion, that it proceeds from a deeper policy than at first sight appears.

Since the revolution of America, and more so since that of France, this preaching up the doctrine of precedents, drawn from times and circumstances antecedent to those events, has been the studied practice of the English government. The generality of those precedents are founded on principles and opinions, the reverse of what they ought; and the greater distance of time they are drawn from, the more they are to be suspected. But by associating those precedents with a superstitious reverence for ancient things, as monks shew relics and call them holy, the generality of mankind are deceived into the design. Governments now act as if they were afraid to awaken a single reflection in man. They are softly leading him to the sepulchre of precedents, to deaden his faculties and call his attention from the scene of revolutions. They feel that he is arriving at knowledge faster than they wish, and their policy of precedents is the barometer of their fears. This political popery, like the ecclesiastical popery of old, has had its day, and is hastening to its exit. The ragged relic and the antiquated precedent, the monk and the monarch, will moulder together.

Government by precedent, without any regard to the principle of the precedent, is one of the vilest systems that can be set up. In numerous instances, the precedent ought to operate as a warning, and not as an example, and requires to be shunned instead of imitated; but instead of this, precedents are taken in the lump, and put at once for constitution and for law.

Either the doctrine of precedents is policy to keep man in a state of ignorance, or it is a practical confession that wisdom degenerates in governments as governments increase in age, and can only hobble along by the stilts and crutches of precedents. How is it that the same persons who would proudly be thought wiser than their predecessors, appear at the same time only as the ghosts of departed wisdom? How strangely is antiquity treated! To answer some purposes it is spoken of as the times of darkness and ignorance, and to answer others, it is put for the light of the world.

If the doctrine of precedents, is to be followed, the expences of government need not continue the same. Why pay men extravagantly, who have but little to do? If every thing that can happen is already in precedent, legislation is at an end, and precedent, like a dictionary, determines every case. Either, therefore, government has arrived at its dotage, and requires to be renovated, or all the occasions for exercising its wisdom have occurred.

We now see all over Europe, and particularly in England, the curious phænomenon of a nation looking one way, and a government the other—the one forward and the other backward. If governments are to go on by precedent, while nations go on by improvement, they must at last come to a final separation; and the sooner, and the more civilly, they determine this point, the better*.

Having thus spoken of constitutions generally, as things distinct from actual governments, let us proceed to consider the parts of which a constitution is composed.

Opinions differ more on this subject, than with respect to the whole. That a nation ought to have a constitution, as a rule for the conduct of its government, is a simple question in which all men, not directly courtiers, will agree. It is only on the component parts that questions and opinions multiply.

---

*In England, the improvements in agriculture, useful arts, manufactures, and commerce, have been made in opposition to the genius of its government, which is that of following precedents. It is from the enterprize and industry of the individuals, and their numerous associations, in which, tritely speaking, government is neither pillow nor bolster, that these improvements have proceeded. No man thought about the government, or who was *in*, or who was *out*, when he was planning or executing those things; and all he had to hope, with respect to government, was, *that it would let him alone*. Three or four very silly ministerial news-papers are continually offending against the spirit of national improvement, by ascribing it to a minister. They may with as much truth ascribe this book to a minister.

But this difficulty, like every other, will diminish when put into a train of being rightly understood.

The first thing is, that a nation has a right to establish a constitution.

Whether it exercises this right in the most judicious manner at first, is quite another case. It exercises it agreeably to the judgment it possesses; and by continuing to do so, all errors will at last be exploded.

When this right is established in a nation, there is no fear that it will be employed to its own injury. A nation can have no interest in being wrong.

Though all the constitutions of America are on one general principle, yet no two of them are exactly alike in their component parts, or in the distribution of the powers which they give to the actual governments. Some are more, and others less complex.

In forming a constitution, it is first necessary to consider what are the ends for which government is necessary? Secondly, what are the best means, and the least expensive, for accomplishing those ends?

Government is nothing more than a national association; and the object of this association is the good of all, as well individually as collectively. Every man wishes to pursue his occupation, and to enjoy the fruits of his labours, and the produce of his property in peace and safety, and with the least possible expence. When these things are accomplished, all the objects for which government ought to be established are answered.

It has been customary to consider government under three distinct general heads. The legislative, the executive, and the judicial.

But if we permit our judgment to act unincumbered by the habit of multiplied terms, we can perceive no more than two divisions of power, of which civil government is composed, namely, that of legislating or enacting laws, and that of executing or administering them. Every thing, therefore, appertaining to civil government, classes itself under one or other of these two divisions.

So far as regards the execution of the laws, that which is called the judicial power, is strictly and properly the executive power of every country. It is that power to which every individual has appeal, and which causes the laws to be executed; neither have we any other clear idea with respect to the official execution of the laws. In England, and also in America and France, this power begins with the magistrate, and proceeds up through all the courts of judicature.

I leave to courtiers to explain what is meant by calling monarchy the executive power. It is merely a name in which acts of government are done; and any other, or none at all, would answer the same purpose. Laws have neither more nor less authority on this account. It must be from the justness of their principles, and the interest which a nation feels therein, that they derive support; if they require any other than this, it is a sign that something in the system of government is imperfect. Laws difficult to be executed cannot be generally good.

With respect to the organization of the *legislative power*, different modes have been adopted in different countries. In America it is generally composed of two houses. In France it consists but of one, but in both countries it is wholly by representation.

The case is, that mankind (from the long tyranny of assumed power) have had so few opportunities of making the necessary trials on modes and principles of government, in order to discover the best, *that government is but now beginning to be known*, and experience is yet wanting to determine many particulars.

The objections against two houses are, first, that there is an inconsistency in any part of a whole legislature, coming to a final determination by vote on any matter, whilst *that matter*, with respect to *that whole*, is yet only in a train of deliberation, and consequently open to new illustrations.

Secondly, That by taking the vote on each, as a separate body, it always admits of the possibility, and is often the case in practice, that the minority governs the majority, and that, in some instances, to a degree of great inconsistency.

Thirdly, That two houses arbitrarily checking or controuling each other is inconsistent; because it cannot be proved, on the principles of just representation, that either should be wiser or better than the other. They may check in the wrong as well as in the right,—and therefore, to give the power where we cannot give the wisdom to use it, nor be assured of its being rightly used, renders the hazard at least equal to the precaution*.

The objection against a single house is, that it is always in a condition of committing itself too soon.—But it should at the same time be remembered, that when there is a constitution which defines the power, and establishes the principles within which a legislature shall act, there is already a more effectual check provided, and more powerfully operating, than any other check can be. For example,

Were a bill to be brought into any of the American legislatures, similar to that which was passed into an act by the English parliament, at the commencement of George the First, to extend the duration of the assemblies to a longer period than they now sit, the check is in the constitution, which in effect says, *Thus far shalt thou go and no further.*

But in order to remove the objection against a single house, (that of acting with too quick an impulse,) and at the same time to avoid the inconsistencies, in some cases absurdi-

*With respect to the two houses, of which the English Parliament is composed, they appear to be effectually influenced into one, and, as a legislature, to have no temper of its own. The minister, whoever he at any time may be, touches it as with an opium wand, and it sleeps obedience.

But if we look at the distinct abilities of the two houses, the difference will appear so great, as to shew the inconsistency of placing power where there can be no certainty of the judgment to use it. Wretched as the state of representation is in England, it is manhood compared with what is called the house of Lords; and so little is this nick-named house regarded, that the people scarcely inquire at any time what it is doing. It appears also to be most under influence, and the furthest removed from the general interest of the nation. In the debate on engaging in the Russian and Turkish war, the majority in the house of peers in favour of it was upwards of ninety, when in the other house, which is more than double its numbers, the majority was sixty-three.

The proceedings on Mr. Fox's bill, respecting the rights of juries, merits also to be noticed. The persons called the peers were not the objects of that bill. They are already in possession of more privileges than that bill gave to others. They are their own jury, and if any of that house were prosecuted for a libel, he would not suffer, even upon conviction, for the first offence. Such inequality in laws ought not to exist in any country. The French constitution says, That *the law is the same to every individual, whether to protect or to punish. All are equal in its sight.*

ties, arising from two houses, the following method has been proposed as an improvement upon both.

First, To have but one representation.

Secondly, To divide that representation, by lot, into two or three parts.

Thirdly, That every proposed bill, shall be first debated in those parts by succession, that they may become the hearers of each other, but without taking any vote. After which the whole representation to assemble for a general debate and determination by vote.

To this proposed improvement has been added another, for the purpose of keeping the representation in a state of constant renovation; which is, that one-third of the representation of each county, shall go out at the expiration of one year, and the number be replaced by new elections.— Another third at the expiration of the second year replaced in like manner, and every third year to be a general election*.

But in whatever manner the separate parts of a constitution may be arranged, there is *one* general principle that distinguishes freedom from slavery, which is, that all *hereditary government over a people is to them a species of slavery, and representative government is freedom.*

Considering government in the only light in which it should be considered, that of a NATIONAL ASSOCIATION; it ought to be so constructed as not to be disordered by any accident happening among the parts; and, therefore, no extraordinary power, capable of producing such an effect, should be lodged in the hands of any individual. The death, sickness, absence, or defection, of any one individual in a government, ought to be a matter of no more consequence, with respect to the nation, than if the same circumstance had taken place in a member of the English Parliament, or the French National Assembly.

Scarcely any thing presents a more degrading character of national greatness, than its being thrown into confusion by any thing happening to, or acted by, an individual; and the

---

*As to the state of representation in England, it is too absurd to be reasoned upon. Almost all the represented parts are decreasing in population, and the unrepresented parts are increasing. A general convention of the nation is necessary to take the whole state of its government into consideration.

ridiculousness of the scene is often increased by the natural insignificance of the person by whom it is occasioned. Were a government so constructed, that it could not go on unless a goose or a gander were present in the senate, the difficulties would be just as great and as real on the flight or sickness of the goose, or the gander, as if it were called a King. We laugh at individuals for the silly difficulties they make to themselves, without perceiving, that the greatest of all ridiculous things are acted in governments*.

All the constitutions of America are on a plan that excludes the childish embarrassments which occur in monarchical countries. No suspension of government can there take place for a moment, from any circumstance whatever. The system of representation provides for every thing, and is the only system in which nations and governments can always appear in their proper character.

As extraordinary power, ought not to be lodged in the hands of any individual, so ought there to be no appropriations of public money to any person, beyond what his services in a state may be worth. It signifies not whether a man be called a president, a king, an emperor, a senator, or by any other name, which propriety or folly may devise, or arrogance assume, it is only a certain service he can perform in the state; and the service of any such individual in the rotine of office, whether such office be called monarchical, presidential, senatorial, or by any other name or title, can never exceed the

*It is related, that in the canton of Berne, in Swisserland, it had been customary, from time immemorial, to keep a bear at the public expence, and the people had been taught to believe, that if they had not a bear they should all be undone. It happened some years ago, that the bear, then in being, was taken sick and died too suddenly to have his place immediately supplied with another. During this interregnum the people discovered, that the corn grew, and the vintage flourished, and the sun and moon continued to rise and set, and every thing went on the same as before, and, taking courage from these circumstances, they resolved not to keep any more bears; for, said they, "a bear is a very voracious, expensive animal, and we were obliged to pull out his claws, lest he should hurt the citizens."

The story of the bear of Berne was related in some of the French newspapers, at the time of the flight of Louis XVI. and the application of it to monarchy could not be mistaken in France; but it seems, that the aristocracy of Berne applied it to themselves, and have since prohibited the reading of French news-papers.

value of ten thousand pounds a year. All the great services that are done in the world are performed by volunteer characters, who accept nothing for them; but the rotine of office is always regulated to such a general standard of abilities as to be within the compass of numbers in every country to perform, and therefore cannot merit very extraordinary recompence. *Government*, says Swift, *is a plain thing, and fitted to the capacity of many heads.*

It is inhuman to talk of a million sterling a year, paid out of the public taxes of any country, for the support of any individual, whilst thousands who are forced to contribute thereto, are pining with want, and struggling with misery. Government does not consist in a contrast between prisons and palaces, between poverty and pomp; it is not instituted to rob the needy of his mite, and increase the wretchedness of the wretched. — But of this part of the subject I shall speak hereafter, and confine myself at present to political observations.

When extraordinary power and extraordinary pay are allotted to any individual in a government, he becomes the center, round which every kind of corruption generates and forms. Give to any man a million a year, and add thereto the power of creating and disposing of places, at the expence of a country, and the liberties of that country are no longer secure. What is called the splendor of a throne is no other than the corruption of the state. It is made up of a band of parasites, living in luxurious indolence, out of the public taxes.

When once such a vicious system is established it becomes the guard and protection of all inferior abuses. The man who is in the receipt of a million a year is the last person to promote a spirit of reform, lest, in the event, it should reach to himself. It is always his interest to defend inferior abuses, as so many out-works to protect the citadel; and in this species of political fortification, all the parts have such a common dependence that it is never to be expected they will attack each other*.

Monarchy would not have continued so many ages in the world, had it not been for the abuses it protects. It is the

---

*It is scarcely possible to touch on any subject, that will not suggest an allusion to some corruption in governments. The simile of *"fortifications,"*

master fraud, which shelters all others. By admitting a participation of the spoil, it makes itself friends; and when it ceases
to do this, it will cease to be the idol of courtiers.

As the principle on which constitutions are now formed
rejects all hereditary pretentions to government, it also rejects
all that catalogue of assumptions known by the name of
prerogatives.

If there is any government where prerogatives might with
apparent safety be entrusted to any individual, it is in the
fœderal government of America. The President of the United
States of America is elected only for four years. He is not only
responsible in the general sense of the word, but a particular
mode is laid down in the constitution for trying him. He cannot be elected under thirty-five years of age; and he must be a
native of the country.

In a comparison of these cases with the government of England, the difference when applied to the latter amounts to an
absurdity. In England the person who exercises prerogative is
often a foreigner; always half a foreigner, and always married
to a foreigner. He is never in full natural or political connection with the country, is not responsible for any thing, and

---

unfortunately involves with it a circumstance, which is directly in point with
the matter above alluded to.

Among the numerous instances of abuse which have been acted or protected
by governments, ancient or modern, there is not a greater than that of quartering a man and his heirs upon the public, to be maintained at its expence.

Humanity dictates a provision for the poor; but by what right, moral or
political, does any government assume to say, that the person called the Duke
of Richmond, shall be maintained by the public? Yet, if common report is
true, not a beggar in London can purchase his wretched pittance of coal,
without paying towards the civil list of the Duke of Richmond. Were the
whole produce of this imposition but a shilling a year, the iniquitous principle
would be still the same; but when it amounts, as it is said to do, to not less
than twenty thousand pounds *per ann.* the enormity is too serious to be
permitted to remain—This is one of the effects of monarchy and aristocracy.

In stating this case, I am led by no personal dislike. Though I think it mean
in any man to live upon the public, the vice originates in the government;
and so general is it become, that whether the parties are in the ministry or in
the opposition, it makes no difference: they are sure of the guarantee of each
other.

becomes of age at eighteen years; yet such a person is permitted to form foreign alliances, without even the knowledge of the nation, and to make war and peace without its consent.

But this is not all. Though such a person cannot dispose of the government, in the manner of a testator, he dictates the marriage connections, which, in effect, accomplishes a great part of the same end. He cannot directly bequeath half the government to Prussia, but he can form a marriage partnership that will produce almost the same thing. Under such circumstances, it is happy for England that she is not situated on the continent, or she might, like Holland, fall under the dictatorship of Prussia. Holland, by marriage, is as effectually governed by Prussia, as if the old tyranny of bequeathing the government had been the means.

The presidency in America, (or, as it is sometimes called, the executive,) is the only office from which a foreigner is excluded, and in England it is the only one to which he is admitted. A foreigner cannot be a member of parliament, but he may be what is called a king. If there is any reason for excluding foreigners, it ought to be from those offices where mischief can most be acted, and where, by uniting every bias of interest and attachment, the trust is best secured.

But as nations proceed in the great business of forming constitutions, they will examine with more precision into the nature and business of that department which is called the executive. What the legislative and judicial departments are, every one can see; but with respect to what, in Europe, is called the executive, as distinct from those two, it is either a political superfluity or a chaos of unknown things.

Some kind of official department, to which reports shall be made from the different parts of a nation, or from abroad, to be laid before the national representatives, is all that is necessary; but there is no consistency in calling this the executive; neither can it be considered in any other light than as inferior to the legislative. The sovereign authority in any country is the power of making laws, and every thing else is an official department.

Next to the arrangement of the principles and the organization of the several parts of a constitution, is the provision to be made for the support of the persons to whom the nation shall confide the administration of the constitutional powers.

A nation can have no right to the time and services of any person at his own expence, whom it may chuse to employ or entrust in any department whatever; neither can any reason be given for making provision for the support of any one part of a government and not for the other.

But, admitting that the honour of being entrusted with any part of a government is to be considered a sufficient reward, it ought to be so to every person alike. If the members of the legislature of any country are to serve at their own expence, that which is called the executive, whether monarchical, or by any other name, ought to serve in like manner. It is inconsistent to pay the one, and accept the service of the other gratis.

In America, every department in the government is decently provided for; but no one is extravagantly paid. Every member of Congress, and of the assemblies, is allowed a sufficiency for his expences. Whereas in England, a most prodigal provision is made for the support of one part of the government, and none for the other, the consequence of which is, that the one is furnished with the means of corruption, and the other is put into the condition of being corrupted. Less than a fourth part of such expence, applied as it is in America, would remedy a great part of the corruption.

Another reform in the American constitutions, is the exploding all oaths of personality. The oath of allegiance in America is to the nation only. The putting any individual as a figure for a nation is improper. The happiness of a nation is the superior object, and therefore the intention of an oath of allegiance ought not to be obscured by being figuratively taken, to, or in the name of, any person. The oath, called the civic oath, in France, viz. the *"nation, the law, and the king,"* is improper. If taken at all, it ought to be as in America, to the nation only. The law may or may not be good; but, in this place, it can have no other meaning, than as being conducive to the happiness of the nation, and therefore is included in it. The remainder of the oath is improper, on the ground, that all personal oaths ought to be abolished. They are the remains of tyranny on one part, and slavery on the other; and the

name of the CREATOR ought not to be introduced to witness
the degradation of his creation; or if taken, as is already mentioned, as figurative of the nation, it is in this place redundant. But whatever apology may be made for oaths at the first
establishment of a government, they ought not to be permitted afterwards. If a government requires the support of oaths,
it is a sign that it is not worth supporting, and ought not to
be supported. Make government what it ought to be, and it
will support itself.

To conclude this part of the subject:—One of the greatest
improvements that has been made for the perpetual security
and progress of constitutional liberty, is the provision which
the new constitutions make for occasionally revising, altering,
and amending them.

The principle upon which Mr. Burke formed his political
creed, that *"of binding and controuling posterity to the end of
time, and of renouncing and abdicating the rights of all posterity for ever,"* is now become too detestable to be made a subject of debate; and, therefore, I pass it over with no other
notice than exposing it.

Government is but now beginning to be known. Hitherto
it has been the mere exercise of power, which forbad all effectual enquiry into rights, and grounded itself wholly on possession. While the enemy of liberty was its judge, the progress of
its principles must have been small indeed.

The constitutions of America, and also that of France, have
either affixed a period for their revision, or laid down the
mode by which improvements shall be made. It is perhaps
impossible to establish any thing that combines principles
with opinions and practice, which the progress of circumstances, through a length of years, will not in some measure
derange, or render inconsistent; and, therefore, to prevent inconveniences accumulating, till they discourage reformations
or provoke revolutions, it is best to provide the means of
regulating them as they occur. The Rights of Man are the
rights of all generations of men, and cannot be monopolized
by any. That which is worth following, will be followed for
the sake of its worth; and it is in this that its security lies, and
not in any conditions with which it may be encumbered.
When a man leaves property to his heirs, he does not connect

it with an obligation that they shall accept it. Why then should we do otherwise with respect to constitutions?

The best constitution that could now be devised, consistent with the condition of the present moment, may be far short of that excellence which a few years may afford. There is a morning of reason rising upon man on the subject of government, that has not appeared before. As the barbarism of the present old governments expires, the moral condition of nations with respect to each other will be changed. Man will not be brought up with the savage idea of considering his species as his enemy, because the accident of birth gave the individuals existence in countries distinguished by different names; and as constitutions have always some relation to external as well as to domestic circumstances, the means of benefiting by every change, foreign or domestic, should be a part of every constitution.

We already see an alteration in the national disposition of England and France towards each other, which, when we look back to only a few years, is itself a revolution. Who could have foreseen, or who would have believed, that a French National Assembly would ever have been a popular toast in England, or that a friendly alliance of the two nations should become the wish of either. It shews, that man, were he not corrupted by governments, is naturally the friend of man, and that human nature is not of itself vicious. That spirit of jealousy and ferocity, which the governments of the two countries inspired, and which they rendered subservient to the purpose of taxation, is now yielding to the dictates of reason, interest, and humanity. The trade of courts is beginning to be understood, and the affectation of mystery, with all the artificial sorcery by which they imposed upon mankind, is on the decline. It has received its death-wound; and though it may linger, it will expire.

Government ought to be as much open to improvement as any thing which appertains to man, instead of which it has been monopolized from age to age, by the most ignorant and vicious of the human race. Need we any other proof of their wretched management, than the excess of debts and taxes with which every nation groans, and the quarrels into which they have precipitated the world?

Just emerging from such a barbarous condition, it is too soon to determine to what extent of improvement government may yet be carried. For what we can foresee, all Europe may form but one great republic, and man be free of the whole.

CHAP. V.

WAYS AND MEANS OF IMPROVING THE CONDITION OF EUROPE, INTERSPERSED WITH MISCELLANEOUS OBSERVATIONS.

IN contemplating a subject that embraces with equatorial magnitude the whole region of humanity, it is impossible to confine the pursuit in one single direction. It takes ground on every character and condition that appertains to man, and blends the individual, the nation, and the world.

From a small spark, kindled in America, a flame has arisen, not to be extinguished. Without consuming, like the *Ultima Ratio Regum*, it winds its progress from nation to nation, and conquers by a silent operation. Man finds himself changed, he scarcely perceives how. He acquires a knowledge of his rights by attending justly to his interest, and discovers in the event that the strength and powers of despotism consist wholly in the fear of resisting it, and that, in order *"to be free, it is sufficient that he wills it."*

Having in all the preceding parts of this work endeavoured to establish a system of principles as a basis, on which governments ought to be erected; I shall proceed in this, to the ways and means of rendering them into practice. But in order to introduce this part of the subject with more propriety, and stronger effect, some preliminary observations, deducible from, or connected with, those principles, are necessary.

Whatever the form or constitution of government may be, it ought to have no other object than the *general* happiness. When, instead of this, it operates to create and encrease wretchedness in any of the parts of society, it is on a wrong system, and reformation is necessary.

Customary language has classed the condition of man under the two descriptions of civilized and uncivilized life. To the one it has ascribed felicity and affluence; to the other hardship and want. But, however, our imagination may be impressed by painting and comparison, it is nevertheless true, that a great portion of mankind, in what are called civilized countries, are in a state of poverty and wretchedness, far below the condition of an Indian. I speak not of one country, but of all. It is so in England, it is so all over Europe. Let us enquire into the cause.

It lies not in any natural defect in the principles of civilization, but in preventing those principles having an universal operation; the consequence of which is, a perpetual system of war and expence, that drains the country, and defeats the general felicity of which civilization is capable.

All the European governments (France now excepted) are constructed not on the principle of universal civilization, but on the reverse of it. So far as those governments relate to each other, they are in the same condition as we conceive of savage uncivilized life; they put themselves beyond the law as well of GOD as of man, and are, with respect to principle and reciprocal conduct, like so many individuals in a state of nature.

The inhabitants of every country, under the civilization of laws, easily civilize together, but governments being yet in an uncivilized state, and almost continually at war, they pervert the abundance which civilized life produces to carry on the uncivilized part to a greater extent. By thus engrafting the barbarism of government upon the internal civilization of a country, it draws from the latter, and more especially from the poor, a great portion of those earnings, which should be applied to their own subsistence and comfort.—Apart from all reflections of morality and philosophy, it is a melancholy fact, that more than one-fourth of the labour of mankind is annually consumed by this barbarous system.

What has served to continue this evil, is the pecuniary advantage, which all the governments of Europe have found in keeping up this state of uncivilization. It affords to them pretences for power, and revenue, for which there would be neither occasion nor apology, if the circle of civilization were rendered compleat. Civil government alone, or the government of laws, is not productive of pretences for many taxes; it operates at home, directly under the eye of the country, and precludes the possibility of much imposition. But when the scene is laid in the uncivilized contention of governments, the field of pretences is enlarged, and the country, being no longer a judge, is open to every imposition, which governments please to act.

Not a thirtieth, scarely a fortieth, part of the taxes which are raised in England are either occasioned by, or applied to, the purposes of civil government. It is not difficult to see, that the whole which the actual government does in this respect, is to enact laws, and that the country administers and executes them, at its own expence, by means of magistrates, juries, sessions, and assize, over and above the taxes which it pays.

In this view of the case, we have two distinct characters of government; the one the civil government, or the government of laws, which operates at home, the other the court or cabinet government, which operates abroad, on the rude plan of uncivilized life; the one attended with little charge, the other with boundless extravagance; and so distinct are the two, that if the latter were to sink, as it were by a sudden opening of the earth, and totally disappear, the former would not be deranged. It would still proceed, because it is the common interest of the nation that it should, and all the means are in practice.

Revolutions, then, have for their object, a change in the moral condition of governments, and with this change the burthen of public taxes will lessen, and civilization will be left to the enjoyment of that abundance, of which it is now deprived.

In contemplating the whole of this subject, I extend my views into the department of commerce. In all my publications, where the matter would admit, I have been an advocate for commerce, because I am a friend to its effects. It is a pacific system, operating to cordialize mankind, by rendering nations, as well as individuals, useful to each other. As to mere theoretical reformation, I have never preached it up. The most effectual process is that of improving the condition of man by means of his interest; and it is on this ground that I take my stand.

If commerce were permitted to act to the universal extent it is capable, it would extirpate the system of war, and produce a revolution in the uncivilized state of governments. The invention of commerce has arisen since those governments began, and is the greatest approach towards universal civilization, that has yet been made by any means not immediately flowing from moral principles.

Whatever has a tendency to promote the civil intercourse of nations, by an exchange of benefits, is a subject as worthy of philosophy as of politics. Commerce is no other than the traffic of two individuals, multiplied on a scale of numbers; and by the same rule that nature intended the intercourse of two, she intended that of all. For this purpose she has distributed the materials of manufactures and commerce, in various and distant parts of a nation and of the world; and as they cannot be procured by war so cheaply or so commodiously as by commerce, she has rendered the latter the means of extirpating the former.

As the two are nearly the opposites of each other, consequently, the uncivilized state of European governments is injurious to commerce. Every kind of destruction or embarrassment serves to lessen the quantity, and it matters but little in what part of the commercial world the reduction begins. Like blood, it cannot be taken from any of the parts, without being taken from the whole mass in circulation, and all partake of the loss. When the ability in any nation to buy is destroyed, it equally involves the seller. Could the government of England destroy the commerce of all other nations, she would most effectually ruin her own.

It is possible that a nation may be the carrier for the world, but she cannot be the merchant. She cannot be the seller and the buyer of her own merchandize. The ability to buy must reside out of herself; and, therefore, the prosperity of any commercial nation is regulated by the prosperity of the rest. If they are poor she cannot be rich, and her condition, be it what it may, is an index of the height of the commercial tide in other nations.

That the principles of commerce, and its universal operation may be understood, without understanding the practice, is a position that reason will not deny; and it is on this ground only that I argue the subject. It is one thing in the counting-house, in the world it is another. With respect to its operation it must necessarily be contemplated as a reciprocal thing; that only one half its powers resides within the nation, and that the whole is as effectually destroyed by destroying the half that resides without, as if the destruction had been committed on that which is within; for neither can act without the other.

When in the last, as well as in former wars, the commerce of England sunk, it was because the general quantity was lessened every where; and it now rises, because commerce is in a rising state in every nation. If England, at this day, imports and exports more than at any former period, the nations with which she trades must necessarily do the same; her imports are their exports, and *vice versa*.

There can be no such thing as a nation flourishing alone in commerce; she can only participate; and the destruction of it in any part must necessarily affect all. When, therefore, governments are at war, the attack is made upon the common stock of commerce, and the consequence is the same as if each had attacked his own.

The present increase of commerce is not to be attributed to ministers, or to any political contrivances, but to its own natural operations in consequence of peace. The regular markets had been destroyed, the channels of trade broken up, the high road of the seas infested with robbers of every nation, and the attention of the world called to other objects. Those interruptions have ceased, and peace has restored the deranged condition of things to their proper order*.

It is worth remarking, that every nation reckons the balance of trade in its own favour; and therefore something must be irregular in the common ideas upon this subject.

The fact, however, is true, according to what is called a balance; and it is from this cause that commerce is universally supported. Every nation feels the advantage, or it would

*In America, the increase of commerce is greater in proportion than in England. It is, at this time, at least one half more than at any period prior to the revolution. The greatest number of vessels cleared out of the port of Philadelphia, before the commencement of the war, was between eight and nine hundred. In the year 1788, the number was upwards of twelve hundred. As the state of Pennsylvania is estimated as an eighth part of the United States in population, the whole number of vessels must now be nearly ten thousand.

abandon the practice: but the deception lies in the mode of making up the accounts, and in attributing what are called profits to a wrong cause.

Mr. Pitt has sometimes amused himself, by shewing what he called a balance of trade from the custom-house books. This mode of calculation, not only affords no rule that is true, but one that is false.

In the first place, Every cargo that departs from the custom-house, appears on the books as an export; and, according to the custom-house balance, the losses at sea, and by foreign failures, are all reckoned on the side of profit, because they appear as exports.

Secondly, Because the importation by the smuggling trade does not appear on the custom-house books, to arrange against the exports.

No balance, therefore, as applying to superior advantages, can be drawn from those documents; and if we examine the natural operation of commerce, the idea is fallacious; and if true, would soon be injurious. The great support of commerce consists in the balance being a level of benefits among all nations.

Two merchants of different nations trading together, will both become rich, and each makes the balance in his own favour; consequently, they do not get rich out of each other; and it is the same with respect to the nations in which they reside. The case must be, that each nation must get rich out of its own means, and increases that riches by something which it procures from another in exchange.

If a merchant in England sends an article of English manufacture abroad, which costs him a shilling at home, and imports something which sells for two, he makes a balance of one shilling in his own favour: but this is not gained out of the foreign nation or the foreign merchant, for he also does the same by the article he receives, and neither has a balance of advantage upon the other. The original value of the two articles in their proper countries were but two shillings; but by changing their places, they acquire a new idea of value, equal to double what they had at first, and that increased value is equally divided.

There is no otherwise a balance on foreign than on domestic

commerce. The merchants of London and Newcastle trade on the same principles, as if they resided in different nations, and make their balances in the same manner: yet London does not get rich out of Newcastle, any more than Newcastle out of London: but coals, the merchandize of Newcastle, have an additional value at London, and London merchandize has the same at Newcastle.

Though the principle of all commerce is the same, the domestic, in a national view, is the part the most beneficial; because the whole of the advantages, on both sides, rests within the nation; whereas, in foreign commerce, it is only a participation of one half.

The most unprofitable of all commerce is that connected with foreign dominion. To a few individuals it may be beneficial, merely because it is commerce; but to the nation it is a loss. The expence of maintaining dominion more than absorbs the profits of any trade. It does not increase the general quantity in the world, but operates to lessen it; and as a greater mass would be afloat by relinquishing dominion, the participation without the expence would be more valuable than a greater quantity with it.

But it is impossible to engross commerce by dominion; and therefore it is still more fallacious. It cannot exist in confined channels, and necessarily breaks out by regular or irregular means, that defeat the attempt; and to succeed would be still worse. France, since the revolution, has been more than indifferent as to foreign possessions; and other nations will become the same, when they investigate the subject with respect to commerce.

To the expence of dominion is to be added that of navies, and when the amount of the two are subtracted from the profits of commerce, it will appear, that what is called the balance of trade, even admitting it to exist, is not enjoyed by the nation, but absorbed by the government.

The idea of having navies for the protection of commerce is delusive. It is putting the means of destruction for the means of protection. Commerce needs no other protection than the reciprocal interest which every nation feels in supporting it—it is common stock—it exists by a balance of advantages to all; and the only interruption it meets, is from the present uncivilized state of governments, and which it is its common interest to reform*.

Quitting this subject, I now proceed to other matters.—As it is necessary to include England in the prospect of a general reformation, it is proper to enquire into the defects of its government. It is only by each nation reforming its own, that the whole can be improved, and the full benefit of reformation enjoyed. Only partial advantages can flow from partial reforms.

France and England are the only two countries in Europe where a reformation in government could have successfully begun. The one secure by the ocean, and the other by the immensity of its internal strength, could defy the malignancy of foreign despotism. But it is with revolutions as with commerce, the advantages increase by their becoming general, and double to either what each would receive alone.

As a new system is now opening to the view of the world, the European courts are plotting to counteract it. Alliances, contrary to all former systems, are agitating, and a common interest of courts is forming against the common interest of man. This combination draws a line that runs throughout Europe, and presents a cause so entirely new, as to exclude all calculations from former circumstances. While despotism warred with despotism, man had no interest in the contest; but in a cause that unites the soldier with the citizen, and nation with nation, the despotism of courts, though it feels the danger, and meditates revenge, is afraid to strike.

No question has arisen within the records of history that pressed with the importance of the present. It is not whether this or that party shall be in or out, or whig or tory, or high or low shall prevail; but whether man shall inherit his rights, and universal civilization take place? Whether the fruits of his labours shall be enjoyed by himself, or consumed by the profligacy of governments? Whether robbery shall be banished from courts, and wretchedness from countries?

---

*When I saw Mr. Pitt's mode of estimating the balance of trade, in one of his parliamentary speeches, he appeared to me to know nothing of the nature and interest of commerce; and no man has more wantonly tortured it than himself. During a period of peace, it has been havocked with the calamities of war. Three times has it been thrown into stagnation, and the vessels unmanned by impressing, within less than four years of peace.

When, in countries that are called civilized, we see age going to the workhouse and youth to the gallows, something must be wrong in the system of government. It would seem, by the exterior appearance of such countries, that all was happiness; but there lies hidden from the eye of common observation, a mass of wretchedness that has scarcely any other chance, than to expire in poverty or infamy. Its entrance into life is marked with the presage of its fate; and until this is remedied, it is in vain to punish.

Civil government does not consist in executions; but in making that provision for the instruction of youth, and the support of age, as to exclude, as much as possible, profligacy from the one, and despair from the other. Instead of this, the resources of a country are lavished upon kings, upon courts, upon hirelings, imposters, and prostitutes; and even the poor themselves, with all their wants upon them, are compelled to support the fraud that oppresses them.

Why is it, that scarcely any are executed but the poor? The fact is a proof, among other things, of a wretchedness in their condition. Bred up without morals, and cast upon the world without a prospect, they are the exposed sacrifice of vice and legal barbarity. The millions that are superfluously wasted upon governments, are more than sufficient to reform those evils, and to benefit the condition of every man in a nation, not included within the purlieus of a court. This I hope to make appear in the progress of this work.

It is the nature of compassion to associate with misfortune. In taking up this subject I seek no recompence—I fear no consequence. Fortified with that proud integrity, that disdains to triumph or to yield, I will advocate the Rights of Man.

It is to my advantage that I have served an apprenticeship to life. I know the value of moral instruction, and I have seen the danger of the contrary.

At an early period, little more than sixteen years of age, raw and adventurous, and heated with the false heroism of a master* who had served in a man of war, I began the carver of my own fortune, and entered on board the Terrible, Privateer,

*Rev. William Knowles, master of the grammar school of Thetford, in Norfolk.

Capt. Death. From this adventure I was happily prevented by
the affectionate and moral remonstrance of a good father,
who, from his own habits of life, being of the Quaker profession, must begin to look upon me as lost. But the impression,
much as it effected at the time, began to wear away, and I
entered afterwards in the King of Prussia Privateer, Capt.
Mendez, and went with her to sea. Yet, from such a beginning, and with all the inconvenience of early life against me, I
am proud to say, that with a perseverance undismayed by difficulties, a disinterestedness that compelled respect, I have not
only contributed to raise a new empire in the world, founded
on a new system of government, but I have arrived at an eminence in political literature, the most difficult of all lines to
succeed and excel in, which aristocracy, with all its aids, has
not been able to reach or to rival.

Knowing my own heart, and feeling myself, as I now do,
superior to all the skirmish of party, the inveteracy of interested
or mistaken opponents, I answer not to falsehood or abuse,
but proceed to the defects of the English government*.

I begin with charters and corporations.

It is a perversion of terms to say, that a charter gives rights.
It operates by a contrary effect, that of taking rights away.
Rights are inherently in all the inhabitants; but charters, by
annulling those rights in the majority, leave the right by ex-

*Politics and self-interest have been so uniformly connected, that the
world, from being so often deceived, has a right to be suspicious of public
characters: but with regard to myself, I am perfectly easy on this head. I did
not, at my first setting out in public life, nearly seventeen years ago, turn my
thoughts to subjects of government from motives of interest; and my conduct from that moment to this, proves the fact. I saw an opportunity, in
which I thought I could do some good, and I followed exactly what my heart
dictated. I neither read books, nor studied other people's opinions. I thought
for myself. The case was this:

During the suspension of the old governments in America, both prior to,
and at the breaking out of hostilities, I was struck with the order and deco-
rum with which every thing was conducted; and impressed with the idea, that
a little more than what society naturally performed, was all the government
that was necessary; and that monarchy and aristocracy were frauds and impositions upon mankind. On these principles I published the pamphlet *Common
Sense*. The success it met with was beyond any thing since the invention of
printing. I gave the copy right up to every state in the union, and the demand
ran to not less than one hundred thousand copies. I continued the subject

clusion in the hands of a few. If charters were constructed so as to express in direct terms, *"that every inhabitant, who is not a member of a corporation, shall not exercise the right of voting,"* such charters would, in the face, be charters, not of

---

in the same manner, under the title of the *Crisis*, till the complete establishment of the revolution.

After the declaration of independence, Congress unanimously, and unknown to me, appointed me secretary in the foreign department. This was agreeable to me, because it gave me the opportunity of seeing into the abilities of foreign courts, and their manner of doing business. But a misunderstanding arising between congress and me, respecting one of their commissioners, then in Europe, Mr. Silas Deane, I resigned the office, and declined, at the same time, the pecuniary offers made me by the ministers of France and Spain, M. Gerard and Don Juan Mirralles.

I had by this time so completely gained the ear and confidence of America, and my own independence was become so visible as to give me a range in political writing, beyond, perhaps, what any man ever possessed in any country; and what is more extraordinary, I held it undiminished to the end of the war, and enjoy it in the same manner to the present moment. As my object was not myself, I set out with the determination, and happily with the disposition, of not being moved by praise or censure, friendship or calumny, nor of being drawn from my purpose by any personal altercation; and the man who cannot do this, is not fit for a public character.

When the war ended, I went from Philadelphia to Borden-Town, on the east bank of the Delaware, where I have a small place. Congress was at this time at Prince-Town, fifteen miles distant; and General Washington had taken his headquarters at Rocky-Hill, within the neighbourhood of Congress, for the purpose of resigning up his commission, (the object for which he accepted it being accomplished,) and of retiring to private life. While he was on this business, he wrote me the letter which I here subjoin.

Rocky-Hill, Sept. 10, 1783.

I have learned since I have been at this place, that you are at Borden-Town. Whether for the sake of retirement or œconomy, I know not. Be it for either, for both, or whatever it may, if you will come to this place, and partake with me, I shall be exceedingly happy to see you at it.

Your presence may remind Congress of your past services to this country; and if it is in my power to impress them, command my best exertions with freedom, as they will be rendered chearfully by one, who entertains a lively sense of the importance of your works, and who, with much pleasure, subscribes himself,   Your sincere friend,

G. WASHINGTON.

During the war, in the latter end of the year 1780, I formed to myself a design of coming over to England; and communicated it to General Greene, who was then in Philadelphia, on his route to the southward, General Washington being then at too great a distance to communicate with immediately.

rights, but of exclusion. The effect is the same under the form they now stand; and the only persons on whom they operate, are the persons whom they exclude. Those whose rights are guaranteed, by not being taken away, exercise no other rights, than as members of the community they are entitled to without a charter; and, therefore, all charters have no other than an indirect negative operation. They do not give rights to A, but they make a difference in favour of A by taking away the right of B, and consequently are instruments of injustice.

But charters and corporations have a more extensive evil

I was strongly impressed with the idea, that if I could get over to England, without being known, and only remain in safety till I could get out a publication, that I could open the eyes of the country with respect to the madness and stupidity of its government. I saw that the parties in parliament had pitted themselves as far as they could go, and could make no new impressions on each other. General Greene entered fully into my views; but the affair of Arnold and André happening just after, he changed his mind, and, under strong apprehensions for my safety, wrote very pressingly to me from Anapolis, in Maryland, to give up the design, which, with some reluctance, I did. Soon after this I accompanied Col. Lawrens, son of Mr. Lawrens, who was then in the Tower, to France, on business from Congress. We landed at L'Orient; and while I remained there, he being gone forward, a circumstance occurred, that renewed my former design. An English packet from Falmouth to New-York, with the government dispatches on board, was brought into L'Orient. That a packet should be taken, is no extraordinary thing; but that the dispatches should be taken with it, will scarcely be credited, as they are always slung at the cabin window, in a bag loaded with cannon-ball, and ready to be sunk at a moment. The fact, however, is as I have stated it, for the dispatches came into my hands, and I read them. The capture, as I was informed, succeeded by the following stratagem:—The captain of the Madame privateer, who spoke English, on coming up with the packet, passed himself for the captain of an English frigate, and invited the captain of the packet on board, which, when done, he sent some of his own hands back, and secured the mail. But be the circumstance of the capture what it may, I speak with certainty as to the government dispatches. They were sent up to Paris, to Count Vergennes, and when Col. Lawrens and myself returned to America, we took the originals to Congress.

By these dispatches I saw into the stupidity of the English cabinet, far more than I otherwise could have done, and I renewed my former design. But Col. Lawrens was so unwilling to return alone; more especially, as among other matters, we had a charge of upwards of two hundred thousand pounds sterling in money, that I gave in to his wishes, and finally gave up my plan. But I am now certain, that if I could have executed it, that it would not have been altogether unsuccessful.

effect, than what relates merely to elections. They are sources of endless contentions in the places where they exist; and they lessen the common rights of national society. A native of England, under the operation of these charters and corporations, cannot be said to be an Englishman in the full sense of the word. He is not free of the nation, in the same manner that a Frenchman is free of France, and an American of America. His rights are circumscribed to the town, and, in some cases, to the parish of his birth; and all other parts, though in his native land, are to him as a foreign country. To acquire a residence in these, he must undergo a local naturalization by purchase, or he is forbidden or expelled the place. This species of feudality is kept up to aggrandize the corporations at the ruin of towns; and the effect is visible.

The generality of corporation towns are in a state of solitary decay, and prevented from further ruin, only by some circumstance in their situation, such as a navigable river, or a plentiful surrounding country. As population is one of the chief sources of wealth, (for without it land itself has no value,) every thing which operates to prevent it must lessen the value of property; and as corporations have not only this tendency, but directly this effect, they cannot but be injurious. If any policy were to be followed, instead of that of general freedom, to every person to settle where he chose, (as in France or America,) it would be more consistent to give encouragement to new comers, than to preclude their admission by exacting premiums from them*.

The persons most immediately interested in the abolition of

---

*It is difficult to account for the origin of charter and corporation towns, unless we suppose them to have arisen out of, or been connected with, some species of garrison service. The times in which they began justify this idea. The generality of those towns have been garrisons; and the corporations were charged with the care of the gates of the towns, when no military garrison was present. Their refusing or granting admission to strangers, which has produced the custom of giving, selling, and buying freedom, has more of the nature of garrison authority than civil government. Soldiers are free of all corporations throughout the nation, by the same propriety that every soldier is free of every garrison, and no other persons are. He can follow any employment, with the permission of his officers, in any corporation town throughout the nation.

corporations, are the inhabitants of the towns where corporations are established. The instances of Manchester, Birmingham, and Sheffield, shew, by contrast, the injury which those Gothic institutions are to property and commerce. A few examples may be found, such as that of London, whose natural and commercial advantage, owing to its situation on the Thames, is capable of bearing up against the political evils of a corporation; but in almost all other cases the fatality is too visible to be doubted or denied.

Though the whole nation is not so directly affected by the depression of property in corporation towns as the inhabitants themselves, it partakes of the consequence. By lessening the value of property, the quantity of national commerce is curtailed. Every man is a customer in proportion to his ability; and as all parts of a nation trade with each other, whatever affects any of the parts, must necessarily communicate to the whole.

As one of the houses of the English parliament is, in a great measure, made up of elections from these corporations; and as it is unnatural that a pure stream should flow from a foul fountain, its vices are but a continuation of the vices of its origin. A man of moral honour and good political principles, cannot submit to the mean drudgery and disgraceful arts, by which such elections are carried. To be a successful candidate, he must be destitute of the qualities that constitute a just legislator: and being thus disciplined to corruption by the mode of entering into parliament, it is not to be expected that the representative should be better than the man.

Mr. Burke, in speaking of the English representation, has advanced as bold a challenge as ever was given in the days of chivalry. "Our representation," says he, "has been found *perfectly adequate to all the purposes* for which a representation of the people can be desired or devised. I defy," continues he, "the enemies of our constitution to shew the contrary."— This declaration from a man, who has been in constant opposition to all the measures of parliament the whole of his political life, a year or two excepted, is most extraordinary; and, comparing him with himself, admits of no other alternative, than that he acted against his judgment as a member, or has declared contrary to it as an author.

But it is not in the representation only that the defects lie, and therefore I proceed in the next place to the aristocracy.

What is called the House of Peers, is constituted on a ground very similar to that, against which there is a law in other cases. It amounts to a combination of persons in one common interest. No reason can be given, why an house of legislation should be composed entirely of men whose occupation consists in letting landed property, than why it should be composed of those who hire, or of brewers, or bakers, or any other separate class of men.

Mr. Burke calls this house, *"the great ground and pillar of security to the landed interest."* Let us examine this idea.

What pillar of security does the landed interest require more than any other interest in the state, or what right has it to a distinct and separate representation from the general interest of a nation? The only use to be made of this power, (and which it has always made,) is to ward off taxes from itself, and throw the burthen upon such articles of consumption by which itself would be least affected.

That this has been the consequence, (and will always be the consequence of constructing governments on combinations,) is evident with respect to England, from the history of its taxes.

Notwithstanding taxes have encreased and multiplied upon every article of common consumption, the land-tax, which more particularly affects this "pillar," has diminished. In 1788, the amount of the land-tax was 1,950,000£. which is half a million less than it produced almost an hundred years ago*, notwithstanding the rentals are in many instances doubled since that period.

Before the coming of the Hanoverians, the taxes were divided in nearly equal proportions between the land and articles of consumption, the land bearing rather the largest share: but since that æra, nearly thirteen millions annually of new taxes have been thrown upon consumption. The consequence of which has been a constant encrease in the number and wretchedness of the poor, and in the amount of the poor-

*See Sir John Sinclair's History of the Revenue. The land-tax in 1646 was £2,473,499.

rates. Yet here again the burthen does not fall in equal proportions on the aristocracy with the rest of the community. Their residences, whether in town or country, are not mixed with the habitations of the poor. They live apart from distress, and the expence of relieving it. It is in manufacturing towns and labouring villages that those burthens press the heaviest; in many of which it is one class of poor supporting another.

Several of the most heavy and productive taxes are so contrived, as to give an exemption to this pillar, thus standing in its own defence. The tax upon beer brewed for sale does not affect the aristocracy, who brew their own beer free of this duty. It falls only on those who have not conveniency or ability to brew, and who must purchase it in small quantities. But what will mankind think of the justice of taxation, when they know, that this tax alone, from which the aristocracy are from circumstances exempt, is nearly equal to the whole of the land-tax, being in the year 1788, and it is not less now, 1,666,152£. and with its proportion of the taxes on malt and hops, it exceeds it.—That a single article, thus partially consumed, and that chiefly by the working part, should be subject to a tax, equal to that on the whole rental of a nation, is, perhaps, a fact not to be paralleled in the histories of revenues.

This is one of the consequences resulting from an house of legislation, composed on the ground of a combination of common interest; for whatever their separate politics as to parties may be, in this they are united. Whether a combination acts to raise the price of any article for sale, or the rate of wages; or whether it acts to throw taxes from itself upon another class of the community, the principle and the effect are the same; and if the one be illegal, it will be difficult to shew that the other ought to exist.

It is to no use to say, that taxes are first proposed in the house of commons; for as the other house has always a negative, it can always defend itself; and it would be ridiculous to suppose that its acquiescence in the measures to be proposed were not understood before hand. Besides which, it has obtained so much influence by borough-traffic, and so many of its relations and connections are distributed on both sides of the commons, as to give it, besides an absolute negative in one house, a preponderancy in the other, in all matters of common concern.

It is difficult to discover what is meant by the *landed interest*, if it does not mean a combination of aristocratical landholders, opposing their own pecuniary interest to that of the farmer, and every branch of trade, commerce, and manufacture. In all other respects it is the only interest that needs no partial protection. It enjoys the general protection of the world. Every individual, high or low, is interested in the fruits of the earth; men, women, and children, of all ages and degrees, will turn out to assist the farmer, rather than a harvest should not be got in; and they will not act thus by any other property. It is the only one for which the common prayer of mankind is put up, and the only one that can never fail from the want of means. It is the interest, not of the policy, but of the existence of man, and when it ceases he must cease to be.

No other interest in a nation stands on the same united support. Commerce, manufactures, arts, sciences, and every thing else, compared with this, are supported but in parts. Their prosperity or their decay has not the same universal influence. When the vallies laugh and sing, it is not the farmer only, but all creation that rejoices. It is a prosperity that excludes all envy; and this cannot be said of any thing else.

Why then does Mr. Burke talk of his house of peers, as the pillar of the landed interest? Were that pillar to sink into the earth, the same landed property would continue, and the same ploughing, sowing, and reaping would go on. The aristocracy are not the farmers who work the land, and raise the produce, but are the mere consumers of the rent; and when compared with the active world, are the drones, a seraglio of males, who neither collect the honey nor form the hive, but exist only for lazy enjoyment.

Mr. Burke, in his first essay, called aristocracy, *"the Corinthian capital of polished society."* Towards compleating the figure, he has now added the *pillar*; but still the base is wanting; and whenever a nation chuses to act a Samson, not blind, but bold, down go the temple of Dagon, the Lords and the Philistines.

If a house of legislation is to be composed of men of one

class, for the purpose of protecting a distinct interest, all the other interests should have the same. The inequality, as well as the burthen of taxation, arises from admitting it in one case, and not in all. Had there been an house of farmers, there had been no game laws; or an house of merchants and manufacturers, the taxes had neither been so unequal nor so excessive. It is from the power of taxation being in the hands of those who can throw so great a part of it from their own shoulders, that it has raged without a check.

Men of small or moderate estates, are more injured by the taxes being thrown on articles of consumption, than they are eased by warding it from landed property, for the following reasons:

First, They consume more of the productive taxable articles, in proportion to their property, than those of large estates.

Secondly, Their residence is chiefly in towns, and their property in houses; and the encrease of the poor-rates, occasioned by taxes on consumption, is in much greater proportion than the land-tax has been favoured. In Birmingham, the poor-rates are not less than seven shillings in the pound. From this, as is already observed, the aristocracy are in a great measure exempt.

These are but a part of the mischiefs flowing from the wretched scheme of an house of peers.

As a combination, it can always throw a considerable portion of taxes from itself; and as an hereditary house, accountable to nobody, it resembles a rotten borough, whose consent is to be courted by interest. There are but few of its members, who are not in some mode or other participaters, or disposers of the public money. One turns a candle-holder, or a lord in waiting; another a lord of the bed-chamber, a groom of the stole, or any insignificant nominal office, to which a salary is annexed, paid out of the public taxes, and which avoids the direct appearance of corruption. Such situations are derogatory to the character of man; and where they can be submitted to, honour cannot reside.

To all these are to be added the numerous dependants, the long list of younger branches and distant relations, who are to be provided for at the public expence: in short, were an estimation to be made of the charge of aristocracy to a nation, it will be found nearly equal to that of supporting the poor. The Duke of Richmond alone (and there are cases similar to his) takes away as much for himself as would maintain two thousand poor and aged persons. Is it, then, any wonder, that under such a system of government, taxes and rates have multiplied to their present extent?

In stating these matters, I speak an open and disinterested language, dictated by no passion but that of humanity. To me, who have not only refused offers, because I thought them improper, but have declined rewards I might with reputation have accepted, it is no wonder that meanness and imposition appear disgustful. Independence is my happiness, and I view things as they are, without regard to place or person; my country is the world, and my religion is to do good.

Mr. Burke, in speaking of the aristocratical law of primogeniture, says, "it is the standing law of our landed inheritance; and which, without question, has a tendency, and I think," continues he, "a happy tendency, to preserve a character of weight and consequence."

Mr. Burke may call this law what he pleases, but humanity and impartial reflection will denounce it a law of brutal injustice. Were we not accustomed to the daily practice, and did we only hear of it as the law of some distant part of the world, we should conclude that the legislators of such countries had not yet arrived at a state of civilization.

As to its preserving a character of *weight and consequence*, the case appears to me directly the reverse. It is an attaint upon character; a sort of privateering on family property. It may have weight among dependent tenants, but it gives none on a scale of national, and, much less of universal character. Speaking for myself, my parents were not able to give me a shilling, beyond what they gave me in education; and to do this they distressed themselves: yet, I possess more of what is called consequence, in the world, than any one in Mr. Burke's catalogue of aristocrats.

Having thus glanced at some of the defects of the two houses of parliament, I proceed to what is called the crown upon which I shall be very concise.

It signifies a nominal office of a million sterling a year, the business of which consists in receiving the money. Whether the person be wise or foolish, sane or insane, a native or a foreigner, matters not. Every ministry acts upon the same idea that Mr. Burke writes, namely, that the people must be hood-winked, and held in superstitious ignorance by some bugbear or other; and what is called the crown answers this purpose, and therefore it answers all the purposes to be expected from it. This is more than can be said of the other two branches.

The hazard to which this office is exposed in all countries, is not from any thing that can happen to the man, but from what may happen to the nation—the danger of its coming to its senses.

It has been customary to call the crown the executive power, and the custom is continued, though the reason has ceased.

It was called the *executive*, because the person whom it signified used, formerly, to fit in the character of a judge, in administering or executing the laws. The tribunals were then a part of the court. The power, therefore, which is now called the judicial, is what was called the executive; and, conse-quently, one or other of the terms is redundant, and one of the offices useless. When we speak of the crown now, it means nothing; it signifies neither a judge nor a general: besides which it is the laws that govern, and not the man. The old terms are kept up, to give an appearance of consequence to empty forms; and the only effect they have is that of increas-ing expences.

Before I proceed to the means of rendering governments more conducive to the general happiness of mankind, than they are at present, it will not be improper to take a review of the progress of taxation in England.

It is a general idea, that when taxes are once laid on, they are never taken off. However true this may have been of late, it was not always so. Either, therefore, the people of former times were more watchful over government than those of the present, or government was administered with less ex-travagance.

It is now seven hundred years since the Norman conquest, and the establishment of what is called the crown. Taking this

portion of time in seven separate periods of one hundred
years each, the amount of the annual taxes, at each period,
will be as follows:—

Annual amount of taxes levied by William the
    Conqueror, beginning in the year 1066, ... £.400,000
Annual amount of taxes at one hundred years
    from the conquest, (1166)   200,000
Annual amount of taxes at two hundred years
    from the conquest, (1266)   150,000
Annual amount of taxes at three hundred years
    from the conquest, (1366)   130,000
Annual amount of taxes at four hundred years
    from the conquest, (1466).   100,000

These statements, and those which follow, are taken from
Sir John Sinclair's History of the Revenue; by which it appears, that taxes continued decreasing for four hundred years,
at the expiration of which time they were reduced three-
fourths, viz. from four hundred thousand pounds to one hundred thousand. The people of England of the present day,
have a traditionary and historical idea of the bravery of their
ancestors; but whatever their virtues or their vices might have
been, they certainly were a people who would not be imposed
upon, and who kept government in awe as to taxation, if not
as to principle. Though they were not able to expel the
monarchical usurpation, they restricted it to a republican
œconomy of taxes.

Let us now review the remaining three hundred years.

Annual amount of taxes at five hundred years
    from the conquest, (1566). . . . . £. 500,000
Annual amount of taxes at six hundred years
    from the conquest, (1666). 1,800,000
Annual amount of taxes at the present
    time, (1791) 17,000,000

The difference between the first four hundred years and the
last three, is so astonishing, as to warrant an opinion, that the
national character of the English has changed. It would have
been impossible to have dragooned the former English, into
the excess of taxation that now exists; and when it is considered that the pay of the army, the navy, and of all the

revenue-officers, is the same now as it was above a hundred years ago, when the taxes were not above a tenth part of what they are at present, it appears impossible to account for the enormous increase and expenditure, on any other ground, than extravagance, corruption, and intrigue*.

With the revolution of 1688, and more so since the

---

*Several of the court newspapers have of late made frequent mention of Wat Tyler. That his memory should be traduced by court sycophants, and all those who live on the spoil of a public, is not to be wondered at. He was, however, the means of checking the rage and injustice of taxation in his time, and the nation owed much to his valour. The history is concisely this:—In the time of Richard the second, a poll-tax was levied, of one shilling per head, upon every person in the nation, of whatever estate or condition, on poor as well as rich, above the age of fifteen years. If any favour was shewn in the law, it was to the rich rather than to the poor; as no person could be charged more than twenty shillings for himself, family, and servants, though ever so numerous; while all other families, under the number of twenty, were charged per head. Poll-taxes had always been odious; but this being also oppressive and unjust, it excited, as it naturally must, universal detestation among the poor and middle classes. The person known by the name of Wat Tyler, whose proper name was Walter, and a tyler by trade, lived at Deptford. The gatherer of the poll-tax, on coming to his house, demanded tax for one of his daughters, whom Tyler declared was under the age of fifteen. The tax-gatherer insisted on satisfying himself, and began an indecent examination of the girl, which enraging the father, he struck him with a hammer, that brought him to the ground, and was the cause of his death.

This circumstance served to bring the discontents to an issue. The inhabitants of the neighbourhood espoused the cause of Tyler, who, in a few days was joined, according to some histories, by upwards of fifty thousand men, and chosen their chief. With this force he marched to London, to demand an abolition of the tax, and a redress of other grievances. The court, finding itself in a forlorn condition, and unable to make resistance, agreed, with Richard at its head, to hold a conference with Tyler in Smithfield, making many fair professions, courtier like, of its dispositions to redress the oppressions. While Richard and Tyler were in conversation on these matters, each being on horseback, Walworth, then mayor of London, and one of the creatures of the court, watched an opportunity, and like a cowardly assassin, stabbed Tyler with a dagger; and two or three others falling upon him, he was instantly sacrificed.

Tyler appears to have been an intrepid disinterested man, with respect to himself. All his proposals made to Richard, were on a more just and public ground, than those which had been made to John by the Barons; and notwithstanding the sycophancy of historians, and men like Mr. Burke, who seek to gloss over a base action of the court by traducing Tyler, his fame will outlive their falsehood. If the Barons merited a monument to be erected in Runnymede, Tyler merits one in Smithfield.

Hanover succession, came the destructive system of continental intrigues, and the rage for foreign wars and foreign dominion; systems of such secure mystery that the expences admit of no accounts; a single line stands for millions. To what excess taxation might have extended, had not the French revolution contributed to break up the system, and put an end to pretences, is impossible to say. Viewed, as that revolution ought to be, as the fortunate means of lessening the load of taxes of both countries, it is of as much importance to England as to France; and, if properly improved to all the advantages of which it is capable, and to which it leads, deserve as much celebration in one country as the other.

In pursuing this subject, I shall begin with the matter that first presents itself, that of lessening the burthen of taxes; and shall then add such matters and propositions, respecting the three countries of England, France, and America, as the present prospect of things appears to justify: I mean, an alliance of the three, for the purposes that will be mentioned in their proper place.

What has happened may happen again. By the statement before shewn of the progress of taxation, it is seen, that taxes have been lessened to a fourth part of what they had formerly been. Though the present circumstances do not admit of the same reduction, yet it admits of such a beginning, as may accomplish that end in less time, than in the former case.

The amount of taxes for the year, ending at Michaelmas 1788, was as follows:

Land-tax, ...	£1,950,000
Customs, ...	3,789,274
Excise, (including old and new malt,) . . .	6,751,727
Stamps, ...	1,278,214
Miscellaneous taxes and incidents,.	1,803,755
	£15,572,970

Since the year 1788, upwards of one million, new taxes, have been laid on, besides the produce from the lotteries; and as the taxes have in general been more productive since than before, the amount may be taken, in round numbers, at £17,000,000.

N. B. The expence of collection and the drawbacks, which together amount to nearly two millions, are paid out of the gross amount; and the above is the nett sum paid into the exchequer.

This sum of seventeen millions is applied to two different purposes; the one to pay the interest of the national debt, the other to the current expences of each year. About nine millions are appropriated to the former; and the remainder, being nearly eight millions, to the latter. As to the million, said to be applied to the reduction of the debt, it is so much like paying with one hand and taking out with the other, as not to merit much notice.

It happened, fortunately for France, that she possessed national domains for paying off her debt, and thereby lessening her taxes: but as this is not the case in England, her reduction of taxes can only take place by reducing the current expences, which may now be done to the amount of four or five millions annually, as will hereafter appear. When this is accomplished, it will more than counterbalance the enormous charge of the American war; and the saving will be from the same source from whence the evil arose.

As to the national debt, however heavy the interest may be in taxes; yet, as it serves to keep alive a capital, useful to commerce, it balances by its effects a considerable part of its own weight; and as the quantity of gold and silver in England is, by some means or other, short of its proper proportion*, (being not more than twenty millions, whereas it should be sixty,) it would, besides the injustice, be bad policy to extinguish a capital that serves to supply that defect. But with respect to the current expence, whatever is saved therefrom is gain. The excess may serve to keep corruption alive, but it has no re-action on credit and commerce, like the interest of the debt.

It is now very probable, that the English government (I do not mean the nation) is unfriendly to the French revolution. Whatever serves to expose the intrigue and lessen the influence of courts, by lessening taxation, will be unwelcome to

*Foreign intrigue, foreign wars, and foreign dominions, will in a great measure account for the deficiency.

those who feed upon the spoil. Whilst the clamour of French intrigue, arbitrary power, popery, and wooden shoes could be kept up, the nation was easily allured and alarmed into taxes. Those days are now past; deception, it is to be hoped, has reaped its last harvest, and better times are in prospect for both countries, and for the world.

Taking it for granted, that an alliance may be formed between England, France, and America, for the purposes hereafter to be mentioned, the national expences of France and England may consequently be lessened. The same fleets and armies will no longer be necessary to either, and the reduction can be made ship for ship on each side. But to accomplish these objects, the governments must necessarily be fitted to a common and correspondent principle. Confidence can never take place, while an hostile disposition remains in either, or where mystery and secrecy on one side, is opposed to candour and openness on the other.

These matters admitted, the national expences might be put back, *for the sake of a precedent*, to what they were at some period when France and England were not enemies. This, consequently, must be prior to the Hanover succession, and also to the revolution of 1688*. The first instance that presents itself, antecedent to those dates, is in the very wasteful and profligate times of Charles the Second; at which time England and France acted as allies. If I have chosen a period of great extravagance, it will serve to shew modern extravagance in a still worse light; especially as the pay of the navy,

---

*I happened to be in England at the celebration of the centenary of the revolution of 1688. The characters of William and Mary have always appeared to me detestable; the one seeking to destroy his uncle, and the other her father, to get possession of power themselves; yet, as the nation was disposed to think something of that event, I felt hurt at seeing it ascribe the whole reputation of it to a man who had undertaken it as a jobb, and who, besides what he otherwise got, charged six hundred thousand pounds for the expence of the little fleet that brought him from Holland. George the First acted the same close-fisted part as William had done, and bought the Duchy of Bremin with the money he got from England, two hundred and fifty thousand pounds over and above his pay as king; and having thus purchased it at the expence of England, added it to his Hanoverian dominions for his own private profit. In fact, every nation that does not govern itself, is governed as a jobb. England has been the prey of jobbs ever since the revolution.

the army, and the revenue officers has not encreased since that time.

The peace establishment was then as follows:—See Sir John Sinclair's History of the Revenue.

Navy,	300,000
Army,	212,000
Ordnance,	40,000
Civil List,	462,115
	£1,014,115

The parliament, however, settled the whole annual peace establishment at 1,200,000*. If we go back to the time of Elizabeth, the amount of all the taxes was but half a million, yet the nation sees nothing during that period, that reproaches it with want of consequence.

All circumstances then taken together, arising from the French revolution, from the approaching harmony and reciprocal interest of the two nations, the abolition of court intrigue on both sides, and the progress of knowledge in the science of government, the annual expenditure might be put back to one million and an half, viz.

Navy,	500,000
Army,	500,000
Expences of government,	500,000
	£1,500,000

Even this sum is six times greater than the expences of government are in America, yet the civil internal government in England, (I mean that administered by means of quarter sessions, juries, and assize, and which, in fact, is nearly the whole, and performed by the nation,) is less expence upon the revenue, than the same species and portion of government is in America.

It is time that nations should be rational, and not be governed like animals, for the pleasure of their riders. To read the history of kings, a man would be almost inclined to suppose that government consisted in stag-hunting, and that every

*Charles, like his predecessors and successors, finding that war was the harvest of governments, engaged in a war with the Dutch, the expence of which encreased the annual expenditure to £1,800,000, as stated under the date of 1666; but the peace establishment was but £1,200,000.

nation paid a million a year to a huntsman. Man ought to
have pride, or shame enough to blush at being thus imposed
upon, and when he feel his proper character, he will. Upon all
subjects of this nature, there is often passing in the mind, a
train of ideas he has not yet accustomed himself to encourage
and communicate. Restrained by something that puts on the
character of prudence, he acts the hypocrite upon himself as
well as to others. It is, however, curious to observe how soon
this spell can be dissolved. A single expression, boldly conceived and uttered, will sometimes put a whole company into
their proper feelings; and whole nations are acted upon in the
same manner.

As to the offices of which any civil government may be
composed, it matters but little by what names they are described. In the rotine of business, as before observed, whether
a man be stiled a president, a king, an emperor, a senator, or
any thing else, it is impossible that any service he can perform,
can merit from a nation more than ten thousand pounds a
year; and as no man should be paid beyond his services, so
every man of a proper heart will not accept more. Public
money ought to be touched with the most scrupulous consciousness of honour. It is not the produce of riches only, but
of the hard earnings of labour and poverty. It is drawn even
from the bitterness of want and misery. Not a beggar passes,
or perishes in the streets, whose mite is not in that mass.

Were it possible that the Congress of America, could be so
lost to their duty, and to the interest of their constituents, as
to offer General Washington, as president of America, a million a year, he would not, and he could not, accept it. His
sense of honour is of another kind. It has cost England almost
seventy millions sterling, to maintain a family imported from
abroad, of very inferior capacity to thousands in the nation;
and scarcely a year has passed that has not produced some
new mercenary application. Even the physicians bills have
been sent to the public to be paid. No wonder that jails are
crowded, and taxes and poor-rates encreased. Under such systems, nothing is to be looked for but what has already happened; and as to reformation, whenever it come, it must be
from the nation, and not from the government.

To shew that the sum of five hundred thousand pounds is

more than sufficient to defray all the expences of government, exclusive of navies and armies, the following estimate is added for any country, of the same extent as England.

In the first place, three hundred representatives, fairly elected, are sufficient for all the purposes to which legislation can apply, and preferable to a larger number. They may be divided into two or three houses, or meet in one, as in France, or in any manner a constitution shall direct.

As representation is always considered, in free countries, as the most honourable of all stations, the allowance made to it is merely to defray the expence which the representatives incur by that service, and not to it as an office.

If an allowance, at the rate of five hundred pounds *per ann.* be made to every representative, deducting for non-attendance, the expence, if the whole number attended for six months, each year, would be . . £. 75,000

The official departments cannot reasonably exceed the following number, with the salaries annexed:

Three offices, at ten thousand pounds each		30,000
Ten ditto,	at £. 5000 each	50,000
Twenty ditto,	at £. 2000 each	40,000
Forty ditto,	at £. 1000 each	40,000
Two hundred ditto,	at £. 500 each	100,000
Three hundred ditto,	at £. 200 each	60,000
Five hundred ditto,	at £. 100 each	50,000
Seven hundred ditto,	at £. 75 each	52,500
		£.497,500

If a nation chuse, it can deduct four *per cent.* from all offices, and make one of twenty thousand *per ann.*

All revenue officers are paid out of the monies they collect, and therefore, are not in this estimation.

The foregoing is not offered as an exact detail of offices, but to shew the number and rate of salaries which five hundred thousand pounds will support; and it will, on experience, be found impracticable to find business sufficient to justify even this expence. As to the manner in which office business is now performed, the Chiefs, in several offices, such as the post-office, and certain offices in the exchequer, &c. do little more than sign their names three or four times a year; and the whole duty is performed by under clerks.

Taking, therefore, one million and an half as a sufficient peace establishment for all the honest purposes of government, which is three hundred thousand pounds more than the peace establishment in the profligate and prodigal times of Charles the Second, (notwithstanding, as has been already observed, the pay and salaries of the army, navy, and revenue officers, continue the same as at that period,) there will remain a surplus of upwards of six millions out of the present current expences. The question then will be, how to dispose of this surplus.

Whoever has observed the manner in which trade and taxes twist themselves together, must be sensible of the impossibility of separating them suddenly.

First. Because the articles now on hand are already charged with the duty, and the reduction cannot take place on the present stock.

Secondly. Because, on all those articles on which the duty is charged in the gross, such as *per* barrel, hogshead, hundred weight, or tun, the abolition of the duty does not admit of being divided down so as fully to relieve the consumer, who purchases by the pint, or the pound. The last duty laid on strong beer and ale, was three shillings *per* barrel, which, if taken off, would lessen the purchase only half a farthing *per* pint, and consequently, would not reach to practical relief.

This being the condition of a great part of the taxes, it will be necessary to look for such others as are free from this embarrassment, and where the relief will be direct and visible, and capable of immediate operation.

In the first place, then, the poor-rates are a direct tax which every house-keeper feels, and who knows also, to a farthing, the sum which he pays. The national amount of the whole of the poor rates is not positively known, but can be procured. Sir John Sinclair, in his History of the Revenue, has stated it at £.2,100,587. A considerable part of which is expended in litigations, in which the poor, instead of being relieved, are tormented. The expence, however, is the same to the parish from whatever cause it arises.

In Birmingham, the amount of the poor-rates is fourteen thousand pounds a year. This, though a large sum, is moderate, compared with the population. Birmingham is said to contain seventy thousand souls, and on a proportion of seventy thousand to fourteen thousand pounds poor-rates, the national amount of poor-rates, taking the population of England at seven millions, would be but one million four hundred thousand pounds. It is, therefore, most probable, that the population of Birmingham is over-rated. Fourteen thousand pounds is the proportion upon fifty thousand souls, taking two millions of poor-rates as the national amount.

Be it, however, what it may, it is no other than the consequence of the excessive burthen of taxes, for, at the time when the taxes were very low, the poor were able to maintain themselves; and there were no poor-rates*. In the present state of things, a labouring man, with a wife and two or three children, does not pay less than between seven and eight pounds a year in taxes. He is not sensible of this, because it is disguised to him in the articles which he buys, and he thinks only of their dearness; but as the taxes take from him, at least, a fourth part of his yearly earnings, he is consequently disabled from providing for a family, especially, if himself, or any of them, are afflicted with sickness.

The first step, therefore, of practical relief, would be to abolish the poor-rates entirely, and in lieu thereof, to make a remission of taxes to the poor of double the amount of the present poor-rates, viz. four millions annually out of the surplus taxes. By this measure, the poor would be benefited two millions, and the house-keepers two millions. This alone would be equal to a reduction of one hundred and twenty millions of the national debt, and consequently equal to the whole expence of the American war.

It will then remain to be considered, which is the most effectual mode of distributing this remission of four millions.

It is easily seen, that the poor are generally composed of large families of children, and old people past their labour. If these two classes are provided for, the remedy will so far reach to the full extent of the case, that what remains will be

---

*Poor-rates began about the time of Henry the Eighth, when the taxes began to encrease, and they have encreased as the taxes encreased ever since.

incidental, and, in a great measure, fall within the compass of benefit clubs, which, though of humble invention, merit to be ranked among the best of modern institutions.

Admitting England to contain seven million of souls; if one-fifth thereof are of that class of poor which need support, the number will be one million four hundred thousand. Of this number, one hundred and forty thousand will be aged poor, as will be hereafter shewn, and for which a distinct provision will be proposed.

There will then remain one million two hundred and sixty thousand, which, at five souls to each family, amount to two hundred and fifty-two thousand families, rendered poor from the expence of children and the weight of taxes.

The number of children under fourteen years of age, in each of those families, will be found to be about five to every two families; some having two, and others three; some one, and others four; some none, and others five; but it rarely happens that more than five are under fourteen years of age, and after this age they are capable of service or of being apprenticed.

Allowing five children (under fourteen years) to every two families,

> The number of children will be 630,000
> The number of parents were they all living,
>   would be 504,000

It is certain, that if the children are provided for, the parents are relieved of consequence, because it is from the expence of bringing up children that their poverty arises.

Having thus ascertained the greatest number that can be supposed to need support on account of young families, I proceed to the mode of relief or distribution, which is,

To pay as a remission of taxes to every poor family, out of the surplus taxes, and in room of poor-rates, four pounds a year for every child under fourteen years of age; enjoining the parents of such children to send them to school, to learn reading, writing, and common arithmetic; the ministers of every parish, of every denomination, to certify jointly to an office, for that purpose, that this duty is performed.

The amount of this expence will be,

For six hundred and thirty thousand children,
    at four pounds *per ann.* each,. . . . . £.2,520,000

By adopting this method, not only the poverty of the parents will be relieved, but ignorance will be banished from the rising generation, and the number of poor will hereafter become less, because their abilities, by the aid of education, will be greater. Many a youth, with good natural genius, who is apprenticed to a mechanical trade, such as a carpenter, joiner, millwright, shipwright, blacksmith, &c. is prevented getting forward the whole of his life, from the want of a little common education when a boy.

I now proceed to the case of the aged.

I divide age into two classes. First, the approach of age beginning at fifty. Secondly, old age commencing at sixty.

At fifty, though the mental faculties of man are in full vigour, and his judgment better than at any preceeding date, the bodily powers for laborious life are on the decline. He cannot bear the same quantity of fatigue as at an earlier period. He begins to earn less, and is less capable of enduring wind and weather; and in those more retired employments where much sight is required, he fails apace, and sees himself, like an old horse, beginning to be turned adrift.

At sixty his labour ought to be over, at least from direct necessity. It is painful to see old age working itself to death, in what are called civilized countries, for daily bread.

To form some judgment of the number of those above fifty years of age, I have several times counted the persons I met in the streets of London, men, women, and children, and have generally found that the average is about one in sixteen or seventeen. If it be said that aged persons do not come much in the streets, so neither do infants; and a great proportion of grown children are in schools, and in work shops as apprentices. Taking then sixteen for a divisor, the whole number of persons, in England, of fifty years and upwards of both sexes, rich and poor, will be four hundred and twenty thousand.

The persons to be provided for out of this gross number will be, husbandmen, common labourers, journeymen of every trade and their wives, sailors, and disbanded soldiers, worn out servants of both sexes, and poor widows.

There will be also a considerable number of middling tradesmen, who having lived decently in the former part of life, begin, as age approaches, to lose their business, and at last fall to decay.

Besides these, there will be constantly thrown off from the revolutions of that wheel, which no man can stop, nor regulate, a number from every class of life connected with commerce and adventure.

To provide for all those accidents, and whatever else may befal, I take the number of persons, who at one time or other of their lives, after fifty years of age, may feel it necessary or comfortable to be better supported, than they can support themselves, and that not as a matter of grace and favour, but of right, at one third of the whole number, which is one hundred and forty thousand, as stated in page 626, and for whom a distinct provision was proposed to be made. If there be more, society, notwithstanding the shew and pomposity of government, is in a deplorable condition in England.

Of this one hundred and forty thousand, I take one half, seventy thousand, to be of the age of fifty and under sixty, and the other half to be sixty years and upwards.—Having thus ascertained the probable proportion of the number of aged persons, I proceed to the mode of rendering their condition comfortable, which is,

To pay to every such person of the age of fifty years, and until he shall arrive at the age of sixty, the sum of six pounds *per ann.* out of the surplus taxes; and ten pounds *per ann.* during life after the age of sixty. The expence of which will be,

Seventy thousand persons at £.6 *per ann.*   420,000
Seventy thousand ditto at £.10 *per ann.* 700,000
                                                    £.1,120,000

This support, as already remarked, is not of the nature of a charity, but of a right. Every person in England, male and female, pays on an average in taxes, two pounds eight shillings and sixpence *per ann.* from the day of his (or her) birth; and, if the expence of collection be added, he pays two pounds eleven shillings and sixpence; consequently, at the end of fifty years he has paid one hundred and twenty-eight pounds fifteen shillings; and at sixty, one hundred and fifty-four pounds ten shillings. Converting, therefore, his (or her) individual tax into a tontine, the money he shall receive after fifty years, is but little more than the legal interest of the nett money he has paid; the rest is made up from those whose circumstances do not require them to draw such support, and the capital in both cases defrays the expences of government. It is on this ground that I have extended the probable claims to one third of the number of aged persons in the nation.—Is it then better that the lives of one hundred and forty thousand aged persons be rendered comfortable, or that a million a year of public money be expended on any one individual, and him often of the most worthless or insignificant character? Let reason and justice, let honour and humanity, let even hypocrisy, sycophancy and Mr. Burke, let George, let Louis, Leopold, Frederic, Catharine, Cornwallis, or Tippoo Saib, answer the question*.

The sum thus remitted to the poor will be,

To two hundred and fifty-two thousand poor families, containing six hundred and thirty thousand children,. . 2,520,000
To one hundred and forty thousand
   aged persons, ... 1,120,000
                                £3,640,000

*Reckoning the taxes by families, five to a family, each family pays on an average, 12*l.* 17*s.* 6*d.* *per ann.* to this sum are to be added the poor-rates. Though all pay taxes in the articles they consume, all do not pay poor-rates. About two millions are exempted, some as not being house-keepers, others as not being able, and the poor themselves who receive the relief. The average, therefore, of poor-rates on the remaining number, is forty shillings for every family of five persons, which makes the whole average amount of taxes and rates, 14*l.* 17*s.* 6*d.* For six persons, 17*l.* 17*s.* For seven persons, 20*l.* 16*s.* 6*d.*

The average of taxes in America, under the new or representative system of government, including the interest of the debt contracted in the war, and taking the population at four million of souls, which it now amounts to, and it is daily encreasing, is five shillings per head, men, women, and children. The difference, therefore, between the two governments, is as under,

	England.			America.		
	l.	*s.*	*d.*	*l.*	*s.*	*d.*
For a family of five persons.	14	17	6	1	5	0
For a family of six persons	17	17	0	1	10	0
For a family of seven persons	20	16	6	1	15	0

There will then remain three hundred and sixty thousand pounds out of the four millions, part of which may be applied as follows:

After all the above cases are provided for, there will still be a number of families who, though not properly of the class of poor, yet find it difficult to give education to their children; and such children, under such a case, would be in a worse condition than if their parents were actually poor. A nation under a well regulated government, should permit none to remain uninstructed. It is monarchical and aristocratical government only that requires ignorance for its support.

Suppose then four hundred thousand children to be in this condition, which is a greater number than ought to be supposed, after the provisions already made, the method will be,

To allow for each of those children ten shillings a year for the expence of schooling, for six years each, which will give them six months schooling each year, and half a crown a year for paper and spelling books.

The expence of this will be annually* £250,000.

There will then remain one hundred and ten thousand pounds.

Notwithstanding the great modes of relief which the best instituted and best principled government may devise, there will still be a number of smaller cases, which it is good policy as well as beneficence in a nation to consider.

Were twenty shillings to be given to every woman immediately on the birth of a child, who should make the demand,

*Public schools do not answer the general purpose of the poor. They are chiefly in corporation towns, from which the country towns and villages are excluded; or if admitted, the distance occasions a great loss of time. Education, to be useful to the poor, should be on the spot; and the best method, I believe, to accomplish this, is to enable the parents to pay the expence themselves. There are always persons of both sexes to be found in every village, especially when growing into years, capable of such an undertaking. Twenty children, at ten shillings each, (and that not more than six months each year) would be as much as some livings amount to in the remote parts of England; and there are often distressed clergymen's widows to whom such an income would be acceptable. Whatever is given on this account to children answers two purposes, to them it is education, to those who educate them it is a livelihood.

and none will make it whose circumstances do not require it, it might relieve a great deal of instant distress.

There are about two hundred thousand births yearly in England; and if claimed, by one fourth,

The amount would be 50,000

And twenty shillings to every new-married couple who should claim in like manner. This would not exceed the sum of £20,000.

Also twenty thousand pounds to be appropriated to defray the funeral expences of persons, who, travelling for work, may die at a distance from their friends. By relieving parishes from this charge, the sick stranger will be better treated.

I shall finish this part of the subject with a plan adapted to the particular condition of a metropolis, such as London.

Cases are continually occurring in a metropolis different to those which occur in the country, and for which a different, or rather an additional mode of relief is necessary. In the country, even in large towns, people have a knowledge of each other, and distress never rises to that extreme height it sometimes does in a metropolis. There is no such thing in the country as persons, in the literal sense of the word, starved to death, or dying with cold from the want of a lodging. Yet such cases, and others equally as miserable, happen in London.

Many a youth comes up to London full of expectations, and with little or no money, and unless he gets immediate employment he is already half undone; and boys bred up in London without any means of a livelihood, and as it often happens of dissolute parents, are in a still worse condition; and servants long out of place are not much better off. In short, a world of little cases are continually arising, which busy or affluent life knows not of, to open the first door to distress. Hunger is not among the postponeable wants, and a day, even a few hours, in such a condition, is often the crisis of a life of ruin.

These circumstances, which are the general cause of the little thefts and pilferings that lead to greater, may be prevented. There yet remain twenty thousand pounds out of the four millions of surplus taxes, which, with another fund hereafter to be mentioned, amounting to about twenty thousand pounds more, cannot be better applied than to this purpose. The plan then will be,

First, To erect two or more buildings, or take some already erected, capable of containing at least six thousand persons, and to have in each of these places as many kinds of employment as can be contrived, so that every person who shall come may find something which he or she can do.

Secondly, To receive all who shall come, without enquiring who or what they are. The only condition to be, that for so much, or so many hours work, each person shall receive so many meals of wholesome food, and a warm lodging, at least as good as a barrack. That a certain portion of what each person's work shall be worth shall be reserved, and given to him, or her, on their going away; and that each person shall stay as long, or as short time, or come as often as he chuse, on these conditions.

If each person staid three months, it would assist by rotation twenty-four thousand persons annually, though the real number, at all times, would be but six thousand. By establishing an asylum of this kind, such persons to whom temporary distresses occur, would have an opportunity to recruit themselves, and be enabled to look out for better employment.

Allowing that their labour paid but one half the expence of supporting them, after reserving a portion of their earnings for themselves, the sum of forty thousand pounds additional would defray all other charges for even a greater number than six thousand.

The fund very properly convertible to this purpose, in addition to the twenty thousand pounds, remaining of the former fund, will be the produce of the tax upon coals, and so iniquitously and wantonly applied to the support of the Duke of Richmond. It is horrid that any man, more especially at the price coals now are, should live on the distresses of a community; and any government permitting such an abuse, deserves to be dismissed. This fund is said to be about twenty thousand pounds *per annum*.

I shall now conclude this plan with enumerating the several particulars, and then proceed to other matters.

The enumeration is as follows:

First, Abolition of two million poor-rates.

Secondly, Provision for two hundred and fifty-two thousand poor families.

Thirdly, Education for one million and thirty thousand children.

Fourthly, Comfortable provision for one hundred and forty thousand aged persons.

Fifthly, Donation of twenty shillings each for fifty thousand births.

Sixthly, Donation of twenty shillings each for twenty thousand marriages.

Seventhly, Allowance of twenty thousand pounds for the funeral expences of persons travelling for work, and dying at a distance from their friends.

Eighthly, Employment, at all times, for the casual poor in the cities of London and Westminster.

By the operation of this plan, the poor laws, those instruments of civil torture, will be superceded, and the wasteful expence of litigation prevented. The hearts of the humane will not be shocked by ragged and hungry children, and persons of seventy and eighty years of age begging for bread. The dying poor will not be dragged from place to place to breathe their last, as a reprisal of parish upon parish. Widows will have a maintenance for their children, and not be carted away, on the death of their husbands, like culprits and criminals; and children will no longer be considered as encreasing the distresses of their parents. The haunts of the wretched will be known, because it will be to their advantage, and the number of petty crimes, the offspring of distress and poverty, will be lessened. The poor, as well as the rich, will then be interested in the support of government, and the cause and apprehension of riots and tumults will cease.—Ye who sit in ease, and solace yourselves in plenty, and such there are in Turkey and Russia, as well as in England, and who say to yourselves, "Are we not well off," have ye thought of these things? When ye do, ye will cease to speak and feel for yourselves alone.

The plan is easy in practice. It does not embarrass trade by a sudden interruption in the order of taxes, but effects the relief by changing the application of them; and the money necessary for the purpose can be drawn from the excise collections, which are made eight times a year in every market town in England.

Having now arranged and concluded this subject, I proceed to the next.

Taking the present current expences at seven millions and an half, which is the least amount they are now at, there will remain (after the sum of one million and an half be taken for the new current expences, and four millions for the beforementioned service) the sum of two millions; part of which to be applied as follows:

Though fleets and armies, by an alliance with France, will, in a great measure, become useless, yet the persons who have devoted themselves to those services, and have thereby unfitted themselves for other lines of life, are not to be sufferers by the means that make others happy. They are a different description of men to those who form or hang about a court.

A part of the army will remain at least for some years, and also of the navy, for which a provision is already made in the former part of this plan of one million, which is almost half a million more than the peace establishment of the army and navy in the prodigal times of Charles the Second.

Suppose then fifteen thousand soldiers to be disbanded, and to allow to each of those men three shillings a week during life, clear of all deductions, to be paid in the same manner as the Chelsea College pensioners are paid, and for them to return to their trades and their friends; and also to add fifteen thousand sixpences per week to the pay of the soldiers who shall remain; the annual expence will be,

To the pay of fifteen thousand disbanded soldiers, at three shillings per week, ...	£117,000
Additional pay to the remaining soldiers, ...	19,500
Suppose that the pay to the officers of the disbanded corps be of the same amount as the sum allowed to the men,.	117,000
To prevent bulky estimations, admit the same sum to the disbanded navy as to the army, and the same increase of pay,.	253,500
Total	£507,000

Every year some part of this sum of half a million (I omit the odd seven thousand pounds for the purpose of keeping the account unembarrassed) will fall in, and the whole of it in time, as it is on the ground of life annuities, except the encreased pay of twenty-nine thousand pounds. As it falls in, a part of the taxes may be taken off; for instance, when thirty thousand pounds fall in the duty on hops may be wholly taken off; and as other parts fall in, the duties on candles and soap may be lessened, till at last they will totally cease.

There now remains at least one million and an half of surplus taxes.

The tax on houses and windows is one of those direct taxes, which, like the poor-rates, is not confounded with trade; and, when taken off, the relief will be instantly felt. This tax falls heavy on the middling class of people.

The amount of this tax by the returns of 1788, was,

		l.	s.	d.
Houses and windows by the act of 1766, ...		385,459	11	7
Ditto ditto by the act of 1779,. . . .		130,739	14	5½
Total		516,199	6	0½

If this tax be struck off, there will then remain about one million of surplus taxes, and as it is always proper to keep a sum in reserve, for incidental matters, it may be best not to extend reductions further, in the first instance, but to consider what may be accomplished by other modes of reform.

Among the taxes most heavily felt is the commutation tax. I shall, therefore, offer a plan for its abolition, by substituting another in its place, which will affect three objects at once:

First, That of removing the burthen to where it can best be borne.

Secondly, Restoring justice among families by a distribution of property.

Thirdly, Extirpating the overgrown influence arising from

the unnatural law of primogeniture, and which is one of the
principal sources of corruption at elections.

    The amount of the commutation tax by
        the returns of 1788, was, ...   £ 771,657   0   0

  When taxes are proposed, the country is amused by the
plausible language of taxing luxuries. One thing is called a
luxury at one time, and something else at another; but the
real luxury does not consist in the article, but in the means of
procuring it, and this is always kept out of sight.

  I know not why any plant or herb of the field should be a
greater luxury in one country than another, but an overgrown
estate in either is a luxury at all times, and as such is the
proper object of taxation. It is, therefore, right to take those
kind tax-making gentlemen up on their own word, and argue
on the principle themselves have laid down, that of *taxing
luxuries*. If they, or their champion Mr. Burke, who, I fear, is
growing out of date like the man in armour, can prove that an
estate of twenty, thirty, or forty thousand pounds a year is not
a luxury, I will give up the argument.

  Admitting that any annual sum, say for instance, one
thousand pounds, is necessary or sufficient for the support of
a family, consequently the second thousand is of the nature
of a luxury, the third still more so, and by proceeding on,
we shall at last arrive at a sum that may not improperly be
called a prohibitable luxury. It would be impolitic to set
bounds to property acquired by industry, and therefore it is
right to place the prohibition beyond the probable acquisition to which industry can extend; but there ought to be a
limit to property, or the accumulation of it, by bequest. It
should pass in some other line. The richest in every nation
have poor relations, and those often very near in consan-
guinity.

  The following table of progressive taxation is constructed
on the above principles, and as a substitute for the commutation tax. It will reach the point of prohibition by a regular
operation, and thereby supercede the aristocratical law of
primogeniture.

TABLE I.

A tax on all estates of the clear yearly value of fifty pounds, after deducting the land tax, and up.

	s.	d.	
To £ 500	0	3	per pound
From 500 to 1000	0	6	per pound
On the second thousand	0	9	per pound
On the third ditto	1	0	per pound
On the fourth ditto	1	6	per pound
On the fifth ditto	2	0	per pound
On the sixth ditto	3	0	per pound
On the seventh ditto	4	0	per pound
On the eighth ditto	5	0	per pound
On the ninth ditto	6	0	per pound
On the tenth ditto	7	0	per pound
On the eleventh ditto.	8	0	per pound
On the twelfth ditto	9	0	per pound
On the thirteenth ditto	10	0	per pound
On the fourteenth ditto.	11	0	per pound
On the fifteenth ditto.	12	0	per pound
On the sixteenth ditto	13	0	per pound
On the seventeenth ditto	14	0	per pound
On the eighteenth ditto.	15	0	per pound
On the nineteenth ditto.	16	0	per pound
On the twentieth ditto	17	0	per pound
On the twenty-first ditto	18	0	per pound
On the twenty-second ditto	19	0	per pound
On the twenty-third ditto	20	0	per pound

The foregoing table shews the progression per pound on every progressive thousand. The following table shews the amount of the tax on every thousand separately, and in the last column, the total amount of all the separate sums collected.

TABLE II.

		d.		l.	s.	d.
An estate of £ 50	*per ann.* at	3	per pd. pays	0	12	6
100		3		1	5	0
200		3		2	10	0
300		3		3	15	0
400		3		5	0	0
500		3		7	5	0

After 500*l.* — the tax of sixpence per pound takes place on the second 500*l.* — consequently an estate of 1000*l. per ann.* pays 21*l.* 15*s.* and so on,

			l.	*s.*	*d.*		*l.*	*s.*	*l.*	*s.*
									Total amount.	
For the	1st	500 at	0	3	per pound		7	5	21	15
	2d	500 at	0	6			14	10		
	2d	1000 at	0	9			37	10	59	5
	3d	1000 at	1	0			50	0	109	5
	4th	1000 at	1	6			75	0	184	5
	5th	1000 at	2	0			100	0	284	5
	6th	1000 at	3	0			150	0	434	5
	7th	1000 at	4	0			200	0	634	5
	8th	1000 at	5	0			250	0	880	5
	9th	1000 at	6	0			300	0	1180	5
	10th	1000 at	7	0			350	0	1530	5
	11th	1000 at	8	0			400	0	1930	5
	12th	1000 at	9	0			450	0	2380	5
	13th	1000 at	10	0			500	0	2880	5
	14th	1000 at	11	0			550	0	3430	5
	15th	1000 at	12	0			600	0	4030	5
	16th	1000 at	13	0			650	0	4680	5
	17th	1000 at	14	0			700	0	5380	5
	18th	1000 at	15	0			750	0	6130	5
	19th	1000 at	16	0			800	0	6930	5
	20th	1000 at	17	0			850	0	7780	5
	21st	1000 at	18	0			900	0	8680	5
	22d	1000 at	19	0			950	0	9630	5
	23d	1000 at	20	0			1000	0	10630	5

At the twenty-third thousand the tax becomes twenty shillings in the pound, and consequently every thousand beyond that sum can produce no profit but by dividing the estate. Yet formidable as this tax appears, it will not, I believe, produce so much as the commutation tax; should it produce more, it ought to be lowered to that amount upon estates under two or three thousand a year.

On small and middling estates it is lighter (as it is intended to be) than the commutation tax. It is not till after seven or eight thousand a year that it begins to be heavy. The object is not so much the produce of the tax, as the justice of the measure. The aristocracy has screened itself too much, and this serves to restore a part of the lost equilibrium.

As an instance of its screening itself, it is only necessary to look back to the first establishment of the excise laws, at what is called the Restoration, or the coming of Charles the Second. The aristocratical interest then in power, commuted the feudal services itself was under by laying a tax on beer brewed for *sale*; that is, they compounded with Charles for an exemption from those services for themselves and their heirs, by a tax to be paid by other people. The aristocracy do not purchase beer brewed for sale, but brew their own beer free of the duty, and if any commutation at that time were necessary, it ought to have been at the expence of those for whom the exemptions from those services were intended*; instead of which it was thrown on an entire different class of men.

But the chief object of this progressive tax (besides the justice of rendering taxes more equal than they are) is, as already stated, to extirpate the overgrown influence arising from the unnatural law of primogeniture, and which is one of the principal sources of corruption at elections.

It would be attended with no good consequences to enquire how such vast estates as thirty, forty, or fifty thousand a year could commence, and that at a time when commerce and manufactures were not in a state to admit of such acquisitions. Let it be sufficient to remedy the evil by putting them in a condition of descending again to the community, by the quiet means of apportioning them among all the heirs and heiresses of those families. This will be the more necessary, because hitherto the aristocracy have quartered their younger children and connections upon the public in useless posts, places, and offices, which when abolished will leave them destitute, unless the law of primogeniture be also abolished or superceded.

A progressive tax will, in a great measure, effect this object, and that as a matter of interest to the parties most immedi-

---

*The tax on beer brewed for sale, from which the aristocracy are exempt, is almost one million more than the present commutation tax, being by the returns of 1788, 1,666,152*l.* and consequently they ought to take on themselves the amount of the commutation tax, as they are already exempted from one which is almost one million greater.

ately concerned, as will be seen by the following table; which shews the nett produce upon every estate, after subtracting the tax. By this it will appear, that after an estate exceeds thirteen or fourteen thousand a year, the remainder produces but little profit to the holder, and consequently will pass either to the younger children, or to other kindred.

TABLE III.

Shewing the nett produce of every estate from one thousand to twenty-three thousand pounds a year.

No. of thousands per ann.	Total tax subtracted. £.	Nett produce. £.
1000	21	979
2000	59	1941
3000	109	2891
4000	184	3816
5000	284	4716
6000	434	5566
7000	634	6366
8000	880	7120
9000	1180	7820
10,000	1530	8470
11,000	1930	9070
12,000	2380	9620
13,000	2880	10,120
14,000	3430	10,570
15,000	4030	10,970
16,000	4680	11,320
17,000	5380	11,620
18,000	6130	11,870
19,000	6930	12,170
20,000	7780	12,220
21,000	8680	12,320
22,000	9630	12,370
23,000	10,630	12,370

N. B. The odd shillings are dropped in this table.

According to this table, an estate cannot produce more than 12,370l. clear of the land tax and the progressive tax, and therefore the dividing such estates will follow as a matter of family interest. An estate of 23,000l. a year, divided into five estates of four thousand each and one of three, will be charged only 1129*l.* which is but five *per cent.* but if held by one possessor will be charged 10,630*l.*

Although an enquiry into the origin of those estates be unnecessary, the continuation of them in their present state is another subject. It is a matter of national concern. As hereditary estates, the law has created the evil, and it ought also to provide the remedy. Primogeniture ought to be abolished, not only because it is unnatural and unjust, but because the country suffers by its operation. By cutting off (as before observed) the younger children from their proper portion of inheritance, the public is loaded with the expence of maintaining them; and the freedom of elections violated by the overbearing influence which this unjust monopoly of family property produces. Nor is this all. It occasions a waste of national property. A considerable part of the land of the country is rendered unproductive by the great extent of parks and chases which this law serves to keep up, and this at a time when the annual production of grain is not equal to the national consumption*.—In short, the evils of the aristocratical system are so great and numerous, so inconsistent with every thing that is just, wise, natural, and beneficent, that when they are considered, there ought not to be a doubt that many, who are now classed under that description, will wish to see such a system abolished.

What pleasure can they derive from contemplating the exposed condition, and almost certain beggary of their younger offspring? Every aristocratical family has an appendage of family beggars hanging round it, which in a few ages, or a few generations, are shook off, and console themselves with telling their tale in alms-houses, work-houses, and prisons. This is the natural consequence of aristocracy. The peer and the beggar are often of the same family. One extreme produces the other: to make one rich many must be made poor; neither can the system be supported by other means.

There are two classes of people to whom the laws of England are particularly hostile, and those the most helpless; younger children and the poor. Of the former I have just

---

*See the reports on the corn trade.

spoken; of the latter I shall mention one instance out of the many that might be produced, and with which I shall close this subject.

Several laws are in existence for regulating and limiting workmen's wages. Why not leave them as free to make their own bargains, as the law-makers are to let their farms and houses? Personal labour is all the property they have. Why is that little, and the little freedom they enjoy to be infringed? But the injustice will appear stronger, if we consider the operation and effect of such laws. When wages are fixed by what is called a law, the legal wages remain stationary, while every thing else is in progression; and as those who make that law, still continue to lay on new taxes by other laws, they encrease the expence of living by one law, and take away the means by another.

But if those gentlemen law-makers and tax-makers thought it right to limit the poor pittance which personal labour can produce, and on which a whole family is to be supported, they certainly must feel themselves happily indulged in a limitation on their own part, of not less than twelve thousand a year, and that of property they never acquired, (nor probably any of their ancestors) and of which they have made so ill a use.

Having now finished this subject, I shall bring the several particulars into one view, and then proceed to other matters.

The first EIGHT ARTICLES are brought forward from page 633.

1. Abolition of two million poor-rates.

2. Provision for two hundred and fifty-two thousand poor families, at the rate of four pounds per head for each child under fourteen years of age; which, with the addition of two hundred and fifty thousand pounds, provides also education for one million and thirty thousand children.

3. Annuity of six pounds (per ann.) each for all poor persons, decayed tradesmen, or others (supposed seventy thousand) of the age of fifty years, and until sixty.

4. Annuity of ten pounds each for life for all poor persons, decayed tradesmen, and others (supposed seventy thousand) of the age of sixty years.

5. Donation of twenty shillings each for fifty thousand births.

6. Donation of twenty shillings each for twenty thousand marriages.

7. Allowance of twenty thousand pounds for the funeral expences of persons travelling for work, and dying at a distance from their friends.

8. Employment at all times for the casual poor in the cities of London and Westminster.

SECOND ENUMERATION:

9. Abolition of the tax on houses and windows.

10. Allowance of three shillings per week for life to fifteen thousand disbanded soldiers, and a proportionable allowance to the officers of the disbanded corps.

11. Encrease of pay to the remaining soldiers of 19,500*l.* annually.

12. The same allowance to the disbanded navy, and the same encrease of pay, as to the army.

13. Abolition of the commutation tax.

14. Plan of a progressive tax, operating to extirpate the unjust and unnatural law of primogeniture, and the vicious influence of the aristocratical system*.

There yet remains, as already stated, one million of surplus

---

*When enquiries are made into the condition of the poor, various degrees of distress will most probably be found, to render a different arrangement preferable to that which is already proposed. Widows with families will be in greater want than where there are husbands living. There is also a difference in the expence of living in different countries; and more so in fuel.

	£.
Suppose then fifty thousand extraordinary cases, at the rate of 10*l.* per family per ann..	500,000
100,000 Families, at 8*l.* per family per ann.	800,000
100,000 Families, at 7*l.* per family per ann.	700,000
104,000 Families, at 5*l.* per family per ann.	520,000
And instead of ten shillings per head for the education of other children, to allow fifty shillings per family for that purpose to fifty thousand families	250,000
	2,770,000
140,000 Aged persons as before,.	1,120,000
	3,890,000

This arrangement amounts to the same sum as stated in page 629, including the 250,000*l.* for education; but it provides (including the aged people) for four hundred and four thousand families, which is almost one third of all the families in England.

taxes. Some part of this will be required for circumstances that do not immediately present themselves, and such part as shall not be wanted, will admit a further reduction of taxes equal to that amount.

Among the claims that justice requires to be made, the condition of the inferior revenue officers will merit attention. It is a reproach to any government to waste such an immensity of revenue in sinecures and nominal and unnecessary places and offices, and not allow even a decent livelihood to those on whom the labour falls. The salary of the inferior officers of the revenue has stood at the petty pittance of less than fifty pounds a year for upwards of one hundred years. It ought to be seventy. About one hundred and twenty thousand pounds applied to this purpose, will put all those salaries in a decent condition.

This was proposed to be done almost twenty years ago, but the treasury-board then in being startled at it, as it might lead to similar expectations from the army and navy; and the event was, that the King, or somebody for him, applied to parliament to have his own salary raised an hundred thousand a year, which being done, every thing else was laid aside.

With respect to another class of men, the inferior clergy, I forbear to enlarge on their condition; but all partialities and prejudices for, or against, different modes and forms of religion aside, common justice will determine, whether there ought to be an income of twenty or thirty pounds a year to one man, and of ten thousand to another. I speak on this subject with the more freedom, because I am known not to be a Presbyterian; and therefore the cant cry of court sycophants, about church and meeting, kept up to amuse and bewilder the nation, cannot be raised against me.

Ye simple men, on both sides the question, do ye not see through this courtly craft? If ye can be kept disputing and wrangling about church and meeting, ye just answer the purpose of every courtier, who lives the while on the spoil of the taxes, and laughs at your credulity. Every religion is good that teaches man to be good; and I know of none that instructs him to be bad.

All the before-mentioned calculations, suppose only sixteen

millions and an half of taxes paid into the exchequer, after the expence of collection and drawbacks at the custom-house and excise-office are deducted; whereas the sum paid into the exchequer is very nearly, if not quite, seventeen millions. The taxes raised in Scotland and Ireland are expended in those countries, and therefore their savings will come out of their own taxes; but if any part be paid into the English exchequer, it might be remitted. This will not make one hundred thousand pounds a year difference.

There now remains only the national debt to be considered. In the year 1789, the interest, exclusive of the tontine, was 9,150,138*l.* How much the capital has been reduced since that time the minister best knows. But after paying the interest, abolishing the tax on houses and windows, the commutation tax, and the poor rates; and making all the provisions for the poor, for the education of children, the support of the aged, the disbanded part of the army and navy, and encreasing the pay of the remainder, there will be a surplus of one million.

The present scheme of paying off the national debt appears to me, speaking as an indifferent person, to be an ill-concerted, if not a fallacious job. The burthen of the national debt consists not in its being so many millions, or so many hundred millions, but in the quantity of taxes collected every year to pay the interest. If this quantity continue the same, the burthen of the national debt is the same to all intents and purposes, be the capital more or less. The only knowledge which the public can have of the reduction of the debt, must be through the reduction of taxes for paying the interest. The debt, therefore, is not reduced one farthing to the public by all the millions that have been paid; and it would require more money now to purchase up the capital, than when the scheme began.

Digressing for a moment at this point, to which I shall return again, I look back to the appointment of Mr. Pitt, as minister.

I was then in America. The war was over; and though resentment had ceased, memory was still alive.

When the news of the coalition arrived, though it was a matter of no concern to me as a citizen of America, I felt it as a man. It had something in it which shocked, by publicly sporting with decency, if not with principle. It was impudence in Lord North; it was want of firmness in Mr. Fox.

Mr. Pitt was, at that time, what may be called a maiden character in politics. So far from being hackneyed, he appeared not to be initiated into the first mysteries of court intrigue. Every thing was in his favour. Resentment against the coalition served as friendship to him, and his ignorance of vice was credited for virtue. With the return of peace, commerce and prosperity would rise of itself; yet even this encrease was thrown to his account.

When he came to the helm the storm was over, and he had nothing to interrupt his course. It required even ingenuity to be wrong, and he succeeded. A little time shewed him the same sort of man as his predecessors had been. Instead of profiting by those errors which had accumulated a burthen of taxes unparalleled in the world, he sought, I might almost say, he advertised for enemies, and provoked means to encrease taxation. Aiming at something, he knew not what, he ransacked Europe and India for adventures, and abandoning the fair pretensions he began with, became the knight-errant of modern times.

It is unpleasant to see character throw itself away. It is more so to see one's-self deceived. Mr. Pitt had merited nothing, but he promised much. He gave symptoms of a mind superior to the meanness and corruption of courts. His apparent candour encouraged expectations; and the public confidence, stunned, wearied, and confounded by a chaos of parties, revived and attached itself to him. But mistaking, as he has done, the disgust of the nation against the coalition, for merit in himself, he has rushed into measures, which a man less supported would not have presumed to act.

All this seems to shew that change of ministers amounts to nothing. One goes out, another comes in, and still the same measures, vices, and extravagance are pursued. It signifies not who is minister. The defect lies in the system. The foundation and the superstructure of the government is bad. Prop it as you please, it continually sinks into court government, and ever will.

I return, as I promised, to the subject of the national debt, that offspring of the Dutch-Anglo revolution, and its hand-maid the Hanover succession.

But it is now too late to enquire how it began. Those to whom it is due have advanced the money; and whether it was well or ill spent, or pocketed, is not their crime. It is, however, easy to see, that as the nation proceeds in contemplating the nature and principles of government, and to understand taxes, and make comparisons between those of America, France, and England, it will be next to impossible to keep it in the same torpid state it has hitherto been. Some reform must, from the necessity of the case, soon begin. It is not whether these principles press with little or much force in the present moment. They are out. They are abroad in the world, and no force can stop them. Like a secret told, they are beyond recall; and he must be blind indeed that does not see that a change is already beginning.

Nine millions of dead taxes is a serious thing; and this not only for bad, but in a great measure for foreign government. By putting the power of making war into the hands of foreigners who came for what they could get, little else was to be expected than what has happened.

Reasons are already advanced in this work shewing that whatever the reforms in the taxes may be, they ought to be made in the current expences of government, and not in the part applied to the interest of the national debt. By remitting the taxes of the poor, *they* will be totally relieved, and all discontent on their part will be taken away; and by striking off such of the taxes as are already mentioned, the nation will more than recover the whole expence of the mad American war.

There will then remain only the national debt as a subject of discontent; and in order to remove, or rather to prevent this, it would be good policy in the stock-holders themselves to consider it as property, subject like all other property, to bear some portion of the taxes. It would give to it both popularity and security, and as a great part of its present inconvenience is balanced by the capital which it keeps alive, a measure of this kind would so far add to that balance as to silence objections.

This may be done by such gradual means as to accomplish all that is necessary with the greatest ease and convenience.

Instead of taxing the capital, the best method would be to tax the interest by some progressive ratio, and to lessen the public taxes in the same proportion as the interest diminished.

Suppose the interest was taxed one halfpenny in the pound the first year, a penny more the second, and to proceed by a certain ratio to be determined upon, always less than any other tax upon property. Such a tax would be subtracted from the interest at the time of payment, without any expence of collection.

One halfpenny in the pound would lessen the interest and consequently the taxes, twenty thousand pounds. The tax on waggons amounts to this sum, and this tax might be taken off the first year. The second year the tax on female servants, or some other of the like amount might also be taken off, and by proceeding in this manner, always applying the tax raised from the property of the debt towards its extinction, and not carry it to the current services, it would liberate itself.

The stockholders, notwithstanding this tax, would pay less taxes than they do now. What they would save by the extinction of the poor-rates, and the tax on houses and windows, and the commutation tax, would be considerably greater than what this tax, slow, but certain in its operation, amounts to.

It appears to me to be prudence to look out for measures that may apply under any circumstance that may approach. There is, at this moment, a crisis in the affairs of Europe that requires it. Preparation now is wisdom. If taxation be once let loose, it will be difficult to re-instate it; neither would the relief be so effectual, as to proceed by some certain and gradual reduction.

The fraud, hypocrisy, and imposition of governments, are now beginning to be too well understood to promise them any long career. The farce of monarchy and aristocracy, in all countries, is following that of chivalry, and Mr. Burke is dressing for the funeral. Let it then pass quietly to the tomb of all other follies, and the mourners be comforted.

The time is not very distant when England will laugh at itself for sending to Holland, Hanover, Zell, or Brunswick for men, at the expence of a million a year, who understood neither her laws, her language, nor her interest, and whose capacities would scarcely have fitted them for the office of a parish constable. If government could be trusted to such hands, it must be some easy and simple thing indeed, and materials fit for all the purposes may be found in every town and village in England.

When it shall be said in any country in the world, my poor are happy; neither ignorance nor distress is to be found among them; my jails are empty of prisoners, my streets of beggars; the aged are not in want, the taxes are not oppressive; the rational world is my friend, because I am the friend of its happiness: when these things can be said, then may that country boast its constitution and its government.

Within the space of a few years we have seen two Revolutions, those of America and France. In the former, the contest was long, and the conflict severe; in the latter, the nation acted with such a consolidated impulse, that having no foreign enemy to contend with, the revolution was complete in power the moment it appeared. From both those instances it is evident, that the greatest forces that can be brought into the field of revolutions, are reason and common interest. Where these can have the opportunity of acting, opposition dies with fear, or crumbles away by conviction. It is a great standing which they have now universally obtained; and we may hereafter hope to see revolutions, or changes in governments, produced with the same quiet operation by which any measure, determinable by reason and discussion, is accomplished.

When a nation changes its opinion and habits of thinking, it is no longer to be governed as before; but it would not only be wrong, but bad policy, to attempt by force what ought to be accomplished by reason. Rebellion consists in forcibly opposing the general will of a nation, whether by a party or by a government. There ought, therefore, to be in every nation a method of occasionally ascertaining the state of public opinion with respect to government. On this point the old government of France was superior to the present government of England, because, on extraordinary occasions, recourse could be had to what was then called the States General. But in England there are no such occasional bodies; and as to those who are now called Representatives, a great part of them are mere machines of the court, placemen, and dependants.

I presume, that though all the people of England pay taxes, not an hundredth part of them are electors, and the members of one of the houses of parliament represent nobody but themselves. There is, therefore, no power but the voluntary will of the people that has a right to act in any matter respecting a general reform; and by the same right that two persons can confer on such a subject, a thousand may. The object, in all such preliminary proceedings, is to find out what the general sense of a nation is, and to be governed by it. If it prefer a bad or defective government to a reform, or chuse to pay ten times more taxes than there is occasion for, it has a right so to do; and so long as the majority do not impose conditions on the minority, different to what they impose on themselves, though there may be much error, there is no injustice. Neither will the error continue long. Reason and discussion will soon bring things right, however wrong they may begin. By such a process no tumult is to be apprehended. The poor, in all countries, are naturally both peaceable and grateful in all reforms in which their interest and happiness is included. It is only by neglecting and rejecting them that they become tumultuous.

The objects that now press on the public attention are, the French revolution, and the prospect of a general revolution in governments. Of all nations in Europe, there is none so much interested in the French revolution as England. Enemies for ages, and that at a vast expence, and without any national object, the opportunity now presents itself of amicably closing the scene, and joining their efforts to reform the rest of Europe. By doing this, they will not only prevent the further effusion of blood, and encrease of taxes, but be in a condition of getting rid of a considerable part of their present burthens, as has been already stated. Long experience however has shewn, that reforms of this kind are not those which old governments wish to promote; and therefore it is to nations, and not to such governments, that these matters present themselves.

In the preceding part of this work, I have spoken of an alliance between England, France, and America, for purposes that were to be afterwards mentioned. Though I have no direct authority on the part of America, I have good reason to conclude, that she is disposed to enter into a consideration of such a measure, provided, that the governments with which she might ally, acted as national governments, and not as courts enveloped in intrigue and mystery. That France as a nation, and a national government, would prefer an alliance with England, is a matter of certainty. Nations, like individuals, who have long been enemies, without knowing each other, or knowing why, become the better friends when they discover the errors and impositions under which they had acted.

Admitting, therefore, the probability of such a connection, I will state some matters by which such an alliance, together with that of Holland, might render service, not only to the parties immediately concerned, but to all Europe.

It is, I think, certain, that if the fleets of England, France, and Holland were confederated, they could propose, with effect, a limitation to, and a general dismantling of all the navies in Europe, to a certain proportion to be agreed upon.

First, That no new ship of war shall be built by any power in Europe, themselves included.

Secondly, That all the navies now in existence shall be put back, suppose to one-tenth of their present force. This will save to France and England at least two millions sterling annually to each, and their relative force be in the same proportion as it is now. If men will permit themselves to think, as rational beings ought to think, nothing can appear more ridiculous and absurd, exclusive of all moral reflections, than to be at the expence of building navies, filling them with men, and then hauling them into the ocean, to try which can sink each other fastest. Peace, which costs nothing, is attended with infinitely more advantage, than any victory with all its expence. But this, though it best answers the purpose of nations, does not that of court governments, whose habited policy is pretence for taxation, places, and offices.

It is, I think, also certain, that the above confederated powers, together with that of the United States of America, can propose with effect, to Spain, the independance of South America, and the opening those countries of immense extent and wealth to the general commerce of the world, as North America now is.

With how much more glory, and advantage to itself, does a nation act, when it exerts its powers to rescue the world from bondage, and to create itself friends, than when it employs those powers to encrease ruin, desolation, and misery. The horrid scene that is now acting by the English government in the East-Indies, is fit only to be told of Goths and Vandals, who, destitute of principle, robbed and tortured the world they were incapable of enjoying.

The opening of South America would produce an immense field of commerce, and a ready money market for manufactures, which the eastern world does not. The East is already a country full of manufactures, the importation of which is not only an injury to the manufactures of England, but a drain upon its specie. The balance against England by this trade is regularly upwards of half a million annually sent out in the East-India ships in silver; and this is the reason, together with German intrigue, and German subsidies, there is so little silver in England.

But any war is harvest to such governments, however ruinous it may be to a nation. It serves to keep up deceitful expectations which prevent a people looking into the defects and abuses of government. It is the *lo here!* and the *lo there!* that amuses and cheats the multitude.

Never did so great an opportunity offer itself to England, and to all Europe, as is produced by the two Revolutions of America and France. By the former, freedom has a national champion in the Western world; and by the latter, in Europe. When another nation shall join France, despotism and bad government will scarcely dare to appear. To use a trite expression, the iron is becoming hot all over Europe. The insulted German and the enslaved Spaniard, the Russ and the Pole, are beginning to think. The present age will hereafter merit to be called the Age of reason, and the present generation will appear to the future as the Adam of a new world.

When all the governments of Europe shall be established on the representative system, nations will become acquainted, and the animosities and prejudices fomented by the intrigue and artifice of courts, will cease. The oppressed soldier will become a freeman; and the tortured sailor, no longer dragged along the streets like a felon, will pursue his mercantile voyage in safety. It would be better that nations should continue the pay of their soldiers during their lives, and give them their discharge and restore them to freedom and their friends, and cease recruiting, than retain such multitudes at the same expence, in a condition useless to society and themselves. As soldiers have hitherto been treated in most countries, they might be said to be without a friend. Shunned by the citizen on an apprehension of being enemies to liberty, and too often insulted by those who commanded them, their condition was a double oppression. But where genuine principles of liberty pervade a people, every thing is restored to order; and the soldier civily treated, returns the civility.

In contemplating revolutions, it is easy to perceive that they may arise from two distinct causes; the one, to avoid or get rid of some great calamity; the other, to obtain some great and positive good; and the two may be distinguished by the names of active and passive revolutions. In those which proceed from the former cause, the temper becomes incensed and sowered; and the redress, obtained by danger, is too often sullied by revenge. But in those which proceed from the latter, the heart, rather animated than agitated, enters serenely upon the subject. Reason and discussion, persuasion and conviction, become the weapons in the contest, and it is only when those are attempted to be suppressed that recource is had to violence. When men unite in agreeing that a *thing is good*, could it be obtained, such as relief from a burden of taxes and the extinction of corruption, the object is more than half accomplished. What they approve as the end, they will promote in the means.

Will any man say, in the present excess of taxation, falling so heavily on the poor, that a remission of five pounds annually of taxes to one hundred and four thousand poor families is not a *good thing*? Will he say, that a remission of seven pounds annually to one hundred thousand other poor families—of eight pounds annually to another hundred thousand poor families, and of ten pounds annually to fifty thousand poor and widowed families, are not *good things*? And to proceed a step farther in this climax, will he say, that to provide against the misfortunes to which all human life is subject, by securing six pounds annually for all poor, distressed, and reduced persons of the age of fifty and until sixty, and of ten pounds annually after sixty is not a *good thing*?

Will he say, that an abolition of two million of poor-rates to the house-keepers, and of the whole of the house and window-light tax and of the commutation tax is not a *good thing*? Or will he say, that to abolish corruption is a *bad thing*?

If, therefore, the good to be obtained be worthy of a passive, rational, and costless revolution, it would be bad policy to prefer waiting for a calamity that should force a violent one. I have no idea, considering the reforms which are now passing and spreading throughout Europe, that England will permit herself to be the last; and where the occasion and the opportunity quietly offer, it is better than to wait for a turbulent necessity. It may be considered as an honour to the animal faculties of man to obtain redress by courage and danger, but it is far greater honour to the rational faculties to accomplish the same object by reason, accommodation, and general consent*.

As reforms, or revolutions, call them which you please, extend themselves among nations, those nations will form connections and conventions, and when a few are thus confederated, the progress will be rapid, till despotism and

*I know it is the opinion of many of the most enlightened characters in France (there always will be those who see farther into events than others) not only among the general mass of citizens, but of many of the principal members of the former National Assembly, that the monarchical plan will not continue many years in that country. They have found out, that as wisdom cannot be made hereditary, power ought not; and that, for a man to merit a million stirling a year from a nation, he ought to have a mind capable of comprehending from an atom to a universe; which, if he had, he would be above receiving the pay. But they wished not to appear to lead the nation faster than its own reason and interest dictated. In all the conversations where I have been present upon this subject, the idea always was, that when such a time, from the general opinion of the nation, shall arrive, that the honourable and liberal method would be, to make a handsome present in fee simple to the person whoever he may be, that shall then be in the monarchical office, and for him to retire to the enjoyment of private life, possessing his share of general rights and privileges, and to be no more accountable to the public for his time and his conduct than any other citizen.

corrupt government be totally expelled, at least out of two quarters of the world, Europe and America. The Algerine piracy may then be commanded to cease, for it is only by the malicious policy of old governments, against each other, that it exists.

Throughout this work, various and numerous as the subjects are, which I have taken up and investigated, there is only a single paragraph upon religion, viz. *"that every religion is good, that teaches man to be good."*

I have carefully avoided to enlarge upon the subject, because I am inclined to believe, that what is called the present ministry wish to see contentions about religion kept up, to prevent the nation turning its attention to subjects of government. It is, as if they were to say, *"Look that way, or any way, but this."*

But as religion is very improperly made a political machine, and the reality of it is thereby destroyed, I will conclude this work with stating in what light religion appears to me.

If we suppose a large family of children, who, on any particular day, or particular circumstance, made it a custom to present to their parent some token of their affection and gratitude, each of them would make a different offering, and most probably in a different manner. Some would pay their congratulations in themes of verse or prose, by some little devices, as their genius dictated, or according to what they thought would please; and, perhaps, the least of all, not able to do any of those things, would ramble into the garden, or the field, and gather what it thought the prettiest flower it could find, though, perhaps, it might be but a simple weed. The parent would be more gratified by such variety, than if the whole of them had acted on a concerted plan, and each had made exactly the same offering. This would have the cold appearance of contrivance, or the harsh one of controul. But of all unwelcome things, nothing could more afflict the parent than to know, that the whole of them had afterwards gotten together by the ears, boys and girls, fighting, scratching, reviling, and abusing each other about which was the best or the worst present.

Why may we not suppose, that the great Father of all is pleased with variety of devotion; and that the greatest offence we can act, is that by which we seek to torment and render each other miserable. For my own part, I am fully satisfied that what I am now doing, with an endeavour to conciliate mankind, to render their condition happy, to unite nations that have hitherto been enemies, and to extirpate the horrid practice of war, and break the chains of slavery and oppression, is acceptable in his sight, and being the best service I can perform, I act it chearfully.

I do not believe that any two men, on what are called doctrinal points, think alike who think at all. It is only those who have not thought that appear to agree. It is in this case as with what is called the British constitution. It has been taken for granted to be good, and encomiums have supplied the place of proof. But when the nation come to examine into its principles and the abuses it admits, it will be found to have more defects than I have pointed out in this work and the former.

As to what are called national religions, we may, with as much propriety, talk of national Gods. It is either political craft or the remains of the Pagan system, when every nation had its separate and particular deity. Among all the writers of the English church clergy, who have treated on the general subject of religion, the present Bishop of Landaff has not been excelled, and it is with much pleasure that I take the opportunity of expressing this token of respect.

I have now gone through the whole of the subject, at least, as far as it appears to me at present. It has been my intention for the five years I have been in Europe, to offer an address to the people of England on the subject of government, if the opportunity presented itself before I returned to America. Mr. Burke has thrown it in my way, and I thank him. On a certain occasion three years ago, I pressed him to propose a national convention to be fairly elected for the purpose of taking the state of the nation into consideration; but I found, that however strongly the parliamentary current was then setting against the party he acted with, their policy was to keep every thing within that field of corruption, and trust to accidents. Long experience had shewn that parliaments would follow any change of ministers, and on this they rested their hopes and their expectations.

Formerly, when divisions arose respecting governments, recourse was had to the sword, and a civil war ensued. That savage custom is exploded by the new system, and reference is had to national conventions. Discussion and the general will arbitrates the question, and to this, private opinion yields with a good grace, and order is preserved uninterrupted.

Some gentlemen have affected to call the principles upon which this work and the former part of *Rights of Man* are founded, "a new fangled doctrine." The question is not whether those principles are new or old, but whether they are right or wrong. Suppose the former, I will shew their effect by a figure easily understood.

It is now towards the middle of February. Were I to take a turn into the country, the trees would present a leafless winterly appearance. As people are apt to pluck twigs as they walk along, I perhaps might do the same, and by chance might observe, that a *single bud* on that twig had begun to swell. I should reason very unnaturally, or rather not reason at all, to suppose *this* was the *only* bud in England which had this appearance. Instead of deciding thus, I should instantly conclude, that the same appearance was beginning, or about to begin, every where; and though the vegetable sleep will continue longer on some trees and plants than on others, and though some of them may not *blossom* for two or three years, all will be in leaf in the summer, except those which are *rotten*. What pace the political summer may keep with the natural, no human foresight can determine. It is, however, not difficult to perceive that the spring is begun.—Thus wishing, as I sincerely do, freedom and happiness to all nations, I close the

SECOND PART.

APPENDIX.

As the publication of this work has been delayed beyond the time intended, I think it not improper, all circumstances considered, to state the causes that have occasioned the delay.

The reader will probably observe, that some parts in the plan contained in this work for reducing the taxes, and certain parts in Mr. Pitt's speech at the opening of the present session, Tuesday, January 31, are so much alike, as to induce a belief, that either the Author had taken the hint from Mr. Pitt, or Mr. Pitt from the Author.—I will first point out the parts that are similar, and then state such circumstances as I am acquainted with, leaving the reader to make his own conclusion.

Considering it almost an unprecedented case, that taxes should be proposed to be taken off, it is equally as extraordinary that such a measure should occur to two persons at the same time; and still more so, (considering the vast variety and multiplicity of taxes) that they should hit on the same specific taxes. Mr. Pitt has mentioned, in his speech, the tax on *Carts* and *Waggons*—that on *Female Servants*—the lowering the tax on *Candles*, and the taking off the tax of three shillings on *Houses* having under seven windows.

Every one of those specific taxes are a part of the plan contained in this work, and proposed also to be taken off. Mr. Pitt's plan, it is true, goes no farther than to a reduction of three hundred and twenty thousand pounds; and the reduction proposed in this work to nearly six millions. I have made my calculations on only sixteen millions and an half of revenue, still asserting that it was "very nearly, if not quite, seventeen millions." Mr. Pitt states it at 16,690,000. I know enough of the matter to say, that he has not *over*stated it. Having thus given the particulars, which correspond in this work and his speech, I will state a chain of circumstances that may lead to some explanation.

The first hint for lessening the taxes, and that as a consequence flowing from the French revolution, is to be found in the ADDRESS and DECLARATION of the Gentlemen who met at the Thatched-House Tavern, August 20, 1791. Among many other particulars stated in that Address, is the following, put as an interrogation to the government opposers of the French Revolution. *"Are they sorry that the pretence for new oppressive taxes, and the occasion for continuing many old taxes will be at an end?"*

It is well known, that the persons who chiefly frequent the Thatched-House Tavern, are men of court connections, and so much did they take this Address and Declaration respecting the French revolution and the reduction of taxes in disgust, that the

Landlord was under the necessity of informing the Gentlemen, who composed the meeting of the twentieth of August, and who proposed holding another meeting, that he could not receive them*.

What was only hinted at in the Address and Declaration, respecting taxes and principles of government, will be found reduced to a regular system in this work. But as Mr. Pitt's speech contains some of the same things respecting taxes, I now come to give the circumstances before alluded to.

The case is: This work was intended to be published just before the meeting of Parliament, and for that purpose a considerable part of the copy was put into the printer's hands in September, and all the remaining copy, as far as page 648, which contains the parts to which Mr. Pitt's speech is similar, was given to him full six weeks before the meeting of parliament, and he was informed of the time at which it was to appear. He had composed nearly the whole about a fortnight before the time of Parliament meeting, and had printed as far as page 617, and had given me a proof of the next sheet, up to page 628. It was then in sufficient forwardness to be out at the time proposed, as two other sheets were ready for striking off. I had before told him, that if he thought he should be straightened for time, I would get part of the work done at another press, which he desired me not to do. In this manner the work stood on the Tuesday fortnight preceding the meeting of Parliament, when all at once, without any previous intimation, though I had been with him the evening before, he sent me, by one of his workmen, all the remaining copy, from page 617, declining to go on with the work *on any consideration*.

*The gentleman who signed the address and declaration as chairman of the meeting, M. Horne Tooke, being generally supposed to be the person who drew it up, and having spoken much in commendation of it, has been jocularly accused of praising his own work. To free him from this embarassment, and to save him the repeated trouble of mentioning the author, as he has not failed to do, I make no hesitation in saying, that as the opportunity of benefiting by the French Revolution easily occurred to me, I drew up the publication in question, and shewed it to him and some other gentlemen; who, fully approving it, held a meeting for the purpose of making it public, and subscribed to the amount of fifty guineas to defray the expence of advertising. I believe there are at this time, in England, a greater number of men acting on disinterested principles, and determined to look into the nature and practices of government themselves, and not blindly trust, as has hitherto been the case, either to government generally, or to parliaments, or to parliamentary opposition, than at any former period. Had this been done a century ago, corruption and taxation had not arrived to the height they are now at.

To account for this extraordinary conduct I was totally at a loss, as he stopped at the part where the arguments on systems and principles of government closed, and where the plan for the reduction of taxes, the education of children, and the support of the poor and the aged begins; and still more especially, as he had, at the time of his beginning to print, and before he had seen the whole copy, offered a thousand pounds for the copy-right, together with the future copy-right of the former part of the Rights of Man. I told the person who brought me this offer that I should not accept it, and wished it not to be renewed, giving him as my reason, that though I believed the printer to be an honest man, I would never put it in the power of any printer or publisher to suppress or alter a work of mine, by making him master of the copy, or give to him the right of selling it to any minister, or to any other person, or to treat as a mere matter of traffic, that which I intended should operate as a principle.

His refusal to complete the work (which he could not purchase) obliged me to seek for another printer, and this of consequence would throw the publication back till after the meeting of Parliament, otherways it would have appeared that Mr. Pitt had only taken up a part of the plan which I had more fully stated.

Whether that gentleman, or any other, had seen the work, or any part of it, is more than I have authority to say. But the manner in which the work was returned, and the particular time at which this was done, and that after the offers he had made, are suspicious circumstances. I know what the opinion of booksellers and publishers is upon such a case, but as to my own opinion, I chuse to make no declaration. There are many ways by which proof sheets may be procured by other persons before a work publicly appear; to which I shall add a certain circumstance, which is,

A ministerial bookseller in Piccadilly who has been employed, as common report says, by a clerk of one of the boards closely connected with the ministry (the board of trade and plantation of which Hawksbury is president) to publish what he calls my Life (I wish his own life and that those of the cabinet were as good) used to have his books printed at the same printing-office that I employed; but when the former part of *Rights of Man* came out, he took his work away in dudgeon; and about a week or ten days before the printer returned my copy, he came to make him an offer of his work again, which was accepted. This would consequently give him admission into the printing-office where the sheets of this work were then lying; and as booksellers and printers are free with each other, he would have the opportunity of seeing what was going on.—Be the case however as it may, Mr. Pitt's plan, little and diminutive as it is, would have had a very awkward appearance, had this work appeared at the time the printer had engaged to finish it.

I have now stated the particulars which occasioned the delay, from the proposal to purchase, to the refusal to print. If all the Gentlemen are innocent, it is very unfortunate for them that such a variety of suspicious circumstances should, without any design, arrange themselves together.

Having now finished this part, I will conclude with stating another circumstance.

About a fortnight or three weeks before the meeting of Parliament, a small addition, amounting to about twelve shillings and six pence a year, was made to the pay of the soldiers, or rather, their pay was docked so much less. Some Gentlemen who knew, in part, that this work would contain a plan of reforms respecting the oppressed condition of soldiers, wished me to add a note to the work, signifying, that the part upon that subject had been in the printer's hands some weeks before that addition of pay was proposed. I declined doing this, lest it should be interpreted into an air of vanity, or an endeavour to excite suspicion (for which, perhaps, there might be no grounds) that some of the government gentlemen, had, by some means or other, made out what this work would contain: and had not the printing been interrupted so as to occasion a delay beyond the time fixed for publication, nothing contained in this appendix would have appeared.

THOMAS PAINE.

THE AGE OF REASON

The Age of Reason

Being an Investigation of
True and of Fabulous Theology

1794

TO MY
FELLOW CITIZENS
OF THE
UNITED STATES OF AMERICA.

I PUT the following work under your protection. It contains my opinion upon Religion. You will do me the justice to remember, that I have always strenuously supported the Right of every Man to his own opinion, however different that opinion might be to mine. He who denies to another this right, makes a slave of himself to his present opinion, because he precludes himself the right of changing it.

The most formidable weapon against errors of every kind is Reason. I have never used any other, and I trust I never shall.

Your affectionate friend and fellow citizen,

THOMAS PAINE.

Luxembourg, 8th Pluvoise,
Second Year of the French Republic, one and indivisible.
January 27, O. S. 1794.

THE AGE OF REASON

IT has been my intention, for several years past, to publish my thoughts upon Religion. I am well aware of the difficulties that attend the subject; and, from that consideration, had reserved it to a more advanced period of life. I intended it to be the last offering I should make to my fellow citizens of all nations; and that at a time, when the purity of the motive that induced me to it, could not admit of a question, even by those who might disapprove the work.

The circumstance that has now taken place in France, of the total abolition of the whole national order of priest-hood, and of every thing appertaining to compulsive systems of

religion, and compulsive articles of faith, has not only precipitated my intention, but rendered a work of this kind
exceedingly necessary; lest, in the general wreck of superstition, of false systems of government, and false theology, we
lose sight of morality, of humanity, and of the theology that is
true.

As several of my colleagues, and others of my fellow citizens of France, have given me the example of making their
voluntary and individual profession of faith, I also will make
mine; and I do this with all that sincerity and frankness with
which the mind of man communicates with itself.

I believe in one God, and no more; and I hope for happiness beyond this life.

I believe the equality of man, and I believe that religious
duties consist in doing justice, loving mercy, and endeavouring to make our fellow creatures happy.

But lest it should be supposed that I believe many other
things in addition to these, I shall, in the progress of this
work, declare the things I do not believe, and my reasons for
not believing them.

I do not believe in the creed professed by the Jewish
church, by the Roman church, by the Greek church, by the
Turkish church, by the Protestant church, nor by any church
that I know of. My own mind is my own church.

All national institutions of churches, whether Jewish, Christian, or Turkish, appear to me no other than human inventions set up to terrify and enslave mankind, and monopolize
power and profit.

I do not mean by this declaration to condemn those who
believe otherwise. They have the same right to their belief as I
have to mine. But it is necessary to the happiness of man, that
he be mentally faithful to himself. Infidelity does not consist
in believing, or in disbelieving: it consists in professing to believe what he does not believe.

It is impossible to calculate the moral mischief, if I may so
express it, that mental lying has produced in society. When a
man has so far corrupted and prostituted the chastity of his
mind, as to subscribe his professional belief to things he does
not believe, he has prepared himself for the commission of
every other crime. He takes up the trade of a priest for the

sake of gain, and in order to *qualify* himself for that trade, he begins with a parjury. Can we conceive any thing more destructive to morality than this?

Soon after I had published the pamphlet, COMMON-SENSE, in America, I saw the exceeding probability that a Revolution in the System of Government, would be followed by a revolution in the system of religion. The adulterous connection of church and state, wherever it had taken place, whether Jewish, Christian, or Turkish, had so effectually prohibited, by pains and penalties, every discussion upon established creeds, and upon first principles of religion, that until the system of government should be changed, those subjects could not be brought fairly and openly before the world: but that whenever this should be done, a revolution in the system of religion would follow. Human inventions and priest-craft would be detected; and man would return to the pure, unmixed, and unadulterated belief of one God, and no more.

Every national church or religion has established itself by pretending some special mission from God communicated to certain individuals. The Jews have their Moses; the Christians their Jesus Christ, their apostles and saints; and the Turks their Mahomet; as if the way to God was not open to every man alike.

Each of those churches show certain books which they call *revelation*, or the word of God. The Jews say that their word of God was given by God to Moses face to face; the Christians say, that their word of God came by divine inspiration; and the Turks say, that their word of God (the Koran) was brought by an angel from heaven. Each of those churches accuses the other of unbelief; and, for my own part, I disbelieve them all.

As it is necessary to affix right ideas to words, I will, before I proceed further into the subject, offer some observations on the word *revelation*. Revelation, when applied to religion, means something communicated *immediately* from God to man.

No one will deny or dispute the power of the Almighty to make such a communication if he pleases. But admitting, for the sake of a case, that something has been revealed to a certain person, and not revealed to any other person, it is revelation to that person only. When he tells it to a second person, a second to a third, a third to a fourth, and so on, it ceases to be a revelation to all those persons. It is revelation to the first person only, and *hearsay* to every other; and consequently, they are not obliged to believe it.

It is a contradiction in terms and ideas to call any thing a revelation that comes to us at second hand, either verbally or in writing. Revelation is necessarily limited to the first communication. After this, it is only an account of something which that person says was a revelation made to him; and though he may find himself obliged to believe it, it cannot be incumbent upon me to believe it in the same manner, for it was not a revelation made to *me*, and I have only his word for it that it was made to *him*.

When Moses told the children of Israel that he received the two tables of the commandments from the hand of God, they were not obliged to believe him, because they had no other authority for it than his telling them so; and I have no other authority for it than some historian telling me so. The commandments carry no internal evidence of divinity with them. They contain some good moral precepts, such as any man qualified to be a law-giver or a legislator could produce himself, without having recourse to supernatural intervention.*

When I am told that the Koran was written in heaven, and brought to Mahomet by an angel, the account comes to near the same kind of hearsay evidence, and second hand authority, as the former. I did not see the angel myself, and therefore I have a right not to believe it.

When also I am told that a woman, called the Virgin Mary, said, or gave out, that she was with child without any cohabitation with a man, and that her betrothed husband, Joseph, said, that an angel told him so, I have a right to believe them or not: such a circumstance required a much stronger evidence than their bare word for it: but we have not even this; for neither Joseph nor Mary wrote any such matter themselves. It is only reported by others that *they said so*. It is hear-

---

*It is, however, necessary to except the declaration which says, that God *visits the sins of the fathers upon the children*. It is contrary to every principle of moral justice.

say upon hearsay, and I do not chuse to rest my belief upon such evidence.

It is, however, not difficult to account for the credit that was given to the story of Jesus Christ being the Son of God. He was born at a time when the heathen mythology had still some fashion and repute in the world, and that mythology had prepared the people for the belief of such a story. Almost all the extraordinary men that lived under the heathen mythology were reputed to be the sons of some of their gods. It was not a new thing at that time to believe a man to have been celestially begotten: the intercourse of gods with women was then a matter of familiar opinion. Their Jupiter, according to their accounts, had cohabited with hundreds: the story, therefore, had nothing in it either new, wonderful, or obscene: it was conformable to the opinions that then prevailed among the people called Gentiles, or mythologists, and it was those people only that believed it. The Jews who had kept strictly to the belief of one God, and no more, and who had always rejected the heathen mythology, never credited the story.

It is curious to observe how the theory of what is called the Christian church, sprung out of the tail of the heathen mythology. A direct incorporation took place in the first instance, by making the reputed founder to be celestially begotten. The trinity of gods that then followed was no other than a reduction of the former plurality, which was about twenty or thirty thousand. The statue of Mary succeeded the statue of Diana of Ephesus. The deification of heroes, changed into the cannonization of saints. The mythologists had gods for every thing; the Christian mythologists had saints for every thing. The church became as crouded with the one, as the pantheon had been with the other; and Rome was the place of both. The Christian theory is little else than the idolatry of the ancient mythologists, accommodated to the purposes of power and revenue; and it yet remains to reason and philosophy to abolish the amphibious fraud.

Nothing that is here said can apply, even with the most distant disrespect, to the *real* character of Jesus Christ. He was a virtuous and an amiable man. The morality that he preached and practised was of the most benevolent kind; and though similar systems of morality had been preached by Confucius, and by some of the Greek philosophers, many years before; by the quakers since; and by many good men in all ages; it has not been exceeded by any.

Jesus Christ wrote no account of himself, of his birth, parentage, or any thing else. Not a line of what is called the New Testament is of his writing. The history of him is altogether the work of other people; and as to the account given of his resurrection and ascension, it was the necessary counterpart to the story of his birth. His historians, having brought him into the world in a supernatural manner, were obliged to take him out again in the same manner, or the first part of the story must have fallen to the ground.

The wretched contrivance with which this latter part is told, exceeds every thing that went before it. The first part, that of the miraculous conception, was not a thing that admitted of publicity; and therefore the tellers of this part of the story, had this advantage, that though they might not be credited, they could not be detected. They could not be expected to prove it, because it was not one of those things that admitted of proof, and it was impossible that the person of whom it was told could prove it himself.

But the resurrection of a dead person from the grave, and his ascension through the air, is a thing very different as to the evidence it admits of, to the invisible conception of a child in the womb. The resurrection and ascension, supposing them to have taken place, admitted of public and occular demonstration, like that of the ascension of a balloon, or the sun at noon day, to all Jerusalem at least. A thing which every body is required to believe, requires that the proof and evidence of it should be equal to all, and universal; and as the public visibility of this last related act was the only evidence that could give sanction to the former part, the whole of it falls to the ground, because that evidence never was given. Instead of this, a small number of persons, not more than eight or nine, are introduced as proxies for the whole world, to say, they *saw it*, and all the rest of the world are called upon to believe it. But it appears that Thomas did not believe the resurrection; and, as they say, would not believe, without having occular and manual demonstration himself. *So neither will I;* and the reason is equally as good for me and for every other person, as for Thomas.

It is in vain to attempt to palliate or disguise this matter. The story, so far as relates to the supernatural part, has every mark of fraud and imposition stamped upon the face of it. Who were the authors of it is as impossible for us now to know, as it is for us to be assured, that the books in which the account is related, were written by the persons whose names they bear. The best surviving evidence we now have respecting this affair is the Jews. They are regularly descended from the people who lived in the times this resurrection and ascension is said to have happened, and they say, *it is not true.* It has long appeared to me a strange inconsistency to cite the Jews as a proof of the truth of the story. It is just the same as if a man were to say, I will prove the truth of what I have told you, by producing the people who say it is false.

That such a person as Jesus Christ existed, and that he was crucified, which was the mode of execution at that day, are historical relations strictly within the limits of probability. He preached most excellent morality, and the equality of man; but he preached also against the corruptions and avarice of the Jewish priests; and this brought upon him the hatred and vengeance of the whole order of priest-hood. The accusation which those priests brought against him, was that of sedition and conspiracy against the Roman government, to which the Jews were then subject and tributary; and it is not improbable that the Roman government might have some secret apprehension of the effects of his doctrine as well as the Jewish priests; neither is it improbable that Jesus Christ had in contemplation the delivery of the Jewish nation from the bondage of the Romans. Between the two, however, this virtuous reformer and revolutionist lost his life.

It is upon this plain narrative of facts, together with another case I am going to mention, that the Christian mythologists, calling themselves the Christian church, have erected their fable, which for absurdity and extravagance is not exceeded by any thing that is to be found in the mythology of the ancients.

The ancient mythologists tell that the race of Giants made

war against Jupiter, and that one of them threw an hundred rocks against him at one throw; that Jupiter defeated him with thunder, and confined him afterwards under Mount Etna; and that every time the Giant turns himself, Mount Etna belches fire. It is here easy to see that the circumstance of the mountain, that of its being a vulcano, suggested the idea of the fable; and that the fable is made to fit and wind itself up with that circumstance.

The Christian mythologists tell that their Satan made war against the Almighty, who defeated him, and confined him afterwards, not under a mountain, but in a pit. It is here easy to see that the first fable suggested the idea of the second; for the fable of Jupiter and the Giants was told many hundred years before that of Satan.

Thus far the ancient and the Christian mythologists differ very little from each other. But the latter have contrived to carry the matter much farther. They have contrived to connect the fabulous part of the story of Jesus Christ, with the fable originating from Mount Etna: and in order to make all the parts of the story tye together, they have taken to their aid the traditions of the Jews; for the Christian mythology is made up partly from the ancient mythology, and partly from the Jewish traditions.

The Christian mythologists, after having confined Satan in a pit, were obliged to let him out again, to bring on the sequel of the fable. He is then introduced into the garden of Eden in the shape of a snake, or a serpent, and in that shape he enters into familiar conversation with Eve, who is no ways surprised to hear a snake talk; and the issue of this tête-à-tête is, that he persuades her to eat an apple, and the eating of that apple, damns all mankind.

After giving Satan this triumph over the whole creation, one would have supposed that the church mythologists would have been kind enough to send him back again to the pit; or, if they had not done this, that they would have put a mountain upon him, (for they say that their faith can remove a mountain) or have put him *under* a mountain, as the former mythologists had done, to prevent his getting again among the women, and doing more mischief. But instead of this, they leave him at large without even obliging him to give his parole. The secret of which is, that they could not do without him; and after being at the trouble of making him, they bribed him to stay. They promised him ALL the Jews, ALL the Turks by anticipation, nine-tenths of the world beside, and Mahomet into the bargain. After this, who can doubt the bountifulness of the Christian mythology?

Having thus made an insurrection and a battle in heaven, in which none of the combatants could be either killed or wounded—put Satan into the pit—let him out again—given him a triumph over the whole creation—damned all mankind by the eating of an apple, these Christian mythologists bring the two ends of their fable together. They represent this virtuous and amiable man, Jesus Christ, to be at once both God and man, and also the Son of God, celestially begotten on purpose to be sacrificed, because, they say, that Eve in her longing had eaten an apple.

Putting aside every thing that might excite laughter by its absurdity, or detestation by its prophaneness, and confining ourselves merely to an examination of the parts, it is impossible to conceive a story more derogatory to the Almighty, more inconsistent with his wisdom, more contradictory to his power, than this story is.

In order to make for it a foundation to rise upon, the inventors were under the necessity of giving to the being, whom they call Satan, a power equally as great, if not greater, than they attribute to the Almighty. They have not only given him the power of liberating himself from the pit, after what they call his fall, but they have made that power increase afterwards to infinity. Before this fall, they represent him only as an angel of limited existence, as they represent the rest. After his fall, he becomes, by their account, omnipresent. He exists every where, and at the same time. He occupies the whole immensity of space.

Not content with this deification of Satan, they represent him as defeating by stratagem, in the shape of an animal of the creation, all the power and wisdom of the Almighty. They represent him as having compelled the Almighty to the *direct necessity* either of surrendering the whole of the creation to the government and sovereignty of this Satan, or of capitulating for its redemption by coming down upon earth, and exhibiting himself upon a cross in the shape of a man.

Had the inventors of this story told it the contrary way, that is, had they represented the Almighty as compelling Satan to exhibit *himself* on a cross in the shape of a snake, as a punishment for his new transgression, the story would have been less absurd, less contradictory. But instead of this, they make the transgressor triumph, and the Almighty fall.

That many good men have believed this strange fable and lived very good lives under that belief (for credulity is not a crime) is what I have no doubt of. In the first place, they were educated to believe it, and they would have believed any thing else in the same manner. There are also many who have been so enthusiastically enraptured by what they conceived to be the infinite love of God to man, in making a sacrifice of himself, that the vehemence of the idea has forbidden and deterred them from examining into the absurdity and prophaneness of the story. The more unnatural any thing is, the more is it capable of becoming the object of dismal admiration.

But if objects for gratitude and admiration are our desire, do they not present themselves every hour to our eyes? Do we not see a fair creation prepared to receive us the instant we were born—a world furnished to our hands that cost us nothing? Is it we that light up the sun; that pour down the rain; and fill the earth with abundance? Whether we sleep or wake, the vast machinery of the universe still goes on. Are these things, and the blessings they indicate in future, nothing to us? Can our gross feelings be excited by no other subjects than tragedy and suicide? Or is the gloomy pride of man become so intolerable, that nothing can flatter it but a sacrifice of the Creator?

I know that this bold investigation will alarm many, but it would be paying too great a compliment to their credulity to forbear it upon that account. The times and the subject demand it to be done. The suspicion that the theory of what is called the Christian church is fabulous, is becoming very extensive in all countries; and it will be a consolation to men staggering under that suspicion, and doubting what to believe and what to disbelieve, to see the subject freely investigated. I therefore pass on to an examination of the books called the Old and the New Testament.

These books, beginning with Genesis and ending with Revelations (which by the bye is a book of riddles that requires a Revelation to explain it) are, we are told, the word of God. It is therefore proper for us to know who told us so, that we may know what credit to give to the report. The answer to this question is, that nobody can tell, except that we tell one another so. The case, however, historically appears to be as follows:

When the church mythologists established their system, they collected all the writings they could find, and managed them as they pleased. It is a matter altogether of uncertainty to us whether such of the writings as now appear, under the name of the Old and the New Testament, are in the same state in which those collectors say they found them; or whether they added, altered, abridged, or dressed them up.

Be this as it may, they decided by *vote* which of the books, out of the collection they had made, should be the WORD OF GOD, and which should not. They rejected several; they voted others to be doubtful, such as the books called the Apocraphy; and those books which had a majority of votes, were voted to be the word of God. Had they voted otherwise, all the people, since calling themselves Christians, had believed otherwise; for the belief of the one comes from the vote of the other. Who the people were that did all this, we know nothing of; they called themselves by the general name of the church; and this is all we know of the matter.

As we have no other external evidence or authority for believing those books to be the word of God than what I have mentioned, which is no evidence or authority at all, I come, in the next place, to examine the internal evidence contained in the books themselves.

In the former part of this essay, I have spoken of revelation. I now proceed further with that subject, for the purpose of applying it to the books in question.

Revelation is a communication of something, which the person, to whom that thing is revealed, did not know before. For if I have done a thing, or seen it done, it needs no revelation to tell me I have done it, or seen it, nor to enable me to tell it, or to write it.

Revelation, therefore, cannot be applied to any thing done upon earth of which man is himself the actor or the witness; and consequently all the historical and anecdotal part of the Bible, which is almost the whole of it, is not within the meaning and compass of the word revelation, and therefore is not the word of God.

When Samson ran off with the gate-posts of Gaza, if he ever did so (and whether he did or not is nothing to us) or when he visited his Delilah, or caught his foxes, or did any thing else, what has revelation to do with these things? If they were facts, he could tell them himself; or his secretary, if he kept one, could write them, if they were worth either telling or writing; and if they were fictions, revelation could not make them true; and whether true or not, we are neither the better nor the wiser for knowing them.—When we contemplate the immensity of that Being, who directs and governs the incomprehensible WHOLE, of which the utmost ken of human sight can discover but a part, we ought to feel shame at calling such paltry stories the word of God.

As to the account of the creation, with which the book of Genesis opens, it has all the appearance of being a tradition which the Israelites had among them before they came into Egypt; and after their departure from that country, they put it at the head of their history, without telling, as it is most probable they did not know, how they came by it. The manner in which the account opens, shews it to be traditionary. It begins abruptly. It is nobody that speaks. It is nobody that hears. It is addressed to nobody. It has neither first, second, nor third person. It has every criterion of being a tradition. It has no voucher. Moses does not take it upon himself by introducing it with the formality that he uses on other occasions, such as that of saying, *"The Lord spake unto Moses, saying."*

Why it has been called the Mosaic account of the creation, I am at a loss to conceive. Moses, I believe, was too good a judge of such subjects to put his name to that account. He had been educated among the Egyptians, who were a people as well skilled in science, and particularly in astronomy, as any people of their day; and the silence and caution that Moses

observes, in not authenticating the account, is a good negative evidence that he neither told it, nor believed it.—The
case is, that every nation of people has been world-makers,
and the Israelites had as much right to set up the trade of
world-making as any of the rest; and as Moses was not an
Israelite, he might not chuse to contradict the tradition. The
account, however, is harmless; and this is more than can be
said for many other parts of the Bible.

When we read the obscene stories, the voluptuous debaucheries, the cruel and torturous executions, the unrelenting vindictiveness, with which more than half the Bible is
filled, it would be more consistent that we called it the word
of a demon, than the word of God. It is a history of wickedness, that has served to corrupt and brutalize mankind; and,
for my own part, I sincerely detest it, as I detest every thing
that is cruel.

We scarcely meet with any thing, a few phrases excepted,
but what deserves either our abhorrence, or our contempt, till
we come to the miscellaneous parts of the Bible. In the
anonymous publications, the Psalms and the book of Job,
more particularly in the latter, we find a great deal of elevated
sentiment reverentially expressed of the power and benignity
of the Almighty; but they stand on no higher rank than many
other compositions on similar subjects, as well before that
time as since.

The proverbs, which are said to be Solomon's, though
most probably a collection, (because they discover a knowlege
of life, which his situation excluded him from knowing) are
an instructive table of ethics. They are inferior in keenness to
the proverbs of the Spaniards, and not more wise and œco-
nomical than those of the American Franklin.

All the remaining parts of the Bible, generally known by
the name of the prophets, are the works of the Jewish poets
and itinerant preachers, who mixed poetry, anecdote, and devotion together; and those works still retain the air and stile
of poetry, though in translation.*

*As there are many readers who do not see that a composition is poetry
unless it be in rhyme, it is for their information that I add this note.

Poetry consists principally in two things: Imagery and composition. The
composition of poetry differs from that of prose in the manner of mixing

There is not, throughout the whole book, called the Bible, any word that describes to us what we call a poet, nor any word that describes what we call poetry. The case is, that the word *prophet*, to which later times have affixed a new idea, was the Bible word for poet, and the word *prophesying* meant the art of making poetry. It also meant the art of playing poetry to a tune upon any instrument of music.

We read of prophesying with pipes, taberets, and horns. Of prophesying with harps, with psalteries, with cymbals, and with every other instrument of music then in fashion. Were we now to speak of prophesying with a fiddle, or with a pipe and tabor, the expression would have no meaning, or would appear ridiculous, and to some people contemptuous, because we have changed the meaning of the word.

We are told of Saul being among the *prophets*, and also that he prophesied; but we are not told what *they prophesied*, nor what *he prophesied*. The case is, there was nothing to tell; for these prophets were a company of musicians and poets; and Saul joined in the concert; and this was called *prophesying*.

The account given of this affair in the book called Samuel,

---

long and short syllables together. Take a long syllable out of a line of poetry, and put a short one in the room of it, or put a long syllable where a short one should be, and that line will lose its poetical harmony. It will have an effect upon the line like that of misplacing a note in a song.

The imagery in those books, called the prophets, appertains altogether to poetry. It is fictitious and often extravagant, and not admissible in any other kind of writing than poetry.

To shew that these writings are composed in poetical numbers, I will take ten syllables as they stand in the book, and make a line of the same number of syllables, (heroic measure) that shall rhyme with the last word. It will then be seen, that the composition of those books is poetical measure. The instance I shall first produce is from Isaiah.

> "*Hear, O ye heavens, and give ear, O earth.*"
> 'Tis God himself that calls attention forth.

Another instance I shall quote is from the mournful Jeremiah, to which I shall add two other lines, for the purpose of carrying out the figure, and shewing the intention of the poet.

> "*O! that mine head were waters, and mine eyes*"
> Were fountains, flowing like the liquid skies;
> Then would I give the mighty flood release,
> And weep a deluge for the human race.

is, that Saul met a *company* of prophets; a whole company of them! coming down with a psaltery, a tabret, a pipe, and a harp, and that they prophesied, and that he prophesied with them. But it appears afterwards, that Saul prophesied badly, that is, he performed his part badly; for it is said, that "*an evil spirit from God*** came upon Saul, and he prophesied."

Now were there no other passage in the book, called the Bible, than this, to demonstrate to us that we have lost the original meaning of the word *prophesy*, and substituted another meaning in its place, this alone would be sufficient; for it is impossible to use and apply the word *prophesy* in the place it is here used and applied, if we give to it the sense which later times have affixed to it. The manner in which it is here used strips it of all religious meaning, and shews that a man might then be a *prophet*, or might *prophesy*, as he may now be a poet, or a musician, without any regard to the morality or the immorality of his character. The word was originally a term of science, promiscuously applied to poetry and to music, and not restricted to any subject upon which poetry and music might be exercised.

Deborah and Barak are called prophets, not because they predicted any thing, but because they composed the poem or song that bears their name in celebration of an act already done: David is ranked among the prophets, for he was a musician; and was also reputed to be (though perhaps very erroneously) the author of the psalms. But Abraham, Isaac, and Jacob, are not called prophets. It does not appear from any accounts we have that they could either sing, play music, or make poetry.

We are told of the greater and the lesser prophets. They might as well tell us of the greater and the lesser God; for there cannot be degrees in prophesying consistently with its modern sense. But there are degrees in poetry, and therefore the phrase is reconcilable to the case, when we understand by it the greater and the lesser poets.

It is altogether unnecessary, after this, to offer any obser-

---

*As those men, who call themselves divines and commentators, are very fond of puzzling one another, I leave them to contest the meaning of the first part of the phrase, that of, *an evil spirit from God*. I keep to my text. I keep to the meaning of the word prophesy.

vations upon what those men, stiled prophets, have written. The axe goes at once to the root, by shewing that the original meaning of the word has been mistaken, and consequently all the inferences that have been drawn from those books, the devotional respect that has been paid to them, and the laboured commentaries that have been written upon them, under that mistaken meaning, are not worth disputing about.—In many things, however, the writings of the Jewish poets, deserve a better fate than that of being bound up, as they now are, with the trash that accompanies them, under the abused name of the word of God.

If we permit ourselves to conceive right ideas of things, we must necessarily affix the idea, not only of unchangeableness, but of the utter impossibility of any change taking place, by any means or accident whatever, in that which we would honour with the name of the word of God; and therefore the word of God cannot exist in any written or human language.

The continually progressive change to which the meaning of words is subject, the want of an universal language which renders translations necessary, the errors to which translations are again subject, the mistakes of copyists and printers, together with the possibility of wilful alteration, are of themselves evidences, that human language, whether in speech or in print, cannot be the vehicle of the word of God.—The word of God exists in something else.

Did the book, called the Bible, excel in purity of ideas and expression, all the books that are now extant in the world, I would not take it for my rule of faith, as being the word of God; because the possibility would nevertheless exist of my being imposed upon. But when I see throughout the greatest part of this book, scarcely any thing but a history of the grossest vices, and a collection of the most paltry and contemptible tales, I cannot dishonour my Creator by calling it by his name.

Thus much for the Bible. I now go on to the book called the New Testament. The *new* Testament! that is, the *new* Will, as if there could be two wills of the Creator.

Had it been the object or the intention of Jesus Christ to establish a new religion, he would undoubtedly have written the system himself, or *procured it to be written* in his life time. But there is no publication extant authenticated with his name. All the books called the New Testament were written after his death. He was a Jew by birth and by profession; and he was the son of God in like manner that every other person is; for the Creator is the Father of All.

The first four books, called Matthew, Mark, Luke, and John, do not give a history of the life of Jesus Christ, but only detached anecdotes of him. It appears from these books, that the whole time of his being a preacher was not more than eighteen months; and it was only during this short time, that those men became acquainted with him. They make mention of him, at the age of twelve years, sitting, they say, among the Jewish doctors, asking and answering them questions. As this was several years before their acquaintance with him began, it is most probable they had this anecdote from his parents. From this time there is no account of him for about sixteen years. Where he lived, or how he employed himself during this interval, is not known. Most probably he was working at his father's trade, which was that of a carpenter. It does not appear that he had any school education, and the probability is that he could not write, for his parents were extremely poor, as appears from their not being able to pay for a bed when he was born.

It is somewhat curious that the three persons, whose names are the most universally recorded, were of very obscure parentage. Moses was a foundling, Jesus Christ was born in a stable, and Mahomet was a mule-driver. The first and the last of these men, were founders of different systems of religion; but Jesus Christ founded no new system. He called men to the practice of moral virtues, and the belief of one God. The great trait in his character is philanthropy.

The manner in which he was apprehended, shews that he was not much known at that time; and it shews also that the meetings he then held with his followers were in secret: and that he had given over, or suspended, preaching publicly. Judas could no otherways betray him than by giving information where he was, and pointing him out to the officers that went to arrest him; and the reason for employing and paying

Judas to do this, could arise only from the causes already mentioned, that of his not being much known, and living concealed.

The idea of his concealment not only agrees very ill with his reputed divinity, but associates with it something of pusillanimity; and his being betrayed, or in other words, his being apprehended, on the information of one of his followers, shews that he did not intend to be apprehended, and consequently that he did not intend to be crucified.

The Christian mythologists tell us, that Christ died for the sins of the world, and that he came on *purpose to die*. Would it not then have been the same if he had died of a fever, or of the small pox, of old age, or of any thing else?

The declaratory sentence which, they say, was passed upon Adam in case he ate of the apple, was not, that *thou shalt surely be crucified, but thou shalt surely die*. The sentence was death, and not the *manner of dying*. Crucifixion, therefore, or any other particular manner of dying, made no part of the sentence that Adam was to suffer, and consequently, even upon their own tactic, it could make no part of the sentence that Christ was to suffer in the room of Adam. A fever would have done as well as a cross, if there was any occasion for either.

This sentence of death which, they tell us, was thus passed upon Adam, must either have meant dying naturally, that is, ceasing to live, or, have meant what these mythologists call damnation: and consequently, the act of dying on the part of Jesus Christ, must, according to their system, apply as a prevention to one or other of these two *things* happening to Adam and to us.

That it does not prevent our dying is evident, because we all die; and if their accounts of longevity be true, men die faster since the crucifixion than before: and with respect to the second explanation, (including with it the *natural death* of Jesus Christ as a substitute for the *eternal death or damnation* of all mankind) it is impertinently representing the Creator as coming off, or revoking the sentence, by a pun or a quibble upon the word *death*. That manufacturer of quibbles, St. Paul, if he wrote the books that bear his name, has helped this quibble on, by making another quibble upon the word

Adam. He makes there to be two Adams; the one who sins in fact, and suffers by proxy; the other who sins by proxy and suffers in fact. A religion thus interlarded with quibble, subterfuge and pun, has a tendency to instruct its professors in the practice of these arts. They acquire the habit without being aware of the cause.

If Jesus Christ was the Being which those mythologists tell us he was, and that he came into this world to *suffer*, which is a word they sometimes use instead of *to die*, the only real suffering he could have endured would have been *to live*. His existence here was a state of exilement or transportation from heaven, and the way back to his original country was to die. — In fine, every thing in this strange system is the reverse of what it pretends to be. It is the reverse of truth, and I become so tired with examining into its inconsistencies and absurdities, that I hasten to the conclusion of it, in order to proceed to something better.

How much, or what parts of the books called the New Testament, were written by the persons whose names they bear, is what we can know nothing of, neither are we certain in what language they were originally written. The matters they now contain may be classed under two heads: anecdote, and epistolary correspondence.

The four books already mentioned, Matthew, Mark, Luke, and John, are altogether anecdotal. They relate events after they had taken place. They tell what Jesus Christ did and said, and what others did and said to him; and in several instances they relate the same event differently. Revelation is necessarily out of the question with respect to those books; not only because of the disagreement of the writers, but because revelation cannot be applied to the relating of facts by the persons who saw them done, nor to the relating or recording of any discourse or conversation by those who heard it. The book, called the Acts of the Apostles, an anonymous work, belongs also to the anecdotal part.

All the other parts of the New Testament, except the book of enigmas, called the Revelations, are a collection of letters under the name of Epistles; and the forgery of letters has been such a common practice in the world, that the probability is, at least, equal, whether they are genuine or forged. One thing, however, is much less equivocal, which is, that out of the matters contained in those books, together with the assistance of some old stories, the church has set up a system of religion very contradictory to the character of the person whose name it bears. It has set up a religion of pomp and of revenue in pretended imitation of a person whose life was humility and poverty.

The invention of a purgatory, and of the releasing of souls therefrom, by prayers, bought of the church with money; the selling of pardons, dispensations, and indulgences, are revenue laws, without bearing that name or carrying that appearance. But the case nevertheless is, that those things derive their origin from the proxysm of the crucifixion, and the theory deduced therefrom, which was, that one person could stand in the place of another, and could perform meritorious services for him. The probability therefore is, that the whole theory or doctrine of what is called the redemption (which is said to have been accomplished by the act of one person in the room of another) was originally fabricated on purpose to bring forward and build all those secondary and pecuniary redemptions upon; and that the passages in the books upon which the idea or theory of redemption is built, have been manufactured and fabricated for that purpose. Why are we to give this church credit, when she tells us that those books are genuine in every part, any more than we give her credit for every thing else she has told us; or for the miracles she says she has performed. That she *could* fabricate writings is certain, because she could write; and the composition of the writings in question, is of that kind that any body might do it; and that she *did* fabricate them is not more inconsistent with probability, than that she should tell us, as she has done, that she could and did work miracles.

Since then no external evidence can, at this long distance of time, be produced to prove whether the church fabricated the doctrine called redemption or not, (for such evidence, whether for or against, would be subject to the same suspicion of being fabricated) the case can only be referred to the internal evidence which the thing carries of itself; and this affords a very strong presumption of its being a fabrication. For the internal evidence is, that the theory or doctrine of redemption has for its basis, an idea of pecuniary justice, and not that of moral justice.

If I owe a person money and cannot pay him, and he threatens to put me in prison, another person can take the debt upon himself, and pay it for me. But if I have committed a crime, every circumstance of the case is changed. Moral justice cannot take the innocent for the guilty, even if the innocent would offer itself. To suppose justice to do this, is to destroy the principle of its existence, which is the thing itself. It is then no longer justice. It is indiscriminate revenge.

This single reflection will shew that the doctrine of redemption is founded on a mere pecuniary idea corresponding to that of a debt which another person might pay; and as this pecuniary idea corresponds again with the system of second redemptions obtained through the means of money given to the church, for pardons, the probability is, that the same persons fabricated both the one and the other of those theories; and that, in truth, there is no such thing as redemption; that it is fabulous; and that man stands in the same relative condition with his Maker he ever did stand since man existed; and that it is his greatest consolation to think so.

Let him believe this, and he will live more consistently and morally than by any other system. It is by his being taught to contemplate himself as an out-law, as an out-cast, as a beggar, as a mumper, as one thrown, as it were, on a dunghill, at an immense distance from his Creator, and who must make his approaches by creeping and cringing to intermediate beings, that he conceives either a contemptuous disregard for every thing under the name of religion, or becomes indifferent, or turns, what he calls, devout. In the latter case, he consumes his life in grief, or the affectation of it. His prayers are reproaches. His humility is ingratitude. He calls himself a worm, and the fertile earth a dunghill; and all the blessings of life by the thankless name of vanities. He despises the choicest gift of God to man, the GIFT OF REASON; and having endeavoured to force upon himself the belief of a system against which reason revolts, he ungratefully calls it *human reason*, as if man could give reason to himself.

Yet with all this strange appearance of humility, and this contempt for human reason, he ventures into the boldest presumptions. He finds fault with every thing. His selfishness is never satisfied; his ingratitude is never at an end. He takes on himself to direct the Almighty what to do, even in the government of the universe. He prays dictatorially. When it is sun-shine, he prays for rain, and when it is rain, he prays for sun-shine. He follows the same idea in every thing that he prays for; for what is the amount of all his prayers, but an attempt to make the Almighty change his mind, and act otherwise than he does. It is as if he were to say—thou knowest not so well as I.

But some perhaps will say, Are we to have no word of God—No revelation? I answer yes. There is a word of God; there is a revelation.

THE WORD OF GOD IS THE CREATION WE BEHOLD: And it is in *this word*, which no human invention can counterfeit or alter, that God speaketh universally to man.

Human language is local and changeable, and is therefore incapable of being used as the means of unchangeable and universal information. The idea that God sent Jesus Christ to publish, as they say, the glad tidings to all nations, from one end of the earth unto the other, is consistent only with the ignorance of those who knew nothing of the extent of the world, and who believed, as those world-saviours believed, and continued to believe, for several centuries, (and that in contradiction to the discoveries of philosophers, and the experience of navigators) that the earth was flat like a trencher; and that a man might walk to the end of it.

But how was Jesus Christ to make any thing known to all nations? He could speak but one language, which was Hebrew; and there are in the world several hundred languages. Scarcely any two nations speak the same language, or understand each other; and as to translations, every man who knows any thing of languages, knows that it is impossible to translate from one language into another not only without losing a great part of the original, but frequently of mistaking the sense: and besides all this, the art of printing was wholly unknown at the time Christ lived.

It is always necessary that the means that are to accomplish any end, be equal to the accomplishment of that end, or the end cannot be accomplished. It is in this, that the difference between finite and infinite power and wisdom discovers itself. Man frequently fails in accomplishing his end, from a natural inability of the power to the purpose; and frequently from the want of wisdom to apply power properly. But it is impossible for infinite power and wisdom to fail as man faileth. The means it useth are always equal to the end: but human language, more especially as there is not an universal language, is incapable of being used as an universal means of unchangeable and uniform information; and therefore it is not the means that God useth in manifesting himself universally to man.

It is only in the CREATION that all our ideas and conceptions of a *word of God* can unite. The creation speaketh an universal language, independently of human speech or human language, multiplied and various as they be. It is an ever existing original, which every man can read. It cannot be forged; it cannot be counterfeited; it cannot be lost; it cannot be altered; it cannot be suppressed. It does not depend upon the will of man whether it shall be published or not; it publishes itself from one end of the earth to the other. It preaches to all nations and to all worlds; and this *word of God* reveals to man all that is necessary for man to know of God.

Do we want to contemplate his power? We see it in the immensity of the creation. Do we want to contemplate his wisdom? We see it in the unchangeable order by which the incomprehensible Whole is governed. Do we want to contemplate his munificence? We see it in the abundance with which he fills the earth. Do we want to contemplate his mercy? We see it in his not withholding that abundance even from the unthankful. In fine, do we want to know what God is? Search not the book called the scripture, which any human hand might make, but the scripture called the Creation.

The only idea man can affix to the name of God, is, that of a *first cause*, the cause of all things. And incomprehensibly difficult as it is for man to conceive what a first cause is, he arrives at the belief of it, from the tenfold greater difficulty of disbelieving it. It is difficult beyond description to conceive that space can have no end; but it is more difficult to conceive an end. It is difficult beyond the power of man to conceive an eternal duration of what we call time; but it is more impossible to conceive a time when there shall be no time. In like manner of reasoning, every thing we behold carries in itself the internal evidence that it did not make itself. Every man is an evidence to himself, that he did not make himself; neither could his father make himself, nor his grandfather, nor any of his race; neither could any tree, plant, or animal, make itself: and it is the conviction arising from this evidence, that carries us on, as it were, by necessity, to the belief of a first cause eternally existing, of a nature totally different to any material existence we know of, and by the power of which all things exist, and this first cause man calls God.

It is only by the exercise of reason, that man can discover God. Take away that reason, and he would be incapable of understanding any thing; and, in this case, it would be just as consistent to read even the book called the Bible, to a horse as to a man. How then is it that those people pretend to reject reason?

Almost the only parts in the book, called the Bible, that convey to us any idea of God, are some chapters in Job, and the 19th psalm. I recollect no other. Those parts are true *deistical* compositions; for they treat of the *Deity* through his works. They take the book of Creation as the word of God; they refer to no other book; and all the inferences they make are drawn from that volume.

I insert, in this place, the 19th psalm, as paraphrased into English verse, by Addison. I recollect not the prose, and where I write this I have not the opportunity of seeing it.

> The spacious fermament on high,
> With all the blue etherial sky,
> And spangled heavens, a shining frame,
> Their great original proclaim.
> The unwearied sun, from day to day,
> Does his Creator's power display,
> And publishes to every land,
> The work of an Almighty hand.
> Soon as the evening shades prevail,
> The moon takes up the wond'rous tale,

And nightly to the list'ning earth
Repeats the story of her birth.
Whilst all the stars that round her burn,
And all the planets in their turn,
Confirm the tidings as they roll,
And spread the truth from pole to pole.
What tho' in solemn silence, all
Move round this dark terrestrial ball,
What tho' no real voice, nor sound,
Amidst their radiant orbs be found,
In reason's ear they all rejoice,
And utter forth a glorious voice;
For ever singing as they shine,
THE HAND THAT MADE US IS DIVINE.

What more does man want to know than that the hand, or power, that made these things is divine, is omnipotent. Let him believe this, with the force it is impossible to repel if he permits his reason to act, and his rule of moral life will follow of course.

The allusions in Job have all of them the same tendency with this psalm; that of deducing or proving a truth, that would be otherwise unknown, from truths already known.

I recollect not enough of the passages in Job to insert them correctly: but there is one that occurs to me that is applicable to the subject I am speaking upon. "Canst thou by searching find out God; canst thou find out the Almighty to perfection."

I know not how the printers have pointed this passage, for I keep no Bible: but it contains two distinct questions that admits of distinct answers.

First, canst thou by *searching* find out God? Yes. Because, in the first place, I know I did not make myself, and yet I have existence; and by *searching* into the nature of other things, I find that no other thing could make itself; and yet millions of other things exist; therefore it is, that I know, by positive conclusion resulting from this search, that there is a power superior to all those things, and that power is God.

Secondly, Canst thou find out the Almighty to *perfection*?

No. Not only because the power and wisdom he has manifested in the structure of the creation that I behold, is to me
incomprehensible; but because even this manifestation, great
as it is, is probably but a small display of that immensity of
power and wisdom, by which millions of other worlds, to
me invisible by their distance, were created and continue to
exist.

It is evident that both these questions were put to the reason of the person to whom they are supposed to have been
addressed; and it is only by admitting the first question to be
answered affirmatively, that the second could follow. It would
have been unnecessary, and even absurd, to have put a second
question more difficult than the first, if the first question had
been answered negatively. The two questions have different
objects, the first refers to the existence of God, the second to
his attributes. Reason can discover the one, but it falls infinitely short in discovering the whole of the other.

I recollect not a single passage in all the writings ascribed to
the men, called apostles, that convey any idea of what God is.
Those writings are chiefly controversial; and the gloominess
of the subject they dwell upon, that of a man dying in agony
on a cross, is better suited to the gloomy genius of a monk in
a cell, by whom it is not impossible they were written, than to
any man breathing the open air of the creation. The only passage that occurs to me, that has any reference to the works of
God, by which only his power and wisdom can be known, is
related to have been spoken by Jesus Christ, as a remedy
against distrustful care. "Behold the lillies of the field, they
toil not, neither do they spin." This, however, is far inferior to
the allusions in Job, and in the nineteenth psalm; but it is
similar in idea, and the modesty of the imagery is correspondent to the modesty of the man.

As to the christian system of faith, it appears to me as a
species of atheism; a sort of religious denial of God. It professes to believe in a man rather than in God. It is a compound made up chiefly of manism with but little deism, and is
as near to atheism as twilight is to darkness. It introduces
between man and his maker an opaque body which it calls a
redeemer; as the moon introduces her opaque self between
the earth and the sun, and it produces by this means a reli-

gious or an irreligious eclipse of light. It has put the whole orb of reason into shade.

The effect of this obscurity has been that of turning every thing upside down, and representing it in reverse; and among the revolutions it has thus magically produced, it has made a revolution in Theology.

That which is now called natural philosophy, embracing the whole circle of science, of which astronomy occupies the chief place, is the study of the works of God and of the power and wisdom of God in his works, and is the true theology.

As to the theology that is now studied in its place, it is the study of human opinions and of human fancies *concerning* God. It is not the study of God himself in the works that he has made, but in the works or writings that man has made; and it is not among the least of the mischiefs that the christian system has done to the world, that it has abandoned the original and beautiful system of theology, like a beautiful innocent to distress and reproach, to make room for the hag of superstition.

The book of Job, and the 19th psalm, which even the church admits to be more ancient than the chronological order in which they stand in the book called the Bible, are theological orations conformable to the original system of theology. The internal evidence of those orations proves to a demonstration, that the study and contemplation of the works of creation and of the power and wisdom of God revealed and manifested in those works, made a great part of the religious devotion of the times in which they were written; and it was this devotional study and contemplation that led to the discovery of the principles upon which, what are now called Sciences, are established; and it is to the discovery of these principles that almost all the Arts that contribute to the convenience of human life, owe their existence. Every principal art has some science for its parent, though the person who mechanically performs the work does not always, and but very seldom, perceive the connection.

It is a fraud of the christian system to call the sciences *human inventions*; it is only the application of them that is human. Every science has for its basis a system of principles as fixed and unalterable as those by which the universe is regulated and governed. Man cannot make principles; he can only discover them:

For example. Every person who looks at an almanack sees an account when an eclipse will take place, and he sees also that it never fails to take place according to the account there given. This shews that man is acquainted with the laws by which the heavenly bodies move. But it would be something worse than ignorance, were any church on earth to say, that those laws are an human invention.

It would also be ignorance, or something worse, to say, that the scientific principles, by the aid of which man is enabled to calculate and fore-know when an eclipse will take place, are an human invention. Man cannot invent any thing that is eternal and immutable; and the scientific principles he employs for this purpose, must, and are, of necessity, as eternal and immutable as the laws by which the heavenly bodies move, or they could not be used as they are, to ascertain the time when, and the manner how, an eclipse will take place.

The scientific principles that man employs to obtain the fore-knowledge of an eclipse, or of any thing else relating to the motion of the heavenly bodies, are contained chiefly in that part of science that is called trigonometry, or the properties of a triangle, which, when applied to the study of the heavenly bodies, is called astronomy; when applied to direct the course of a ship on the ocean, it is called navigation; when applied to the construction of figures drawn by a rule and compass, it is called geometry; when applied to the construction of plans of edifices, it is called architecture; when applied to the measurement of any portion of the surface of the earth, it is called land-surveying. In fine, it is the soul of science. It is an eternal truth: it contains the *mathematical demonstration* of which man speaks, and the extent of its uses are unknown.

It may be said, that man can make or draw a triangle, and therefore a triangle is an human invention.

But the triangle, when drawn, is no other than the image of the principle: it is a delineation to the eye, and from thence to the mind, of a principle that would otherwise be imperceptible. The triangle does not make the principle, any more than a candle taken into a room that was dark, makes the chairs and tables that before were invisible. All the properties of a triangle exist independently of the figure, and existed before any triangle was drawn or thought of by man. Man had no more to do in the formation of those properties, or principles, than he had to do in making the laws by which the heavenly bodies move; and therefore the one must have the same divine origin as the other.

In the same manner as it may be said, that man can make a triangle, so also may it be said, he can make the mechanical instrument, called a lever. But the principle by which the lever acts, is a thing distinct from the instrument, and would exist if the instrument did not: it attaches itself to the instrument after it is made; the instrument therefore can act no otherwise than it does act; neither can all the effort of human invention make it act otherwise. That which, in all such cases, man calls the *effect*, is no other than the principle itself rendered perceptible to the senses.

Since then man cannot make principles, from whence did he gain a knowledge of them, so as to be able to apply them, not only to things on earth, but to ascertain the motion of bodies so immensely distant from him as all the heavenly bodies are? From whence, I ask, *could* he gain that knowledge, but from the study of the true theology?

It is the structure of the universe that has taught this knowledge to man. That structure is an ever existing exhibition of every principle upon which every part of mathematical science is founded. The offspring of this science is mechanics; for mechanics is no other than the principles of science applied practically. The man who proportions the several parts of a mill, uses the same scientific principles, as if he had the power of constructing an universe: but as he cannot give to matter that invisible agency, by which all the component parts of the immense machine of the universe have influence upon each other, and act in motional unison together without any apparent contact, and to which man has given the name of attraction, gravitation, and repulsion, he supplies the place of that agency by the humble imitation of teeth and cogs. All the parts of man's microcosm must visibly touch. But could he gain a knowledge of that agency, so as to be able to apply it in practice, we might then say, that another *canonical book* of the word of God had been discovered.

If man could alter the properties of the lever, so also could he alter the properties of the triangle: for a lever (taking that sort of lever, which is called a steel-yard for the sake of explanation) forms, when in motion, a triangle. The line it descends from (one point of that line being in the fulcrum) the line it descends to, and the chord of the arc, which the end of the lever describes in the air, are the three sides of a triangle. The other arm of the lever describes also a triangle; and the corresponding sides of those two triangles, calculated scientifically or measured geometrically; and also the sines, tangents, and secants generated from the angles, and geometrically measured, have the same proportions to each other, as the different weights have that will balance each other on the lever, leaving the weight of the lever out of the case.

It may also be said that man can make a wheel and axis, that he can put wheels of different magnitudes together, and produce a mill. Still the case comes back to the same point, which is, that he did not make the principle that gives the wheels those powers. That principle is as unalterable as in the former cases, or rather it is the same principle under a different appearance to the eye.

The power that two wheels, of different magnitudes, have upon each other, is in the same proportion as if the semi-diameter of the two wheels were joined together and made into that kind of lever I have described, suspended at the part where the semi-diameters join; for the two wheels, scientifically considered, are no other than the two circles generated by the motion of the compound lever.

It is from the study of the true theology that all our knowledge of science is derived, and it is from that knowledge that all the arts have originated.

The Almighty lecturer, by displaying the principles of science in the structure of the universe, has invited man to study and to imitation. It is as if he had said to the inhabitants of this globe that we call ours, "I have made an earth for man to dwell upon, and I have rendered the starry heavens visible, to teach him science and the arts. He can now provide for his own comfort, AND LEARN FROM MY MUNIFICENCE TO ALL, TO BE KIND TO EACH OTHER."

Of what use is it, unless it be to teach man something, that his eye is endowed with the power of beholding, to an incomprehensible distance, an immensity of worlds revolving in the ocean of space? Or of what use is it that this immensity of worlds is visible to man? What has man to do with the Pleiades, with Orion, with Sirius, with the star he calls the north star, with the moving orbs he has named Saturn, Jupiter, Mars, Venus, and Mercury, if no uses are to follow from their being visible? A less power of vision would have been sufficient for man, if the immensity he now possesses were given only to waste itself, as it were, on an immense desart of space glittering with shows.

It is only by contemplating what he calls the starry heavens, as the book and school of science, that he discovers any use in their being visible to him, or any advantage resulting from his immensity of vision. But when he contemplates the subject in this light, he sees an additional motive for saying that *nothing was made in vain*; for in vain would be this power of vision if it taught man nothing.

As the christian system of faith has made a revolution in theology, so also has it made a revolution in the state of learning. That which is now called learning was not learning originally. Learning does not consist, as the schools now make it to consist, in the knowledge of languages, but in the knowledge of things to which language gives names.

The Greeks were a learned people; but learning with them, did not consist in speaking Greek, any more than in a Roman's speaking Latin, or a Frenchman's speaking French, or an Englishman's speaking English. From what we know of the Greeks, it does not appear that they knew or studied any language but their own; and this was one cause of their becoming so learned; it afforded them more time to apply themselves to better studies. The schools of the Greeks were schools of science and philosophy, and not of languages; and it is in the knowledge of the things that science and philosophy teach, that learning consists.

Almost all the scientific learning that now exists, came to us from the Greeks, or the people who spoke the Greek language. It therefore became necessary to the people of other nations, who spoke a different language, that some among them should learn the Greek language, in order that the learning the Greeks had, might be made known in those nations, by translating the Greek books of science and philosophy into the mother tongue of each nation.

The study therefore of the Greek language, (and in the same manner for the Latin) was no other than the drudgery business of a linguist; and the language thus obtained, was no other than the means, or as it were, the tools, employed to obtain the learning the Greeks had. It made no part of the learning itself; and was so distinct from it, as to make it exceedingly probable, that the persons who had studied Greek sufficiently to translate those works, such, for instance, as Euclid's Elements, did not understand any of the learning the works contained.

As there is now nothing new to be learned from the dead languages, all the useful books being already translated, the languages are become useless, and the time expended in teaching and in learning them is wasted. So far as the study of languages may contribute to the progress and communication of knowledge (for it has nothing to do with the *creation* of knowledge) it is only in the living languages that new knowledge is to be found: and certain it is, that, in general, a youth will learn more of a living language in one year, than of a dead language in seven; and it is but seldom that the teacher knows much of it himself. The difficulty of learning the dead languages does not arise from any superior abstruseness in the languages themselves, but in their *being dead*, and the pronunciation entirely lost. It would be the same with any other language when it becomes dead. The best Greek linguist, that now exists, does not understand Greek so well as a Grecian plowman did, or a Grecian milkmaid; and the same for the Latin, compared with a plowman or a milkmaid of the Romans; and with respect to pronunciation, and idiom, not so well as the cows that she milked. It would therefore be advantageous to the state of learning, to abolish the study of the dead languages, and to make learning consist, as it originally did, in scientific knowledge.

The apology that is sometimes made for continuing to teach the dead languages is, that they are taught at a time when a child is not capable of exerting any other mental faculty than that of memory. But this is altogether erroneous. The human mind has a natural disposition to scientific knowledge, and to the things connected with it. The first and favourite amusement of a child, even before it begins to play, is that of imitating the works of man. It builds houses with cards or sticks; it navigates the little ocean of a bowl of water with a paper boat; or dams the stream of a gutter, and contrives something which it calls a mill; and it interests itself in the fate of its works with a care that resembles affection. It afterwards goes to school, where its genius is killed by the barren study of a dead language, and the philosopher is lost in the linguist.

But the apology that is now made for continuing to teach the dead languages, could not be the cause at first of cutting down learning to the narrow and humble sphere of linguistry; the cause, therefore, must be sought for elsewhere. In all researches of this kind, the best evidence that can be produced, is the internal evidence the thing carries with itself, and the evidence of circumstances that unites with it, both of which, in this case, are not difficult to be discovered.

Putting then aside, as matter of distinct consideration, the outrage offered to the moral justice of God, by supposing him to make the innocent suffer for the guilty, and also the loose morality and low contrivance of supposing him to change himself into the shape of a man, in order to make an excuse to himself for not executing his supposed sentence upon Adam; putting, I say, those things aside, as matter of distinct consideration, it is certain, that what is called the christian system of faith, including in it the whimsical account of the creation; the strange story of Eve, the snake, and the apple; the amphibious idea of a man-god; the corporeal idea of the death of a god; the mythological idea of a family of gods; and the christian system of arithmetic, that three are one, and one is three, are all irreconciliable, not only to the divine gift of reason that God has given to man, but to the knowledge that man gains of the power and wisdom of God, by the aid of the sciences, and by studying the structure of the universe that God has made.

The setters up, therefore, and the advocates of the christian system of faith, could not but foresee that the continually

progressive knowledge that man would gain by the aid of science, of the power and wisdom of God, manifested in the
structure of the universe, and in all the works of creation,
would militate against, and call into question, the truth of
their system of faith; and therefore it became necessary to
their purpose to cut learning down to a size less dangerous
to their project, and this they effected by restricting the idea
of learning to the dead study of dead languages.

They not only rejected the study of science out of the christian schools, but they persecuted it; and it is only within
about the last two centuries that the study has been revived.
So late as 1610 Galileo, a Florentine, discovered and introduced the use of telescopes, and by applying them to observe
the motions and appearances of the heavenly bodies, afforded
additional means for ascertaining the true structure of the
universe. Instead of being esteemed for these discoveries, he
was sentenced to renounce them, or the opinions resulting
from them, as a damnable heresy. And prior to that time
Vigilius was condemned to be burned for asserting the antipodes, or in other words, that the earth was a globe, and
habitable in every part where there was land; yet the truth of
this is now too well known even to be told.

If the belief of errors not morally bad did no mischief, it
would make no part of the moral duty of man to oppose and
remove them. There was no moral ill in believing the earth
was flat like a trencher, any more than there was moral virtue
in believing it was round like a globe; neither was there any
moral ill in believing that the creator made no other world
than this, any more than there was moral virtue in believing
that he made millions, and that the infinity of space is filled
with worlds. But when a system of religion is made to grow
out of a supposed system of creation that is not true, and to
unite itself therewith in a manner almost inseparable therefrom, the case assumes an entirely different ground. It is then
that errors, not morally bad, become fraught with the same
mischiefs as if they were. It is then that the truth, though
otherwise indifferent in itself, becomes an essential, by becoming the criterion, that either confirms by corresponding
evidence, or denies by contradictory evidence, the reality of
the religion itself. In this view of the case it is the moral duty

of man to obtain every possible evidence, that the structure of the heavens, or any other part of creation affords, with respect to systems of religion. But this, the supporters or partizans of the christian system, as if dreading the result, incessantly opposed, and not only rejected the sciences, but persecuted the professors. Had Newton or Descartes lived three or four hundred years ago, and pursued their studies as they did, it is most probable they would not have lived to finish them; and had Franklin drawn lightning from the clouds at the same time, it would have been at the hazard of expiring for it in flames.

Latter times have laid all the blame upon the Goths and Vandals, but, however unwilling the partizans of the Christian system may be to believe or to acknowledge it, it is nevertheless true, that the age of ignorance commenced with the Christian system. There was more knowledge in the world before that period than for many centuries afterwards; and as to religious knowledge, the christian system, as already said, was only another species of mythology; and the mythology to which it succeeded, was a corruption of an ancient system of theism.*

*It is impossible for us now to know at what time the heathen mythology began; but it is certain, from the internal evidence that it carries, that it did not begin in the same state or condition in which it ended. All the gods of that mythology, except Saturn, were of modern invention. The supposed reign of Saturn was prior to that which is called the heathen mythology, and was so far a species of theism that it admitted the belief of only one God. Saturn is supposed to have abdicated the government in favour of his three sons and one daughter, Jupiter, Pluto, Neptune and Juno: after this, thousands of other gods and demi-gods were imaginarily created, and the calendar of gods increased as fast as the calendar of saints, and the calendar of courts have increased since.

All the corruptions that have taken place in theology, and in religion, have been produced by admitting of what man calls *revealed religion*. The mythologists pretended to more revealed religion than the christians do. They had their oracles and their priests, who were supposed to receive and deliver the word of God verbally on almost all occasions.

Since then all corruptions, down from Moloch to modern predestinarianism, and from the human sacrifices of the heathens to the christian sacrifice of the Creator, have been produced by admitting what is called *revealed religion*, the most effectual means to prevent all such evils and impositions, is not to admit of any other revelation than that which is manifested in the book of Creation; and to contemplate the Creation, as the only true and real word of God that ever did or ever will exist, and that every thing else, called the word of God is fable and imposition.

It is owing to this long interregnum of science, *and to no other cause*, that we have now to look back through a vast chasm of many hundred years to the respectable characters we call the ancients. Had the progression of knowledge gone on proportionably with the stock that before existed, that chasm would have been filled up with characters rising superior in knowledge to each other; and those ancients, we now so much admire, would have appeared respectably in the back ground of the scene. But the christian system laid all waste; and if we take our stand about the beginning of the sixteenth century, we look back through that long chasm, to the times of the ancients, as over a vast sandy desart, in which not a shrub appears to intercept the vision to the fertile hills beyond.

It is an inconsistency, scarcely possible to be credited, that any thing should exist under the name of a *religion*, that held it to be *irreligious* to study and contemplate the structure of the universe that God had made. But the fact is too well established to be denied. The event that served more than any other, to break the first link in this long chain of despotic ignorance, is that known by the name of the reformation by Luther. From that time, though it does not appear to have made any part of the intention of Luther, or of those who are called reformers, the Sciences began to revive, and Liberality, their natural associate, began to appear. This was the only public good the reformation did; for with respect to religious good, it might as well not have taken place. The mythology still continued the same; and a multiplicity of national popes grew out of the downfal of the Pope of Christendom.

Having thus shewn, from the internal evidence of things, the cause that produced a change in the state of learning, and the motive for substituting the study of the dead languages in the place of the Sciences, I proceed, in addition to the several observations already made in the former part of this work, to compare, or rather to confront, the evidence that the structure of the universe affords, with the christian system of religion. But as I cannot begin this part better than by referring to the ideas that occurred to me at an early part of life, and which I doubt not have occurred in some degree to almost every other person at one time or other, I shall state what those ideas were, and add thereto such other matter as shall arise out of the subject, giving to the whole, by way of preface, a short introduction.

My father being of the quaker profession, it was my good fortune to have an exceedingly good moral education, and a tolerable stock of useful learning. Though I went to the grammar school*, I did not learn Latin, not only because I had no inclination to learn languages, but because of the objection the quakers have against the books in which the language is taught. But this did not prevent me from being acquainted with the subjects of all the Latin books used in the school.

The natural bent of my mind was to science. I had some turn, and I believe some talent, for poetry; but this I rather repressed than encouraged, as leading too much into the field of imagination. As soon as I was able I purchased a pair of globes, and attended the philosophical lectures of Martin and Ferguson, and became afterwards acquainted with Dr. Bevis, of the society, called the Royal Society, then living in the Temple, and an excellent astronomer.

I had no disposition for what was called politics. It presented to my mind no other idea than is contained in the word Jockeyship. When, therefore, I turned my thoughts towards matters of government, I had to form a system for myself, that accorded with the moral and philosophic principles in which I had been educated. I saw, or at least I thought I saw, a vast scene opening itself to the world in the affairs of America; and it appeared to me, that unless the Americans changed the plan they were then pursuing, with respect to the government of England, and declare themselves independent, they would not only involve themselves in a multiplicity of new difficulties, but shut out the prospect that was then offering itself to mankind through their means. It was from these motives that I published the work known by the name of *Common sense*, which is the first work I ever did publish: and so far as I can judge of myself, I believe I never should have

---

*The same school, Thetford in Norfolk, that the present counsellor Mingay went to, and under the same master.

been known in the world as an author on any subject whatever, had it not been for the affairs of America. I wrote *Common sense* the latter end of the year 1775, and published it the
first of January 1776. Independence was declared the fourth of
July following.

Any person who has made observations on the state and
progress of the human mind, by observing his own, cannot
but have observed, that there are two distinct classes of what
we call Thoughts: those that we produce in ourselves by reflection and the act of thinking, and those that bolt into the
mind of their own accord. I have always made it a rule to
treat those voluntary visitors with civility, taking care to examine, as well as I was able, if they were worth entertaining;
and it is from them I have acquired almost all the knowledge
that I have. As to the learning that any person gains from
school education, it serves only, like a small capital, to put
him in the way of beginning learning for himself afterwards.
Every person of learning is finally his own teacher; the reason of which is, that principles, being of a distinct quality to
circumstances, cannot be impressed upon the memory. Their
place of mental residence is the understanding, and they are
never so lasting as when they begin by conception. Thus
much for the introductory part.

From the time I was capable of conceiving an idea, and
acting upon it by reflection, I either doubted the truth of the
christian system, or thought it to be a strange affair; I scarcely
know which it was: but I well remember, when about seven
or eight years of age, hearing a sermon read by a relation of
mine, who was a great devotee of the church, upon the subject of what is called *Redemption by the Death of the Son of
God*. After the sermon was ended I went into the garden, and
as I was going down the garden steps (for I perfectly recollect
the spot) I revolted at the recollection of what I had heard,
and thought to myself that it was making God Almighty act
like a passionate man that killed his son when he could not
revenge himself any other way; and as I was sure a man would
be hanged that did such a thing, I could not see for what
purpose they preached such sermons. This was not one of
those kind of thoughts that had any thing in it of childish
levity; it was to me a serious reflection arising from the idea I

had, that God was too good to do such an action, and also too Almighty to be under any necessity of doing it. I believe in the same manner to this moment; and I moreover believe, that any system of religion that has any thing in it that shocks the mind of a child, cannot be a true system.

It seems as if parents of the christian profession were ashamed to tell their children any thing about the principles of their religion. They sometimes instruct them in morals, and talk to them of the goodness of what they call Providence; for the christian mythology has five deities: there is God the Father, God the Son, God the Holy Ghost, the God Providence, and the Goddess Nature. But the christian story of God the Father putting his son to death, or employing people to do it (for that is the plain language of the story) cannot be told by a parent to a child; and to tell him that it was done to make mankind happier and better is making the story still worse, as if mankind could be improved by the example of murder; and to tell him that all this is a mystery, is only making an excuse for the incredibility of it.

How different is this to the pure and simple profession of Deism! The true deist has but one Deity; and his religion consists in contemplating the power, wisdom, and benignity of the Deity in his works, and in endeavouring to imitate him in every thing moral, scientifical, and mechanical.

The religion that approaches the nearest of all others to true deism, in the moral and benign part thereof, is that professed by the quakers, but they have contracted themselves too much by leaving the works of God out of their system. Though I reverence their philanthropy, I cannot help smiling at the conceit, that if the taste of a quaker could have been consulted at the creation, what a silent and drab-coloured creation it would have been! Not a flower would have blossomed its gaieties, nor a bird been permitted to sing.

Quitting these reflections, I proceed to other matters. After I had made myself master of the use of the globes and of the orrery,* and conceived an idea of the infinity of space, and of

---

*As this book may fall into the hands of persons who do not know what an orrery is, it is for their information I add this note, as the name gives no idea of the uses of the thing. The orrery has its name from the person who invented it. It is a machinery of clock-work representing the universe in minia-

the eternal divisibility of matter, and obtained, at least, a general knowledge of what is called natural philosophy, I began to compare, or, as I have before said, to confront, the internal evidence those things afford with the christian system of faith.

Though it is not a direct article of the christian system that this world that we inhabit is the whole of the habitable creation, yet it is so worked up therewith, from what is called the Mosaic account of the creation, the story of Eve and the apple, and the counterpart of that story, the death of the son of God, that to believe otherwise, that is, to believe that God created a plurality of worlds, at least as numerous as what we call stars, renders the christian system of faith at once little and ridiculous; and scatters it in the mind like feathers in the air. The two beliefs cannot be held together in the same mind; and he who thinks that he believes both, has thought but little of either.

Though the belief of a plurality of worlds was familiar to the ancients, it is only within the last three centuries that the extent and dimensions of this globe that we inhabit, have been ascertained. Several vessels, following the tract of the ocean, have sailed entirely round the world, as a man may march in a circle, and come round by the contrary side of the circle to the spot he set out from. The circular dimensions of our world in the widest part, as a man would measure the widest round of an apple or a ball, is only twenty five thousand and twenty English miles, reckoning sixty nine miles and an half to an equatorial degree, and may be sailed round in the space of about three years.*

A world of this extent may, at first thought, appear to us to be great; but if we compare it with the immensity of space in

---

ture; and in which the revolution of the earth round itself and round the sun, the revolution of the moon round the earth, the revolution of the planets round the sun, their relative distances from the sun as the center of the whole system, their relative distances from each other, and their different magnitudes, are represented as they really exist in what we call the heavens.

*Allowing a ship to sail, on an average, three miles in an hour, she would sail entirely round the world in less than one year, if she could sail in a direct circle; but she is obliged to follow the course of the ocean.

which it is suspended, like a bubble or a balloon in the air, it is infinitely less in proportion than the smallest grain of sand is to the size of the world, or the finest particle of dew to the whole ocean; and is therefore but small; and, as will be hereafter shewn, is only *one* of a system of worlds, of which the universal creation is composed.

It is not difficult to gain some faint idea of the immensity of space in which this and all the other worlds are suspended, if we follow a progression of ideas. When we think of the size or dimensions of a room, our ideas limit themselves to the walls, and there they stop. But when our eye, or our imagination, darts into space, that is, when it looks upward into what we call the open air, we cannot conceive any walls or boundaries it can have; and if for the sake of resting our ideas, we suppose a boundary, the question immediately renews itself, and asks, what is beyond that boundary? and in the same manner, what is beyond the next boundary? and so on, till the fatigued imagination returns and says, *there is no end.* Certainly, then, the Creator was not pent for room when he made this world no larger than it is; and we have to seek the reason in something else.

If we take a survey of our own world, or rather of this, of which the Creator has given us the use, as our portion in the immense system of creation, we find every part of it, the earth, the waters, and the air that surround it, filled, and, as it were, crouded with life, down from the largest animals that we know of, to the smallest insects the naked eye can behold, and from thence to others still smaller, and totally invisible without the assistance of the microscope. Every tree, every plant, every leaf, serves not only as an habitation, but as a world to some numerous race, till animal existence becomes so exceedingly refined, that the effluvia of a blade of grass would be food for thousands.

Since then no part of our earth is left unoccupied, why is it to be supposed, that the immensity of space is a naked void, lying in eternal waste. There is room for millions of worlds as large or larger than ours, and each of them millions of miles apart from each other.

Having now arrived at this point, if we carry our ideas only one thought further, we shall see, perhaps, the true reason, at least a very good reason for our happiness, why the Creator, instead of making one immense world, extending over an immense quantity of space, has preferred dividing that quantity of matter into several distinct and separate worlds, which we call planets, of which our earth is one. But before I explain my ideas upon this subject, it is necessary (not for the sake of those that already know, but for those who do not) to shew what the system of the universe is.

That part of the universe, that is called the solar system (meaning the system of worlds to which our earth belongs, and of which Sol, or in English language the Sun, is the center) consists, besides the Sun, of six distinct orbs, or planets, or worlds, besides the secondary bodies, called satellites, or moons, of which our earth has one that attends her in her annual revolution round the sun, in like manner as the other satellites, or moons, attend the planets, or worlds, to which they severally belong, as may be seen by the assistance of the telescope.

The Sun is the center, round which those six worlds, or planets, revolve at different distances therefrom, and in circles concentric to each other. Each world keeps constantly in nearly the same tract round the Sun, and continues, at the same time, turning round itself, in nearly an upright position, as a top turns round itself when it is spinning on the ground, and leans a little sideways.

It is this leaning of the earth, ($23\frac{1}{2}$ degrees) that occasions summer and winter, and the different length of days and nights. If the earth turned round itself in a position perpendicular to the plane or level of the circle it moves in round the Sun, as a top turns round when it stands erect on the ground, the days and nights would be always of the same length, twelve hours day, and twelve hours night, and the season would be uniformly the same throughout the year.

Every time that a planet (our earth for example) turns round itself, it makes what we call day and night; and every time it goes entirely round the Sun, it makes what we call a year, consequently our world turns three hundred and sixty-five times round itself, in going once round the Sun.*

The names that the ancients gave to those six worlds, and which are still called by the same names, are Mercury, Venus, this world that we call ours, Mars, Jupiter, and Saturn. They appear larger to the eye than the stars, being many million miles nearer to our earth than any of the stars are. The planet Venus is that which is called the evening star, and sometimes the morning star, as she happens to set after, or rise before, the Sun, which, in either case, is never more than three hours.

The Sun, as before said, being the center, the planet, or world, nearest the Sun, is Mercury; his distance from the Sun is thirty-four million miles, and he moves round in a circle always at that distance from the Sun, as a top may be supposed to spin round in the tract in which a horse goes in a mill. The second world is Venus; she is fifty seven million miles distant from the Sun, and consequently moves round in a circle much greater than that of Mercury. The third world is this that we inhabit, and which is eighty eight million miles distant from the Sun, and consequently moves round in a circle greater than that of Venus. The fourth world is Mars; he is distant from the Sun one hundred and thirty four million miles, and consequently moves round in a circle greater than that of our earth. The fifth is Jupiter; he is distant from the Sun five hundred and fifty seven million miles, and consequently moves round in a circle greater than that of Mars. The sixth world is Saturn; he is distant from the Sun seven hundred and sixty three million miles, and consequently moves round in a circle that surrounds the circles or orbits of all the other worlds or planets.

The space, therefore, in the air, or in the immensity of space, that our solar system takes up for the several worlds to perform their revolutions in round the sun, is of the extent in a strait line of the whole diameter of the orbit or circle, in which Saturn moves round the Sun, which being double his

---

*Those who supposed that the Sun went round the earth every 24 hours, made the same mistake in idea, that a cook would do in fact, that should make the fire go round the meat, instead of the meat turning round itself towards the fire.

distance from the Sun, is fifteen hundred and twenty six million miles; and its circular extent is nearly five thousand million, and its globical content is almost three thousand five hundred million times three thousand five hundred million square miles.*

But this, immense as it is, is only one system of worlds. Beyond this, at a vast distance into space, far beyond all power of calculation, are the stars called the fixed stars. They are called fixed, because they have no revolutionary motion as the six worlds or planets have that I have been describing. Those fixed stars continue always at the same distance from each other, and always in the same place, as the Sun does in the center of our system. The probability therefore is, that each of those fixed stars is also a sun, round which another system of worlds or planets, though too remote for us to discover, performs its revolutions, as our system of worlds does round our central sun.

By this easy progression of ideas, the immensity of space will appear to us to be filled with systems of worlds; and that no part of space lies at waste, any more than any part of our globe of earth and water is left unoccupied.

Having thus endeavoured to convey, in a familiar and easy manner, some idea of the structure of the universe, I return to explain what I before alluded to, namely, the great benefits arising to man in consequence of the Creator having made a *plurality* of worlds, such as our system is, consisting of a

---

*If it should be asked, how can man know these things? I have one plain answer to give, which is, that man knows how to calculate an eclipse, and also how to calculate, to a minute of time, when the planet Venus, in making her revolutions round the sun, will come in a strait line between our earth, and the sun, and will appear to us about the size of a large pea passing across the face of the sun. This happens but twice in about an hundred years, at the distance of about eight years from each other, and has happened twice in our time, both of which were foreknown by calculation. It can also be known when they will happen again for a thousand years to come, or to any other portion of time. As, therefore, man could not be able to do those things if he did not understand the solar system, and the manner in which the revolutions of the several planets or worlds are performed, the fact of calculating an eclipse or a transit of Venus, is a proof in point that the knowledge exists; and as to a few thousand, or even a few million miles more or less, it makes scarcely any sensible difference in such immense distances.

central sun and six worlds, besides satellites, in preference to that of creating one world only of a vast extent.

It is an idea I have never lost sight of, that all our knowledge of science is derived from the revolutions (exhibited to our eye, and from thence to our understanding) which those several planets, or worlds, of which our system is composed, make in their circuit round the Sun.

Had then the quantity of matter which these six worlds contain been blended into one solitary globe, the consequence to us would have been, that either no revolutionary motion would have existed, or not a sufficiency of it, to give us the ideas and the knowledge of science we now have; and it is from the sciences that all the mechanical arts that contribute so much to our earthly felicity and comfort are derived.

As therefore the Creator made nothing in vain, so also must it be believed that he organized the structure of the universe in the most advantageous manner for the benefit of man; and as we see, and from experience feel, the benefits we derive from the structure of the universe, formed as it is, which benefits we should not have had the opportunity of enjoying, if the structure, so far as relates to our system, had been a solitary globe, we can discover, at least, one reason why a *plurality* of worlds has been made, and that reason calls forth the devotional gratitude of man, as well as his admiration.

But it is not to us, the inhabitants of this globe, only, that the benefits arising from a plurality of worlds are limited. The inhabitants of each of the worlds, of which our system is composed, enjoy the same opportunities of knowledge as we do. They behold the revolutionary motions of our earth, as we behold theirs. All the planets revolve in sight of each other; and therefore the same universal school of science presents itself to all.

Neither does the knowledge stop here. The system of worlds, next to us, exhibits in its revolutions, the same principles and school of science, to the inhabitants of their system, as our system does to us, and in like manner throughout the immensity of space.

Our ideas, not only of the Almightyness of the Creator, but of his wisdom and his beneficence, become enlarged in proportion as we contemplate the extent and the structure of the universe. The solitary idea of a solitary world rolling, or at rest, in the immense ocean of space, gives place to the chearful idea of a society of worlds, so happily contrived, as to administer, even by their motion, instruction to man. We see our own earth filled with abundance; but we forget to consider how much of that abundance is owing to the scientific knowledge the vast machinery of the universe has unfolded.

But, in the midst of those reflections, what are we to think of the christian system of faith that forms itself upon the idea of only one world, and that of no greater extent, as is before shewn, than twenty five thousand miles. An extent, which a man walking at the rate of three miles an hour, for twelve hours in the day, could he keep on in a circular direction, would walk entirely round in less than two years. Alas! what is this to the mighty ocean of space, and the Almighty power of the Creator!

From whence then could arise the solitary and strange conceit that the Almighty, who had millions of worlds equally dependent on his protection, should quit the care of all the rest, and come to die in our world, because, they say, one man and one woman had eaten an apple. And, on the other hand, are we to suppose that every world, in the boundless creation, had an Eve, an apple, a serpent, and a redeemer. In this case, the person who is irreverently called the Son of God, and sometimes God himself, would have nothing else to do than to travel from world to world, in an endless succession of death, with scarcely a momentary interval of life.

It has been, by rejecting the evidence, that the word, or works of God in the creation, affords to our senses, and the action of our reason upon that evidence, that so many wild and whimsical systems of faith, and of religion, have been fabricated and set up. There may be many systems of religion, that so far from being morally bad, are in many respects morally good: but there can be but ONE that is true; and that one, necessarily must, as it ever will, be in all things consistent with the ever existing word of God that we behold in his works. But such is the strange construction of the Christian system of faith, that every evidence the heavens affords to man, either directly contradicts it, or renders it absurd.

It is possible to believe, and I always feel pleasure in encouraging myself to believe it, that there have been men in the world who persuaded themselves that, what is called *a pious fraud*, might, at least under particular circumstances, be productive of some good. But the fraud being once established, could not afterwards be explained; for it is with a pious fraud, as with a bad action, it begets a calamitous necessity of going on.

The persons who first preached the christian system of faith, and in some measure combined with it the morality preached by Jesus Christ, might persuade themselves that it was better than the heathen mythology that then prevailed. From the first preachers, the fraud went on to the second, and to the third, till the idea of its being a pious fraud became lost in the belief of its being true; and that belief came again encouraged by the interest of those who made a livelihood by preaching it.

But though such a belief might, by such means, be rendered almost general among the laity, it is next to impossible to account for the continual persecution carried on by the church, for several hundred years, against the sciences and against the professors of science, if the church had not some record or some tradition, that it was originally no other than a pious fraud, or did not foresee, that it could not be maintained against the evidence that the structure of the universe afforded.

Having thus shewn the irreconcileable inconsistencies between the real word of God existing in the universe, and that which is called, *the word of God*, as shewn to us in a printed book, that any man might make, I proceed to speak of the three principal means that have been employed in all ages, and perhaps in all countries, to impose upon mankind.

Those three means are, Mystery, Miracle, and Prophecy. The two first are incompatible with true religion, and the third ought always to be suspected.

With respect to mystery, every thing we behold is, in one sense, a mystery to us. Our own existence is a mystery: the whole vegetable world is a mystery. We cannot account how it is that an acorn, when put into the ground, is made to develop itself, and become an oak. We know not how it is that the seed we sow unfolds and multiplies itself, and returns to us such an abundant interest for so small a capital.

The fact, however, as distinct from the operating cause, is not a mystery because we see it; and we know also the means we are to use, which is no other than putting the seed in the ground. We know therefore as much as is necessary for us to know; and that part of the operation that we do not know, and which if we did, we could not perform, the Creator takes upon himself and performs it for us. We are therefore better off than if we had been let into the secret, and left to do it for ourselves.

But though every created thing is in this sense a mystery, the word mystery cannot be applied to *moral truth*, any more than obscurity can be applied to light. The God in whom we believe is a God of moral truth, and not a God of mystery or obscurity. Mystery is the antagonist of truth. It is a fog of human invention, that obscures truth and represents it in distortion. Truth never invelops *itself* in mystery; and the mystery in which it is at any time inveloped, is the work of its antagonist, and never of itself.

Religion, therefore, being the belief of a God, and the practice of moral truth, cannot have connection with mystery. The belief of a God, so far from having any thing of mystery in it, is of all beliefs the most easy, because it arises to us, as is before observed, out of necessity. And the practice of moral truth, or in other words, a practical imitation of the moral goodness of God, is no other than our acting towards each other, as he acts benignly towards all. We cannot *serve* God in the manner we serve those who cannot do without such service; and, therefore, the only idea we can have of serving God, is that of contributing to the happiness of the living creation that God has made. This cannot be done by retiring ourselves from the society of the world, and spending a recluse life in selfish devotion.

The very nature and design of religion, if I may so express it, prove even to demonstration, that it must be free from every thing of mystery, and unincumbered with every thing that is mysterious. Religion, considered as a duty, is incumbent upon every living soul alike, and therefore must be on a level to the understanding and comprehension of all. Man does not learn religion as he learns the secrets and mysteries of a trade. He learns the theory of religion by reflection. It arises out of the action of his own mind upon the things which he sees, or upon what he may happen to hear or to read, and the practice joins itself thereto.

When men, whether from policy or pious fraud, set up systems of religion incompatible with the word or works of God in the creation, and not only above, but repugnant to human comprehension, they were under the necessity of inventing, or adopting, a word that should serve as a bar to all questions, enquiries, and speculations. The word *mystery* answered this purpose; and thus it has happened, that religion, which, in itself, is without mystery, has been corrupted into a fog of mysteries.

As *mystery* answered all general purposes, *miracle* followed as an occasional auxilary. The former served to bewilder the mind, the latter to puzzle the senses. The one was the lingo; the other the legerdemain.

But before going further into this subject, it will be proper to enquire what is to be understood by a miracle.

In the same sense that every thing may be said to be a mystery, so also may it be said, that every thing is a miracle, and that no one thing is a greater miracle than another. The elephant, though larger, is not a greater miracle than a mite; nor a mountain a greater miracle than an atom. To an Almighty power, it is no more difficult to make the one than the other, and no more difficult to make a million of worlds than to make one. Every thing therefore is a miracle in one sense; whilst, in the other sense, there is no such thing as a miracle. It is a miracle when compared to our power, and to our comprehension. It is not a miracle compared to the power that performs it. But as nothing in this description conveys the idea that is affixed to the word miracle, it is necessary to carry the enquiry further.

Mankind have conceived to themselves certain laws by which, what they call, nature, is supposed to act; and that a miracle is something contrary to the operation and effect of those laws. But unless we know the whole extent of those laws, and of what are commonly called, the powers of nature, we are not able to judge whether any thing that may appear to us wonderful, or miraculous, be within, or be beyond, or be contrary to, her natural power of acting.

The ascension of a man several miles high into the air, would have every thing in it that constitutes the idea of a miracle, if it were not known that a species of air can be generated several times lighter than the common atmospheric air, and yet possess elasticity enough to prevent the balloon, in which that light air is enclosed, from being compressed into as many times less bulk, by the common air that surrounds it. In like manner, extracting flashes or sparks of fire from the human body, as visibly as from a steel struck with a flint, and causing iron or steel to move without any visible agent, would also give the idea of a miracle, if we were not acquainted with electricity and magnatism: so also would many other experiments in natural philosophy, to those who are not acquainted with the subject. The restoring persons to life, who are to appearance dead, as is practiced upon drowned persons, would also be a miracle, if it were not known that animation is capable of being suspended without being extinct.

Besides these, there are performances by slight of hand, and by persons acting in concert, that have a miraculous appearance, which, when known, are thought nothing of. And besides these, there are mechanical and optical deceptions. There is now an exhibition in Paris of ghosts or spectres, which, though it is not imposed upon the spectators as a fact, has an astonishing appearance. As therefore we know not the extent to which either nature or art can go, there is no positive criterion to determine what a miracle is; and mankind, in giving credit to appearances, under the idea of their being miracles, are subject to be continually imposed upon.

Since then appearances are so capable of deceiving, and things not real have a strong resemblance to things that are, nothing can be more inconsistent, than to suppose, that the Almighty would make use of means, such as are called miracles, that would subject the person who performed them to the suspicion of being an impostor, and the persons who related them to be suspected of lying, and the doctrine intended to be supported thereby, to be suspected as a fabulous invention.

Of all the modes of evidence that ever were invented to

obtain belief to any system or opinion, to which the name of religion has been given, that of *miracle*, however successful the imposition may have been, is the most inconsistent. For, in the first place, whenever recourse is had to show, for the purpose of procuring that belief, (for a miracle, under any idea of the word, is a show) it implies a lameness or weakness in the doctrine that is preached. And, in the second place, it is degrading the Almighty into the character of a show-man, playing tricks to amuse and make the people stare and wonder. It is also the most equivocal sort of evidence that can be set up; for the belief is not to depend upon the thing called a miracle, but upon the credit of the reporter, who says that he saw it; and therefore the thing, were it true, would have no better chance of being believed than if it were a lie.

Suppose, I were to say, that when I sat down to write this book, a hand presented itself in the air, took up the pen, and wrote every word that is herein written; would any body believe me? certainly they would not. Would they believe me a whit the more if the thing had been a fact? certainly they would not. Since then, a real miracle, were it to happen, would be subject to the same fate as the falshood, the inconsistency becomes the greater, of supposing the Almighty would make use of means that would not answer the purpose for which they were intended, even if they were real.

If we are to suppose a miracle to be something so entirely out of the course of what is called nature, that she must go out of that course to accomplish it; and we see an account given of such miracle by the person who said he saw it, it raises a question in the mind very easily decided, which is, Is it more probable that nature should go out of her course, or that a man should tell a lie? We have never seen, in our time, nature go out of her course, but we have good reason to believe that millions of lies have been told in the same time; it is therefore at least millions to one, that the reporter of a miracle tells a lie.

The story of the whale swallowing Jonah, though a whale is large enough to do it, borders greatly on the marvellous; but it would have approached nearer to the idea of a miracle, if Jonah had swallowed the whale. In this case, which may serve for all cases of miracles, the matter would decide itself as before stated, namely, Is it more probable that a man should have swallowed a whale, or told a lie?

But supposing that Jonah had really swallowed the whale, and gone with it in his belly to Nineveh, and to convince the people that it was true, have cast it up in their sight of the full length and size of a whale, would they not have believed him to have been the devil instead of a prophet? or, if the whale had carried Jonah to Nineveh, and cast him up in the same public manner, would they not have believed the whale to have been the devil, and Jonah one of his imps?

The most extraordinary of all the things called miracles, related in the New Testament, is that of the devil flying away with Jesus Christ, and carrying him to the top of a high mountain; and to the top of the highest pinacle of the temple, and showing him, and promising to him *all the kingdoms of the world*. How happened it that he did not discover America? or is it only with *kingdoms* that his sooty highness has any interest?

I have too much respect for the moral character of Christ, to believe that he told this whale of a miracle himself; neither is it easy to account for what purpose it could have been fabricated, unless it were to impose upon the connoisseurs of miracles, as is sometimes practised upon the connoisseurs of Queen Ann's farthings, and collectors of relics and antiquities; or to render the belief of miracles ridiculous, by outdoing miracle, as Don Quixote outdid chivalry; or to embarrass the belief of miracles by making it doubtful by what power, whether of God, or of the devil, any thing called a miracle was performed. It requires, however, a great deal of faith in the devil to believe this miracle.

In every point of view, in which those things called miracles can be placed and considered, the reality of them is improbable, and their existence unnecessary. They would not, as before observed, answer any useful purpose, even if they were true; for it is more difficult to obtain belief to a miracle, than to a principle evidently moral, without any miracle. Moral principle speaks universally for itself. Miracle could be but a thing of the moment, and seen but by a few; after this, it requires a transfer of faith, from God to man, to believe a miracle upon man's report. Instead therefore of admitting the recitals of miracles, as evidence of any system of religion being true, they ought to be considered as symptoms of its being fabulous. It is necessary to the full and upright character of truth, that it rejects the crutch; and it is consistent with the character of fable, to seek the aid that truth rejects. Thus much for mystery and miracle.

As mystery and miracle took charge of the past and the present, prophecy took charge of the future, and rounded the tenses of faith. It was not sufficient to know what had been done, but what would be done. The supposed prophet was the supposed historian of times to come; and if he happened, in shooting with a long bow of a thousand years, to strike within a thousand miles of a mark, the ingenuity of posterity could make it point-blank; and if he happened to be directly wrong, it was only to suppose, as in the case of Jonah and Nineveh, that God had repented himself, and changed his mind. What a fool do fabulous systems of religion make of man!

It has been shewn in a former part of this work, that the original meaning of the words *prophet* and *prophesying* has been changed, and that a prophet, in the sense the word is now used, is a creature of modern invention; and it is owing to this change in the meaning of the words, that the flights and metaphors of the Jewish poets, and phrases and expressions now rendered obscure by our not being acquainted with the local circumstances to which they applied at the time they were used, have been erected into prophesies, and made to bend to explanations at the will and whimsical conceits of sectaries, expounders, and commentators. Every thing unintelligible was prophetical, and every thing insignificant was typical. A blunder would have served for a prophecy; and a dish-clout for a type.

If by a prophet we are to suppose a man, to whom the Almighty communicated some event that would take place in future, either there were such men, or there were not. If there were, it is consistent to believe that the event, so communicated, would be told in terms that could be understood; and not related in such a loose and obscure manner as to be out of the comprehension of those that heard it, and so equivocal as to fit almost any circumstance that might happen afterwards. It is conceiving very irreverently of the Almighty to suppose he would deal in this jesting manner with mankind: yet all the things called prophesies, in the book called the Bible, come under this description.

But it is with prophesy, as it is with miracle. It could not answer the purpose even if it were real. Those to whom a prophecy should be told, could not tell whether the man prophesied or lied, or whether it had been revealed to him or whether he conceited it: and if the thing that he prophesied, or pretended to prophesy, should happen, or something like it among the multitude of things that are daily happening, nobody could again know whether he foreknew it, or guessed at it, or whether it was accidental. A prophet, therefore, is a character useless and unnecessary; and the safe side of the case is, to guard against being imposed upon by not giving credit to such relations.

Upon the whole, mystery, miracle, and prophesy, are appendages that belong to fabulous and not to true religion. They are the means by which so many *Lo heres!* and *Lo theres!* have been spread about the world, and religion been made into a trade. The success of one impostor gave encouragement to another, and the quieting salvo of doing *some good* by keeping up a *pious fraud,* protected them from remorse.

Having now extended the subject to a greater length than I first intended, I shall bring it to a close by abstracting a summary from the whole.

First, that the idea or belief of a word of God existing in print, or in writing, or in speech, is inconsistent in itself for the reasons already assigned. These reasons, among many others, are the want of an universal language; the mutability of language; the errors to which translations are subject; the possibility of totally suppressing such a word; the probability of altering it, or of fabricating the whole, and imposing it upon the world.

Secondly, That the creation we behold is the real and ever existing word of God, in which we cannot be deceived. It proclaimeth his power, it demonstrates his wisdom, it manifests his goodness and beneficence.

Thirdly, That the moral duty of man consists in imitating the moral goodness and beneficence of God manifested in the creation towards all his creatures. That seeing, as we daily do, the goodness of God to all men, it is an example calling upon all men to practice the same towards each other; and consequently that every thing of persecution and revenge between man and man, and every thing of cruelty to animals, is a violation of moral duty.

I trouble not myself about the manner of future existence. I content myself with believing, even to positive conviction, that the power that gave me existence is able to continue it, in any form and manner he pleases, either with or without this body; and it appears more probable to me that I shall continue to exist hereafter, than that I should have had existence, as I now have, before that existence began.

It is certain that, in one point, all nations of the earth, and all religions agree. All believe in a God. The things in which they disagree, are the redundancies annexed to that belief; and therefore, if ever an universal religion should prevail, it will not be believing any thing new, but in getting rid of redundancies, and believing as man believed at first. Adam, if ever there were such a man, was created a Deist; but in the mean time let every man follow, as he has a right to do, the religion and the worship he prefers.

———————

Thus far I had written on the 28th of December, 1793. In the evening I went to the Hotel Philadelphia (formerly White's Hotel) passage des Petits Pères, where I lodged when I came to Paris, in consequence of being elected a member of the Convention, but had left the lodging about nine months, and taken lodgings in the Rue Fauxbourg St. Denis, for the sake of being more retired than I could be in the middle of the town.

Meeting with a company of Americans at the Hotel Philadelphia, I agreed to spend the evening with them, and, as my lodging was distant about a mile and half, I bespoke a bed at the hotel. The company broke up about twelve o'clock, and I went directly to bed. About four in the morning I was awakened by a rapping at my chamber door: when I opened it, I saw a guard, and the master of the hotel with them. The guard told me they came to put me under arrestation, and to demand the key of my papers. I desired them to walk in, and I would dress myself, and go with them immediately.

It happened that Achilles Audibert, of Calais, was then in the hotel; and I desired to be conducted into his room. When we came there, I told the guard that I had only lodged at the hotel for that night;—that I was printing a work, and that part of that work was at the Maison Bretagne, Rue Jacob; and desired they would take me there first, which they did.

The printing office, at which the work was printing, was near to the Maison Bretagne, where Colonel Blackden and Joel Barlow, of the United States of America, lodged; and I had desired Joel Barlow to compare the proof sheets with the copy, as they came from the press. The remainder of the manuscript, from page 32 to 76, was at my lodging. But besides the necessity of my collecting all the parts of the work together, that the publication might not be interrupted by my imprisonment, or by any event that might happen to me, it was highly proper that I should have a fellow citizen of America with me during the examination of my papers, as I had letters of correspondence in my possession of the President of congress General Washington; the minister of foreign affairs to congress Mr. Jefferson; and the late Benjamin Franklin; and it might be necessary for me to make a proces verbal to send to congress.

It happened that Joel Barlow had received only one proof sheet of the work, which he had compared with the copy, and sent it back to the printing-office.

We then went, in company with Joel Barlow, to my lodging; and the guard, or commissaires, took with them the interpreter to the committee of surety general. It was satisfactory to me, that they went through the examination of my papers with the strictness they did; and it is but justice that I say, they did it not only with civility, but with tokens of respect to my character.

I shewed them the remainder of the manuscript of the foregoing work. The interpreter examined it, and returned it to me, saying, *"it is an interesting work; it will do much good."* I also shewed him another manuscript, which I had intended for the committee of public safety; it is intitled, "Observations on the Commerce between the United States of America and France."

After the examination of my papers was finished, the guard

conducted me to the prison of the Luxembourg, where they left me as they would a man whose undeserved fate they regretted. I offered to write under the proces-verbal they had made, that they had executed their orders with civility, but they declined it.

THOMAS PAINE.

POSTSCRIPT.

THE matters contained in this Postscript would not have appeared, at least at this time, had it not been for the extraordinary circumstance of my being put into a state of arrestation, and deprived of my liberty, by the committee of surety-general.

A motion was made in the convention to exclude foreigners from the convention. Bourdon de l'Oise said, "We have heard a great deal of the patriotism of Thomas Paine; but it is said (on dit) that he intrigues with an ancient agent of the office of foreign affairs."

I wish that Bourdon de l'Oise had been prudent enough to have informed himself better of things than he has done, before he said any thing about me. It ought to have occurred to him, that I have a reputation in the world of more years standing than he has of months. It is more than eighteen years since I proposed the independence and the establishment of the American Republic. He should also have recollected that as I am a citizen of a country in alliance with France, it might be in my power to render some services to France, which himself could not. But since he has dragged me into an explanation of what, it would have been better, should not yet be made public, I will state the whole as concisely, but at the same time as prudently, as I can.

I know but one person in the office of foreign affairs. He is adjoint in the American department of that office. He is married to a citizenne of the United States of America, and consequently my acquaintance with him was very natural. Thus much by way of preface. I now come to the point.

I met Barrère, of the committee of public safety, one day on the Boulevards; I believe it was in August last. He asked me something in French, which I did not understand; and we went together to the office of foreign affairs. The agent in the

American department served as interpreter. Barrère then asked me, "If I could furnish him with the plan of constitution I had presented to the Committee of Constitution. The plan, he said, contained some things he wished had been adopted*." I told him that I could, and that I would send the plan to him the next morning, which I did; and it is still in his possession.

Barrère then asked me my opinion about sending commissioners from the convention to the congress of the United States of America? I told him that I thought it would be very proper. But as verbal interpretation was tedious, I offered to give him my opinion in writing, and leave it at the office of foreign affairs to be translated for him. Barrère thanked me, and desired that I would; and said also, that he should be glad of any information or observations I could give him. He then asked me if an hundred ship loads of flour could be procured from America? I told him that it could; and that I would give him an account of the quantity of flour, grain, Indian corn, and rice, annually exported from America, by which he would see that an hundred ship loads was but a small quantity compared with the annual exports of that country.

In two or three days after this, I carried to the office of foreign affairs, to be translated for Barrère, an account of the annual quantity of American exports, distinguishing the several articles of flour, wheat, rye, Indian corn, and rice, amounting in the whole to upwards of twelve hundred ship loads, allowing each ship to carry two thousand barrels of flour, each barrel weighing 184 pounds French.

I then gave, as I had promised, my opinion, in writing, on the subject of sending commissioners from the convention to congress. I introduced the matter, by saying that I intended to return to America the latter end of the year; that any service I could render to France, when I arrived in America, I would do voluntarily, and without any recompence; but that it would be inconsistent that I should be one of the commissioners; for though my fellow citizens of America might be pleased at my being elected a member of the convention, they

---

*Barrère and myself were both members of the Committee of Constitution.

would not like to see me return among them in any other character than as one of themselves.

I then communicated to Barrère such matters respecting America as might be proper for the commissioners to know. After this, I gave him an account of the different parties in England for and against the war with France. I then entered extensively into the confederacy of foreign powers formed against France, and shewed, from a variety of reasons and circumstances, that the confederacy could not long hold together, and that the parties would quarrel among themselves.

I concluded my correspondence, which extended to upwards of twenty pages, with giving to Barrère my opinion upon the internal affairs of France, and the best measures to be adopted. I told him very freely, and that also, in the most affectionate manner, that liberty and the revolution were incomplete until the constitution was established and in practice.

All these papers were translated, and sent to Barrère, and the originals were returned to me, and are now in my possession. They were among the papers that the commissaries of the committee of general surety examined. The commissaries did me the justice to tell me, that every thing they found in my papers, (which took up almost the whole day to examine) shewed me to be a man of good morals and good principles, and as such they gave the key of my apartments into my own care, and did not, as the public news-papers have said, put the seals upon my papers.

While I was communicating the abovementioned matters to Barrère, the agent at the foreign office said to me one day, that *salt-petre was becoming scarce.*

The next morning I gave him a written paper, beginning with the following words — "You tell me, *that salt-petre is becoming scarce. I here communicate to you a plan of the late Captain Paul Jones, which if successfully put in practice, will supply France with that article.*" I then stated what the plan was, enjoining the agent to translate it himself, and send it to the committee of public safety, which he did.

Though Bourdon de l'Oise has been so imprudent as to force me into an explanation of many things that would (as I have already said) been better not to have been told at present, I will so far guard against that imprudence, as not to tell what the plan was, because the success depends upon secrecy, which was my reason for enjoining the agent to translate it himself. But as Danton reads English, and I cannot write French, I have sent a copy of the plan to him, that he may compare it with the plan sent to the committee of public safety.

I come now to speak of the last paper that has been translated for me at the office of foreign affairs, which was in September last, since which I have not been there.

Every man who has any knowledge of national politics must see the difficulty of bringing the present war to a conclusion, even after the belligerent powers are tired of carrying it on. The difficulty arises partly from the nature of the war, and partly from the circumstances that attend it. Almost all the European powers are involved in the war, and there is scarcely any power left to offer its services for the purpose of bringing about a peace.

This being the case, I wrote to Mr. Jefferson, late minister from the United States of America to France, and now minister foreign affairs to congress, to engage him to propose to congress, to send commissioners to Europe, to confer with the ministers of all the neutral nations on the means of bringing about a peace, and of establishing the revolution and the constitution at once.

I wrote and sent at the same time a letter to be inserted in the news papers of the United States of America, for the purpose of giving to my fellow citizens of that country a just idea of the heterogeneous confederacy formed against France, and also to promote the object of sending commissioners to Europe. I also printed five hundred copies here, (Paris) at my own expence; I gave some of them among such of the members of the convention as understood English. I sent fifty to Calais; and I made a present of twenty-five to the office of foreign affairs. I desired the agent at that office to translate the letter into French, which he did, and the translation is now in my possession. One of the objects of this letter is, to shew to the confederacy (as well as to the rest of the world) the folly of their attempt against France, in all the points of view in which it can be politically placed. Here follows the letter. It will speak for itself. The reader will see in it the ideas of a man who looks above all local parties, and who employs his mind (as he did throughout the whole of the American revolution) only upon national and capital objects.

A Citizen of the United States of America,
To the Citizens of Europe.

PHILADELPHIA, July 28, 1793
18th Year of Independence.

"UNDERSTANDING that a proposal is intended to be made at the ensuing meeting of the Congress of the United States of America, 'to send Commissioners to Europe to confer with the Ministers of all the Neutral Powers, for the purpose of negociating preliminaries of Peace,' I address this letter to you on that subject, and on the several matters connected therewith.

"In order to discuss this subject through all its circumstances, it will be necessary to take a review of the state of Europe, prior to the French revolution. It will from thence appear, that the powers leagued against France are fighting to attain an object, which, were it possible to be attained, would be injurious to themselves.

"This is not an uncommon error in the history of wars and governments, of which the conduct of the English government in the war against America is a striking instance. She commenced that war for the avowed purpose of subjugating America; and after wasting upwards of one hundred millions sterling, and then abandoning the object, she discovered, in the course of three or four years, that the prosperity of England was increased, instead of being diminished, by the independence of America. In short, every circumstance is pregnant with some natural effect, upon which intentions and opinions have no influence; and the political error lies in misjudging what the effect will be. England misjudged it in the American war, and the reasons I shall now offer will shew, that she misjudges it in the present war.—In discussing this subject, I leave out of the question every thing respecting forms and systems of government; for as all the governments of Europe differ from each other, there is no reason that the government of France should not differ from the rest.

"OF THE STATE OF EUROPE PRIOR TO THE FRENCH REVOLUTION.

"The clamours continually raised in all the countries of Europe were, that the family of the Bourbons was become too powerful; that the intrigues of the court of France endangered the peace of Europe. Austria saw with a jealous eye the connection of France with Prussia; and Prussia, in her turn, became jealous of the connection of France with Austria; England had wasted millions unsuccessfully in attempting to prevent the family compact with Spain; Russia disliked the alliance between France and Turkey; and Turkey became apprehensive of the inclination of France towards an alliance with Russia. Sometimes the quadruple alliance alarmed some of the powers, and at other times a contrary system alarmed others, and in all those cases the charge was always made against the intrigues of the Bourbons.

"Admitting those matters to be true, the only thing that could have quieted the apprehensions of all those powers with respect to the interference of France, would have been her entire NEUTRALITY in Europe; but this was impossible to be obtained, or if obtained was impossible to be secured, because the genius of her government was repugnant to all such restrictions.

"It now happens that by entirely changing the genius of her government, which France has done for herself, this neutrality, which neither wars could accomplish nor treaties secure, arises naturally of itself, and becomes the ground upon which the war should terminate. It is the thing that approaches the nearest of all others to what ought to be the political views of all the European powers; and there is nothing that can so effectually secure this neutrality, as that the genius of the French government should be different from the rest of Europe.

"But if their object is to restore the Bourbons and monarchy together, they will unavoidably restore with it all the evils of which they have complained; and the first question of discord will be, whose ally is that monarchy to be?

"Will England agree to the restoration of the family compact against which she has been fighting and scheming ever since it existed? Will Prussia agree to restore the alliance between France and Austria, or will Austria agree to restore the former connection between France and Prussia, formed on purpose to oppose herself; or will Spain or Russia, or any of the maritime powers, agree that France and her navy should be allied to England? In fine, will any of the powers agree to strengthen the hands of the other against itself? Yet all these cases involve themselves in the original question of the restoration of the Bourbons; and on the other hand, all of them disappear by the neutrality of France.

"If their object is not to restore the Bourbons, it must be the impracticable project of a partition of the country. The Bourbons will then be out of the question, or, more properly speaking, they will be put in a worse condition: for as the preservation of the Bourbons made a part of the first object, the extirpation of them makes a part of the second. Their pretended friends will then become interested in their destruction, because it is favourable to the purpose of partition that none of the nominal claimants should be left in existence.

"But however the project of a partition may at first blind the eyes of the confederacy, or however each of them may hope to outwit the other in the progress or in the end, the embarrassments that will arise are insurmountable. But even were the object attainable, it would not be of such general advantage to the parties as the neutrality of France, which costs them nothing, and to obtain which they would formerly have gone to war.

OF THE PRESENT STATE OF EUROPE, AND THE CONFEDERACY.

In the first place the confederacy is not of that kind that forms itself originally by concert and consent. It has been forced together by chance—a heterogeneous mass, held only by the accident of the moment; and the instant that accident ceases to operate, the parties will retire to their former rivalships.

I will now, independently of the impracticability of a partition project, trace out some of the embarrassments which will arise among the confederated parties; for it is contrary to the interest of a majority of them that such a project should succeed.

To understand this part of the subject it is necessary, in the first place, to cast an eye over the map of Europe, and observe the geographical situation of the several parts of the confederacy; for however strongly the passionate politics of the moment may operate, the politics that arise from geographical situation are the most certain, and will in all cases finally prevail.

The world has been long amused with what is called the *"balance of power."* But it is not upon armies only that this balance depends. Armies have but a small circle of action. Their progress is slow and limited. But when we take maritime power into the calculation, the scale extends universally. It comprehends all the interests connected with commerce.

The two great maritime powers are England and France. Destroy either of those, and the balance of naval power is destroyed. The whole world of commerce that passes on the Ocean would then lie at the mercy of the other, and the ports of any nation in Europe might be blocked up.

The geographical situation of those two maritime powers comes next under consideration. Each of them occupies one entire side of the channel from the straits of Dover and Calais to the opening into the Atlantic. The commerce of all the northern nations, from Holland to Russia, must pass the straits of Dover and Calais, and along the Channel, to arrive at the Atlantic.

This being the case, the systematical politics of all the nations, northward of the straits of Dover and Calais, can be ascertained from their geographical situation; for it is necessary to the safety of their commerce that the two sides of the Channel, either in whole or in part, should not be in the possession either of England or France. While one nation possesses the whole of one side, and the other nation the other side, the northern nations cannot help seeing that in any situation of things their commerce will always find protection on one side or the other. It may sometimes be that of England and sometimes that of France.

Again, while the English navy continues in its present condition, it is necessary that another navy should exist to controul the universal sway the former would otherwise have over the commerce of all nations. France is the only nation in Europe where this balance can be placed. The navies of the North, were they sufficiently powerful, could not be sufficiently operative. They are blocked up by the ice six months in the year. Spain lies too remote; besides which, it is only for the sake of her American mines that she keeps up her navy.

Applying these cases to the project of a partition of France, it will appear, that the project involves with it a DESTRUCTION OF THE BALANCE OF MARITIME POWER; because it is only by keeping France entire and indivisible that the balance can be kept up. This is a case that at first sight lies remote and almost hidden. But it interests all the maritime and commercial nations in Europe in as great a degree as any case that has ever come before them.—In short, it is with war as it is with law. In law, the first merits of the case become lost in the multitude of arguments; and in war they become lost in the variety of events. New objects arise that take the lead of all that went before, and everything assumes a new aspect. This was the case in the last great confederacy in what is called the succession war, and most probably will be the case in the present.

I have now thrown together such thoughts as occurred to me on the several subjects connected with the confederacy against France, and interwoven with the interest of the neutral powers. Should a conference of the neutral powers take place, these observations will, at least, serve to generate others. The whole matter will then undergo a more extensive investigation than it is in my power to give; and the evils attending upon either of the projects, that of restoring the Bourbons, or of attempting a partition of France, will have the calm opportunity of being fully discussed.

On the part of England, it is very extraordinary that she should have engaged in a former confederacy, and a long expensive war, to *prevent* the family compact, and now engage in another confederacy to *preserve* it. And on the part of the other powers, it is as inconsistent that they should engage in a partition project, which, could it be executed, would immediately destroy the balance of maritime power in Europe, and would probably produce a second war, to remedy the political errors of the first.

A CITIZEN OF THE UNITED STATES OF AMERICA.

The Age of Reason
Part the Second

1795

PREFACE.

I HAVE mentioned in the former part of the *Age of Reason*, that it had long been my intention to publish my thoughts upon religion, but that I had originally reserved it to a later period in life, intending it to be the last work I should undertake. The circumstances, however, which existed in France in the latter end of the year 1793, determined me to delay it no longer. The just and humane principles of the revolution, which philosophy had first diffused, had been departed from. The idea, always dangerous to society as it is derogatory to the Almighty, that priests could forgive sins, though it seemed to exist no longer, had blunted the feelings of humanity, and callously prepared men for the commission of all crimes. The intolerant spirit of church persecution had transferred itself into politics; the tribunals, stiled revolutionary, supplied the place of an inquisition, and the guillotine of the stake. I saw many of my most intimate friends destroyed; others daily carried to prison; and I had reason to believe, and had also intimations given me, that the same danger was approaching myself.

Under these disadvantages, I began the former part of the *Age of Reason*; I had, besides, neither bible nor testament to refer to, though I was writing against both, nor could I procure any; notwithstanding which, I have produced a work that no bible believer, though writing at his ease, and with a library of church books about him, can refute. Towards the latter end of December of that year, a motion was made and carried to exclude foreigners from the convention. There were but two, Anacharsis Clootz, and myself; and I saw I was particularly pointed at by Bourdon de l'Oise in his speech on that motion. Conceiving, after this, that I had but a few days of liberty, I set down and brought the work to a close as speedily as possible; and I had not finished it more than six hours, in the state it has since appeared, before a guard came, about three in the morning, with an order signed by the two committees of public safety and surety general for putting me in arrestation as a foreigner, and conveying me to the prison of the Luxembourg. I contrived, in my way there, to call on Joel Barlow, and I put the manuscript of the work into his hands, as more safe than in my possession in prison; and not knowing what might be the fate in France, either of the writer or the work, I addressed it to the protection of the citizens of the United States.

It is justice that I say, that the guard who executed this order, and the interpreter to the committee of general surety, who accompanied them to examine my papers, treated me not only with civility, but with respect. The keeper of the Luxembourg, Benoit, a man of good heart, shewed to me every friendship in his power, as did also all his family, while he continued in that station. He was removed from it, put into arrestation, and carried before the tribunal upon a malignant accusation, but acquitted.

After I had been in the Luxembourg about three weeks, the Americans, then in Paris, went in a body to the convention, to reclaim me as their countryman and friend; but were answered by the president, Vadier, who was also president of the committee of surety general, and had signed the order for my arrestation, that I was born in England. I heard no more after this from any person out of the walls of the prison, till the fall of Robespierre on the 9th of Thermidor, 27th July 1794.

About two months before this event, I was seized with a fever that in its progress had every symptom of becoming mortal, and from the effects of which I am not recovered. It was then that I remembered with renewed satisfaction, and congratulated myself most sincerely, on having written the former part of the *Age of Reason*. I had then but little expectation of surviving, and those about me had less. I know therefore, by experience, the conscientious trial of my own principles.

I was then with three chamber comrades, Joseph Vanheule of Bruges, Charles Bastini and Michael Robyns of Louvain. The unceasing and anxious attention of these three friends to me by night and day, I remember with gratitude and mention with pleasure. It happened that a physician (Dr. Graham) and a surgeon (Mr. Bond) part of the suite of General O'Hara, were then in the Luxembourg. I ask not myself whether it be convenient to them, as men under the English government, that I express to them my thanks, but I should reproach myself if I did not, and also to the physician of the Luxembourg, Dr. Markoski.

I have some reason to believe, because I cannot discover any other, that this illness preserved me in existence. Among the papers of Robespierre that were examined and reported upon to the convention by a committee of deputies, is a note in the hand writing of Robespierre in the following words:

"Démander que Thomas Paine soit décrété d'accusation, pour l'intérêt de l'Amérique autant que de la France."

"Demand that Thomas Paine be decreed of accusation, for the interest of America as well as of France."

From what cause it was that the intention was not put in execution, I know not, and cannot inform myself; and therefore I ascribe it to impossibility on account of that illness.

The Convention, to repair as much as lay in their power the injustice I had sustained, invited me publicly and unanimously to return into the Convention, and which I accepted, to shew I could bear an injury without permitting it to injure my principles or my disposition. It is not because right principles have been violated that they are to be abandoned.

I have seen, since I have been at liberty, several publications written, some in America and some in England, as answers to the former part of the *Age of Reason*. If the authors of these can amuse themselves by so doing, I shall not interrupt them. They may write against the work and against me as much as they please. They do me more service than they intend, and I can have no objection that they write on. They will find, however, by this second part, without its being written as an answer to them, that they must return to their work, and spin their cobweb over again. The first is brushed away by accident.

They will now find that I have furnished myself with a bible and testament; and I can say also that I have found them to be much worse books than I had conceived. If I have erred in any thing in the former part of the *Age of Reason*, it has been by speaking better of some parts than they deserved.

I observe that all my opponents resort, more or less, to what they call scripture evidence and bible authority to help them out. They are so little masters of the subject as to confound a dispute about authenticity, with a dispute about doctrines. I will, however, put them right, that if they should be disposed to write any more, they may know how to begin.

October, 1795.   THOMAS PAINE.

THE AGE OF REASON.

IT has often been said that any thing may be proved from the bible; but before any thing can be admitted as proved from the bible, the bible itself must be proved to be true; for if the bible be not true, or the truth of it be doubtful, it ceases to have authority and cannot be admitted as proof of any thing.

It has been the practice of all Christian commentators on the bible, and of all Christian priests and preachers, to impose the bible on the world as a mass of truth, and as the word of God. They have disputed and wrangled, and have anathematised each other about the supposeable meaning of particular parts and passages therein: one has said and insisted that such a passage meant such a thing; another that it meant directly the contrary; and a third that it meant neither one nor the other, but something different from both; and this they have called *understanding* the bible.

It has happened that all the answers that I have seen to the former part of *the Age of Reason*, have been written by priests; and these pious men, like their predecessors, contend and wrangle and *understand* the bible. Each understands it differently, but each understands it best, and they have agreed in nothing, but in telling their readers that Thomas Paine understands it not.

Now, instead of wasting their time and heating themselves in fractious disputations about doctrinal points drawn from the bible, these men *ought to know*, and if they do not it is civility to inform them, that the first thing to be *understood* is, whether there is sufficient authority for believing the bible to be the word of God, or whether there is not?

There are matters in that book said to be done by the *express command of God*, that are as shocking to humanity, and to every idea we have of moral justice, as any thing done by Robespierre, by Carrier, by Joseph Lebon, in France, by the English government in the East-Indies, or by any other assassin in modern times. When we read in the books ascribed to Moses, Joshua, &c. that they (the Israelites) came by stealth upon whole nations of people, who, as the history itself shews, had given them no offence, that they put *all those nations to the sword — that they spared neither age nor infancy — that they utterly destroyed men, women, and children — that they left not a soul to breathe,* expressions that are repeated over and over again in those books, and that too with exulting ferocity, are we sure these things are facts? Are we sure that the Creator of man commissioned these things to be done? Are we sure that the books that tell us so were written by his authority?

It is not the antiquity of a tale that is any evidence of its truth, on the contrary it is a symptom of its being fabulous; for the more ancient any history pretends to be, the more it has the resemblance of fable. The origin of every nation is buried in fabulous tradition, and that of the Jews is as much to be suspected as any other.

To charge the commission of things upon the Almighty, which in their own nature, and by every rule of moral justice, are crimes, as all assassination is, and more especially the assassination of infants, is a matter of serious concern. The bible tells us, that those assassinations were done by the *express command of God.* To believe therefore the bible to be true, we must *unbelieve* all our belief in the moral justice of God; for wherein could crying or smiling infants offend? And to read the bible without horror, we must undo every thing that is tender, sympathising, and benevolent in the heart of man. Speaking for myself, if I had no other evidence that the bible is fabulous than the sacrifice I must make to believe it to be true, that alone would be sufficient to determine my choice.

But in addition to all the moral evidence against the bible, I will, in the progress of this work, produce such other evidence as even a priest cannot deny, and shew from that evidence, that the bible is not entitled to credit as being the word of God.

But before I proceed to this examination, I will shew wherein the bible differs from all other ancient writings with respect to the nature of the evidence necessary to establish its authenticity; and this is the more proper to be done because the advocates of the bible in their answers to the former part of *the Age of Reason*, undertake to say, and they put some stress thereon, that the authenticity of the bible is as well established as that of any other ancient book, as if our belief of the one could become any rule for our belief of the other.

I know, however, but of one ancient book that authoritatively challenges universal consent and belief, and that is *Euclid's Elements of Geometry**; and the reason is, because it is a book of self-evident demonstration, entirely independent of its author, and of every thing relating to time, place, and circumstance. The matters contained in that book would have the same authority they now have, had they been been written by any other person, or had the work been anonymous, or had the author never been known; for the identical certainty of who was the author, makes no part of our belief of the matters contained in the book.

But it is quite otherwise with respect to the books ascribed to Moses, to Joshua, to Samuel, &c. Those are books of *testimony*, and they testify of things naturally incredible; and therefore the whole of our belief, as to the authenticity of those books, rests, in the first place, upon the *certainty* that they were written by Moses, Joshua, and Samuel; secondly, upon the credit we give to their testimony. We may believe the first, that is, we may believe the certainty of the authorship, and yet not the testimony; in the same manner, that we may believe that a certain person gave evidence upon a case and yet not believe the evidence that he gave. But if it should be found that the books ascribed to Moses, Joshua, and Samuel, were not written by Moses, Joshua, and Samuel, every part of the authority and authenticity of those books is gone at once, for there can be no such thing as forged or invented

*Euclid, according to chronological history, lived three hundred years before Christ, and about one hundred before Archimedes. He was of the city of Alexandria, in Egypt.

testimony, neither can there be anonymous testimony, more especially as to things naturally incredible, such as that of talking with God face to face, or that of the sun and moon standing still at the command of a man.

The greatest part of the other ancient books are works of genius; of which kind are those ascribed to Homer, to Plato, to Aristotle, to Demosthenes, to Cicero, &c. Here again the author is not an essential in the credit we give to any of those works; for as works of genius they would have the same merit they have now were they anonymous. Nobody believes the Trojan story, as related by Homer, to be true; for it is the poet only that is admired, and the merit of the poet will remain though the story be fabulous. But if we disbelieve the matters related by the bible authors, Moses for instance, as we disbelieve the things related by Homer, there remains nothing of Moses in our estimation but an impostor. As to the ancient historians, from Herodotus to Tacitus, we credit them as far as they relate things probable and credible, and no further; for if we do, we must believe the two miracles which Tacitus relates were performed by Vespasian, that of curing a lame man and a blind man in just the same manner as the same things are told of Jesus Christ by his historians. We must also believe the miracle cited by Josephus, that of the sea of Pamphilia opening to let Alexander and his army pass, as is related of the red sea in Exodus. These miracles are quite as well authenticated as the bible miracles, and yet we do not believe them. —Consequently the degree of evidence necessary to establish our belief of things naturally incredible, whether in the bible or elsewhere, is far greater than that which obtains our belief to natural and probable things; and therefore the advocates for the bible have no claim to our belief of the bible, because that we believe things stated in other ancient writings; since that we believe the things stated in those writings no further than they are probable and credible, or because they are self-evident like Euclid, or admire them because they are elegant like Homer, or approve them because they are sedate like Plato, or judicious like Aristotle.

Having premised those things, I proceed to examine the authenticity of the bible, and I begin with what are called the five books of Moses; *Genesis, Exodus, Leviticus, Numbers,* and

Deuteronomy. My intention is to shew, that those books are spurious, and that Moses is not the author of them; and still further, that they were not written in the time of Moses, nor till several hundred years afterwards, that they are no other than an attempted history of the life of Moses, and of the times in which he is said to have lived; and also of the times prior thereto, written by some very ignorant and stupid pretenders to authorship several hundred years after the death of Moses; as men now write histories of things that happened, or are supposed to have happened, several hundred or several thousand years ago.

The evidence that I shall produce in this case, is from the books themselves; and I will confine myself to this evidence only. Were I to refer for proofs to any of the ancient authors, whom the advocates of the bible call prophane authors, they would controvert that authority as I controvert theirs. I will therefore come on their own ground, and oppose them with their own weapon, the bible.

In the first place, there is no affirmative evidence that Moses is the author of those books; and that he is the author, is altogether an unfounded opinion got abroad nobody knows how. The style and manner in which those books are written, give no room to believe, or even to suppose, they were written by Moses; for it is altogether the style and manner of another person speaking of Moses. In Exodus, Leviticus, and Numbers (for every thing in Genesis is prior to the time of Moses, and not the least allusion is made to him therein) the whole, I say, of these books is in the third person: it is always, *the Lord said unto Moses, or Moses said unto the Lord; or Moses said unto the people, or the people said unto Moses;* and this is the style and manner that historians use in speaking of the persons whose lives and actions they are writing. It may be said that a man may speak of himself in the third person, and therefore it may be supposed that Moses did; but supposition proves nothing; and if the advocates for the belief that Moses wrote those books himself, have nothing better to advance than supposition, they may as well be silent.

But granting the grammatical right that Moses might speak of himself in the third person, because any man might speak of himself in that manner, it cannot be admitted as a fact in those books, that it is Moses who speaks, without rendering Moses truly ridiculous and absurd.—For example, Numb. chap. xii. v. 3. *"Now the man Moses was* VERY MEEK *above all the men which were on the face of the earth."* If Moses said this of himself, instead of being the meekest of men, he was one of the most vain and arrogant of coxcombs; and the advocates for those books may now take which side they please, for both sides are against them. If Moses was not the author, the books are without authority; and if he was the author, the author is without credit; because, to boast of *meekness* is the reverse of meekness, and is a *lie in sentiment.*

In Deuteronomy the style and manner of writing marks more evidently than in the former books that Moses is not the writer. The manner here used is dramatical. The writer opens the subject by a short introductory discourse, and then introduces Moses as in the act of speaking, and when he has made Moses finish his harangue, he (the writer) resumes his own part and speaks till he brings Moses forward again, and at last closes the scene with an account of the death, funeral, and character of Moses.

This interchange of speakers occurs four times in this book. From the first verse of the first chapter to the end of the fifth verse it is the writer who speaks, he then introduces Moses as in the act of making his harangue, and this continues to the end of the 40th verse of the fourth chapter. Here the writer drops Moses and speaks historically of what was done in consequence of what Moses, when living, is supposed to have said, and which the writer had dramatically rehearsed.

The writer opens the subject again in the first verse of the fifth chapter, though it is only by saying that Moses, called the people of Israel together; he then introduces Moses as before, and continues him as in the act of speaking to the end of the 26th chapter. He does the same thing at the beginning of the 27th chapter, and continues Moses, as in the act of speaking, to the end of the 28th chapter. At the 29th chapter the writer speaks again through the whole of the first verse and the first line of the second verse, where he introduces Moses for the last time, and continues him as in the act of speaking to the end of the 33d chapter.

The writer having now finished the rehearsal on the part of Moses, comes forward and speaks through the whole of the last chapter. He begins by telling the reader that Moses went up to the top of Pisgah, that he saw from thence the land which (the writer says) had been promised to Abraham, Isaac and Jacob—that he, Moses died there in the land of Moab— that *he* buried him in a valley in the land of Moab, but that no man knoweth of his sepulchre unto this day; that is, unto the time in which the writer lived who wrote the book of Deuteronomy. The writer then tells, that Moses was one hundred and ten years of age when he died—that his eye was not dim nor his natural force abated; and he concludes by saying, that there arose not a prophet *since* in Israel like unto Moses, whom, says this anonymous writer, the Lord knew face to face.

Having thus shewn, as far as grammatical evidence applies, that Moses was not the writer of those books, I will after making a few observations on the inconsistencies of the writer of the book of Deuteronomy, proceed to shew, from the historical and chronological evidence contained in those books, that Moses *was not*, because *he could not be*, the writer of them; and consequently, that there is no authority for believing, that the inhuman and horrid butcheries of men, women, and children, told of in those books, were done, as those books say they were, at the command of God. It is a duty incumbent on every true deist, that he vindicates the moral justice of God against the calumnies of the bible.

The writer of the book of Deuteronomy, whoever he was, for it is an anonymous work, is obscure and also contradictory with himself in the account he has given of Moses.

After telling that Moses went to the top of Pisgah (and it does not appear from any account that he ever came down again) he tells us that Moses died *there* in the land of Moab, and that *he* buried him in a valley in the land of Moab: but as there is no antecedent to the pronoun *he*, there is no knowing who the *he* was that did bury him. If the writer meant that *he* (God) buried him, how should *he*, the writer, know it, or why should we (the readers), believe him, since we know not who the writer was that tells us so; for certainly Moses could not himself tell where he was buried.

The writer also tells us, that no man knoweth where the sepulchre of Moses is *unto this day*, meaning the time in which this writer lived, how then should he know that Moses was buried in a valley in the land of Moab? for as the writer lived long after the time of Moses, as is evident from his using the expression *unto this day*, meaning a great length of time after the death of Moses, he certainly was not at his funeral. And on the other hand it is impossible that Moses himself could say, that *no man knoweth where his sepulchre is unto this day*. To make Moses the speaker would be an improvement on the play of a child that hides itself and cries, *nobody can find me*. Nobody can find Moses.

This writer has no where told us how he came by the speeches that he has put into the mouth of Moses to speak, and therefore we have a right to conclude that he either composed them himself or wrote them from oral tradition. One or other of these is the more probable, since he has given, in the fifth chapter, a table of commandments, in which that called the fourth commandment is different from the fourth commandment in the twentieth chapter of Exodus. In that of Exodus, the reason given for keeping the seventh day is, because (says the commandment) God made the heavens and the earth in six days, and rested on the seventh; but in that of Deuteronomy, the reason given is, that it was the day on which the children of Israel came out of Egypt, and *therefore* says this commandment, *the Lord thy God commanded thee to keep the sabbath-day. This* makes no mention of the creation, nor *that* of the coming out of Egypt. There are also many things given as laws of Moses in this book, that are not to be found in any of the other books, among which is that inhuman and brutal law, ch. xxi, v. 18, 19, 20, 21, which authorises parents, the father, and the mother, to bring their own children to have them stoned to death, for what it is pleased to call stubbornness. But priests have always been fond of preaching up Deuteronomy, for Deuteronomy preaches up tythes; and it is from this book, ch. xxv, v. 4, they have taken the phrase, and applied it to tything, that *thou shalt not muzzle the ox when he treadeth out the corn*. And that this might not escape observation, they have noted it in the table of contents, at the head of the chapter, though it is only a single verse of less than two lines. O priests! priests! ye are willing to be compared to an ox for the sake of tythes. Though it is impossible for us to know *identically* who the writer of Deuteronomy was, it is not difficult to discover him *professionally*, that he was some Jewish priest, who lived, as I shall shew in the course of this work, at least three hundred and fifty years after the time of Moses.

I come now to speak of the historical and chronological evidence. The chronology that I shall use is the bible chronology, for I mean not to go out of the bible for evidence of any thing, but to make the bible itself prove, historically and chronologically, that Moses is not the author of the books ascribed to him. It is therefore proper that I inform the reader (such at least as may not have the opportunity of knowing it) that in the larger bibles, and also in some smaller ones, there is a series of chronology printed in the margin of every page, for the purpose of shewing how long the historical matters stated in each page happened, or are supposed to have happened, before Christ, and consequently the distance of time between one historical circumstance and another.

I begin with the book of Genesis.—In the 14th chapter of Genesis, the writer gives an account of Lot being taken prisoner, in a battle between the four kings against five, and carried off; and that when the account of Lot being taken came to Abraham, that he armed all his houshold, and marched to rescue Lot from the captors; and that he pursued them unto *Dan.* (v. 14.)

To shew in what manner this expression of pursuing *them unto Dan*, applies to the case in question, I will refer to two circumstances, the one in America, the other in France. The city now called New-York in America, was originally New-Amsterdam; and the town in France lately called Havre-Marat, was before called Havre-de-Grace. New-Amsterdam was changed to New-York in the year 1664, and Havre-de-Grace to Havre-Marat in the year 1793. Should, therefore, any writing be found, though without date, in which the name of *New-York* should be mentioned, it would be certain evidence that such a writing could not have been written before, and must have been written after, New-Amsterdam was changed to New-York, and consequently not till after the year 1664, or at least during the course of that year. And in like manner any dateless writing, with the name of Havre-Marat would be certain evidence that such a writing must have been written after Havre-de-Grace became Havre-Marat, and consequently not till after the year 1793, or at least during the course of that year.

I now come to the application of those cases, and to shew that there was no such place as *Dan* till many years after the death of Moses, and consequently that Moses could not be the writer of the book of Genesis where this account of pursuing them unto *Dan* is given.

The place that is called Dan in the bible, was originally a town of the Gentiles called Laish, and when the tribe of Dan seized upon this town, they changed its name to Dan, in commemoration of Dan, who was the father of that tribe, and the great grandson of Abraham.

To establish this in proof, it is necessary to refer from Genesis to the 18th chapter of the book, called the Book of Judges. It is there said, (verse 27) that *they* (the Danites) *came unto Laish to a people that were quiet and secure, and they smote them with the edge of the sword* (the bible is filled with murder) *and burned the city with fire — and they built a city* (verse 28) *and dwelt therein — and they called the name of the city Dan, after the name of Dan their father, howbeit the name of the city was Laish at the first.*

This account of the Danites taking possession of Laish and changing it to Dan, is placed in the book of Judges immediately after the death of Samson. The death of Samson is said to have happened 1120 years before Christ, and that of Moses 1441 before Christ; and therefore according to the historical arrangement, the place was not called Dan till 331 years after the death of Moses.

There is a striking confusion between the historical and the chronological arrangement in the book of Judges. The five last chapters, as they stand in the book 17, 18, 19, 20, 21, are put chronologically before all the preceding chapters. They are made to be 28 years before the 16th chapter, 266 before the 15th — 245 before the 13th — 195 before the 9th — 90 before the 4th — and 15 years before the first chapter. This shews the uncertain and fabulous state of the bible. According to the chronological arrangement, the taking of Laish and giving it the name of Dan, is made to be twenty years after the death of Joshua, who was the successor of Moses; and by the historical order, as it stands in the book, it is made to be three hundred and six years after the death of Joshua, and three hundred and thirty-one after that of Moses. But they both exclude Moses from being the writer of Genesis; because, according to either of the statements, no such a place as Dan existed in the time of Moses; and therefore the writer of Genesis must have been some person that lived after the town of Laish had the name of Dan, and who that person was nobody knows, and consequently the book of Genesis is anonymous and without authority.

I come now to state another point of historical and chronological evidence, and to shew therefrom, as in the preceding case, that Moses is not the author of the book of Genesis.

In the 36th chapter of Genesis, there is given a genealogy of the sons and descendants of Esau, who are called Edomites, and also a list by name of the kings of Edom; in enumerating of which, it is said, verse 31, "and these are the kings that reigned in Edom *before there reigned any king over the children of Israel.*"

Now, were any dateless writing to be found, in which, speaking of any past events, the writer should say, these things happened before there was any congress in America, or before there was any convention in France, it would be evidence that such writing could not have been written before, and could only be written after, there was a congress in America, or a convention in France, as the case might be; and consequently that it could not be written by any person who died before there was a congress in the one country, or a convention in the other.

Nothing is more frequent, as well in history as in conversation, than to refer to a fact in the room of a date. It is most natural so to do, first, because a fact fixes itself in the memory better than a date; secondly, because the fact includes the date, and serves to give two ideas at once; and this manner of speaking by circumstances, implies as positively that the fact alluded to *is past*, as if it was so expressed. When a person, in speaking upon any matter, says, it was before I was married

—or before my son was born—or before I went to America
—or before I went to France, it is absolutely understood and
intended to be understood, that he has been married—that
he has had a son—that he has been in America, or been in
France. Language does not admit of using this mode of expression in any other sense; and whenever such an expression
is found any where, it can only be understood in the sense in
which only it could have been used.

The passage, therefore, that I have quoted—"that these are
the kings that reigned in Edom before there reigned *any* king
over the children of Israel," could only have been written
after the first king began to reign over them; and consequently that the book of Genesis, so far from having been
written by Moses, could not have been written till the time of
Saul at least. This is the positive sense of the passage, but the
expression *any* king, implies more kings than one, at least it
implies two; and this will carry it to the time of David, and if
taken in a general sense, it carries itself through all times of
the Jewish monarchy.

Had we met with this verse in any part of the bible that
professed to have been written after kings began to reign in
Israel, it would have been impossible not to have seen the
application of it. It happens then that this is the case. The two
books of Chronicles, which give a history of *all* the kings of
Israel, are *professedly*, as well as in fact, written after the Jewish
monarchy began, and this verse that I have quoted, and all
the remaining verses of the 36th chapter of Genesis are, word
for word, in the first chapter of Chronicles beginning at the
43d verse.

It was with consistency that the writer of the Chronicles
could say, as he has said, 1 Chron. ch. i. ver. 43, *These are the
kings that reigned in Edom before there reigned any king over
the children of Israel*; because he was going to give, and has
given, a list of the kings that had reigned in Israel. But as it is
impossible that the same expression could have been used before that period, it is as certain as any thing can be proved
from historical language, that this part of Genesis is taken
from Chronicles, and that Genesis is not so old as Chronicles;
and probably not so old as the book of Homer or as Æsop's
fables; admitting Homer to have been, as the tables of

chronology state, contemporary with David or Solomon, and Æsop to have lived about the end of the Jewish monarchy.

Take away from Genesis the belief that Moses was the author, on which only the strange belief that it is the word of God has stood, and there remains nothing of Genesis but an anonymous book of stories, fables, and traditionary or invented absurdities, or of down-right lies. The story of Eve and the serpent, and of Noah and his ark, drops to a level with the Arabian tales, without the merit of being entertaining; and the account of men living to eight and nine hundred years, becomes as fabulous as the immortality of the giants of the mythology.

Besides, the character of Moses, as stated in the bible, is the most horrid that can be imagined. If those accounts be true, he was the wretch that first began and carried on wars on the score, or on the pretence, of religion; and under that mask, or that infatuation, committed the most unexampled atrocities that are to be found in the history of any nation, of which I will state only one instance.

When the Jewish army returned from one of their plundering and murdering excursions, the account goes on as follows, Numbers, chap. xxxi, ver. 13.

"And Moses and Eleazar the priest, and all the princes of the congregation, went forth to meet them without the camp.—And Moses was *wroth* with the officers of the host, with the captains over thousands, and captains over hundreds, which came from the battle.—And Moses said unto them, *Have ye saved all the women alive?*—Behold these caused the children of Israel, through the council of Balaam, to commit trespass against the Lord in the matter of Peor, and there was a plague among the congregation of the Lord.—Now, therefore, *kill every male among the little ones, and kill every woman that hath known a man by lying with him.—But all the women-children that hath not known a man by lying with him, keep alive for yourselves.*"

Among the detestable villains that in any period of the world have disgraced the name of man, it is impossible to find a greater than Moses if this account be true. Here is an order to butcher the boys, to massacre the mothers, and debauch the daughters.

Let any mother put herself in the situation of those moth-ers:—one child murdered—another destined to violation, and herself in the hands of an executioner; let any daughter put herself in the situation of those daughters, destined as prey to the murderers of a mother and a brother, and what will be their feelings? It is in vain that we attempt to impose upon nature, for nature will have her course, and the religion that tortures all her social ties is a false religion.

After this detestable order, follows an account of the plun-der taken, and the manner of dividing it; and here it is that the prophaneness of priestly hypocrisy encreases the catalogue of crimes—verse 37,—"And *the Lord's tribute* of the sheep was six hundred and threescore and fifteen;—and the beeves were thirty and six thousand, of which *the Lord's tribute* was threescore and twelve—and the asses were thirty thousand, of which *the Lord's tribute* was threescore and one—and the persons were sixteen thousand, of which *the Lord's tribute* was thirty and two." In short, the matters contained in this chap-ter, as well as in many other parts of the bible, are too horrid for humanity to read, or for decency to hear; for it appears from the 35th verse of this chapter, that the number of women-children consigned to debauchery by the order of Moses was thirty-two thousand.

People in general know not what wickedness there is in this pretended word of God. Brought up in habits of superstition, they take it for granted, that the bible is true, and that it is good. They permit themselves not to doubt of it; and they carry the ideas they form of the benevolence of the Almighty to the book which they have been taught to believe was writ-ten by his authority. Good heavens, it is quite another thing! It is a book of lies, wickedness, and blasphemy; for what can be greater blasphemy than to ascribe the wickedness of man to the orders of the Almighty.

But to return to my subject, that of shewing that Moses is not the author of the books ascribed to him, and that the bible is spurious.—The two instances I have already given should be sufficient, without any additional evidence, to in-validate the authenticity of any book that pretended to be four or five hundred years more ancient than the matters it speaks of, or refers to, as facts; for in the case of *pursuing them unto Dan*, and of the *kings that reigned over the children of Israel*, not even the flimsy pretence of prophecy can be pleaded. The expressions are in the preter-tense, and it would be down-right idiotism to say, that a man could prophesy in the preter-tense.

But there are many other passages scattered throughout those books that unite in the same point of evidence. It is said in Exodus (another of the books ascribed to Moses) chap. xvi, v. 34. "And the children of Israel did eat manna *until they came to a land inhabited*; they did eat manna *until they came unto the borders of the land of Canaan.*"

Whether the children of Israel eat manna or not, or what manna was, or whether it was any thing more than a kind of fungus, or small mushroom, or other vegetable substance, common to that part of the country, makes no part of my argument. All that I mean to shew is, that it is not Moses that could write this account, because the account extends itself beyond the life time of Moses. Moses, according to the bible, (but it is such a book of lies and contradictions, there is no knowing which part to believe, or whether any) died in the wilderness, and never came upon the borders of the land of Canaan, and consequently it could not be he that said what the children of Israel did or what they eat when they came there. This account of eating manna, which they tell us was written by Moses, extends itself to the time of Joshua, the successor of Moses, as appears by the account given in the book of Joshua after the children of Israel had passed the river Jordan and came into the borders of the land of Canaan. Joshua, chap. v, ver. 12. *"And the manna ceased on the morrow after they had eaten of the old corn of the land; neither had the children of Israel manna any more, but they did eat of the fruit of the land of Canaan that year."*

But a more remarkable instance than this occurs in Deuteronomy, which, while it shews that Moses could not be the writer of that book, shews also the fabulous notions that prevailed at that time about giants. In the third chapter of Deuteronomy, among the conquests said to be made by Moses, is an account of the taking of Og, king of Basan, verse 12. "For only Og, king of Basan, remained of the race of giants. Behold his bedstead was a bedstead of iron; is it not in *Rabbath* of the children of Ammon? Nine cubits was the length thereof, and four cubits the breadth of it after the cubit of a man." A cubit is 1 foot $9\frac{888}{1000}$ inches. The length, therefore, of the bed was 16 feet 4 inches, and the breadth 7 feet 4 inches. Thus much for this giant's bed. Now for the historical part, which though the evidence is not so direct and positive as in the former cases; it is, nevertheless, very presumeable and corroborating evidence, and is better than the *best* evidence on the contrary side.

The writer, by way of proving the existence of this giant, refers to his bed, as to an *ancient relic*, and says, is it not in *Rabbath* (or Rabbah) of the children of Ammon? meaning, that it is; for such is frequently the bible method of affirming a thing. But it could not be Moses that said this, because Moses could know nothing about Rabbah nor of what was in it. Rabbah was not a city belonging to this giant king, nor was it one of the cities that Moses took. The knowledge, therefore, that this bed was at Rabbah, and of the particulars of its dimensions must be referred to the time when Rabbah was taken, and this was not till four hundred years after the death of Moses; for which see 2 Sam. ch. xii, ver. 26, "And Joab (David's general) fought against *Rabbah of the children of Ammon*, and took the royal city, &c."

As I am not undertaking to point out all the contradictions in time, place, and circumstance, that abound in the books ascribed to Moses, and which prove to demonstration, that those books could not be written by Moses, nor in the time of Moses, I proceed to the book of Joshua; and to shew that Joshua is not the author of that book, and that it is anonymous and without authority. The evidence I shall produce is contained in the book itself. I will not go out of the bible for proof against the supposed authenticity of the bible. False testimony is always good against itself.

Joshua, according to the first chapter of Joshua, was the immediate successor of Moses. He was moreover a military man, which Moses was not; and he continued as chief of the people of Israel twenty-five years, that is, from the time that Moses died, which, according to the bible chronology, was 1451 years before Christ, until 1426 years before Christ, when, according to the same chronology, Joshua died. If therefore we find in this book, said to have been written by Joshua, references to *facts done* after the death of Joshua, it is evidence that Joshua could not be the author; and also that the book could not have been written till after the time of the latest fact which it records. As to the character of the book, it is horrid. It is a military history of rapine and murder, as savage and brutal, as those recorded of his predecessor in villany and hypocrisy, Moses; and the blasphemy consists, as in the former books, in ascribing those deeds to the orders of the Almighty.

In the first place, the book of Joshua, as is the case in the preceding books, is written in the third person. It is the historian of Joshua that speaks; for it would have been absurd and vain glorious, that Joshua should say of himself, as is said of him, in the last verse of the 6th chapter, that *his fame was noised throughout all the country*. I now come more immediately to the proof.

In the 24th chapter, ver. 31, it is said, "And Israel served the Lord all the days of Joshua, and *all the days of the elders that over-lived Joshua*." How in the name of common sense, can it be Joshua that relates what people had done after he was dead? This account must not only have been written by some historian that lived after Joshua, but that lived also after the Elders that had out-lived Joshua.

There are several passages, of a general meaning with respect to time, scattered throughout the book of Joshua, that carries the time in which the book was written to a distance from the time of Joshua, but without marking by exclusion any particular time as in the passage above quoted. In that passage the time that intervened between the death of Joshua and the death of the Elders, is excluded descriptively and absolutely, and the evidence substantiates that the book could not have been written till after the death of the last.

But though the passages to which I allude, and which I am going to quote, do not designate any particular time by exclusion, they imply a time far more distant from the days of Joshua, than is contained between the death of Joshua and the death of the Elders. Such is the passage, chap. x. v. 14. where, after giving an account that the sun stood still upon Gibeon, and the moon in the valley of Ajalon at the command of Joshua (a tale fit only to amuse children)* the passage says—"And there was no day like that, before it, nor *after it*, that the Lord harkened to the voice of a man."

The time implied by the expression, *after it*, that is after *that* day, being put in comparison with all the time that passed *before it*, must, in order to give any expressive signification to the passage, mean a *great length of time.*—For example, it would have been ridiculous to have said so the next day, or the next week, or the next month, or the next year. To give therefore meaning to the passage, comparative with the wonder it relates, and the prior time it alludes to, it must mean centuries of years. Less however than one would be trifling; and less than two would be barely admissible.

A distant but general time is also expressed in the 8th chapter, where, after giving an account of the taking the city of Ai, it is said, ver. 28, "And Joshua burned Ai and made it an heap for ever, a desolation *unto this day.*" And again, ver. 29, where speaking of the king of Ai, whom Joshua had hanged, and buried at the entering of the gate, it is said, "And he raised thereon a great heap of stones, which remaineth *unto this day*," that is, unto the day or time in which the writer of the book of Joshua lived. And again, in the 10th chapter,

---

*This tale of the sun standing still upon mount Gibeon, and the moon in the valley of Ajalon, is one of those fables that detects itself. Such a circumstance could not have happened without being known all over the world. One half would have wondered why the sun did not rise, and the other why it did not set, and the tradition of it would be universal; whereas there is not a nation in the world that knows any thing about it. But why must the moon stand still? What occasion could there be for moon-light in the day time, and that too while the sun shined? As a poetical figure, the whole is well enough; it is a-kin to that in the song of Deborah and Barak, *The stars in their courses fought against Sisera*; but it is inferior to the figurative declaration of Mahomet to the persons who came to expostulate with him on his goings on; *Wert thou*, said he, *to come to me with the sun in thy right hand and the moon in thy left, it should not alter my career*. For Joshua, to have exceeded Mahomet, he should have put the sun and moon one in each pocket, and carried them as Guy Faux carried his dark lanthorn, and taken them out to shine as he might happen to want them. The sublime and the ridiculous are often so nearly related, that it is difficult to class them separately. One step above the sublime makes the ridiculous, and one step above the ridiculous makes the sublime again. The account, however, abstracted from the poetical fancy, shews the ignorance of Joshua, for he should have commanded the earth to have stood still.

where, after speaking of the five kings, whom Joshua had hanged on five trees, and then thrown in a cave, it is said, "And he laid great stones on the cave's mouth, which remain unto this *very* day."

In enumerating the several exploits of Joshua and of the tribes and of the places which they conquered or attempted, it is said, chap. xv, v. 63, "As for the Jebusites, the inhabitants of Jerusalem, the children of Judah, could not drive them out; but the Jebusites dwell with the children of Judah AT JERUSA-LEM *unto this day.*"—The question upon this passage is, at what time did the Jebusites and the children of Judah dwell together at Jerusalem? As this matter occurs again in the first chapter of Judges, I shall reserve my observations till I come to that part.

Having thus shewn from the book of Joshua itself, without any auxiliary evidence whatever, that Joshua is not the author of that book, and that it is anonymous, and consequently without authority, I proceed as before-mentioned to the book of Judges.

The book of Judges is anonymous on the face of it, and therefore even the pretence is wanting to call it the word of God. It has not so much as a nominal voucher. It is alto-gether fatherless.

This book begins with the same expression as the book of Joshua. That of Joshua begins, chap. i. ver. 2. *Now after the death of Moses,* &c. And this of Judges begins; *Now after the death of Joshua,* &c. This and the similarity of style between the two books, indicate that they are the work of the same author; but who he was is altogether unknown. The only point that the book proves, is, that the author lived long after the time of Joshua; for though it begins as if it followed im-mediately after his death, the second chapter is an epitome or abstract of the whole book, which, according to the bible chronology, extends its history through a space of three hun-dred and six years; that is, from the death of Joshua 1426 years before Christ, to the death of Samson 1720 years before Christ, and only twenty five years before Saul went *to seek his father's asses, and was made king;* but there is good reason to believe that it was not written till the time of David at least, and that the book of Joshua was not written before the same time.

In the first chapter of Judges, the writer, after announcing the death of Joshua, proceeds to tell what happened between the children of Judah and the native inhabitants of the land of Cannan. In this statement, the writer, having abruptly mentioned *Jerusalem* in the 7th verse, says immediately after, in the 8th verse, by way of explanation, "Now the children of Judah *had* fought against Jerusalem and *taken it.*" Consequently this book could not have been written before Jerusalem had been taken. The reader will recollect the quotation I have just before made from the 15th chapter of Joshua, ver. 63, where it is said, that *the Jebusites dwell with the children of Judah at Jerusalem at this day,* meaning the time when the book of Joshua was written.

The evidence I have already produced to prove that the books I have hitherto treated of were not written by the persons to whom they are ascribed, nor till many years after their death, if such persons ever lived, is already so abundant, that I can afford to admit this passage with less weight than I am entitled to draw from it. For the case is, that so far as the bible can be credited as an history, the city of Jerusalem was not taken till the time of David, and consequently that the book of Joshua and of Judges were not written till after the commencement of the reign of David, which was 370 years after the death of Joshua.

The name of the city that was afterwards called Jerusalem, was originally Jebus or Jebusi, and was the capital of the Jebusites. The account of David's taking this city is given in 2 Samuel, chap. v, ver. 4, &c. also in 1 Chron. chap. xiv, v. 4, &c. There is no mention in any part of the bible that it was ever taken before, nor any account that favours such an opinion. It is not said, either in Samuel or in Chronicles, that they *utterly destroyed men, women and children — that they left not a soul to breathe,* as is said of their other conquests; and the silence here observed, implies that it was taken by capitulation, and that the Jebusites, the native inhabitants, continued to live in the place after it was taken. The account therefore given in Joshua, that *the Jebusites dwell with the children of*

Judah at Jerusalem at this day, corresponds to no other time than after the taking the city by David.

Having now shewn that every book in the bible, from Genesis to Judges, is without authenticity, I come to the book of *Ruth*—an idle bundling story, foolishly told, nobody knows by whom, about a strolling country girl creeping slily to bed to her cousin Boaz. Pretty stuff indeed to be called the word of God! It is, however, one of the best books in the bible, for it is free from murder and rapine.

I come next to the two books of Samuel; and to shew that those books were not written by Samuel, nor till a great length of time after the death of Samuel, and that they are, like all the former books, anonymous, and without authority.

To be convinced that these books have been written much later than the time of Samuel, and consequently not by him, it is only necessary to read the account which the writer gives of Saul going to seek his father's asses, and of his interview with Samuel, of whom Saul went to enquire about those lost asses, as foolish people now-a-days go to a conjurer to enquire after lost things.

The writer, in relating this story of Saul, Samuel, and the asses, does not tell it as a thing that had just then happened, but as an *ancient story in the time this writer lived*; for he tells it in the language or terms used at the time that *Samuel* lived, which obliges the writer to explain the story in the terms or language used in the time the *writer* lived.

Samuel, in the account given of him in the first of those books, chap. ix. is called *the Seer*; and it is by this term that Saul enquires after him, ver. 11. "And as they (Saul and his servant) went up the hill to the city, they found young maidens going out to draw water; and they said unto them, *Is the Seer here?*" Saul then went according to the direction of these maidens, and met Samuel without knowing him, and said to him, ver. 18, "Tell me, I pray thee, where the *Seer's house is?*" And Samuel answered Saul, and said, *I am the Seer.*

As the writer of the book of Samuel relates these questions and answers in the language or manner of speaking used in the time they are said to have been spoken; and as that manner of speaking was out of use when this author wrote, he found it necessary, in order to make the story understood, to explain the terms in which these questions and answers are spoken. And he does this in the 9th verse, where he says—"*Before-time* in Israel, when a man went to enquire of God, thus he spake, come let us go to the Seer; for he that is now called a prophet, was *before-time* called a Seer." This proves, as I have before said, that this story of Saul, Samuel, and the asses was an antient story at the time the book of Samuel was written, and consequently that Samuel did not write it, and that the book is without authenticity.

But if we go further into those books, the evidence is still more positive, that Samuel is not the writer of them; for they relate things that did not happen till several years after the death of Samuel. Samuel died before Saul; for the 1st of Samuel, chap. xxviii. tells, that Saul and the witch of Endor conjured Samuel up after he was dead; yet the history of matters contained in those books is extended through the remaining part of Saul's life, and to the latter end of the life of David, who succeeded Saul. The account of the death and burial of Samuel, (a thing which he could not write himself) is related in the 25th chapter of the first book of Samuel; and the chronology affixed to this chapter, makes this to be 1060 years before Christ; yet the history of this *first* book is brought down to 1056 years before Christ, that is, to the death of Saul, which was not till four years after the death of Samuel.

The second book of Samuel begins with an account of things that did not happen till four years after Samuel was dead; for it begins with the reign of David, who succeeded Saul, and it goes on to the end of David's reign, which was forty-three years after the death of Samuel; and therefore the books are in themselves positive evidence that they were not written by Samuel.

I have now gone through all the books in the first part of the bible to which the names of persons are affixed as being the authors of those books, and which the church, stiling itself the Christian church, have imposed upon the world as the writings of Moses, Joshua, and Samuel, and I have detected and proved the falshood of this imposition.—And now ye priests of every description, who have preached and written against the former part of the *Age of Reason*, what have ye to say? Will ye, with all this mass of evidence against you, and staring you in the face, still have the assurance to march into your pulpits, and continue to impose these books on your congregations as the works of *inspired penmen*, and the word of God; when it is as evident as demonstration can make truth appear, that the persons who, ye say, are the authors, are *not* the authors, and that ye know not who the authors are. What shadow of pretence have ye now to produce for continuing the blasphemous fraud? What have ye still to offer against the pure and moral religion of Deism, in support of your system of falshood, idolatry, and pretended revelation?

Had the cruel and murdering orders with which the bible is filled, and the numberless torturing executions of men, women, and children, in consequence of those orders, been ascribed to some friend, whose memory you revered, you would have glowed with satisfaction at detecting the falshood of the charge, and gloried in defending his injured fame. It is because ye are sunk in the cruelty of superstition, or feel no interest in the honour of your Creator, that we listen to the horrid tales of the bible, or hear them with callous indifference. The evidence I have produced, and shall still produce, in the course of this work, to prove that the bible is without authority, will, whilst it wounds the stubbornness of a priest, relieve and tranquilize the mind of millions. It will free them from all those hard thoughts of the Almighty, which priestcraft and the bible had infused into their mind, and which stood in everlasting opposition to all their ideas of his moral justice and benevolence.

I come now to the two books of Kings, and the two books of Chronicles. Those books are altogether historical, and are chiefly confined to the lives and actions of the Jewish kings, who in general were a parcel of rascals: but these are matters with which we have no more concern than we have with the Roman emperors, or Homer's account of the Trojan war. Besides which, as those books are anonymous, and as we know nothing of the writer, or of his character, it is impossible for us to know what degree of credit to give to the matters related therein. Like all other ancient histories, they appear to be a jumble of fable and of fact, and of probable and of improbable things, but which distance of time and place, and change of circumstances in the world, have rendered obsolete, and uninteresting.

The chief use I shall make of those books will be that of comparing them with each other, and with other parts of the bible, to shew the confusion, contradiction, and cruelty, in this pretended word of God.

The first book of Kings begins with the reign of Solomon, which, according to the bible chronology, was 1015 years before Christ; and the second book ends 588 years before Christ, being a little after the reign of Zedekiah, whom Nebuchadnezzar, after taking Jerusalem, and conquering the Jews, carried captive to Babylon. The two books include a space of four hundred and twenty-seven years.

The two books of Chronicles are an history of the same times, and in general of the same persons by another author; for it would be absurd to suppose that the same author wrote the history twice over. The first book of Chronicles (after giving the genealogy from Adam to Saul which takes up the first nine chapters) begins with the reign of David, and the last book ends as in the last book of Kings, soon after the reign of Zedekiah, about 588 years before Christ. The two last verses of the last chapter bring the history fifty-two years more forward, that is, to 536. But these verses do not belong to the book, as I shall shew when I come to speak of the book of Ezra.

The two books of Kings, besides the history of Saul, David, and Solomon, who reigned over *all* Israel, contain an abstract of the lives of seventeen kings and one queen, who are stiled kings of Judah, and of nineteen who are stiled kings of Israel; for the Jewish nation, immediately on the death of Solomon, split into two parties, who chose separate kings, and who carried on most rancourous wars against each other.

These two books are little more than a history of assassinations, treachery, and wars. The cruelties that the Jews had accustomed themselves to practice on the Canaanites, whose country they had savagely invaded under a pretended gift from God, they afterwards practised as furiously on each other. Scarcely half their kings died a natural death, and in some instances whole families were destroyed to secure possession to the successor, who, after a few years, and sometimes only a few months, or less, shared the same fate. In the tenth chapter of the second book of Kings, an account is given of two baskets full of children's heads, seventy in number, being exposed at the entrance of the city; they were the children of Ahab, and were murdered by the orders of Jehu, whom Elisha, the pretended man of God, had anointed to be king over Israel, on purpose to commit this bloody deed, and assassinate his predecessor. And in the account of the reign of Manaham, one of the kings of Israel, who had murdered Shallum, who had reigned but one month, it is said, 2 Kings, chap. xv, ver. 16, that Manaham smote the city of Tiphsah, because they opened not the city to him, *and all the women therein that were with child, he ript up.*

Could we permit ourselves to suppose that the Almighty would distinguish any nation of people by the name of *his chosen people*, we must suppose that people to have been an example to all the rest of the world of the purest piety and humanity; and not such a nation of ruffians and cut-throats as the ancient Jews were. A people who, corrupted by, and copying after, such monsters and impostors as Moses and Aaron, Joshua, Samuel, and David, had distinguished themselves above all others, on the face of the known earth, for barbarity and wickedness. If we will not stubbornly shut our eyes, and steel our hearts, it is impossible not to see, in spite of all that long-established superstition imposes upon the mind, that the flattering appellation of *his chosen people*, is no other than a LIE, which the priests and leaders of the Jews had invented to cover the baseness of their own characters, and which Christian priests, sometimes as corrupt, and often as cruel, have professed to believe.

The two books of Chronicles are a repetition of the same crimes; but the history is broken in several places by the author leaving out the reign of some of their kings; and in this as well as in that of Kings, there is such a frequent transition from kings of Judah to kings of Israel, and from kings of Israel to kings of Judah, that the narrative is obscure in the reading. In the same book the history sometimes contradicts itself. For example, in the second book of Kings, chap. i. ver. 17, we are told, but in rather ambiguous terms, that after the death of Ahaziah, king of Israel, Jehoram or Joram (who was of the house of Ahab) reigned in his stead in the *second year* of Jehoram or Joram, son of Jehoshaphat, king of Judah;— and in chap. viii. ver. 16, of the same book, it is said, "And in the *fifth year* of Joram, the son of Ahab, king of Israel, Jehoshaphat being then king of Judah, Jehoram the son of Jehoshaphat, king of Judah, began to reign;" that is, one chapter says, that Joram of Judah began to reign in the *second* year of Joram of Israel; and the other chapter says, that Joram of Israel began to reign in the *fifth* year of Joram of Judah.

Several of the most extraordinary matters related in one history, as having happened during the reign of such or such of their kings, are not to be found in the other in relating the reign of the same king. For example, the two first rival kings after the death of Solomon, were Rehoboam and Jeroboam; and in I Kings, chap. xii. and xiii. an account is given of Jeroboam making an offering of burnt-incense, and that a man, who is there called a man of God, cried out against the altar, ch. xiii. ver. 2. "O altar, altar, thus saith the Lord, behold a child shall be born unto the house of David, Josiah by name, and upon thee shall he offer the priests of the high places that burn incense upon thee, and men's bones shall be burned upon thee."—Verse 3, "And it came to pass, when king Jeroboam heard the saying of the man of God, which had cried against the altar in Bethel, that he put forth his hand from the altar, saying, *Lay hold on him;* and his hand which he put out against him, *dried up, so that he could not pull it in again to him.*"

One would think that such an extraordinary case as this, (which is spoken of as a judgment) happening to the chief of one of the parties, and that at the first moment of the separation of the Israelites into two nations would, if it had been true, been recorded in both histories. But though men in later times have believed *all that the prophets have said unto them*, it does not appear that those prophets or historians believed each other. They knew each other too well.

A long account also is given in Kings about Elijah. It runs through several chapters, and concludes with telling, 2 Kings, chap. ii, ver. 11, "And it came to pass as they (Elijah and Elisha) still went on, and talked, that behold there appeared *a chariot of fire, and houses of fire,* and parted them both

asunder, and Elijah *went up by a whirlwind into heaven.*"
Hum! This the author of Chronicles, miraculous as the story
is, makes no mention of, though he mentions Elijah by name.
Neither does he say any thing of the story related in the second chapter of the same book of Kings, of a parcel of children
calling Elisha, *bald-head, bald-head*; and that this *man of God*,
ver. 24, "turned back, and looked upon them, and *cursed
them in the name of the Lord*; and there came forth two she-
bears out of the wood, and tare forty and two children of
them." He also passes over in silence the story told, 2 Kings,
chap. xiii. that when they were burying a man in the sepulchre
where Elisha had been buried, it happened that the dead man,
as they were letting him down, (ver. 21.) "touched the bones
of Elisha, and he (the dead man) *revived, and stood upon his
feet.*" The story does not tell us, whether they buried the
man, notwithstanding he revived and stood upon his feet, or
drew him up again. — Upon all these stories, the writer of the
Chronicles is as silent as any writer of the present day, who
did not chuse to be accused of *lying*, or at least of *romancing*,
would be about stories of the same kind.

But, however these two historians may differ from each
other with respect to the tales related by either, they are silent
alike with respect to those men stiled prophets, whose writings
fill up the latter part of the bible. Isaiah, who lived in the time
of Hezekiah, is mentioned in Kings, and again in Chronicles,
when these histories are speaking of that reign; but except in
one, or two instances at most, and those very slightly, none of
the rest are so much as spoken of, or even their existence
hinted at, though, according to the bible chronology, they
lived within the time those histories were written, and some of
them long before. If those prophets, as they are called, were
men of such importance in their day, as the compilers of the
bible and priests and commentators have since represented
them to be, how can it be accounted for, that not one of those
histories should say any thing about them?

The history in the books of Kings and of Chronicles is
brought forward, as I have already said, to the year 588 before
Christ. It will therefore be proper to examine which of those
prophets lived before that period. Here follows a table of all

the prophets, with the times in which they lived before Christ, according to the chronology affixed to the first chapter of each of the books of the prophets, and also of the number of years they lived before the books of Kings and Chronicles were written.

TABLE of the prophets, with the time in which they lived before Christ, and also before the books of Kings and Chronicles were written.

Names.	Years before Christ	Years before Kings and Chron.	Observations.
Isaiah.	760	172	⎧ mentioned.
Jeremiah.	629	41	mentioned only in the last chap. of Chronicles.
Ezekiel	595	7	not mentioned.
Daniel.	607	19	not mentioned.
Hosea.	785	97	not mentioned.
Joel.	800	212	not mentioned.
Amos.	789	199	not mentioned.
Obadiah.	789	199	not mentioned.
Jonah.	862	274	see the note.*
Micah.	750	162	not mentioned.
Nahum.	713	125	not mentioned.
Habbakuk.	626	38	not mentioned.
Zephaniah.	630	42	not mentioned.
Haggai ⎫ after the Zechariah ⎬ year 588 Malachi. ⎭			

This table is either not very honourable for the bible historians, or not very honourable for the bible prophets; and

*In 2 Kings, chap. xiv, ver. 25, the name of Jonah is mentioned on account of the restoration of a tract of land by Jeroboam; but nothing further is said of him, nor is any allusion made to the book of Jonah, nor to his expedition to Nineveh, nor to his encounter with the whale.

I leave it to priests and commentators, who are very learned in little things, to settle the point of *etiquette* between the two; and to assign a reason why the authors of Kings and of Chronicles have treated those prophets, whom, in the former part of the Age of Reason, I have considered as poets, with as much degrading silence as an historian of the present day would treat Peter Pindar.

I have one more observation to make on the book of Chronicles, after which I shall pass on to review the remaining books of the bible.

In my observations on the book of Genesis, I have quoted a passage from the 36th chapter, ver. 31, which evidently refers to a time *after* that kings began to reign over the children of Israel; and I have shewn, that as this verse is verbatim the same as in 1 Chron. chap. i. ver. 43, where it stands consistently with the order of history, which in Genesis it does not, that the verse in Genesis and a great part of the 36th chapter, have been taken from Chronicles; and that the book of Genesis, though it is placed first in the bible, and ascribed to Moses, has been manufactured by some unknown person after the book of Chronicles was written, which was not until at least eight hundred and sixty years after the time of Moses.

The evidence I proceed by to substantiate this is regular, and has in it but two stages. First, as I have already stated, that the passage in Genesis refers itself for *time* to Chronicles. Secondly, that the book of Chronicles to which this passage refers itself, was not *began* to be written until at least eight hundred and sixty years after the time of Moses. To prove this, we have only to look into the thirteenth verse of the third chapter of the first book of Chronicles, where the writer, in giving the genealogy of the descendants of David, mentions *Zedekiah*: and it was in the time of Zedekiah that Nebuchadnezzar conquered Jerusalem 588 years before Christ, and consequently more than 860 years after Moses. Those who have superstitiously boasted of the antiquity of the bible, and particularly of the books ascribed to Moses, have done it without examination and without any other authority than that of one credulous man telling it to another; for, so far as historical and chronological evidence applies, the very first book in the bible is not so ancient as the book of Homer, by more than three hundred years, and is about the same age with Æsop's fables.

I am not contending for the morality of Homer; on the contrary, I think it to be a book of false glory and tending to instil immoral and mischievous notions of honour; and with respect to Æsop, though the moral is in general just, the fable is often cruel; and the cruelty of the fable does more injury to the heart, especially in a child, than the moral does good to the judgment.

Having now dismissed Kings and Chronicles, I come to the next in course, the book of Ezra.

As one proof, among others I shall produce to shew the disorder in which this pretended word of God, the bible, has been put together, and the uncertainty of who the authors were, we have only to look at the three first verses in Ezra, and the two last in Chronicles; for by what kind of cutting and shuffling has it been, that the three first verses in Ezra should be the two last verses in Chronicles, or that the two last in Chronicles should be the three first in Ezra. Either the authors did not know their own works, or the compilers did not know the authors.

Two last verses of Chronicles.

Three first verses of Ezra.

Verse 22. Now in the first year of Cyrus, king of Persia, that the word of the Lord, spoken by the mouth of Jeremiah, might be accomplished, the Lord stirred up the spirit of Cyrus, king of Persia, that he made a proclamation throughout all his kingdom, and put it also into writing, saying,

23. Thus saith Cyrus, king of Persia, all the kingdoms of the earth hath the Lord God of heaven given me; and he hath charged me to build him an house in Jerusalem, which is in

Verse 1. Now in the first year of Cyrus, king of Persia, that the word of the Lord, by the mouth of Jeremiah, might be fulfilled, the Lord stirred up the spirit of Cyrus, king of Persia, that he made a proclamation throughout all his kingdom, and put it also into writing, saying,

2. Thus saith Cyrus, king of Persia, the Lord God of heaven hath given me all the kingdoms of the earth; and he hath charged me to build him an house at Jerusalem, which is in Judah.

Judah. Who is there among you of all his people? The Lord his God be with him, and let him go up.

3. Who is there among you of all his people? His God be with him; and let him go up *to Jerusalem which is in Judah, and build the house of the Lord God of Israel (he is the God) which is in Jerusalem.*

The last verse in Chronicles is broken abruptly, and ends in the middle of a phrase with the word *up*, without signifying to what place. This abrupt break, and the appearance of the same verses in different books, shew, as I have already said, the disorder and ignorance in which the bible has been put together, and that the compilers of it had no authority for what they were doing, nor we any authority for believing what they have done.*

*I observed, as I passed along, several broken and senseless passages in the bible without thinking them of consequence enough to be introduced in the body of the work; such as that, 1 Samuel, chap. xiii, ver. 1, where it is said, "Saul reigned *one year*, and when he had reigned *two* years over Israel, Saul chose him three thousand men," etc. The first part of the verse, that Saul reigned *one year*, has no sense, since it does not tell us what Saul did, nor say any thing of what happened, at the end of *that one* year; and it is, besides, mere absurdity to say he reigned *one year* when the very next phrase says he had reigned two, for if he had reigned two it was impossible not to have reigned one.

Another instance occurs in Joshua, chap. v, where the writer tells a story of an angel (for such the table of contents at the head of the chapter calls him) appearing unto Joshua, and the story ends abruptly and without any conclusion. The story is as follows—Verse 13. "And it came to pass when Joshua was by Jericho, that he lift up his eyes and looked, and behold, there stood a man over against him with his sword drawn in his hand: and Joshua went unto him and said unto him, art thou for us or for our adversaries? Verse 14. And he said, nay; but as captain of the host of the Lord am I now come. And Joshua fell on his face to the earth and did *worship*, and said unto him, *What saith my Lord unto his servant?* Verse 15. And the captain of the Lord's host said unto Joshua, loose thy shoe from off thy foot; for the place whereon thou standest is holy. And Joshua did so."—And what then? nothing; for here the story ends, and the chapter too.

Either this story is broken off in the middle, or it is a story told by some Jewish humourist in ridicule of Joshua's pretended mission from God; and the compilers of the bible not perceiving the design of the story, has told it as a serious matter. As a story of humour and ridicule, it has a great deal of point; for it pompously introduces an angel in the figure of a man, with a drawn sword in his hand, before whom Joshua *falls on his face to the earth*

The only thing that has any appearance of certainty in the book of Ezra is the time in which it was written, which was immediately after the return of the Jews from the Babylonian captivity, about 536 years before Christ. Ezra (who according to the Jewish commentators, is the same person as is called Esdras in the Apocrypha) was one of the persons who returned, and who it is probable wrote the account of that affair. Nehemiah, whose book follows next to Ezra, was another of the returned persons, and who it is also probable wrote the account of the same affair in the book that bears his name. But those accounts are nothing to us, nor to any other person, unless it be to the Jews, as a part of the history of their nation; and there is just as much of the word of God in those books as there is in any of the histories of France, or Rapïn's history of England or the history of any other country.

But even in matters of historical record, neither of those writers are to be depended upon. In the second chapter of Ezra the writer gives a list of the tribes and families, and of the precise number of souls of each, that returned from Babylon to Jerusalem; and this enrollment of the persons so returned, appears to have been one of the principal objects for writing the book; but in this there is an error that destroys the intention of the undertaking.

The writer begins his enrollment in the following manner, chap. ii. ver. 3. "The children of Parosh two thousand one hundred seventy and four." Ver. 4. "The children of Shephatiah three hundred seventy and two." And in this manner he proceeds through all the families; and in the 64th verse, he makes a total, and says, "The whole congregation together was *forty and two thousand, three hundred and threescore.*"

But whoever will take the trouble of casting up the several

---

and worships (which is contrary to their second commandment) and then this most important embassy from heaven ends, in telling Joshua to *pull off his shoe.* It might as well have told him to pull up his breeches.

It is certain, however, that the Jews did not credit every thing their leaders told them, as appears from the cavalier manner in which they speak of Moses when he was gone into the mount, "As for *this* Moses, say they, *we wot not what is become of him.*" Ex. chap. xxxii. ver. 1.

particulars, will find that the total is but 29,818; so that the error is 12,542.* What certainty then can there be in the bible for any thing?

Nehemiah, in like manner, gives a list of the returned families, and of the number of each family. He begins, as in Ezra, by saying, chap. vii. ver. 8, "The children of Parosh two thousand three hundred and seventy-two;" and so on through all the families. This list differs in several of the particulars from that of Ezra. In the 66th verse, Nehemiah makes a total, and says, as Ezra had said, "The whole congregation together was forty and two thousand three hundred and threescore." But the particulars of this list make a total but of 31,080, so that the error here is 11,271. These writers may do well enough for bible-makers; but not for any thing where truth and exactness is necessary.

The next book in course is the book of Esther. If Madam Esther thought it any honour to offer herself as a kept mistress to Ahasuerus, or as a rival to queen Vashti, who had refused to come to a drunken king, in the midst of a drunken company, to be made a shew of (for the account says, they had been drinking seven days and were merry) let Esther and Mordecai look to that. It is no business of ours, at least it is none of mine; besides which, the story has a great deal the appearance of being fabulous, and is also anonymous. I pass on to the book of Job.

The book of Job differs in character from all the books we have hitherto passed over. Treachery and murder make no

*Particulars of the families from the second chapter of Ezra.

Chap. ii.		Bᵗ forᵈ 11,577		Bᵗ forᵈ 15,783		Bᵗ forᵈ 19,444
Ver.3 . . . 2172	v. 13 . . . 666	v. 23 . . . 128	v. 33 . . . 725
4 . . . 372	14 . . . 2056	24 . . . 42	34 . . 345
5 . . . 775	15 . . . 454	25 . . . 743	35 . . 3630
6 . . . 2812	16 . . . 98	26 . . . 621	36 . . 973
7 . . . 1254	17 . . . 323	27 . . . 122	37 . . 1052
8 . . . 945	18 . . . 112	28 . . . 223	38 . . 1247
9 . . . 760	19 . . . 223	29 . . . 52	39 . . 1017
10 . . . 642	20 . . . 95	30 . . . 156	40 . . 74
11 . . . 623	21 . . . 123	31 . . . 1254	41 . . 128
12 . . . 1222	22 . . . 56	32 . . . 320	42 . . 139
11,577	15,783	19,444	58 . . 392
			60 . . 652
			Total 29,818

part of this book. It is the meditations of a mind strongly impressed with the vicissitudes of human life, and by turns sinking under, and struggling against, the pressure. It is a highly wrought composition between willing submission and involuntary discontent; and shews man as he sometimes is, more disposed to be resigned than he is capable of being. Patience has but a small share in the character of the person of whom the book treats; on the contrary, his grief is often impetuous; but he still endeavours to keep a guard upon it, and seems determined, in the midst of accumulating ills, to impose upon himself the hard duty of contentment.

I have spoken in a respectful manner of the book of Job in the former part of the *Age of Reason*, but without knowing at that time what I have learned since, which is, that from all the evidence that can be collected, the book of Job does not belong to the bible.

I have seen the opinion of two Hebrew commentators, Abenhezra and Spinosa, upon this subject. They both say that the book of Job carries no internal evidence of being an Hebrew book; that the genus of the composition, and the drama of the piece, are not Hebrew; that it has been translated from another language into Hebrew, and that the author of the book was a Gentile; that the character represented under the name of Satan (which is the first and only time this name is mentioned in the bible) does not correspond to any Hebrew idea; and that the two convocations which the Deity is supposed to have made of those whom the poem calls sons of God, and the familiarity which this supposed Satan is stated to have with the Deity, are in the same case.

It may also be observed, that the book shews itself to be the production of a mind cultivated in science, which the Jews, so far from being famous for, were very ignorant of. The allusions to objects of natural philosophy are frequent and strong, and are of a different cast to any thing in the books known to be Hebrew. The astronomical names Pleiades, Orion, and Arcturus, are Greek, and not Hebrew names; and as it does not appear from any thing that is to be found in the bible, that the Jews knew any thing of astronomy, or that they studied it, they had no translation for those names into their own language, but adopted the names as they found them in the poem.

That the Jews did translate the literary productions of the Gentile nations into the Hebrew language, and mix them with their own, is not a matter of doubt. The 31st chapter of Proverbs is an evidence of this. It is there said, ver. 1. *The words of king Lemuel, the prophesy which his mother taught him.* This verse stands as a preface to the proverbs that follow, and which are not the proverbs of Solomon, but of Lemuel; and this Lemuel was not one of the kings of Israel, nor of Judah, but of some other country, and consequently a Gentile. The Jews, however, have adopted his proverbs; and as they cannot give any account who the author of the book of Job was, nor how they came by the book, and as it differs in character from the Hebrew writings, and stands totally unconnected with every other book and chapter in the bible before it, and after it, it has all the circumstantial evidence of being originally a book of the Gentiles.*

The bible-makers, and those regulators of time, the bible chronologists, appear to have been at a loss where to place, and how to dispose of, the book of Job; for it contains no one historical circumstance, nor allusion to any, that might serve to determine its place in the bible. But it would not have answered the purpose of these men to have informed the world of their ignorance; and therefore they have affixed to it the æra of 1520 years before Christ, which is during the time the Israelites were in Egypt, and for which they have just as

---

*The prayer known by the name of *Augur's prayer*, in the 30th chapter of Proverbs, immediately preceding the Proverbs of Lemuel, and which is the only sensible, and well conceived, and well expressed, prayer in the bible, has much the appearance of being a prayer taken from the Gentiles. The name of Augur occurs on no other occasion than this; and he is introduced, together with the prayer ascribed to him, in the same manner, and nearly in the same words, that Lemuel and his proverbs are introduced in the chapter that follows. The first verse of the 30th chapter says, *"The words of Augur, the son of Jakeh even the prophecy."* Here the word prophecy is used with the same application it has in the following chapter of Lemuel, unconnected with any thing of prediction. The prayer of Augur is in the 8th and 9th verses— *"Remove far from me vanity and lies; give me neither riches nor poverty, but feed me with food convenient for me: Lest I be full and deny thee, and say who is the Lord? or lest I be poor and steal, and take the name of my God in vain."* This has not any of the marks of being a Jewish prayer; for the Jews never prayed but when they were in trouble, and never for any thing but victory, vengeance or riches.

much authority, and no more, than I should have for saying it was a thousand years before that period. The probability, however, is, that it is older than any book in the bible; and it is the only one that can be read without indignation or disgust.

We know nothing of what the ancient Gentile world (as it is called) was before the time of the Jews, whose practice has been to calumniate and blacken the character of all other nations; and it is from the Jewish accounts that we have learned to call them heathen. But as far as we know to the contrary, they were a just and a moral people, and not addicted, like the Jews, to cruelty and revenge, but of whose profession of faith we are unacquainted. It appears to have been their custom to personify both virtue and vice by statues and images, as is done now-a-days both by statuary and by painting; but it does not follow from this, that they worshipped them any more than we do. I pass on to the book of,

PSALMS, of which it is not necessary to make much observation. Some of them are moral, and others are very revengeful, and the greater part relates to certain local circumstances of the Jewish nation at the time they were written, with which we have nothing to do. It is, however, an error or an imposition to call them the Psalms of David. They are a collection, as song-books are now-a-days, from different song-writers, who lived at different times. The 137th Psalm could not have been written till more than four hundred years after the time of David, because it is written in commemoration of an event, the captivity of the Jews in Babylon, which did not happen till that distance of time. *"By the rivers of Babylon we sat down; yea, we wept when we remembered Zion. We hanged our harps upon the willows, in the midst thereof; for there they that carried us away captive, required of us a song, saying, sing us one of the songs of Zion."* As a man would say to an American, or to a Frenchman, or to an Englishman, sing us one of your American songs, or your French songs, or your English songs. This remark, with respect to the time this psalm was written, is of no other use than to shew (among others already mentioned) the general imposition the world has been under with respect to the authors of the bible. No regard has been paid to time, place, and circumstance, and the names of persons have been affixed to the several books, which it was as impossible they should write as that a man should walk in procession at his own funeral.

THE BOOK OF PROVERBS. These, like the Psalms, are a collection, and that from authors belonging to other nations than those of the Jewish nation, as I have shewn in the observations upon the book of Job: besides which, some of the proverbs ascribed to Solomon did not appear till two hundred and fifty years after the death of Solomon; for it is said in the first verse of the 25th chapter, *"These are also proverbs of Solomon, which the men of Hezekiah, king of Judah copied out."* It was two hundred and fifty years from the time of Solomon to the time of Hezekiah. When a man is famous, and his name is abroad, he is made the putative father of things he never said or did, and this most probably has been the case with Solomon. It appears to have been the fashion of that day to make proverbs, as it is now to make *Jest-books*, and father them upon those who never saw them.

The book of *Ecclesiastes*, or the *Preacher*, is also ascribed to Solomon, and that with much reason if not with truth. It is written as the solitary reflexions of a worn out debauchee, such as Solomon was, who looking back on scenes he can no longer enjoy, cries out, *all is vanity!* A great deal of the metaphor and of the sentiment is obscure, most probably by translation, but enough is left to shew they were strongly pointed in the original.* From what is transmitted to us of the character of Solomon, he was witty, ostentatious, dissolute, and at last melancholy. He lived fast, and died, tired of the world, at the age of fifty-eight years.

Seven hundred wives, and three hundred concubines, are worse than none; and however it may carry with it the appearance of heightened enjoyment, it defeats all the felicity of affection, by leaving it no point to fix upon. Divided love is never happy. This was the case with Solomon; and if he could not, with all his pretensions to wisdom discover it before hand, he merited, unpitied, the mortification he afterwards endured. In this point of view his preaching is unnecessary,

---

* *Those that look out of the window shall be darkened;* is an obscure figure in translation for loss of sight.

because to know the consequences, it is only necessary to know the case. Seven hundred wives, and three hundred concubines would have stood in place of the whole book. It was needless after this to say, that all was vanity and vexation of spirit; for it is impossible to derive happiness from the company of those whom we deprive of happiness.

To be happy in old age, it is necessary that we accustom ourselves to objects that can accompany the mind all the way through life, and that we take the rest as good in their day. The mere man of pleasure is miserable in old age, and the mere drudge in business is but little better: whereas natural philosophy, mathematical, and mechanical science, are a continual source of tranquil pleasure; and in spite of the gloomy dogma of priests and of superstition, the study of those things is the study of the true theology. It teaches man to know and to admire the Creator, for the principles of science are in the creation, and are unchangeable, and of divine origin.

Those who knew Benjamin Franklin will recollect that his mind was ever young; his temper ever serene. Science, that never grows grey, was always his mistress. He was never without an object; for when we cease to have an object, we become like an invalid in an hospital waiting for death.

SOLOMON'S SONGS, amorous and foolish enough, but which wrinkled fanaticism, has called divine. The compilers of the bible have placed these songs after the book of Ecclesiastes; and the chronologists have affixed to them the æra of 1014 years before Christ, at which time Solomon, according to the same chronology, was nineteen years of age, and was then forming his seraglio of wives and concubines. The bible-makers and the chronologists should have managed this matter a little better, and either have said nothing about the time, or chosen a time less inconsistent with the supposed divinity of those songs; for Solomon was then in the honey-moon of *one thousand* debaucheries.

It should also have occurred to them, that as he wrote, if he did write, the book of Ecclesiastes long after these songs, and in which he exclaims, that all is vanity and vexation of spirit, that he included those songs in that description. This is the more probable, because he says, or somebody for him, Ecclesiastes, chap. ii. ver. 8, *I got me men-singers and women-singers* (most probably to sing those songs) *and musical instruments of all sorts*, and behold (v. 11) *all was vanity and vexation of spirit*. The compilers, however, have done their work but by halves; for as they have given us the songs, they should have given us the tunes that we might sing them.

The books called the books of the Prophets fill up all the remaining part of the bible. They are sixteen in number, beginning with Isaiah and ending with Malachi, of which I have given a list in the observations up on Chronicles. Of these sixteen prophets, all of whom, except the three last, lived within the time the books of Kings and Chronicles were written, two only, Isaiah and Jeremiah, are mentioned in the history of those books. I shall begin with those two, reserving what I have to say on the general character of the men called prophets, to another part of the work.

Whoever will take the trouble of reading the book ascribed to Isaiah, will find it one of the most wild and disorderly compositions ever put together. It has neither beginning, middle, nor end; and except a short historical part, and a few sketches of history in two or three of the first chapters, is one continued incoherent bombastical rant, full of extravagant metaphor, without application, and destitute of meaning. A school-boy would scarcely have been excuseable for writing such stuff. It is (at least in translation) that kind of composition and false taste, that is properly called prose run mad.

The historical part begins at the 36th chapter, and is continued to the end of the 39th chapter. It relates some matters that are said to have passed during the reign of Hezekiah, king of Judah, at which time Isaiah lived. This fragment of history begins and ends abruptly. It has not the least connection with the chapter that precedes it, nor with that which follows it, nor with any other in the book. It is probable that Isaiah wrote this fragment himself, because he was an actor in the circumstances it treats of; but except this part, there are scarcely two chapters that have any connection with each other. One is entitled, at the beginning of the first verse, the Burden of Babylon; another, the Burden of Moab; another, the Burden of Damascus; another, the Burden of Egypt; another, the Burden of the Desart of the Sea; another, the Burden of the Valley of Vision: as you would say, the story of the knight of the burning mountain; the story of Cinderella or the glassen slipper; the story of the sleeping beauty in the wood, &c. &c.

I have already shewn in the instance of the two last verses of Chronicles, and the three first in Ezra, that the compilers of the bible mixed and confounded the writings of different authors with each other; which alone, were there no other cause, is sufficient to destroy the authenticity of any compilation, because it is more than presumptive evidence that the compilers are ignorant who the authors were. A very glaring instance of this occurs in the book ascribed to Isaiah. The latter part of the 44th chapter and the beginning of the 45th, so far from having been written by Isaiah, could only have been written by some person who lived at least an hundred and fifty years after Isaiah was dead.

These chapters are a compliment to *Cyrus*, who permitted the Jews to return to Jerusalem from the Babylonean captivity, to rebuild Jerusalem and the Temple, as is stated in Ezra. The last verse of the 44th chapter and the beginning of the 45th, are in the following words: *That saith of Cyrus, he is my shepherd and shall perform all my pleasure: even saying to Jerusalem, Thou shalt be built; and to the Temple, thy foundations shall be laid. Thus saith the Lord to his anointed, to Cyrus, whose right hand I have holden to subdue nations before him, and I will loose the loins of kings to open before him the two-leaved gates, and the gates shall not be shut. I will go before thee, &c.*

What audacity of church and priestly ignorance it is to impose this book upon the world as the writing of Isaiah, when Isaiah, according to their own chronology, died soon after the death of Hezekiah, which was six hundred and ninety-eight years before Christ; and the decree of Cyrus in favour of the Jews returning to Jerusalem, was, according to the same chronology, 536 years before Christ, which is a distance of time between the two of one hundred and sixty-two years. I do not suppose that the compilers of the bible made these books, but rather that they picked up some loose anonymous essays, and put them together under the names of such authors as best suited their purpose. They have encouraged the imposition, which is next to inventing it; for it was impossible but they must have observed it.

When we see the studied craft of the scripture-makers, in making every part of this romantic book of school-boy's eloquence, bend to the monstrous idea of a son of God, begotten by a ghost on the body of a virgin, there is no imposition we are not justified in suspecting them of. Every phrase and circumstance are marked with the barbarous hand of superstitious torture, and forced into meanings it was impossible they could have. The head of every chapter, and the top of every page, are blazoned with the names of Christ and the church, that the unwary reader might suck in the error before he began to read.

Behold, a virgin shall conceive, and bear a son, Isaiah, chap. vii. ver. 14, has been interpreted to mean the person called Jesus Christ, and his mother Mary, and has been echoed through Christendom for more than a thousand years: and such has been the rage of this opinion, that scarcely a spot in it but has been stained with blood, and marked with desolation in consequence of it. Though it is not my intention to enter into controversy on subjects of this kind, but to confine myself to shew that the bible is spurious, and thus, by taking away the foundation to overthrow at once the whole structure of superstition raised thereon; I will, however, stop a moment to expose the fallacious application of this passage.

Whether Isaiah was playing a trick with Ahaz, king of Judah, to whom this passage is spoken, is no business of mine. I mean only to shew the misapplication of the passage, and that it has no more reference to Christ and his mother, than it has to me and my mother. The story is simply this:

The king of Syria, and the king of Israel, (I have already mentioned that the Jews were split into two nations, one of which was called Judah, the capital of which was Jerusalem, and the other Israel) made war jointly against Ahaz, king of Judah, and marched their armies towards Jerusalem. Ahaz and his people became alarmed, and the account says, ver. 2, *"Their hearts were moved as the trees of the wood are moved with the wind."*

In this situation of things, Isaiah addresses himself to Ahaz, and assures him in the *name of the Lord*, the cant phrase of all the prophets, that these two kings should not succeed against him; and to satisfy Ahaz that this should be the case, tells him to ask a sign: this, the account says, Ahaz declined doing, giving as a reason, that he would not tempt the Lord; upon which, Isaiah, who is the speaker, says, ver. 14, "Therefore the Lord himself shall give you a sign, *Behold, a virgin shall conceive and bear a son;*" and the 16th verse says, *"And before this child shall know to refuse the evil and chuse the good, the land which thou abhorrest* (or dreadest, meaning Syria and the kingdom of Israel) *shall be forsaken of both her kings."* Here then was the sign, and the time limited for the completion of the assurance or promise; namely, before this child should know to refuse the evil and chuse the good.

Isaiah having committed himself thus far, it became necessary to him, in order to avoid the imputation of being a false prophet, and the consequences thereof, to take measures to make this sign appear. It certainly was not a difficult thing in any time of the world, to find a girl with child, or to make her so; and perhaps Isaiah knew of one before hand; for I do not suppose that the prophets of that day were any more to be trusted than the priests of this. Be that, however, as it may, he says in the next chapter, ver. 2, "And I took unto me faithful witnesses to record, Uriah the priest, and Zechariah the son of Jeberechiah, and *I went unto the prophetess, and she conceived and bare a son."*

Here then is the whole story, foolish as it is, of this child and this virgin. And it is upon the barefaced perversion of this story, that the book of Matthew, and the impudence and sordid interest of priests in later times, have founded a theory which they call the gospel; and have applied this story to signify the person they call Jesus Christ, begotten, they say, by a ghost whom they call holy, on the body of a woman engaged in marriage and afterwards married, whom they call a virgin, seven hundred years after this foolish story was told: a theory which, speaking for myself, I hesitate not to believe and to say, is as fabulous and as false as God is true.*

But to shew the imposition and falshood of Isaiah, we have only to attend to the sequel of this story, which though it is

---

*In the 14th verse of the 7th chapter, it is said, that the child should be called Immanuel. But this name was not given to either of the children, otherwise than as a character which the word signifies. That of the prophetess was called Maher-shalal-hash-baz, and that of Mary was called Jesus.

passed over over in silence in the book of Isaiah, is related in the 28th chapter of 2 Chronicles, and which is, that instead of these two kings failing in their attempt against Ahaz, king of Judah, as Isaiah had pretended to foretel in the name of the Lord, they *succeeded*: Ahaz was defeated and destroyed, an hundred and twenty thousand of his people were slaughtered, Jerusalem was plundered, and two hundred thousand women, and sons and daughters, carried into captivity. Thus much for this lying prophet and impostor Isaiah, and the book of falshoods that bears his name. I pass on to the book of

JEREMIAH. This prophet, as he is called, lived in the time that Nebuchadnezzar besieged Jerusalem, in the reign of Zedekiah, the last king of Judah, and the suspicion was strong against him, that he was a traitor in the interest of Nebuchadnezzar. Every thing relating to Jeremiah shews him to have been a man of an equivocal character. In his metaphor of the potter and the clay, chap. xviii, he guards his prognostications in such a crafty manner, as always to leave himself a door to escape by, in case the event should be contrary to what he had predicted.

In the 7th and 8th verses of that chapter, he makes the Almighty to say, "At what instant I shall speak concerning a nation, and concerning a kingdom, to pluck up, and to pull down and destroy it; if that nation, against whom I have pronounced, turn from their evil, *I will repent me of the evil that I thought to do unto them.*" Here was a proviso against one side of the case: now for the other side.

Verses 9 and 10. "At what instant I shall speak concerning a nation, and concerning a kingdom, to build and to plant it, if it do evil in my sight that it obey not my voice, then *I will repent me of the good wherewith I said I would benefit them.*" Here is a proviso against the other side; and according to this plan of prophesying, a prophet could never be wrong, however mistaken the Almighty might be. This sort of absurd subterfuge, and this manner of speaking of the Almighty, as one would speak of a man, is consistent with nothing but the stupidity of the bible.

As to the authenticity of the book, it is only necessary to read it, in order to decide positively, that, though some passages recorded therein may have been spoken by Jeremiah, he is not the author of the book. The historical parts, if they can be called by that name, are in the most confused condition. The same events are several times repeated, and that in a manner different, and sometimes in contradiction to each other, and this disorder runs even to the last chapter, where the history, upon which the greater part of the book has been employed, begins a-new, and ends abruptly. The book has all the appearance of being a medley of unconnected anecdotes, respecting persons and things of that time, collected together in the same rude manner as if the various and contradictory accounts that are to be found in a bundle of news-papers respecting persons and things of the present day, were put together without date, order, or explanation. I will give two or three examples of this kind.

It appears from the accounts of the 37th chapter, that the army of Nebuchadnezzar, who are called the army of the Chaldeans, had besieged Jerusalem sometime, and on their hearing that the army of Pharoah of Egypt were marching against them, they raised the siege and retreated for a time. It may here be proper to mention, in order to understand this confused history, that Nebuchadnezzar had besieged and taken Jerusalem during the reign of Jehoiakin, the predecessor of Zedekiah, and that it was Nebuchadnezzar who had made Zedekiah king, or rather vice-roy; and that this second siege, of which the book of Jeremiah treats, was in consequence of the revolt of Zedekiah against Nebuchadnezzar. This will in some measure account for the suspicion that affixes itself to Jeremiah, of being a traitor, and in the interest of Nebuchadnezzar, whom Jeremiah calls in the 43d chapter, ver. 10, the servant of God.

The 11th verse of this chapter (the 37th) says, "And it came to pass, that, when the army of the Chaldeans was broken up from Jerusalem for fear of Pharoah's army, that Jeremiah went forth out of Jerusalem to go (as this account states) into the land of Benjamin, to separate himself thence in the midst of the people. And when he was in the gate of Benjamin, a captain of the ward was there, whose name was Irijah, and he took Jeremiah the prophet, saying, *Thou fallest away to the Chaldeans.* Then Jeremiah said, *it is false, I fall not away to the Chaldeans.*"—Jeremiah being thus stopt and accused, was, after being examined, committed to prison on suspicion of being a traitor, where he remained, as is stated in the last verse of this chapter.

But the next chapter gives an account of the imprisonment of Jeremiah, which has no connection with *this* account, but ascribes his imprisonment to another circumstance, and for which we must go back to the 21st chapter. It is there stated, ver. 1, that Zedekiah sent Pashur, the son of Melchiah, and Zephaniah the son of Maasciah the priest, to Jeremiah, to enquire of him concerning Nebuchadnezzar, whose army was then before Jerusalem; and Jeremiah said to them, ver. 8, "Thus saith the Lord, Behold I set before you the way of life and the way of death. He that abideth in this city, shall die by the sword and by the famine, and by the pestilence, *but he that goeth out and falleth to the Chaldeans that besiege you, he shall live, and his life shall be unto him for a prey.*"

This interview and conference breaks off abruptly at the end of the 10th verse of the 21st chapter; and such is the disorder of this book, that we have to pass over sixteen chapters upon various subjects, in order to come at the continuation and event of this conference; and this brings us to the first verse of the 38th chapter, as I have just mentioned.

The 38th chapter opens with saying, "Then Shephatiah the son of Mattan, and Gedaliah the son of Pashur, and Jucal the son of Shelemiah, and Pashur the son of Malchiah (here are more persons mentioned than in the 21st chapter) heard the words that Jeremiah spoke unto the people saying, *Thus saith the Lord, he that remaineth in this city, shall die by the sword, by famine, and by the pestilence; but he that goeth forth to the Chaldeans shall live; for he shall have his life for a prey, and shall live.*" (which are the words of the conference) "Therefore (say they to Zedekiah) we beseech thee, let this man be put to death, *for thus he weakeneth the hands of the men of war that remaineth in this city, and the hands of all the people in speaking such words unto them; for this man seeketh not the welfare of the people but the hurt;*" and at the 6th verse it is said, "Then they took Jeremiah, and put him into the dungeon of Malchiah."

These two accounts are different and contradictory. The

one ascribes his imprisonment to his attempt to *escape out of the city*, the other to his *preaching and prophesying in the city*. The one to his being seized by the guard at the gate, the other to his being accused before Zedekiah by the conferees.*

In the next chapter (the 39th,) we have another instance of the disordered state of this book; for notwithstanding the siege of the city by Nebuchadnezzar has been the subject of several of the preceding chapters, particularly the 37th and 38th; the 39th chapter begins as if not a word had been said upon the subject, and as if the reader was still to be informed of every particular respecting it; for it begins with saying, ver. I, *"In the ninth year of Zedekiah, king of Judah, in the tenth*

---

*I observed two chapters, 16th and 17th, in the 1st book of Samuel, that contradict each other with respect to David, and the manner he became acquainted with Saul, as the 37th and 38th chapter of the book of Jeremiah contradict each other with respect to the cause of Jeremiah's imprisonment.

In the 16th chapter of Samuel, it is said, that an evil spirit from God troubled Saul, and that his servants advised him (as a remedy) "to seek out a man who was a cunning player upon the harp:" and Saul said, ver. 17, "provide me now a man that can play well, and bring him to me." Then answered one of his servants, and said, "Behold, I have seen a son of Jesse, the Bethlehemite, that is cunning in playing, and a mighty man, and a man of war, and prudent in matters, and a comely person, and the Lord is with him: wherefore Saul sent messengers unto Jesse, and said, send me David thy son. And (ver. 21) David came to Saul, and stood before him, and he loved him greatly, and he became his armour bearer; and when the evil spirit from God was upon Saul (ver. 23.) David took his harp, and played with his hand, and Saul was refreshed, and was well."

But the next chapter (17.) gives an account, all different to this, of the manner that Saul and David became acquainted. Here it is ascribed to David's encounter with Goliah, when David was sent by his father to carry provision to his brethren in the camp. In the 55th verse of this chapter, it is said, "And when Saul saw David go forth against the Philistine (Goliah) he said to Abner the captain of the host, Abner, whose son is this youth? And Abner said, as thy soul liveth, O king, I cannot tell. And the king said, enquire thou whose son the stripling is. And as David returned from the slaughter of the Philistine, Abner took him and brought him before Saul, with the head of the Philistine in his hand. And Saul said unto him, whose son art thou, thou young man? And David answered, I am the son of thy servant Jesse, the Bethlemite." These two accounts belie each other, because each of them supposes Saul and David not to have known each other before. This book, the bible, is too ridiculous even for criticism.

month, came Nebuchadnezzar, king of Babylon, and all his army, against Jerusalem, and besieged it." &c. &c.

But the instance in the last chapter (the 52d) is still more glaring: for though the story has now been told over and over again, this chapter still supposes the reader not to know any thing of it; for it begins by saying, ver. 1, *"Zedekiah was one and twenty years old when he began to reign, and he reigned eleven years in Jerusalem: and his mother's name was Hamutal; the daughter of Jeremiah of Libnath. Ver. 4. And it came to pass in the ninth year of his reign, in the tenth month, that Nebuchadnezzar, king of Babylon came, he and all his army, against Jerusalem, and pitched against it, and built forts against it,"* &c. &c.

It is not possible that any one man, and more particularly Jeremiah, could have been the writer of this book. The errors are such as could not have been committed by any person setting down to compose a work. Were I or any other man to write in such a disordered manner, nobody would read what was written, and every one would suppose that the writer was in a state of insanity. The only way therefore to account for the disorder is, that the book is a medley of detached unauthenticated anecdotes, put together by some stupid bookmaker, under the name of Jeremiah, because many of them refer to him, and to the circumstances of the times he lived in.

Of the duplicity and of the false prediction of Jeremiah, I shall mention two instances, and then proceed to review the remainder of the bible.

It appears from the 38th chapter, that when Jeremiah was in prison, Zedekiah sent for him, and at this interview, which was private, Jeremiah pressed it strongly on Zedekiah to surrender himself to the enemy. If, says he, v. 17, *Thou wilt assuredly go forth unto the king of Babylon's princes, then thy soul shall live, &c.* Zedekiah was apprehensive that what passed at this conference should be known; and he said to Jeremiah, ver. 25, "If the princes, meaning those of Judah, hear that I have talked with thee, and they come unto thee, and say unto thee, declare unto us now what thou hast said unto the king; hide it not from us, and we will not put thee to death, and also what the king said unto thee; then thou shalt say unto them, I presented my supplication before the king, that he would not cause me to return to Jonathan's house to die there. Then came all the princes unto Jeremiah, and asked him, and *he told them according to all the words the king had commanded.*" Thus this man of God, as he is called, could tell a lie, or very strongly prevaricate, when he supposed it would answer his purpose; for certainly he did not go to Zedekiah to make this supplication, neither did he make it; he went because he was sent for; and he employed that opportunity to advise Zedekiah to surrender himself to Nebuchadnezzar.

In the 34th chapter is a prophesy of Jeremiah to Zedekiah in these words; ver. 2, "Thus saith the Lord, Behold I will give this city into the hand of the king of Babylon, and he will burn it with fire, and thou shalt not escape out of his hand; but shalt surely be taken and delivered into his hand; and thine eyes shall behold the eyes of the king of Babylon, and he shall speak with thee mouth to mouth, and thou shalt go to Babylon; *yet hear the word of the Lord, O Zedekiah, king of Judah. Thus saith the Lord, thou shalt not die by the sword: but thou shalt die in peace, and with the burnings of thy fathers, the former kings that were before thee, so shall they burn odours for thee; and they will lament thee, saying, Ah, Lord!* FOR I HAVE PRONOUNCED THE WORD, SAITH THE LORD."

Now, instead of Zedekiah beholding the eyes of the king of Babylon, and speaking with him mouth to mouth, and dying in peace; and with the burning of odours, as at the funeral of his fathers (as Jeremiah had declared the Lord himself had pronounced,) the reverse, according to the 52th chapter, was the case; it is there said, verse 10, *"That the king of Babylon slew the sons of Zedekiah before his eyes; then he put out the eyes of Zedekiah, and bound him in chains, and carried him to Babylon, and put him in prison till the day of his death."* What then can we say of these prophets, but that they are impostors and lyars?

As for Jeremiah he experienced none of those evils. He was taken into favour by Nebuchadnezzar, who gave him in charge to the captain of the guard, chap. xxxix, ver. 12, *"Take him (said he) and look well to him, and do him no harm; but do unto him even as he shall say unto thee."* Jeremiah joined himself afterwards to Nebuchadnezzar, and went about prophesying for him against the Egyptians who had marched to the relief of Jerusalem while it was besieged. Thus much for another of the lying prophets, and the book that bears his name.

I have been the more particular in treating of the books ascribed to Isaiah and Jeremiah, because those two are spoken of in the books of Kings and of Chronicles, which the others are not. The remainder of the books, ascribed to the men called prophets, I shall not trouble myself much about, but take them collectively into the observations I shall offer on the character of the men styled prophets.

In the former part of the *Age of Reason* I have said, that the word prophet was the bible word for poet, and that the flights and metaphors of the Jewish poets, have been foolishly erected into what are now called prophecies. I am sufficiently justified in this opinion, not only because the books called the Prophecies are written in poetical language; but because there is no word in the bible, except it be the word prophet, that describes what we mean by a poet. I have also said that the word signified a performer upon musical instruments, of which I have given some instances; such as that of a company of prophets prophesying with psalteries, with tabrets, with pipes, with harps, &c. and that Saul prophesied with them, 1 Sam. chap. x, ver. 5. It appears from this passage, and from other parts in the book of Samuel, that the word prophet was confined to signify poetry and music; for the person who was supposed to have a visionary insight into concealed things was not called a prophet but a *Se-er*,* 1 Sam. chap. ix, ver. 9; and it was not till after the word *Seer*, went out of use (which most probably was when Saul banished those he called wizards) that the profession of the Seer, or the art of seeing, became incorporated into the word prophet.

According to the *modern* meaning of the word prophet and prophesying, it signifies foretelling events to a great distance of time; and it became necessary to the inventors of the gospel to give it this latitude of meaning, in order to apply or to stretch what they call, the prophesies of the old testament, to the times of the new. But according to the old testament, the

---

*I know not what is the Hebrew word that corresponds to the word *Seer* in English; but I observe it is translated into French by *le Voyant*, from the verb *voir*, to see, and which means the person who sees or the Se-er.

prophesying of the Seer, and afterwards of the Prophet, so far as the meaning of the word Seer was incorporated into that of Prophet, had reference only to things of the time then passing, or very closely connected with it; such as the event of a battle they were going to engage in, or of a journey, or of any enterprize they were going to undertake, or of any circumstance then pending, or of any difficulty they were then in, all of which had immediate reference to themselves, (as in the case already mentioned of Ahaz and Isaiah, with respect to the expression, *Behold a virgin shall conceive and bear a son*) and not to any distant future time. It was that kind of prophesying that corresponds to what we call fortune-telling, such as casting nativities, predicting riches, fortunate or unfortunate marriage, conjuring for lost goods, &c. and it is the fraud of the Christian church, not that of the Jews, and the ignorance and superstition of modern, not that of ancient times, that have elevated those poetical-musical-conjuring-dreaming-strolling gentry, into the rank they have since had.

But besides this general character of all the prophets, they had also a particular character. They were in parties; and they prophesied for, or against, according to the party they were with, as the political and poetical writers of the present day write in defence of the party they associate with against the other.

After the Jews were divided into two nations, that of Judah and that of Israel, each party had its prophets who abused and accused each other of being false prophets, lying prophets, impostors, &c. The prophets of the party of Judah prophesied against the prophets of the party of Israel, and those of the party of Israel against those of Judah. This party-prophesying shewed itself immediately on the separation under the first two rival kings Rehoboam and Jeroboam. The prophet that cursed, or prophesied against, the altar that Jeroboam had built in Bethel was of the party of Judah where Rehoboam was king; and he was way-laid on his return home by a prophet of the party of Israel, who said unto him, (1 Kings, chap. x.) *Art thou the man of God that came from Judah? and he said I am.* Then the prophet of the party of Israel said to him, *I am a prophet also as thou art* (signifying of Judah) *and an angel spake unto me by the word of the Lord, saying, bring him back with thee unto thine house, that he may eat bread and drink water: but,* says the 18th verse, *he lyed unto him.* The event, however, according to the story, is, that the prophet of Judah never got back to Judah; for he was found dead on the road by the contrivance of the prophet of Israel, who no doubt was called a true prophet by his own party, and the prophet of Judah a lying prophet.

In the 3d chapter of the 2d of Kings, a story is related of prophesying, or conjuring, that shews in several particulars the character of a prophet. Jehoshaphat, king of Judah, and Joram, king of Israel, had, for a while, ceased their party animosity, and entered into an alliance; and those two, together with the king of Edom, engaged in a war against the king of Moab. After uniting and marching their armies, the story says, they were in great distress for water, upon which Jehoshaphat said, *"Is there not here a prophet of the Lord, that we may enquire of the Lord by him? And one of the servants of the king of Israel said, here is Elisha* (Elisha was of the party of Judah) *and Jehoshaphat the king of Judah said, The word of the Lord is with him."* The story then says, that these three kings went down to Elisha; and when Elisha (who, as I have said, was a Judahmite prophet) saw the king of Israel, *he said unto him, "What have I to do with thee, get thee to the prophets of thy father, and the prophets of thy mother. Nay, but said the king of Israel, the Lord hath called these three kings together to deliver them into the hand of the king of Moab."* (meaning, because of the distress they were in for water). Upon which Elisha said, *"As the Lord of hosts liveth, before whom I stand, surely, were it not that I regard the presence of Jehoshaphat, king of Judah, I would not look towards thee, nor see thee."* Here is all the venom and vulgarity of a party prophet. We have now to see the performance or manner of prophesying.

Verse 15. *"Bring me,* said Elisha, *a minstrel. And it came to pass, when the minstrel played, that the hand of the Lord came upon him."* Here is the farce of the conjurer. Now for the prophesy. *"And Elisha said,* (singing most probably to the tune he was playing,) *Thus saith the Lord — make this valley full of ditches,"* which was just telling them what every countryman could have told them, without either fiddle or farce, that the way to get water was to dig for it.

But as every conjuror is not famous alike for the same thing, so neither were those prophets; for though all of them, at least those I have spoken of, were famous for lying, some of them excelled in cursing. Elisha, whom I have just mentioned, was a chief in this branch of prophesying. It was he that cursed the forty-two children in the name of the Lord, whom the two she-bears came and devoured. We are to suppose that those children were of the party of Israel. But as those who will curse will lye, there is just as much credit to be given to this story of Elisha's two she-bears, as there is to that of the dragon of Wantley, of whom it is said,

> Poor children three, devoured he,
> That could not with him grapple;
> And at one sup, he eat them up,
> As a man would eat an apple.

There were another description of men called prophets, that amused themselves with dreams and visions but whether by night or by day we know not. These, if they were not quite harmless, were but little mischievous. Of this class are,

EZEKIEL and DANIEL; and the first question upon those books, as upon all the others, is, are they genuine? that is, were they written by Ezekiel and Daniel?

Of this there is no proof; but so far as my own opinion goes, I am more inclined to believe they were than that they were not. My reasons for this opinion are as follow:

First, because those books do not contain internal evidence to prove they were *not* written by Ezekiel and Daniel, as the books ascribed to Moses, Joshua, Samuel, etc. etc. prove they were not written by Moses, Joshua, Samuel, etc. etc.

Secondly, because they were not written till after the Babylonish captivity began; and there is good reason to believe, that not any book in the bible was written before that period; at least it is proveable, from the books themselves, as I have already shewn, that they were not written till after the commencement of the Jewish monarchy.

Thirdly, because the manner in which the books ascribed to Ezekiel and Daniel are written, agrees with the condition those men were in at the time of writing them.

Had the numerous commentators and priests who have

foolishly employed or wasted their time in pretending to expound and unriddle those books, been carried into captivity as Ezekiel and Daniel were, it would greatly have improved their intellects in comprehending the reason for this mode of writing; and have saved them the trouble of racking their invention, as they have done, to no purpose; for they would have found that themselves would be obliged to write, whatever they had to write, respecting their own affairs, or those of their friends, or of their country, in a concealed manner as those men have done.

These two books differ from all the rest; for it is only these that are filled with accounts of dreams and visions; and this difference arose from the situation the writers were in as prisoners of war or prisoners of state in a foreign country, which obliged them to convey even the most trifling information to each other, and all their political projects or opinions in obscure and metaphorical terms. They pretended to have dreamed dreams, and seen visions, because it was unsafe for them to speak facts or plain language. We ought however to suppose that the persons to whom they wrote understood what they meant, and that it was not intended any body else should. But these busy commentators and priests have been puzzling their wits to find out what it was not intended they should know, and with which they have nothing to do.

Ezekiel and Daniel were carried prisoners to Babylon, under the first captivity, in the time of Jehoiachim, nine years before the second captivity in the time of Zedekiah. The Jews were then still numerous, and had considerable force at Jerusalem; and as it is natural to suppose that men, in the situation of Ezekiel and Daniel, would be meditating the recovery of their country and their own deliverance, it is reasonable to suppose, that the accounts of dreams and visions, with which these books are filled, are no other than a disguised mode of correspondence to facilitate those objects. It served them as a cypher or secret alphabet. If they are not this, they are tales, reveries, and nonsense; or at least a fanciful way of wearing off the wearisomeness of captivity; but the presumption is, they are the former.

Ezekiel begins his book by speaking of a vision of *cheru-*

bims, and of a vision of a *wheel within a wheel,* which he says he saw by the river Chebar in the land of his captivity. Is it not reasonable to suppose that by the cherubims he meant the temple at Jerusalem, where they had figures of cherubims; and by a wheel within a wheel (which as a figure has always been understood to signify political contrivance) the project or means of recovering Jerusalem. In the latter part of his book he supposes himself transported to Jerusalem, and into the temple; and he refers back to the vision on the river Chebar, and says, chap. xliii. ver. 3, that this last vision was like the vision on the river Chebar; which indicates that those pretended dreams and visions had for their object the recovery of Jerusalem, and nothing further.

As to the romantic interpretations and applications, wild as the dreams and visions they undertake to explain, which commentators and priests have made of those books, that of converting them into things which they call prophesies, and making them bend to times and circumstances, as far remote even as the present day, it shews the fraud or the extreme folly to which credulity or priest-craft can go.

Scarcely any thing can be more absurd than to suppose, that men situated as Ezekiel and Daniel were, whose country was over-run and in the possession of the enemy, all their friends and relations in captivity abroad, or in slavery at home, or massacred, or in continual danger of it; scarcely any thing, I say, can be more absurd than to suppose, that such men should find nothing to do, but that of employing their time and their thoughts about what was to happen to other nations a thousand or two thousand years after they were dead: at the same time nothing more natural than that they should meditate the recovery of Jerusalem, and their own deliverance, and that this was the sole object of all the obscure and apparently frantic writing contained in those books.

In this sense, the mode of writing used in those two books, being forced by necessity, and not adopted by choice, is not irrational. But if we are to view the books as prophesies, they are false. In the 29th chapter of Ezekiel, speaking of Egypt, it is said, ver. 11, "No foot of man shall pass through it, nor foot of beast shall pass through it; *neither shall it be inhabited for forty years.*" This is what never came to pass, and consequently it is false as all the books I have already reviewed are. I here close this part of the subject.

In the former part of the *Age of Reason*, I have spoken of Jonah, and of the story of him and the whale. A fit story for ridicule, if it was written to be believed; or of laughter, if it was intended to try what credulity could swallow; for if it could swallow Jonah and the whale, it can swallow any thing.

But, as is already shewn in the observations on the book of Job and of Proverbs, it is not always certain which of the books in the bible are originally Hebrew, or only translations from books of the Gentiles into Hebrew; and as the book of Jonah, so far from treating of the affairs of the Jews, says nothing upon that subject, but treats altogether of the Gentiles, it is more probable that it is a book of the Gentiles than of the Jews; and that it has been written as a fable to expose the nonsense, and satyrize the vicious and malignant character of a bible prophet or a predicting priest.

Jonah is represented, first, as a disobedient prophet, running away from his mission, and taking shelter on board a vessel of the Gentiles bound from Joppa to Tarshish; as if he ignorantly supposed, by such a paltry contrivance, he could hide himself where God could not find him. The vessel is overtaken by a storm at sea, and the mariners, all of whom are Gentiles, believing it to be a judgment on account of someone on board who had committed a crime, agreed to cast lots to discover the offender, and the lot fell upon Jonah: But before this, they had cast all their wares and merchandize over-board, to lighten the vessel, while Jonah, like a stupid fellow, was fast asleep in the hold.

After the lot had designated Jonah to be the offender, they questioned him to know who and what he was? and he told them *he was an Hebrew*; and, the story implies, that he confessed himself to be guilty. But these Gentiles, instead of sacrificing him at once, without pity or mercy, as a company of bible prophets or priests would have done by a Gentile in the same case, and as it is related Samuel had done by Agag, and Moses by the women and children, they endeavoured to save him, though at the risk of their own lives: for the account says, "*Nevertheless*, (that is, though Jonah was a Jew and a foreigner, and the cause of all their misfortunes, and the loss of their cargo) *the men rowed hard to bring the boat to land, but they could not, for the sea wrought, and was tempestuous against them."* Still, however, they were unwilling to put the fate of the lot into execution, and they cried, says the account, unto the Lord, saying, *"We beseech thee, O Lord, let us not perish for this man's life, and lay not upon us innocent blood; for thou, O Lord, has done as it pleased thee."* Meaning thereby, that they did not presume to judge Jonah guilty, since that he might be innocent, but that they considered the lot that had fallen upon him, as a decree of God, or as it *pleased God.* The address of this prayer shews that the Gentiles worshipped *one Supreme Being,* and that they were not idolaters as the Jews represented them to be. But the storm still continuing, and the danger encreasing they put the fate of the lot into execution, and cast Jonah into the sea, where, according to the story, a great fish swallowed him whole and alive.

We have now to consider Jonah securely housed from the storm in the fish's belly. Here we are told that he prayed; but the prayer is a made up prayer, taken from various parts of the psalms, without connection or consistency, and adapted to the distress, but not at all to the condition, that Jonah was in. It is such a prayer as a Gentile, who might know something of the Psalms, could copy out for him. This circumstance alone, were there no other, is sufficient to indicate that the whole is a made up story. The prayer however is supposed to have answered the purpose, and the story goes on, (taking off at the same time the cant language of a bible prophet) saying, *"The Lord spake unto the fish,* and it vomited out Jonah upon dry land."

Jonah then receives a second mission to Nineveh, with which he sets out, and we have now to consider him as a preacher. The distress he is represented to have suffered, the remembrance of his own disobedience as the cause of it, and the miraculous escape he is supposed to have had, were sufficient, one would conceive, to have impressed him with sympathy and benevolence in the execution of his mission: but instead of this, he enters the city with denunciation and malediction in his mouth, crying— *"Yet forty days, and Nineveh shall be overthrown."*

We have now to consider this supposed missionary in the last act of his mission; and here it is that the malevolent spirit of a bible prophet, or of a predicting priest, appears in all that blackness of character that men ascribe to the Being they call the Devil.

Having published his prediction, he withdrew, says the story, to the east side of the city. But for what? Not to contemplate in retirement the mercy of his Creator to himself or to others, but to wait with malignant impatience the destruction of Nineveh. It came to pass, however, as the story relates, that the Ninevites reformed, and that God, according to the bible phrase, repented him of the evil he had said he would do unto them, and did it not. This, saith the first verse of the last chapter, *displeased Jonah exceedingly, and he was very angry*. His obdurate heart would rather that all Nineveh should be destroyed, and every soul, young and old, perish in its ruins, than that his prediction should not be fulfilled. To expose the character of a prophet still more, a gourd is made to grow up in the night that promises him an agreeable shelter from the heat of the sun, in the place to which he is retired, and the next morning it dies. Here the rage of the prophet becomes excessive, and he is ready to destroy himself. *"It is better said he for me to die than to live."* This brings on a supposed expostulation between the Almighty and the prophet, in which the former says, *"Dost thou well to be angry for the gourd? And Jonah said I do well to be angry even unto death. Then said the Lord, thou hast had pity on the gourd for which thou hast not laboured, neither madest it to grow, which came up in a night and perished in a night, and should not I spare Nineveh that great city in which are more than three score thousand persons that cannot discern between their right hand and their left."*

Here is both the winding up of the satire and the moral of the fable. As a satire it strikes against the character of *all the bible prophets*, and against all the indiscriminate judgments upon men, women and children, with which this lying book, the bible, is crowded; such as Noah's flood, the destruction of the cities of Sodom and Gomorrah, the extirpation of the Canaanites even to sucking infants and women with child; because the same reflection, *that there are more than threescore thousand persons that cannot discern between their right hand and their left,* meaning young children, apply to all the cases. It satyrizes also the supposed partiality of the Creator for one nation more than for another.

As a moral, it preaches against the malevolent spirit of prediction; for as certainly as a man predicts ill he becomes inclined to wish it. The pride of having his judgment right hardens his heart, till at last, he beholds with satisfaction, or sees with disappointment, the accomplishment or the failure of his predictions.—This book ends with the same kind of strong and well directed point against prophets, prophesies, and indiscriminate judgments, as the chapter that Benjamin Franklin made for the bible, about Abraham and the stranger, ends against the intolerant spirit of religious persecution. Thus much for the book of Jonah.

Of the poetical parts of the bible, that are called prophesies, I have spoken in the former part of the *Age of Reason*, and already in this; where I have said that the word *Prophet* is the bible word for *poet*, and that the flights and metaphors of those poets, many of which are become obscure by the lapse of time, and the change of circumstances, have been ridiculously erected into things called prophesies, and applied to purposes the writers never thought of. When a priest quotes any of those passages, he unriddles it agreeably to his own views, and imposes that explanation upon his congregation as the meaning of the writer. The *whore of Babylon* has been the common whore of all the priests, and each has accused the other of keeping the strumpet. So well do they agree in their explanations.

There now remains only a few books, which they call the books of the *lesser* prophets; and as I have already shewn that the *greater* are imposters, it would be cowardice to disturb the repose of the little ones. Let them sleep then in the arms of their nurses the priests, and both be forgotten together.

I have now gone through the bible as a man would go through a wood with an axe on his shoulder, and fell trees. Here they lie, and the priests, if they can, may replant them. They may, perhaps, stick them in the ground, but they will never make them grow.—I pass on to the books of the New Testament.

_____

THE NEW TESTAMENT.

THE NEW TESTAMENT they tell me is founded upon the prophesies of the Old; if so, it must follow the fate of its foundation.

As it is nothing extraordinary that a woman should be with child before she was married, and that the son she might bring forth should be executed even unjustly, I see no reason for not believing that such a woman as Mary, and such men as Joseph, and Jesus, existed. Their mere existence is a matter of indifference, about which there is no ground either to believe or to disbelieve, and which comes under the common head of, *"It may be so,"* and *what then?* The probability, however, is, that there were such persons, or at least such as resembled them in part of the circumstances, because almost all romantic stories have been suggested by some actual circumstance; as the adventures of Robinson Crusoe, not a word of which is true, was suggested by the case of Alexander Selkirk.

It is not then the existence or the non-existence of the persons that I trouble myself about. It is the fable of Jesus Christ, as told in the new testament, and the wild and visionary doctrine raised thereon, against which I contend. The story, taking it as it is told, is blasphemously obscene. It gives an account of a young woman engaged to be married, and while under this engagement, she is, to speak plain language, debauched by a ghost, under the impious pretence (Luke chap. i, ver. 35.) that *"the holy ghost shall come, upon thee, and the power of the highest shall over-shadow thee."* Notwithstanding which, Joseph afterwards marries her, cohabits with her as his wife, and in his turn rivals the ghost. This is putting the story into intelligible language, and when told in this manner, there is not a priest but must be ashamed to own it.*

Obscenity in matters of faith, however wrapped up, is always a token of fable and imposture; for it is necessary to our serious belief in God, that we do not connect it with stories, that run, as this does, into ludicrous interpretations. This

_____

*Mary, the supposed virgin mother of Jesus, had several other children, sons and daughters. See Matth. chap. xiii, ver. 55, 56.

story is, upon the face of it, the same kind of story as that of Jupiter and Leda, or Jupiter and Europa, or any of the amorous adventures of Jupiter; and shews, as is already stated in the former part of the *Age of Reason*, that the Christian faith is built upon the heathen mythology.

As the historical parts of the new testament, so far as concern Jesus Christ, are confined to a very short space of time, less than two years, and all within the same country, and nearly to the same spot, the discordance of time, place, and circumstance, which detect the fallacy of the books of the old testament, and proves them to be impositions, cannot be expected to be found here in the same abundance. The new testament, compared with the old, is like a farce of one act, in which there is not room for very numerous violations of the unities. There are, however, some glaring contradictions, which exclusive of the fallacy of the pretended prophecies, are sufficient to shew the story of Jesus Christ to be false.

I lay it down as a position which cannot be controverted; First, that the *agreement* of all the parts of a story does not prove that story to be true, because the parts may agree and the whole may be false: Secondly, that the *disagreement* of the parts of a story proves the *whole cannot be true.* The agreement does not prove truth, but the disagreement proves falshood positively.

The history of Jesus Christ is contained in the four books ascribed to Matthew, Mark, Luke, and John. The first chapter of Matthew begins with giving a genealogy of Jesus Christ; and in the third chapter of Luke, there is also given a genealogy of Jesus Christ. Did these two agree, it would not prove the genealogy to be true, because it might nevertheless be a fabrication; but as they contradict each other in every particular, it proves falshood absolutely. If Matthew speak truth, Luke speaks falshood; and if Luke speak truth, Matthew speaks falshood; and as there is no authority for believing one more than the other, there is no authority for believing either: and if they cannot be believed, even in the very first thing they say, and set out to prove, they are not entitled to be believed in any thing they say afterwards. Truth is an uniform thing; and as to inspiration and revelation, were we to admit it, it is impossible to suppose it can be contradictory. Either then the men called apostles were impostors, or the books ascribed to them have been written by other persons and fathered upon them, as is the case in the old testament.

THE BOOK OF MATTHEW gives, chap. i, ver. 6, a geneology by name from David, up, through Joseph the husband of Mary to Christ, and makes there to be *twenty-eight* generations. The book of Luke gives also a genealogy by name from Christ, through Joseph the husband of Mary, down to David, and makes there to be *forty-three* generations. Besides which there is only the two names of David and Joseph that are alike in the two lists. I here insert both genealogical lists, and for the sake of perspicuity and comparison, have placed them both in the same direction, that is, from Joseph down to David.

	Genealogy according to Matthew.		Genealogy according to Luke.
	Christ		Christ
2	Joseph	2	Joseph
3	Jacob	3	Heli
4	Matthan	4	Matthat
5	Eleazar.	5	Levi
6	Eliud	6	Melchi
7	Achim	7	Janna
8	Sadoc	8	Joseph
9	Azor.	9	Mattathias
10	Eliakim	10	Amos
11	Abiud	11	Naum
12	Zorobabel	12	Esli
13	Salathiel	13	Nagge
14	Jechonias.	14	Maath
15	Josias	15	Mattathias
16	Amon	16	Semei
17	Manasses	17	Joseph
18	Ezekias	18	Juda
19	Achaz	19	Joanna
20	Joatham	20	Rhesa
21	Ozias	21	Zorobabel
22	Joram	22	Salathiel
23	Josaphat	23	Neri

24	Asa	24	Melchi
25	Abia	25	Addi
26	Roboam	26	Cosam
27	Solomon	27	Elmodam
28	DAVID*	28	Er
		29	Jose
		30	Eliezer
		31	Johim
		32	Matthat
		33	Levi
		34	Simeon
		35	Juda
		36	Joseph
		37	Jonan
		38	Eliakim
		39	Melea
		40	Menan
		41	Mattatha
		42	Nathan
		43	DAVID

Now if these men, Matthew and Luke, set out with a falshood between them (as these two accounts shew they do) in the very commencement of their history of Jesus Christ, and of who, and of what he was, what authority (as I have before asked) is there left for believing the strange things they tell us afterwards? If they cannot be believed in their account of his natural genealogy, how are we to believe them when they tell us he was the son of God, begotten by a ghost, and

*From the birth of David to the birth of Christ is upwards of 1080 years, and as the life-time of Christ is not included, there is but 27 full generations. To find therefore the average age of each person mentioned in the list at the time his first son was born, it is only necessary to divide 1080 by 27, which gives 40 years for each person. As the life-time of man was then but of the same extent it is now, it is an absurdity to suppose that 27 following generations should all be old bachelors before they married; and the more so, when we are told, that Solomon, the next in succession to David, had a house-full of wives and mistresses before he was twenty-one years of age. So far from this genealogy being a solemn truth, it is not even a reasonable lie. The list of Luke gives about twenty-six years for the average age, and this is too much.

that an angel announced this in secret to his mother? If they lied in one genealogy, why are we to believe them in the other? If his natural genealogy be manufactured, which it certainly is, why are we not to suppose, that his celestial genealogy is manufactured also; and that the whole is fabulous? Can any man of serious reflection hazard his future happiness upon the belief of a story, naturally impossible, repugnant to every idea of decency, and related by persons already detected of falshood? Is it not more safe that we stop ourselves at the plain, pure, and unmixed belief of one God, which is Deism, than that we commit ourselves on an ocean of improbable, irrational, indecent and contradictory tales?

The first question, however, upon the books of the new testament, as upon those of the old, is, are they genuine? were they written by the persons to whom they are ascribed? for it is upon this ground only that the strange things related therein have been credited. Upon this point there is no *direct* proof *for* or *against*; and all that this state of a case proves, is *doubtfulness*, and doubtfulness is the opposite of belief. The state, therefore, that the books are in prove against themselves as far as this kind of proof can go.

But exclusive of this, the presumption is, that the books called the evangelists, and ascribed to Matthew, Mark, Luke, and John, were not written by Matthew, Mark, Luke, and John, and that they are impositions. The disordered state of the history in these four books, the silence of one book upon matters related in the other, and the disagreement that is to be found among them, implies that they are the productions of some unconnected individuals, many years after the things they pretend to relate, each of whom made his own legend; and not the writings of men living intimately together, as the men called apostles are supposed to have done. In fine, that they have been manufactured as the books of the old testament have been by other persons than those whose names they bear.

The story of the angel announcing, what the church calls, the *immaculate conception*, is not so much as mentioned in the books ascribed to Mark and John, and is differently related in Matthew and Luke. The former says the angel appeared to Joseph; the latter says it was to Mary; but either

Joseph or Mary was the worst evidence that could have been thought of; for it was others that should have testified *for them*, and not they for themselves. Were any girl, that is now with child, to say, and even to swear it, that she was gotten with child by a ghost, and that an angel told her so, would she be believed? Certainly she would not. Why then are we to believe the same thing of another girl whom we never saw, told by nobody knows who, nor when, nor where. How strange and inconsistent is it, that the same circumstances that would weaken the belief even of a probable story, should be given as a motive for believing this one that has, upon the face of it, every token of absolute impossibility and imposture?

The story of Herod destroying all the children under two years old, belongs altogether to the writer of the book of Matthew; not one of the rest mentions any thing about it. Had such a circumstance been true, the universality of it must have made it known to all the writers, and the thing would have been too striking to have been omitted by any. This writer tells us, that Jesus escaped this slaughter, because Joseph and Mary were warned by an angel to flee with him into Egypt: but he forgot to make provision for John, who was then under two years of age. John, however, who staid behind fared as well as Jesus who fled; and therefore the story circumstantially belies itself.

Not any two of those writers agree in reciting *exactly in the same words*, the written inscription, short as it is, which they tell us was put over Christ when he was crucified; and besides this, Mark says, he was crucified at the third hour (nine in the morning) and John says, it was at the sixth hour, twelve at noon.*

The inscription is thus stated in those books.

Matthew . . . This is Jesus the king of the Jews.
Mark . . . . The king of the Jews.
Luke . . . . This is the king of the Jews.
John. . . Jesus of Nazareth the king of the Jews.

---

*According to John, the sentence was *not passed* till about the sixth hour (noon) and consequently the execution could not be till the afternoon. But Mark says expressly, that he was *crucified* at the third hour. Nine in the morning, chap. xv, ver. 25. John, chap. xix, ver. 14.

We may infer from these circumstances, trivial as they are, that those writers, whoever they were, and in whatever time they lived, were not present at the scene. The only one of the men, called apostles, who appears to have been near to the spot, was Peter, and when he was accused of being one of Jesus's followers, it is said, (Matt. chap. xxvi, ver. 74) "then Peter began to *curse* and to *swear*, saying, I know not the man." Yet we are now called upon to believe this same Peter, convicted by their own account of perjury. For what reason or on what authority should we do this?

The accounts that are given of the circumstances that, they tell us, attended the crucifixion, are differently related in those four books.

The book ascribed to Matthew says, *there was darkness over all the land, from the sixth hour unto the ninth hour—that the veil of the temple was rent in twain from the top to the bottom—that there was an earthquake—that the rocks rent—that the graves opened—that the bodies of many of the saints that slept, arose, and came out of their graves after the resurrection, and went into the holy city, and appeared unto many.* Such is the account which this dashing writer of the book of Matthew gives, but in which he is not supported by the writers of the other books.

The writer of the book ascribed to Mark, in detailing the circumstances of the crucifixion, makes no mention of any earthquake, nor of the rocks rending, nor of the graves opening, nor of the dead men walking out. The writer of the book of Luke is silent also upon the same points. And as to the writer of the book of John, though he details all the circumstances of the crucifixion down to the burial of Christ, he says nothing about either the darkness—the veil of the temple—the earthquake—the rocks—the graves, nor the dead men.

Now if it had been true that these things had happened, and if the writers of these books had lived at the time they *did* happen, and had been the persons they are said to be, namely, the four men called apostles, Matthew, Mark, Luke and John, it was not possible for them, as true historians, even without the aid of inspiration, not to have recorded them. The things, supposing them to have been facts, were of too much notoriety not to have been known, and of too much importance not to have been told. All these supposed apostles must have been witnesses of the earthquake, if there had been any; for it was not possible for them to have been absent from it. The opening of the graves and the resurrection of the dead men, and their walking about the city, is of still greater importance than the earthquake. An earthquake is always possible and natural, and proves nothing: but this opening of the graves is supernatural and directly in point to their doctrine, their cause, and their apostleship. Had it been true, it would have filled up whole chapters of those books, and been the chosen theme, and general chorus of all the writers: but instead of this, little and trivial things, and mere prattling conversations of *he said this*, and *she said that*, are often tediously detailed, while this most important of all, had it been true, is passed off in a slovenly manner, by a single dash of the pen, and that by one writer only, and not so much as hinted at by the rest.

It is an easy thing to tell a lie, but it is difficult to support the lie after it is told. The writer of the book of Matthew should have told us who the saints were that came to life again and went into the city, and what became of them afterwards, and who it was that saw them; for he is not hardy enough to say that he saw them himself—whether they came out naked and all in natural buff, he-saints, and she-saints, or whether they came full dressed, and where they got their dresses—whether they went to their former habitations and reclaimed their wives, their husbands, and their property, and how they were received—whether they entered ejectments for the recovery of their possessions, or brought actions of *crim. con.* against the rival interlopers—whether they remained on earth, and followed their former occupations of preaching or working, or whether they died again, or went back to their graves alive, and buried themselves.

Strange indeed that an army of saints should return to life, and nobody know who they were, nor who it was that saw them, and that not a word more should be said upon the subject, nor these saints have any thing to tell us! Had it been the prophets who (as we are told) had formerly prophesied of these things, *they* must have had a great deal to say. They could have told us every thing; and we should have had posthumus prophecies, with notes and commentaries upon the first, a little better, at least, than we have now. Had it been Moses and Aaron, and Joshua, and Samuel and David, not an unconverted Jew had remained in all Jerusalem. Had it been John the Baptist, and the saints of the times then present, every body would have known them, and they would have out-preached and out-famed all the other apostles. But instead of this, these saints are made to pop up like Jonah's gourd in the night, for no purpose at all but to wither in the morning. Thus much for this part of the story.

The tale of the resurrection follows that of the crucifixion; and in this, as well as in that, the writers, whoever they were, disagree so much as to make it evident that none of them were there.

THE BOOK OF MATTHEW states, that when Christ was put in the sepulchre, the Jews applied to Pilate for a watch or a guard to be placed over the sepulchre to prevent the body being stolen by the disciples, and that in consequence of this request, the sepulchre was *made sure, sealing the stone*, that covered the mouth, *and setting a watch*. But the other books say nothing about this application, nor about the sealing, nor the guard, nor the watch; and according to their accounts there were none. Matthew, however, follows up this part of the story of the guard or the watch, with a second part, that I shall notice in the conclusion, as it serves to detect the fallacy of those books.

THE BOOK OF MATTHEW continues its account and says, (chap. xxviii, v. 1,) that at the end of the sabbath as it began to *dawn*, towards the first day of the week came *Mary Magdalene* and the *other Mary* to see the sepulchre. — Mark says it was *sun rising*, and John says it was *dark*. Luke says it was *Mary Magdalene*, and *Joanna*, and *Mary the mother* of James, and *other women* that came to the sepulchre; and John states that Mary Magdalene came alone. So well do they agree about their first evidences! They all, however, appear to have known most about *Mary Magdalene*; she was a woman of a large acquaintance; and it was not an ill conjecture that she might be upon the stroll.

THE BOOK OF MATTHEW goes on to say—(ver. 2) And behold there was a great earthquake, for the angel of the Lord descended from heaven, and came and rolled back the stone from the door and *sat upon it*. But the other books say nothing about any earthquake, nor about the angel rolling back the stone and *sitting upon it*; and according to their accounts there was no angel *sitting there*. Mark says the angel was *within the sepulchre sitting* on the right side. Luke says there were *two* and they were both *standing up*; and John says they were both *sitting down, one at the head and the other at the feet*.

Matthew says, that the angel that was *sitting upon the stone on the outside* of the sepulchre, told the two Maries that Christ was risen, and that the women went *away quickly*. Mark says that the women, upon seeing the stone rolled away, and wondering at it, went *into* the sepulchre, and that it was the angel that was *sitting within* on the right side that told them so. Luke says it was the two angels that were standing up, and John says it was Jesus Christ himself that told it to Mary Magdalene, and that she did not go into the sepulchre, but only stooped down and looked in.

Now if the writers of these four books had gone into a court of justice to prove an *alibi*, (for it is of the nature of an alibi that is here attempted to be proved, namely, the absence of a dead body by supernatural means) and had they given their evidence in the same contradictory manner as it is here given, they would have been in danger of having their ears cropt for perjury, and would have justly deserved it. Yet this is the evidence, and these are the books, that have been imposed upon the world as being given by divine inspiration, and as the unchangeable word of God.

The writer of the book of Matthew, after giving this account, relates a story that is not to be found in any of the other books, and which is the same I have just before alluded to.

"Now, says he, (that is after the conversation the women had had with the angel sitting upon the stone) behold some of the watch (meaning the watch that he had said had been placed over the sepulchre) came into the city, and shewed unto the chief priests all the things that were done, and when they were assembled with the elders, and had taken council, they gave large money unto the soldiers, saying, say ye, that his disciples came by night and stole him away while we *slept*;

and if this come to the governor's ears, we will persuade him and secure you. So they took the money and did as they were taught. And this saying (that his disciples stole him away) is commonly reported among the Jews *until this day*."

The expression, *until this day*, is an evidence that the book ascribed to Matthew, was not written by Matthew; and that it has been manufactured long after the times and things of which it pretends to treat; for the expression implies a great length of intervening time. It would be inconsistent in us to speak in this manner of any thing happening in our own time. To give therefore intelligible meaning to the expression, we must suppose a lapse of some generations at least; for this manner of speaking carries the mind back to an ancient time.

The absurdity also of the story is worth noticing; for it shews the writer of the book of Matthew to have been an exceeding weak and foolish man. He tells a story that contradicts itself in point of possibility; for though the guard, if there were any, might be made to say, that the body was taken away while they were *asleep*; and to give that as a reason for their not having prevented it, that same sleep must also have prevented their knowing how, and by whom it was done; and yet they are made to say that it was the disciples who did it. Were a man to tender his evidence of something that he should say was done, and of the manner of doing it, and of the persons who did it, while he was asleep, and could know nothing of the matter, such evidence could not be received. It will do well enough for testament evidence, but not for any thing where truth is concerned.

I come now to that part of the evidence in those books that respects the pretended appearance of Christ after this pretended resurrection.

The writer of the book of Matthew relates, that the angel that was sitting on the stone at the mouth of the sepulchre, said to the two Maries, chap. xxviii, ver. 7, *"Behold Christ is gone before you into Galilee, there ye shall see him; lo, I have told you."* And the same writer, at the two next verses (8,9) makes Christ himself to speak to the same purpose to these women, immediately after the angel had told it to them, and that they *ran quickly* to tell it to the disciples. And at the 16th verse it is said, *"Then the eleven disciples went away into*

Galilee, into a mountain where Jesus had appointed them; and when they saw him, they worshipped him."

But the writer of the book of John tells a story very different to this; for he says, chap. xx, ver. 19, *"Then the same day at evening, being the first day of the week*, (that is, the same day that Christ is said to have risen) *when the doors were shut, where the disciples were assembled for fear of the Jews, came Jesus and stood in the midst of them."*

According to Matthew, the eleven were marching to Galilee, to meet Jesus in a mountain by his own appointment, at the very time, when, according to John, they were assembled in another place; and that not by appointment, but in secret for fear of the Jews.

The writer of the book of Luke contradicts that of Matthew more pointedly than John does; for he says expressly that the meeting was *in Jerusalem*, the evening of the same day that he, Christ, rose, and that the *eleven* were *there*. See Luke, chap. xxiv, verses 13, 33.

Now it is not possible (unless we admit these supposed disciples the right of wilful lying) that the writers of these books could be any of the eleven persons called disciples. For if, according to Matthew, the eleven went into Galilee to meet Jesus in a mountain by his own appointment on the same day that he is said to have risen, Luke and John must have been two of that eleven; yet the writer of Luke says, expressly, and John implies as much, that the meeting was that same day in a house in Jerusalem. And on the other hand, if, according to Luke and John, the *eleven* were assembled in a house in Jerusalem, Matthew must have been one of that eleven, yet Matthew says, the meeting was in a mountain in Galilee, and consequently the evidence given in those books destroy each other.

The writer of the book of Mark says nothing about any meeting in Galilee; but he says, chap. xvi, ver. 12, that Christ, after his resurrection, appeared in *another form* to two of them, as they walked into the country; and that these two told it to the residue who would not believe them. Luke also tells a story, in which he keeps Christ employed the whole of the day of this pretended resurrection, until the evening, and which totally invalidates the account of going to the mountain in Galilee. He says that two of them, without saying which two, went that *same day* to a village called Emmaus, threescore furlongs (seven miles and an half) from Jerusalem, and that Christ, in disguise, went with them and staid with them unto the evening, and supped with them, and then vanished out of their sight, and re-appeared that same evening at the meeting of the eleven in Jerusalem.

This is the contradictory manner in which the evidence of this pretended re-appearance of Christ is stated. The only point in which the writers agree is the skulking privacy of that re-appearance; for whether it was in the recess of a mountain in Galilee, or in a shut-up house in Jerusalem it was still skulking. To what cause then are we to assign this skulking? On the one hand it is directly repugnant to the supposed or pretended end, that of convincing the world that Christ was risen; and on the other hand to have asserted the publicity of it would have exposed the writers of those books to public detection; and therefore they have been under the necessity of making it a private affair.

As to the account of Christ being seen by more than five hundred at once, it is Paul only who says it, and not the five hundred who say it for themselves. It is therefore the testimony but of one man, and that too of a man who did not, according to the same account, believe a word of the matter himself at the time it is said to have happened. His evidence, supposing him to have been the writer of the 15th chapter of Corinthians, where this account is given, is like that of a man who comes into a court of justice to swear that what he had sworn before is false. A man may often see reason, and he has too always the right, of changing his *opinion*, but this liberty does not extend to matters of fact.

I now come to the last scene, that of the ascension into heaven. Here all fear of the Jews, and of every thing else, must necessarily have been out of the question. It was that which, if true, was to seal the whole, and upon which the reality of the future mission of the disciples was to rest for proof. Words, whether declarations or promises, that passed in private, either in the recess of a mountain in Galilee or in a shut-up house in Jerusalem, even supposing them to have been spoken, could not be evidence in public. It was therefore neccessary that this last scene should preclude the possibility of denial and dispute, and that it should be, as I have stated in the former part of the *Age of Reason*, as public and as visible as the sun at noon-day: at least, it ought to have been as public as the crucifixion is reported to have been. But to come to the point —

In the first place, the writer of the book of Matthew does not say a syllable about it; neither does the writer of the book of John. This being the case, is it possible to suppose that those writers, who affect to be even minute in other matters, would have been silent upon this, had it been true? The writer of the book of Mark passes it off in a careless slovenly manner, with a single dash of the pen, as if he was tired of romancing, or ashamed of the story; so also does the writer of Luke: and even between these two there is not an apparent agreement as to the place where this final parting is said to have been.

THE BOOK OF MARK says, that Christ appeared to the eleven as they sat at meat, alluding to the meeting of the eleven at Jerusalem; he then states the conversation that he says passed at that meeting; and immediately after says (as a school-boy would finish a dull story) "*So then*, after the Lord had spoken unto them, he was received up into heaven, and sat on the right hand of God." But the writer of Luke says, that the ascension was from Bethany; that he, Christ, *led them out as far as Bethany, and was parted from them there, and was carried up into heaven.* — So also was Mahomet: and as to Moses, the *apostle* Jude says, ver. 9, *that Michael and the devil disputed about his body.* While we believe such fables as these, or either of them, we believe unworthily of the Almighty.

I have now gone through the examination of the four books ascribed to Matthew, Mark, Luke, and John: and when it is considered that the whole space of time, from the crucifixion to what is called the ascension, is but a few days, apparently not more than three or four, and that all the circumstances are reported to have happened nearly about the same spot, Jerusalem, it is, I believe, impossible to find, in any story upon record, so many and such glaring absurdities, contradictions, and falshoods, as are in those books. They are more numerous and striking than I had any expectation of finding when I began this examination, and far more so than

I had any idea of when I wrote the former part of the *Age of Reason*. I had then neither bible nor testament to refer to, nor could I procure any. My own situation, even as to existence, was becoming every day more precarious; and as I was willing to leave something behind me upon the subject, I was obliged to be quick and concise. The quotations I then made were from memory only, but they are correct; and the opinions I have advanced in that work, are the effect of the most clear, and long established conviction, that the bible and the testament are impositions upon the world—that the fall of man—the account of Jesus Christ being the son of God—and of his dying to appease the wrath of God—and of salvation by that strange means, are all fabulous inventions dishonourable to the wisdom and power of the Almighty—that the only true religion is deism, by which I then meant and now mean the belief of one God, and an imitation of his moral character, or the practice of what are called moral virtues—and that it was upon this only (so far as religion is concerned) that I rested all my hopes of happiness hereafter. So say I now—and so help me God.

But to return to the subject.—Though it is impossible, at this distance of time to ascertain as a fact who were the writers of those four books (and this alone is sufficient to hold them in doubt, and where we doubt we do not believe) it is not difficult to ascertain negatively, that they were not written by the persons to whom they are ascribed. The contradictions in those books demonstrate two things.

First, that the writers cannot have been eye-witnesses and ear-witnesses of the matters they relate, or they would have related them without those contradictions; and consequently that the books have not been written by the persons called apostles, who are supposed to have been witnesses of this kind.

Secondly, That the writers, whoever they were, have not acted in concerted imposition; but each writer separately and individually for himself, and without the knowledge of the other.

The same evidence that applies to prove the one, applies equally to prove both those cases, that is, that the books were not written by the men called apostles, and also that they are not a concerted imposition. As to inspiration it is altogether out of the question. We may as well attempt to unite truth and falshood as inspiration and contradiction.

If four men are eye-witnesses and ear-witnesses to a scene, they will, without any concert between them, agree as to the time and place when and where that scene happened. Their individual knowlege of the thing, each one knowing it for himself, renders concert totally unnecessary. The one will not say it was in a mountain in the country, and the other, at a house in town. The one will not say it was at sun-rise, and the other that it was dark; for in whatever place it was, and at whatever time it was, they know it equally alike.

And on the other hand, if four men concert a story, they will make their separate relations of that story agree and cor-roborate with each other to support the whole. *That* concert supplies the want of fact in the one case, as the knowlege of the fact supersedes, in the other case, the necessity of concert. The same contradictions therefore that prove there has been no concert, prove also that the reporters had not knowledge of the fact; (or rather of that which they relate as a fact;) and detect also the falshood of their reports. Those books, there-fore, have neither been written by the men called apostles, nor by imposters in concert. How then have they been written?

I am not one of those who are fond of believing there is much of that which is called wilful lying, or lying originally, except in the case of men setting up to be prophets, as in the old testament, for prophesying is lying professionally. In al-most all other cases it is not difficult to discover the progress by which even simple supposition with the aid of credulity will in time grow into a lye, and at last be told as a fact: and whenever we can find a charitable reason for a thing of this kind we ought not to indulge a severe one.

That story of Jesus Christ appearing after he was dead is the story of an apparition; such as timid imagination can always create in vision and credulity believe. Stories of this kind had been told of the assassination of Julius Cæsar not many years before, and they generally have their origin in violent deaths or in execution of innocent persons. In cases of this kind, compassion lends its aid and benevolently stretches the story.

It goes on a little and a little farther, till it becomes a *most certain truth*. Once start a ghost and credulity fills up the history of its life, and assigns the cause of its appearance. One tells it one way, another another way, till there are as many stories about the ghost, and about the proprietor of the ghost, as there are about Jesus Christ in these four books.

The story of the appearance of Jesus Christ is told with that strange mixture of the natural and the impossible that distinguishes legendary tale from fact. He is represented as suddenly coming in and going out when the doors are shut, and of vanishing out of sight, and appearing again, as one would conceive of an unsubstantial vision; then again he is hungry, sits down to meat, and eats his supper. But as those who tell stories of this kind never provide for all the cases, so it is here. They have told us that when he arose he left his grave cloaths behind him, but they have forgotten to provide other cloaths for him to appear in afterwards; or to tell us what he did with them when he ascended. Whether he stripped all off, or went up cloaths and all. In the case of Elijah, they have been careful enough to make him throw down his mantle. How it happened not to be burnt in the chariot of fire, *they* also have not told us. But as imagination supplies all deficiencies of this kind, we may suppose, if we please, that it was made of Salamander's wool.

Those who are not much acquainted with ecclesiastical history may suppose, that the book called the new testament has existed ever since the time of Jesus Christ, as they suppose that the books ascribed to Moses have existed ever since the time of Moses. But the fact is historically otherwise. There was no such book as the new testament till more than three hundred years after the time that Christ is said to have lived.

At what time the books ascribed to Matthew, Mark, Luke, and John, began to appear is altogether a matter of uncertainty. There is not the least shadow of evidence of who the persons were that wrote them, nor at what time they were written; and they might as well have been called by the names of any of the other supposed apostles as by the names they are now called. The originals are not in the possession of any Christian church existing, any more than the two tables of stone written on, they pretend, by the finger of God upon mount Sinai and given to Moses, are in the possession of the Jews; and even if they were, there is no possibility of proving the hand writing in either case. At the time those four books were written there was no printing, and consequently there could be no publication otherwise than by written copies, which any man might make or alter at pleasure, and call them originals. Can we suppose it is consistent with the wisdom of the Almighty to commit himself and his will to man upon such precarious means as these, or that it is consistent we should pin our faith upon such uncertainties? We cannot make, nor alter, nor even imitate, so much as a blade of grass that he has made, and yet we can make or alter *words of God*, as easily as words of man.*

About three hundred and fifty years after the time that Christ is said to have lived, several writings of the kind I am speaking of were scattered in the hands of divers individuals, and as the church had began to form itself into a hierarchy or church government with temporal powers, it set itself about collecting them into a code as we now see them, called, the *New Testament*. They decided by vote, as I have before said, in the former part of the *Age of Reason*, which of those writings, out of the collection they had made, should be the *word of God*, and which should not. The rabbins of the Jews had decided, by vote, upon the books of the bible before.

As the object of the church, as is the case in all national establishment of churches, was power and revenue, and terror the means it used, it is consistent to suppose that the most

---

*The former part of the *Age of Reason* has not been published two years, and there is already an expression in it that is not mine. The expression is, *The book of Luke was carried by a majority of one vote only*. It may be true, but it is not I that have said it. Some person who might know of that circumstance has added it in a note at the bottom of the page of some of the editions printed either in England or in America, and the printers after that have erected it into the body of the work, and made me the author of it. If this has happened within such a short space of time, notwithstanding the aid of printing, which prevents the alteration of copies individually, what may not have happened in a much greater length of time when there was no printing and when any man who could write could make a written copy and call it an original by Matthew, Mark, Luke, or John.

miraculous and wonderful of the writings they had collected, stood the best chance of being voted; and as to the authenticity of the books the *vote stands in the place of it*; for it can be traced no higher.

Disputes, however, ran high among the people then calling themselves Christians, not only as to points of doctrine, but as to the authenticity of the books. In the contest between the person called Saint Augustine and Fauste, about the year 400, the latter says, "The books called the evangelists have been composed long after the times of the apostles by some obscure men, who fearing that the world would not give credit to their relation of matters, of which they could not be informed, have published them under the names of the apostles; and which are so full of sottishness and discordant relations, that there is neither agreement nor connection between them."

And in another place, addressing himself to the advocates of those books, as being the word of God, he says, "It is thus that your predecessors have inserted in the scriptures of our Lord many things which, though they carry his name, agree not with his doctrine. This is not surprising, *since that we have often proved*, that these things have not been written by himself nor by his apostles, but that, for the greatest part, they are founded upon *tales, upon vague reports*, and put together by I know not what half-Jews, with but little agreement between them, and which they have, nevertheless, published under the name of the apostles of our Lord, and have thus attributed to them their own *errors and their lies*."*

The reader will see by those extracts that the authenticity of the books of the new testament was denied, and the books treated as tales, forgeries, and lies, at the time they were voted to be the word of God. But the interest of the church, with the assistance of the faggot, bore down the opposition, and at last suppressed all investigation. Miracles followed upon miracles, if we will believe them, and men were taught to say they believed whether they believed or not. But (by way of throwing in a thought) the French revolution has excommu-

*I have taken those two extracts from Boulanger's life of Paul, written in French. Boulanger has quoted them from the writings of Augustin against Fauste, to which he refers.

nicated the church from the power of working miracles. She has not been able, with the assistance of all her saints, to work *one* miracle since the revolution began; and as she never stood in greater need than now, we may, without the aid of divination, conclude, that all her former miracles are tricks and lies.*

When we consider the lapse of more than three hundred years intervening between the time that Christ is said to have lived and the time the new Testament was formed into a book, we must see, even without the assistance of historical evidence, the exceeding uncertainty there is of its authenticity. The authenticity of the book of Homer, so far as regards the authorship, is much better established than that of the new testament, though Homer is a thousand years the most ancient. It was only an exceeding good poet that could have written the book of Homer, and therefore few men only could have attempted it; and a man capable of doing it would not have thrown away his own fame by giving it to another. In like manner, there were but few that could have composed Euclid's Elements, because none but an exceeding good geometrician could have been the author of that work.

*Boulanger in his life of Paul has collected from the ecclesiastical histories and the writings of the fathers as they are called, several matters which shew the opinions that prevailed among the different sects of Christians at the time the testament, as we now see it, was voted to be the word of God. The following extracts are from the second chapter of that work.

"The Marcionists (a Christian sect) assured that the evangelists were filled with falsities. The Manichéens, who formed a very numerous sect at the commencement of Christianity, *rejected as false all the New Testament*, and shewed other writings quite different, that they gave for authentic—The Cérinthiens, like the Marcionistes, admitted not the Acts of the Apostles—The Encratites and the Sévénians adopted neither the Acts nor the Epistles of Paul—Chrysostom, in a homily which he made upon the Acts of the Apostles, says, that in his time, about the year 400, many people knew nothing either of the author nor of the book—St. Irénée, who lived before that time, reports, that the Valentinians, like several other sects of the Christians, accuse the scriptures of being filled with errors, imperfections and contradictions—The Ebionites, or Nazareans, who were the first Christians, rejected all the Epistles of Paul, and regarded him as an impostor. They report, among other things, that he was originally a Pagan, that he came to Jerusalem, where he lived some time, and that having a mind to marry the daughter of the high-priest, he had himself circumcised; but that not being able to obtain her, he quarrelled with the Jews, and wrote against circumcision, and against the observation of the sabbath, and against all the legal ordinances."

But with respect to the books of the new testament, particularly such parts as tell us of the resurrection and ascension of Christ, any person who could tell a story of an apparition, or of a *man's walking*, could have made such books; for the story is most wretchedly told. The chance, therefore, of forgery in the testament, is millions to one greater than in the case of Homer or Euclid. Of the numerous priests or parsons of the present day, bishops and all, every one of them can make a sermon or translate a scrap of latin, especially if it has been translated a thousand times before; but is there any amongst them that can write poetry like Homer, or science like Euclid? The sum total of a parson's learning, with very few exceptions, is *a*, *b*, *ab*, and *hic*, *hæc*, *hoc*; and their knowledge of science is three times one is *one*; and this is more than sufficient to have enabled them, had they lived at the time, to have written all the books of the new testament.

As the opportunities of forgery were greater, so also was the inducement. A man could gain no advantage by writing under the name of Homer or Euclid. If he could write equal to them, it would be better that he wrote under his own name; if inferior, he could not succeed. Pride would prevent the former, and impossibility the latter. But with respect to such books as compose the new testament, all the inducements were on the side of forgery. The best imagined history that could have been made at the distance of two or three hundred years after the time, could not have passed for an original under the name of the real writer. The only chance of success lay in forgery; for the church wanted pretence for its new doctrine, and truth and talents were out of the question.

But as it is not uncommon (as before observed) to relate stories of persons *walking* after they are dead, and of ghosts and apparitions of such as have fallen by some violent or extraordinary means; and as the people of that day were in the habit of believing such things, and of the appearance of angels, and also of devils, and of their getting into people's insides, and shaking them like a fit of an ague, and of their being cast out again as if by an emetic, (Mary Magdalene, the book of Mark tells us, had brought up, or been brought to bed of, seven devils) it was nothing extraordinary that some story of this kind should get abroad, of the person called Jesus Christ, and become afterwards the foundation of the four books ascribed to Matthew, Mark, Luke, and John. Each writer told the tale as he heard it, or thereabouts, and gave to his book the name of the saint, or the apostle, whom tradition had given as the eye-witness. It is only upon this ground that the contradictions in those books can be accounted for; and if this be not the case, they are down-right impositions, lies, and forgeries, without even the apology of credulity.

That they have been written by a sort of half-Jews, as the foregoing quotations mention, is enough discernable. The frequent references made to that chief assassin and impostor Moses, and to the men called prophets, establish this point; and on the other hand the church has complimented the fraud by admitting the bible and the testament to reply to each other. Between the Christian-Jew and the Christian-Gentile, the thing called a prophesy, and the thing prophesied of; the type and the thing typified; the sign and the thing signified; have been industriously rummaged up, and fitted together like old locks and picklock keys. The story, foolishly enough told, of Eve and the serpent, and naturally enough as to the enmity between men and serpents (for the serpent always bites about the *heel*, because it cannot reach higher; and the man always knocks the serpent about the *head* as the most effectual way to prevent its biting*): this foolish story, I say, has been made into a prophecy, a type, and a promise to begin with: and the lying imposition of Isaiah to Ahaz, that *a virgin shalt conceive and bear a son*, as a sign that Ahaz should conquer, when the event was that he was defeated (as already noticed in the observations on the book of Isaiah) has been perverted and made to serve as a winder-up.

Jonah and the whale are also made into a sign and type. Jonah is Jesus, and the whale is the grave; for it is said (and they have made Christ to say it of himself,) Matth. chap. xvii, ver. 40, "For as Jonah was *three days* and *three nights* in the whale's belly, so shall the son of man be *three days* and *three*

---

*It shall bruise thy *head*, and thou shalt bruise his *heel*. Genesis, chap. iii, ver. 15.

nights in the heart of the earth." But it happens awkwardly enough, that Christ, according to their own account, was but one day and two nights in the grave; about 36 hours instead of 72; that is, the friday night, the saturday, and the saturday night; for, they say, he was up on the sunday morning by sun-rise or before. But as this fits quite as well as the *bite* and the *kick* in Genesis, and the *virgin* and her *son* in Isaiah, it will pass in the lump of *orthodox* things. — Thus much for the historical part of the testament and its evidences.

THE EPISTLES OF PAUL.

The Epistles ascribed to Paul, being fourteen in number, almost fill up the remaining part of the testament. Whether those epistles were written by the person to whom they are ascribed, is a matter of no great importance, since that the writer, whoever he was, attempts to prove his doctrine by argument. He does not pretend to have been witness to any of the scenes told of the resurrection and the ascension, and he declares that he had not believed them.

The story of his being struck to the ground as he was journeying to Damascus, has nothing in it miraculous or extraordinary. He escaped with life, and that is more than many others have done who have been struck with lightning; and that he should lose his sight for three days and be unable to eat or drink during that time, is nothing more than is common in such conditions. His companions that were with him, appear not to have suffered in the same manner, for they were well enough to lead him the remainder of the journey; neither did they pretend to have seen any vision.

The character of the person called Paul, according to the accounts given of him, has in it a great deal of violence and fanaticism. He had persecuted with as much heat as he preached afterwards. The stroke he had received, had changed his thinking without altering his constitution; and either as a Jew or a Christian he was the same zealot. Such men are never good moral evidences of any doctrine they preach. They are always in extremes, as well of action as of belief.

The doctrine he sets out to prove by argument, is the resurrection of the same body, and he advances this as an evidence of immortality. But so much will men differ in their manner of thinking, and in the conclusions they draw from the same premises, that this doctrine of the resurrection of the same body, so far from being an evidence of immortality, appears to me to furnish an evidence against it: for, if I have already died in this body, and am raised again in the same body in which I have died, it is presumptive evidence that I shall die again. That resurrection no more secures me against the repetition of dying, than an ague fit, when past, secures me against another. To believe therefore in immortality, I must have a more elevated idea than is contained in this gloomy doctrine of the resurrection.

Besides, as a matter of choice, as well as of hope, I had rather have a better body and a more convenient form, than the present. Every animal in the creation excels us in something. The winged insects, without mentioning doves or eagles, can pass over more space, and with greater ease, in a few minutes, than man can in an hour. The glide of the smallest fish, in proportion to its bulk, exceeds us in motion almost beyond comparison, and without weariness. Even the sluggish snail can ascend from the bottom of a dungeon, where man by the want of that ability would perish, and a spider can launch itself from the top as a playful amusement. The personal powers of man are so limited, and his heavy frame so little constructed to extensive enjoyment, that there is nothing to induce us to wish the opinion of Paul to be true. It is too little for the magnitude of the scene; too mean for the sublimity of the subject.

But all other arguments apart, the *consciousness of existence* is the only conceivable idea we can have of another life, and the continuance of that consciousness is immortality. The consciousness of existence, or the knowing that we exist, is not necessarily confined to the same form, nor to the same matter, even in this life. We have not in all cases the same form, nor in any case the same matter, that composed our bodies twenty or thirty years ago, and yet we are conscious of being the same persons. Even legs and arms, which make up almost half the human frame, are not necessary to the consciousness of existence. These may be lost or taken away, and the full consciousness of existence remain, and were their place supplied by wings, or other appendages, we cannot conceive that it could alter our consciousness of existence. In short, we know not how much, or rather how little, of our composition it is, and how exquisitely fine that little is, that creates in us this consciousness of existence, and all beyond that is like the pulp of a peach, distinct and separate from the vegetative speck in the kernel.

Who can say by what exceeding fine action of fine matter it is, that a thought is produced in what we call the mind; and yet that thought, when produced, as I now produce the thought I am writing, is capable of becoming immortal, and is the only production of man that has that capacity. Statues of brass or marble will perish, and statues made in imitation of them are not the same statues, nor the same workmanship, any more than a copy of a picture is the same picture. But print and reprint a thought a thousand times over, and that, with materials of any kind, carve it in wood, or engrave it in stone, the thought is eternally and identically the same thought in every case. It has a capacity of unimpaired exist-ence, unaffected by change of matter, and is essentially dis-tinct, and of a nature different, from every thing else that we know of, or can conceive. If then the thing produced has in itself a capacity of being immortal, it is more than a token that the power that produced it, which is the self-same thing as consciousness of existence, can be immortal also; and that as independently of the matter it was first connected with, as the thought is of the printing or writing it first appeared in. The one idea is not more difficult to believe than the other; and we can see that one is true.

That the consciousness of existence is not dependant on the same form or the same matter, is demonstrated to our senses in the works of the creation, as far as our senses are capable of receiving that demonstration. A very numerous part of the animal creation preaches to us, far better than Paul, the belief of a life hereafter. Their little life resembles an earth and a heaven, a present and a future state; and com-prises, if it may be so expressed, immortality in miniature.

The most beautiful part of the creation to our eye, are the winged insects, and they are not so originally. They ac-quire that form and that inimitable brilliancy by progressive changes. The slow and creeping caterpillar-worm of to-day, passes in a few days to a torpid figure and a state resembling death; and in the next change comes forth in all the miniature magnificence of life, a splendid butterfly. No resemblance of the former creature remains; every thing is changed; all his powers are new, and life is to him another thing. We cannot conceive that the consciousness of existence is not the same in this state of the animal as before; why then must I believe that the resurrection of the same body is necessary to continue to me the consciousness of existence hereafter?

In the former part of the *Age of Reason* I have called the creation the true and only real word of God; and this instance, or this text, in the book of creation, not only shews to us that this thing may be so, but that it is so; and that the belief of a future state is a *rational belief*, corroborated by facts visible in the creation: for it is not more difficult to believe that we shall exist hereafter in a better state and form than at present, than that a worm should become a butterfly, and quit the dunghill for the atmosphere, if we did not know it as a fact.

As to the doleful jargon ascribed to Paul in the 15th chapter of 1 Corinthians, which makes part of the burial service of some Christian sectaries, it is as destitute of meaning as the tolling of the bell at the funeral. It explains nothing to the understanding; it illustrates nothing to the imagination; but leaves the reader to find any meaning if he can.

"All flesh, says he, is not the same flesh. There is one flesh of men, another of beasts, another of fishes, and another of birds." And what then? Nothing. A cook could have said as much. "There are also, says he, bodies celestial and bodies terrestrial. The glory of the celestial is *one*, and the glory of the terrestrial is the *other*." And what then? Nothing. And what is the difference? Nothing that he has told. "There is, says he, one glory of the sun, and another glory of the moon, and another glory of the stars." And what then? Nothing; except that he says that *one star differeth from another star in glory*, instead of distance; and he might as well have told us that the moon did not shine so bright as the sun. All this is nothing better than the jargon of a conjurer, who picks up phrases he does not understand, to confound the credulous people who come to have their fortune told. Priests and conjurers are of the same trade.

Sometimes Paul affects to be a naturalist, and to prove his system of resurrection from the principles of vegetation. *"Thou fool, says he, that which thou sowest is not quickened except it die."* To which one might reply in his own language, and say, Thou fool, Paul, that which thou sowest is not quickened except it die *not*; for the grain that dies in the ground never does and cannot vegetate. It is only the living grains that produce the next crop. But the metaphor, in any point of view, is no simile. It is succession and resurrection. The progress of an animal, from one state of Being to another, as from a worm to a butterfly, applies to the case, but this of the grain does not; and shews Paul to have been, what he says of others, a FOOL.

Whether the fourteen epistles ascribed to Paul were written by him or not is a matter of indifference. They are either argumentative or dogmatical; and as the argument is defective, and the dogmatical part is merely presumptive, it signifies not who wrote them; and the same may be said for the remaining parts of the testament. It is not upon the epistles, but upon what is called the gospel, contained in the four books ascribed to Matthew, Mark, Luke, and John, and upon the pretended prophesies, that the theory of the church, calling itself the Christian church, is founded. The epistles are dependant upon those, and must follow their fate: for if the story of Jesus Christ be fabulous, all reasoning founded upon it as a supposed truth, must fall with it.

We know from history, that one of the principal leaders of this church, Athanasius, lived at the time the new testament was formed, and we know also from the absurd jargon he has left us, under the name of a creed, the character of the men who formed the new testament*; and we know also from the same history, that the authenticity of the books of which it is composed, was denied at the time. It is upon the vote of such men as Athanasius, that the testament was decreed to be the word of God, and nothing can present to us a more strange

---

*Athanasius died, according to the church chronology, in the year 371.

idea than that of decreeing the word of God by vote. Those who rest their faith upon such authority, put man in the place of God, and have no true foundation for future happiness. Credulity, however, is not a crime; but it becomes criminal by resisting conviction. It is strangling in the womb of the conscience the efforts it makes to ascertain truth. We should never force belief upon ourselves in any thing.

I here close the subject on the old testament and the new. The evidence I have produced to prove them forgeries, are extracted from the books themselves, and acts, like a two-edged sword, either way. If the evidence be denied, the authenticity of the scriptures is denied with it, for it is scripture evidence; and if the evidence be admitted, the authenticity of the books is disproved. The contradictory impossibilities contained in the old testament and the new, put them in the case of a man who swears *for* and *against.* Either evidence convicts him of perjury, and equally destroys reputation.

Should the bible and testament hereafter fall, it is not I that have done it. I have done no more than extracted the evidence from the confused mass of matters with which it is mixed, and arranged that evidence in a point of light to be clearly seen and easily comprehended; and having done this, I leave the reader to judge for himself, as I have judged for myself.

CONCLUSION.

In the former part of the *Age of Reason,* I have spoken of the three frauds, *mystery, miracle,* and *prophesy;* and as I have seen nothing in any of the answers to that work that in the least affects what I have there said upon those subjects, I shall not encumber this second part with additions that are not necessary.

I have spoken also in the same work upon what is called *revelation,* and have shewn the absurd misapplication of that term to the books of the old testament and the new; for certainly revelation is out of the question in reciting any thing of which man has been the actor or the witness. That which a man has done or seen, needs no revelation to tell him he has done it or seen it, for he knows it already, nor to enable him to tell it or to write it. It is ignorance or imposition to apply the term revelation in such cases; yet the bible and testament are classed under this fraudulent description of being all *revelation*.

Revelation then, so far as the term has relation between God and man, can only be applied to something which God reveals of his *will* to man. But though the power of the Almighty to make such a communication is necessarily admitted, because to that power all things are possible, yet the thing so revealed, (if any thing ever was revealed, and which, by the bye, it is impossible to prove) is revelation to the person *only to whom it is made*. His account of it to another is not revelation; and whoever puts faith in that account, puts it in the man from whom the account comes; and that man may have been deceived, or may have dreamed it, or he may be an impostor and may lie. There is no possible criterion whereby to judge of the truth of what he tells; for even the morality of it would be no proof of revelation. In all such cases, the proper answer would be, *"When it is revealed to me, I will believe it to be revelation, but it is not and cannot be incumbent upon me to believe it to be revelation before; neither is it proper that I should take the word of man as the word of God, and put man in the place of God."*

This is the manner in which I have spoken of revelation in the former part of the *Age of Reason*; and which, whilst it reverentially admits revelation as a possible thing, because, (as before said) to the Almighty all things are possible, it prevents the imposition of one man upon another, and precludes the wicked use of pretended revelation.

But though, speaking for myself, I thus admit the possibility of revelation, I totally disbelieve that the Almighty ever did communicate any thing to man by any mode of speech in any language, or by any kind of vision or appearance, or by any means which our senses are capable of receiving; otherwise than by the universal display of himself in the works of the creation, and by that repugnance we feel in ourselves to bad actions, and disposition to good ones.

The most detestable wickedness, the most horrid cruelties, and the greatest miseries that have afflicted the human race, have had their origin in this thing called revelation or revealed religion. It has been the most dishonourable belief against the character of the divinity, the most destructive to morality and the peace and happiness of man, that ever was propagated since man began to exist. It is better, far better, that we admitted, if it were possible, a thousand devils to roam at large, and to preach publicly the doctrine of devils, if there were any such, than that we permitted one such impostor and monster as Moses, Joshua, Samuel, and the bible prophets, to come with the pretended word of God in his mouth, and have credit among us.

Whence arose all the horrid assassination of whole nations of men, women, and infants, with which the bible is filled, and the bloody persecutions and tortures unto death, and religious wars, that since that time, have laid Europe in blood and ashes? Whence arose they, but from this impious thing called revealed religion: and this monstrous belief that God had spoken to man. The lies of the bible have been the cause of the one, and the lies of the testament, of the other.

Some Christians pretend that Christianity was not established by the sword. But of what period of time do they speak? It was impossible that *twelve* men could *begin* with the sword; they had not the power; but no sooner were the professors of Christianity sufficiently powerful to employ the sword, than they did so; and the stake and the faggot too; and Mahomet could not do it sooner. By the same spirit that Peter cut off the ear of the high priest's servant, (if the story be true) he would have cut off his head and the head of his master had he been able. Besides this, Christianity founds itself originally upon the bible, and the bible was established altogether by the sword, and that in the worst use of it; not to terrify, but to extirpate. The Jews made no converts; they butchered all. The bible is the sire of the testament, and both are called the *word of God*; the Christians read both books; the ministers preach from both books; and this thing, called Christianity, is made up of both. It is then false to say that Christianity was not established by the sword.

The only sect that has not persecuted, are the Quakers, and the only reason that can be given for it is, that they are rather Deists than Christians. They do not believe much about Jesus

Christ, and they call the scriptures a dead letter. Had they called them by a worse name, they had been nearer the truth.

It is incumbent on every man who reverences the character of the Creator, and who wishes to lessen the catalogue of artificial miseries, and remove the cause that has sown persecutions thick among mankind, to expel all ideas of a revealed religion, as a dangerous heresy, and an impious fraud. What is it that we have learned from this pretended thing called *revealed religion*? Nothing that is useful to man, and every thing that is dishonourable to his Maker. What is it the bible teaches us? Rapine, cruelty, and murder. What is it the testament teaches us? To believe that the Almighty committed debauchery with a woman engaged to be married; and the belief of this debauchery is called faith.

As to the fragments of morality that are irregularly and thinly scattered in those books, they make no part of this pretended thing, revealed religion. They are the natural dictates of conscience, and the bonds by which society is held together, and without which it cannot exist, and are nearly the same in all religions and in all societies. The testament teaches nothing new upon this subject, and where it attempts to exceed, it becomes mean and ridiculous. The doctrine of not retaliating injuries is much better expressed in Proverbs, which is a collection as well from the Gentiles as the Jews, than it is in the testament. It is there said, Proverbs xxiv, ver. 21, *If thine enemy be hungry give him bread to eat, and if he be thirsty give him water to drink.** But when it is said, as in the

---

*According to what is called Christ's sermon on the mount, (in the book of Matthew) where, among some other good things, a great deal of this feigned morality is introduced; it is there expressly said, that the doctrine of forbearance, or of not retaliating injuries, was *not any part of the doctrine of the Jews*; but as this doctrine is found in Proverbs, it must, according to that statement, have been copied from the Gentiles, from whom Christ had learned it. Those men, whom Jewish and Christian idolaters have abusively called heathen, had much better and clearer ideas of justice and morality than are to be found in the old testament, so far as it is Jewish, or in the new. The answer of Solon on the question, "Which is the most perfect popular government?" has never been exceeded by any man since his time, as containing a maxim of political morality. *"That, says he, where the least injury done to the meanest individual is considered as an insult on the whole constitution."* Solon lived above 500 years before Christ.

testament, *if a man smite thee on the right cheek, turn to him the other also*; it is assassinating the dignity of forbearance and sinking man into a spaniel.

Loving of enemies is another dogma of feigned morality, and has besides no meaning. It is incumbent on man as a moralist that he does not revenge an injury; and it is equally as good in a political sense; for there is no end to retaliation; each retaliates on the other, and calls it justice. But to love in proportion to the injury, if it could be done, would be to offer a premium for crime. Besides, the word *enemies* is too vague and general to be used in a moral maxim, which ought always to be clear and defined like a proverb. If a man be the enemy of another from mistake and prejudice, as in the case of religious opinions, and sometimes in politics, that man is different to an enemy at heart with a criminal intention, and it is incumbent upon us, and contributes also to our own tranquility, that we put the best construction upon a thing it will bear; but even this erroneous motive in him makes no motive for love on the other part; and to say that we can love voluntarily, and without a motive, is morally and physically impossible.

Morality is injured by prescribing to it duties, that, in the first place, are impossible to be performed, and if they could be, would be productive of evil; or, as before said, be premiums for crime. The maxim of *doing as we would be done unto*, does not include this strange doctrine of loving enemies; for no man expects to be loved himself for his crime or for his enmity.

Those who preach this doctrine of loving their enemies, are in general the greatest persecutors, and they act consistently by so doing; for the doctrine is hypocritical, and it is natural that hypocrisy should act the reverse of what it preaches. For my own part I disown the doctrine, and consider it as feigned or fabulous morality: yet the man does not exist that can say I have persecuted him or any man, or any set of men, either in the American revolution or in the French revolution; or that I have in any case returned evil for evil; but it is not incumbent on man to reward a bad action with a good one, or to return good for evil, and wherever it is done, it is a voluntary act and not a duty. It is also absurd to suppose that such doctrine can make any part of a revealed religion. We imitate the moral character of the Creator by forbearing with each other; for he forbears with all; but this doctrine would imply that he loved man not in proportion as he was good, but as he was bad.

If we consider the nature of our condition here, we must see there is no occasion for such thing as a *revealed religion*. What is it we want to know? Does not the creation, the universe we behold, preach to us the existence of an Almighty power, that governs and regulates the whole; and is not the evidence that this creation holds out to our senses infinitely stronger than any thing we can read in a book, that any impostor might make, and call it the word of God. As for morality, the knowledge of it exists in every man's conscience.

Here we are. The existence of an Almighty power is sufficiently demonstrated to us, though we cannot conceive, as it is impossible we should, the nature and manner of its existence. We cannot conceive how we came here ourselves, and yet we know for a fact that we are here. We must know also that the power that called us into being, can, if he please, and when he please, call us to account for the manner in which we have lived here; and therefore, without seeking any other motive for the belief, it is rational to believe that he will, for we know before hand that he can. The probability or even possibility of the thing, is all that we ought to know; for if we knew it as a fact, we should be the mere slaves of terror. Our belief would have no merit, and our best actions no virtue.

Deism then teaches us, without the possibility of being deceived, all that is necessary or proper to be known. The creation is the bible of the deist. He there reads, in the hand writing of the Creator himself, the certainty of his existence, and the immutability of his power; and all other bibles and testaments are to him forgeries. The probability that we *may be* called to account hereafter, will, to reflecting minds, have the influence of belief; for it is not our belief or our disbelief, that can make or unmake the fact. As this is the state we are in, and which it is proper we should be in as free agents, it is the fool only, and not the philosopher, nor even the prudent man, that will live as if there were no God.

But the belief of a God is so weakened by being mixed with the strange fable of the Christian creed, and with the wild adventures related in the bible, and the obscurity and obscene nonsense of the testament, that the mind of man is bewildered as in a fog. Viewing all these things in confused mass, he confounds fact with fable, and, as he cannot believe all, he feels a disposition to reject all. But the belief of a God is a belief distinct from all other things, and ought not to be confounded with any. The notion of a trinity of gods has enfeebled the belief of *one* God. A multiplication of beliefs acts as a division of belief, and in proportion as any thing is divided it is weakened.

Religion, by such means, becomes a thing of form instead of fact; of notion instead of principle; morality is banished to make room for an imaginary thing called faith, and this faith has its origin in a supposed debauchery. A man is preached instead of a God; an execution as an object for gratitude; the preachers daub themselves with the blood like a troop of assassins and pretend to admire the brilliancy it gives them. They preach a hum-drum sermon on the merits of the execution; praise Jesus Christ for being executed; and condemn the Jews for doing it. A man, by hearing all this nonsense lumped and preached together, confounds the God of the creation with the imagined God of the Christians, and lives as if there were none.

Of all the systems of religion that ever were invented, there is none more derogatory to the Almighty, more unedifying to man, more repugnant to reason, and more contradictory in itself than this thing called Christianity. Too absurd for belief, too impossible to convince, and too inconsistent for practice, it renders the heart torpid, or produces only atheists and fanatics. As an engine of power it serves the purpose of despotism; and as a means of wealth, the avarice of priests; but so far as respects the good of man in general, it leads to nothing here or hereafter.

The only religion that has not been invented, and that has in it every evidence of divine originality, is pure and simple deism. It must have been the first, and will probably be the last that man believes: but pure and simple deism does not answer the purpose of despotic governments. They cannot lay hold of religion as an engine, but by mixing it with human inventions, and making their own authority a part; neither does it answer the avarice of priests, but by incorporating themselves and their functions with it, and becoming, like the government, a party in the system. It is this that forms the otherwise mysterious connection of church and state. The church human, and the state tyrannic.

Were man impressed as fully and as strongly as he ought to be with the belief of a God, his moral life would be regulated by the force of that belief. He would stand in awe of God and of himself, and would not do the thing that could not be concealed from either. To give this belief the full opportunity of force, it is necessary that it acts alone; this is deism: but when, according to the Christian trinitarian scheme, one part of God is represented by a dying man, and another part, called the holy ghost, by a flying pigeon, it is impossible that belief can attach itself to such wild conceits.*

It has been the scheme of the Christian church, and of all other invented systems of religion, to hold man in ignorance of the Creator, as it is of governments to hold him in ignorance of his rights. The systems of the one are as false as those of the other, and are calculated for mutual support. The study of theology, as it stands in Christian churches, is the study of nothing. It is founded in nothing; it rests on no principles; it proceeds by no authorities; it has no data; it can demonstrate nothing; and admits of no conclusion. Not any thing can be studied as a science without our being in possession of the principles upon which it is founded; and as this is not the case with Christian theology, it is, therefore, the study of nothing.

Instead then of studying theology, as is now done, out of the bible and testament, the meanings of which books are always controverted, and the authenticity of which is disproved, it is necessary that we refer to the bible of the creation. The principles we discover there are eternal and of divine origin. They are the foundation of all the science that exists in the world, and must be the foundation of theology.

*The book called the book of Matthew, says, chap. iii, ver. 16, that *the holy ghost descended in the shape of a dove*. It might as well have said, a goose. The creatures are equally harmless, and the one is as much a nonsensical lie as the other. The 2d of Acts, ver. 2, 3, says, that it descended in *a mighty rushing wind*, in the shape of *cloven tongues*. Perhaps it was cloven feet. Such absurd stuff is fit only for tales of witches and wizards.

We can know God only through his works. We cannot have a conception of any one attribute but by following some principle that leads to it. We have only a confused idea of his power, if we have not the means of comprehending something of its immensity. We can have no idea of his wisdom but by knowing the order and manner in which it acts. The principles of science lead to this knowledge; for the creator of man is the creator of science, and it is through that medium that man can see God, as it were, face to face.

Could a man be placed in a situation, and endowed with power of vision, to behold at one view, and to contemplate deliberately, the structure of the universe, to mark the movements of the several planets, the cause of their varying appearances, the unerring order in which they revolve even to the remotest comet, their connection and dependence on each other, and to know the system of laws, established by the Creator, that governs and regulates the whole, he would then conceive, far beyond what any church theology can teach him, the power, the wisdom, the vastness, the munificence of the Creator. He would then see that all the knowledge man has of science, and that all the mechanical arts by which he renders his situation comfortable here are derived from that source. His mind exalted by the scene, and convinced by the fact, would increase in gratitude as it encreased in knowledge. His religion or his worship would become united with his impovement as a man; and any employment he followed, that had connection with the principles of the creation, as every thing of agriculture, of science, and of the mechanical arts has, would teach him more of God, and of the gratitude he owes to him, than any theological Christian sermon he now hears. Great objects inspire great thoughts; great munificence excites great gratitude; but the groveling tales and doctrines of the bible and testament are fit only to excite contempt.

Though man cannot arrive, at least in this life, at the actual scene I have described, he can demonstrate it; because he has knowledge of the principles upon which the creation is constructed. We know that the greatest works can be represented in model, and that the universe can be represented by the same means. The same principles by which we measure an inch or an acre of ground will measure to millions in extent.

A circle of an inch diameter has the same geometrical properties as a circle that would circumscribe the universe. The same properties of a triangle that will demonstrate upon paper the course of a ship, will do it on the ocean; and when applied to what are called the heavenly bodies, will ascertain to a minute the time of an eclipse, though those bodies are millions of miles distant from us. This knowledge is of divine origin; and it is from the bible of the creation that man has learned it, and not from the stupid bible of the church that teaches man nothing.*

All the knowledge man has of science and of machinery, by the aid of which his existence is rendered comfortable upon earth, and without which he would be scarcely distinguishable in appearance and condition from a common animal, comes from the great machine and structure of the universe. The constant and unwearied observations of our ancestors upon the movements and revolutions of the heavenly bodies, in what are supposed to have been the early ages of the world, has brought this knowledge upon earth. It is not Moses and the prophets, nor Jesus Christ, nor his apostles, that have done it. The Almighty is the great mechanic of the creation; the first philosopher and the original teacher of all science. Let us then learn to reverence our master, and not forget the labours of our ancestors.

Had we at this day no knowledge of machinery, and were it

*The bible-makers have undertaken to give us, in the first chapter of Genesis, an account of the creation, and in doing this they have demonstrated nothing but their ignorance. They make there to have been three days and three nights, evenings and mornings, before there was a sun, when it is the presence or absence of the sun that is the cause of day and night; and, what is called, his rising and setting, that of morning and evening. Besides, it is a puerile and pitiful idea to suppose the Almighty to say, *Let there be light*. It is the imperative manner of speaking that a conjurer uses, when he says to his cups and balls, *Presto, be gone*; and most probably has been taken from it; as Moses and his rod is a conjurer and his wand. Longinus calls this expression, the *sublime*; and by the same rule that of the conjurer is sublime too, for the manner is expressively and grammatically the same. When authors and critics talk of the sublime, they see not how nearly it borders on the ridiculous. The sublime of the critics, like some parts of Edmund Burke's *"Sublime and beautiful,"* is like a windmill just visible in a fog, which imagination might distort into a flying mountain, an arch angel, or a flock of wild geese.

possible that man could have a view, as I have before described, of the structure and machinery of the universe, he would soon conceive the idea of constructing some, at least, of the mechanical works we now have, and the idea so conceived, would progressively advance in practice. Or could a model of the universe, such as is called an orrery, be presented before him and put in motion, his mind would arrive at the same idea. Such an object and such a subject would, whilst it improved him in knowledge useful to himself as a man and a member of society, as well as entertaining, afford far better matter for impressing him with a knowledge of, and a belief in, the Creator, and of the reverence and gratitude that man owes to him, than the stupid texts of the bible and the testament, from which, be the talents of the preacher what they may, only stupid sermons can be preached. If man must preach, let him preach something that is edifying, and from texts that are known to be true.

The bible of the creation is inexhaustible in texts. Every part of science, whether connected with the geometry of the universe, with the systems of animal and vegetable life, or with the properties of inanimate matter, is a text as well for devotion as for philosophy; for gratitude, as for human improvement. It will perhaps be said, that if such a revolution in the system of religion take place, that every preacher ought to be a philosopher. *Most certainly;* and every house of devotion, a school of science.

It has been by wandering from the immutable laws of science, and the light of reason, and setting up an invented thing, called *revealed religion*, that so many wild and blasphemous conceits have been formed of the Almighty. The Jews have made him the assassin of the human species, to make room for the religion of the Jews; the Christians have made him the murderer of himself, and the founder of a new religion to supercede and expel the Jewish religion; and to find pretence and admission for these things, they must have supposed his power or his wisdom imperfect, or his will changeable; and the changeableness of the will is the imperfection of the judgment. The philosopher knows that the laws of the Creator have never changed, with respect either to the principles of science or the properties of matter. Why then is it to be supposed they have changed with respect to man?

I here close the subject. I have shewn in all the foregoing part of this work, that the bible and testament are impositions and forgeries; and I leave the evidence, I have produced in proof of it, to be refuted, if any one can do it: and I leave the ideas that are suggested in the conclusion of the work, to rest on the mind of the reader; certain as I am, that when opinions are free, either in matters of government or religion, truth will finally and powerfully prevail.

END OF THE SECOND PART.

Chronology

1737   Born January 29 in Thetford, Norfolk, England, the son of Joseph Pain and Frances Cocke Pain. (Joseph Pain, born 1708, a Quaker, was a corsetmaker who also worked a small farm. In 1734 he married Frances Cocke, born c. 1697, an Anglican and the daughter of a Thetford attorney.) Christened Thomas Pain and baptized in the Church of England (will later be confirmed in the Church of England, although he will frequently attend Quaker meetings with father).

1738   Sister Elizabeth born August 29. She dies in infancy.

1743   Begins attending grammar school in Thetford. Enjoys studying history, mathematics, and science.

1750   Leaves school to begin apprenticeship as a corsetmaker in his father's shop.

1756   Enlists on privateer *Terrible*, but is persuaded not to sail by father.

1757   Serves on privateer *King of Prussia* for six months of the Seven Years War. Works in London for a master corsetmaker. Attends philosophical and scientific lectures given by Benjamin Martin and James Ferguson, and becomes acquainted with astronomer John Bevis.

1758   Moves to Dover, Kent, where he continues working as a journeyman corsetmaker.

1759   Becomes master corsetmaker, opening his own shop in Sandwich, Kent, in April. Marries Mary Lambert, an orphan who works as a maid, on September 27. They move to Margate, Kent.

1760   Wife dies.

1761   Abandons corsetmaking and returns to Thetford to study for position in the excise service.

1762–63	Appointed to excise service as a supernumerary officer on December 1, 1762, through the patronage of Frederic Falkland. Assigned to Grantham, Lincolnshire, where he gauges brewers' casks.
1764	Appointed on August 8 as a permanent excise officer, with annual salary of £50, and assigned to the Alford Out-Ride, coastal district in Lincolnshire.
1765	Dismissed from excise service on August 29 for clearing consignment of merchandise without inspecting the goods, an offense commonly committed by excise officers. Returns to corsetmaking in Diss, Norfolk.
1766	Moves to London and teaches in private academy at Goodman's Fields for £25 a year. Successfully petitions in July for reinstatement as an excise officer, but is unable to find a vacant position.
1767	Begins teaching at school in Kensington in January.
1768	Appointed to excise position in Lewes, Sussex, in February. Lodges in the home of Samuel Ollive, a tobacconist and one of the town's leading citizens. Becomes involved in town and parish affairs and joins a social club that meets in the White Hart Inn. Writes poems and political satires from a Whig viewpoint.
1769–70	Moves to new lodgings after Samuel Ollive dies in July 1769. Begins running tobacco shop with Ollive's widow while continuing his excise duties.
1771	Marries the Ollives' daughter, Elizabeth (b. 1749), on March 26.
1772–73	Joins other excise officers in petitioning Parliament for higher salaries. Begins work on pamphlet *The Case of the Officers of Excise* during summer 1772, and has 4,000 copies printed (costs are paid by subscription of excise officers). Spends winter 1772–73 in London distributing pamphlet to members of Parliament, and presents copy to playwright Oliver Goldsmith. Parliament takes no action on petition.
1774	Dismissed from excise service on April 8 for being absent from his post without permission. Tobacco shop fails, and

on April 14 Pain sells his household possessions and shop stock at public auction to pay his debts. Signs formal separation agreement with wife on June 4 and receives £35 in return for renouncing future claims against her property. Goes to London, where his friend George Lewis Scott, a scientist and member of the excise board, introduces him to Benjamin Franklin. Pain sails for Philadelphia in early October, carrying letter of introduction from Franklin to his son-in-law, Richard Bache. Falls ill, possibly with typhus, during voyage. Lands on November 30 and is cared for by Dr. John Kearsley, a friend of Franklin.

1775   Writes essay for the January number of *The Pennsylvania Magazine; or American Monthly Museum*, published by printer Robert Aitken, then becomes its editor in February. Contributes poems and articles on science and politics to the magazine under pseudonyms and publishes other writers, including John Witherspoon and Francis Hopkinson (there is no evidence that Pain wrote essay condemning slavery that appeared in the *Pennsylvania Journal* in March, although it is often attributed to him). Revolutionary War begins with fighting between Massachusetts militia and British troops at Lexington and Concord on April 19. Becomes friends with several Philadelphia advocates of the American cause, including Dr. Benjamin Rush, mathematician and astronomer David Rittenhouse, retired druggist Christopher Marshall, former brewer Timothy Matlack, Dr. Thomas Young, and teacher James Cannon. Meets John Adams. Leaves editorship of *Pennsylvania Magazine* in September. Writes newspaper articles with Thomas Pryor encouraging the home manufacture of saltpeter (potassium nitrate), a gunpowder ingredient.

1776   Publishes *Common Sense*, a pamphlet calling for the creation of an independent American republic, in Philadelphia on January 10 (pamphlet is attributed to "an Englishman"). Directs that his share of the profits from its sale be used to buy mittens for American troops in Quebec. Begins spelling his name "Paine." Expanded second edition of *Common Sense* is published on February 14; the pamphlet is read throughout the colonies and sells tens of thousands of copies (Paine later estimates that

150,000 copies were sold in 1776). Using pseudonym "The Forester," Paine publishes series of letters in the Pennsylvania press in April and May defending American independence and republicanism and attacking critics of *Common Sense*. Shortly after Congress adopts Declaration of Independence on July 4, Paine joins the Associators, a Pennsylvania militia, and becomes secretary to General Daniel Roberdeau. Serves with the "Flying Camp," a militia force defending Perth Amboy, New Jersey, against possible British seaborne attack; when it disbands in September, becomes aide-de-camp to General Nathanael Greene at Fort Lee, New Jersey. Writes reports on the war for the Pennsylvania press. British forces cross the Hudson River on November 20, forcing evacuation of Fort Lee. Paine joins American troops under George Washington in their retreat across New Jersey, then leaves the army at Trenton and returns to Philadelphia in early December to write. Pamphlet *The American Crisis, Number I*, intended to rally American morale after series of defeats in New York and New Jersey, published in Philadelphia on December 19. Encouraged by victory of Washington's army at Trenton on December 26.

1777   Publishes *The American Crisis, Number II* in January, continuing series championing the American cause (pamphlets are signed "Common Sense"; Paine's authorship of series becomes widely known). Appointed secretary to commission sent by Congress to negotiate with several Indian tribes and meets with them at Easton, Pennsylvania, in late January. Elected to the Committee of Correspondence of the Whig Society of Philadelphia on April 1. Publishes *The American Crisis, Number III* in April. Congress creates Committee for Foreign Affairs on April 17; on nomination of John Adams, Paine is appointed as its secretary at salary of $70 a month. Plans to write history of the American Revolution. Publishes *The American Crisis, Number IV* in September as British army approaches Philadelphia, then flees the city. Pennsylvania executive council appoints Paine as its observer with Washington's army on October 10; Paine frequently visits the army at its camps in Pennsylvania, including Valley Forge. Spends the remainder of the year at the Bordentown, New Jersey, home of his friend Joseph Kirkbride.

1778   France and the United States sign treaties of alliance and
            commerce on February 6 (news reaches Congress on May
            2). Paine travels to Lancaster, Pennsylvania, in February to
            resume duties as secretary to the Committee for Foreign
            Affairs (Congress is meeting in nearby York). Publishes
            fifth *Crisis* in March. Returns to Philadelphia with Con-
            gress in early July after the British army leaves the city.
            Publishes sixth *Crisis* in October and seventh in Novem-
            ber. Writes four articles defending the 1776 Pennsylvania
            state constitution, which had created a unicameral legisla-
            ture, replaced the governor with an executive council, and
            extended the vote to all male taxpayers (constitution con-
            tinues to be subject of intense struggle within the state).
            In December Paine becomes involved in factional contro-
            versy surrounding the conduct of Silas Deane, a Con-
            necticut merchant sent by Congress to France in 1776 to
            purchase war supplies, now under suspicion of improperly
            profiting from his mission (Deane's supporters include
            John Jay, Gouverneur Morris, and leading Philadelphia
            merchant Robert Morris, who is a business partner of
            Deane; among his opponents are Samuel Adams, Richard
            Henry Lee, and Paine's friend Henry Laurens). After
            Deane publicly accuses his critics in Congress of unfair
            treatment, Paine writes series of articles attacking Deane
            for making unfounded charges and for failing to account
            for his financial dealings in France.

1779   Paine publishes more articles on Deane in which he refers
            to secret diplomatic correspondence proving that military
            supplies sent to America from France before treaty of alli-
            ance were gifts from the French government, not pur-
            chases made by Deane. Conrad Alexandre Gérard, French
            minister to the United States, writes to Congress protest-
            ing Paine's articles (disclosure of covert aid to the U.S.
            while France was at peace with Britain is potentially em-
            barrassing to Louis XVI). Paine asks for opportunity to
            defend himself before Congress against charge of indis-
            cretion; when his request is denied, he resigns as secretary
            of the Committee for Foreign Affairs on January 8. Con-
            gress adopts resolution on January 12 disavowing Paine's
            articles and declaring that Louis XVI had not sent aid to
            the United States before the treaty of alliance was signed.
            Paine refuses offer from Gérard to become paid writer of

material promoting close American ties with France. Publishes series of articles and letters defending his conduct in Deane affair, which has angered Deane's influential supporters. Takes low-paying position as a clerk with merchant Owen Biddle in April. Becomes increasingly involved in effort to control prices in Pennsylvania as inflation worsens. On May 25 Paine is elected to two extra-legal citizens' committees, one charged with regulating the price of staple goods, the other with investigating the affairs of Robert Morris, who is accused of profiting excessively from his dealings in military supplies. Publishes three articles in June and July urging Congress to make the securing of American fishing rights off Newfoundland a condition of peace with Britain and warning against excessive deference to French interests. After a series of hostile articles appear in press questioning Paine's loyalty to the American cause, a mass meeting held in Philadelphia on July 27 adopts resolution in his support. By late September refusal of merchants and farmers to sell goods at regulated prices causes collapse of efforts to implement price controls; Paine becomes opponent of price regulation and advocate of currency reform as means of controlling inflation. Seeks financial support for his writing from the Pennsylvania executive council. Appointed clerk of the Pennsylvania assembly on November 2.

1780   Publishes *The Crisis, No. VIII* in February and *The Crisis, No. IX* in June. Proposes system of voluntary private contributions to support American troops; idea is successfully implemented by Robert Morris. Receives an honorary master's degree from the newly created University of Pennsylvania on July 4. Paine writes in September to Joseph Reed, president of the Pennsylvania executive council, proposing that the state secretly send him to England to publish articles advocating peace with an independent America; Reed rejects the plan as too dangerous. Publishes pamphlet *The Crisis Extraordinary* in October, calling for the states to levy and collect taxes to finance the war. Resigns position as clerk of the assembly in November. Meets Marquis de Lafayette and Marquis de Chastellux. Using documents supplied by the Indiana Company, a land-speculation company, Paine writes *Public Good*, pamphlet published December 30, contesting Virginia's claim to territory northwest of the Ohio River and urging cession of the claim to Congress. (Dispute over western land claims had caused Maryland to withhold ratification of the Articles of Confederation; in 1781 the Virginia legislature conditionally cedes its western lands to Congress, and Maryland ratifies the Articles.)

1781   Accompanies Colonel John Laurens, an aide to George Washington and son of Henry Laurens, to France on mission to obtain further loans and supplies. Travels at his own expense after opposition in Congress prevents him from serving as Laurens' official secretary. Sails from Boston on February 11 and lands in France on March 9. Sees Franklin, now serving as American minister to France (Franklin plays major role in securing further aid from French government). Disillusioned by his treatment in the United States, Paine considers staying in Europe, but decides to return to America. Sails with Laurens on June 1 and arrives in Boston on August 25. Returns to Philadelphia in severe financial hardship. Surrender of Lord Cornwallis at Yorktown, Virginia, on October 19 ends major fighting in the Revolutionary War. Silas Deane is discredited by publication of letters urging reconciliation with Britain. Paine discusses with Robert Morris, now superintendent of finance, the possibility of his writing public letters and articles in support of measures to finance the war and restore national credit.

1782   In February Paine, Washington, secretary for foreign affairs Robert R. Livingston, and Robert Morris make clandestine agreement under which Paine will receive $800 a year from a secret fund controlled by Morris in return for writing in support of new financial measures. Publishes articles on taxation in March and April after showing them to Morris. Paid 1,530 livres (about $300) by the Chevalier de la Luzerne, Gérard's successor as French minister to the United States, for writing in *The Crisis, No. XI* in May that the United States and France should jointly negotiate peace with Britain. In response to Abbé Guillaume Raynal's *The Revolution of America*, Paine publishes *Letter Addressed to the Abbé Raynal* in August, insisting on the unique nature of the American Revolution and praising the American alliance with France. Sends copies to France for distribution and receives 50 guineas from La Luzerne. Writes series of public letters urging Rhode Island to grant Congress power to levy a 5 percent impost on imports (Rhode Island legislature had rejected measure, which requires unanimous consent of the states, after 11 other states had approved it). Travels to Providence, Rhode Island, in December to work for the impost.

1783   Publishes additional letters in the Rhode Island press, then returns to Philadelphia in February after Virginia's repeal of its earlier ratification of the impost causes the measure to lapse. Paine's visit is denounced by advocates of state sovereignty, who accuse Congress of improperly attempting to influence Rhode Island's decision. Congress ratifies preliminary peace treaty with Britain on April 15. Paine publishes *The Last Crisis, No. XIII* on April 19, the eighth anniversary of the battles of Lexington and Concord. Appeals to Congress in June for remuneration for his contribution to the Revolution. Spends summer in Bordentown with the Kirkbride family. Goes to New York in December, where he appeals to the state legislature for compensation. Writes public letter urging American states to form a closer union in response to British exclusion of American ships from the West Indies.

1784   Returns to Philadelphia in January, then goes in February to Bordentown, where he now owns a house and five acres of land. New York legislature approves compensation for Paine in April, and in June he receives the confiscated estate of a Tory in New Rochelle. Despite support from Washington, Thomas Jefferson, and James Madison, bill to award Paine a land grant is rejected by the Virginia legislature in June; its defeat is ascribed to resentment against Paine for challenging Virginia land claims in *Public Good*.

1785   Elected to American Philosophical Society in January. Awarded £500 by the Pennsylvania assembly in April and $3,000 by Congress in October for his services during the Revolution (may never have received the money from Pennsylvania). Works on series of inventions, including smokeless candles and innovative design for a single-arch iron bridge using principles of stone vaulting (Paine writes that design was inspired by pattern of spider's web). Hires mechanic John Hall in November as workshop assistant. Publishes letter in December criticizing recent decision of the Pennsylvania assembly to repeal state charter of the Bank of North America, founded in 1782 by Robert Morris and his associates.

1786   Publishes widely circulated pamphlet *Dissertations on Government; the Affairs of the Bank; and Paper Money* in February, arguing in favor of rechartering the bank and opposing the issue of paper money not backed by specie. (Pennsylvania assembly had issued £150,000 in paper money in March 1785, and the bank's refusal to accept it at face value had contributed to the revocation of its charter in September 1785.) Discusses steamboat development with inventor John Fitch in March. Continues writing public letters in defense of the bank during the spring and is criticized by its opponents, including assemblyman John Smilie, who accuses Paine of writing for hire. Exhibits wooden and cast-iron models of single-arch bridge in the garden of Franklin's house in June. Publishes letter in September arguing that party prejudice has made unicameral legislature established by the 1776 Pennsylvania constitution dangerous to liberty. Works in the fall on a wrought-iron bridge model. Denounces paper money in letter published in November. Shows new bridge model to Franklin and David Rittenhouse in late December.

1787   Exhibits wrought-iron bridge model in State House Yard in Philadelphia in January. Tries unsuccessfully to secure funding from the Pennsylvania assembly for building bridge across the Schuylkill River. Attends weekly meetings of the newly formed Society for Political Enquiries, whose members include Franklin, Gouverneur Morris, Benjamin Rush, and James Wilson. Hoping to gain endorsements for his iron bridge, Paine sails for France on April 26, carrying letters of introduction from Franklin to leading French scientific and political figures. Lands in France on May 26 and goes to Paris. Begins friendship with Jefferson, now serving as American minister to France, and sees Lafayette. Presents bridge model to the French Academy of Sciences in July and receives its endorsement in August. Travels to London in September, seeking endorsement of the Royal Society. Sees mother in Thetford and provides annuity for her (father died in 1786). Publishes pamphlet *Prospects on the Rubicon*, urging Britain not to go to war with France over the factional struggle in the Netherlands. Becomes friends with writer and member of Parliament Edmund Burke, who had supported American colonists in the 1770s; through Burke, Paine meets leaders of Whig opposition, including Charles James Fox and the Duke of Portland. Meets painters John Trumbull and Benjamin West. Made honorary member of the Society for Constitutional Information, English political reform group whose leading members include John Frost, Thomas Hollis, John Cartwright, Thomas Holcraft, and John Horne Tooke. Returns to Paris in December to pursue plans for bridging the Seine.

1788   Paine, Jefferson, and Lafayette follow ratification controversy over the proposed United States constitution and debate the constitution among themselves. Returns to London in June to seek investors for bridge. Sends reports on British politics to Jefferson (position of American minister to Britain has been vacant since John Adams returned to the U.S. in the spring). Goes to ironworks at Rotherham, Yorkshire, in fall to supervise construction of 90-foot bridge arch.

1789   Continues working on bridge, moving between London and Rotherham. Tours English factories. Tests weight-bearing capacity of bridge in April and begins planning construction of 110-foot span. Continues correspondence with Jefferson, sending reports on British politics and receiving accounts of events in France. Estates General convene at Versailles on May 5 after being summoned by Louis XVI to address worsening financial and political situation in France. On June 17 the Third Estate declares itself to be a National Assembly, and after a majority of the clergy join them, the members of the Assembly vow on June 20 not to disperse until France has been given a written constitution. Alarmed by royalist troop movements, Paris crowd storms the Bastille, fortress used as a prison, on July 14. In August the National Assembly abolishes feudal system and adopts the Declaration of the Rights of Man and Citizen, drafted in part by Lafayette. Paine travels to Paris in November and sees Lafayette, now commander of the Paris National Guard.

1790   Corresponds with Edmund Burke on French Revolution in January. Burke gives speech in Parliament in February denouncing the Revolution and begins writing *Reflections on the Revolution in France*. Paine returns to England in March. Sees Gouverneur Morris, now in London as President Washington's personal envoy. Writes to Lafayette, urging French support for Spain in its confrontation with Britain over Nootka Sound (France remains neutral, and Spain avoids war by making concessions). Bridge components are shipped to London in May; Paine hires workers and begins supervising assembly of demonstration span in field near village of Paddington. Writes essay on establishing a mint in the United States. Bridge assembly is completed in fall; despite praise from members of the Royal Society, Paine is unable to find a buyer. *Reflections on the Revolution in France* is published November 1 and sells 12,000 copies within a month.

1791   *Rights of Man: Being an Answer to Mr. Burke's Attack on the French Revolution* published by Paine in London on February 22 and then withdrawn, possibly due to printer Joseph Johnson's fear of government prosecution. Pamphlet is reissued by printer J. Jordan on March 16 and sells tens of thousands of copies in several editions, including cheap editions authorized by Paine, for which he receives no royalties. Paine returns to Paris in the spring. After unsuccessful attempt by Louis XVI and Marie Antoinette to flee the country, June 20–22, Paine joins with Etienne Claivière, the Marquis de Condorcet, Jacques Pierre Brissot de Warville, and Achille François Duchastelet to form the Republican Club. Writes broadside manifesto calling for Louis XVI to be deposed; it is translated by Duchastelet and distributed on July 1. First number of *Le Républicain*, journal of the Republican Club, appears July 2 with article by Paine. Continues his advocacy of a republican government for France in public letter to Abbé Sieyès, published on July 9 (Paine's publications are among earliest calling for overthrow of the monarchy). Returns to London in mid-July. *Life of Thomas Pain*, hostile biography subsidized by the Pitt ministry and written by George Chalmers under the pseudonym "Francis Oldys," is published July 19, making public details of Paine's early life, including his two marriages. Paine attends meetings of the Society for Constitutional Information and other political reform groups. On September 14 Louis XVI agrees to first written French constitution, instituting a limited monarchy. In London, Paine sees American poet Joel Barlow, John Horne Tooke, writer and political thinker William Godwin, and woman's rights advocate Mary Wollstonecraft, author of *A Vindication of the Rights of Men*, an earlier response to Burke. Proposes toast to the "Revolution of the World" at dinner held November 4 to commemorate the Glorious Revolution of 1688. Experimental bridge arch in Paddington is disassembled when Paine is unable to find a buyer or investors. (Paine's design is further developed by Rowland Burdon, who builds 236-foot single-arch iron bridge over the Wear at Sunderland, England, in 1793–96, the longest bridge of its kind yet built. Ironwork for Sunderland Bridge is cast at Rotherham under supervision of foreman William Yates, who had earlier worked with Paine on his demonstration span. Although Paine holds patent on his design, he receives no compensation for the Wear bridge.)

1792   Paine publishes *Rights of Man, Part the Second, Combining Principle and Practice* in London on February 16. Pamphlet discusses possible forms of republican government and proposes government programs to alleviate plight of the poor; it goes through four printings within two weeks, and sales of both parts of *Rights of Man* exceed 200,000 copies by end of 1792. France declares war on Austria on April 20 (Prussia enters war as Austrian ally early in summer). Paine receives summons on May 21 to stand trial on June 8 for misdemeanor offense of seditious libel; Pitt ministry also issues proclamation ordering magistrates to investigate writers and printers of seditious literature. Home secretary Henry Dundas tells Parliament on May 25 that proclamation is directed against *Rights of Man*, which Dundas links to increasing agitation by reform and workingmen's societies. Paine responds in public letter to Dundas, praising American example of representative government. Trial is postponed until December. Paine stays in London with Thomas (Clio) Rickman, a friend from Lewes. Insurrection in Paris on August 10 leads to final overthrow of the monarchy and summoning of National Convention. Lafayette, a supporter of constitutional monarchy, flees France (captured by the Austrians, he is imprisoned until 1797). National Assembly confers honorary French citizenship on Paine and 16 other foreigners on August 26. Electoral assembly in Pas-de-Calais elects Paine to the National Convention on September 6 (he is also elected by three other departments). Paine finishes pamphlet *Letter Addressed to the Addressers on the Late Proclamation*, in which he calls for the election by universal manhood suffrage of a national convention to establish a new constitution in Britain. Accepts Convention seat and arrives in Calais to enthusiastic welcome on September 13. Travels to Paris and votes with the Convention on September 21 to formally abolish the monarchy and proclaim the French Republic. Follows sessions and speaks in the Convention through an interpreter (Paine never becomes proficient in spoken French). Opposes proposal by Danton to allow election of judges regardless of their lack of legal training. Appointed on October 11 to nine-man committee charged with drafting new republican constitution (only Paine and two other members of the committee survive the Terror of 1793–94). Lives at White's Hotel in Paris and associates almost exclusively with people who speak English. Sees Joel Barlow, Gouverneur Morris (now American minister to France), Condorcet, Brissot, Clavière, Jean-Marie and Manon Roland, Edmond Genêt (who becomes French minister to the U.S. in 1793), printer Nicolas de Bonneville, and François Xavier Lanthenas; most of his close associates in the Convention are leaders of the Girondin faction, who favor spreading the Revolution throughout Europe. Paine meets in October with Irish revolutionary Lord Edward Fitzgerald and recommends that France financially support an insurrection in Ireland. Supports trial of Louis XVI for treason (proceedings begin December 11). Loyalist crowds in Britain hang and burn Paine in effigy and government supporters circulate hostile tracts and broadsides. On December 18 Paine is convicted in absentia of seditious libel and is outlawed for failing to stand trial (outlawry makes him subject to indefinite imprisonment and the forfeiture of his property). Pitt ministry begins prosecuting printers and sellers of *Rights of Man*.

1793   Convention debates fate of Louis XVI. Paine becomes leading opponent of his execution, arguing that Louis should be imprisoned for the duration of the war and then exiled to the United States. Convention approves death sentence on January 17. Paine speaks in support of granting a reprieve, but motion is defeated and Louis is guillotined on January 21. France declares war on Great Britain and the Netherlands on February 1 (President Washington proclaims American neutrality in the conflict on April 22). Paine moves into house on Faubourg St. Denis. Plays cards and chess with friends and sees Mary Wollstonecraft, Joel Barlow, and Clio Rickman, who had fled England to avoid prosecution for selling Paine's work. After Girondin leaders have Jean-Paul Marat indicted in April for inciting violence against members of the Convention, Paine helps Brissot attack Marat in the press and testifies against him at his trial. Marat is acquitted amid popular acclaim; episode discredits Girondins and increases influence of Jacobins. Paine writes pessimistically to Jefferson on April 20 about course of the French Revolution and warns Danton in letter of May 6 about "spirit of denunciation." Paris crowds force suspension of 22 leading Girondins from Convention on June 2. Paine avoids the Convention during the summer; begins to drink heavily. Meets with Jacobin leader Bertrand Barère in late August and advises him to send commissioners to the United States to strengthen Franco-American relations. Assists Barère in purchasing food from the United States. Brissot, and 9 other Girondins are guillotined on October 31 (Clavière and Duchastelet commit suicide later to avoid execution and Condorcet dies in prison in spring 1794, possibly after taking poison). Paine works during autumn on pamphlet *The Age of Reason*, deistic examination of religion. On December 25 Barère criticizes letting foreigners serve in the Convention; Paine is then denounced by name, and Convention expels him and its other foreign member, Prussian-born Anacharsis Cloots. Paine and Cloots are arrested on December 28 on orders of the Committee of General Security and imprisoned in the former Luxembourg Palace.

1794   *The Age of Reason; Being an Investigation of True and of Fabulous Theology* published in Paris in January. Paine appeals to Gouverneur Morris for help with his case. In February Morris writes to French foreign minister Deforgues that Paine is an American citizen and inquiring into the reasons for his arrest. Deforgues responds that Paine has made himself subject to French law by accepting

French citizenship and a seat in the Convention, and Morris does not pursue the matter (Morris writes to Jefferson that bringing attention to Paine's case would increase the likelihood of his execution). In prison Paine debates religion with Cloots, an atheist, until Cloots is guillotined on March 24. Sees Danton in prison before his execution on April 5. Falls seriously ill with fever in mid-June as executions in Paris rapidly increase. Robespierre is guillotined on July 28 along with many of his followers. Paine partially recovers from his illness and writes appeal to the Convention and to the Committee of Public Safety on August 6, but receives no response. Learns that James Monroe has replaced Morris as American minister in August. Appeals to Monroe in letter in which he describes Morris as "my inveterate enemy," and receives encouraging reply on October 4. Monroe formally petitions Committee of General Security on November 1, asserting Paine's American citizenship, praising his role in the American Revolution, and asking that he be either released or tried. Paine is released from prison on November 4, in poor health and suffering from abscess in his side; Monroe and his wife, Elizabeth, care for him in their home in Paris. Convention votes on December 8 to reinstate him as a member.

1795   Writes letter to Washington on February 22, reproaching the President for failing to aid him during his imprisonment, but at Monroe's urging does not send it. In June the Convention begins considering new constitution that establishes indirectly elected bicameral legislature and a five-man executive Directory, and limits voting to payers of direct taxes and soldiers who served under the Republic. Paine publishes *Dissertation on First Principles of Government*, pamphlet defending universal manhood suffrage, and appears before the Convention on July 7 for the first time since 1792 to oppose property qualifications for voting (suffrage limitation is not changed, and constitution is approved by Convention in August). In early August Paine finishes second part of *The Age of Reason*, containing detailed attack on the authority of the Bible (published in autumn). Falls dangerously ill in September with recurrence of abscess and is cared for by Elizabeth Monroe. Writes and sends letters in late September to Washington and to James Madison, now a leader of Republican opposition to the Federalist administration, accusing Washington of "treachery" for failing to aid him. Convention dissolves in October as new constitution takes effect (Paine does not seek election to new legislature). Continues to suffer from abscess. During the winter writes pamphlet *Agrarian Justice*, calling for the taxation of landed property and the creation of a public fund to compensate persons for their lost natural inheritance of land.

1796   Directory tells Monroe that it considers restrictive definition of neutral maritime rights contained in Jay's Treaty, the Anglo-American agreement negotiated in 1794 and ratified in 1795, to be hostile to France. In April Paine publishes *The Decline and Fall of the English System of Finance*, predicting that the cost of war against France will cause the Bank of England to collapse. Directory pays for pamphlet to be translated and printed throughout Europe. Relations between Paine and Monroe are strained by Paine's open hostility toward Washington's administration and his ties to Jean-François Reubell and other members of the Directory. Paine moves out of Monroe's house during spring and into rooms in Paris suburb of Suresnes. Writes lengthy public letter to Washington, accusing him of treachery and hypocrisy, criticizing his generalship in the Revolution, and denouncing Jay's Treaty as a betrayal of American interests and a breach of faith with France. Completes letter on July 30 and sends it to Benjamin Franklin Bache, Franklin's grandson and publisher of the Philadelphia *Aurora*, who prints excerpts in October and November (letter is published as pamphlet in February 1797). Washington administration recalls Monroe and sends Charles Cotesworth Pinckney to replace him. Directory authorizes seizure of American ships trading with Britain and refuses to receive Pinckney as new American minister.

1797   Paine joins French deists in newly organized Society of Theophilanthropists in January. Meets Irish revolutionary Theobald Wolfe Tone. Leaves Paris in March and goes to Le Havre intending to return to America, but does not sail for fear of capture by British frigates blockading the port. Pamphlet *Agrarian Justice, Opposed to Agrarian Law, and to Agrarian Monopoly* published. Paine returns to Paris in May and moves in with printer Nicolas de Bonneville, his wife, Marguerite, and their children. Writes articles for Bonneville's paper, *Bien Informé*. In response to increasingly frequent French seizures of American ships, President John Adams appoints three commissioners to negotiate with the Directory. Paine writes public letter in September protesting printer Thomas Williams' conviction for blasphemy for selling *The Age of Reason* in England. American commissioners arrive in Paris in October. Paine advises French foreign minister Talleyrand and the commissioners to work for international agreement on neutral maritime rights. Publishes pamphlet in November defending the Directory's use of the army on September 4 to purge the legislature of royalist members. Writes articles in December proposing construction of fleet of shallow-draft gunboats to be used in an invasion of England.

1798   Continues advocating invasion scheme, hoping that it will lead to revolution in England; sends detailed memorandum on plan to General Napoleon Bonaparte. Becomes friends with American inventor Robert Fulton. Assists British and American citizens living in France in their dealings with the government. Writes to Directory in June advocating French assistance to revolutionary uprising in Ireland (Directory sends several small expeditions, which are defeated; Tone is captured and commits suicide to avoid being hanged). Publication in the United States of dispatches from American commissioners revealing that three French diplomatic agents had solicited them for $240,000 bribe as precondition for negotiation ("XYZ Affair") causes public furor, and during the summer United States begins waging undeclared naval war against France. Talleyrand and the Directory distance themselves from Paine, who is intensely disliked by the Adams administration.

1799   Works on essays on international commerce. Bonaparte overthrows Directory in coup d'etat on November 9. Paine spends winter in Bruges, Belgium, with Joseph Vanhuele, one of his cellmates in Luxembourg prison. *Bien Informé* is suppressed after it compares Bonaparte to Oliver Cromwell.

1800   Paine returns to Paris in spring and resumes living with
            Bonneville family. Tells Oliver Ellsworth, member of new
            commission sent by President Adams, that Jay's Treaty
            and the recall of Monroe have made negotiating a
            Franco-American agreement extremely difficult. French
            authorities warn Paine that he will be deported if he
            continues to behave "irregularly." Speaks critically of
            Bonaparte in conversations with British and American
            friends. Publishes *Pacte Maritime*, essays on international
            commerce and neutral maritime rights. Builds five-foot-
            long bridge models and writes proposal for linking re-
            gions of France through series of canals and iron bridges.
            American commissioners sign treaty on September 30
            ending naval conflict with France. Encouraged by news of
            Jefferson's presidential candidacy, Paine writes to him in
            October, enclosing copies of trade essays (published in
            1801 as *Compact Maritime*) and expressing wish to return
            to the United States.

1801   Jefferson, now president, writes to Paine in March, offer-
            ing him passage on an American warship returning from
            France (Paine continues to fear capture by the Royal
            Navy). Paine decides to wait for ship bearing Robert R.
            Livingston, the new American minister to France.
            Jefferson's offer becomes public and is denounced by the
            Federalist press. Paine works on inventions, including a
            crane and a planing machine. Sees Livingston when he
            arrives in December.

1802   Britain and France sign armistice in March, suspending
            British blockade. Paine sails from Le Havre in early Sep-
            tember and lands in Baltimore on October 30. Federalist
            press widely attacks him as an infidel and a drunkard.
            Goes to Washington, D.C., where Jefferson receives him
            at the executive mansion. Publishes series of letters "To
            the Citizens of the United States" in the Republican
            press, in which he bitterly attacks Washington and John
            Adams. After port of New Orleans is closed to American
            navigation, Paine writes to Jefferson proposing that the
            United States purchase Louisiana Territory from France
            with the consent of its inhabitants (Jefferson is already
            considering purchasing New Orleans). Receives letter
            from Samuel Adams, who writes that he is "grieved" by
            Paine's "defence of infidelity."

1803   Writes and publishes a response to Adams defending his religious beliefs. Travels in February to Philadelphia; Benjamin Rush, angered by *The Age of Reason*, refuses to see him. Goes to Bordentown, where he sees Joseph Kirkbride for the last time (Kirkbride dies in autumn). Encounters hostile reception from pro-Federalist crowd in Trenton. Travels to New York in early March and sees Monroe, who is about to sail for France as a special envoy with instructions to purchase New Orleans and the Floridas (Monroe and Livingston are unexpectedly offered entire Louisiana Territory by the French, and sign treaty for its purchase on May 2). Attends dinner for 70 people held in his honor on March 18. Returns to Bordentown. Marguerite de Bonneville and her three sons arrive in Bordentown (Nicolas de Bonneville, who is under surveillance by the French police, is unable to leave France). Writes public letter criticizing Federalist proposals to seize New Orleans by force. Corresponds with Jefferson on constitutional implications of Louisiana Purchase. Travels to Stonington, Connecticut, to visit Nathan Haley, a sea captain he had known in France. Discusses current events with neighboring farmers and fishermen. Goes to his New Rochelle farm in autumn, but falls ill and lodges in village.

1804   Returns to New York in January. Marguerite de Bonneville, unhappy in Bordentown, comes to New York with her sons, and Paine assumes responsibility for their schooling. Paine becomes friends with physician Nicholas Romaine, philanthropist John Pintard, auctioneer John Fellows (who had published *The Age of Reason* in the United States), veterinarian and blacksmith William Carver, and deist Elihu Palmer, publisher of *The Prospect, or View of the Moral World*. Writes frequently for *The Prospect*, mainly on religious subjects. Publishes article predicting successful invasion of England by Bonaparte. Returns to cottage on New Rochelle farm in spring. Sells 60 acres of farm for $4,020 to pay his debts. Writes article in September denying right of Louisiana's inhabitants to immediate statehood and to continue importing slaves.

1805   Recommends to Jefferson that the United States mediate between France and the rebels in Haiti. Begins collecting his works for projected five-volume edition. Goes to New

York in January and stays with William Carver until April, when he returns to New Rochelle. Contributes pieces to *The American Citizen*, Republican newspaper edited by English political exile James Cheetham, including last in series of letters "To the Citizens of the United States," criticizing Federalist hostility toward France. Publishes pamphlet *Constitutions, Governments, and Charters* in June, advocating new procedures for legislative grants of state charters. Writes three-part letter to the *Aurora*, criticizing the gubernatorial veto established by the 1790 Pennsylvania state constitution and calling for extensive legal reform, including use of arbitration wherever possible in civil cases. Begins to drink heavily as health declines.

1806   Angered when New Rochelle election officials question his American citizenship and refuse to count his ballot. Moves in spring into home of William Carver at 36 Cedar Street in New York. Writes widely reprinted essay attributing yellow fever to putrid air rising from stagnant mud and recommending rebuilding of wharves as a preventive measure. Becomes friends with Irish exile Thomas Addis Emmet, brother of executed revolutionary leader Robert Emmet. Suffers apoplectic fit on July 25 and is confined to bed for weeks. Moves in November into home of portrait painter John Wesley Jarvis at 85 Church Street. Becomes friends with Jarvis. Quarrels with Carver over boarding bill.

1807   Writes series of articles advocating construction of a gunboat fleet to defend American coasts. Quarrels with Cheetham and begins publishing his writing in *Public Advertiser*, Republican paper printed by Jacob Frank. Moves in April to home of baker Zakarias Hitt on Broome Street. Builds model gunboats and sends them along with written proposal to Jefferson in September. Writes articles attacking Cheetham and Chief Justice John Marshall.

1808   Moves to cheap tavern at 63 Partition (later Fulton) Street after Hitt raises rent to $7 a week in January. Friends persuade him to sell house and land in Bordentown, and in July he begins boarding in house on Herring Street (now 293 Bleecker Street) in Greenwich Village, north of the city. Loses use of his legs. Last known published piece, attack on Cheetham and the Federalists, appears on August 25.

1809   Makes out will on January 18, leaving most of estate to Marguerite de Bonneville and her sons (Benjamin Bonneville later becomes an army officer, western explorer, and subject of an 1837 book by Washington Irving). Requires constant care as his condition worsens. Develops severe swelling and painful skin sores in March. Society of Friends denies his request to be buried in a Quaker cemetery, claiming that Paine's followers might try to build a monument, which Quaker rules forbid. Visited by Secretary of the Treasury Albert Gallatin. Carried on May 4 to nearby house (now site of 59 Grove Street) rented by Bonneville family. Refuses entreaties that he recant deism and accept Christianity. Dies on morning of June 8. Buried on New Rochelle farm on June 9. (In 1819 English journalist William Cobbett has Paine's remains exhumed and sent to England, intending to build a memorial to him; the plan fails and remains are eventually lost.)

Note on the Texts

This volume contains a selection of pamphlets, articles, addresses, and letters written by Thomas Paine, arranged chronologically, followed by his two books, *Rights of Man* and *The Age of Reason*. The texts of the items published during Paine's lifetime are taken from their original sources, whether pamphlet, newspaper, or book. Because Paine's writings were often immediately reprinted by others, many of the pieces included have a complex printing history, and extensive research, therefore, underlies the discovery of the facts of that history and the determination of the best choice of texts for inclusion in this volume. Letters not published during Paine's lifetime are taken from the best modern texts, and items originally published in French are taken from the best English translations. The articles that make up what became known as *The American Crisis* are not grouped together; because they appeared sporadically from 1776 to 1783, they are presented in this volume according to the date of their first publication. The specific texts of the works included here are described in the following annotated list (which also identifies the descriptive titles supplied in this volume for some of the pieces).

Common Sense was first published by Richard Bell on January 10, 1776. An expanded edition, prepared by Paine, was published by William and Thomas Bradford on February 14, 1776. Because of the huge demand for the pamphlet, the Bradfords gave the work to two printing firms, the shop of Melchior Styner and Charles Cist, and the shop of Benjamin Towne. Collation shows that the work of Towne is more accurate, and the text of that version is printed here.

The four numbered Forester letters were published in more than one Philadelphia newspaper. The texts of the letters here are from the first printings: "Letter I. To Cato," *Pennsylvania Packet*, April 1, 1776; "Letter II. To Cato," *Pennsylvania Gazette*, April 10, 1776; "Letter III. To Cato," *Pennsylvania Packet*, April 22, 1776; "Letter IV," *Pennsylvania Journal*, May 8, 1776. The text of one other letter, unnumbered and untitled (here given the title "Reply to Cato's Eighth Letter"), comes from the *Pennsylvania Evening Post*, April 30, 1776, its only appearance.

The American Crisis comprises a group of articles published and numbered by Paine over a period of seven years. After publishing articles numbered I–IX, Paine did not assign number X, though in its place he published *The Crisis Extraordinary*, which was followed by number XI. He skipped number XII, and he called the final article in the series *The Last Crisis, Number XIII* (published on the anniversary of the Lexington-Concord battle, April 19, and perhaps numbered in honor of the thirteen states). Without Paine's authorization, James Carey of Philadelphia published in 1797 an edition of Paine's collected works, in which he grouped together various articles under the heading "The American Crisis"; besides including the numbered pieces, he combined three articles under the number X, chose another to be labeled XII, and added others under the titles "Supernumerary Crisis I" and "Supernumerary Crisis II." Later editors adopted this classification, but since it did not originate with Paine it is not adopted here.

The first publication of *The American Crisis, Number I* was in a pamphlet printed by Styner and Cist in Philadelphia on December 19, 1776; a second printing, bearing this date on the last page, followed soon after. Publication in newspapers followed. Though for many years it was thought that the first appearance was in the *Philadelphia Journal* on December 19, 1776, that paper had temporarily suspended its publication. Paine himself wrote in a letter to Henry Laurens on January 14, 1779, that he gave "that piece to the printer gratis, and confined him to the price of two coppers, which was sufficient to defray his charges." His statement confirms that the first publication of the work was as a pamphlet. The text presented here is that of the first printing.

The American Crisis, Number II was published in pamphlet form by Styner and Cist in Philadelphia on January 17, 1777, before it appeared in any newspapers. The text of that edition is printed here.

The American Crisis, Number III was published in pamphlet form by Styner and Cist in Philadelphia on April 25, 1777. No newspaper versions are known to have appeared. The text printed here is of the first edition.

The American Crisis, Number IV was published in pamphlet form by Styner and Cist in Philadelphia on September 13, 1777, and on the same day in the *Pennsylvania Evening Post*. The text of the pamphlet version is printed here.

The American Crisis, Number V was published as a pamphlet by John Dunlap on March 23, 1778, in Lancaster, Pennsylvania, where Paine had gone during the British occupation of Philadelphia. No newspaper publication has been located. The text of the first edition is printed here.

"Prospects for War Between Britain and France" (the descriptive title supplied here for an item headed only "To the People of America"), appeared in the *Pennsylvania Gazette*, June 10, 1778, published in York Town (York, Pennsylvania) during the British occupation of Philadelphia; that text is printed here.

"The Crisis, Number VI" appeared first in the *Pennsylvania Packet*, published by John Dunlap, in Philadelphia on October 22, 1778, and that text is printed here.

"The Crisis, Number VII" was published in the *Pennsylvania Packet* on November 12, 1778, and that text is printed here.

"Portion of a Letter to Henry Laurens" (1778?) appeared untitled in the New York *Public Advertiser* on May 30, 1807 (Paine contributed articles to this journal during this period). That text is printed here.

"Response to *Observations on the American Revolution*" appeared under the heading "To the *Pennsylvania Packet*" and was published in that paper on March 20, 1779. That text is printed here.

"Response to the Riot Outside James Wilson's House" appeared under the heading "To the printer of the *Pennsylvania Packet*," and was published there on October 16, 1779. That text is printed here.

"The Crisis, Number VIII" appeared in the *Pennsylvania Packet* on February 26, 1780; a line at the end stated: "To be concluded in a subsequent paper," but no subsequent installment was published. That text is printed here.

"The Crisis, No IX" was first published in the *Pennsylvania Packet* on June 10, 1780, but a corrected version was published there on June 13, 1780, with a note apologizing for the errors of the earlier version. The text printed here is that of the June 13, 1780, printing.

The Crisis Extraordinary was published as a pamphlet by William Harris in Philadelphia on October 7, 1780. Other pamphlet versions later appeared, as well as newspaper texts. The text printed here is that of the first edition.

Public Good, Being an Examination Into the Claim of Virginia to the Vacant Western Territory, and Of the Right of The United States to the Same. To which is added, Proposals for laying off a new State, to be applied as a fund for carrying on the war, or redeeming the national debt. By the author of Common Sense was published as a pamphlet by John Dunlap in Philadelphia on December 30, 1780. That text is printed here.

"Common Sense, on the King of England's Speech," appeared in two installments. The first was printed in the *Pennsylvania Packet* on February 19, 1782, ending with the note "To be continued in a future paper." The second part was printed in the *Pennsylvania Gazette*, February 27, 1782. The printings of the *Gazette* and *Packet* are from the same typesetting (the *Gazette* printing of the first part appeared on February 20, and the second part appeared in the *Pennsylvania Packet* on February 28). Other newspaper appearances are derived from these two. The texts printed here are those of the *Pennsylvania Packet* and *Pennsylvania Gazette*, February 19 and February 27, 1782.

"Common Sense, on Financing the War" was published in the *Pennsylvania Gazette* and the *Pennsylvania Journal* on March 6, 1782 (the text which appeared in the *Pennsylvania Packet* on March 7 is from the same typesetting as that of the *Gazette*). The *Journal* version omits most of Paine's quotation from the congressional resolution. The article was carried by other papers, but the earliest and most complete printings are those of the *Gazette* and the *Packet*. The text printed here is that of the *Pennsylvania Gazette*. (Paine's three articles, published on February 19, 27, and March 6, 1782, were gathered together and titled "Crisis X," without his authorization, by James Carey in *The Works of Thomas Paine,* published in 1797.)

"The Necessity of Taxation" appeared in the *Pennsylvania Gazette* and the *Pennsylvania Journal* on April 3, 1782 (it appeared in the *Packet* on April 4, 1782, printed from the same typesetting as the *Gazette*). Because the text of the *Gazette* seems more accurate than that of the *Journal,* that text is printed here.

"Response to an Accusation of Bribery," written for the *Freeman's Journal,* was published in that newspaper on May 1, 1782, and does not seem to have appeared elsewhere; that text is printed here.

"The Crisis, No. XI" was first published in the *Pennsylvania Packet* and the *Pennsylvania Journal* on May 11, 1782 (other newspaper versions are derived from them). There are very few variants between the *Packet* and the *Journal* texts. The text printed here is that of the *Pennsylvania Packet*.

"To Sir Guy Carleton" was published in the *Pennsylvania Packet,* June 1, 1782, and was later reprinted in five other papers. (In Carey's 1797 edition of the *The Works of Thomas Paine,* this piece was retitled "Supernumerary Crisis I"; Paine himself had no part in preparing that collected edition.) The text printed here is that of the *Pennsylvania Packet*.

"To the Earl of Shelburne" was published in the *Pennsylvania Gazette* and in the *Pennsylvania Journal* on October 30; the *Pennsylvania Packet* version, published on October 31, is identical to that of the *Gazette*. The article was later printed in other papers. (Carey's collected edition prints this piece as "Crisis XII," but no contemporary version used that title.) The text printed here is that of the *Pennsylvania Gazette*.

"The Last Crisis, No. XIII," dated Philadelphia, April 19, 1783, was published in the *Pennsylvania Packet* and in the *Pennsylvania Journal* on that day (the *Gazette* and *Freeman's Journal* versions appeared on April 23). The text of the *Packet* seems the most accurate, and that text is printed here.

"Commerce with Britain and the Necessity of Union" was dated December 9, 1783, by Paine and published in *Rivington's New-York*

Gazette, under the title "To the People of America" on December 10, 1783. The letter was written in response to an article that had appeared in the *Gazette* on December 6, and it was later reprinted in other papers. (This letter was published as "The Supernumerary Crisis II" by Carey in his edition of *The Works of Thomas Paine.*) The text printed here is that of *Rivington's New-York Gazette.*

"On the Affairs of Pennsylvania," dated by Paine "Philad. Sept. 15, 1786," was published in the *Pennsylvania Gazette,* September 20, 1786, as the fifth in his series of articles defending the Bank of North America. It was also published in the *Pennsylvania Packet* on September 21, with no variants. The text printed here is that of the *Gazette.*

"Attack on Paper Money Laws," dated by Paine "Philadelphia, Nov. 3, 1786," is number VI in his series on the Bank. It was published in the *Pennsylvania Packet,* November 7, 1786, and on November 8 in the *Gazette.* The text printed here is that of the *Packet.*

"To Thomas Jefferson," February? 1788, was not published during Paine's lifetime. The text of the letter printed here is that of *The Papers of Thomas Jefferson,* vol. 13, edited by Julian P. Boyd, Princeton University Press, 1956. Used with permission.

"To George Washington," October 16, 1789, was not published during Paine's lifetime. The text of the letter printed here is that of *The Papers of George Washington, Presidential Series,* vol. 4, edited by W. W. Abbot and Dorothy Twohig, University Press of Virginia, 1993. Used with permission of the University Press of Virginia.

"To Benjamin Rush," March 16, 1790, was not published during Paine's lifetime. (A portion of the letter, addressed to "A Friend in Philadelphia," appeared in *Miscellaneous Letters and Essays on Various Subjects, by Thomas Paine,* published in London by R. Carlile in 1819.) The text printed here is that of the holograph manuscript in the Library of Congress.

"To George Washington," May 1, 1790, was not published during Paine's lifetime. The text of the letter printed here is that of the typescript transcription prepared by the staff of *The Papers of George Washington,* edited by W. W. Abbot and Dorothy Twohig, for a forthcoming volume in the *Presidential Series.* Used with permission of the University Press of Virginia.

"To the Authors of *The Republican*" was published in the London *Morning Post,* July 19, 1791, the earliest printing in English of the letter written by Paine and translated into French by Condorcet for publication in the first number of *Le Républicain, ou le Défenseur du gouvernement représentatif, par une société de républicains,* Paris, July 2, 1791. The *Morning Post* text is printed here.

"To the Abbé Sieyès," July 8, 1791 was published in Moncure Con-

way, *The Writings of Thomas Paine,* vol. 3, New York, G. P. Putnam's
Sons, 1895. That text is printed here. The letter was first published in
French in the Paris *Moniteur Universel* on July 8, 1791; Paine's En-
glish text has not been found.

*Reasons for Wishing to Preserve the Life of Louis Capet. As delivered
to the National Convention, January 15, 1793,* was first published in a
pamphlet printed for James Ridgway from Paine's original English
holograph version, and that text is printed here.

"Shall Louis XVI Have Respite? Speech in the Convention, January 19, 1793 (read in French by Deputy Bancal)," did not appear in
English. The text printed here is from Moncure Conway, *The Writings of Thomas Paine,* vol. 3, the first publication in English of this
speech. Conway derived his text from contemporary French sources,
with emendations based on Paine's quotation of several sentences in
a memorial to James Monroe.

"To Danton, Paris, May 6, 2d year of the Republic (1793)," was
not published during Paine's lifetime. The text of the letter printed
here is from John Durand, *New Materials for the History of the
American Revolution,* New York, Henry Holt & Co., 1889. This
letter was discovered in the French archives by Hippolyte Taine;
Durand was Taine's translator and the first to publish the letter.

*Agrarian Justice, Opposed to Agrarian Law, and to Agrarian Mo-
nopoly,* appeared in a pamphlet published by W. Adlard, Rue Me-
nilmontant, Paris, and reprinted and sold by J. Adlard and J. Parsons,
London, 1797. It was probably printed in late March or early April
1797; collations against three other contemporary editions, printed in
England and America, show that this text is most accurate and was
probably an earlier printing than the other three; that text is printed
here. Some sentences were suppressed in all the English editions;
Conway, in his edition of Paine, used the earlier French version as his
source to retrieve and translate some of the missing material, and
these passages are given in the notes to this volume.

"To Samuel Adams, January 1, 1803" includes an introduction by
Paine, the letter from Samuel Adams, and Paine's reply, all published
by Paine in *The National Intelligencer,* Washington, D.C., on January 26, 1803; that text is printed here.

"The Construction of Iron Bridges" was published in the *Aurora,*
Philadelphia, June 17, 1803, and signed "Thomas Paine, Bordentown
on the Delaware, June 13, 1803"; that text is printed here.

"Of the Term 'Liberty of the Press' " was published in *The American Citizen,* New York, October 20, 1806, and that text is printed
here.

*Rights of Man: Being an Answer to Mr. Burke's Attack on the
French Revolution* was first printed for J. Johnson in London, on

February 22, 1791. After selling only a few copies, Johnson sold the remaining sheets to J. S. Jordan. Copies with the imprint of J. Jordan were issued in London on March 16, 1791, with a preface that had not been in the first issue. Jordan brought out a second edition on March 19, 1791, which incorporated revisions possibly made by friends of Paine after he had left England for France. The text printed here is that of the March 16, 1791, issue.

Rights of Man. Part The Second. Combining Principle and Practice, was brought out in London by J. S. Jordan on February 16, 1792. This edition is the one from which all others are derived. Paine prepared two editions that combined both parts of *Rights of Man.* The first was a cheap edition, published by H. D. Symonds in London in 1792, but because the risk of prosecution at the time was greater for cheaper editions, passages were omitted and replaced by asterisks. Paine's other edition was prepared during his imprisonment in France, and described by him as "stripped of its national and personal references"; it was published in London by Daniel Isaac Eaton in 1795. The text printed here is that of the February 16, 1792, edition.

The Age of Reason. Being an Investigation of True and of Fabulous Theology, was printed in Paris for Barrois, senior, in February 1794. This first printing contains a final section (not available in any other version, including other Barrois printings), in which Paine gives a detailed description of his arrest and an account of his activities in France. Copies of this printing are extremely rare. The text printed here is that of the copy in the Library of Congress, from which the last three pages are missing. The text of these pages (727.24–730.6 in the present volume) is taken from Moncure Conway's edition, *The Writings of Thomas Paine,* volume 3, published by G. P. Putnam's Sons in New York, 1895.

The Age of Reason. Part the Second. Being an Investigation of True and of Fabulous Theology, was printed for the author in Paris, in late fall, 1795. Two other editions appeared in London: one was set from a faulty transcript bought from the French printer by H. D. Symonds, and published by him on October 25, 1795; the second was published on January 1, 1796, by Daniel Isaac Eaton, who set his edition from a copy of the edition printed in France sent to him by Paine. The text used in this volume is that of the 1795 edition printed in France under Paine's supervision (15,000 copies of this edition were sent to Benjamin Franklin Bache for distribution in America).

This volume presents the texts of the original printings (and in one case original holograph) chosen for inclusion here; it does not attempt to reproduce features of 18th-century typography and handwriting, such as the long letter "s" or the use of quotation marks at the beginning of every line of a quotation. Page numbers referred to within the original texts have been changed to the pagination of the present volume. The texts are printed without other changes, except for the correction of typographical errors. Spelling, punctuation, and capitalization are often expressive features, and they are not altered, even when inconsistent or irregular. The following is a list of typographical errors corrected, cited by page and line number: 15.10, DAY."; 16.17, ever.; 21.3, *they*; 24.7, Willam; 29.11, far of; 32.4, as man; 32.5, of of; 32.14, dictinctions; 33.28, may he; 35.22, remaims; 36.3–4, extirpated the; 47.35, crawl; 48.38, on Britain; 50.25, charge; 51.28, says; 57.19, sitting; 57.40, governmeats; 62.27, M'Cloed; 62.36, thought; 64.33, Alass; 75.39, *self.*; 79.36, *thus*; 80.16, becase; 80.17, *Nineteen*; 87.22, unavoidable; 87.35, there *own*; 97.23, stuped; 115.25, pendent; 119.10, declareing; 119.12, createing; 120.22, odjections; 130.30, makeing; 143.22, pound; 161.23, Pensylvania; 163.14, and authority; 183.36, gentlement; 184.7, *you.**; 184.18, throat; 184.32, threaten; 185.9–10, strange! That; 188.1, france; 192.9, favoutable; 209.40, Stafford; 212.34, 7th; 218.28, or once; 222.24, Has; 223.13, rediculed; 223.30, loses; 225.9, and will; 225.14, it is not; 226.38, misfortunes; 229.1, benifit; 229.2, philanthrophy; 230.36, leiusurely; 232.28, ourseves; 238.8, by own; 264.6, *"space*; 264.10, greator; 267.25, seas,; 269.23, of of; 271.11, say; 272.4, subject; 274.21, crown; 279.13–14, impor-portance; 279.34, opulated; 281.9, adaquate; 284.14, exportsd own; 291.4, of a a; 291.16, at it; 291.38, dulisive; 305.23, misfortue; 306.3, it the; 314.40, face our; 322.14, mouth; 326.19, number, not; 326.36, and and; 327.36, ar; 330.6, referencies; 336.31, merderer; 345.34, *treaty,*; 353.13, parly; 357.10, well-centured; 383.20, Duchetclet; 383.25, Malonet; 384.1, grevious; 405.17, 1,850,000; 422.7, Schuykill; 422.14, contemtemplation; 424.12, the the; 424.25, being n; 425.14, Aurerica; 426.37, greattest; 434.10, miseires; 437.32, period "yet; 451.12, Lewis; 454.5, Bertheir; 472.5, author "On; 486.25, Parliament;; 490.34, Quisne; 491.5, Quisne; 512.3, are; 513.16, Ignorance of; 520.32, of of; 547.30, *Londdon*; 570.11, the the; 573.23, conferrees; 584.14, occured; 584.16, curions; 603.40, unmaned; 607.17, Andrè; 607.42, into; 668.37, This is; 677.29, keeness; 682.20, npon; 689.16, taht; 718.37, end; 762.33, tine; 763.18, Chronilces; 768.11, author the; 773.28, Isaiah?; 776.35, sthi; 782.30, ld; 783.3, ot; 783.15, chh, noturcthat; 784.35, *hiim*; 797.9, inconsisent; 799.32, themselves,. Errors corrected second printing: 666.3, left (*LOA*); 810.28, *lies.** (*LOA*).

Notes

In the notes below, the reference numbers denote page and line of this volume (the line count includes headings). No note is made for material included in standard desk-reference books such as Webster's *Collegiate, Biographical,* and *Geographical* dictionaries. Footnotes in the text are Paine's own. Paine's references to page numbers within the texts printed here have been changed to correspond with this volume. Biblical quotations are keyed to the King James Version. Quotations from Shakespeare are keyed to *The Riverside Shakespeare,* ed. G. Blakemore Evans (Boston: Houghton Mifflin, 1974). For references to other studies and further biographical background, see Alfred Owen Aldridge, *Man of Reason: The Life of Thomas Paine* (Philadelphia: J. P. Lippincott, 1959); Audrey Williamson, *Thomas Paine, His Life, Work, and Times* (New York: St. Martin's Press, 1973); David Freeman Hawke, *Paine* (New York: Harper & Row, 1974); and Eric Foner, *Tom Paine and Revolutionary America* (New York: Oxford University Press, 1976).

COMMON SENSE, THE CRISIS, AND OTHER PAMPHLETS, ARTICLES, AND LETTERS

5.4–6   Man . . . THOMSON.] James Thomson, *Liberty: A Poem* (1736), part IV, lines 636–37.

13.4   Gideon . . . prophet Samuel] Judges 6–8, especially 8:22–23; I Samuel 8:5–20, 12:17–19.

17.29   Saul . . . lot] I Samuel 10:17–24.

19.39–40   Sir William Meredith] Meredith (d. 1790) was a Whig Member of Parliament, 1754–80, and author of several pamphlets on British politics.

20.38   Mr. Pelham] Henry Pelham (1695?–1754), first lord of the treasury (prime minister) and chancellor of the exchequer from 1743 until his death.

22.29   miseries of Hanover] The German electorate of Hanover, whose ruling dynasty had also reigned in Britain since 1714, was invaded by the French during the Seven Years War (1756–63).

26.10   Boston] British troops had occupied Boston since June 1774. The city was besieged by American forces from April 19, 1775, until the British evacuation on March 17, 1776.

27.27–29   Milton . . . deep."] *Paradise Lost* (1667), Book IV, lines 98–99.

28.1–2   repeal . . . undeceived us] Parliament repealed the Stamp Act in
March 1766 after widespread colonial resistance, but in 1767 again asserted its
right to tax the American colonies by enacting import duties on glass, lead,
paint, paper, and tea that had been proposed by chancellor of the exchequer
Charles Townshend. At the same time Parliament established an American
board of customs commissioners, based in Boston and answering to the British treasury board, which would become highly resented by the American
colonists.

28.40–29.2   temporary stoppage . . . acts] In response to the Boston
Tea Party of 1773, Parliament passed four laws in spring 1774 that became
known in the American colonies as the Coercive, or Intolerable, Acts. The
acts closed Boston harbor until "obedience to the laws" was restored in the
town and the destroyed tea paid for, increased the Crown's power over Massachusetts government, permitted the trials of persons accused of committing
capital crimes while enforcing the law or collecting revenue in the colonies to
be removed to Britain or Nova Scotia, and allowed the quartering of troops
in occupied domestic dwellings throughout the colonies. Widespread opposition to the acts resulted in the meeting of the First Continental Congress in
Philadelphia on September 5, 1774, and the creation by Congress on October
18 of the Continental Association. The articles of the Association pledged the
colonies to discontinue the slave trade and cease importing goods from Great
Britain, Ireland, and the East and West Indies after December 1, 1774, to
cease consuming British goods after March 1, 1775, and, if necessary, to cease
all exports (excluding rice) to Britain, Ireland, and the West Indies after September 10, 1775. The Association was enforced by elected town, city, and
county committees, which punished violators by publicity and boycott.

34.19   *Dragonetti . . . rewards.*"] Giacinto Dragonetti (1738–1818),
Trattorio delle virtù et de' primi (1765).

35.16   Indians and Negroes] In 1775 Lord Dunmore, royal governor of
Virginia, attempted to enlist Indians from the northwest frontier as allies
against the American patriots. Dunmore also issued a proclamation in November 1775 offering to free slaves of rebel masters if they would fight with
British forces.

37.39   *Entic's naval history*] John Entick, *A new naval history; or, Compleat view of the British marine . . .* (1757).

38.3   Mr. Burchett] Josiah Burchett (1666?–1746), secretary of the Ad-
miralty, 1698–1742, and writer on British naval history.

38.27   bombs] Small naval vessels used for shore bombardment.

39.12   Terrible . . . Death] Captain William Death commanded the privateer *Terrible*, 26 guns, in its engagement with the French privateer *Vengeance*, 36 guns, at the western entrance to the English Channel on
December 27, 1756. After a battle lasting three hours, Captain Death was
fatally wounded and the *Terrible* surrendered. Paine later wrote in *Rights of*

Man that he had briefly enlisted onboard the *Terrible;* see 604.34–605.4 in this volume.

41.32–33   Pennsylvania . . . lands]   Royal charters granted to Connecticut colonists in 1662 and to William Penn in 1681 resulted in conflicting territorial juridiction over the Wyoming Valley in present-day northeastern Pennsylvania. In 1769 Connecticut settlers began moving into the valley, and in 1774–75 the Connecticut colonial government organized the region as a township, and then as a separate county, in Connecticut. After Pennsylvania militia unsuccessfully attempted to drive the Connecticut settlers from the valley late in 1775, the Continental Congress mediated an agreement allowing the settlers to remain for the duration of hostilities with Britain. A commission appointed by Congress awarded permanent jurisdiction to Pennsylvania in 1782.

44.3–5   Associators petition . . . twenty-eight]   A committee of privates serving in the Military Association (the Pennsylvania militia) submitted two petitions to the assembly in October 1775. The first called for the adoption of a law making militia service compulsory for all freemen; the second asserted that it would not violate liberty of conscience to levy fines on Quakers who refused to serve. On November 17, 1775, the assembly divided 14–14 on the question of requiring 20 days of compulsory militia drill a year. The speaker cast the deciding vote in the affirmative, and on November 25 the assembly passed a militia law that levied fines on "Non-Associators."

44.37–39   Mr. Cornwall . . . Assembly]   Charles Wolfram Cornwall (1735–89) was a junior lord of the treasury in the North government, 1774–80, and then Speaker of the House of Commons, 1780–89. The New York general assembly adopted a remonstrance to the House of Commons in early 1775 that protested several parliamentary measures, including the Declaratory, Coercive, and Quebec Acts (sees notes 91.15–16, 28.40–29.2, and 49.37). On May 15, 1775, the House of Commons debated the petition, and after voting 186–67 that it claimed rights inconsistent with the legislative authority of Parliament, refused it further consideration.

45.38   Burgh's political Disquisitions]   James Burgh (1714–75), British political writer whose *Political Disquisitions* (1774), criticizing the structure of government in Great Britain, was widely influential in the American colonies.

46.19–20   same day . . . Speech]   On January 10, 1776, copies of the speech delivered by George III at the opening of Parliament on October 26, 1775, reached Philadelphia.

47.19   Sir John Dalrymple]   Dalrymple (1726–1810) was the author of several works on historical and scientific subjects, including *The Address of the people of Great-Britain to the inhabitants of America* (1775), which reaffirmed Britain's political authority over the colonies.

49.37   unjust extention . . . Canada]   The Quebec Act of 1774 extended the boundaries of Quebec southward to the Ohio River, thereby including territory claimed by Virginia, Massachusetts, and Connecticut. It was also resented by many colonists for establishing civil government in Quebec without an elected legislature and for granting the Roman Catholic Church the right to collect tithes in the province.

51.12–13   letter . . . New-York papers] An extract from a letter "from a Gentleman in London, to his friend in this city, dated July 26, 1775" appeared in *Rivington's New-York Gazetteer* on October 12, 1775, and was reprinted in the *New-York Gazette and the Weekly Mercury* the following week. The letter described the North ministry as sincerely pursuing reconciliation with the colonists and urged Americans to negotiate a settlement with Britain that recognized parliamentary supremacy over the colonies. A reply printed in the *New York Journal* on November 14, 1775, attributed the letter to Dr. Myles Cooper (1737–85), a Loyalist clergymen who had served as president of King's College in New York from 1763 until May 1775, when he fled the city.

51.28   footing . . . sixty-three] Before the end of the Seven Years War in 1763, Britain had rarely imposed taxes on the American colonies, or enforced those legally in effect, which were designed primarily for the regulation of trade and not the raising of revenue.

54.20–24   "The ANCIENT . . . GENERAL."] The Quaker petition, written by John Pemberton (1727–95), clerk of the Monthly Meeting of Philadelphia, was dated January 20, 1776.

60.4   CATO] Writing under the name "Cato," the Rev. Dr. William Smith (1727–1803), an Anglican clergyman and provost of the College of Philadelphia, published four letters in the Philadelphia press in March 1776 opposing American independence and criticizing *Common Sense*. Smith published four more "Cato" letters in April 1776.

61.20   *Cassandra*] An essay published under the name "Cassandra" had appeared in the Philadelphia press in late March 1776 criticizing "Cato's" arguments. It has been attributed to James Cannon, a mathematician, teacher, and friend of Paine.

62.1–2   Committee . . . Convention] The Philadelphia Committee of Inspection and Observation, an elected body established in 1774 to carry out the resolves of the First Continental Congress, called on February 28, 1776, for a provincial convention to take into consideration "the present state of the province," including the underrepresentation of the western counties in the assembly. In March the assembly agreed to add 13 new seats in the western counties and four in Philadelphia, and scheduled a special election for May 1, 1776.

62.26–27   body of M'Leod.] Captain Donald McLeod, a British officer killed at the battle of Moore's Creek Bridge in North Carolina on February 27, 1776, while leading Loyalist forces. He was reported to have been hit by nine musket balls and 24 pieces of shot.

63.21 Commissioners] Under the Prohibitory Act passed by Parliament on December 22, 1775, George III was authorized to appoint commissioners with the power to grant pardons and restore the king's protection to regions of the colonies that had ceased to be in rebellion. On May 3, 1776, the king named Admiral Richard Howe, commander of the Royal Navy in America, and his brother, General William Howe, commander of the British Army in America, as commissioners.

65.13 thy soliloquy] "Cato" had prefaced one of his letters with a ten-line parody of *Hamlet*, III.i.69–77, that contained the phrase ". . . Who would endure this Pain"; the mock soliloquy also referred to advocates of independence John Adams, Christopher Marshall, Thomas Young, James Cannon, and Benjamin Rush.

67.17–18 Gentleman . . . *principles*] David Rittenhouse (1732–96), Philadelphia scientist and advocate of independence.

68.39–40 Oration . . . Montgomery] *An Oration in memory of General Montgomery, and of the Officers who fell with him, December 31, 1775, before Quebec*, delivered on February 19, 1776, by the Rev. Dr. William Smith, the author of the "Cato" letters, and subsequently printed as a pamphlet.

69.27–30 "*my dear* . . . MacDonald's commission] The Rev. Dr. William Smith was born in Aberdeen, Scotland. Lieutenant Colonel Donald MacDonald was sent to North Carolina in 1775 by General Gage to recruit immigrants from the Scottish Highlands for the king's service. MacDonald was later commissioned as a brigadier-general of militia by Josiah Martin, the royal governor of North Carolina, and assembled a force of 1,400 Loyalists, approximately two-thirds of whom were Highlanders. He was captured by Patriot forces after the battle of Moore's Creek Bridge, February 27, 1776.

69.31–32 *Plain Truth*] *Plain Truth: addressed to the inhabitants of America, containing remarks on a late pamphlet, entitled Common sense . . .*, published in Philadelphia in March 1776 under the name "Candidus." Although its authorship has been attributed by some to the Rev. Dr. William Smith, it is now believed to have been written by James Chalmers, a Maryland Loyalist.

72.33–34 act . . . pirates] The Prohibitory Act of December 22, 1775, made ships involved in commerce with the American colonies subject to seizure by the Royal Navy.

75.17 *Allen*] William Allen (1704–80), chief justice of Pennsylvania, 1750–74, and his son, Andrew (1740–1825), a Pennsylvania delegate to the Continental Congress, 1775–76, were both opponents of independence.

80.32 *Rosseau*] Jean Jacques Rousseau, *Projet de paix perpétuelle* (1761).

81.15 The charter] Magna Charta, signed by King John in 1215.

82.15 scripture . . . Ez 35.] In his fifth letter, "Cato" criticized the use of scripture in *Common Sense,* and then wrote that the only modern king rejected by God in the Bible was "*Mounsier,* the King of *France,*" citing the prophecy concerning Mount Seir in Ezekiel 35. "Cato" interpreted Ezekiel 35 as a warning against Protestant America allying itself with Catholic France, and wrote that this "application is much more natural" than that which *Common Sense* had made of I Samuel 8.

83.27   *Common Man*]   "A Common Man" was the signature used in a letter addressed to "Cato, Cassandra, and All the Writers on the Independence Controversy" that appeared in the Philadelphia press in late March 1776. The letter called for the press debate on independence to be conducted with less personal acrimony and greater attention to the economic consequences of independence.

84.15–16   Gentleman . . . instructions]   John Dickinson (1732–1808) drafted instructions, adopted by the assembly on November 9, 1775, that enjoined Pennsylvania's delegates in Congress to "utterly reject" proposals for independence from Britain.

88.17   before . . . Quebec]   American troops besieged Quebec until the arrival of a British relief expedition on May 6, 1776.

89.9   Clymer and Allen]   George Clymer (1739–1813), the leading "Independent" candidate, and later a signer of the Declaration of Independence; Andrew Allen (1740–1825), Pennsylvania attorney general and delegate to Congress, who later swore allegiance to the king and emigrated to England. Samuel Howell and Alexander Wilcox, candidates on the "Dependent" or "Moderate" ticket with Allen, were also elected on May 1, receiving 941 and 921 votes respectively.

90.14–15   odium . . . Assembly]   In January 1775 the New York assembly refused to appoint delegates to the Second Continental Congress. The New York Committee of Sixty, formed in 1774 to enforce the nonimportation Association (see note 28.40–29.2), then called for the election of a provincial convention, which met on April 20, 1775, and appointed delegates to Congress. In May 1775 legislative power in New York passed to the newly elected provincial congress.

91.15–16   declared, . . . WHATSOEVER,"]   The Declaratory Act of 1766, passed after the repeal of the Stamp Act, reaffirmed Parliament's authority to legislate for the American colonies.

95.39   this city]   Philadelphia.

100.4   LORD HOWE]   Vice Admiral Richard Howe (1727–99), 4th Viscount Howe.

100.5–6   "What's . . . CHURCHILL.]   Cf. Charles Churchill (1731–64), "The Author," lines 113–14: "What's in this name of *Lord,* that I should fear / To bring their vices to the public ear?"

100.22–23   published a proclamation]   On November 30, 1776, the

Howe brothers offered pardons and papers of protection to colonists who would swear an oath of allegiance to the king within 60 days.

101.4–5   deceased brother's]   George Augustus Howe (1724–58), older brother of Richard and William, had been killed fighting the French at Ticonderoga during the Seven Years War. The General Court (legislature) of Massachusetts appropriated £250 for a monument to him in Westminster Abbey.

102.7   14th . . . September]   In their declaration of July 14, 1776, the Howes announced their authority to grant pardons. Their declaration of September 19, 1776, asserted that the king would "direct a revision" of royal instructions and "concur in the revisal" of parliamentary acts adverse to colonial interests if the Americans would cease fighting and renew their allegiance to the crown.

102.18   the gentlemen . . . business]   Benjamin Franklin, John Adams, and Edward Rutledge were appointed by Congress on September 6, 1776, to confer with Lord Howe. They met with him on Staten Island, New York, on September 11.

106.9–10   Quakers . . . *Pemberton,*"]   The address urged Quakers to resist military service, special taxes in support of the war, and oaths of loyalty to the new revolutionary governments. (For John Pemberton, see note 54.20–24 in this volume.)

107.21   Colonel Rohl's]   Colonel Johann Gottlieb Rall (c. 1720–76), killed during Washington's surprise attack on the Hessian garrison at Trenton, New Jersey, December 26, 1776.

108.29–30   butcherly . . . St. Vincents]   After gaining possession of St. Vincent from France in the peace treaty of 1763, Britain became the first European power to make a concerted effort to settle the island against the resistance of its Carib population. In 1797 the surviving Caribs were deported.

113.32–33   "*We . . . back.*"]   Cf. Luke 9:62.

114.10–11   Hugh Gaine's . . . paper]   The *New-York Gazette and the Weekly Mercury,* a Loyalist newspaper.

114.29   duke of Gloucester]   William Henry (1743–1805), Duke of Gloucester, younger brother of George III.

118.29–30   the Colonies . . . rebellion]   George III proclaimed the colonies to be in rebellion on August 23, 1775.

118.32–34   FIRST. . . petitioned]   In October 1774 the First Continental Congress adopted a resolution repudiating the Declaratory Act of 1766, a nonimportation agreement (see note 28.40–29.2), a petition to the king, and an address to the people of Great Britain.

123.21–23   Poland . . . French]   In 1772 nearly 30 percent of Poland's territory was partitioned among Russia, Austria, and Prussia. Genoa sold Corsica to France in 1768.

123.28   treaty . . . Hessians] Early in 1776 Britain concluded a treaty with the prince of Hesse-Kassel to hire mercenary soldiers for service in America. Eventually 30,000 mercenaries from six German states fought in the Revolutionary War, 17,000 of whom were from Hesse-Kassel. Over 7,500 German mercenaries were killed or died from disease, and another 5,000 deserted.

128.10   Lord North's motion] Lord North proposed that Parliament refrain from laying revenue taxes upon the colonies if the colonial assemblies agreed to levy their own taxes to support imperial defense and colonial government. Parliament approved the proposal on February 27, 1775.

129.28   East-India . . . TEA] In 1773 Parliament attempted to rescue the East India Company from bankruptcy by giving it a monopoly of the tea trade in the American colonies. The measure led to widespread colonial resistance, including the Boston Tea Party of December 16, 1773.

130.12   second petition] The "Olive Branch" petition, drafted by John Dickinson, was adopted by Congress on July 5, 1775, and signed on July 8. It criticized the conduct of the ministry since 1763 and appealed to the king's "royal magnanimity and benevolence" in seeking reconciliation with Britain. George III refused to receive the petition when it reached London and, on August 23, 1775, proclaimed the colonies to be in rebellion.

133.14–15   charge . . . DRAYTON] In his charge, delivered on April 23, 1776, Drayton (1742–79) reviewed the events leading to the adoption of a temporary constitution by the South Carolina provincial congress on March 26, 1776. Drayton said that both the recent actions of George III and those of James II in 1688 had broken "the original contract between king and people" by violating fundamental laws, and asserted that the American revolution was as justified as the 1688 revolution in England. He concluded his charge by declaring, "The Almighty created America to be independent of Britain."

133.16–17   ADDRESS . . . New-York] *An Address of the Convention of the Representatives of the State of New-York, to their Constituents,* written by John Jay and printed in Fishkill, New York, on December 23, 1776.

133.39–40   sister . . . society] George III was alleged to have secretly married Hannah Lightfoot, a Quaker woman, while he was Prince of Wales.

135.4   20th of November] The Quaker address appeared December 20, 1776; see note 106.9–10.

152.13   Knight . . . Post] A Knight of the Windmill is one who fights chimeras, from Cervantes' *Don Quixote* (1605–15), Part I, chapter 8, in which Quixote attacks a windmill that he has mistaken for a giant. A Knight of the Post was a person who earned a living as a perjurer, so named from the signposts outside court where such persons could be found waiting to be bribed. The term was also used as a variant of "Knight of the Whipping Post"—a swindler, cheat, or otherwise notorious person.

158.14   General Carleton . . . lakes.] In October 1776, after encountering determined resistance on Lake Champlain from American naval forces led by Benedict Arnold, General Guy Carleton (1724–1808) decided to withdraw his troops into Canada.

162.10   attack . . . Mud-Island.] Mud Island, on the Pennsylvania shore of the Delaware below the mouth of the Schuylkill, was the site of Fort Mifflin, which withstood British attack from September 26 to November 16, 1777.

162.12   fable of Bender] After his defeat by the Russians at Poltava in 1709, Charles XII of Sweden sought refuge in Ottoman territory, eventually making his camp on the Dniester River at Bender (now Bendery, Moldova). For diplomatic reasons Sultan Ahmed III ordered Charles taken into custody, and on February 1, 1713, several thousand Janissaries attacked his encampment. For eight hours Charles and his personal guards fought the Turks from inside a stone house, fleeing only after the roof was set on fire. While running to another building, Charles fell and was captured (he returned to Swedish territory in 1714).

164.35–36   Charles of Sweden] Presumably, Charles XII of Sweden (1682–1718).

168.11   My official situation] In April 1777 Paine had been elected by Congress to the post of secretary to the Committee for Foreign Affairs.

177.16   treaty with France] France and the United States concluded a treaty of alliance on February 6, 1778, in which France recognized the United States and promised, in the event of war between France and Britain, to fight with the United States until Britain accepted American independence.

179.27   burning . . . Mr. Borden's] A British raiding party sailed up the Delaware to Bordentown, New Jersey, on May 8, 1778, and burned the house of Mr. Borden. The next day it burned the nearby house of Colonel Joseph Kirkbride, a friend of Paine.

181.4–5   CARLISLE . . . EDEN] Frederick Howard, Earl of Carlisle, and William Eden were members of a British peace commission authorized by Parliament in March 1778; Sir Henry Clinton succeeded Sir William Howe as commander of the British Army in America in May 1778. The Carlisle commission was instructed to accede to nearly all American demands except independence, but Congress refused to meet with the commissioners and voted on April 22, 1778, not to negotiate with Britain unless it recognized American independence.

181.15   last proclamation] The proclamation was issued in New York by Carlisle and Eden on October 3, 1778.

189.14   expedition to Egg-Harbour] On October 14, 1778, British forces raided Little Egg Harbor, New Jersey, and burned several houses and ten privateering vessels. The next day they killed 50 men of Pulaski's Legion on nearby Minock Island before withdrawing.

198.4   Admiral Saunders]   Sir Charles Saunders (1713?–75) commander-in-chief of the Royal Navy in the Mediterranean, 1760–63 and 1773–75.

206.5   Mr.   Banks   and   Dr.   Solander]   Naturalists   Joseph   Banks (1743–1820) and Daniel Solander (1736–82) sailed aboard the *Endeavour* with Captain James Cook on his first voyage around the world, 1768–71.

208.33–36   "*yet . . . wither*]   Cf. Jonah 3:4–4:7.

216.18   *Admiral*]   While serving as president of the South Carolina provincial congress, Drayton was onboard the schooner *Defence* when it exchanged fire with the British vessels *Tamar* and *Cherokee* off Charleston on November 11, 1775. The South Carolina council of safety then appointed Drayton to command the ship *Prosper* on December 16, despite his lack of maritime experience. Drayton saw no action with the *Prosper,* but remained its commander until March 27, 1776, when he was elected chief justice of the state by the general assembly.

216.38–39   Mr. Deane's impositions]   For Paine's involvement in the controversy over Silas Deane's conduct, see Chronology, 1778 and 1779.

218.10   affair of the fourth]   A group of militiamen gathered in Philadelphia on October 4, 1779, for the purpose of driving from the city "disaffected persons and those who supported them." The militia expelled several opponents of extralegal price controls and then marched toward the house of James Wilson, a leading opponent of price controls and the 1776 state constitution, and a prominent legal defender of Tories accused of treason. Wilson had meanwhile gathered about 20 friends and political allies, including financier Robert Morris, inside his house. When the militia arrived outside shots were exchanged between the two groups. Four militiamen were killed, along with one man inside the house and an onlooker who had joined in the attack. The fighting ended when Joseph Reed, president of the Pennsylvania executive council, arrived with a mounted militia unit and dispersed the crowd. Although arrests were made, no one was ever tried for the shootings, and in March 1780 the executive council pardoned all persons involved in the "Fort Wilson Riot."

222.11–12   Confederated . . . Europe]   Spain declared war against Britain on June 21, 1779.

230.29   fate of Charlestown]   On May 12, 1780, the British captured over 5,000 prisoners when the American garrison at Charleston, South Carolina, surrendered.

235.1   *The Crisis Extraordinary*]   On May 28, 1780, George Washington sent a letter from his camp at Morristown, New Jersey, to Joseph Reed, president of the Pennsylvania executive council, describing the army's need for provisions and asking for help from the state authorities in obtaining supplies. In the letter, Washington wrote: "The crisis in every point of view is extraordinary and extraordinary expedients are necessary."

243.26   emissions stopt]   On September 1, 1779, Congress resolved to limit emissions of Continental paper money at $200 million, and on March 18, 1780, it approved a plan for retiring the existing Continental currency and replacing it with $10 million in new paper money.

246.2   forty to one]   The financial measures adopted by Congress valued the existing paper currency at 40–1 against specie.

246.26–27   pamphlet . . . Dalrymple]   See note 47.19.

253.3–7   VIRGINIA . . . UNITED STATES]   The draft Articles of Confederation submitted in July 1776 gave Congress power to set the boundaries of states, including those whose colonial charters claimed lands extending to the South Sea (Pacific Ocean). This provision was opposed by delegates from Virginia and other states with western land claims and was removed from the revised Articles approved by Congress on November 15, 1777, and submitted to the state legislatures for ratification (the Articles had to be ratified by all 13 states before they could take effect). By February 1779 ratification had been approved in every state except Maryland, whose legislature insisted on restoring to Congress power to set state boundaries (many prominent Maryland political leaders had made speculative land purchases in the western territory which they feared the Virginia legislature would invalidate). On January 2, 1781, the Virginia legislature offered to cede to Congress its lands northwest of the Ohio River on condition that new states be eventually formed out of the territory and that purchases made from the Indians by land companies be voided. Under pressure from the Chevalier de la Luzerne, French minister to the United States, the Maryland legislature approved the Articles of Confederation on February 2 and their ratification was completed on March 1, 1781.

255.39   sir Dalby . . . account]   *An historical account of the rise and growth of the West-India collonies, and of the great advantage they are to England, in respect to trade* (London, 1690).

257.38   Oldmixon's . . . Virginia.]   John Oldmixon (1673–1742), *The British Empire in America*, 2 vols. (1708).

259.10–11   cape . . . Comfort]   Located at the end of the peninsula between the York and James rivers, where Hampton Roads flows into Chesapeake Bay; later the site of Fort Monroe.

266.8–9   Stith's . . . Virginia.]   The Rev. William Stith (1707–55), *The History of the First Discovery and Settlement of Virginia* (Williamsburg, 1747).

266.21   Hutchinson . . . New England]   Thomas Hutchinson, *The History of the Province of Massachusetts Bay* (1764–67).

287.22   the speech]   In his speech at the opening of Parliament on

November 27, 1781, George III pledged to continue the war despite the surrender of British forces under Lord Cornwallis at Yorktown on October 19.
News of the capitulation had reached London on November 25.

288.4   expression . . . used]   In the first "Forester" letter; see page 60 in
this volume.

293.19   Smollet's . . . England]   Tobias George Smollett, *A Complete
History of England* (1757–65).

297.5   Colonel . . . myself]   Paine and Colonel John Laurens traveled to
France in 1781 and, with the help of Benjamin Franklin, obtained additional
financial aid from the French government.

297.16   Commissioners in Paris]   Congress appointed Benjamin Franklin,
Silas Deane, and Thomas Jefferson to serve as diplomatic commissioners in
Europe on September 26, 1776. Jefferson declined the appointment and was
replaced by Arthur Lee, who quarreled with Deane and accused him of misconduct.

315.20   New-York papers]   New York City remained under British occupation until November 1783.

319.37   major Trent]   William Trent (1715–1787) joined George Morgan
(1743–1810) and other land speculators in unsuccessfully petitioning the Virginia legislature and Congress to validate their title to a northwestern land
grant made by the Six Nations in 1768 as compensation for losses incurred by
traders during the Pontiac Indian War of 1763–65.

325.9   cabinet and councils]   Lord George Germain, secretary of state for
the American colonies since November 1775, resigned on February 11, 1782.
On February 27 the House of Commons voted to cease offensive operations
in America and on March 5 it authorized peace negotiations. Lord North
resigned on March 20 and on March 22 the Marquis of Rockingham agreed
to form a new ministry with the Earl of Shelburne serving as secretary for
colonial affairs. The Rockingham administration then moved to negotiate
peace with the United States while seeking to split the Franco-American
alliance.

334.13–34   Huddy . . . Asgil]   Joshua Huddy, a militia artillery captain,
was captured on March 24, 1782, by members of the Associated Loyalists and
imprisoned on a British ship at New York. Captain Richard Lippencott of the
Associated Loyalists removed Huddy from the ship under pretense of using
him in a prisoner exchange and took him under guard to Middletown, New
Jersey, where he was hanged on April 12. A placard placed on Huddy's body
announced that his death was in retaliation for the alleged murder of New
Jersey Loyalist Philip White on March 30 (Monmouth County patriots
claimed White had been killed while trying to escape). Washington wrote to
Clinton on April 21 demanding that Lippencott be surrendered to American
authorities; Clinton, who had already ordered Lippencott court-martialed,

replied on April 25 that he would try the person responsible for Huddy's death. Washington then ordered the selection of a British officer for possible retaliation, and on May 26 Charles Asgill, a 19-year-old officer who had surrendered at Yorktown in 1781, was chosen by lot.

337.31   murderer . . . officer]   In August 1782 Carleton informed Washington that the court-martial had acquitted Lippencott on the grounds that he had executed Huddy under orders from William Franklin, commander of the Associated Loyalists and former royal governor of New Jersey (Franklin was a natural son of Benjamin Franklin). Washington referred the matter to Congress with the recommendation that Asgill not be hanged (executing Asgill would have violated the Yorktown capitulation agreement, which protected British prisoners against retaliatory measures). After learning that Louis XVI and Marie Antoinette hoped that Asgill would be spared, Congress ordered his release on November 7, 1782. Lippencott emigrated to Canada at the end of the war.

338.1   *Earl of Shelburne*]   Following the death of the Marquis of Rockingham on July 1, 1782, the Earl of Shelburne had become first lord of the treasury (prime minister) in a new cabinet.

341.10–11   Mr. Wedderburne]   Alexander Wedderburn (1733–1805) was solicitor general, 1771–78, and attorney general, 1778–80, in the North ministry.

342.8–9   Augustine]   St. Augustine, capital of the British province of East Florida, 1763–83, and a refuge for Loyalists during the Revolution.

343.33   20,000 Russians]   In 1775 the North ministry sought to hire Russian mercenaries to fight in America. After Empress Catherine II rejected the proposal, agreements were negotiated with several German princes; see note 123.28.

344.33   Mungo]   A black slave and servant in *The Padlock* (1768), comic opera by Isaac Bickerstaffe (1733–?1808), music by Charles Dibdin (1745–1814).

345.17–18   Admiral Digby]   Robert Digby (1732–1815), commander-in-chief of the Royal Navy in North America, 1781.

347.7   pamphlet . . . Reynal]   *Letter addressed to the Abbe Raynal on the affairs of North-America. In which the mistakes in the abbe's account of the Revolution of America are corrected and cleared up* (Philadelphia, 1782) was Paine's reply to *Révolution de l'Amérique* (translation, *The Revolution of America*, Boston and New York, 1781) by l'Abbé Guillaume Thomas François Raynal (1713–96).

355.23–24   Lord Sheffield]   John Baker Holroyd (1735–1821), Earl of Sheffield, whose *Observations on the commerce of the American states with Europe and the West Indies* was published in 1783.

357.2   certain State]   Rhode Island.

357.18   the Fisheries]   The peace treaty of 1783 secured American fishing
rights off Newfoundland and Nova Scotia. In three articles published in
Philadelphia, June–July 1779, Paine had urged Congress to protect the fisheries.

359.3–5   present constitution . . . parties]   The Pennsylvania state constitution adopted on September 28, 1776, vested legislative powers in a unicameral general assembly, elected annually by all male taxpayers over 21 and by
non-taxpaying sons of freeholders over 21 (this was the widest suffrage
adopted by any state). Executive power was given to a 12-member council
elected by the freemen; the council had no veto power. Supreme court judges
were to serve for seven-year terms. After its adoption the constitution became
the focus of a continuing political struggle within the state between its "Con-
stitutionalist" supporters, who were strongest in the western counties, and its
"Republican" or "Anti-Constitutionalist" opponents, who were led by Philadelphia commercial interests.

359.10–11   "A serious . . . affairs."]   The piece appeared in the *Pennsylvania Packet* in four parts in early December 1778.

361.29–31   attack . . . *North-America*]   On September 13, 1785, the Pennsylvania assembly repealed the charter it had granted to the Bank on April 1,
1782. The Bank was rechartered by the assembly in March 1787.

365.11–12   legal tenders . . . state]   In March 1785 the Pennsylvania assembly issued £150,000 in bills of credit which could be used to buy land
from, and to pay debts, taxes, and custom and import duties owed to, the
state; the paper money was not, however, legal tender for paying private
debts. By the end of 1786 paper money had been issued as full legal tender in
North Carolina, Georgia, New Jersey, and Rhode Island.

368.2   February? 1788]   This letter was probably written in February 1788,
when Paine, Jefferson, and the marquis de Lafayette were meeting regularly in
Paris to discuss the proposed federal constitution of the United States.

369.4   Mr. Wilson]   Paine refers to James Wilson's speech at the Pennsylvania ratifying convention, November 24, 1787, subsequently issued as a pamphlet, *The Substance of a Speech Delivered by James Wilson, Esq. Explanatory of
the General Principles of the Proposed Federal Constitution . . .* (1787).

370.22–23   Walkers . . . Yorkshire]   The Walker brothers owned a large
ironworks.

371.9   Christie]   Thomas Christie (1761–96) wrote essays on literature,
history, medicine, theology, and philosophy, and was the author of *Miscella-
nies, Philosophical, Medical, and Moral* (1789), and, in opposition to Burke,
*Letters on the Revolution in France and the New Constitution established by the
National Assembly* (1791).

371.23   Dr. Purcival]   Dr. Thomas Percival, 1740–1804, a Manchester
physician and writer on medical, scientific, and ethical subjects.

371.27   Rutlege] John Rutledge, Jr. (1766–1819), a planter and attorney, was a member of the South Carolina house of representatives (1788–94; 1811), and later a Federalist U.S. representative (1797–1803).

372.26–27   Convention . . . Constitution] In September 1789 opponents of the 1776 Pennsylvania constitution succeeded in having the assembly call a new constitutional convention. It met from November 24, 1789, until February 26, 1790, and drafted a constitution which established a bicameral legislature, a single executive with a limited veto, and judges who served for good behavior (for life, unless removed for misconduct). Suffrage was given to all freemen over 21 who paid taxes. The new constitution was adopted on September 2, 1790.

374.21–22   King's Speech] Louis XVI pledged to maintain constitutional freedom in his speech to the National Assembly on February 4, 1790.

376.6   *Republican.*] *Le Républicain, ou le Défenseur du gouvernement représentatif, par une société de républicains,* newspaper published by the Republican Club, founded in 1791 by Paine and four French admirers of the American Revolution, all of whom perished during the Jacobin Terror: Jean-Pierre Brissot de Warville (1754–93); Etienne Clavière (1735–93); Marie Jean Antoine Nicolas Caritat de Condorcet (1743–94); and Achille François Duchastelet (1760–94).

380.1   *To . . . Sieyès*] A French text of this letter was published in the *Moniteur Universel* on July 8, 1791.

382.11   Louis . . . tried] The National Convention had abolished the monarchy on September 21, 1792, and after prolonged debate, voted on December 5 to place Louis XVI on trial. The trial began on December 11, 1792, and the former king was convicted of treason by a unanimous vote on January 15, 1793.

383.5–6   flight . . . Louis XVI.] Louis XVI attempted to flee Paris in disguise on June 20, 1791, but was captured at Varennes on June 21 and returned to Paris under guard.

383.9   French Citizen] Paine was voted honorary French citizenship by the National Assembly on August 26, 1792.

383.25   Malouet] Pierre-Victor Malouet (1740–1814), former intendant of the French fleet and a royalist who emigrated from France in August 1792 and returned in 1801.

386.5   *****] The text printed here is taken from a pamphlet version of Paine's address published in London in 1793, a time when the Pitt ministry was prosecuting printers and sellers of *Rights of Man* for seditious libel. It is probable that fear of prosecution caused the printer to use asterisks at this point in the text, which reads "George III" in the French version.

387.8   Two . . . Louis Capet] The Comte d'Artois (1757–1836), later Charles X, fled France on July 16, 1789; the Comte de Provence (1755–1824), later Louis XVIII, left the country on June 29, 1791. Both became leaders of émigré Royalists.

387.21   Ci-devant Monsieur] "Ex-Monsieur"; the eldest brother of the king of France was often referred to as "Monsieur."

389.8   being a Quaker] Paine's father was a Quaker.

389.28–29   appeal . . . people] Some Girondin leaders had proposed that the king's fate be decided by a national referendum. The Convention rejected the proposal by a 424–283 vote on January 15, 1793.

390.28–31   THURIOT . . . GARRAN] Jacques-Alexandre Thuriot de la Rosiere (1753–1829), and Comte Jean-Philippe Garran-Coulon (1748–1816), members of the National Convention.

392.23   the war.] By May 1793 France was at war with Austria, Prussia, Great Britain, the Netherlands, and Spain.

393.29   fixing . . . provisions] In 1779 Paine had been involved in the movement to combat inflation in Philadelphia by having extralegal citizens' committees regulate prices.

395.14–15   denunciation . . . deputies] The revolutionary Paris Commune had divided the city into 48 sections. In early 1793 militant revolutionary committees in many of the sections began to demand the arrest of 22 leading Girondins in the Convention. On June 2, 1793, the proscribed Girondins were arrested after a large mob surrounded the Convention; almost all of them were subsequently guillotined.

396.10   the present war] France and Great Britain had been at war since 1793.

396.14   WATSON. . . Landaff.] Richard Watson (1737–1816) taught chemistry at Cambridge before becoming Bishop of Llandaff. His works on religion included An Apology for the Bible (1796), a response to Paine's The Age of Reason.

396.29–36   * . . . *] The text printed here is taken from a pamphlet version published in London in 1797. It is probable that fear of prosecution by the Pitt ministry for seditious libel caused the printer to suppress portions of the text.

399.37   Agrarian Law.] Originally a Roman law governing the division of captured lands; in the 18th century, the redistribution of landed property in the interest of greater social equality.

401.36   emprunts] Loans.

403.16   Bourbon kings.] British war aims included the restoration of the monarchy in France.

403.22   France . . . Belgia.] France annexed Belgium in 1795.

405.31–32   * . . . *] See note 396.29–36. Translated, these passages in the 1797 French pamphlet version read "as odious as it is unjust" and "it is necessary that a revolution be made in it."

410.38   Horsley . . . Bishop] Samuel Horsley (1733–1806), Bishop of Rochester and member of the House of Lords.

412.18   numeraire] Specie.

415.32   Felix qui cautus] Happy is he who is cautious.

419.26   Dr. Emmons] Nathanael Emmons (1745–1840), Massachusetts Congregational minister known for his support of the Federalist party. On April 9, 1801, he delivered a sermon comparing Jefferson to Jeroboam, the sinful ruler described in I Kings and II Chronicles.

419.32–33   four letters . . . Adams.] The letters, written between September 12 and November 20, 1790, discussed the nature of government; they were published as a pamphlet in 1802.

420.29–30   third . . . States] Paine's letter appeared in the *National Intelligencer*, November 29, 1802, and described his imprisonment in Paris during the Jacobin Terror of 1793–94.

RIGHTS OF MAN

433.26   Mr. Burke . . . speech] Burke delivered his speech attacking the French Revolution in the House of Commons on February 9, 1790.

433.31   the Pamphlet] *Reflections on the Revolution in France, and on the Proceedings in Certain Societies in London Relative to that Event; in a Letter intended to have been sent to a Gentleman in Paris* was published in London on November 1, 1790.

434.24–25   Archbishop . . . Minister] Etienne Charles de Loménie de Brienne (1727–94), Archbishop of Toulouse, was controller-general of finance, the senior ministerial position in the French government, from May 1787 to August 1788. Brienne took an oath of allegiance to the Revolution in 1790, but was arrested in November 1793 during the Jacobin Terror and died in prison.

436.24–25   Revolution . . . Societies.] The Revolution Society was established in 1788 to commemorate the Glorious Revolution of 1688. The Society for Constitutional Information, established in 1780, advocated annual parliamentary elections, equal representation in the House of Commons according to population, and universal manhood suffrage.

436.26   Dr. Price . . . sermon] The sermon was published as *A Discourse on the Love of Our Country* (1789).

447.3   "*Othello's . . . gone!*"] Shakespeare, *Othello*, III.iii.357.

447.16–17   revenge . . . 1745.] Paine described the suppression of the
1745 Jacobite uprising in a newspaper article published in February 1782; see
293.27–295.2 in this volume.

447.25   Lord George Gordon] Gordon (1751–93), a prominent anti-
Catholic agitator who helped inspire the London "No Popery" riots of 1780
(see note 454.40–455.1), was convicted in 1787 of libeling Marie Antoinette,
the French ambassador in London, and the "Judges and Administration of
the Laws of England." In 1788 he was sentenced to five years imprisonment
and incarcerated in Newgate, where he received guests and held dinners and
dances in his cell. Unable to post bond for his future good behavior, Gordon
remained in Newgate at the expiration of his sentence and died there of
typhus. Many of his contemporaries questioned his sanity.

449.4   Bunyan's . . . Despair.] Giant Despair is the master of Doubting
Castle in John Bunyan's *The Pilgrim's Progress from this World to that which is
to come,* Part I (1678).

449.30   Count de Broglio] Victor François, duc de Broglie (1718–1804),
appointed war minister by Louis XVI on July 11, 1789. He resigned and fled
the country soon after the fall of the Bastille.

450.3–4   parliament of Paris.] The parlement was a law court whose
judges were drawn from the nobility and which exercised appellate, trial, and
administrative jurisdiction over a large region of central and northern France.
Its powers included registering royal edicts, and it sometimes delayed their
registration as a remonstrance against the crown. In the spring of 1788 it
refused to implement a new land tax and on May 3, 1788, proclaimed that
new taxes required the assent of the Estates General, which had not met since
1614. On May 6 troops arrested two of the judges, and a series of royal edicts
were issued on May 8 curtailing the parlement's powers.

450.13   archbishop of Vienne] Jean-George le Franc de Pompignan
(1715–90).

454.14   Temple-bar] Gateway built in 1670 that marked the western
boundary of the City of London. It was removed in 1878.

454.40–455.1   burnings . . . 1780] In 1778 Parliament passed a Catholic
Relief Act which allowed Catholics who swore allegiance to the king to purchase and inherit land, teach school, and serve in the military. On June 2,
1780, Lord George Gordon, president of the London Protestant Association,
led a crowd of approximately 50,000 people to the Houses of Parliament,
where he presented a petition calling for repeal of the 1780 act. Although the
crowd dispersed after the House of Commons refused immediate consideration of the petition, rioting broke out in London later that night. The riots
continued for a week as mobs destroyed Catholic chapels and ransacked
Catholic neighborhoods, broke open and burned Newgate and several other
prisons, and attacked the Inns of Court, the Bank of England, and the homes
of prominent persons, including magistrate Sir John Fielding and Lord Chief

Justice Mansfield. By June 9 order was restored with the deployment of 15,000 troops. At least 285 and possibly as many as 850 people were killed during the riots, and 21 persons were later hanged.

457.9   *fourth of August*]   On August 4, 1789, the National Assembly abolished feudal privileges, including the aristocracy's exemption from taxation.

463.22–24   "And God . . . them."]   Cf. Genesis 1:26–27.

469.29–30   act . . . seven years]   The Septennial Act of 1716 allowed a parliament to last for seven years unless dissolved earlier. It superseded the Triennial Act of 1694, which required that a new parliament be summoned and elected within three years of the first meeting of its predecessor.

469.33–34   Bill . . . reform parliament]   In 1785 Pitt proposed disfranchising 36 small boroughs and giving their 72 seats to London and the counties, as well as a limited extension of suffrage in the county constituencies. The bill was defeated in the House of Commons, 248–174.

472.5   author . . . Nations,"]   Scottish philosopher and economist Adam Smith (1723–90).

472.25   *Loaves* and *fishes*]   An expression for the emoluments of office. Cf. John 6:1–14, 24–27.

477.2–4   writer . . . things."]   Cf. Paul the Apostle, I Corinthians 13:11.

480.38   *Sternhold* and *Hopkins*]   Thomas Sternhold (d. 1549) and John Hopkins (d. 1570) were versifiers of psalms; the first edition of the *Sternhold and Hopkins Psalter* appeared in 1562.

481.17   dissenter's bill]   In 1787, 1789, and 1790, unsuccessful attempts were made in Parliament to repeal the Corporation and Test Acts, 17th-century laws that required civil and military officeholders in England and Wales, including members of the House of Commons, to take Anglican communion and to renounce the Catholic doctrine of transubstantiation. Burke abstained from voting on the repeal motions in 1787 and 1789, but actively opposed repeal in 1790, arguing that many Dissenters (non-Anglican Protestants) sought to destroy the Church of England.

484.5   burnings in Smithfield]   During the reigns of Henry VIII and, especially, Queen Mary (1553–58) dozens of Protestants were burned at the stake at Smithfield, just outside the walls of London, for their religious convictions.

484.21   edict of Nantz]   The Edict of Nantes, signed by Henry IV in 1598, granted freedom of conscience, full civil rights, and limited freedom of worship to French Huguenots (Protestants). Its revocation by Louis XIV in 1685 led thousands of Huguenots to emigrate.

487.40–488.1   "to . . . Capulets."]   In *Reflections on the Revolution in France,* Burke wrote, with reference to the writings of early 18th-century

"Freethinkers": "In as few years, their few successors will go to the family vault of 'all the Capulets.' " Cf. Shakespeare's *Romeo and Juliet,* IV.i.111–12.

490.29   Abbé Raynal] See note 347.7.

511.38–39   wise-men of Gotham] The proverbial stupidity of the inhabitants of Gotham, Nottinghamshire, was the subject of English tales and rhymes.

513.5   Regency Bill] After George III became physically and mentally ill in the autumn of 1788, the Pitt ministry introduced a Regency Bill in Parliament that would have allowed the Prince of Wales to exercise limited royal powers. Burke and other Whigs, who hoped that the Prince of Wales would ask the Whigs to form a new ministry, opposed the bill, arguing that restricting the regent's sovereign authority would unconstitutionally infringe upon the hereditary succession of the monarchy. The bill was withdrawn when the king recovered in February 1789.

519.18–19   Fortunatus's . . . sword] In German folklore and Thomas Dekker's dramatic comedy *Old Fortunatus* (1600), Fortunatus's wishing-cap transports him wherever he wishes to go. In Italian drama, Harlequin's wooden sword, like a magic wand, transforms everything it touches.

522.40   coalition . . . champions] Charles James Fox and Lord North, who had long been political adversaries, formed a coalition ministry in April 1783 in which Fox served as secretary for foreign affairs and North as secretary for home and colonial affairs. The Fox-North administration lasted until December 1783, when George III intervened to defeat Fox's bill to reform the East India Company in the House of Lords and then dismissed the coalition and asked William Pitt to form a new ministry.

533.8   Carlton-House] The London residence of the Prince of Wales.

542.36–37   published two works] The pamphlets *A Letter to a Member of the National Assembly,* published May 21, 1791, and *An Appeal from the New to the Old Whigs,* published August 3, 1791.

580.7   Bill of Rights] In February 1689 Parliament offered the throne to William of Orange and his wife Mary on the condition that they agreed to a declaration of right. William and Mary accepted, and the provisions of the declaration were incorporated in an act, commonly known as the Bill of Rights, which became law on December 16, 1689. The Bill of Rights barred Catholics from the throne, denounced the abuses of James II, and declared that the Crown could not legally suspend or dispense with laws, levy money, or keep a standing army in peacetime without the consent of Parliament. It also called for free elections to Parliament, frequent holdings of Parliament, freedom of speech in Parliament, proclaimed the right of subjects to petition the king, and declared that excessive bail and fines ought not to be imposed and that cruel and unusual punishments ought not to be inflicted.

580.14   convention parliament] After James II fled to France in December 1688, Prince William asked all persons who had served in Parliament under Charles II to meet in London. This gathering then asked William to summon a "Convention" of the Lords and Commons, and to issue writs for elections to the Commons (because William was not yet king, he could not summon a Parliament). The Convention met on January 22, 1689, and on February 12 conditionally offered the throne to William and Mary. On February 23 William, now king, gave royal assent to a bill declaring the Convention to be a legitimate Parliament.

580.37   quoz] A peculiar or absurd person or thing; it was also used as an ejaculation or retort to express incredulity or contempt.

581.20–21   St. Stephen's] St. Stephen's Chapel in the Palace of Westminster, where the House of Commons met at the time.

587.32   Russian and Turkish war] Fearful of Russian expansion in the Black Sea region, the Pitt ministry sent Empress Catherine an ultimatum in March 1791 demanding an end to the Russo-Turkish War on terms favorable to the Ottoman Empire. Despite having his policy endorsed by Parliament, Pitt began to doubt that a war with Russia would be financially supported by the Commons, and in April 1791 the ministry withdrew the ultimatum.

587.36   Fox's bill . . . juries] The Libel Act of 1792 allowed juries to determine whether a publication was libelous under the law, as well as whether the defendant had published it; previously juries were restricted to determining the facts of publication, while the power of determining its libelous nature was reserved for the judge trying the case.

610.38   Sinclair's . . . Revenue] Sir John Sinclair, *History of the Public Revenues of the British Empire* (1785–90).

612.34   Burke . . . essay] *Reflections on the Revolution in France.*

634.26   Chelsea College] Chelsea Hospital, an institution for invalid old soldiers, was built in the late 17th century on the site of a theological college.

635.29   commutation tax] A graduated tax on windows in houses, imposed by the Pitt ministry in 1784 in addition to previous window taxes, to compensate for revenue lost by a reduction in the import duty on tea.

656.23   Bishop of Landaff] See note 396.14.

658.7–8   January 31] January 31, 1792.

660.32–34   clerk . . . Life] Under the pseudonym Francis Oldys, George Chalmers had published a hostile and somewhat inaccurate biography of Paine in 1791, paid for by the British government. Paine cites an earlier work by Chalmers in Part One of *Rights of Man;* see 527.4–11 in this volume.

THE AGE OF REASON

665.20   *Luxembourg*] The former Luxembourg Palace in Paris, where Paine was imprisoned from December 28, 1793, until November 4, 1794.

669.28   Diana of Ephesus] Ephesus was the site of the cult of Diana, virgin goddess of childbearing, described at the advent of Christianity in Acts 19:24–35.

698.19   Vigilius] Virgilius, or Virgil, or Ferghil (d. 784), Irish abbot of a monastery in Salzburg, was denounced as a heretic by Boniface and cautioned by Pope Zacharias that he would endanger his salvation if he persisted in teaching that an inhabited world, with its own sun and moon, existed under the known world. He became Bishop of Salzburg after Boniface's death and was canonized in 1233.

701.17–18   Martin . . . Dr. Bevis] Benjamin Martin (1704–82), mathematician and traveling scientific lecturer; James Ferguson (1710–76), Scottish astronomer and lecturer; John Bevis (1693–1771), noted astronomer.

721.13   Bourdon de l'Oise] François-Louis Bourdon de l'Oise (1758?–97), prominent Jacobin who had voted for the execution of the king. In 1797 he was deported by the Directory to French Guiana, where he died.

721.30–32   one . . . citizenne] Louis-Guillaume Otto (1754–1817), French diplomat who served in the United States between 1779 and 1792. An ally of the Girondins, he was imprisoned by the Jacobins, 1793–94. In 1787 he married Elizabeth Livingston of New York; after her death, he married America-Françes Crèvecoeur, the American-born daughter of writer Michel-Guillaume-Jean de (J. Hector St. John) Crèvecoeur, in 1790.

721.35   Barrère] Bertrand Barère de Vieuzac (1755–1841), member of the Committee of Public Safety, 1793–94.

733.2   General O'Hara] O'Hara, a British officer, was captured at Toulon in November 1793 and exchanged in August 1795. He had presented Cornwallis' sword to George Washington in the surrender ceremony at Yorktown.

735.4   Carrier . . . Lebon] Jean-Baptiste Carrier (1756–94) presided over thousands of executions at Nantes, October 1793–February 1794, including the mass drownings of prisoners in barges. Joseph Le Bon (1765–95) represented the Committee of General Security in the Somme and Pas-de-Calais, November 1793–July 1794, and carried out numerous public executions at Arras and Cambrai. Both men were guillotined after the fall of Robespierre.

765.15   Rapin's . . . England] Paul de Rapin de Thoyras (1661–1725), a Huguenot who fled to The Hague after the revocation of the Edict of Nantes and accompanied William of Orange to England; author of *Histoire d'Angleterre* (1724; English translation, *History of England*, 1726–31, by Nicolas Tindal).

767.18   Abenhezra] Abraham ben Meir Ibn Ezra (c. 1090–1164), Spanish Jewish scholar, poet, and writer.

785.11–15   dragon . . . apple.] Cf. the ballad of the Dragon of Wantley, lines 21–24, in Thomas Percy's *Reliques of Ancient English Poetry* (1765–94).

810.8   Fauste]   Faustus was a Manichaean priest, probably from Africa, whom Augustine met in Carthage (*Confessions,* Bk. 5, chap. 6–7); cf. Augustine's treatise *Against Faustus the Manichaean* and *Retractations.*

810.38   Boulanger's life of Paul]   Nicolas-Antoine Boulanger (1722–59), *Critical Examination of the Life of St. Paul.*

812.13   *hic, hæc, hoc;*]   Latin: masculine, feminine, and neuter for the adjective "this"; as pronouns, "he, she, it."

Index

criticism of, 63, 94
danger from, 142
different kinds of, 106
hope Indians will subdue back
counties, 98
and occupation of American cities
by British, 110
people must join or oppose, 119,
142, 144–45
pessimism of, 117
prostitutes are, 132
reaction of to battle of Lexington,
127
responsible for inflation, 143–44
should favor independence for their
own safety, 53
strength of in Middle Colonies, 90,
94
called traitors, 119
weakness of in New England, 90,
94
welcome General Howe, 101
distinction from Whigs, 181
Whigs protect, 124
Whigs threaten, 104, 105, 109–10,
219
Whigs too lenient toward, 134
See also American Revolution;
Whigs
Townshend, George, 1st Marquis, 139
Traquair, Earl of, 294
Treason
of Benedict Arnold, 250
and Silas Deane, 296–97
definition of, 138
Louis XVI charged with, 384–85
Trent, William, 319
Trenton, battle of, 157, 215
Trumbull, John, 374
Tryon, William, 163
Tullibardine, Marquis of, 294
Turgot, Anne-Robert Jacques, Baron
de, 490, 491
Turkey, 377, 726
Tyler, Wat, 617
Tyranny
English kings rule with, 579–80
likely if independence is not de-
clared, 35
not easily conquered, 91
monarchy degenerates into, 377

uncontrolled power leads to, 235
See also Despotism; Oppression

Unicameralism
danger from, 360–63, 587
Union
America's strength lies in, 36–37, 61,
118, 166, 280, 350
God brings about, 254
necessity of, 303–5, 351–53, 355–58,
357, 358
strengthening of called for, 51, 112,
350
is strengthening, 159
United States. See America; American
Revolution; Independence of
America
Universal philanthropy, 419–20
Universe, 703–8, 827

Vadier, Marc-Guillaume Alexis, 732
Vanheule, Joseph, 732
Vaughan, Benjamin, 370, 375
Vaughan, General John, 163
Venice, not a true republic, 378
Vergennes, Charles Gravier, Comte de,
443, 607
despotism of, 491
opposes French publication of
American constitutions, 492
unfriendly to America, 491
Versailles, march to, 456–61
Vespasian, 737
Veto power of king criticized, 10,
29–30
See also Executive power
Vice, man subject to, 7–8
See also Corruption
Vienna, Congress of, 330
Virgilius (Ferghil), 698
Virginia
claims western lands, 253–86, 319–24
commerce with west, 284
original territory designated by
name of, 256
Voltaire, 94, 490, 491

Wages, should not be set artificially
low, 642
Walker Brothers, Rotherham, 370, 371,
423

CATALOGING INFORMATION

Paine, Thomas, 1737–1809.
    Collected Writings / Thomas Paine.
    Edited by Eric Foner.

    (The Library of America ; 76)
    Contents: Common Sense, The American crisis, and other articles,
pamphlets, and letters—Rights of man—The age of reason.
    1. Political science. I. Title: Common sense. II. Title: The American crisis.
III. Title: Rights of man. IV. Title: The age of reason. V. Series.

JC177.A5   1995   94–25756
320.5′1—dc20
ISBN 1–883011–03–5

THE LIBRARY OF AMERICA SERIES

*This book is set in 10 point Linotron Galliard,
a face designed for photocomposition by Matthew Carter
and based on the sixteenth-century face Granjon. The paper is
acid-free Ecusta Nyalite and meets the requirements for permanence
of the American National Standards Institute. The binding
material is Brillianta, a woven rayon cloth made by
Van Heek-Scholco Textielfabrieken, Holland.
The composition is by The Clarinda
Company. Printing and binding by
R. R. Donnelley & Sons Company.
Designed by Bruce Campbell.*